Finland

Andy Symington
George Dunford

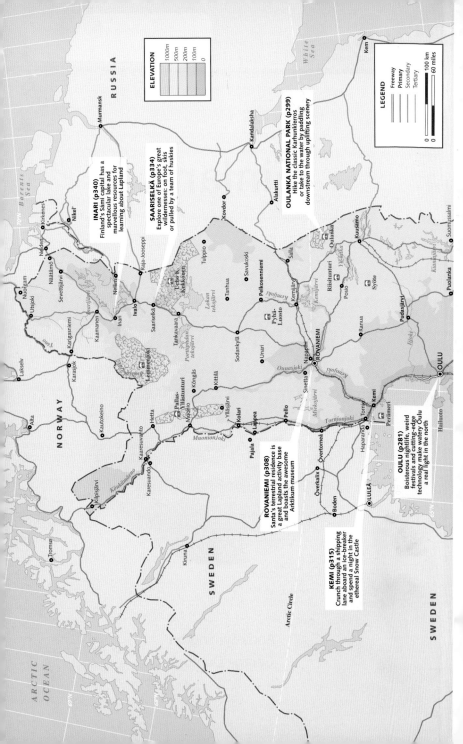

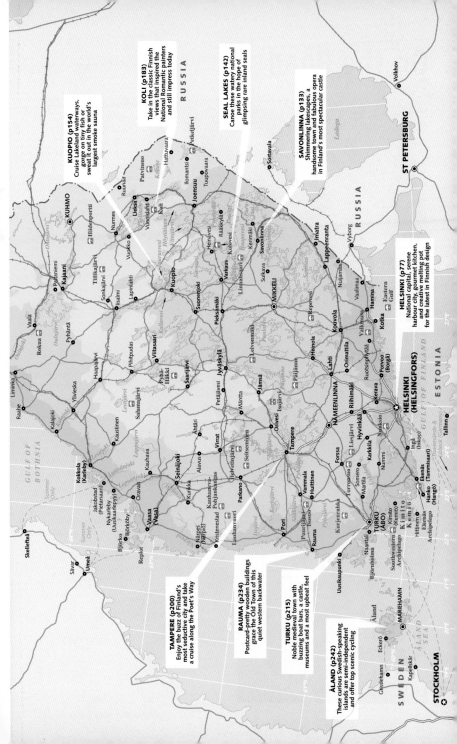

KUOPIO (p154)
Cruise Lakeland waterways, gorge on tiny fish or sweat it out in the world's largest smoke sauna

KOLI (p183)
Take in the classic Finnish National Romantic painters that inspired the and still impress today

SEAL LAKES (p142)
Canoe these watery national parks in the hope of glimpsing rare inland seals

SAVONLINNA (p133)
Shimmering lakescapes, a handsome town and fabulous opera in Finland's most spectacular castle

HELSINKI (p77)
National capital, serene harbour city, gourmet kitchen, and creative melting pot for the latest in Finnish design

TAMPERE (p200)
Enjoy the buzz of Finland's most seductive city and take a cruise along the Poet's Way

RAUMA (p234)
Postcard-pretty wooden buildings grace the Old Town of this quiet western backwater

TURKU (p215)
Noble medieval town with buzzing boat bars, castle, museums and a most upbeat feel

ÅLAND (p242)
These curious Swedish-speaking islands are semi-independent and offer top scenic cycling

RUSSIA

RUSSIA

GULF OF BOTHNIA

GULF OF FINLAND

ESTONIA

SWEDEN

ÅLAND SEA

STOCKHOLM

ST PETERSBURG

HELSINKI (HELSINGFORS)

On the Road

ANDY SYMINGTON
Coordinating Author
One of the simple pleasures of a Finland summer is gathering some of nature's harvest from the forests and mires. You've never tasted berries and mushrooms like them; this successful hunt has yielded wild strawberries, little rubies of perfect fruity sweetness.

GEORGE DUNFORD This is a *vihta* I made (with a lot of help from my host Raili) before a traditional sauna. It's the famous birch twigs that you whack yourself with during a real sauna. It was followed (with much encouragement from Raili) with the traditional swim in the freezing lake.

For full author biographies see p379.

SUOMI SEASONS

Finland's mighty latitudes mean its seasons contrast utterly and are marked with full force and majesty. As the snow melts, life races to reassert itself, and the glory of the never-setting summer sun blesses the land with festivity and fertility. Then, as the last calls of the migratory birds fade into the south, the short, spectacular autumn bathes Lapland in golden colours, an artistic caprice of nature before the winter's harsh glory. As the bear sleeps, sparkling summer lakes become snowmobile highways, and otherworldly temples are raised in ice. Only the undaunted spruces and pines, poking above their snowy blankets, can be recognised.

Winter Finland

It's cold and it's dark, but winter is something magical. Finns are far from cowed by the conditions; they strap on the skis and skates, start up the snowmobiles, and head out to enjoy the subzero temperatures. There's a real magic in the air – especially in Lapland, where there's snow on the ground for seven months of the year.

1 Reindeer

Whether pulling you on a sleigh adventure, racing along the ice with their tongues lolling, hanging out with Santa, or supplying you with cheese or meat for a traditional Lapland meal, these goofy antlered beasts are ubiquitous in Finland's far north. See p65 for more on the reindeer.

2 Christmas Spirit

Old, bearded Joulupukki (as Santa calls himself in these parts; see p310) makes his home here. There's guaranteed snow, plenty of local festive tradition, and the forests are full of Christmas trees, so where better to bring the family for a bit of December romance?

3 Northern Lights

Whether caused by the collision of charged particles, or sparked by a giant snow fox running across the Arctic tundra, the haunting, humbling splendour of the aurora borealis (p322) never leaves those fortunate to have witnessed it.

4 Husky Voices

Fizzing over the snow behind a team of huskies under the low winter sun is tough to beat. Short jaunts are great, but overnight safaris give you time to feed and bond with your loveable dogs, and try out a wood-fired sauna in the middle of the winter wilderness. If you're more of a cat person, you can enjoy similar trips on a snowmobile or behind reindeer.

5 Ice-Fishing

Finns love to fish, so when their lakes freeze over they have to find an angle. Taking their lead from the polar bear, they cut a hole in the ice, bring something warm (or warming) to drink, and hope for a bite – before getting frostbitten. See p75 for more on ice-fishing.

6 Snow Hotels

Even reading the words can shoot a shiver up your spine, but spending a night in one of these ethereally beautiful, extravagantly artistic snow buildings is a marvellous experience. Heavy-duty sleeping bags ensure a relatively cosy slumber, and a morning sauna banishes any lingering chills. For some of the best see p73.

Summer Finland

The sun makes up for its winter neglect by spending some quality time with the Finns in summer: in the north it hangs in the sky for 10 weeks without setting. Sparkling waters reflect spruce forests and people revel in nature alongside remote lakesides. It's also party time, with terraces packed, kauppatoris humming with life, and Midsummer celebrations emptying the breweries.

① Tastes of Summer

Summer kauppatoris (market squares) burst with straight-from-the-garden vegetables, and berries and mushrooms foraged in the forests and fells. The glorious sweetness of tiny wild strawberries; the delicate pepperiness of chanterelles; melt-in-the-mouth new potatoes glorified with fresh dill; the tangy, creamy splendour of a Lapland cloudberry – all are tastes of nature that define the Finnish summer.

② Back to Nature

It's almost compulsory to spend some downtime each summer at a *mökki*, or summer cottage. Take a wood-burning sauna, a skinny dip in the shimmering lake, a rowboat, darts, and the smell of sausages on the grill, and you have a pretty good definition of Nordic peace.

③ All Aboard!

With so much water, it'd be a crime not to get out on it. Hire a canoe and meet freshwater seals, go rafting on the frisky northern rivers, pull on the waders and cast for salmon, or cruise one of the classic lake routes aboard a steamer.

④ Freaky Festivals

However offbeat or classical your tastes, there's a festival for you in Finland. Music on offer ranges from marvellous opera in a castle setting, to melancholic Finnish tango, to the biggest names in heavy rock. Heading up the more bizarre offerings are wife-carrying, playing air guitar, and voting for the town's laziest resident then throwing them in the sea. See p21 for more on Finnish festivals.

⑤ Island-hopping

Nipping out for a crayfish lunch at a restaurant in the middle of Helsinki harbour (p77), chugging across Inarijärvi (p340) to a Sámi holy place or exploring the Swedish-speaking semi-independent Åland archipelago (p242) by bike: one of Finland's nearly 200,000 islands will suit you.

Hiking Finland

Though hiking's great in summer (so long as you pack repellent), September is a magical time to go walking, as the autumn colours of the *ruska* season paint the northern landscape with a fairy-tale palette of gold, russet and bronze. Finland's *jokamiehenoikeus* (everyman) rule means you've got the right to walk anywhere in the countryside, so strike off and enjoy the freedom!

3

❶ Top Corner Climbs

The very northwestern tip of Finland, Kilpis-järvi (p328), has some mighty scenic day walks, and the stout bulk of Saana Fell invites ascent for a 'king-of-the-castle' thrill. If you like the views, consider the long, tough trek to Finland's highest peak, Halti, a round trip of at least five days.

❷ Karhunkierros

The 'Bear's Ring' (p299) is Finland's most popular trek, and deservedly so for its striking terrain of hills and sharp gorges. While you won't be alone, it's a memorable and satisfying walk that gets even better during the *ruska* period.

❸ Spirit of Karelia

This eastern slice of the nation (p161) has a mystic aura, and its wilderness is said to hold the soul of Finnishness. Bears and wolves prowl the forests, through which over 1000km of marked trails exist; you are also pacing through terrain that saw some of the harshest fighting of the Winter War (p36).

❹ Wilderness Huts

All the major trekking routes in Finland's protected areas are well supplied with simple but sociable huts where you can unroll your sleeping bag and cook a meal. As well as handy stopovers, they're a great spot to meet Finns and swap some trekking tales.

❺ Saariselkä Wilderness

One of Europe's great redoubts of nature, the Urho K Kekkonen National Park (p293) offers limitless possibilities for a strategic escape from urban life. Epic Lapland scenery, DIY trekking routes, magical autumn colours, and space, space and more space, are the drawcards for hikers with a bit of experience.

❻ Kevo Strict Nature Reserve

You've got to stay on the path in this heavily protected area (p344), but the dramatic gorge scenery through which you pace means there's no call to stray in any case.

Contents

CONTENTS 15

Regional Map Contents

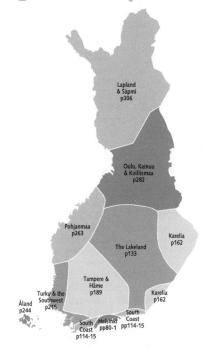

Lapland
& Sápmi
p306

Oulu, Kainuu
& Koillismaa
p282

Pohjanmaa
p263

Karelia
p162

The Lakeland
p133

Tampere &
Häme
p189

Karelia
p162

Turku & the
Southwest
p215

Åland
p244

South
Coast
p114-15

Helsinki
pp80-1

South
Coast
pp114-15

Destination Finland

Remote, forested, sparsely populated Finland has had a hell of a last hundred years. It's propelled itself from an agricultural backwater of the Russian Empire to one of the world's most prosperous and forward-looking nations, with a great standard of living and education, low crime and corruption, and a booming technology industry. Although socially and economically part of the vanguard of nations, parts of Finland remain gloriously remote. Its trendsetting capital, Helsinki, is counterbalanced by vast forested wildernesses in the north and east.

There's something pure in both the Finnish air and spirit that's incredibly vital and exciting. It's an invitation to get out and active year-round, whether by whooshing across the snow behind a team of huskies or shooting rapids on a frisky Lapland river. A post-sauna dip in an ice-hole under the majestic aurora borealis isn't a typical winter's day just anywhere. Nor is hiking or canoeing under the midnight sun through pine forests populated by wolves and bears your typical tanning-oil summer.

Nordic peace in a lakeside cottage, summer sunshine on a convivial beer terrace, avant-garde Helsinki design, dark melodic music, and cafes warm with baking cinnamon aromas, are just the beginning of Suomi seduction. And the real bonus? The Finns themselves, who tend to do their own thing and are much the better for it. Independent, loyal, warm and welcoming – a memorable people in an inspirational country.

But Finland, like everyone, has issues. The devastating 2007 school shooting was followed within a year by an almost identical college massacre. Peaceful Suomi was horrified. Always keen for a bit of introspection, Finns wondered if it revealed something rotten at their society's core; some hang over from the war years perhaps, or a dramatic manifestation of those seasonal depressive tendencies that seem to boost alcoholism and suicide stats? Or is it just too easy for angry youths to buy a gun? As usual there are no clear answers, but tightening gun laws is a likely first step towards preventing a reoccurrence.

Since the 12th century, Russia has loomed large. Finland's long experience with the Bear has stood it in good stead, and the two countries have a strong relationship, with much exchange of commerce and tourism. Nevertheless, Finns on the street are understandably nervous of what some view as an increasingly nationalistic Moscow. Memories of the bitter fights for freedom are too painful for national service and the army not to be taken seriously here.

However, climate change upstages even Russia on the agenda. Southern Finland has already noticed dramatically changed weather patterns, and the almost unthinkable prospect of a nonwhite Christmas in Helsinki looks everlikelier. Though Finland will reap corn sown by bigger nations, its people and government are very environmentally conscious. Definitely realistic rather than idealistic, they prefer managed forestry and a nuclear power sector to back-to-basics pipedreams.

Finland has seen a great growth in tourism in recent years and is well placed, with its magnificent wildernesses, healthy tree cover and tradition of cottage culture, to offer a sustainable ecological experience to travellers looking for a new type of low-impact holiday. It's perhaps Europe's finest destination for getting outdoors and revelling in nature's bounty while treading lightly.

FAST FACTS

Capital: Helsinki

Population: 5,300,484

Cups of coffee drunk per day: over 20 million

Size: 338,145 sq km

Percentage of country covered in water: 10%

GDP per capita: €30,978

Unemployment rate: 6.9%

Number of reindeer: 193,000

Number of days of no sun in Nuorgam: 51

Number of days of constant sun in Nuorgam: 72

Getting Started

For somewhere offering such awesome wildernesses and off-the-beaten track opportunities, travel in Finland is gloriously easy. Buses and trains run on time, tourist offices are eager to please and full of at-your-fingertips information, and you can get by easily enough without even dipping into a Finnish dictionary. It's not cheap, but neither are prices as elevated as sometimes imagined, and accommodation in particular can be excellent value, with hotels chopping their prices in summer and plenty of cosy wooden cabins at bargain rates.

WHEN TO GO

The tourist season in southern Finland and the Lakeland is early June to late August. This is when all attractions and summer accommodation options are open, steamboats and ferries ply the lakes and rivers and there's always some event or other in full swing. Attractions, though not towns and cities, are at their busiest during Finnish holidays from late June until the end of July. This is the time of long, light nights, when Finland doesn't seem to sleep and numerous festivals (p21) offer everything from chamber music to wife-carrying.

Northern Finland, including Lapland, is different. Mosquitoes can be unbearably annoying in July – and we do mean unbearable – but they tail off in August, and then September is delightful with its autumn *ruska* colours. October, and February to April are good times to visit Lapland to view the aurora borealis (Northern Lights) and enjoy winter activities such as skiing and dog-sledding. The Christmas holiday period is also prime time up north, and charter flights bring thousands of families eager for snow, reindeer and some Christmas spirit – after all, this is where Santa Claus makes his home…

See Climate Charts (p350) for more information.

COSTS & MONEY

Finland is expensive, but not quite as much as its reputation would suggest. With a bit of planning, you can have a great time here on almost any budget.

Summer is generally the cheapest time to visit. Nearly all the hotels drop their prices – a twin room in a three-star hotel, for example, might drop from €120 to €70 – and student apartments are repurposed as budget accommodation. This is also the time when camp sites, with their cheap wooden cabins, are open.

After accommodation, transport will likely be your biggest expenditure, especially if you move around a lot. Buses and trains are expensive – think €25 to €30 for a ride of a couple of hours – and taxis have an horrendous flag fall. Car hire costs €200 to €350 a week, and petrol is pricier than almost anywhere else in the world.

A couple using public transport, travelling in summer, staying in good midrange hotels and eating out, will spend €130 to €160 per day per person, a little more in pricier Helsinki. If you nab a decent car-hire deal, this figure wouldn't be increased greatly. Solo travellers will pay more, as single hotel rooms are often almost the same price as a double.

Two shoe-stringers, using hostels and cabins and mostly self-catering, could get by comfortably on €60 to €70 each per day, less if not taking too many long trips.

There are numerous ways to reduce the amount you spend in Finland. It's worth being an HI member, as you'll save €2.50 a night in many places.

HOW MUCH?

Bus ride (200km) €33.40

Sauna free-€20

Bottle of cheap red in a restaurant €30

Day's bike hire €10-20

Simple log cabin for two €30-40

DON'T LEAVE HOME WITHOUT...

You can buy virtually anything you need in Finland, but be sure to carry these:

- Insect repellent (double the strength and double the quantity)
- A sleeping sheet and a pillowcase for cabins and hostels (p347)
- Eye-mask; if daylight at 2am will keep you from sleeping
- Seriously warm clothing for winter or a water- and windproof jacket for summer
- A passport: EU citizens still need it for day trips to Estonia. And a Russian visa if you'll be tempted across that border
- A swimsuit; even if it's winter, there are great water parks and ice-holes for post-sauna dips in the lakes
- A mobile phone; public phones are nonexistent and SIM cards are cheap (see p355)

Group and family accommodation in hotels and cottages is excellent value, and there's a discount on buses for four or more tickets booked together. Camping grounds nearly always have some sort of cabin accommodation sleeping four or more, ranging from simple huts with bunks to luxurious wooden houses: always excellent value.

Many hotels offer weekend discounts similar to their summer ones; similarly, car-hire companies have a good-value weekend rate. It's much cheaper to eat in restaurants at lunchtime, when there are daily specials and often a groaning buffet table – a filling meal can be as little as €7 on weekdays.

Students with valid ID and seniors receive substantial discounts on museum admission prices quoted in this book, as well as on transport.

TRAVELLING RESPONSIBLY

Finland is a rather environmentally friendly country, and things like recycling and sustainable forestry have been institutionalised for a long time now. The outdoorsy focus of much travel in the country means it's easy to travel responsibly by picking minimal-impact activities like hiking or reindeer-sledding, using public transport and following basic guidelines such as those detailed on www.environment.fi. The website www.outdoors.fi outlines ways to avoid impact when visiting protected areas. See the Greendex (p394), Environment (p63) and Accommodation (p347) sections of this book for more specific details of ecofriendly travel in Finland.

But travelling responsibly doesn't just mean treading lightly in nature. It includes endeavouring to spend your money in a way that will benefit the local community; trying to stay in family-owned places and eat sustainable, locally produced food; making the effort to at least learn how to say 'please' and 'thank you' in Finnish (OK, Finnish doesn't have a word for 'please' but you know what we mean); and respecting local cultures. This is particularly important in Lapland, where Sámi communities are a focus of touristic interest but don't always reap the benefit from it. If you're going to buy a colourful Sámi hat as a memento, for example, buy it in Inari from a local craftsperson, not from the souvenir stand at Helsinki airport.

TRAVEL LITERATURE

House of Orphans, by Helen Dunmore, is a gloriously evocative historical novel, with excellent background on early-20th-century Finnish rural life, the class divide, workers' movement and burgeoning nationalism, through the eyes of sympathetic characters.

TOP 10

Sweden
Norway
FINLAND
Gulf of Bo...
Helsinki

BOOKS

Finns are among the world's most voracious readers and the local literature scene is an active one, although relatively few novels are translated. See p43 for more on Finnish literature.

1 *Kalevala*, by Elias Lönnrot, translation by Keith Bosley, is Finland's epic, compiled from the songs of bards. It tells everything from the history of the world to how to make decent homebrew.

2 *The Year of the Hare*, by Arto Paasilinna, is an offbeat tale telling how a Finnish journalist revolutionises his life and sees things in a new way while travelling around the countryside with a hare.

3 *The Canine Kalevala* is a doggy take on the *Kalevala* by Mauri Kunnas, successful and much-loved children's author and illustrator.

4 *Finn Family Moomintroll*, by Tove Jansson, is one of the earliest and best of the loveable Moomin books.

5 *Seven Brothers*, by Aleksis Kivi, is one of the Finnish classics, and allegorises the birth of Finnish consciousness with a story about

brothers escaping from conventional life by heading to the forest.

6 *Tummien Perhosten Koti* (The Home of Dark Butterflies), by Leena Lander, is a successful and challenging novel about a teenager growing up in a strict boys' home.

7 *The Egyptian*, by Mika Waltari, was a worldwide blockbuster success for this prolific novelist.

8 *Fallen Asleep While Young*, by 1939 Nobel laureate Frans Eemil Sillanpää, is a portrayal of a peasant girl.

9 *The Position of the Sun*, by Ranya El Ramly (now Paasonen), is a recently translated first novel that won critical acclaim.

10 *Not Before Sundown*, by Johanna Sinisalo, is called Troll – A Love Story in the USA, and tells the story of a photographer who rescues a wounded troll.

FILMS

The Kaurismäki brothers Aki and Mika put Finnish cinema on the map, but there are several other promising young directors on the scene these days. See p54 for more on Finnish cinema.

1 *Drifting Clouds*, directed by Aki Kaurismäki, is a marvellous film, full of awkward, stilted emotions, about a couple forced to seek new jobs.

2 *Man Without a Past* is another excellent work from Aki Kaurismäki.

3 *Musta jää* (Black Ice) is a 2007 film that won many plaudits for its portrayal (with little left to the imagination) of a middle-aged love triangle.

4 *Tuntematon Sotilas* (Unknown Soldier), directed by Rauni Mollberg, is a good film about the Continuation War, based on the book by Väinö Linna.

5 *The Winter War* (Talvisota) is another good film about the fight against the Russians.

6 *Tummien Perhosten Koti* (The Home of Dark Butterflies) is a successful film adaptation of Leena Lander's novel.

7 *Mannerheim*, due out in late 2009 and directed by Finnish Hollywood director Renny Harlin, is an eagerly awaited biopic about this complex figure who played such a major role in the Finnish Civil War and WWII.

8 *Näkkälä* is a documentary film about a Swiss man who goes to live as a reindeer herder in a remote Sámi community.

9 *Pahat Pojat* (Bad Boys) is a Finnish gang film, about four infamous brothers who terrorised the nation by robbing petrol pumps and worse.

10 *LA Without A Map*, a touching love story, is perhaps Mika Kaurismäki's best solo work.

Travels through Sweden, Finland, and Lapland to the North Cape (Vol II), by Giuseppe Acerbi, has recently been republished. This late-18th-century traveller's account is a gem, full of keen observations on the places visited, and the customs of the Sámi.

Bad Wisdom, by Bill Drummond and Mark Manning, is a visionary and disturbing rock 'n' roll road trip through Finland, taking an icon of Elvis to the North Pole. If it were a film, it'd cop an X-rating for kinky sexual content and substance abuse.

Though set just over the river in Sweden, *Popular Music*, by Mikael Niemi, is an area with much Finnish influence and has plenty to say about contemporary Lapland through the eyes of a boy liberated from the constraints of small-town life by discovering rock music.

Palace of the Snow Queen, by Barbara Sjoholm, is a winter travelogue that spends more time in Norway and Sweden, but is good on Lapland and the Sámi in general. It has much detail on the building of snow hotels, and pays a visit to Inari's film festival.

Let the Northern Lights Erase Your Name, by Vendela Vida, is a woman's voyage to discover her roots and evokes Finnish and Norwegian Lapland through her vulnerable visitor's eyes. The emotional journey is powerful, but the setting's just an exotic backdrop here and let down by inaccuracies.

See p43 for information on Finnish literature.

INTERNET RESOURCES

Almost every town in Finland has a website chock-full of information, nearly always: www.(townname).fi. See also Accommodation (p347) for relevant sites.

Aurora Forecast (www.gedds.alaska.edu/AuroraForecast/) The best predictor of aurora borealis activity. Based in Alaska, but you can change the view to Europe.

Cosy Finland (www.cosyfinland.com) Organisation that sets up dinners and homestays with Finnish host families.

Finnish Tourist Board (www.visitfinland.com) Official site full of excellent information from the practical to the whimsical.

FMI (www.fmi.fi) The Finnish weather forecast.

Forest and Park Service (www.outdoors.fi) Truly excellent resource, with detailed information on all Finland's national parks and protected areas, as well as activities listings.

Helsingin Sanomat (www.hs.fi/english) International edition of Finland's best daily newspaper.

Lonely Planet (www.lonelyplanet.com) Check recent postings for the very latest recommendations and tips on travelling in Finland.

Virtual Finland (virtual.finland.fi) Maintained by the Ministry of Foreign Affairs, this is an excellent, informative and entertaining website.

Events Calendar

JANUARY–FEBRUARY

SKÁBMAGOVAT 3rd weekend in Jan
Sámi film festival in Inari with collaboration from international indigenous groups (www.siida.fi).

RUNEBERG DAY 5 Feb
This day commemorates Finland's national poet. Flags are at half mast and people eat 'Runeberg tarts' (p111).

LASKIAINEN 7 weeks before Easter
Coinciding with Carnaval in other countries, people ski and toboggan down hills and enjoy other winter sports during this festival.

MARCH–APRIL

TAR SKI RACE early Mar
Long-distance cross-country ski race held in Oulu (www.tervahiihto.fi).

TAMPEREEN ELOKUVAJUHLAT early Mar
Respected international short-film festival in Tampere (www.tamperefilmfestival.fi).

LAHTI SKI GAMES early Mar
Ski-jumping and other winter shenanigans in the southern city of Lahti (www.lahtiskigames.com).

ICE-ANGLING MARATHON late Mar
Forty-eight hours of nonstop ice-fishing (www.oulutourism.fi).

REINDEER RACING FINAL last weekend in Mar or 1st weekend in Apr
The King's Cup in Inari is the highlight of the reindeer-racing season (www.paliskunnat.fi).

PÄÄSIÄINEN EASTER
On Easter Sunday people go to church, paint eggs, and eat *mämmi* (pudding of rye and malt).

APRIL JAZZ ESPOO
Jazz with big-name artists and big crowds, held in Espoo (www.apriljazz.fi, in Finnish).

TAMPERE BIENNALE
Festival featuring new Finnish music, held in even-numbered years only (www.tampere.fi/festival/music).

MAY

VAPPU 1 May
Traditionally a festival of students and workers, this also marks the beginning of summer, and is celebrated with plenty of alcohol and merrymaking.

IJAHIS IDJA last weekend in May
The annual Sámi music festival in Inari (www.ijahisidja.fi, in Finnish).

JUNE

PISPALA SCHOTTISCHE early Jun
International folk-dance festival held in Tampere (www.sottiisi.net).

HELSINKI DAY 12 Jun
Celebrations of the city's anniversary (www.hel.fi/helsinkipaiva, in Finnish).

KUOPIO TANSSII JA SOI mid-Jun
International dance festival held in Kuopio (www.kuopiodancefestival.fi).

PROVINSSIROCK mid-Jun
Big three-day rock festival held in Seinäjoki (www.provinssirock.fi).

MIDNIGHT SUN FILM FESTIVAL mid-Jun
Sodankylä hosts a big range of Finnish and international screenings (www.msfilmfestival.fi).

MIDSUMMER'S EVE & DAY weekend closest to 22 June
Juhannus (Midsummer) is the most important annual event for Finns. Celebrated with bonfires and dancing, and ornate poles are decorated and raised in Åland. People head to summer cottages to celebrate the longest day of the year.

JUTAJAISET late Jun
Celebration of Lapland folklore held in Rovaniemi (www.jutajaiset.fi).

WOODCARVING SYMPOSIUM late Jun or early Jul
Held every odd year in Kemijärvi (www.kemijarven-kuvanveistoviikot.fi).

MIKKELI MUSIC FESTIVAL   late Jun or early Jul
A week-long celebration of classical music (www
.mikkelimusic.net).

PRAASNIEKKA
These Orthodox celebrations are day-long religious and folk festivals held in North Karelia
and other eastern provinces between May and
September, most notably at the end of June.

JULY

SAVONLINNA OPERA FESTIVAL
A whole month of fabulous opera in a spectacular
castle setting (www.operafestival.fi).

IMATRA BIG BAND FESTIVAL   early Jul
Imatra, near the Russian border, draws international big bands for this festival (www.ibbf.fi).

RUISROCK   early Jul
Finland's oldest and arguably its best rock festival,
held in Turku (www.ruisrock.fi).

KIHAUS FOLK   early Jul
Rääkkylä's widely acclaimed festival of modern
and experimental Finnish folk music and dancing
(www.kihaus.fi).

TANGOMARKKINAT   early Jul
Finland's older generations converge on Seinäjoki
in this massive celebration of the tango (www
.tangomarkkinat.com).

**WIFE-CARRYING WORLD
CHAMPIONSHIPS**   early Jul
An unusual husband-and-wife team competition
in Sonkajärvi, with international participants and
beer prizes (www.sonkajarvi.fi).

SULKAVAN SUURSOUDUT   2nd Sun in Jul
Massive rowing festival and even bigger party
held in Sulkava (www.suursoudut.net).

JYVÄSKYLÄN KESÄ   mid-July
Jyväskylä's multifaceted arts festival (www.jy
vaskylankesa.fi).

PORI JAZZ FESTIVAL   mid-Jul
The port town of Pori springs to life with one of
Finland's most notable festivals (www.porijazz.fi).

ALANDIA JAZZ FESTIVAL   mid-Jul
Jazz greats play at waterside venues in Mariehamn
(www.alandiajazz.aland.fi).

TAMMERFEST   mid-Jul
Four days of rock concerts in various venues
around Tampere (www.tammerfest.fi).

GARLIC FESTIVAL   mid-Jul
Oulu's most pungent celebration, with everything
from garlic beer to garlic ice cream on offer (www
.oulunliikekeskus.fi).

RAUMA LACE WEEK   mid-Jul
Rauma hosts lace-making demonstrations and a
carnival (www.rauma.fi).

**KAUSTINEN FOLK MUSIC
FESTIVAL**   3rd week of Jul
A massive folk music and dance extravaganza in
Kaustinen (www.kaustinen.fi).

KOTKA MARITIME FESTIVAL   late Jul
Kotka's festival features music, sailing races and
cruises (www.meripaivat.com).

KUHMO CHAMBER MUSIC FESTIVAL   late Jul
An excellent fortnight of concerts featuring a fist-
ful of young and talented performers from around
Europe (www.kuhmofestival.fi).

SLEEPYHEAD DAY   27 Jul
After a vote by the townspeople, Naantali's laziest
person is rudely awakened by being dragged from
bed and thrown into the sea.

DOWN BY THE LAITURI   late Jul
Rock music festival held in Turku (www.dbtl.fi,
in Finnish).

AUGUST

HAMINA TATTOO   early Aug
Hamina's parade of military music, held in even
years only (www.haminatattoo.com).

NESTE RALLY FINLAND   most years early Aug
The Finnish leg of the World Rally Championship,
in Jyväskylä (www.nesteoilrallyfinland.fi).

LAPPEENRANTA MUSIC FESTIVAL   early Aug
Festival of international music, held in both
Lappeenranta and Lemi (www.lemi.fi).

GOLDPANNERS' FESTIVAL   early Aug
Tankavaara hosts its Goldpanning championships
and more (www.tankavaara.fi).

RAUMAN FESTIVO RAUMA   early Aug
Rauma hosts a chamber music festival (www.rau
manfestivo.fi, in Finnish).

ANKKAROCK VANTAA   early Aug
Big rock festival held in Vantaa (www.ankka
rock.fi).

SAVONLINNA BALLET FESTIVAL   early Aug
Four days of ballet in the Savonlinna castle (www
.savonlinnaballet.net, in Finnish).

**MOBILE PHONE THROWING WORLD
CHAMPIONSHIPS**   late Aug
Savonlinna's quirkiest festival allows participants
to indulge in a spot of Nokia-hurling (www.savon
linnafestivals.com).

**AIR GUITAR WORLD
CHAMPIONSHIPS**   late Aug
Oulu hosts this festival as part of a music video
festival (www.airguitarworldchampionships.com).

HELSINKI FESTIVAL   late Aug–early Sep
Head to the capital for this all-arts festival (www
.helsinginjuhlaviikot.fi).

SEPTEMBER

RUSKA SWING   early Sep
Kemijärvi's festival of swing music and dancing
(www.ruskaswing.fi, in Finnish).

SIBELIUS FESTIVAL   mid-Sep
Performances by the famous Lahti Symphony
Orchestra, honouring composer Jean Sibelius
(www.sinfonialahti.fi).

OCTOBER, NOVEMBER & DECEMBER

BALTIC HERRING MARKET   1st week of Oct
Traditional outdoor herring market, held in
Helsinki (www.portofhelsinki.fi).

**TAMPERE JAZZ
HAPPENING**   late Oct or early Nov
Finnish and international jazz musicians flock to
Tampere (www.tampere.fi).

ITSENÄISYYSPÄIVÄ   6 Dec
Finland celebrates its independence with torch-
light processions, fireworks and concerts.

LUCIA PARADE   13 Dec
Helsinki hosts a big parade for St Lucia's feast day.

JOULU
Pikkujoulu (little Christmas) parties, with plenty
of *glögi* (hot punch) consumed, dot the lead-up
to the main event, which features a family meal
on Christmas Eve.

Itineraries
CLASSIC ROUTES

ESSENTIAL SUOMI
Two to Three Weeks / Helsinki to Rovaniemi

Kick off in **Helsinki** (p77), prowling its buzzing design district. See the harbour – hit **Suomenlinna** (p87) or eat at an island restaurant – before hitting historic **Porvoo's** (p108) enchanting wooden buildings.

Next head towards **Lappeenranta** (p162) on the shores of Finland's largest lake, and home to an enormous sandcastle.

Gorgeous **Savonlinna** (p133) comes next. Its stunning castle hosts a magical opera festival and even if your trip doesn't coincide, it's a memorable town with plenty to do in the area: take your time.

You're in Lakeland, so why not continue by boat? A leisurely day's cruising gets you to **Kuopio** (p154), famous for *kalakukko* (rye loaf filled with tasty lakefish), and its convivial smoke sauna.

The high latitudes are in evidence once you get to **Oulu** (p281) – depending on the season, the sun barely sets or barely rises. It's one of Finland's liveliest towns, with a great summer marketplace.

From Oulu, head to **Kemi** (p315) to see the winter snow castle. Finally, to **Rovaniemi** (p308), base for any number of activities. Then off to explore Lapland or get the sleeper train back to Helsinki.

This highlights trip takes in the capital and a wide selection of Finnish landscapes and towns, from the pretty southern lakelands right up to Lapland's Arctic climes. This journey is about 1200km.

LAPP GOLD
One to Two Weeks / Rovaniemi Loop

In Rovaniemi, capital of Lapland, visit the excellent **Arktikum museum** (p308) to learn about these northern latitudes. Further south in Ranua, you can see some of the region's fauna at its **zoo** (p314).

Cut eastwards to **Ruka** (p298), a lively winter ski resort, and a trailhead of the **Karhunkierros** (p299), one of Finland's best trekking routes.

From here, go via **Kemijärvi** (p329) to **Sodankylä** (p330). Don't miss the wonderful old wooden church.

Heading north, you'll reach **Urho K Kekkonen (UKK) National Park** (p336), where you can try gold panning before striking out on a trek across the spectacular fells in this vast wilderness. Nearby **Saariselkä** (p334) is a good base for summer and winter activities.

One of the most intriguing towns in this region is **Inari** (p340), the capital of Finland's Sámi. It's a handicrafts centre and home to the memorable **Siida museum** (p340).

Next, head to **Lemmenjoki National Park** (p343), where treks and river trips call. Continue the loop towards northwest Finland, ending up at **Hetta** (p324), another Sámi town, with plenty of local walks. From here, if you have time, take a detour up the 'arm' of Finland to remote **Kilpisjärvi** (p328), in the shadow of fearsome Norwegian mountains and the smaller bulk of Saana Fell, a rewarding climb with some memorable views over three nations.

Then, onwards to **Muonio** (p323). In winter you can go husky-sledding, but even in summer it's worth meeting the loveable dogs. From here, return to Rovaniemi, perhaps stopping to ski or rent a summer cottage at busy **Levi** (p321) or peaceful **Pyhä** (p332).

A thorough exploration of the wonders of Lapland and its landscapes, with plenty of opportunity for trekking, skiing or sledding as well as learning about Sámi culture and the Arctic environment. This journey totals around 1600km.

ROADS LESS TRAVELLED

THE WEST COAST   One to Two Weeks / Helsinki to Oulu

Popular with locals, Finland's west coast doesn't attract many foreign visitors, who tend to prefer the charms of the lakes and reindeer.

After Helsinki, stop at **Lohja** (p115) for its church and mining museum. The industrial theme continues with the pretty ironworks at **Fagervik** (p116) and **Fiskars** (p119), which are both near the family-friendly seaside town of **Ekenäs** (p215). Then head southwest to the noble wooden villas of **Hanko** (p121), where St Petersburg society once summered.

Turku (p215) has many drawcards, as does the surrounding **archipelago** (p229) and picturesque **Naantali** (p224).

Uusikaupunki (p231) has a museum that deserves a prize for ironic humour, while **Rauma's Old Town** (p234) features charming wooden buildings. Moving north, busy **Pori** (p237) hosts a pumping jazz festival.

The next bit of coast is known as 'Parallel Sweden': **Kristinestad** (p269) is one of several places in Finland with a Swedish-speaking majority. **Kaskinen** (p270) or **Närpes** (p271) are other tranquil stops. **Vaasa** (p263) has an excellent museum, and is popular for its spa complex and adventure park.

Nykarleby (p276), famous for its waffles and painted church, is a good stop on the way to **Jakobstad** (p274), whose old town rivals Rauma's for beauty. Reaching **Kokkola** (p277), with its boat bar and fascinating mineral museum, you'll definitely feel back in Finnish Finland. Beyond here, a stretch of beautiful coastline runs north to **Oulu** (p281), with **Kalajoki** (p278), one of the world's most northerly beach resorts, on the way.

This 1100km coastal trip is an excellent way to appreciate the differences between the Swedish- and Finnish-speaking communities, not to mention the chance to see picture-perfect wooden towns, sparkling blue water and several more-than-decent beaches.

BORDERLANDS   One to Two Weeks / Helsinki to Kuusamo

Russia's presence looms large in Finnish history and consciousness. This trip takes in areas that have been affected by this relationship.

From Helsinki, head to little **Ruotsinpyhtää** (p126), an attractive village whose river once marked the boundary between the Swedish empire and Russia. Then **Kotka** (p126), a busy port near one of the tsar's favourite fishing spots. Heading towards the modern-day border, the fortress at **Hamina** (p129) was erected by the Swedes to halt the Russian advance in the early 18th century. The plan ultimately failed.

Lappeenranta (p162) suffered a similar fate, with the Russians adding the finishing touches to a fortress originally designed to keep them out. This is the beginning of Karelia, an area where a lot of the most bitter fighting of the 1939 Winter War took place; you'll see numerous memorials on this route.

Heading north, you'll pass through cities largely destroyed during the Winter and Continuation Wars. At **Imatra** (p168), you can see Russia from the Valtionhotelli's top floor, while at **Joensuu** (p171), visit the Carelicum museum to learn more about the area.

From **Ilomantsi** (p174), in deepest Karelia, head out to **Hattuvaara** (p177), a very Orthodox area. You can access the border zone here – Finland's easternmost point. Further north, **Kuhmo** (p291) was where artists and writers set out from, seeking inspiration in the deep forest wilderness further east, which is now part of Russia and much mourned by the Finns. North of here, more deadly Winter War battles took place on the Raate Rd around **Suomussalmi** (p296) where there's an exhibition and moving memorial to the fallen. Then to **Kuusamo** (p295), from which you can fly back to Helsinki.

A 1000km exploration of Finland's eastern zone, shadowing the border with Russia, whose influence has always been very important. This heads through the heartland of divided Karelia, a symbol of Finnish independence, wilderness and loss.

TAILORED TRIPS

OUT & ABOUT

Finland's wonderful portfolio of protected wilderness areas makes for perfect exploration, and its comprehensive network of camping grounds, complete with tent pitches, simple cabins, and full-service cottages with sauna, means that heading out of town is the wallet-friendly way to go too.

While many of the great treks, canoeing routes and national parks are in the north, you can start with a taste of things to come while you are still in Helsinki. In Espoo, a short trip from the capital, is the **Nuuksio National Park** (p112), a haven for several rare bird species and a great place to go for a stroll in the woods. While you're in the south, you could also investigate one of the four maritime parks, such as the **Southwestern Archipelago National Park** (p229). You can visit the archipelago on regular boat trips from Turku or Hanko, but to really explore it you should charter a boat.

In the central belt of Finland, the sheer quantity of lakes invites watery exploration. Grab a canoe for a couple of hours, or go the whole hog and take a week out to explore the **Kolovesi** (p143) and **Linnansaari National Parks** (p142). If you are lucky, you may even glimpse the rare Saimaa ringed seal, which adapted to a freshwater environment after being cut off from the sea by the rising land.

East of here, head to Karelia: the **Patvinsuo National Park** (p180) for excellent trekking, or hit the **Nurmes** (p184) area for a wide choice of activities including excellent rafting.

The Kainuu and Koillismaa areas of northeastern Finland are made for the active. The ski resort of **Ruka** (p298) is one of Finland's major ski resorts but has huge scope for outdoor activity year-round. It's the finishing point for Finland's most popular single trek, the Karhunkierros (Bear's Ring). While to do it in its entirety will take you up to five days, you can easily shorten it to three days, or just try the Little Bear's Ring day walk. The **Oulankajoki** (p302) and **Kitkajoki** (p302) also draw canoeists and kayakers to the area, with routes ranging from gentle to hairy. Bear-watching excursions depart from nearby **Kuusamo** (p295) to the forests near the Russian border.

Lapland's wide expanses are the location of Finland's park heavyweights; superb destinations for multiday treks, with regularly spaced wilderness huts and camping grounds if you wish to stay overnight.

One of the most important and popular areas is the **Urho K Kekkonen (UKK) National Park** (p336), a place of classic Lappish fells – a magnet for trekkers of all abilities. Although the well-known routes get busy in summer, there's some awesome wilderness here where few people venture.

In the northwest is the lovely **Pallas-Yllästunturi National Park** (p325), with comparatively easy trekking southwards from the Sámi town of Hetta. You have to be taken by boat to the starting point, so it feels like you're kissing civilisation goodbye for good, but the trek ends happily at a very hospitable hotel.

Finland's northernmost park is **Lemmenjoki** (p343). This has an excellent network of trails, some decent places to stay, and the chance to make your fortune (or at least dirty your clothes) by panning for gold. Not far away, the **Kevo Reserve** (p344) offers a spectacular gorge walk where you are free to carry a tent on your back.

FINLAND FOR KIDS

In **Helsinki** (p82) options are many, with boat trips on the harbour to see Suomenlinna's submarine, a day at Linnanmäki amusement park, or a short bus ride to the great Serena waterpark at **Espoo** (p111).

Other attractions and theme parks designed specifically with the young in mind include Wasalandia and Tropiclandia in **Vaasa** (p263), Särkänniemi in **Tampere** (p203) and Rauhalahti estate in **Kuopio** (p154). And that's not to mention the Moomins, who have their World at **Naantali** (p224) as well as a museum in Tampere, where kids will also enjoy the Spy Museum. **Oulu** (p281) has the enticing Tietomaa science museum, while the magnificent castle at **Savonlinna** (p133) should appeal to the young 'uns. If it gets the thumbs-down, there's always the world's biggest sandcastle down the road in **Lappeenranta** (p162).

Getting active, the **Oravareitti** (p144), or 'Squirrel Route', is a great two-day canoeing trip, one of many river and lake routes across the country suitable for juvenile paddlers.

Lapland is winter wonderland for the young, with the snow castle in **Kemi** (p315), and sled trips, tobogganing, plenty of material for snowball fights and children's runs at ski resorts like **Levi** (p321). In summer, pan for gold in **Lemmenjoki** (p343) or **Tankavaara** (p336), or meet **reindeer** (p330) and **huskies** (p323) at many places across the region. And the most famous resident of **Napapiiri** (p314), Santa, is in his grotto year-round.

WRITERS & ARTISTS

In the exciting decades leading up to independence writers, painters and composers explored the meaning of Finland, many travelling to the wilderness for inspiration.

Start in Helsinki, where the **Ateneum** (p83) will acquaint you with some of these fascinating characters' work. Grab a copy of the *Kalevala* while in town, and have a drink at the **Hotel Kämp** (p96), where artists thrashed out the nature of Finnishness during epic piss-ups.

Porvoo (p108), home to many artists, and Espoo's **Gallen-Kallela Museum** (p111) are musts, as is the journey to **Sibelius' home** (p106) near Järvenpää. Not far away is **Lohja**, close to the rustic cottage (p116) where Lönnrot, creator of the *Kalevala*, was born.

Sibelius' birthplace in Hämeenlinna (p196) is now a museum, and some memorable interpretations of his music can be heard at **Lahti** (p190).

Definitely investigate **Visavuori** (p199) and **Kalela** (p211), studios of sculptor Emil Wickström and painter Akseli Gallen-Kallela respectively, as well as the wonderful art gallery at **Mänttä** (p212).

Then on to Karelia, from which these women and men drew inspiration. From **Nurmes** (p184) you can plan expeditions of your own, exploring the wilderness by foot, canoe or husky-drawn sled. Nearby **Koli** (p183) enchanted Sibelius, while further north, **Kuhmo** (p291) is the place to learn more about the *Kalevala* and its massive impact on Finnish history, and catch the great chamber music festival.

History

Finnish history is the story of a people who for centuries were a wrestling mat between two heavyweights, Sweden and Russia, and the nation's eventful emergence from their grip to become one of the world's most progressive and prosperous nations.

EARLY DAYS

For more details on Finnish history, http://virtual .finland.fi has excellent essays written by experts on various periods.

What is now Finland was inhabited way back in the mists of time: pre-Ice Age remains have been found at Susiluola cave, near Kristiinankaupunki, dating from some 120,000 years ago. But the big chill erased most traces and sent folk scurrying south to warmer climes. Only at the retreat of the formidable glaciers, which had blanketed the country 3km deep, was a human presence re-established.

One of the best places to learn about the Stone Age in Finland is the Kierikki museum near Oulu, p288

The first post-thaw inhabitants had spread themselves over most of Finland by about 9000 BC. At this period too, the Baltic was formed, as the sea breached into what was once a huge freshwater lake. The people used stone tools and hunted elk and beaver in the fertile forests.

Archaeologists generally find it easier to identify broad groups of people once pottery starts appearing in excavated sites, and it's now clear that a new influence arrived from the east into southern Finland about 5000 years ago. Because Finland was the furthest point west that this culture reached, it's widely suggested that they brought a Finnic language with them from Russia. If so, the people living in Finland at this time are the ancestors of the Finns and the Sámi.

Even as early as the Bronze Age, a sharp differentiation in culture between the agricultural south and west is evident, with strong trade contacts across the Baltic, and between the hunters of the east and north. In this, it's tempting to see the beginnings of a pattern that has characterised all of Finnish history: Finland as meeting point (and sometimes a flashpoint) between Russian and north European cultural influences.

In the 1st century AD, the Roman historian Tacitus mentioned a tribe called the Fenni, whom he basically described as wild savages who had neither homes nor horses. He might have been referring to the Sámi or their forebears, whose nomadic existence better fits this description than that of the agricultural peoples of the south. Genetic studies indicate that today's Sámi are descended mostly from a small original group, and some claim that a divergence of pre-Finnish and Sámi cultures can be seen as far back as 700 BC. Nomadic cultures leave little archaeological evidence, but it seems the Sámi migrated gradually northwards, probably having been displaced by

TIMELINE

120,000 BC	10,000 BC	3000 BC
Present-day Finland is inhabited, but its residents, of whom we know little, are eventually evicted by the last Ice Age.	The retreat of the last Ice Age's glaciers open up the northern lands once more to human habitation. The forests and lakes that replace the ice provide tempting hunting and fishing grounds.	The appearance of distinctive 'Comb Ware' pottery indicates the presence of a new culture that seems to come from the Volga region to the east, perhaps bringing a pre-Finnish language with it.

the southerners and the advance of agriculture into former hunting lands. Verses of the *Kalevala* (see boxed text, p44), which is derived from ancient oral tradition, seem to refer to this conflictual relationship.

In the south, two main Finnish tribes led a warring coexistence in the 1st millennium AD. The Karelians in the east had extensive cultural contact with Russia, while the Häme tribe of the west had trading contacts with Viking groups in Sweden and Åland, as well as other Baltic peoples. Many forts and burial grounds from this period remain, and Hämeenlinna, Turku and Halikko were important trading posts.

SWEDISH RULE

The nascent kingdom of Sweden saw the territory today occupied by Finland as a natural direction for extending its influence in the Baltic and countering the growing power of Novgorod in the east (later to become Russia). Missionary activity had begun in the 12th century, and legend tells of an Englishman, Bishop Henry, leading an expedition of baptism that ended stickily when he was murdered by Lalli, a disgruntled peasant. Swedish and Christian influence continued to spread in Finland, which had a population of around 50,000 at the time.

Things started to heat up in the 13th century. The Pope called a crusade against the Häme tribe, which was increasingly influenced both religiously and politically from Novgorod, and Russian and Swedish forces clashed several times in the first battles of an ongoing saga.

Swedish settlement began in earnest around the middle of the century when Birger Jarl established fortifications at Häme and Turku, among other places. The cathedral at Turku was also under construction and this city was to be Finland's pre-eminent centre for most of its history. The Swedish knights and nobles in charge of these operations set a pattern for a Swedish-speaking bourgeoisie in Finland, which lasted well into the 20th century, but other Swedes, including farmers and fishers, gradually settled, mainly along Finland's Baltic coast. A number of incentives were given to encourage new settlers, many of whom were veterans of the Swedish army.

Sweden's squabbles with Novgorod went on for two centuries, but it was the treaties drawn up by the two powers that defined the spheres of influence. Sweden gained control of southwest Finland and much of the west coast, while Novgorod controlled Karelia, spreading the Orthodox faith and Byzantine culture in the region.

In 1527 King Gustav Vasa of Sweden adopted the Lutheran faith and confiscated much of the property of the Catholic Church. The Finnish Reformation was ushered in by Mikael Agricola (born 1510), who studied with Martin Luther in Germany, and returned to Finland in 1539 to translate parts of the Bible into Finnish. He was also the first person to properly record the traditions and animist religious rites of ethnic Finns. However,

Duke Karl, regent of Finland, didn't care much for the family business. Campaigning against his nephew the king, he encouraged a peasant mutiny in 1596 and finally deposed the king, exacting brutal revenge on his opponents.

AD 100	**1155**	**1323**
The Roman historian Tacitus refers to the 'Fenni', most likely the Sámi, in the first known historical mention of the area. He isn't especially complimentary about their lack of permanent housing arrangements.	The first Christianising expedition is launched from Sweden against the pagan Finns. Further expeditions follow, and Finland is effectively under Swedish dominion for over six centuries.	The Peace of Oreshek, signed by Sweden and Novgorod at Pähkinäsaari, establishes a frontier in the Karelian Isthmus, and delineates permitted spheres of influence still evident in present-day Finland.

his hardline Protestant attitudes meant that most of the frescoes in medieval churches were whitewashed (only to be rediscovered some 400 years later in relatively good condition).

Sweden started another chess game with Russia in Savo and Kainuu, using its Finnish subjects as pawns to settle areas well beyond the agreed boundaries. Russia retaliated, and most of the new settlements were razed in the bloody Kainuu War of the late 16th century.

The 17th century was Sweden's golden age, when it controlled much of the Baltic. Finland was put under the control of various governors.

During the Thirty Years' War in Europe, political power in Finland was exercised by Count Per Brahe, who travelled around the country at this time and founded many towns. He was a larger-than-life figure who made his own rules: once censured for having illegally bagged an elk, he responded curtly that it had been on its last legs and he had killed it out of mercy.

In the middle of the century, Sweden decreed modernisation in Finland. A chain of castle defences was built to protect against Russian attacks, and new factory areas were founded. The *bruk* (ironworks precinct) was often a self-contained society, which harvested the power of water, built ironworks, and built systems for the transportation of firewood. Social institutions, such as schools and churches, were also established.

As well as being the biggest landowner in Sweden, Per Brahe was a gourmet and wrote his own cookbook, which he used to take with him on his travels and insist it was followed to the letter.

Although Finland never experienced feudal serfdom to the extent seen in Russia, ethnic Finns were largely peasant farmers forced to lease land from Swedish landlords.

In 1697 the Swede Karl XII ascended the throne. Within three years he was drawn into the Great Northern War (1700–21), which marked the beginning of the end of the Swedish empire.

FROM SWEDEN TO RUSSIA

Peter the Great took advantage of Sweden's troubles on other fronts, and, though losing early engagements, soon stormed through Finland, a land that had recently been decimated by famine. From 1714 to 1721 Russia occupied Finland, a time still referred to as the Great Wrath, when several thousand Finns were killed and many more were taken into slavery. The 1721 Treaty of Uusikaupunki brought peace at a cost – Sweden lost south Karelia to Russia.

Finland again paid the price for thwarted Swedish ambitions in the war of 1741–43; Russia again occupied Finland, for a period called the Lesser Wrath. The Treaty of Turku in 1743 ended the conflict by ceding parts of Savo to Russia.

Only after the 1740s did the Swedish government decide to impose measures which were designed to improve Finland's socioeconomic situation. Defences were strengthened by building fortresses off Helsinki's coast (Sveaborg, now Suomenlinna) and at Loviisa, and new towns were founded.

1527	1637	1640
The Reformation begins. King Gustav Vasa of Sweden adopts the Lutheran faith and confiscates much of the property of the Catholic Church. Finland's main Reformation figure, Mikael Agricola, returns from Germany in 1539.	Per Brahe becomes governor of Finland and goes on to found many towns. 'I was well pleased with the land and the land with me' was his modest assessment. Meanwhile, Finnish cavalry earn a fearsome reputation in the Thirty Years' War.	Finland's first university is founded in Turku, which was the country's principal city, until Helsinki was made capital in 1812.

Later, Sweden and Russia were to clash repeatedly under King Gustav III, until he was murdered by a group of Swedish aristocrats in 1792. Gustav IV Adolf, who reigned from 1796, was drawn into the disastrous Napoleonic Wars and lost his crown in 1809.

Tsar Alexander I signed a treaty with Napoleon and then attacked Finland in 1808. Following a bloody war, Sweden ceded Finland to Russia in 1809. Alexander pledged to respect Finnish customs and institutions; Finland kept its legal system and its Lutheran faith, and became a semi-autonomous grand duchy with its own senate. At first, Russia encouraged development, and Finland benefited from the annexation. The capital was transferred to Helsinki, as it was felt that Turku was too close to Sweden.

Finland was still very much an impoverished rural society in the 19th century, and travel to the interior, especially in Lapland, could be an arduous journey of weeks by riverboat and overland. The tar and paper industries produced revenue from the vast forests, but were controlled by magnates in Baltic and Bothnian ports such as Oulu, which flourished while the hinterland remained poor. As part of the Russian Empire, Finland was involved in the Crimean War (1853–56), with British troops destroying fortifications at Loviisa, Helsinki and Bomarsund.

> Tar, used to caulk sailing ships, was a major 19th-century Finnish export, produced by burning pine trees in a tar pit; the trees had had their bark removed four years earlier to stimulate resin production.

During the second half of the 19th century, the Finnish independence movement gained credibility, and increasing attempts at Russification led to growing unrest.

A NATION BORN

Early stirrings of Finnish nationalism could be heard in the 19th century. Dissatisfaction with the Swedish administration came to a head with a letter written from officers of the Finnish army to the queen of Sweden questioning the legality of the war they were pursuing against Russia. Meanwhile, academic studies of Finnish cultural traditions were creating a base on which future nationalistic feelings could be founded.

The famous phrase 'Swedes we are not, Russians we will not become, so let us be Finns', though of uncertain origin, encapsulated the growing sense of Finnishness. The Fennoman movement aimed to embrace Finnish culture as a way of maintaining identity despite the heavy arm of Russia around Suomi shoulders: artistic achievements like Lönnrot's *Kalevala* and Runeberg's poem *Our Land*, which became the national anthem, acted as standards to rally around. As Russia tightened its grip with a policy of Russification, workers, and artists such as Sibelius, began to be inspired against the growing oppression, and the nation became emotionally ripe for independence.

> Though still part of Russia, Finland issued its first postage stamps in 1856 and its own currency, the markka, in 1860.

In 1906, the Eduskunta parliament was introduced in Finland with universal and equal suffrage (Finland was the first country in Europe to grant women full political rights); however, Russian political oppression continued and poverty was endemic. In search of work and a better life, many Finns

1700	1714	1741–43
Karl XII of Sweden is drawn into the Great Northern War, which is to mark the beginning of the end for the Swedish empire.	Russia occupies Finland, marking the beginning of the seven years known as the Great Wrath. When peace is made, it retains southern Karelia.	Russian again occupies Finland, in a period known as the Lesser Wrath.

LENIN IN FINLAND

One man who spent plenty of time in Finland was none other than Vladimir Ilyich Lenin, father of the Russian Revolution. Having had a Finnish cellmate during his exile in Siberia, he then regularly visited the country for conferences of the Social Democratic Party. At one of these, in 1905, he met Stalin for the first time. Lenin then lived near Helsinki for a period in 1907 before he was forced to flee the Russian Empire. In a Hollywood-style escape, he jumped off a moving train to avoid tsarist agents, and was then sheltered in Turku, before being moved to the remote island communities of the southwest. Lenin found shelter on Parainen, but fearing capture, he walked across thin ice with a local guide to Nauvo (there's a famous painting of this in the Hermitage in St Petersburg), from which he finally jumped on a steamer to Stockholm.

Lenin entered Finland again via Tornio in 1917. He returned pretty sharply after the abortive first revolution, living in a tent for a while in Iljitsevo, before going back to Russia and destiny.

Lenin, even before having visited Finland, had always agitated for Finnish independence from Russia, a conviction which he maintained. In December 1917, he signed the declaration of Finnish independence, and, without his support, it is doubtful that the nation would have been born at that time. The Lenin Museum in Tampere (p203) is the place to visit to learn more about Lenin in Finland.

---

moved south to Helsinki or emigrated to North America in the first decades of the 20th century.

The Russian Revolution of October 1917 enabled the Finnish parliament to declare independence on 6 December of that year. Although Russia recognised the new nation, it hoped for a parallel workers' uprising, fomenting dissent and supplying arms to that end.

Following an attack by Russian-armed Finnish Reds on the civil guards in Vyborg, the Finnish Civil War flared in late January 1918. During 108 days of heavy fighting, approximately 30,000 Finns were killed. The Reds, comprising the rising working class, aspired to a Russian-style socialist revolution while retaining independence. The nationalist Whites, led by CGE Mannerheim, dreamed of monarchy and sought to emulate Germany.

The Whites, with substantial German help, eventually gained victory and the war ended in May 1918. Friedrich Karl, Prince of Hessen, was elected king of Finland by the Eduskunta on 9 October 1918, but the defeat of imperial Germany a month later made Finland choose a republican state model, under its first president, KJ Ståhlberg. Relations with the Soviets were normalised by the Treaty of Tartu in 1920, which saw Finnish territory expand to its largest point ever, including the other 'arm', the Petsamo region in the far northeast.

Though internal struggles continued, and despite the crushing blows of WWII, the young Finland wasn't to be suppressed and it gained fame internationally as a brave new nation. However minor they may appear, events such as Finland's Winter War heroics, Paavo Nurmi's distinguished career as

> In the first elections in 1907, 19 female members were elected to the Eduskunta, the first woman MPs in the world. Finland has been a trailblazer for equality in politics ever since.

> Mannerheim had a fascinating life divided into several distinct phases. Check out www .mannerheim.fi for an online biography.

1808	**1827**	**1853**
Finland is invaded and occupied by Russia, with Sweden powerless to resist. Finland becomes a grand duchy of the Russian Empire in 1809; Tsar Alexander I promises to respect its autonomy at the Diet of Porvoo.	Elias Lönnrot makes the first of his song-collecting journeys into remote Karelian forests, which would culminate in the publication of *Kalevala*, the national epic.	The Crimean War sees British forces mix with Russian-owned Finland. Strategic coastal fortresses on the Baltic are destroyed.

a long-distance runner, Ester Toivonen's Miss Europe title in 1933, Artturi Virtanen winning the Nobel Prize for Chemistry in 1945, the successful Helsinki Olympics of 1952, and the plaudits won by Finnish designers in international expositions, are all events that fostered national confidence, helped Finland to feel that it belonged at the dinner table of international nations, and gave it strength to keep its head above water during the difficult Cold War period that followed.

THE COLD WAR

The year of the Helsinki Olympics, 1952, was also the year that Finland completed paying its heavy war reparations to the Soviet Union. These were mostly rendered in machinery and ships, and in fact had a positive effect, as they established the heavy engineering industry that eventually stabilised the Finnish postwar economy.

Finnish society changed profoundly during this period. In the 1940s, Finland's was still a predominantly agricultural population, but the privations of the war, which sent people to the towns and cities in search of work, as well as nearly half a million Karelian refugees, sparked an acute housing crisis. The old wooden town centres were mostly demolished to make way for apartment blocks, and roads were widened to allow for motor-vehicle traffic. New suburbs appeared almost overnight around Helsinki; conversely, areas in the north and east lost most of their young people (often half their population) to domestic emigration.

From the end of the war until the early '90s, the overriding political issue was a familiar one: balance between east and west. Stalin's 'friendship and co-operation' treaty of 1948, though explicitly referring to mutual defence in the event of German aggression, was used by the USSR throughout the Cold War period as a coercion tool, in an attempt to limit Finland's interaction with the West.

A savvy political head was needed to negotiate these choppy waters, and Finland found it in the astute if controversial figure of Urho K Kekkonen, president from 1956 to 1981 and a master of diplomacy. He believed that Finland would be more likely to achieve its aims of closer links with Western Europe by maintaining close ties with the Soviets.

Canny and unorthodox, Kekkonen realised that he was the devil the Kremlin knew, and he used this to his advantage. Similarly, he did so with the West's fear that Finland would fall completely under the sway of the USSR. For example, he signed a free-trade agreement with EFTA in 1961 which brought Finland closer to a European orbit, but also signed a parallel agreement for preferential trade with the Soviets. Neither side liked it, but neither wanted to risk 'losing' Finland to the other side.

Kekkonen and his government had a close relationship with many of the KGB's big men in Finland, and political nominations were submitted to

1899	1917	1939
The Tsar implements a policy of Russification in Finland, attempting to impose the Russian language on the country, among other moves. Widespread protests result and campaigns for independence gain strength.	Finland declares independence from the Soviet Union. Shortly afterwards, the Finnish Civil War breaks out between the communist Reds and the establishment Whites.	The Winter War sees the Soviet Union invade Finland. Fifteen weeks of fighting in bitter subzero conditions sees Finland defeated and forced to cede a substantial amount of territory.

THE WINTER WAR AND ITS CONTINUATION

Diplomatic manoeuvrings in Europe in the 1930s meant that Finland, inexperienced in the sinuous negotiations of Great Power politics, had a few difficult choices to make. The security threat posed by the Soviet Union meant that some factions were in favour of developing closer ties with Nazi Germany, while others favoured rapprochement with Moscow. On 23 August 1939, the Soviet and German foreign ministers, Molotov and Ribbentrop, stunned the world by signing a nonaggression pact, which gave the Soviet Union a free hand in Estonia, Latvia and Finland. In a series of talks with JK Paasikivi, later to become Finnish president, the USSR argued that its security required a slice of southeastern Karelia and the right to build some Baltic bases on Finnish soil. Finland refused, and the Red Army was on the march. On 30 November 1939, the Winter War between Finland and the Soviet Union began.

This was a harsh winter – temperatures reached -40°C and soldiers died in their thousands. To its people, Finland resisted heroically, with its mobile skiing troops conducting successful guerrilla-style assaults in small groups. Stalin, to his surprise, was forced to send more and more divisions to the front, with some 600,000 eventually being committed. After 105 days of fighting in the harshest imaginable conditions, Finnish forces were defeated. In the Treaty of Moscow (March 1940), Finland was forced to cede the Karelian Isthmus, together with the eastern Salla and Kuusamo regions and some islands: in total nearly one-tenth of its territory. Over 400,000 Karelian refugees flooded across the new border into Finland.

In the following months, the Soviet Union attempted to persuade Finland for more territory. Isolated from Western allies, Finland turned to Germany for help and allowed the transit of German troops. When hostilities broke out between Germany and the Soviets in June 1941, German troops were already on Finnish soil, and the Continuation War between Finland and the Red Army followed. In the fighting that followed, the Finns began to resettle Karelia. When Soviet forces staged a huge comeback in the summer of 1944, Finnish president Risto Ryti, who had promised Ribbentrop that Finland would not negotiate peace with Russia without German agreement, then resigned with Mannerheim taking his place. Mannerheim negotiated an armistice with the Russians, ceding Finland's 'other arm', the Petsamo area of the Kola peninsula, and ordered the evacuation of German troops. Finland then waged a bitter war in Lapland to oust the Germans, who staged a 'scorched earth' retreat from the country until the general peace in the spring of 1945.

Against the odds, Finland had remained independent, but at a heavy price: the territorial losses of 1940 and 1944 were ratified at the Peace of Paris in February 1947, and heavy war reparations were ordered to be paid to the Soviet Union. Many in Finland are still bitter about the loss of these territories. Nevertheless, the resistance against the might of the Red Army is something of which many Finns are still proud.

Moscow for approval within a framework of 'friendly coexistence'. Many Finns regard his era with embarrassment, believing that Kekkonen abased the country by such close contact with the Bear, and that his grip on power and web of behind-the-scenes manoeuvrings were uncomfortably reminiscent of the Kremlin itself. Press and public seemed unwilling to criticise the USSR

1948	**1950**	**1952**
The 'friendship and co-operation' treaty is signed between Finland and the Soviet Union.	Urho K Kekkonen becomes prime minister for the first time. In 1956, he is elected to the position of president, which he holds for 25 years.	Helsinki hosts the summer Olympic Games. Finland completes its war reparation payments of US$300,000,000 to the USSR as decreed by the Peace of Paris in 1947.

too much, or ask the thorny questions about the real nature of Finland's relationship with it. Conversely, Kekkonen presided over a period in which the nation moved from an impoverished agricultural state to a modern European democracy with a watertight welfare system and healthy economy, all in the shadow of a great power whose actions in Eastern Europe had given ample reason for Finland to tread with extreme caution.

After Kekkonen's resignation due to ill health at 81, the Soviets continued to dabble in Finnish politics, mostly with the aim of reducing US influence and preventing Finland joining what is now the EU. That particular chapter of Finland's long and complicated relationship with its eastern neighbour came to a close with the collapse of the USSR.

MODERN FINLAND

Following the USSR's collapse, a load was lifted from Finland, and the government quickly recognised the Baltic countries of Estonia, Latvia and Lithuania when they declared independence (since then its proximity to and linguistic links with Estonia have established a 'special relationship'). But the early 1990s weren't the easiest of times. The economy, like many in the Western world, went through a cooling-off period. The bubble of the 1980s had burst, the Soviet Union disappeared with debts unpaid, the markka was devalued, unemployment jumped from 3% to 20% and the tax burden grew alarmingly.

However, Finland could finally integrate itself fully with Europe. In a national referendum on 16 October 1994, 57% of voters gave the go-ahead to join the EU. Since January 1995, Finland has prospered, and was one of the first countries to adopt the euro in January 2002.

Balancing power between the president and the parliament had long been on the agenda since Kekkonen's monarchlike presidency and in 1999 a new constitution was approved limiting certain presidential powers. The first to take the wheel under the new order was Tarja Halonen of the Social Democratic Party, elected Finland's first female president in 2000. Referred to affectionately as Muumi Mamma (Moominmummy), she is well loved by many Finns, and was re-elected in 2006 for a further six years. The prime minister since 2003, Matti Vanhanen, of the Centre Party, heads a centre-right coalition government that was formed in 2007.

In the new millennium, Finland has boomed on the back of a strong technology sector, the traditionally important forestry industry, design and manufacturing, and, increasingly, tourism. It's a major success story of the new Europe with a strong economy, robust social values, and superlow crime and corruption. It consistently ranks highly in quality-of-life indices and has in recent years outperformed its traditionally superior neighbour Sweden in many areas.

Russia is, as ever, still high on the agenda. Finland's geographical proximity and close historical relationship with its neighbour gave it a head start

A *kotiryssä*, or Russian contact, was crucial for politicians of ambition in Cold War Finland, when much career advancement was under Moscow's control. But those friendly dinners on the Kremlin's tab could look a little treasonous if the vodka loosened your tongue...

David Kirby's recently published *A Concise History of Finland* is a thorough overview, focused on dispassionately (though never dully) analysing political contexts rather than discussing social history or bringing to life key personalities.

1973	1995	2000
The Delegation for Sámi affairs, the beginnings of the Sámi parliament, convenes for the first time. Finland signs a trade agreement with the EEC despite Soviet pressure.	After a referendum with a 57% 'yes' vote, Finland joins the EU in January.	Finland elects Tarja Halonen as its first female president. She proves a popular figure and is re-elected in 2006 for a further six years.

in dealing with post-Soviet Moscow, and the trade relationship remains close between the two countries. Many Finnish companies contract much of their business to Russia, where wages and overheads are lower, while Russian labour and tourism both make important contributions to the Finnish economy. Nevertheless, many Finns are still suspicious of Russia and Vladimir Putin's brand of nationalism: the Winter War has not been forgotten. National service, border patrols, and the army in general are taken seriously in Finland.

Though Finland has experienced far less immigration than most European countries, immigration has increased in recent years and has been an issue that has raised headlines.

In some parts of the country, relations between Finns and minority groups can be somewhat strained; however, when compared with similar countries, Finland experiences few serious racist incidents.

Finland's own indigenous people, the Sámi, have been afforded greater recognition in the last three decades, with the establishment of a Finnish Sámi parliament and the enshrinement of their languages in regional laws. However, disputes between reindeer herders and forestry firms in the north have ignited debate as to whether Sámi interests continue to come second to those of the country's timber industry.

Despite the challenges ahead, Finland has a right to feel just a wee bit pleased with itself. For a cold and remote, sparsely populated forest nation, it's done rather well. Though there has been concern that Finland's powerful economy is overly reliant on the success of Nokia (p41), the rise of this humble manufacturer of rubber tyres and cable insulation to communications giant parallels the transformation of Finland from war-ravaged farming nation to wealthy technological innovator.

Finland's commitment to nuclear power has divided opinion in northern Europe, with 29% of its energy supplied by the reactors, with more in production. Hydroelectricity is also important, supplying some 15% of production.

Finland's charismatic, outspoken but highly intelligent foreign minister, Alexander Stubb (www .alexstubb.com), has both impressed and ruffled a few feathers in Europe, and is tipped for higher office in the future.

2002

Along with several other European countries, Finland adopts the euro, bidding farewell to the markka after 142 years.

2006

The nation celebrates as outrageous horror metal band Lordi blow away the syrupy competition to win the Eurovision Song Contest.

2008

In the second such incident in less than a year, Matti Saari, aged 22, goes on a shooting spree in a vocational college, killing 10 before turning the gun on himself.

The Culture

THE NATIONAL PSYCHE

Finns define themselves by *sisu*, often translated as 'guts', or resilience to survive hardship. This toughness is down to the ongoing struggles with a harsh environment and a history of Russian and Swedish border disputes. While both Russia and Sweden have influenced Finland, Finns are staunchly independent. Any school child will proudly tell you that Suomi (the Finnish word for Finland) is not a part of Scandinavia, but is a Nordic country.

Many Finns joke that they invented text messaging so they didn't have to talk to each other – so the 'silent Finn' stereotype does have some truth to it. Certainly Finns believe in comfortable silences, so you may find yourself in a conversation that dies off naturally without the need to jumpstart it with talk of the weather. A quiet spell of 20 minutes in a sauna with your best friend is perfectly normal. This is not to say Finns don't talk. Finnish women are known for their ability to talk as they inhale and in conversation you'll find that Finnish words will fly by far too quickly for you to pick up their meaning. Finns generally have a dark, self-deprecating sense of humour and may just be saving their words for a well-timed jibe.

But there is a depressive streak to Finns. The bleakness of winter can strain even the most optimistic soul with many Finns succumbing to seasonal affective disorder (SAD). Some use drink as a crutch, with alcohol becoming the biggest killer of Finns in 2006, overtaking even heart disease. Many try to pep themselves up with coffee (see p58) with Finns among the world's highest consumers of caffeine. Others look to metal music (see p55) so you'll see librarians in Metallica T-shirts and soccer mums whose clutch purses have skull and inverted crucifix details.

Much of the Finnish identity is tied to the lakes and woods. Finns head en masse to their *mökki* (summer cottage; see boxed text, p63) from Midsummer until the end of the July holidays. There, you'll find even the most urbanised Euro-executives chopping wood, lighting the sauna fire and DIY-ing. Many Finns enjoy *jokamiehenoikeus*, which mean's 'everyman's right' and allows Finns to gather berries and mushrooms in summer from public land. This localisation has meant that domestic tourism isn't popular in Finland with Finns snowbirding south to the warmer climes of the Mediterranean in winter.

LIFESTYLE

Consistently you'll see Finland topping the charts on social scales. Average income is good and, because taxation is high, social services are excellent. In 2008, OECD studies rated Finland the number-one country for literacy, and the nation consistently rates 11th in the UN Human Development Index of most liveable countries.

So what's their secret? Some of their success lies in an interventionist state, which is unafraid of taxing alcohol and subsidising education. Salary and workplace negotiation is known for the 'three-way bargaining' structure which

---

LITTLE SATURDAY

Finns love the weekend, when they can get away to their cottages, play sport and party in the evening. But the working week is also broken up in the middle. On Wednesday nights restaurants are busy, music is playing at all the nightspots, bars are full – Finns are celebrating *pikku Lauantai*, which means 'little Saturday'.

includes business, unions and the government. While economists may fear that this would significantly limit business, the successes of Nokia (see boxed text, opposite) and other businesses would seem to argue the contrary.

Ever since 1906 when Finland became the first European state to give women the vote, women have been politically empowered. They were particularly active in the post-WWII years, and were instrumental in welfare reforms, including increased educational opportunity, better child care and encouraging employment outside the home. Today Finland's first woman president, Tarja Halonen, is an exemplar of the kind of work–life balance that many other nations are struggling to achieve.

Finland's divorce rate however is high, with 50% of marriages ending in divorce. The birth rate, as in much of the EU, is low. Finns' traditional love of family is struggling to adapt to the many commitments of the modern world. In 2002, the definition of family expanded to include gays and lesbians when civil unions extended many of the rights of marriage to same-sex couples (although not adoption or the use of common surnames).

Finland's welfare state is under threat as an ageing population leaves the workforce (see opposite). Newspaper reports suggest that the appearance of Romanian beggars in Helsinki and Turku has shocked many Finns, as the country's welfare system has traditionally meant that begging has been rare.

Cosy Finland (www .cosyfinland.com) offers an excellent chance to meet Finns hosting dinners with locals and homestays.

GETTING NAKED & SWEATY

No matter where you are in Finland, you'll never be far from a sauna (pronounced *sah*-oo-nah, not *saw*-nuh). With over 1.6 million in homes, hotels, bars and even on ferries, saunas are prescribed to cure almost every ailment, used to seal business deals or just socialise over a few beers.

Traditionally saunas were used as a family bathhouse as well as having functions like smoking meat and places to give birth. The earliest references to the Finnish sauna date from the chronicles of Ukrainian historian Nestor in 1113 and there are numerous mentions of sauna-going in the *Kalevala*.

Most saunas are private, in Finnish homes, but public saunas are common and almost every hotel has one. An invitation to bathe in a family's sauna is an honour, just as it is to be invited to a person's home for a meal. The sauna is taken naked, a fact that some people find uncomfortable and confronting, but Finns consider perfectly natural. While a Finnish family will often take the sauna together, in mixed gatherings it is usual for the men and women to go separately.

Public saunas are usually separated by gender and if there is just one sauna, the hours are different for men and women. In unisex saunas you will be given some sort of wrap or covering to wear. Finns strictly observe the nonsexual character of the sauna and this point should be respected. The sauna was originally a place to bathe and meditate.

The most common sauna is the electric sauna stove, which produces a fairly dry harsh heat compared with the much-loved chimney sauna, driven by a log fire and the staple of life at summer cottages. Even rarer is the true *savusauna* (smoke sauna), without a chimney. The smoke is let out just before entry and the soot-blackened walls are part of the experience. Although the top of a sauna can get to well over 120°C, many Finns consider the most satisfying temperature for a sauna to be around 80°C. At this temperature you'll sweat and, some Finns claim, feel the wood-smoke in your lungs.

Proper sauna etiquette dictates that you use a *kauha* (ladle) to throw water on the *kiuas* (sauna stove), which then gives off the *löyly* (sauna steam). At this point, at least in summer in the countryside, you might take the *vihta* or *vasta* (a bunch of fresh, leafy birch twigs) and lightly strike yourself. This improves circulation, has cleansing properties and gives your skin a pleasant smell. When you are sufficiently warmed, you'll jump in the sea, a lake, river or pool, then return to the sauna to warm up and repeat the cycle several times. If you're indoors, a cold shower will do. The swim and hot-cold aspect is such an integral part of the sauna experience that in the dead of winter, Finns cut a hole in the ice and jump right in.

YOU WANT TO INVEST IN WHAT?

There must have been a few near executive heart attacks when a company with a history in forestry, paper, rubber and dabbling in computers decided to sell off other operations to concentrate on the dawning mobile-phone market of the 1990s. Confidence wouldn't have been high as the new technology came out of the loss-making research area dubbed the 'cancer ward' for its 17 years of poor economic performance. Previous experiments in car phones had been less than successful.

But Nokia showed real Finnish *sisu* by taking on the new telecommunications technology. Today more than 2 billion people worldwide own a Nokia handset and the telecommunications giant accounts for 20% of the nation's exports. As Nokia moves into new areas such as the web and online music, Finnish economists are experiencing palpitations that the nation's economy may be too dependent on Nokia.

ECONOMY

Is there life outside of Nokia for Finnish exports? Finland's economy was actually founded on forestry (the so-called 'green gold') and three of the nation's top-five earning companies are all about timber. Nokia itself began life as a pulp mill in the 1860s before diversifying into other industries and eventually mobile phones (see boxed text, above). Finnish innovation has created several other global brands like the design favourite **Marimekko** (www .marimekko.fi/eng), furniture designers **Artek** (www.artek.fi/en) and geek-friendly operating system **Linux** (www.linux.org).

Add to this healthy industry a famously high tax rate and you have a nation that's well equipped to look after its citizenry with some of the world's best health care and education. Though Finns grumble about the high excise on alcohol they appreciate the reliable public transport and world-class universities and libraries that these same taxes afford. Like much of the world, Finland is holding its breath as ageing baby-boomers retire and it attempts to maintain high pensions.

POPULATION

In Europe only Iceland and Norway are less sparsely populated than Finland. The country has only 17 people per sq km though in areas of Lapland this can be as lonely as two people per sq km. But the majority of Finns cluster around the greater Helsinki area, Tampere and Turku accounting for a quarter of the population. The further from the south you head, the thinner the population becomes.

Both Finnish and Swedish are official languages, and account for the two main language groups. Some 5.5% of Finns speak Swedish as their first language especially on the west coast in the Pohjanmaa (Ostrobothnia) region and the semi-autonomous region of Åland. These areas have also been popular with immigrants who see Swedish as an easier language to learn than Finnish (see p42).

In the far north, Finland's indigenous people, the Sámi, are an important minority (see boxed text, p326). Another minority group you may see are the Roma people, who are distinguished by the black traditional dress (often set off with lace) of women. There are more than 6000 Roma people in Finland today.

Many Finns regard Karelians in the east as holders of true Finnish culture (the *Kalevala* was inspired by this region) though few speak Karelian as their first language. Karelia was divided by the Finland-Russia border and you'll notice different traditions and a particularly strong Orthodox Church as you travel through the area.

MULTICULTURALISM

Just over 2% of all Finnish residents are foreigners, one of the lowest percentages of any country in Europe. The largest group is Russian (almost 23,000), who tend to settle in Helsinki. Other large groups include Estonian, Swedish and Somali, with the latter part of Finland's ongoing commitment to refugees. Romanians have become a small but visible group in Helsinki and Turku and, although overt racism is uncommon, some disturbing instances have occurred in smaller towns in central Finland. In Helsinki, there have been a few reports of violence between Somali refugees and Finnish youth, though generally, the capital has few incidents of racist violence.

RELIGION

Four out of every five Finns are Lutherans. Many would only go to church twice a year (Christmas and Easter are always popular services), though private prayer is common. Although closely tied to Finnish national identity throughout history, the national church is relatively progressive, ordaining its first female priests as early as the 1980s and revising a Finnish translation of the Bible in 1992.

Just over 1% of Finns belong to the Orthodox Church of Finland with dioceses in Helsinki, Oulu and Karelia. The religion reflects its strong Karelian and Russian influences and you'll see the 'onion-dome' architecture and icon art closest to the border. Other religious groups coexist with little tension including over 20,000 Muslims, 8000 Catholics and around a thousand Jews.

SPORT

Ice hockey is Finland's national passion. Finns regularly play for Canadian and US leagues, and the Leijonat (Lions), Finland's national team, is consistently one of the world's best. Ice hockey season starts in late September and finishes in March. You can see the ice cut and hear the thud of collisions in national league matches at Tampere (home of the ice-hockey museum), Oulu and Helsinki. Turku and Rovaniemi also have major teams. The best way to find out when and where games are on is to ask at the tourist office, or contact the national ticketing outlet **Lippupalvelu** (www.ticketservicefinland.fi).

Winter sports are huge: cross-country skiing was invented in Finland. Downhill skiing is popular but better experienced than watched (see p73). You can watch flying Finns at the ski-jumping centres in Lahti, Kuopio and Jyväskylä. Even a practice session in summer can be impressive (see boxed text, p192).

Pesäpallo, or simply *pesis,* is the Finnish version of baseball based on older Finnish sports such as kingball or longball. The popular summer team sport has the ball pitched up in the air rather than thrown at the batter as in US baseball. Check out www.pesis.fi for more tips on this oddly familiar spectacle.

Athletics (track and field) is very popular in Finland, as a result of the country's long-distance runners and javelin-throwers such as 2008 Olympic medallist Tero Pitkämäki. Paavo Nurmi's nine Olympic golds in running make him one of Finland's greats (see p219).

Rally driving sends Finns wild with legends four-time world champion Tommi Mäkinen and Champion of Champions winner Marcus Grönholm. In Formula One, too, Finland punches well above its weight, with Keke Rosberg and Mika Häkkinen previous world champions, and Kimi Räikkönen and Heikki Kovalainen keeping the legend alive.

Part stunts, part extreme sports, all pranksters, the Dudesons (www .dudesons.com) are Finland's *Jackass*-style troupe with a TV show full of car crashes, 'I heart Suomi' T-shirts and a pig called Britney.

MEDIA
Newspapers
Finns are among the world's most voracious readers of broadsheets and tabloids. *Helsingin Sanomat* is the largest daily in Finland with a circulation of nearly half a million, and an English edition (www.hs.fi/english). *The Helsinki Times* (€3) distils the week's news into English and is known for its positive coverage, while *Ilta-Sanomat* and *Ilta-Lehti* are evening tabloids complete with trashy celebrity gossip. Turku's *Turun Sanomat* and Tampere's *Aamulehti* are significant regional papers.

Radio & TV
The major player is YLE (also called the Finnish Broadcasting Corporation) with four national public radio stations. An English summary of world news is broadcast daily at 10.55pm on YLE 3 and YLE 4. In Helsinki, YLE X plays Finnish and international rock, while Radio Nova is more poppy, and Kiss FM fairly cheesy. Stations like Radio Vega and Radio Extrem broadcast in Swedish.

Finland switched to digital TV in 2007, which means that at the time of research there were 14 free-to-air channels and 19 pay TV (or cable) channels available. YLE has several channels including YLE TV1 (known for news and current affairs), YLE TV2 (home of children and teen programming) and YLE FST5 (Swedish-language broadcasting news and entertainment). Of the commercial stations the most popular channels are MTV3 (entertainment) and SubTV (entertainment, especially US imports) though pay TV channels such as French-owned Canal+ have swiped some of their audiences.

ARTS
Literature
Finland has a rich oral tradition of folklore, which explains why the first alphabet wasn't written until the 16th century by Mikael Agricola (1510–57). In fact many early Finnish stories were written in Swedish. All that changed in the early 19th century with the penning of the *Kalevala* (see boxed text, p44) by Elias Lönnrot, who gathered together many songs, poems and tales. It was the beginning of a nationalistic renaissance. Poet JL Runeberg wrote *Tales of the Ensign Ståhl* capturing Finland at war with Russia, while Aleksis Kivi wrote *Seven Brothers,* the nation's first novel, about brothers escaping education and civilisation in the forest. Finns say the novel has never been successfully translated from the Finnish with the same nuances.

This theme is continued in *The Year of the Hare,* looking at a journalist's escape into the wilds by Arto Paasilinna in the 1970s. Other 20th-century novelists include Mika Waltari who gained fame with *The Egyptian,* and FE Sillanpää who received the Nobel Prize for Literature in 1939. The national bestseller during the postwar period was *The Unknown Soldier* by Väinö Linna. The seemingly endless series of autobiographical novels by Kalle Päätalo and the witty short stories by Veikko Huovinen are also very popular in Finland. Finland's most internationally famous author is the late Tove Jansson (see boxed text, p225), whose books about the fantastic Moomin family have long captured the imagination.

Today many Finns relate to Jussi 'Juba' Tuomola's comic adventures of Viivi and Wagner, which recount the marriage between a feminist and a pig. *Sikspäkki ja salmiakkia* (Six Pack and Salt Liquorice) captures some of the best moments, but a new volume appears each year. Leena Lander is a contemporary Finnish novelist whose *Tummien Perhosten Koti* (The Home of the Dark Butterflies) was made into a popular film.

There's an excellent index of Finnish and other Nordic authors at www .kirjasto.sci.fi

FINLAND'S NATIONAL EPIC

Intrepid country doctor Elias Lönnrot trekked eastern Finland during the first half of the 19th century in order to collect traditional poems, oral runes and folk stories. Over 11 long tours, he compiled this material with his own writing to form the *Kalevala*.

The epic mythology of the book blends creation stories, wedding poems and classic struggles between good and evil. The main narrative, however, focuses on two legendary countries, *Kalevala* (southern Finland, often identified as Karelia) and *Pohjola* (the north). Many commentators feel that the epic echoes ancient territorial conflicts between the Finns and the Sámi.

The first version appeared in 1833, with another following in 1835 and yet another, the final version, *Uusi-Kalevala* (New Kalevala), in 1849. Its influence on generations of Finnish artists, writers and composers is immense, particularly painter Akseli Gallen-Kallela and composer Jean Sibelius, who returned to the work repeatedly for inspiration. See p29 for some destinations in Finland related to the *Kalevala*. Beyond Finland the epic has influenced the Estonian epic *Kalevipoeg* and American poet Longfellow, and JRR Tolkien based significant parts of his mythos on the *Kalevala,* including the language of Elves.

Although it is impossible to accurately reproduce the *Kalevala* in anything other than Finnish, poet Keith Bosley's English translation makes for a lyrical read.

Architecture

For more on design, see Finnish Design, opposite. The high standard of Finnish architecture was established by the works of Alvar Aalto (1898–1976) and Eliel Saarinen (1873–1950). People interested in architecture make pilgrimages to Finland to see superb examples of modern buildings.

Wood has long been the dominant building material in Finland. Some of the best early examples of wooden architecture are churches on Finland's southern and western coasts, such as those at Kerimäki, Keuruu and Ruotsinpyhtää.

Eastern influences date back to 1812 when Helsinki was made the capital under Russian rule. The city centre was created by German-born CL Engel, who combined neoclassical and St Petersburg features in designing the cathedral, the university and other buildings around Senaatintori. Engel also designed a huge number of churches and town halls throughout Finland. After the 1850s National Romanticism emerged in response to pressure from the Russians.

The art nouveau period, which reached its apogee at the turn of the 20th century, combined Karelian ideals with rich ornamentation. Materials used were wood and grey granite. After independence in 1917, rationalism and functionalism emerged, as exemplified by some of Alvar Aalto's work.

Emerging regional schools of architecture include the Oulu School, featuring small towers, porticoes and combinations of various elements, most evident in the region around Oulu. Erkki Helasvuo, who died in 1995, did plenty of work in North Karelia, providing the province with several public buildings that hint at modern Karelianism. The most famous of these is Nurmes Talo, the cultural centre in Nurmes.

Design

For information on design see Finnish Design, opposite.

Painting & Sculpture

Modern Finnish art and sculpture plays with disaffection with technological society (think warped Nokias) and reinterprets the 'Finnishness' (expect parodies of sauna, birches and blonde stereotypes). Vaasa's new Kunsti (see p264) and Helsinki's Kiasma (see p82) are among the best places to spot the next big thing.

(Continued on page 53)

Finnish
Design

Fokus Fabrik cushion covers

The Roots of Creativity

Its inhabitants' almost mystical closeness to nature has always underpinned design in Finland, and it's rarely been a self-conscious art. However high Finland may climb on the lifestyle indexes these days, its design still has its roots in practicality. Indeed, it is a practicality originally born of poverty: the inventiveness of a hand-to-mouth rural population made life easier in very small steps.

Finland's location, and its historical role as a pawn in the figurative Russia-Sweden chess championship, have given it a variety of influences and a certain flexibility. As a meeting point between east and west, it has traditionally been a place of trade, a point of tension and, therefore, a point of change and innovation. Its climate, too, is a key factor, as it has meant that efficiency has always been the primary feature for design of everyday objects. In bald terms, if that axe didn't chop enough wood for the winter, you wouldn't survive it.

For the forest is much more present in Finnish life than in that of other European countries. From its role as a shelter in times of trouble to a provider of the wood that housed and heated the people, it's always been a place of power, commanding respect. So it's no surprise to find that nature is the dominant and enduring motif in the country's designs, from Lapland's sheath knives to the seasonal flower-and-forest colours of Marimekko's palette (p51). Timber itself has remained an important material, and reassuringly chunky wooden objects adorn almost every Finnish home and summer cottage.

ALVAR AALTO

Born in 1898, Alvar Aalto was for many the 20th century's number one architect, and not just in the Yellow Pages. In an era of increasing urbanisation, postwar rebuilding and immense housing pressure, Aalto found elegant solutions for public and private edifices that embraced functionalism but never at the expense of humanity. Viewed from the next

The Finlandia Talo, designed by Alvar Aalto and completed in 1972

DAVID BORLAND

Kaija Aarikka–designed wooden rams (1973).

AARIKKA

century, his work still more than holds its own, and his huge contributions in other areas of art and design make him a mighty figure indeed.

Aalto had a democratic, practical view of his field: he saw his task as 'a question of making architecture serve the wellbeing and prosperity of millions of citizens' where it had previously been the preserve of a wealthy few. But he was no utilitarian; beauty was always a concern, and he was adamant that a proper studio environment was essential for the creativity of the architect to flower.

Born in Kuortane near Seinäjoki, he worked in Jyväskylä, Turku and Helsinki before gaining an international reputation for his pavilions at the World Fairs of the late '30s. His 1925 marriage to Aino Marsio created a dynamic team that pushed boundaries in several fields, including glassware and furniture design. Their work on bending and laminating wood revolutionised the furniture industry, and the classic forms they produced for their company, Artek, are still Finnish staples. His use of rod-shaped ceramic tiles, undulated wood, woven cane, brick and marble was particularly distinctive.

Aalto's notable buildings are dotted throughout Finland (and a few other countries too). Helsinki's Finlandia Talo (p91), built between 1967 and 1972, is a signature work, as is Otaniemi University (1953–66; p112) in Espoo, commonly known as the TKK. Jyväskylä is chock-a-block with Aalto-designed buildings including the Workers' Club (1952; p149) and the Alvar Aalto Museum (1971–73; p149). A comparison of the Aalto Centre in Seinäjoki (p271) with the Kolmen Ristin Kirkko (1955–58; p169) in Imatra highlights the range of Aalto's work. Aalto's work was seminal and hugely influential, and he was much loved as a person too.

Charmingly, Aalto's favourite design was his own wooden boat (on show at his summer house near Jyväskylä, p153), which he planned and built with great love, but little skill. It was barely seaworthy at the best of times, and regularly capsized and sank.

DESIGN OLD & NEW
The classics

If the early 21st century is a new golden age for Finnish design, the original one was in the 1950s and 1960s. The freelance designers producing marvels in glass for Iittala, ceramics for Arabia, cookware for Hackman and furniture for Artek won international recognition and numerous prestigious awards, particularly at the Triennale di Milano shows. Though times were still tough after the war, and the country was still struggling to house refugees from occupied Karelia, the successes of these firms, together with the Helsinki Olympic Games of 1952, helped put a still-young nation on the map and build confidence and national pride, which had weakened after the gruelling battles with Russia and Germany (p33).

The story of the Iittala glass company could be a metaphor for the story of Finnish design. Still producing to models imported from Sweden in the early 20th century, the company began to explore more home-grown options. Glass design competitions were an outward-looking source of ideas: from one of these came Alvar Aalto's famous Iittala vase, which he described as 'an Eskimo woman's leather trousers'. Then two giants of postwar design, Tapio Wirkkala (1915–85) and Timo Sarpaneva (1926–2006), began to explore textures and forms gleaned from Finnish lakescapes. Coloured glass fell from use and the classic Iittala ranges were born, with sand-scouring creating the appearance of cut ice, and Wirkkala's impossibly fluid forms seemingly melting away. The opaque look, which resembled ceramics, was a later creation as a new generation took the field. Harri Koskinen and Annaleena Hakatie were among the leading lights, though the company has never been afraid to commission foreign designers. Iittala is today under the same ownership as Hackman, the long-established cutlery and cookware producers, and Arabia, who roughly paralleled Iittala's glassware trajectory with ceramics.

Alvar Aalto Artek chair

AINO HUOVIO

FINNISH DESIGN CLASSICS

- Artek's Aalto chairs. To think that we take bent wood for granted in our furniture these days.

- The Iittala vase. Yes, Aalto again. Whether or not it actually resembles an Inuit woman's leather pants, it's undeniably a classic.

- An Unikko bedsheet from Marimekko. Who doesn't dream better under those upbeat red poppies?

- 1930s ringed tumblers designed by Aino Aalto (Alvar's wife) – you'll drink your breakfast juice out of one of them within a couple of days of your arrival.

- Marttiini knives, which are made way up north at Rovaniemi and are still first choice for outdoors folk 80 years after they were first produced.

An Iittala store stocking a mind-boggling range of Scandinavian-designed glassware

ANNA WATSON

Other well-established Finnish names include Aarikka, whose wooden jewellery and other accessories have always had a cheerily reassuring solidity and honesty, and Kalevala Koru, a byword for quality silver and gold jewellery, that recently acquired the respected Lapponia company. Pentik's wide range of interior design and homeware products include the recent Saaga range, inspired by the designs of Sámi shaman drums.

The newcomers

A strong design tradition tends to produce good young designers and Finland's education system is strong on fostering creativity, so Suomi is churning them out at a fair rate. New names, ranges and shops crop up in the 'Sinki's design district like mushrooms overnight, and exciting contemporary design is being produced on all fronts. Fennofolk is the name for one broad movement that seeks, like the original giants of Finnish design, to take inspiration from Suomi's natural and cultural heritage, adding a typically Finnish injection of weirdness along the way.

Still one of the biggest names on the Finnish design scene is Stefan Lindfors, whose reptile- and insect-inspired work has been described as a warped updating of Aalto's own nature-influenced work. A recent creation of his is the Plup, a doughnut-shaped drinking bottle forged from recyclable plastic and fit for perpetual refilling from Finland's crystal-clear waters. Its design is a simple but practical rethink of an everyday item that also recalls the traditional shape of Finnish rye-bread loaves.

Also check out Helga Lahtinen's and Anna Salonen's 'Blind Me' Braille ceramic tiles from the offbeat How About Viktor collective; Jukka Korpihete's lights and lamps; Janne Kyttänen's pioneering digital fabrication industrial designs; Fokus Fabrik's unique textiles; and whatever boutique piece Harri Koskinen has produced recently.

Now that designs are offered up to a global audience the question is, is there still a Finnish soul to them? Hopefully the answer is yes. Finland's pre-eminence in design was born of

Onitsuka Tiger Shoe (Strawberry Frog) display by Janne Kyttänen

JANNE KYTTÄNEN

NEW THINGS THAT'LL FIT IN YOUR BAG

- A Plup water bottle. Looks good hanging on your belt and refilling it strikes a blow for the planet.
- One of Sami Rinne's engagingly quirky ceramics – maybe that mug with a handle like a reindeer's antlers?
- A pair of Minna Parikka's shoes – 21st-century style straight from a smoky '30s nightclub.
- One of Jani Martikainen's birch trivets (pot-plant bases) from his Majamoo company. The only trouble is that the plant hides it.
- A Queen of Go-Go T-shirt by talented young graphic designers Antti Hinkula & Teemu Suviala. And it even comes in Finnish colours.

Genelec's current 6010A speakers are still heavily based on the 1022A model first released in 1985
HARRI KOSKINEN

a creativity that was harnessed to, but never separate from, practical concerns. Though as the latest darlings of 21st-century Euro-fashion, Finnish design is in danger of becoming an end in itself, rather than an aesthetically pleasing solution to everyday needs, and the best designers know that function still comes first: those scissors had better cut straight, and that jumper keep the autumn chills away. The rest is detail. But what glorious detail.

DRESSING THE PART

Finnish clothing lines have raised their international profile dramatically in recent years but fashion is a fickle creature and, in many ways Finland, unlike its Nordic neighbours, has tended to beat its own path. Finland has traditionally been a place where teenagers can wear a jumper knitted by Granny to school, and though new and exciting ideas are constantly created here, they tend to be built on solid traditional foundations.

The godfather of Finnish design, Kaj Franck took ideas from traditional rustic clothing for his pared-back creations, but it was the birth and rapid rise to prominence of Marimekko, founded in 1951, that made an international impact. Optimistic, colourful and well-made, it bucked contemporary trends, focusing on a simple and unashamed beauty. Though the company went through a difficult period, it's back at the top these days, as the retro appeal of its classic shirts, bags, curtains and fabrics fills wardrobes with flowers once again.

Thirty-something designer Paola Suhonen's IVANAhelsinki label has set tongues wagging around the world in recent years but remains resolutely Finnish, with iconic references to getting back to nature and a commitment to producing the clothes locally in an environmentally responsible manner. Hanna Sarén's confident range of shoes and clothing is also inspired by the classic Finnish landscapes of forests, lakes and flowering meadows.

A range of clothing by Kaj Franck's Marimekko label

JAN SUTTL

London-based Julia Lundsten's elegant Finsk range of shoes and Minna Parikka's sensuous and provocative footwear have placed these two young Finns firmly in the limelight in recent years, while Janne Lax strikes a blow for the street with his Saint Vacant range of designer sneakers.

(Continued from page 44)

It's a long way from the pagan prehistoric rock paintings found across Finland, including discoveries at Hossa (p296) and Ristiina (p146). Medieval churches in Åland, such as Sankt Mikael Church (in Finström), Sankta Maria Church (in Saltvik) and Sankta Birgitta Church (in Lemland), and in southern Finland have enchanting frescoes.

The golden age of Finnish art is often seen as the National Romantic painters who featured virgin forests and pastoral landscapes. The most comprehensive collections are displayed by the Ateneum and National Museum in Helsinki, and the Turku Art Museum. The luminary of this scene was definitely Akseli Gallen-Kallela, who enjoyed a distinguished and prolific career as creator of *Kalevala*-inspired paintings. Other distinguished painters of this movement include the brothers von Wright, Magnus and Willhelm, who became famous for their depictions of birds; Pekka Halonen, who worked in winter scenery; and Victor Westerholm, who was famous for his Åland landscapes. Eero Järnefelt painted Koli (see p183), ensuring that

SATU NATUNEN

Sámi culture to me means the very act of staying and being alive – it's a life source. It's been my roots; what has bound me to something. When I was a child, I spent a lot of time in my grandmother's house in Karigasniemi. I was a strange child, too much hair, so I was sent to spend time with my grandfather rather than the other kids. He showed me the flowers, nature, told me things. Later I understood how valuable it had been to have heard even short parts of the stories. I asked to tape them but he said no, there must be a possibility for mistakes. I fill the missing parts in and that's how these tales have always developed and grown.

Do parents still maintain the oral tradition? Unfortunately not so much, but there's still something like that going on. Mostly you see it in attitude, the way of behaving in nature, respect for animals. Stories and beliefs have disappeared more, partly because of Christianity, partly because of the school system. People don't explain things in the same way these days.

There was a creator who made too many children. Suddenly he realised he couldn't take care of them all so he negotiated with Mother Earth and asked her to take half. She put them under the ground. Those people have everything better. They're more beautiful, have better boats, better reindeer. Sometimes, if we feel that we are seeking or searching it could be that the person we seek is one of those under the earth. If you go to the fells, it is said it's possible to meet one of these under-earth people. For they have the same curiosity about us. When they appear, if you throw a piece of silver over them they'll stay visible in our world.

In my art the fox is a sign animal to human beings. In the beginning of times, the fox was given this role. When you meet a fox, you meet your animal side. There is a connection both ways. The fox reads you and you must read the fox. Someone once asked me why I had foxes and not human beings in my art and I realised that to me all my foxes somehow seem human beings.

There'll never be a united Sámi people, but self-confidence is stronger all the time. Politically, we are weak: 7000 in Finland, divided in three groups. But Sámi people are respecting their roots more and are finding positives from their own culture, not depressed and overburdened as before. Even young people have traditional clothes, or some jewellery to indicate their Sámi origin. But we are somehow in danger of being hugged into destruction. So many subsidies are sort of destroying the culture. And the Sámi parliament is kind of a fake thing, we have no real political power. But at least you can study Sámi in school these days.

Sámi women have always been strong women. They needed to run the home – the men were always somewhere else, away with the reindeer and so on. It's been quite a maternal culture and still is in most ways. I think feminist movements are a little bit childish. If we want something, we have the strength as women to just take it.

Satu Natunen is a Sámi artist

landmark's place in the national culture, while Juho Rissanen depicted the everyday life of Finns. Helene Schjerfbeck remains the most famous female painter of her age and is known for her self-portraits, which reflect the situation of Finnish women 100 years ago.

Dance & Theatre

Dance is nurtured in Finland. The Finnish National Opera has its own ballet school, and there is a handful of small dance groups in Helsinki and other large towns. The annual Kuopio Dance Festival always features the latest moves.

Ceremonial holidays and festivals are your best chance to see *kansan-tanssit* (folk dances). Old-style dancing in general remains very popular, with a hall in most towns where humppa (Finnish jazz music) or melancholy Finnish tango accompanies twirling couples.

Helsinki is the home of the National Theatre. Finnish theatre is very well attended and heavily subsidised. The most famous dramatist is perhaps Aleksis Kivi, who wrote plays as well as novels.

> The website www.tanssi .net encourages visitors to participate in a night of Finnish dancing and has an English page explaining the etiquette.

Cinema

Although around 20 films are produced in Finland annually, few make it onto screens beyond the Nordic countries. The 1990s saw a flowering, but with a limited domestic audience government funding has always been limited. Recent home-grown hits include *Päätalo* (2008), the story of one of Finland's most successful writers, and *Tummien Perhosten Koti* (The Home of Dark Butterflies; 2008), a stark look at a Finnish boys' home that at the time of writing was Finland's hope for an Academy Award™.

The glory days of Finnish cinema were ushered in by Aki Kaurismäki, who has seen international success with *Leningrad Cowboys Go America* (1989) and *The Man Without a Past* (2002), which won the Grand Prix at Cannes Film Festival. His early film *Calamari Union* (1985) makes for an idiosyncratic portrait of Helsinki's Kallio district. He collaborated on the Leningrad Cowboy films with his brother, Mika, who has a reputation for insightful documentaries like *Sonic Mirror* (2008), as well as international features such as *LA Without A Map* (1998) and *Honey Baby* (2004).

> The Finnish Film Archive has a good overview of Finnish cinema on its website, www.sea.fi.

Finland's biggest export to Hollywood is Renny Harlin (real name Lauri Harjola). After directing the staunchly anticommunist action film *Born American*, which was banned in Finland, Harlin found himself directing box-office hits including *Die Hard II, Cliffhanger* and *Deep Blue Sea*. Harlin famously includes a reference to Finland in all his films, but in 2009 he's slated to return home to produce the biopic *Mannerheim*, based on the life of Finland's wartime leader.

> *Musta jää* (Black Ice; 2007) is a characteristically complex Finnish film of infidelity, which scored that year's Berlin International Film Festival's Golden Bear award.

Music

It's probably the cold that makes Finns dance or crowd into the heat of metal gigs. Summer is all about music festivals from Imatra's Big Band to a plethora of rock festivals. As well as traditional dance bands, you'll find plenty of rock, jazz, folk and classical playing across the country.

CLASSICAL MUSIC

Composer Jean Sibelius' (see boxed text, p197) work dominates Finland's music, particularly the celebrated *Finlandia*. Sibelius is said to have composed the music for the *Kalevala* saga, while Gallen-Kallela painted it.

Sibelius' inheritance has been taken up over the years by a string of talented composers such as Magnus Lindberg and Kaija Saariaho. Thanks to Helsinki's Sibelius Academy, Finnish musical education is among the best in the world, with Finnish conductors, such as Leif Segerstam, Esa-Pekka Salonen and

PLAYLIST

Pack your iPod with these tunes to sample some of Finland's finest:

- *Hard Rock Hallelujah*, Lordi
- *Bad Luck Charm*, Disco Ensemble
- *I'm Not Jesus*, Apocalyptica (featuring Corey Taylor)
- *Máttaráhku Askái* (In Our Foremothers' Arms), Ulla Pirttijärvi
- *Missä Olet Laila*, Scandinavian Music Group
- *Freedom Fighter*, Von Hertzen Brothers
- *Diamonds for Tears*, Poets of the Fall
- *Liquid*, The Rasmus
- *Right Here in my Arms*, HIM
- *Sandstorm*, Darude
- *Happy Being Miserable*, Leningrad Cowboys

Susanna Mälkki, performing in some of the world's best orchestras. There are always some excellent classical music festivals in Finland (see p21).

POPULAR MUSIC

In case 2006 Eurovision Song Contest winners Lordi didn't convince you, Finland's music scene is heavier than anywhere else in the world. Metal has several subgenres in Finland. The biggest export is HIM, who make 'love metal', and their 'heartagram' logo can be seen on T-shirts from Berlin to Boston. Nightwish continues to sell its brand of symphonic metal internationally despite the departure of Tarja Turunen, who has gone on to a successful solo career in Finland and Russia. Catchy light-metal rockers The Rasmus released their album *Black Roses* in 2008, which continued their success. Almost every band markets themselves with their own subgenre, including Finntroll's folk metal (blending metal and humppa), The 69 Eyes' gothic, Apocalyptica's classical metal and Turisas' Viking metal (expect swords and war paint at gigs).

But there is lighter music, such as the Von Hertzen Brothers (see boxed text, p56), rising indie band Disco Ensemble, emo-punks Poets of the Fall and melodic Husky Rescue. Then there are unstoppable legends like Hanoi Rocks, 22-Pistepirkko and, of course, the unicorn-quiffed Leningrad Cowboys. While singing in English appeals to an international audience, several groups sing in Finnish including Zen Café, Apulanta and mellow folk rockers Scandinavian Music Group.

Electronic and hip hop are underground scenes in Finland. Trance DJ and producer Darude is well known while rappers Bomfunk MCs and Kwan have strong followings.

You can see many of these acts at Finland's rock festivals throughout summer including **Ruisrock** (www.ruisrock.fi), **Provinssirock** (www.provinssirock.fi), **Ankkarock** (www.ankkarock.fi) and **Ilosaarirock** (www.ilosaarirock.fi), while Tavastia (see p102) is Helsinki's legendary rock venue. For more on events, see p21.

Jazz is big in Finland, as you can be seen by the huge jazz festivals at Pori, Espoo and Kajaani or at jazz clubs in major cities. Notable Finnish jazz musicians include Raoul Björkenheim, Juhani Aaltonen and Trio Töykeät (now disbanded). Finns have created humppa, a jazz-based music that's synonymous with social dances.

The Sámi use the traditional *yoik* (also called *joiks* or *juoiggus*) to create atmospheric world music that has been compared to Native American

The website www.fimic .fi is an excellent resource for finding out about Finnish music, while www.moremusic.fi has hard-to-get Finnish CDs online.

MIKKO VON HERTZEN

The Von Hertzen Brothers had a good 2008. Their third studio album, *Love Remains The Same*, hit number one in Finland and they supported Neil Young. Lead singer and guitarist, Mikko von Hertzen, joined his brothers Kie and Jonne in 2000 to create the epic rock band that has become a uniquely Finnish success. He spoke to George Dunford just before the band's gig at Ruisrock (see p220).

How would you describe your music for people who've never heard it before? In Finland they tried to put this progressive rock label on us, which is a little bit inaccurate. It doesn't really tell what we are all about, because progressive rock is like nerds playing this difficult stuff and long songs. OK we have long songs but we have rock attitude, which we push forward. I would say that Queen is a good example. I'm not Freddy Mercury [laughs], but the music has similar things in it. We try to be really broad.

Metal is so huge in Finland – why is that? I think because Finnish metal is doing so well in the charts. This is not happening in other parts of the world, but in Finland metal is mainstream. Forget about hip hop and R'n'B – they have it on MTV all the time, but people don't buy it. When some big R'n'B artist gets released it's hardly in the charts in Finland – everyone buys Slayer. That's what goes up in the top five. It must be because there's so many Finnish bands who are doing great internationally in this genre of music. So all the kids when they start to play, they start with metal. It doesn't mean that we don't have other kinds of good band like funk bands, but it's just because the mainstream is metal and hardcore.

But Von Hertzen Brothers music is very different isn't it? Yeah, I'm not into metal much myself. I like the early heavy bands like Black Sabbath and Zeppelin. They're my number-one bands, but where heavy metal went in the thrash direction in the early '80s I never went there with Metallica or Anthrax. I went to the easier side like Pink Floyd. I'm kind of more melodic.

Helsinki is such a big music town these days – where does it come from? There's the Sibelius High School. If you check the bands which have made it big, many of the people are from that high school. It's where talented people from all across Finland apply to this same high school which is a perfect place for people to form band(s). That's where all of us three brothers went, that's where a couple of guys from HIM went, that's where The Rasmus guys went.

You're about to play Ruisrock – what makes this festival so special? It's situated on an island which is surrounded by this bird-nesting area so it's a natural environment. There's been a controversy about whether you can have a rock concert here or not because it interferes with nesting, but it's all over by this time. The location is beautiful, there is water everywhere and these old buildings. The camping area is big and they have the facilities because it's a camping area year-round. It's the oldest festival in Finland; it started in the same year as Woodstock. So it has real history.

chants. The *yoik* is traditionally sung a capella, often invoking a person or place with immense spiritual importance in Sámi culture. Wimme Saari has several *yoik*-based albums including with jazz-collaborators RinneRadio, while Angelit produces dance-based Sámi music. And if you think you escaped the metal, Korpiklaani (formerly known as Shaman) plays metal that includes *yoiks* and reindeer-antler mic stands.

Food & Drink

Italy's big cheese Silvio Berlusconi may have famously crowed in 2005 that 'The Finns don't even know what Parma ham is!' but Finnish food has been undergoing a quiet renaissance. While bulky heavy foods (yes, there's a substantial meat and potato history here) have been traditional winter chow, summer glows with berries and other goodies gathered from the wilds.

The secret ingredient in Finnish food is playfulness. When Finnish chain Koti Pizza beat Italy in the 2008 America's Plate pizza competition, the reindeer-topped rye-dough creation answered the Parma ham taunt, and was cheekily named the 'Berlusconi'.

STAPLES & SPECIALITIES

Finland has borrowed from neighbours Russia and Sweden to create its own cuisine. Seas and lakes offer great fish that's often finished with garden-fresh dill, plus the a long tradition of hunting makes for some interesting game. Potatoes and heavy rye breads also feature strongly. However, during the 1990s, Finnish cuisine met international flavours, with Italian, Chinese and Mexican proving particularly popular. More recently, a reawakening of interest in Finnish foods has seen top chefs reinterpreting local ingredients, by sweetening flavours with local berries or enriching them with reindeer meats or freshly gathered mushrooms.

Berries are more than an ingredient in Finnish food; they also announce the arrival of summer after carb-heavy winters. As well as strawberries, blueberries and raspberries being made into jams and mousses, you'll find tart lingonberry complementing reindeer or red and white currants sprinkled through porridge. For many Finns, the serving of light fruit soups is a clearer sign of summer's arrival than sunshine itself. Rhubarb is also popular, and keep an eye out for rarer berries such as *lakka* (p58) and sea buckthorn.

Like many of their Scandinavian neighbours, Finns love fish. *Lohi* (salmon) is ubiquitous, both fresh and smoked, and is often served with a creamy wild-mushroom sauce. Snack-wise there's *silli*, jars of pickled herring in a variety of sauces. Other traditional fish include the lakefish *siika*, that is something of a delicacy and, in the north, Arctic char. In Savonia, the tastiest fish is baked in a loaf of rye to make the regional speciality, *kalakukko* (fish bread).

With a long heritage of hunting, Finns are partial to game and meat. Reindeer is a staple for the Sámi in the north but also appears further south

If you're seduced by all the delicious pastries in cafes here, *The Great Scandinavian Baking Book*, by Beatrice A Ojakangas, will help you reproduce some of them at home.

FINLAND'S TOP FIVE

- Surrounded by Aalto and with sustainably sourced local produce, **Savoy** (p98) proves you can do it ethically and brilliantly

- Sample *sapas* (Suomi tapas) for a little bit of reindeer and never too much crayfish at **Juuri** (p97), one of the best of the smart new generation of Helsinki restaurants

- Unique twists on Finnish classics like reindeer fillet with cranberry butter or a Bloody Mary soup swimming with crayfish tails make Turku's **Linnankatu 3** (p222) a good pick

- Welcoming service, great flavour combinations, and a generous chef make **Figaro** (p152) dinner destination number one in Finland's architecture capital, Jyväskylä

- Seductive wines, super Suomi flavours, and a darkly romantic brick-vaulted dining room allow Kuopio's **Musta Lammas** (Black Sheep; p159) to stand out from the flock

---

TASTY TRAVEL

Tired of fish? It might be time to try some bear. Grizzly-bear steaks are a delicacy and usually only available during the strictly managed hunting season in autumn, but in finer restaurants you'll find potted and preserved bear meats adding a rich, almost-nutty, flavour to stews and soups year-round.

For something lighter, try *lakka* (cloudberries), which grow best in the swamps of the north and enjoy a brief season in summer. You'll see their golden colour in jams, juices and the liqueur *lakkalikööri* – their distinctively sharp taste means they're used sparingly. Many Finns swear by the *lakka* with *leipäjuusto* (bread cheese), a subtle flavour to set off the stronger fruit. If you're after something really rare try to track down arctic bramble, a tiny berry that is sometimes made into liqueurs.

---

on pizzas and in sausages and salamis. It's a must-try as a sautéed steak with lingonberries. Two other meaty favourites you'll see are grilled liver with bacon, and meatballs, generally both served with mashed potatoes. During hunting season you might even find elk as a special.

Falling Cloudberries, by Tessa Kiros, sees Finnish food meets Mediterranean influence, reflecting the author's Finnish-Greek-Cypriot heritage.

Thick soups are close to the Finnish heart, often served at lunch as part of a long tradition of hearty worker's fare. Creamy fish, hearty pea and smoky mushroom are common with meaty stews, which may include crayfish, elk or bear (see above).

And then there's the pastries. Finns definitely have a sweet tooth and you'd expect a country so insane about coffee to have a few good accompaniments. Look out for *pulla* (a cardamom-flavoured bun), *munkki* (large doughnuts sometimes jam filled) and Runeberg tart (a small tower cake that's topped with raspberry jam; see p110). As for savouries there's usually the rice-filled pastry from Karelia, *karjalanpiirakka* (best with egg butter), though some prefer the potato- or sweet potato–filled varieties.

The famous salty liquorice, *salmiakki*, is an acquired taste as are tar-flavoured gumdrops. Finnish chocolates, however, are excellent, especially those made by Fazer.

The biggest meal of the day is usually lunch, so many restaurants put on all-you-can-eat buffet meals, usually between 11am and 3pm Monday to Friday. These generally cost €7 to €14 and usually include coffee refills and sometimes even dessert. Most hotels offer a free continental-style buffet breakfast, which may consist of breads, cheeses, pastries, more fish, sometimes fruit or cereal and litres of coffee. Finns have dinner as early as 5pm – often just a light meal.

DRINKS

If you think you've got a caffeine habit the Finns will put it in perspective. As a nation they drink 20 million cups per day and you'll most likely find a pot boiling in bus stations, offices and homes, as well as cafes. If coffee's not your brew, you'll find tea in most cafes and opting for tap water (rather than bottled water) is more affordable and saves on plastic.

When it comes to alcohol, Finland is still hungover from a history of prohibition. In 2004 alcohol taxes were relaxed, but in 2007 the sale of bulk alcohol was limited. Strong beers, wines and spirits are still sold by the state network, the aptly named **Alko** (www.alko.fi, ☺ 9am-8pm Mon-Thu, 9am-8pm Fri, 9am-4pm Sat). You'll see its round logo in almost every town. Drinks containing more than 20% alcohol are not sold to those aged under 20; for beer and wine purchases the age limit is 18. Beer and cider under 4.7% alcohol are readily available in supermarkets. Restaurants are pricey places to enjoy a drink, usually adding around €20 per bottle to the retail price of wine.

THE KAHVI DRINKING CAPITAL OF EUROPE

If you ever wondered why there are so many cafes in Finland, wonder no more. It's because Finns are among the world's highest consumers of coffee, a love affair that sees the average person down almost 10kg of the stuff annually – some four to five cups a day each!

Even outside the bustling big cities, coffee is what drives Finland. There are dozens of cafes in every town and village; even petrol stations have cafes, and a cup of coffee is included with the lunch special at most restaurants.

Seldom will you visit a house without being served coffee. Traditionally you say 'no' and then accept, by saying 'OK, just half a cup', which in reality turns out to be four or five cups.

To do as the Finns do, pour your *kahvi* into a *kuppi* and add some *maito* (milk) or *kerma* (cream). It is traditionally accompanied by a *pulla* (cinnamon bun).

Finnish *olut* (beer) is generally light-coloured lager, although Guinness stout and other dark brews have gained in popularity in recent years (alongside a proliferation of Irish pubs). Major brands of lager include Lapin Kulta, Olvi and Koff. There's also a growing number of microbreweries in Finland (look for the word *panimo*), which generally make summery pilsners and thick porters. Such places worthy of a visit include Huvila in Savonlinna, Plevna in Tampere, Koulu and Herman in Turku, Teerenpeli in Lahti and Beer Hunters in Pori.

The strongest beer, containing more than 5% alcohol, is called *A-olut*, or *nelos olut*. More popular is III-beer (called *keskiolut* or *kolmonen*) and I-beer (called *mieto olut* or *pilsneri*), with less than 2% alcohol. Ciders made from apple and pear are also popular on terraces in summer.

The Finnish spirit of choice is the traditional Koskenkorva, a clear grain spirit often affectionately known as *kossu*. To make it more flavoursome liquorice is dissolved into a bottle to make *salmiakkikossu*, a tar-black shot that goes down smoothly. Another variation is *fisu*, which tastes like a Fisherman's Friend cough lolly and will keep you warm on a winter walk home.

Also look out for *Lakka*, a tasty cloudberry liqueur, and *sahti*, a sweet, high-alcohol beer traditionally made at home on the farm, though pubs in Lahti and Savonlinna may also have it. At Christmas time, *glögi* is a heart-warming mulled wine. Finlandia vodka, although owned by a multinational company, is still produced in Altia and comes in flavours like lime and cranberry.

Alcohol is taxed by content, so the stronger it is, the more expensive. The basic measure is 4cl for spirits, 8cl for fortified wines and 12cl for table wines when ordered by the glass. Unless you ask for more when you order at a *baari* or *ravintola*, you'll get the basic measure. If you're buying bottles and cans elsewhere the price includes a small deposit (about €0.20) which is redeemed at recycling stations in supermarkets.

Another classic is *lonkero*, or 'gin long drink', a premixed blend of gin and grapefruit juice, popular after a sauna. It's fairly light and refreshing.

HABITS & CUSTOMS

Finns eat their main meal at lunchtime and will usually only eat a big dinner on a social occasion. If invited to dinner in a Finnish home, it's appropriate to take a gift. Coffee and pastries are almost a Finnish cliché; wine, flowers or chocolates always go down well. The rules when visiting a Finnish home are quite simple; take your shoes off at the door, and never refuse the offer of a sauna or a cup of coffee.

Jokamiehenoikeus translates to every man's rights, but in practice means that Finns are free to collect berries, mushrooms and other produce on public lands – making for a good picnic basket.

CELEBRATIONS

Christmas is Finland's biggest holiday with Joulupukki (Santa Claus; p310) often making a doorstop appearance on Christmas Eve. The day itself is marked by the proclamation of Christmas Peace in Turku's historic centre at midday. The evening is lit by thousands of candle-bearing Finns visiting the graves of family members. On the Yule table, baked ham, supersalted to bring out its flavour, holds pride of place, and is accompanied by *rosolli*, a salad of beetroot, carrot and pickle.

The other big occasion is Midsummer, held on the weekend closest to the summer solstice, when Finns escape to lakeside cottages for barbecues and traditional saunas. Midsummer Eve is marked by bonfires and copious consumption of beer and *kossu*, and often followed by a misguided rowboat trip across the lake to visit friends.

Keen to make the most of summer, crayfish parties have Finns donning the bibs to slurp down the crustacean garnished with dill. There's usually a finger bowl to keep it clean.

WHERE TO EAT & DRINK

Taste of Finland (www .finfood.fi/tasteoffinland) is a good place to start your gourmet gallivanting with recipes, ingredients and details of celebrations.

In the more remote parts of the country dining in the evening is unpopular, so you may struggle to find a meal after 9pm. Opt instead to have your main meal of the day at the definitively Finnish *lounasravintola* (lunch restaurant), which serve large buffets and/or hot specials on weekdays between about 11am and 3pm. They are good value for budget and family travellers. Most other restaurants also offer lunch specials and reopen for evening meals. A few stay open between meals, though most stop food service between meals. *Ravintola* are a curious mix: sometimes restaurants, but often pubs, that may not serve full meals.

Between meals cafes serve light snacks and desserts, with three o'clock coffee and cake almost a compulsory break. Whether you have it at a *kahvila* (cafe), *kahvio* (cafe inside a supermarket or petrol station) or *baari* (bar), the coffee always flows and refills are often free.

Finns eat dinner early, often stopping for a bite on the way home from work. Metropolitan and hotel restaurants open much later than cheap diners, though the Finnish grilli is an exception (see opposite). In this guide, 'lunch' is at least 11am to 3pm, and 'dinner' at least 5pm to 9pm. Restaurants tend to open slightly later and shut earlier on Sundays. In many restaurants you are expected to seat yourself on arrival, and tips are only added for exceptional service.

Helsinki's culinary culture is cosmopolitan but still has great local menus, while Turku, Tampere, Jyväskylä and Oulu also have good dining scenes. Smaller towns suffer from the great Finnish love affair with globalised versions of Mexican, Italian and Chinese cuisine, so finding authentic Finnish grub can be a struggle.

Finns appear to dine earlier so there's more time for drinking. You'll find pubs and bars in most towns, but Helsinki's bar scene is one of the best north of Berlin, and attracts a hip young crowd. Older patrons are catered for in jazz bars and humppa music places. In summer, many of Finland's youth drink in public parks and squares, buying their beer in long squat packs of 12 beers that are called *mäyräkoira* (dachshunds).

The Fifty Best Restaurants (http://50bestrestaurants .fi) is an annual book covering Finland's top eateries, and its website offers an excellent preview.

As summer warms up, chairs and tables spill out the front of cafes in Helsinki, Oulu, Tampere and Turku to create terraces that heave until late with boozing.

Quick Eats

Not every meal in Finland has to be a pricey sit-down affair. In summer a town's kauppatori (market square) sells fresh produce, particularly in-season berries, which make good walking snacks. Finns also buy crisp peas to eat raw as they stroll – look out for discarded skins. Larger towns feature a kauppahalli (covered market), which are cornucopias of oven-fresh pastries, smoked smallgoods, meat and produce. For good buys check out Staples & Specialities (see p57).

At the other end of the health scale, there are grillis. These fast-food stands sell burgers, sausages and kebabs for the after-pub crowd waiting for taxis or buses home. There are several restaurant chains, which may be the only options in small towns. With their bright signage and main street locations, we don't think it's necessary to include listings for most of these places in this guide as you'll be able to find them all-too easily:

Amarillo (www.amarillo.fi) Tex-Mex food with lively bar.

Café Picnic (www.picnic.fi) A healthy sandwich chain with wi-fi.

Fransmanni (www.fransmanni.fi) Fast French.

Golden Rax (www.rax.fi, in Finnish & Swedish) All-you-can-eat pizza and pasta buffet.

Hesburger (www.hesburger.fi) Finland's very-own hamburger chain.

Koti Pizza (www.kotipizza.fi, in Finnish & Swedish) Good-value pizzas available to eat-in or have home-delivered.

Rosso (www.rosso.fi) Large kid-friendly menu of pasta, pizza, steaks and more.

VEGETARIANS & VEGANS

With a long-held love of fish and flesh, Finland is a difficult country for vegetarians. If you're in Helsinki, then there are a few dedicated restaurants, but outside of the capital you'll be trawling menus for pizzas or pastas. Strict vegetarians need to look out for pea soups with a meaty stock and fish-based pastes and dips.

Lunchtime buffets are a good bet for a main meal as they'll often include several fresh salad options, soups and filling rye bread. As well as Asian restaurants (Thai, Vietnamese and Chinese have good options), nonvegans should look out for local delicacies like *karjalanpiirakka* (Karelian pastries), breads like the pudding-rich *mammy* or cheesy *leipäjuusto*, and the wide selection of delicious farm cheeses. In some places there'll be plenty of fresh fruit particularly berries, which are sold in every kauppatori – the best places to stock up for self-catering.

The Finnish vegan society keeps a list of vegetarian and vegan restaurants on its website, www .vegaaniliitto.fi.

EAT YOUR WORDS

Most restaurants will have a menu in English, but if not the Swedish menu may be easier to decipher. The following phrases will help; see the Language chapter (p373) for more details including pronunciation.

Useful Phrases

The bill, please.	*Saisinko laskun.*
The menu/drinks menu, please.	*Saisinko ruokalistan/juomalistan.*
Do you have ...?	*Onko teillä ...?*
I'm a vegetarian.	*Olen kasvissyöjä.*
Nothing else, thanks.	*Ei muuta, kiitos.*
I'd like ...	*Saisinko ...*
I don't eat ...	*En syö ...*
Table (for one/two/four) please?	*Saisinko pöydän (yhdelle/kahdelle/neljälle)?*
Another one, please.	*Saisinko toisen.*

Food Glossary

These 'root' forms are as they would appear on a menu; other endings apply for them to be used correctly in phrases.

aamiainen	breakfast
alkuruoka	starter
appelsiini	orange

illallinen	dinner
juusto	cheese
jälkiruoka	dessert
kahvi	coffee
kala	fish
kana	chicken
kananmuna	egg
keitto	soup
kinkku	ham
lammas	lamb
leipä	(some) bread
liha	meat
lohi	salmon
lounas	lunch
maito	milk
makkara	sausage
mehu	juice
nauta	beef
olut	beer
omena	apple
peruna	potato
pihvi	steak/patty of meat
pippuri	pepper
poro/poronkäristys	reindeer/sautéed reindeer stew
pääruoka	main course
suola	salt
(iso/pieni) tuoppi	(lg/sm) tap beer
vesi	water
viini	wine
voi	butter

Environment

Finland tends to feel that it doesn't need to be told too much about the environment, and likes to do things its own way. With vast reserves of carefully managed forestry, it manages to produce reams of pulp and paper while maintaining its pine-scented green blanket intact. While this doesn't exactly stimulate biodiversity, it's hard to argue with seventy-odd per cent tree coverage. The Finns are environmentally conscious in a very unselfconscious way and favour practical, workable solutions over idealism. It's a country that carefully culls its large mammal population, and that regards nuclear power as a viable green alternative, in the hands of Finns at any rate: Chernobyl wasn't exactly at a healthy distance from Suomi. The average Finnish household, despite above-average carbon emissions, is fairly environmentally friendly, and pilot carbon-neutrality projects are in place in various municipalities.

THE LAND

Without thinking too much about it, people often describe Finland offhand as a country of 'forests and lakes', and the truth is that they are spot on. Some 10% of Suomi is taken up by bodies of water, and nearly 70% is forested with birch, spruce, and pine. It's a fairly flat expanse of territory: though the fells of Lapland add a little height to the picture, they are small change compared to the muscular mountainscapes across the border in Norway.

Measuring 338,145 sq km and weighing in as Europe's seventh-largest nation, Finland hits remarkable latitudes: even its southernmost point is comparable with Anchorage in Alaska, or the lower reaches of Greenland. Its watery vital statistics are also impressive, with 187,888 large lakes and numerous further wetlands and smaller bodies of water. Geographers estimate that its total coastline, including riverbanks and lakeshores, measures 315,000km, not far off the distance to the moon.

The nation's geography owes much to the last Ice Age, which came to an end some 10,000 years ago. Powerful masses of moving ice ground down the bedrock and produced classic glacial features such as eskers, ridges of sand

Lappajärvi, northeast of Seinäjoki, is one of Europe's biggest meteorite impact sites. The crater measures 23km in diameter and was created some 70 to 80 million years ago.

THE MÖKKI

Tucked away in Finland's forests and lakelands are nearly half a million *kesämökkejä*, or summer cottages. Part holiday house, and part sacred place, the *mökki* is the spiritual home of the Finn and you don't know the country until you've spent time in one. The average Finn spends less than two days in a hotel per year, but several weeks in a cottage.

These are the places where people get back to nature. Amenities are often basic – the gloriously genuine ones have no electricity or running water – but even the highest-flying Nokia executives are in their element here, chopping wood, picking chanterelles, rowing on the water, and selecting young birch twigs for the *vihta*, or sauna whisk. There's no better sauna than a lakeside *mökki* one: the soft steam of the wood stove caresses rather than burns, and the nude dash down to the wooden jetty for an invigorating spring into the chilly lake is a Finnish summer icon. As is the post-sauna can of beer, cooled in the lake or an underground dugout, the new potatoes with fresh dill, and the sausages grilled over pinecones on the barbecue. It's hard not to feel at peace when gazing out at the silent lake, pines perfectly reflected in it by the midnight sun, and anything of consequence miles away.

The best way to experience a *mökki* is to be invited to one by a Finnish friend, but failing that, there are numerous ones that you can rent (see p349), particularly in the Lakeland (p134) area.

and gravel that were formed by streams of meltwater under the main body of the glacier, and kettle holes, lumps of ice left behind in depressions by the retreating glaciers that became lakes. The predominant flow of Finland's waterways is northwest to southeast, mirroring the path of the glaciers' retreat.

Released from the oppressive weight of the ice, the crust in these parts began to slowly spring back, in a process known as isostasis. This bounceback still continues today at a rate of some 6mm per year. The Baltic, which in fact was a lake until the saltwater came pouring in via Denmark at about the same period, is decreasing in size as land rises from the sea.

Eskers and wooded hills are the main elevated areas through much of the country, and only in the far north do things start to get a little loftier. Typical of Lapland is the *tunturi*, or fell: these hills dot the region, giving way across the border to the higher chains in Norway and Sweden. Finland's highest point, Halti Fell, on the Norwegian frontier, rises only 1328m above sea level.

WILDLIFE

Finland's short summers and harsh winters call for a series of adaptive measures from its living population. Plants harden for winter and lose water to concentrate their liquid content, thus lowering their freezing temperature. Animals may grow fatty deposits, a white winter coat, or hibernate through it. When the snow melts, a rapid, intense explosion of life is concentrated into the growing season, which is only four months in northern Finland. A spring cold snap, or *takatalvi*, can have devastating effects on the year's brood.

Animals

Finland's vast expanses of forest and wide network of protected areas are important habitats for a large number of bird and animal species. These include a number of large mammals, among them the formidable *karhu*, or brown bear. You're unlikely to see bears even if trekking in their demesne, but various guides around Karelia and Kuusamo offer you a decent chance of watching them in the wild. More common is the *hirvi*, elk (moose), a solitary, shy animal that's a real treat to see unless it's crashing through your car windscreen. Another hazard on the northern highways are the quarter-million or so reindeer (opposite); domesticated beasts pastured and herded mostly by the Sámi in Lapland. Though once extinct in Finland, the wild, or forest, reindeer has returned in small numbers to the country's northeast.

Apart from the bear, the other major carnivores are the fox, the *ilves* (lynx), a mostly nocturnal wild cat that chiefly hunts hares, rodents and birds, the *susi* (wolf), mostly concentrated in the country's east, and the *ahma*, or wolverine, a real wilderness creature whose solitary patrols are nourished by carrion and occasional reindeer hunting. Apart from the fox, you are unlikely to see any of these creatures unless you head out with specialist nature guides.

Other interesting mammals include the rare Saimaa ringed seal, a freshwater dweller that lost its saltwater cousins as the land rose, the flying squirrel, a resident of the taiga, and the famous lemming, an Arctic resident. Other animals include hedgehogs, muskrats, martens, beavers, otters and hares.

There are more than 300 bird species in Finland (see p76 for more information). Large species include black grouse, capercaillies, whooper swans and birds of prey such as the golden eagle, eagle owl and osprey. Chaffinches and willow warblers are the two most common forest species, and their songs are almost synonymous with the Finnish summer. Sparrows are quite common in inhabited areas. Crested-tits, black woodpeckers, black-throated divers, ravens and many owls are common throughout the country; the glorious red-throated diver (*kaakkuri*) is also present, as are many other

The brown bear was once so feared that even mentioning its name (*karhu*) was taboo; numerous synonyms, such as *mesikämmen*, or 'honeypaw', exist in Finnish.

REINDEER ROADBLOCKS

While you'll be lucky to see an elk, and extremely so to see a wolf or lynx, you are guaranteed to see reindeer if you head to the country's north, for there are some 230,000 wandering around Lapland, and you won't have to go trekking in the wilderness to find them.

The reindeer you see are not wild. Reindeer herding has been an essential part of the Sámi culture for centuries, and reindeer are semidomesticated but wander freely. The herders identify their beasts using a complex system of notches cut into the reindeer's ear when it's a calf. Some 10,000 different earmarks exist. The herders' income comes from the meat, although some skins are sold too, and milk is used for Lappish cheeses. Reindeer research studies have found that the meat is of much better quality and healthier when the reindeer has been left to forage freely rather than have its diet supplemented by pellets.

Reindeer get driven mad by the voracious insects in summer. Though many reindeer die from, or as a result of, so many bites (though medicating them has helped in recent years), the *räkkä* season also helps the herders, as the reindeer tend to club together, reasoning that there are less insects per head when they're in a group.

With so many wandering about, it's inevitable that some will find their way onto the Lapland roads and they are very blasé about traffic. Some 3000 to 4500 reindeer die annually on Finnish roads, and trains kill an additional 600.

The best way to avoid an accident is to slow down immediately when you spot a reindeer, regardless of its location, direction or speed. Reindeer move slowly and do not respond to car horns. Nor do they seem to feel that vehicles deserve right of way. If a calf is on one side of the road and its mother on the other, it will almost always try and dash across.

Elk are not as common but are much larger animals and tend to dart onto the road if panicked by traffic. There are around 2000 accidents each year involving elk and generally neither the vehicle nor the animal come out of it looking too good. Be particularly vigilant when driving in the morning or evening, especially in autumn, when elk accidents are a very real and potentially fatal danger. Respect the warning signs!

waterbirds. The people-loving Siberian jay is a common sight in Lapland. There are numerous migrating birds present in spring and summer, including the common crane, a spectacular sight in the fields. Finns who watch migratory birds arrive from the south have a saying for how to determine when summer will come: it is one month from sighting a skylark, half a month from a chaffinch, just a little from a white wagtail and not a single day from a swift. Less popular creatures include the viper (*kyy*), which is the most common poisonous snake.

Plants

Finnish plant life has developed relatively recently, having been wiped out by the last Ice Age, and is specially adapted either to survive the harsh winters, or to take advantage of the short summers.

Although coastal areas support a more diverse tree population, nearly all of Finland's blanket forest cover is made up of pine, spruce and birch. The Scots pine is now the most common forest tree, and is a very hardy species whose symbiotic relationship with a fungus dramatically increases the efficiency of its root system. It generally grows on dryish ground and sandy soils, conditions that don't foster undergrowth. The spruce (Christmas tree) dominates in natural forests, which are dark and dense. The slender, deciduous birch is a symbol of the Finnish summer, and can be found throughout. Most forests in Finland are logged every 80 years or so and forestry management is a big thing here (see p66).

Finnish flora sparkle during the dynamic period between late May and September. Flowers bloom riotously and berries are gathered; you'll see

Lemmings are not really suicidal. While they do migrate in large numbers in years of overpopulation, the image of them jumping en masse over a cliff comes from the Disney film *Wild Wilderness*, when the beasts took a dive in the name of Hollywood.

cars all over the place and families filling buckets with wild mushrooms, blueberries, wild strawberries, and in the north, the delicious Arctic cloudberries (bakeapples).

The website of Finland's environmental authority, www.environment.fi, is a good resource for keeping up to date with the latest policies and measures in the country.

ENVIRONMENTAL ISSUES

As a general model for environmentally sustainable nationhood, Finland does very well. Though it has a high per-capita carbon-emission rate, this is largely due to its abnormal heating requirements and is offset in many ways. As in much of northern Europe, cycling and recycling were big here decades ago, littering and waste-dumping don't exist, and sensible solutions for keeping houses warm and minimising heat loss were a question of survival not virtue. Its tree cover of nearly 70% is the world's highest, and Finns in general have a deep respect for, and understanding of, nature and have always trodden lightly in it, seeing the forest as friend not foe.

Finns are dedicated users of bicycles (at least in summer) and, like much of northern Europe, public transport is seen as the obvious option rather than a last resort. Holidays are still spent at the *mökki* (summer cottage) or out in the countryside; foraging for berries and mushrooms significantly reduces packaging and food miles, and many people grow their own vegetables. There's no need for expensive, attention-grabbing environmental campaigning in Finland; the traditionally close relationship to the natural world here has combined with a Nordic tendency for common-good urban practices with optimum results. High levels of education and low poverty play their parts here too.

FORESTRY IN FINLAND

Whether producing tar for caulking ships in the days of sail, timber for furniture, or paper and pulp for our endless demands for them, forestry has a long and important history in Finland. While the technology boom has meant that it now accounts for only 21% of total exports, down from nearly 90% in the late 1950s, it's still a highly significant, and sometimes controversial, business. It's a huge source of income and employment, but also the nation's major cause of pollution and the main topic of environmental debate.

Finland is the second-largest exporter of paper products in the world and is dependent on paper manufacturing. Around 64% of the country is 'exploitable' forest – government- or privately owned – that is harvested for cutting on a long-term, cyclical basis. While this is indubitably well managed – the forest lobby feel that they are criticised because they've done such a good job in preserving it in the first place – it has an unavoidable impact on local ecosystems, with ecological diversity lowered. However, the main problem it causes in Finland is water pollution, especially from use of fertilisers on the forest areas.

While Finland may look idyllic and pristine, things are not always as they seem. In a recent government survey, only 43% of the country's rivers were rated 'good' or better while about 80% of lakes were given the nod of approval. The pulp and paper industry uses vast quantities of water, although improved technology is leading to better water conservation and lowered emissions into the lakes and rivers. Worryingly, though, Finland's sea areas had markedly declined in water quality in the early years of the 21st century. While massive emissions from Russian St Petersburg and Vyborg contribute heavily to this, it's a disquieting trend.

The forestry industry is also fighting battles up in the north, where Sámi reindeer herders complain that the companies are erecting fences that jeopardise traditional movement between pasturing areas, and logging old-growth forests in the region. The Sámi are seeking legislation to prevent this, while the forestry companies and Metsähallitus claim that only a minimal area is affected and the reindeer have more than enough space anyway. As always, the truth lies somewhere in between, but it's an ugly confrontation between powerful commercial interests and an indigenous minority.

But they're not a nation of tree-huggers. Most of the forests (see opposite) are periodically logged, and privately owned plots are long-term investments for many Finns. Hunting is big here, and animals are kept at an 'optimum' population level. The elk population reaches around 130,000 in autumn, and is reduced by some 50,000 by the keen shooting contingent.

Despite the rushing rivers and clean air, Finland only manages to produce some 16% of its energy needs from hydro- and wind-generated sources. It has a firm commitment to nuclear energy, which is routinely either praised or bemoaned by various environmental thinktanks.

The Finnish Forest and Park Service, **Metsähallitus** (www.outdoors.fi), is the main domestic conservation body. As well as overseeing 120,000 sq km of land, it also works to protect endangered species and promote biodiversity on forest lands that are used for commercial purposes. Though it has a double role, being responsible for much of the managed logging of Finland's forests, it is also the number-one reference point for travellers looking to minimise their own environmental impact in Finland's forests and protected areas, and its website outlines codes of conduct that, while mostly common sense, are respected far more here than in many other nations. For more information about the National Park Service and protected wilderness areas, see p68.

While environmental consciousness is high in Finland, an impact from tourism is inevitable, particularly in destinations that attract an amount of visitors disproportionate to their existing population. The ski resort is the classic example of this, and a recent study by Landscape Lab (www .arcticcentre.org/landscapelab) on their impact produced predictable but concerning results. It used a variety of markers, such as the presence of urban birds, to measure urbanisation, and found their population to be high in several of northern Finland's tourist centres, with a corresponding withdrawal of more sensitive species from those areas.

Another hypothesis it posited was that perhaps the changing nature of tourism towards more ecological, nature-focused experiences could in fact have a detrimental effect on the ecosystem as a whole, as tourism spread thinly over a large area, rather than concentrated in a few key destinations, might have a larger overall impact on nature. Balanced against this is the positive effect on traditional communities, with more local employment, a key factor in remote areas. For tips on how to minimise your impact see p18.

The Finnish branch of the World Wildlife Fund runs week-long volunteer programs every summer where you participate in a work camp on a conservation project. Email info@wwf.fi for details of upcoming camps.

It's not going to pull the kids away from Counter-strike, but if you want to have a crack at managing your own pine forest, check out the simulator that you can download at http://sokl.joensuu .fi/saima/pume_eng.htm

The Great Outdoors

Finland's beauty and appeal lie in its fantastic natural environment, with vast forests, long waterways and numerous lakes to explore, as well as the harsh Arctic wilderness in the north. Getting outdoors is the best way to experience the country and Finland is remarkably well set-up for any type of activity, from all-included safari-style packages to map-and-compass do-it-yourself adventures. There's almost unlimited scope in both summer and winter.

NATIONAL PARKS

One of the best websites we know is www.outdoors.fi, with comprehensive information on all of Finland's parks and protected areas. An invaluable resource.

Finland's excellent network of national parks and other protected areas is maintained by **Metsähallitus** (Finnish Forest and Park Service; www.outdoors.fi). At last count, there were 35 national parks that made up a total area of over 8000 sq km. A similar amount of territory is protected under other categories, while further swathes of land are designated wilderness reserves. In total, over 30,000 sq km, some 9% of the total area, is in some way protected land.

The Metsähallitus website provides wonderful information on all these spots; the organisation also publishes individual leaflets on each park, as well as *Finland's National Parks*, a booklet listing all national parks, with information on trails and accommodation, and notes on flora and fauna. This can be obtained at any Metsähallitus office or nature centre; the website also has details on how to get the brochures you need posted out to you.

The largest and most pristine national parks are in northern Finland, particularly Lapland, where vast swathes of wilderness invite trekking, cross-country skiing, fishing and canoeing. See the Lapland chapter (p306) for more details.

Linnansaari and Kolovesi National Parks, near Savonlinna, are the best parks in the Lakeland area and home to the extremely endangered Saimaa ringed seal. To see larger mammals – such as the shy and elusive elk – it's best

NATIONAL PARKS

Great National Parks	Features	Activities	Best Time to Visit
Lemmenjoki (p343)	Broad rivers and old-growth forests; golden eagles, reindeer	Trekking, boating, gold-panning	Aug-Sep
Linnansaari & Kolovesi (p142)	Luscious lakes and freshwater seals	Canoeing	May-Sep
Oulanka (p299)	Pine forests and river valleys; elk, white-tailed eagles; calypso flowers	Trekking the Bear's Ring, canoeing, rafting	late Jun-Sep
Urho K Kekkonen (p336)	Fells, mires and old Sámi settlements; reindeer, flying squirrels	Trekking, cross-country skiing, fishing	Jul-Sep & Nov-Apr
Ekenäs Archipelago (Southwestern Archipelago; p119)	Strings of islets and skerries; seals, eider ducks, greylag geese	Boating, fishing	May-Sep
Nuuksio (p112)	Forest within striking distance of Helsinki; woodpeckers, elk, divers	Nature trails	May-Oct
Patvinsuo (p180)	Broad boglands and old forest; bears, beavers, cranes	Hiking	Jun-Oct
Pallas-Yllästunturi (p325)	Undulating fells; bears, snow buntings, ptarmigans	Hiking, trekking, skiing	Jul-Sep & Nov-Apr

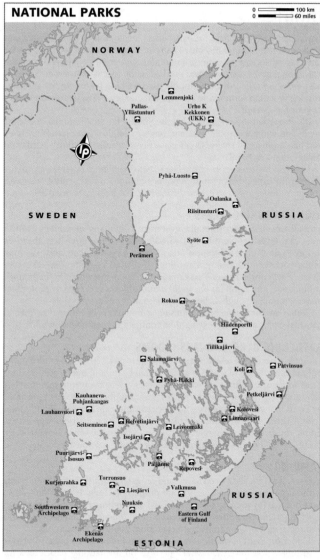

NATIONAL PARKS

0 — 100 km
0 — 60 miles

NORWAY

Lemmenjoki

Pallas-
Yllästunturi

Urho K
Kekkonen
(UKK)

Pyhä-Luosto

Oulanka

Riisitunturi

SWEDEN

RUSSIA

Syöte

Perämeri

Rokua

Hiidenportti

Tiilikajärvi

Salamajärvi

Koli

Patvinsuo

Pyhä-Häkki

Petkeljärvi

Kauhaneva-
Pohjankangas

Lauhanvuori

Kolovesi

Linnansaari

Seitseminen

Helvetinjärvi

Leivonmäki

Isojärvi

Puurijärvi-
Isosuo

Päljänne

Repovesi

Kurjenrahka

Torronsuo

Liesjärvi

Valkmusa

RUSSIA

Nuuksio

Southwestern
Archipelago

Eastern Gulf
of Finland

Ekenäs
Archipelago

ESTONIA

If heading off trekking on your own, always advise someone of your route and intended arrival date, or note these details in trekkers' books in huts and hostels.

to visit one of the national parks in the northeast, such as Oulanka National Park, or further north in Lapland, such as Lemmenjoki, Pallas-Yllästunturi and Urho K Kekkonen National Parks. These parks are vast and services and facilities are few; to make the most of a visit you should be prepared to spend several days trekking and camping. Many of the national parks have excellent networks of wilderness huts that provide cosy free places to overnight on hiking routes. See p70 for trail recommendations and more information about trekking.

HIKING

The superb system of national parks offers memorable trekking throughout Finland in the summer months. The routes are backed up by resources for camping, so it's easy to organise a multiday wilderness adventure.

National parks offer excellent marked trails, and most forest and wilderness areas are crisscrossed by locally used walking paths. Nights are short or nonexistent in summer, so you can walk for as long as your heart desires or your feet permit.

It's important to remember what the Finnish landscape does and doesn't offer. You will get scented pine and birch forest, low hills, jewel-like lakes and brisk, powerful rivers. Don't expect epic mountains, fjords, cliffs and valleys; that's not Finland.

The trekking season runs from late May to September in most parts of the country. In Lapland the ground is not dry enough for hiking until mid-June, and mosquitoes are an irritation during July. For highlights, see p10.

RIGHT OF PUBLIC ACCESS

The *jokamiehenoikeus* (literally 'everyman's right') is an ancient Finnish code that gives people the right to walk, ski or cycle anywhere they like in forests and other wilderness areas – even across private land – as long as they behave responsibly. Canoeing, rowing and kayaking on lakes and rivers is also unrestricted. You can rest and swim anywhere in the Finnish countryside, and camp for one night *almost* anywhere. Travel by motorboat or snowmobile, though, is heavily restricted.

Watch out for stricter regulations regarding access in nature reserves and national parks where access might be confined to marked paths.

GATHERING BERRIES & MUSHROOMS

Except in strict nature reserves, it's permissible to pick berries and mushrooms – but not other kinds of plants – under Finland's right of public access. Finns do so with gusto, filling pails with blueberries, which come into season in late July, and delicious little wild strawberries. Cloudberries are so appreciated by Finns that you may not have a chance to sample this orange, slightly sour, creamy berry in the wild. In some parts of Lapland, cloudberries are protected. Edible mushrooms are numerous in Finnish forests, as are poisonous ones; make sure you have a mushroom guide or know what you are doing!

> Prepare to be bewildered by the number of different types of berries on offer. Cloudberries are the prize, but bilberries (blueberries), bearberries, cowberries (lingonberries), crowberries, cranberries, whortleberries, wild strawberries and more are there to look out for…

CAMPING

Everyman's right allows you to rest and camp temporarily in the countryside without permission, even on private property as long as you don't do so near homes. Try to camp on already-used sites to preserve the environment. Camping is not permitted in town parks or on beaches and in national parks and reserves it may be restricted to certain designated areas.

Under the right of public access, you cannot make a campfire on private land unless you have the owner's permission. In national parks, look for designated campfire areas (*nuotiopaikka*), and watch for fire warning signs – *metsäpalovaroitus* means the fire risk is very high. Felling trees or cutting brush to make a campfire is forbidden; use fallen wood instead.

HUTS & SHELTERS

Metsähallitus operates a huge network of free, properly maintained wilderness huts across its swathe of national parks and protected areas. Huts typically have basic bunks, cooking facilities, a pile of dry firewood and a compost toilet. You are required to leave the hut as it was – ie replenish the firewood and carry away your rubbish. The Finns' 'wilderness rule' states that the last one to arrive will be given the best place to sleep, but, on busy treks in peak season, it's good to have a tent, because someone usually ends up sleeping outside.

Some huts require advance booking, or have a separate, lockable section that must be booked ahead (usually €9 per bed). This is called a *varaustupa*.

Various other structures, including tepee-style *kotas* in Lapland, are designed for cooking and for temporary or emergency shelter from the weather. In a *laavu* (simple log shelter), you can pitch your tent inside or just roll out your sleeping bag.

The website www.outdoors.fi has invaluable information on huts and hiking routes; a 1:50,000 trekking map is recommended for finding wilderness huts. These are published by Karttakeskus and cost €19 from tourist offices, national park visitor centres or map shops.

WHAT TO BRING
Food
You will have to carry all food when you walk in wilderness areas. If you plan to walk between huts, you generally won't need cooking equipment, but it's best to have a camp stove in case of fire bans.

Insect Repellent
Mosquitoes are a big problem here, particularly in summer and particularly in Lapland. They are accompanied by hoards of other biting creatures from midges to horseflies. Skimp on protection at your own peril. Some trekkers use a head net; they may look comical, but so does a nose swollen with bites.

WHERE TO TREK
You can hike anywhere in Finland, but national parks and reserves have marked routes, designated campfire places, well-maintained wilderness huts and boardwalks over the boggy bits.

Lapland is the main trekking region, with huge national parks that have well-equipped huts and good, long hiking routes. See p306 for details. There are other classic trekking areas in the Kainuu and Koillismaa regions, and in North Karelia.

Some recommended treks are described here. Excellent trekking maps are available in Finland for all of these routes.

Hetta–Pallastunturi (p325) One of western Lapland's best walks heads through light forest with an easy gradient for 55km through national park.

Karhunkierros (Bear's Ring; p299) The most famous of all Finnish trekking routes, this trail in northern Finland covers 80km of rugged cliffs, gorges and suspension bridges.

Karhunpolku (Bear's Trail; p179) This 133km marked hiking trail of medium difficulty leads north from Lieksa through a string of stunning national parks and nature reserves.

Kevo Route (p344) A fabulous point-to-point or loop walk of 64km to 78km through a memorable gorge in far-north Lapland.

UKK Route (p293) The nation's longest trekking route is this 240km route through northern Finland. It starts at Koli Hill, continues along the western side of Lake Pielinen and ends at Iso-Syöte Hill. Further east, there are more sections.

CYCLING

Riding a bike in Finland is one of the best ways to explore parts of the country in summer. What sets Finland apart from both Sweden and Norway is the almost total lack of mountains. Main roads are in good condition and traffic is very light compared to elsewhere in Europe. Bicycle tours are further facilitated by the liberal camping regulations, excellent cabin accommodation at camping grounds, and the long hours of daylight in June and July.

The drawback is this: distances in Finland are vast. And let's face it, a lot of the Finnish scenery can get repetitive at a bicycle's pace. It's best to look at planning shorter explorations in particular areas, combining cycling with bus and train trips – Finnish buses and trains are very bike-friendly.

Even if your time is limited, don't skip a few quick jaunts in the countryside. There are very good networks of cycling paths in and around most major cities and holiday destinations (for instance, the networks around Oulu and Turku).

In most towns bicycles can be hired from sports shops, tourist offices, camping grounds or hostels for €10 to €20 per day, or €50 to €80 a week.

BRINGING YOUR BICYCLE

Most airlines will carry a bike free of charge, so long as the bike and panniers don't exceed the weight allowance per passenger. Other airlines, including many budget ones, levy a small charge. Inform the airline that you will be bringing your bike when you book your ticket. Depending on the airline, you may have to dismantle it.

Bikes can be carried on long-distance buses for €3 to €10 (often free in practice) if there is space available (and there usually is).

Bikes can accompany passengers on most normal train journeys, with a surcharge of up to €10. Inter-City (IC) trains have spaces for bikes, which should be booked in advance; you'll have to take your bike to the appropriate space in the double-decker wagon – you can lock it in with a 50-cent coin. You can take your bike on regional trains that have a suitcase symbol on the timetable; put it in the luggage van.

WHERE TO CYCLE

You can cycle on all public roads except motorways. Many public roads in southern Finland have a dedicated cycling track running alongside.

Åland

The Åland islands are the most bicycle-friendly region in Finland, and (not surprisingly) are the most popular region for bicycle tours.

Southern Finland

Southern Finland has more traffic than other parts of the country, but with careful planning you can find quiet roads that offer pleasant scenery. Around Turku, the Archipelago route (p228) offers excellent coastal scenery and island-hopping, while the Ox Rd runs through rural areas from Turku to Hämeenlinna (see p200).

The Lakeland & Karelia

Two theme routes cover the whole eastern frontier, from the south to Kuusamo in the north. *Runon ja rajan tie* (Road of the Poem and Frontier) consists of secondary sealed roads, and passes several typical Karelian villages before ending in Lieksa. Some of the smallest and most remote villages along the easternmost roads have been lumped together to create the *Korpikylien tie* (Road of Wilderness Villages). This route starts at Saramo village in northern Nurmes and ends at Hossa in the northeastern Kainuu region.

A recommended loop takes you around Lake Pielinen, and may include a ferry trip across the lake. Another good loop is around Viinijärvi, west of Joensuu.

Western Finland

This flat region, known as Pohjanmaa, is generally good for cycling, except that distances are long. The scenery is mostly agricultural, with picturesque wooden barns amid fields of grain in this breadbasket of Finland. The 'Swedish Coast' around Vaasa and north to Kokkola is the most scenic part of this region.

WINTER SPORTS

Winter's a wonderful time in Finland: see p6 for inspiration.

SLED SAFARIS & SNOWMOBILING

Whether you head out for an hour, or on an epic week-long adventure, being whisked across the snow by an enthusiastic team of huskies or reindeer is an experience like no other. Lapland (see p306) is the best place to do this, but it's also available further south in places like Nurmes (p185) and Lieksa (p179).

Similar excursions can be made on snowmobiles (skidoos). Operators in the same locations offer these trips. You'll need a valid driver's licence to use one. You normally share a machine, and take turns to drive it: you pay extra if you want one all to yourself. The basic prices are also increased for more powerful snowmobiles.

DOWNHILL SKIING & SNOWBOARDING

Finnish slopes are generally quite low and so are well suited to beginners and families. The best resorts are in Lapland, where the fells allow for longer runs. In central and southern Finland, ski runs are much shorter, averaging about 1km in length.

The ski season in Finland runs from late November to early May and slightly longer in the north, where it's possible to ski from October to May. Beware of the busy Christmas, mid-February and Easter holiday periods – they can get very crowded, and accommodation prices go through the roof.

You can rent all skiing or snowboarding equipment at major ski resorts for about €30/110 a day/week. A one-day lift pass costs around €30/160 a day/week (slightly less in the shoulder and off-peak seasons), although it is possible to pay separately for each ride. Skiing lessons are also available starting at around €60 for an hour's lesson for two.

The best resorts are Levi (p321), Ruka (p298), Pyhä-Luosto (p332) and Ylläs (p318), but Syöte, Koli, Pallas, Ounasvaara and Saariselkä are also good.

THE BEST: SNOW HOTELS

Are we suckers for paying top dollar to sleep in subzero temperatures or is a night in the icy splendour of a snow hotel a passport to frosty paradise? You decide; Finland has several places to try out the ultimate in wintry sleeping. These are our favourites:

- **Lumilinna** (p315) In the centre of Kemi, the romantic snow castle offers stylish chateau sleeping.
- **Snow Village** (p319) Down vodkas from icy glasses in the igloo bar, then snuggle up atop your icy mattress.
- **Hotel Kakslauttanen** (p336) Traditional ice igloos for a Lapland sleep or high-tech heated ones for cracking aurora borealis (Northern Lights) views.

FORGET YOUR SKIS, DID YA?

Finland is proud of having invented the burgeoning sport of Nordic Walking, originally devised as a training method for cross-country skiers during the summer months. Basically, it involves using two specially designed hand-held poles while briskly walking; it may look a little weird at first, but involves the upper body in the activity and results in a 20% to 45% increase in energy consumption, and an increase in heart rate, substantially adding to the exercise value of the walk. Nordic Blading is a speedier version, using poles while on in-line skates – some pretty scary velocities can be reached!

CROSS-COUNTRY SKIING

Cross-country skiing is one of the simplest and most pleasant things to do outdoors in winter in Finland. It's the ideal way to explore the beautiful, silent winter countryside of lakes, fells, fields and forests, and is widely used by Finns for fitness and as a means of transport.

Practically every town and village has a network of ski tracks (*latu* or *ladut*) around the urban centre, in many cases illuminated (*valaistu*). The one drawback to using these tracks is that you'll need to bring your own equipment (or purchase some), as rentals often aren't possible.

Cross-country skiing at one of Finland's many ski resorts is an easier option. Tracks get much longer but also are better maintained. Ski resorts offer excellent instruction and rent out equipment. The best cross-country skiing is in Lapland, where resorts offer hundreds of kilometres of trails. Keep in mind that there are only about five hours of daylight each day in northern Lapland during winter – if you're planning on a longer trek, spring is the best time. Cross-country skiing is best during January and February in southern Finland, and from December to April in the north.

WATER SPORTS

ROWING, CANOEING & RAFTING

With 10% water coverage, Finland has long been a boating country, and until relatively recently boata were an important form of transport on the lakes and rivers. Every waterside town has a place (most frequently the camping ground) where you can rent a canoe, kayak, or row boat by the hour or day. Rental cottages often have row boats that you can use free of charge to investigate the local lake and its islands.

Canoes and kayaks are suitable for longer adventures lasting several days or weeks. For these, you'll need a plastic barrel for your gear, a life jacket and waterproof route maps. Route maps and guides may be purchased at local or regional tourist offices and at **Karttakeskus map shop** (www.kart takeskus.fi; Vuorikatu 14, Helsinki), which takes orders via its website. Canoe and kayak rentals range in price from €15 to €30 per day, and €80 to €200 per week, more if you need overland transportation to the start or end point of your trip.

Where To Row & Paddle

The sheltered bays and islands around the Turku archipelago and Åland in southwest Finland are good for canoeing in summer.

Finland's system of rivers, canals and linked waterways means there are some extensive canoeing routes. In the Lakeland, the Kolovesi and Linnansaari National Parks (p142) are excellent waters for canoeing, and offer plenty of exploration opportunities. North Karelia, particularly around Lieksa and Ruunaa, also offers good paddling. Rivers further north, in the Kuusamo area and in Lapland, are very steep and fast-flowing, with tricky rapids, making them suitable for experienced paddlers only.

Rapids are classified according to a scale from I to VI: I is very simple, II will make your heart beat faster, III is dangerous for your canoe, IV may be fatal for the inexperienced. Rapids classified as VI are just short of Niagara Falls and will probably kill you. Unless you're an experienced paddler you shouldn't negotiate anything above a class I rapid on your own. Always be prepared to carry your canoe or kayak around an unsafe stretch of river.

The website www.canoeinfinland.com has details of several Lakeland routes.

Ivalojoki Route (easy) A 70km route along the Ivalojoki, in northeast Lapland, that starts at the village of Kuttura and finishes in Ivalo, crossing 30 rapids along the way.

Lakeland Trail (easy to medium) This 350km route travels through the heart of the lake district (Kangaslampi, Enonkoski, Savonranta, Kerimäki, Punkaharju, Savonlinna and Rantasalmi) and takes 14 to 18 days.

Oravareitti (easy to medium) In the heart of the Lakeland, the 'Squirrel Route' is a well-marked two-day trip from Juva to Sulkava.

Oulankajoki and Kitkajoki (easy to difficult) A variety of choices on these neighbouring rivers in a spectacular wilderness area of northeast Finland.

Savonselkä Circuit (easy to difficult) The circuit, near Lahti, has three trails that are 360km, 220km and 180km in length. There are many sections that can be done as day trips and that are suitable for novice paddlers.

Seal Trail (easy) Explore the watery national parks of Kolovesi and Linnansaari, maybe spotting a rare ringed seal from your canoe.

Plenty of operators offer whitewater rafting expeditions in canoes or rubber rafts. The Ruunaa area (p181) is one of the best of many choices for this adrenalin-packed activity.

FISHING

Finnish waters are teeming with fish, and with people trying to catch them; per capita, Finns must be among the Earth's most enthusiastic anglers. Commonly caught fish include salmon (both river and landlocked), trout, grayling, perch, pike, zander (pike-perch), whitefish and Arctic char.

With so many bodies of water there is no shortage of places to cast a line, and not even the lakes freezing over stops the Finns (see boxed text, below). Lapland has the greatest concentration of quality fishing spots, but the number of designated places in southern Finland is also increasing. Some of the most popular fishing areas are the spectacular salmon-rich Tenojoki in the furthest north, the Torniojoki, the Kainuu region around Kajaani, Ruovesi, Hossa, Ruunaa, Lake Saimaa around Mikkeli, Lake Inari, and the Kymijoki near Kotka.

The website www.fishing.fi has plenty of useful information in English on fishing throughout the country.

ICE-FISHING

Nothing stops a Finn on a mission for fish. Not even when the winter closes in, the lakes freeze over, and the finny tribes below grow sluggish and hope for a breather from those pesky hooks.

No, the intrepid locals just walk or drive out to a likely spot on the ice, carve a hole using a hand-drill, unfold the campstool, and drop in a line. And wait, though the temperature be around -30°C. Seriously warm clothes and your choice of a flask of coffee or a bottle of Koskenkorva complete the picture.

Many tour operators offering winter activities organise ice-fishing excursions. In other places, ask at the tourist office or buy a beer for a likely looking type in the local pub.

Tourist offices can direct you to the best fishing spots in the area, and usually can provide some sort of regional fishing map and put you in touch with local guides. Fishing equipment of varying quality is widely available for hire from camp sites and other accommodation providers in fishy areas.

Permits

Several permits are required of foreigners (between the ages of 18 and 64) who wish to go fishing in Finland, but they are very easy to arrange. The website www.mmm.fi has all the details. Simple angling with hook and line requires no permit; neither does ice-fishing, unless you are doing these at rapids or other salmon waterways.

For other types of fishing, first you will need a national fishing permit, known as a 'fishing management fee'. A permit is €6/20 per week/year; they're payable at any bank or post office. Second, fishing with a lure requires a regional permit (€6/27), also available at banks and post offices. In addition to this a local permit may be required. There are often automatic permit machines; tourist offices, sports shops and camping grounds can also supply permits. The waters in Åland are regulated separately and require a separate regional permit.

The Metsähallitus website (www.outdoors.fi) details fishing restrictions in protected areas.

OTHER ACTIVITIES

BIRD-WATCHING

Bird-watching is increasingly popular in Finland, in no small part because many bird species migrate to northern Finland in summer to take advantage of the almost continuous daylight for breeding and rearing their young. The best months for watching birds are May to June or mid-July, and late August to September or early October.

Liminganlahti (Liminka Bay), near Oulu, is a wetlands bird sanctuary and probably the best bird-watching spot in Finland. Other good areas include Puurijärvi-Isosuo National Park in Western Finland, Siikalahti in the Lakeland, Oulanka National Park near Kuusamo, the Porvoo area east of Helsinki and the Kemiö Islands. D Gosney's *Finding Birds in Finland* is a field handbook on birding sites with many practical tips.

Check out www.birdlife.fi for a good introduction and a few links for bird-watching in Finland.

Helsinki

Created on land torn by sea and arm-wrestled over by Sweden and Russia, Helsinki spans the broken coast, hacked-out bays and rocky islands to have a rugged allure. Beyond the spectacular scenery, the Daughter of the Baltic has built herself with true Finnish *sisu* (guts) against invading neighbours and some truly diabolical weather to quietly become a world city.

Since its days as a trading centre, Helsinki was where Finland spoke to the world and, with eloquent whispers from Alvar Aalto and Jean Sibelius, the world liked what it heard. Recently it's been Aki Kaurismäki's gritty realist postcards or the metal salutes of Lordi that have been raising the volume, but if the Nordic capital keeps its neighbours up past their bedtime, no-one's complaining.

Because Helsinki is a night city, even when it's light. In summer the days stretch out until midnight and it feels like the whole population has moved out onto terraces. There's plenty to lift a glass to with art nouveau meeting classic Russian architecture overlaid with some uniquely Finnish reinvention, but the ever-humble Finns would never lift a glass to their own city.

Even in winter when the dark hangover seems to catch up with the city, Helsinki makes the best of flipping its Rautatientori into an ice-skating rink that squeals with joy. And it means that the bar and club culture has flourished. Maybe the stereotypical shyness of Helsinki's people is just a cover – they're trying to keep their city a secret from the rest of the world.

HIGHLIGHTS

- Walloping yourself with fresh birch leaves as you bake in **Kotiharjun Sauna** (p89)
- Pottering around the ruins of **Suomenlinna** (p87) to discover forgotten history
- Finding your perfect pitch in the city's excellent nightlife, from moshing at **Heavy Corner** (p101) to swilling a *lakka* (cloudberry) cocktail at **A21** (p100)
- Donning a beret and a thoughtful look to ponder the weird works at **Espoo Museum of Modern Art** (p111), one of Europe's best
- Drawing your own artistic inspiration from a circuit of **Tuusulanjärvi** (p106), the lake where Sibelius and other artists lived
- Hopping on the **ferry to Tallinn** (p109) to drink yourself… errr absorb the culture of the Old Town
- Mooching in **Porvoo's cafes** (p111) or getting a street history lesson in **Old Town** (p108)

- TELEPHONE CODE: 09
- POPULATION: 568,531

HISTORY

Founded in 1550 by King Gustav Vasa, Helsinki was to be a rival to the Hansa trading town of Tallinn. Earlier trials at Ekenäs were fruitless, so by royal decree traders from Ekenäs and a few other towns were shanghaied to the newly founded Helsingfors (the Swedish name for Helsinki).

For more than 200 years it remained a backwater market town on a windy, rocky peninsula. The Swedes built their fortress named Sveaborg in 1748 to protect the eastern part of the empire against Russian attack. In the war of 1808, the Russians took the theoretically impenetrable fortress and annexed Finland as an autonomous grand duchy. A capital closer to St Petersburg was necessary to keep a closer eye on Finland's domestic politics, and a really big fort would come in handy. In 1812 sophisticated Turku lost its standing as Finland's capital and premier town to what was once a trading outpost.

In the 19th and early 20th centuries, Helsinki grew rapidly in all directions. German architect CL Engel was called on to dignify the city centre, which resulted in the neoclassical Senaatintori (Senate Square). The city suffered heavy Russian bombing during WWII, but in the postwar period Helsinki recovered and went on to host the Summer Olympic Games in 1952.

In the 1970s and '80s, many new suburbs were built around Helsinki and residents celebrated their 'Helsinki Spirit', a term used for Cold War détente. It remains the seat of national parliament and official home to the president. Pride in the city peaked in 2007 when it hosted the Eurovision Song Contest, an opportunity for Helsinki to show off its dynamic cultural life to the world.

ORIENTATION

Helsinki is built on a peninsula surrounded by an archipelago of islets; there are links to many of them by bridge and ferry. Surrounding satellite cities include Espoo to the west and Vantaa, with the international airport, to the north.

The city itself has two centres based around its transport: Rautatientori (Railway Square) and Kauppatori (Market Square) at the city's port. From Kauppatori, Esplanadi Park runs west with popular strolling streets Eteläesplanadi and Pohjoisesplanadi on either side. Several ferries depart to the islands and Estonia from the port. You can get almost anywhere from Rautatientori thanks to the Metro links, intercity trains and bus stops around the square. A block west is Mannerheimintie, a major road that heads out to the Kallio district.

Maps

The city tourist office can supply a good free map of Helsinki, as well as walking, cycling and public-transport maps. *See Helsinki On Foot* (€2) is a good walking guide, while *Helsinki Your Way* (free) is a valuable booklet of events and listings.

INFORMATION

Bookshops

Akateeminen Kirjakauppa (Academic Bookshop; Map p86; ☎ 12141; Pohjoisesplanadi 39; ⊙ 9am-9pm Mon-Fri, 9am-6pm Sat, noon-6pm Sun) Finland's biggest bookshop with a huge travel section, maps, Finnish literature and impressively large English section including magazines and newspapers.

Hagelstams Bokhandel (Map p86; ☎ 649 291; Fredrikinkatu 35; ⊙ 10am-6pm Mon-Fri, 10am-3pm Sat) Antiquarian and secondhand bookshop with English paperbacks.

Discount Cards

To do some serious sightseeing, the **Helsinki Card** (☎ 2288 1200; www.helsinkicard.fi; adult 24/48/72hr €33/43/53, child €11/14/17) entitles you to urban travel, entry to more than 50 attractions in and around Helsinki, and discounts on day tours to Porvoo and Tallinn. The card (and a brochure outlining the discounts) is available at the city tourist office or at hotels, kiosks and transport terminals.

Emergency

General Emergency (☎ 112)
Police (☎ 122)

Internet Access

As well as those listed here, several of the city's cafes and bars have at least one terminal. Wi-fi is found at various points and many cafes will allow you to sit with a laptop and use their network.

Ateneum (Map p86; ☎ 173 361; www.ateneum.fi; Kaivokatu 2; ⊙ 9am-6pm Tue & Fri, 9am-8pm Wed & Thu, 11am-5pm Sat & Sun) The art gallery has a peaceful reading room with two free internet terminals. Access the rear entrance off Yliopistonkatu.

Level 7 (Map p86; ☎ 673 327; www.cafelevel7.fi; Vilhonkatu 5B; per hr €4; ⊙ 1-10pm) Quick access in venue popular with LAN gamers.

HELSINKI IN...

One Day

You should kick off with a strong coffee (the rest of caffeine-addicted Finland will) at one of the town's cafes (p99) before grabbing a *pulla* (cardamom bun) at the **kauppahalli** (p99). Stretch your legs over to **Tuomiokirkko** (p85) while waiting for a ferry to **Suomenlinna** (p87). Grab lunch at an **island restaurant** (p97) before the boat back to town. You can spend the afternoon in **Kiasma** (p82), the always-brain-bending home of new art, before dinner in the even odder **Zetor** (p100). Finish the night with a high-altitude drink at **Ateljee Bar** (p100), so you can say you've seen the whole city.

Two Days

With a weekend you can take your time on day one by browsing longer in Senate Square and head to **Katajanokka Island** (p86), especially stunning Orthodox **Uspenski Cathedral** (p85). Spend the afternoon at **Suomenlinna** (p87). On your second day hit the galleries: the **Ateneum** (p83) showcases the Golden Age of Finnish Art. Contradict it with **Kiasma**, then recharge with a sauna at **Yrjönkadun Uimahalli** (p88) before hitting classy Kallio bars like **Tokio** (p100).

Four Days

With two more days, you can delve deep into Helsinki's jagged coastline. Head past Hietaniemi Beach to pay homage to music at the **Sibelius monument** (p91), then take in some traditional architecture at the **Seurasaari Open-air Museum** (p88). At night, scat at **Storyville** (p102) if you're a jazz person, or rock out at **Tavastia** (p102). On your last day, take a trip to **Porvoo** (p108) for its beautiful wooden buildings and gorgeous riverside, then return for a triumphant dinner at **Savoy** (p98), Alvar Aalto's gift to dining.

Library 10 (Map p86; ☎ 3108 5000; Elielinkatu 2; ⏰ 10am-10pm Mon-Thu, 10am-6pm Fri, noon-6pm Sat & Sun, shorter hours in summer) Music and IT library on the 1st floor of the main post office, by the railway station. Several half-hour terminals and others bookable by phone.

mbar (Map p86; ☎ 6124 5420; Mannerheimintie 22; per hr €5; ⏰ 9am-midnight, later at weekends) In the Lasipalatsi complex. Offers good-quality internet access with heaps of terminals.

Rikhardinkatu Library (Map p86; ☎ 3108 5013; Rikhardinkatu 3; ⏰ 10am-8pm Mon-Thu, 10am-6pm Fri & Sat) The most central of Helsinki's public libraries has a good English-language selection and free internet terminals.

TeleCenter (Map p86; ☎ 670 612; Vuorikatu 8; per hr €2; ⏰ 10am-9pm Mon-Fri, 11am-7pm Sat, noon-7pm Sun) Slowish connection but cheap and friendly. Also sells its own brand of international phonecards.

Internet Resources

City of Helsinki (www.hel.fi) Excellent Helsinki City website, with links to all the information you might need.

Helsinki Expert (www.helsinkiexpert.fi) Sightseeing tours, accommodation bookings, tickets and events listings.

Helsinki Finland (www.visithelsinki.fi) Helsinki City Tourist & Convention Bureau official website.

HKL HST (www.hkl.fi) Public transportation routes and fares.

Visit Finland (www.visitfinland.com) Information pages of the Finnish Tourist Board.

Laundry

Most Helsinki hotels offer laundry service and some hostels have self-service facilities.

Easywash (☎ 406 982; per load €6-8; ⏰ 10am-8pm Mon-Thu, 10am-6pm Fri & Sat) city centre (Map pp80-1; Topeliuksenkatu 21); Kamppi (Map pp80-1; Kalevankatu 45) Self-service laundrette.

Left Luggage

At the bus and train station it costs €4 for a large locker, big enough to hold most backpacks. There are similar lockers and left-luggage counters at the ferry terminals.

Medical Services

Maria Hospital (Map pp80-1; ☎ 3106 3231; Lapinlah-denkatu 16; ⏰ 24hr) For emergency medical assistance.

Töölö Health Station (Map pp80-1; ☎ 310 5015; Sibeliuksenkatu 14; ⏰ 8am-6pm Mon, 8am-4pm Tue-Fri) A medical centre for nonemergencies.

Yliopiston Apteekki Mannerheimintie (Map pp80-1; ☎ 4178 0300; Mannerheimintie 96; ⏰ 24hr); city centre (Map p86; Mannerheimintie 5; ⏰ 7am-midnight) The branch in the city centre is more convenient.

HELSINKI

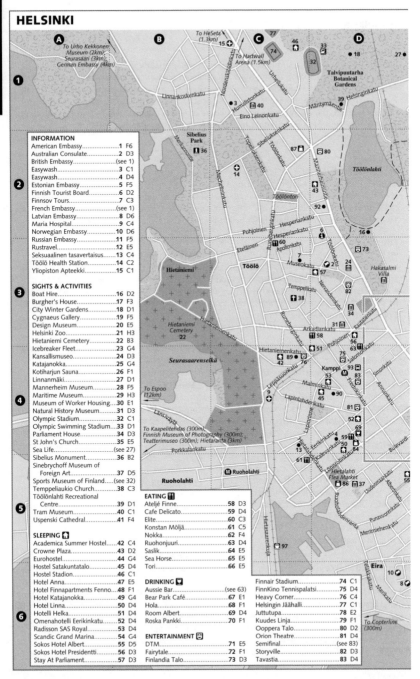

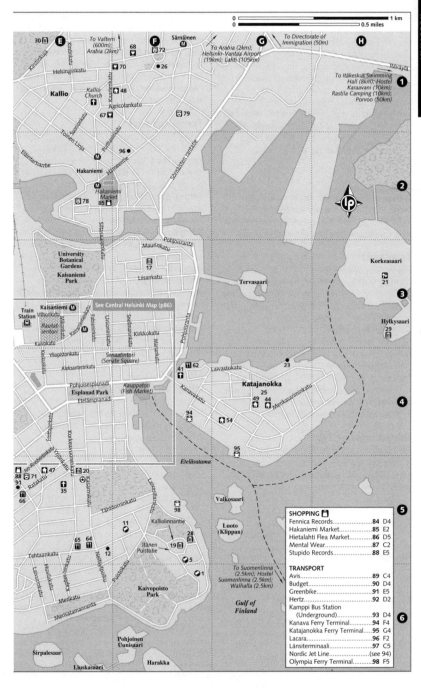

SHOPPING 🛍
Fennica Records.....................**84** D4
Hakaniemi Market...................**85** E2
Hietalahti Flea Market............**86** D5
Mental Wear..........................**87** C2
Stupido Records.....................**88** E5

TRANSPORT
Avis...**89** C4
Budget....................................**90** D4
Greenbike...............................**91** E5
Hertz......................................**92** D2
Kamppi Bus Station
  (Underground)....................**93** D4
Kanava Ferry Terminal............**94** F4
Katajanokka Ferry Terminal.....**95** G4
Lacara.....................................**96** F2
Länsiterminaali.......................**97** C5
Nordic Jet Line.................(see 94)
Olympia Ferry Terminal..........**98** F5

Money

Major banks (with international ATMs) are easy to find throughout the city, but the best place to exchange cash or travellers cheques is at the official moneychangers, who charge a lower commission. At the airport there's an exchange counter and a 24-hour exchange machine.

Forex (www.forex.fi; ☼ 8am-9pm summer, 8am-7pm Mon-Sat rest of the year) city centre (Map p86; Mannerheimintie 10); Esplanadi Park (Map p86; Pohjoisesplanadi 23) Has good rates, with a flat €2 fee on travellers cheques and no commission. There is another office at the train station (Map p86).

Post

Main post office (Map p86; ☎ 020-451 4400; Mannerheiminaukio 1; ☼ 7am-9pm Mon-Fri, 10am-6pm Sat & Sun) The post office is in the large building between the bus and train stations with the poste restante office adjacent.

Telephone

Public telephones are a rarity, with most Finns owning mobile phones. The railway station and some hostels have internet phone booths that allow you to use Skype either using your account or by inserting money.

Main telephone office (Map p86; ☼ 9am-5pm Mon-Fri) On the 2nd floor of the main post office building. You can place calls from here, but it's cheaper to call overseas using a prepaid phonecard.

TeleCenter (Map p86; ☎ 670 612; Vuorikatu 8; ☼ 9am-9pm Mon-Sat, noon-8pm Sun) A call centre with cabins and cheap international rates, starting from about €0.10 per minute to other European countries.

Tourist Information

In summer you'll probably see uniformed 'Helsinki Helpers' wandering around in their green bibs – collar these useful multilinguals for any tourist information.

Apart from the tourist office publications, free tourist publications include *Helsinki This Week* (published monthly) and *City in English* which are available at tourist offices, bookshops and other points around the city.

Helsinki City Tourist Office (Map p86; ☎ 169 3757; www.hel.fi/tourism; Pohjoisesplanadi 19; ☼ 9am-8pm

---

HELSINKI ON A HANDSET

Packed your mobile or cell phone? Helsinki Tourism has a cut-down version of their tourism site designed to be delivered to your mobile at www.helsinki.mobi.

Mon-Fri, 9am-6pm Sat & Sun May-Sep, 9am-6pm Mon-Fri, 10am-4pm Sat & Sun Oct-Apr) Busy multilingual office with a great quantity of information on the city.

Helsinki Expert (Map p86; www.helsinkiexpert.fi) Book hotel rooms and purchase tickets for train, bus and ferry travel around Finland and for travel to Tallinn and St Petersburg; also sells Helsinki Card (see p78) and is located in the tourist office.

Travel Agencies

From Helsinki you can easily arrange trips to the Baltic countries, Russia and beyond.

Finnsov Tours (Map pp80-1; ☎ 436 6960; finnsov.fi; Museokatu 15) One of the more established operators, providing tours, travel arrangements and help with visas.

Helsinki Expert (Map p86; ☎ 2288 1200; www.helsinkiexpert.fi) An agency handling travel around Finland and to Tallinn and St Petersburg.

Kilroy Travels (Map p86; ☎ 020-354 5769; www.kilroytravels.com; Kaivokatu 10C) Specialises in student and budget travel.

Rustravel (Map pp80-1; ☎ 611 520; www.rustravel.fi; Tehtaankatu 12) Great for Russian visas, given its proximity to the Russian embassy, but also helpful with tours to Ukraine.

Traveller (Map p86; ☎ 660 002; www.traveller.fi; Kasarmikatu 26) Specialises in train routes from Helsinki to Russia and beyond on the Trans-Siberian and Trans-Mongolian.

SIGHTS

Museums & Galleries

Helsinki has over 50 museums but some are too obscure to interest all but enthusiasts. For a full list, pick up the *Museums* booklet (free) from the tourist office.

KIASMA

The quirky curves of **Kiasma** (Museum of Contemporary Art Kiasma; Map p86; ☎ 1733 6501; www.kiasma.fi; Mannerheiminaukio 2; adult/under 18yr €7/free; ☼ 10am-8.30pm Wed-Sun, 9am-5pm Tue) have been a part of Helsinki for more than 10 years, but the contemporary art space still surprises with exciting new exhibits. American architect Steven Holl designed the unique structure to mimic the Greek letter *chi*, which represents an intersection. The building has become a meeting point for art as well as drinkers on its popular terrace, while skateboarders tear up the area around the nearby **Mannerheim statue**.

As well as regular contemporary exhibitions in kinetic sculpture, cross media or installation, there's a rapidly growing collection of Finnish and international modern art from the 1960s to the present. Focusing on the left of field, there's a permanent collection on the 3rd floor and an experimental theatre with a changing program (tickets usually cost extra) on the ground floor, known for the handwritten clock outside the arty museum shop.

Behind Kiasma is **Sanomatalo** (Map p86), the HQ of the famous Helsinki daily, *Helsingin Sanomat*. Designed by Sarlotta Narjus and Antti-Matti Sikula, it's a glassy, cool space that has exhibitions as well as popular shops, bars and cafes.

KANSALLISMUSEO

Impressive **Kansallismuseo** (National Museum of Finland; Map pp80-1; ☎ 4050 9544; www.kansallismuseo .fi; Mannerheimintie 34; adult/child €5.50/free; ☺ 11am-8pm Tue-Wed, 11am-6pm Thu-Sun) resembles a Gothic church with its heavy stonework and tall-steeple tower, but actually opened in 1916. Inside the museum is divided into rooms covering different periods of Finnish history, including a large collection of prehistoric finds, church relics and cultural exhibitions. Look up for the vivid frescoes by Akseli Gallen-Kallela depicting scenes from the epic *Kalevala*, including one of the hero Väinämöinen plunging a stake into the giant pike.

ATENEUM

The **Ateneum** (Ateneum Art Museum; Map p86; ☎ 1733 6401; www.ateneum.fi; Kaivokatu 2; adult/student/child €8/6.50/free; ☺ 9am-6pm Tue & Fri, 9am-8pm Wed & Thu, 11am-5pm Sat & Sun) is an ideal crash course in Finnish art. It houses Finnish paintings and sculptures from the heyday of the 18th century to the 1950s including works by Albert Edelfelt, Akseli Gallen-Kallela, the Von Wright brothers and Pekka Halonen. Pride of place goes to the prolific Gallen-Kallela's triptych from the *Kalevala* depicting Väinämöinen's pursuit of the maiden Aino. There's also a small but interesting collection of 19th- and early-20th-century foreign art. Downstairs is a cafe, good bookshop and reading room. The building itself dates from 1887 and once held the Design Museum (right) until its collection grew too large in the 1970s.

NATURAL HISTORY MUSEUM

Recently renovated, the **Natural History Museum** (Luonnontieteellinen Museo; Map pp80-1; ☎ 1912 8800; www.fmnh.helsinki.fi; Pohjoinen Rautatiekatu 13; adult/ child €5/2.50; ☺ 9am-5pm Tue-Fri, 11am-4pm Sat & Sun) is

known for its controversial weather vane of a sperm impregnating an ova. New exhibitions like Story of the Bones, which puts skeletons in an evolutionary context, bring new life to the University of Helsinki's extensive collection of mammals, birds and other creatures, including all Finnish species. The dinosaur skeletons and the saggy African elephant in the foyer are hits with kids.

KAAPELITEHDAS

The sprawling **Kaapelitehdas** (Cable Factory; off Map pp80-1; ☎ 4763 8300; www.kaapelitehdas.fi; Tallberginkatu 1C) once manufactured sea cable and later became Nokia's main factory until the 1980s. It's now a bohemian cultural centre featuring studios, galleries, concerts, and theatre and dance performances. Take tram 8, bus 15, 20, 21V, 65A or 66A, or the metro to the Ruoholahti stop; it's off Porkkalankatu.

There are several museums here, including the **Finnish Museum of Photography** (off Map pp80-1; ☎ 6866 3622; www.fmp.fi; Tallberginkatu 1G; adult/child €6/free; ☺ noon-7pm Tue-Sun), which has interesting studies of both photojournalism and artistic practice. **Teatterimuseo** (off Map pp80-1; ☎ 020-796 1670; www.teatterimuseo.fi; Tallberginkatu 1G; admission €6; ☺ 11am-6pm Tue-Sun, closed Jul) is a campy look behind Finland's dramatic scene including costumes and sets.

MANNERHEIM MUSEUM

This fascinating **museum** (Map pp80-1; ☎ 635 443; www.mannerheim-museo.fi; Kalliolinnantie 14; adult/child €8/free; ☺ 11am-4pm Fri-Sun & by appointment) in Kaivopuisto Park was the home of Baron Gustav Mannerheim, former president, Commander in Chief of the Finnish army and Finnish Civil War victor. The great Field Marshal never owned the building; he rented it from chocolate magnate, Karl Fazer, until his death. The house tells of Mannerheim's intrepid life with hundreds of military medals and photographs from his Asian expedition travelling 14,000km along the Silk Road from Samarkand to Beijing. Entry includes an informative one-hour guided tour in six languages, plus free plastic booties to keep the hallowed floor clean.

DESIGN MUSEUM

This **museum** (Map pp80-1; ☎ 622 05421; www .designmuseum.fi; Korkeavuorenkatu 23; adult/child €7/free; ☺ 11am-6pm Tue-Sun, also Mon Jun-Aug, 11am-8pm Tue Sep-May) has a permanent collection that

PAOLA SUHONEN

Over 10 years ago, designer Paola Suhonen started the fashion design company IvanaHelsinki and in 2007 it was Finland's first label to be selected for Paris Fashion Week. In 2008 the Design Museum hosted her Fennofolk show, which showcased the hottest new Finnish artists who were playing with their traditional icons to create new work.

How did the Fennofolk show happen? I came up with the name Fennofolk so I could put together a show about today's movement in art and in design. It was supposed to be IvanaHelsinki's 10-year exhibition but as usually happens I go further and further and that's what we have now. I wanted to have good people – that was the main point, not their work but cool people and friends and people that I know that do great stuff.

How does the Fennofolk use Finnish national culture? You can freely use something that's really authentic for you. It might be something that you want to differentiate from the crowd of what everyone else is doing, something that's from your roots, from your culture, then you have another level to your design because everyone has the same trends, but something authentic gives more edge to the design.

Where do your designs come from? What I call my designs or artwork I think of them as souvenirs of my soul world. They are something really unique and from my head. The designs I'm doing are a reflection of that world. I always have a story or a theme.

Where can people shop in Helsinki for great design and art? The Punavuori where we are now. There are a lot of little shops and vintage stores and galleries and workshops of young designers where they also sell their stuff that they're doing.

looks at the uniqueness of Finnish design, particularly the recent Fennofolk movement (see boxed text, above). Changing exhibitions focus on contemporary design – everything from clothing to household furniture.

SPORTS MUSEUM OF FINLAND

The **sports museum** (Urheilumuseo; Map pp80-1; ☎ 434 2250; Olympiastadion; admission €5; ⏰ 11am-5pm Mon-Fri, noon-4pm Sat & Sun), in the 1952 Olympic Stadium, houses Finland's sporting hall of fame including the triumph of runner Paavo Nurmi and Matti Nykänen, one of the most successful ski jumpers of all time. There are good simulations that let you compete in the 200m race against champions and there's a novel exhibition about Pesäpallo, Finland's own baseball-like game.

Also here is the **Stadium Tower** (Stadion Torni; admission €2; ⏰ 9am-8pm Mon-Fri, 9am-6pm Sat & Sun) with a 72m-high viewing platform that looks back to the city.

Trams 3B, 3T, 4, 7A, 7B and 10 from the city centre all run past it.

KAUPUNGINMUSEO

A group of small museums scattered around the city centre constitute the **Kaupunginmuseo** (www.helsinkicitymuseum.fi), which all have free entry. All buildings focus on an aspect of the city's past or present.

The must-see of the bunch is **Helsinki City Museum** (Map p86; ☎ 3103 6630; Sofiankatu 4; admission free; ⏰ 9am-5pm Mon-Fri, 11am-5pm Sat & Sun), which has historical exhibitions of photographs, rare books and films that piece together the city's transition from Russian to Swedish hands and into independence.

Other good museums in this group:

Burgher's House (Ruiskumestarintalo; Map pp80-1; ☎ 3107 1549; Kristianinkatu 12; ⏰ 11am-4pm Sun-Thu Jun-Aug & Dec) Built in 1818, this is central Helsinki's oldest wooden townhouse.

Museum of Worker Housing (Työväenasuntomuseo; Map pp80-1; ☎ 3107 1548; Kirstinkuja 4; ⏰ 11am-4pm Sun-Thu Jun-Aug) Shows how industrial workers lived in the early 20th century.

Sederholm House (Map p86; ☎ 3103 6529; Aleksanterinkatu 18; ⏰ 11am-4pm Sun-Thu Aug-Jun) Helsinki's oldest brick building dating from 1757 is furnished to suit a wealthy 18th-century merchant.

Tram Museum (Raitioliikennemuseo; Map pp80-1; ☎ 169 3576; Töölönkatu 51A; ⏰ 11am-4pm Sun-Thu Aug-May) This delightful museum displays vintage trams and depicts daily life in Helsinki's streets in past decades.

Tuomarinkylä Museum & Children's Museum (Lastenmuseo; Map p107; ☎ 3107 1568; Tuomarinkylä; ⏰ 11am-4pm Sun-Thu mid-Mar–Jul & Sep-Dec) Not far from the airport, these museums occupy an 18th-century manor house perceiving the city through the eyes of a modern family. From central Helsinki take bus 64 to its terminus and walk 1km.

OTHER GALLERIES & MUSEUMS

The **Post Museum** (Postimuseo; Map p86; ☎ 020-451 4908; Asema-aukio 5; adult/child €6/free; ☑ 9am-6pm Mon-Fri, 11am-4pm Sat & Sun) was closed for renovations at the time of research but the collection offers a fascinating insight into stamps, computerised data banks and the role postcards have played in Finland's history.

The **Amos Anderson Art Museum** (Map p86; ☎ 684 4460; Yrjönkatu 27; adult/child €7/free; ☑ 10am-6pm Mon-Fri, 11am-5pm Sat & Sun) houses the collection of publishing magnate Amos Anderson, one of the wealthiest Finns of his time. It includes Finnish and European paintings and sculptures from the 15th century to the present.

Finnish art from the 19th century is showcased at **Cygnaeus gallery** (Map pp80-1; ☎ 4050 9628; www.nba.fi; Kalliolinnantie 8; adult/child €4/free; ☑ 11am-7pm Wed, 11am-4pm Thu-Sun). It opened in 1882 and is one of Finland's oldest art galleries in an attractive wooden building (built in 1870) in Kaivopuisto Park.

The largest collection of classic European paintings in Finland is in the former brewery called **Sinebrychoff Museum of Foreign Art** (Map pp80-1; ☎ 1733 6460; Bulevardi 40; admission €5, with special exhibitions €7.50; ☑ 10am-6pm Tue & Fri, 10am-8pm Wed-Thu, 11am-5pm Sat & Sun). The main collection is Italian, Flemish and Swedish in origin. The Empire room is an impressive re-creation that drips with chandeliers and opulence.

Churches

One of CL Engel's finest creations, the chalk-white neoclassical **Tuomiokirkko** (Lutheran Cathedral; Map p86; ☎ 709 2455; Unioninkatu 29; ☑ 9am-6pm Mon-Sat, noon-6pm Sun Sep-May, 9am-midnight Jun-Aug), presides over Senate Square, though as it was not completed until 1852, the architect, who died in 1840, never saw it. Given Finland's Lutheran sensibilities, it was created to serve as a reminder of God's supremacy over the square. Its high flight of stairs, however, has become a meeting place for canoodling couples, and a setting for New Year's revelry. The interior features statues of the Reformation heroes Luther, Melanchthon and Mikael Agricola; true to their ideals, there is little other ornamentation under the lofty dome. There's a cafe in the brick-vaulted crypt in summer.

The eye-catching red-brick **Uspenski Cathedral** (Map pp80-1; ☎ 634 267; Kanavakatu 1; ☑ 9.30am-4pm Mon-Fri, 9.30am-2pm Sat, noon-3pm Sun, closed Mon Oct-Apr) is equally imposing on nearby Katajanokka

Island. The two opposing cathedrals face each other off high above the city in a contest for its soul. Built as a Russian Orthodox church in Byzantine-Slavonic style in 1868, it features classic onion-topped domes and now serves the Finnish Orthodox congregation. The high, square interior has a lavish icon-ostasis with the Evangelist flanking panels depicting the Last Supper and the Ascension. Orthodox services held at 6pm on Saturday and 10am Sunday are well worth attending as a discreet visitor for the fabulous chorals and candlelit atmosphere.

Hewn into solid rock, **Temppeliaukio Church** (Map pp80-1; ☎ 494 698; Lutherinkatu 3; ☑ 10am-8pm Mon-Fri, 10am-6pm Sat, noon-1.45pm & 3.30-6pm Sun) was designed by Timo and Tuomo Suomalainen in 1969 and remains one of Helsinki's foremost attractions. The church symbolises the modern innovativeness of Finnish religious architecture and features a stunning 24m-diameter roof covered in 22km of copper stripping. There are regular concerts, with great acoustics; the entrance is at the northern end of Fredrikinkatu.

Helsinki's oldest church is the white wood **Vanha Kirkko** (Map p86; Lönnrotinkatu), designed by CL Engel. Opposite the church is a **memorial** to Elias Lönnrot, compiler of the *Kalevala* epic, depicting the author flanked by his most famous character, 'steady old Väinämöinen'.

Helsinki's largest church is the soaring twin-spired neo-Gothic **St John's Church** (Map pp80-1; St John's Park), off Korkeavuorenkatu.

Hietaranta

Helsinki has several city beaches and **Hietaranta** is the best. It's a likeable stretch of sand just west of the centre, and ideal in summer for either swimming or enjoying the terrace.

The nicest way to get here is to stroll from Mechelininkatu west through the **Hietaniemi cemetery** (Map pp80-1). Finnish cemeteries are beautiful and designed to be walked in; this one has Orthodox, Jewish and Muslim, as well as Lutheran, sections.

Parks & Gardens

A good cure for seasonal blues can be the **City Winter Gardens** (Talvipuutarha; Map pp80-1; Hammarskjöldintie 1; admission free; ☑ noon-3pm Tue-Fri, noon-4pm Sat & Sun), which are elaborate greenhouses, founded in 1893, and containing cacti, palms, and other sun-loving plants foreign to Finnish soil. They are surrounded by

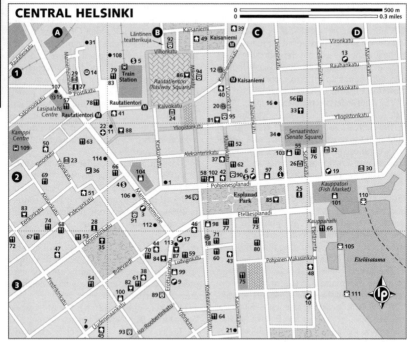

CENTRAL HELSINKI

botanical gardens, including a spectacular display of roses. Take tram 8 from Ruoholahti metro or Töölö.

Closer to the centre, the **Kaisaniemi Botanical Gardens** (☎ 1912 8856; Unioninkatu 44; admission free, greenhouses €5; ⊙ 9am-8pm Apr-Sep, 9am-5pm Oct-Mar) is run by the university and comprises Finland's largest botanical collection, with classic 19th-century greenhouses, a cafe and a park.

LINNANMÄKI

This **amusement park** (Map pp80-1; ☎ 020-385 677; www.linnanmaki.fi; Tivolikuja 1; 1-day adult/child ride pass from €33/21, entry-only free; ⊙ 11am-10pm May-early Sep) is a real kid-pleaser with rides, a roller-coaster and nightly fireworks. Its profits are donated to child-welfare organisations.

Nearby, **Sea Life** ((Map pp80-1; ☎ 565 8200; www .sealife.fi; Tivolitie 10; adult/child €13.50/9.50; ⊙ 10am-7pm Mon-Sat, 10am-8pm Wed, 10am-5pm Sun Jun-Sep, 10am-5pm Oct-May) is an awesome aquarium complex with walk-through tunnels that let you spot sharks, rays and a myriad of fish up close.

Bus 23, and trams 3B, 3T and 8, take you to Linnanmäki and Sea Life.

Helsinki Zoo

Spacious **Helsinki Zoo** (Map pp80-1; ☎ 169 5969; adult/child €7/4, with ferry ride €12/6; ⊙ 10am-8pm May-Aug, 10am-4pm Oct-Feb, 10am-6pm Sep-Apr) is located on Korkeasaari, best reached by ferry from Kauppatori. Established in 1889, it has animals and birds from Finland and around the world housed in large natural enclosures, as well as a tropical house, a small farm and a good cafe and terrace.

Ferries leave from Kauppatori and from Hakaniemi every 30 minutes or so in summer and zoo bus 11 goes from Herttoniemi metro station. This bus also runs at weekends in winter, otherwise it's bus 16 or the metro to Kulosaari and walk 1.5km through the island of Mustikkamaa.

Katajanokka Island

Just east of Kauppatori, this **island** (Map pp80-1) is divided from the mainland by a narrow canal and makes for an enjoyable stroll. It's a paradise of upmarket Jugendstil residential buildings with extravagant turrets and curious carvings galore. While the south side of the island has two of the major ferry terminals, the other side is more peaceful, with the Engel-designed Foreign Ministry looking out over the impressively functional fleet of ice-breakers. At the western end of the island, the Uspenski Cathedral looks over a leisure harbour and a series of warehouses attractively converted into enticing restaurants and bars.

The tourist office's excellent brochure *See Helsinki on Foot* (€2) has a self-guided walk around Katajanokka.

Suomenlinna
Just a 15-minute ferry ride from Kauppatori, this 'fortress of Finland' (off Map pp80–1)

is the must-do half-day trip from the city. Set on a tight cluster of islands, the Unesco World Heritage Site has been hotly contested real estate ever since the Swedes built here in 1748 to stave off Russian attacks, naming their bastion Sveaborg (Swedish fortress). It rivalled Turku as Finland's largest town until the vicious battles of 1808, which led to the Russians taking the fortifications and moving the capital to Helsinki in 1812. It remained in Russian hands until independence but during the Finnish Civil War it served as a prison for communist prisoners.

Suomenlinna actually spans two islands, Iso Mustaari in the north and Susisaari in the south, which are connected by a small bridge. Most visits to the island begin at the bridge with the **Inventory Chamber Visitor Centre** (☎ 668 800; www.suomenlinna.fi; walking tours €6.50, free with Helsinki Card; ☒ 10am-6pm May-Sep, walking tours depart 11am & 2pm Jun-Aug), which has tourist information, maps and guided walking tours in summer. You can also hop off at the King's Gate Quay on Susisaari, if you want to explore for yourself. There's a blue-sign-posted walking path that takes in many of the main attractions.

For transport to Suomenlinna see p106.

MUSEUMS

At the visitors centre is **Suomenlinna Museum** (☎ 684 1880; admission €5; ☒ 10am-6pm May-Sep, 10am-4pm Oct-Apr), featuring a scale model of Suomenlinna as it looked in 1808, and an illuminating 30-minute audiovisual display.

Two museums retell Suomenlinna's military history and can be visited with a combination ticket (€6). **Manege** (☎ 1814 5296; admission €4; ☒ 11am-6pm mid-May–Aug) commemorates WWII and displays heavy artillery. Finland was forbidden to possess submarines by the 1947 Treaty of Paris and the WWII-era U-boat **Vesikko** (☎ 1814 6238; admission €4; ☒ 11am-6pm mid-May–Aug) is one of the few submarines remaining in the country. You climb inside and see how it all worked – it's not for the claustrophobic.

Ehrensvärd Museum (☎ 684 1850; adult/child €3/1; ☒ 10am-5pm May-Aug, 11am-4pm Sep, 11am-4pm Sat & Sun Apr & Oct) preserves an 18th-century officer's home with dozens of model ships, sea charts, portraits and blue-and-white-tile Swedish stoves. Opposite Ehrensvärd Museum is the **shipyard** where sailmakers and other workers have been building ships since the 1750s. As many as two dozen ships are in the dry dock at any given time. They can be from 12m to 32m long and from as far away as the UK.

The delightful **Toy Museum** (☎ 668 417; admission €4; ☒ 11am-4pm Sat & Sun Apr & Sep, 11am-5pm daily May-Aug, 11am-6pm Jul) is a private collection of hundreds of dolls and almost as many teddy bears – the personal achievement of Piippa Tandefelt. The cafe here serves delicious homemade apple pie.

OTHER SIGHTS

Exploring the old bunkers, crumbling fortress walls and cannons at the southern end of Susisaari will give you an insight into this fortress. Young children should beware of the sudden drops and uncovered ruins. A torch will come in handy if you fancy exploring some of the tunnels.

Monumental **King's Gate** was built in 1753–54 as a two-storey fortress wall, which had a double drawbridge and a stairway, the 'King's Steps', added.

Next to the main quay, the distinctive pink **Jetty Barracks Gallery** (☎ 673 140; ☒ 10am-6pm Tue-Sun) is one of the best-preserved remaining buildings of the Russian era, and now has various exhibitions.

The **church** on Iso Mustasaari island was built by the Russians in 1854 and served as a Russian-Orthodox place of worship until the 1920s when it became Lutheran. It's the only church in the world to double as a lighthouse – the beacon was originally gaslight but is now electric and still in use.

Seurasaari

West of the centre, this island is best known for **Seurasaari Open-Air Museum** (☎ 484 511; www.kolumbus .fi/seurasaarisaatio; adult/child €6/free; ☒ 11am-5pm mid-Sep–mid-May, 11am-7pm Wed Jun-Aug, 9am-3pm Mon-Fri, 11am-5pm Sat & Sun late May & early Sep) with 18th- and 19th-century traditional houses, manors and outbuildings from around Finland. Guides dressed in traditional costume demonstrate folk-dancing and crafts such as spinning, embroidery and troll-making. While you'll see other museums like this across Finland, Seurasaari definitely has the best. There are guided tours in English at 11.30am and 3.30pm.

Worth visiting on a trip to Seurasaari, the **Urho Kekkonen Museum** (☎ 4050 9650; www.nba.fi/en /ukk_museum; Seurasaarentie 15, Tamminiemi; adult/child €6/ free, free with Helsinki Card; ☒ 11am-5pm Thu-Sun, 11am-7pm Wed, 11am-5pm Mon & Tue mid-May–mid-Aug) gives a glimpse into the life of Finland's greatest president. A guided tour wanders through the magnificent villa, its surrounding park and peeks into the traditional sauna that hosted diplomatic chinwags with Nikita Khrushchev.

It's also a venue for Helsinki's biggest Midsummer bonfires and a popular area for picnicking. Take bus 24 from the central train station. From central Helsinki, take bus 24, or tram 4 and walk.

ACTIVITIES

Enjoy a sauna and swim at the **Yrjönkadun Uimahalli** (Map p86; ☎ 3108 7401; Yrjönkatu 21; admission

€4-11; ⊗ men 6.30am-9pm Tue, Thu & Sat, women noon-9pm Sun & Mon, 6.30pm-9pm Wed & Fri) or **Kotiharjun Sauna** (Map pp80-1; ☎ 753 1535; Harjutorinkatu 1; admission €7; ⊗ 2-8pm Tue-Fri, 1-7pm Sat, sauna time until 10pm), two of the city's favourite institutions. Yrjönkadun is a sleek art-deco complex that first opened in 1928 while Kotiharjun is more working-class in the Kallio district. Another Kallio sauna is **Arla** (☎ 719 218; www.arlansauna.net; Kaarlenkatu 15; saunas €7; ⊗ 2pm-8am Wed-Sun), which enjoys a younger crowd thanks to the handy bars.

Helsinki has several affordable public swimming pools with inexpensive admission. Most convenient is the outdoor **Olympic Swimming Stadium** (Map pp80-1; ☎ 3108 7854; Hammarskjöldintie; admission €3.20; ⊗ May-Sep). There are also saunas here and you can rent towels and swimwear. However, the most impressive pool is the **Itäkeskus swimming hall** (Map p107; ☎ 3108 7202; Olavinlinnantie 6; admission €4.80; ♿). Take the metro to Itäkeskus station, walk east for a block and turn left at Olavinlinnantie. The entirely underground complex is carved from rock and was designed to double as a bomb shelter. In summer there are good **beaches** at Hietaniemi, Seurasaari and Suomenlinna, though some don't let the winter chill stop them – ice-swimming is popular.

Cycling is a great way to experience Helsinki's parks and sights. The bike and skate route map, *Pyöräilyreittejä Helsingissä* (Cycling Routes in Helsinki), is free at the city tourist office. For information on bike rental see p105.

Rollerblading is popular, especially in Kaivopuisto park and around Töölönlahti, the pretty bay north of the station. Skates can be hired at **Töölönlahti Recreational Centre** (Map pp80-1; ☎ 4776 9760; Mäntymäentie 1).

In winter Rautatientori becomes **Jääpuisto** (Ice Park; Map pp80-1; ☎ 3108 7934; www.jaapuisto .fi; admission €5, skate rental €5; ⊗ 10am-9pm Mon-Thu, 10am-9pm Fri & Sat, 10am-8pm Sun, late Nov–mid-Mar), an outdoor ice-skating area where you can hire skates and get involved.

HELSINKI WALKING & CYCLING TOUR

This tour requires a combination of walking and cycling – if you're on foot you'll probably want to stick to the central Helsinki area unless you want to hop on a tram for a rest, but with a bike it's a breeze to get out to Seurasaari, west of the city.

The starting point for any Helsinki tour is the bustling **Kauppatori (1**; p103), also known as the market square. It is flanked by stately 19th-century buildings – some of only a few remaining in the city after the devastation of WWII. The stone obelisk topped by a golden eagle is **The Stone of the Empress (2)**, Helsinki's oldest monument, unveiled in 1835 in honour of a visit by Tsar Nicholas I and Tsarina Alexandra.

Havis Amanda (3), the female nude statue dipping in a fountain just west of the market, was designed in 1908 by Finnish sculptor Ville Vallgren, who called the work *Merenneito* (Mermaid). The statue, known to most Finns as 'Manta', is commonly regarded as the symbol of Helsinki. During Vappu (May Day) students gather here to celebrate the coming of spring.

Across from Kauppatori is the **Presidential Palace (4)**, guarded by colourfully uniformed sentries. This is the president's official Helsinki residence – at the time of writing it's home to Tarja Halonen, Finland's first woman president and known for her resemblance to American chat-show host, Conan O'Brien.

Heading east, cross the footbridge onto Katajanokka Island to visit the Orthodox **Uspenski Cathedral (5**; p85) on a hill above the harbour. This very photogenic red-brick church is one of the most recognisable landmarks in Helsinki. Katajanokka itself is well worth a stroll if you have the time – many of its narrow streets have fine art nouveau residential buildings.

Back on the mainland, turn right along Sofiankatu, a narrow cobbled street with interpretive boards explaining early Helsinki history. It leads to **Senaatintori (6)**, Helsinki's 'official' centre. The statue of Tsar Alexander II in Senaatintori was cast in 1894, marking the strong Russian influence in 19th-century Helsinki.

Engel's stately chalk-white, blue-domed Tuomiokirkko (Lutheran Cathedral; p85), completed in 1852, is the square's most prominent feature and Helsinki's most recognisable building. The main University of Helsinki building is on the west side of Senaatintori and the magnificent National Library is a little further north along Unioninkatu. Two of Helsinki's museums, Helsinki City Museum (p84) and Sederholm House (p84) are along the south side of the square.

Walking back to Pohjoisesplanadi, you're in the pleasant **Esplanadi Park (7)**, with a cobbled avenue and grassy verges. It's a

HELSINKI

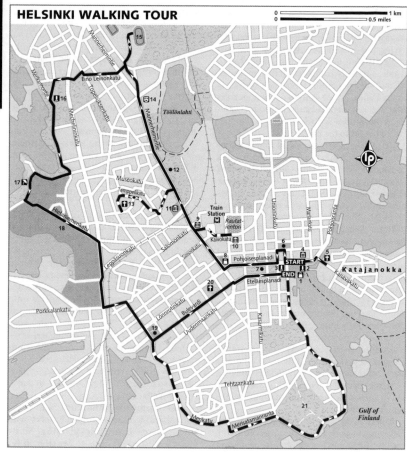

HELSINKI WALKING TOUR

WALK FACTS

Start Kauppatori
Finish Kauppatori
Distance 8km
Duration 3 hours

favourite summer spot and there's often live music here. The Esplanadi leads to the city's broad main thoroughfare, Mannerheimintie. On the northeast corner is the famous **Stockmann department store** (**8**; p104), where seemingly every Helsinkian buys everything.

Continue two blocks north on Mannerheimintie to **Kiasma** (**9**; p82), the daring museum of contemporary art. An **eques-**

trian statue of Marshal CGE Mannerheim, Finland's most revered military leader, dominates the square next to the museum.

Detour two blocks east to the Soviet-sized Rautatientori (Railway Square), which serves as a transport hub, but also boasts the national gallery, **Ateneum** (**10**; p83). The museum building, long a work-in-progress, was completed in 1991. The train station itself is a masterpiece of the Finnish National Romantic style.

Return to Mannerheimintie and continue walking northwest. The monolithic 1931 **Parliament House** (**11**; ☎ 4321; Mannerheimintie 30; admission free; ⏰ guided tours 11am & noon Sat, noon & 1pm Sun, also 1pm Mon-Fri Jul-Aug) dominates this stretch. A little further up Mannerheimintie, on the right, is one of Alvar Aalto's most famous works, the angular **Finlandia Talo** (12; ☎ visiting info 40241, box office 402 4400; Mannerheimintie 13; guided tours €6), a concert hall built between 1967 and 1972. Opening hours depend on events, so ring for information.

At this point you can detour west along Museokatu and Aurorankatu to Temppelikatu where you'll find **Temppeliaukio Church** (13; p85), a modern church hewn from solid rock.

A few blocks further to the north, on Mannerheimintie, is the 1993 **Ooppera Talo** (14; p102), home of the Finnish National Opera. Continue a short distance north on Mannerheimintie to the 1952 **Olympic Stadium** (15; p84). For some of the best views of Helsinki, take a lift to the top of the 72m Stadium Tower.

From the stadium, walk or cycle west to Sibelius park and the **Sibelius monument (16)**. This kinetic sculpture was created by artist Eila Hiltunen in 1967 to honour Finland's most famous composer, Jean Sibelius. Bus 24 from the park can take you northwest to the Seurasaari Open-Air Museum (p88), or south to the intersection of Mannerheimintie and Pohjoisesplanadi, its terminus.

Alternatively, continue walking or riding around the coast road to **Hietaranta beach** (17; p85), Helsinki's most popular beach. Heading back towards the city centre through the peaceful **Hietaniemi Cemetery** (18; p85), you'll reach **Hietalahti square (19)**, which has its own kauppahalli (covered market) that serves as a popular antique and flea market (p99). From here you can return to the city centre along Bulevardi, pausing in the summer park where there's a lovely church, **Vanha Kirkko** (20; p85).

Alternatively, continue around past the West Harbour to the south of the peninsula, following the waterfront to **Kaivopuisto Park (21)**, a favourite place for Finns to picnic and laze around in summer. Note the small wooden jetties, erected for households to wash their rugs, a very typical and traditional ritual of the Finnish summer. Continuing along the waterfront you pass the Olympia ferry terminal and eventually arrive back at Kauppatori.

HELSINKI FOR CHILDREN

Helsinki has a lot to offer kids, with summer boat trips, amusement parks and outdoor events all up and running year-round. Finland is a child-friendly society and just about every hotel and restaurant will be keen to help out with cots or highchairs. Prams and strollers with smaller wheels may have problems in the older paved parts of town, but trams and other public transport accommodate them well. Family rooms are available even in business hotels which can make the trip a little more affordable.

There's plenty to keep rug rats busy. As well as a harbour, ferry destinations like the zoo and Suomenlinna can make for good excursions. Linnanmäki amusement park (p86) is as hard to resist as fairy floss, while Sea Life (p86) has a little more educational substance. The Serena Water Park (p112) in Espoo is good clean splashy fun.

The pick of the museums is Kiasma (p82), which has loads of interaction and freaky fun, though check that special exhibits won't raise any 'adult themes'. On Suomenlinna (p87), visiting the toy museum and crawling through the submarine are always a hit, while the Tram Museum, Children's Museum and Sports Museum will also appeal to various ages. The Heureka science centre (p112) in Vantaa is also a winner. Pre-teens will get a kick out of the dinosaurs at the Natural History Museum (p83), though you might have some explaining to do about the weather vane. Most museums are free to under 18-year-olds.

The beaches on Suomenlinna and at Hietaniemi are particularly safe, while there are playgrounds in both Kaivopuisto and Töölönlahti bay. In winter, the kids can tackle ice skating at Jääpuisto (p89), while you stay snug in a nearby coffee shop.

TOURS

Helsinki Expert (☎ 2288 1600; www.helsinkiexpert.fi; adult/child €25/15, with Helsinki Card €11; ⏱ on the hour 10am-2pm summer, 11am winter) runs 90-minute sightseeing tours in its bright orange bus. They depart from Esplanadi, near the tourist office and include a taped commentary (in 11 languages) via a headset. A similar route runs from the Olympic ferry terminal daily at 10.30am via the Katajanokka terminal (10.45am). The same company offers walking tours and tailored group tours.

Other good tours that operate in summer include:

BizarreOne (☎ 424 0606; www.bizarreone.fi) Does excellent tours (one/two days €70) including shopping, ice

HELSINKI

GAY & LESBIAN HELSINKI

Helsinki has an active scene, which may not be as massive as Copenhagen or Stockholm, but has several dedicated venues and a host of gay-friendly spots. Every June Helsinki's GLBTI community gathers around **Helsinki Pride** (www.helsinkipride.fi), which includes balls, karaoke and picnics. The hyper-hip clubs are in Punavuori,. while Kallio has more grungy venues.

Voltti (www.voltti-lehti.fi) is a Finnish-language magazine available at most newstands (€7.50). They also produce the *Gay Guide,* which is available from the tourist office and on the website with updated listings of bars, club nights, cruise spots, saunas and shops. Another good online guide is **QLife** (www.qlife.fi), an English-language site that includes an events calendar and venues throughout Finland.

For more information, contact **HeSeta** (☎ 681 2580; www.heseta.fi, in Finnish; Mannerheimintie 170), the Helsinki branch of the national GLBTI organisation located about 4km north of the centre. See also p353 for more information.

Bars & Clubs

DTM (Map pp80-1; ☎ 676 315; www.dtm.fi; Iso Roobertinkatu 28; door charge €2-10, cafe free; 🕑 9am-4am Mon-Sat, noon-4am Sun; 🖳) Scandinavia's biggest gay club is a multilevel complex with an early-opening cafe-bar. There are a couple of club areas opening at 9pm (with a minimum age of 22) and regular club nights, as well as drag shows or women-only sessions.

Hercules (Map p86; ☎ 612 1776; www.herculesgayclub.com; Lönnrotinkatu 4; 🕑 9pm-4am) A busy disco, aimed at men aged 30-plus, but dance-floor classics and campy karaoke attract everyone.

Room Albert (Map pp80-1; ☎ 643 626; Kalevankatu 36; www.roombar.fi; 🕑 2pm-2am) A slick bar for gay men, with laid-back tunes.

Bear Park Café (Map pp80-1; ☎ 044-576 0679; www.bearparkcafe.net; Karhupuisto; 🕑 daylight) Not just for the hairy, this is a relaxed spot for a post-Kallio cruise that sometimes features cabaret or jazz.

Fairytale (Map pp80-1; ☎ 870 3226; www.fairytale.fi; Helsinginkatu 7; 🕑 4pm-2am Mon-Fri, 2pm-2am Sat & Sun; 🖳) One of Kallio's dark drinking dens for men.

---

swimming, pub tours and, our personal fave, the Heavy Helsinki, which includes hard-rocking karaoke and entry to a gig.

Bike Tours (☎ 045 1296850; www.biketours.fi) Starting from Havis Amanda fountain (at 11am, 2pm and 5pm in summer), near the tourist office, these two-wheel tours (per 1½/2½ hr €15/20) will get you further around the city; you'll need to grab a bike (see p105).

Open Top Tours (☎ 050-430 2050; with Helsinki Card all tours €10) A hop-on hop-off tour (adult/child €24/10) aboard an open-top double-decker bus that leaves from the Senate Square, taking in the major sights. The Helsinki in a Nutshell tour (€29/12) includes a quick boat tour if you're short on time.

Rudolf City (☎ 050-307 5000; www.rudolfcity.com) Takes excellent half-/full-day tours (from €29/49) as far out as Turku and Porvoo, with an emphasis on activity,and can include a Finnish barbecue or picnic. They collect from Eurohostel (see opposite), Olympic Tower (see p84) and the Mannerheim Statue.

A good budget alternative is to catch the 3T tram and pick up the free *Take the Tram For Helsinki Sightseeing* brochure as a guide around the city centre and out to Kallio.

Cruises

Strolling through Kauppatori in summer, you won't have to look for cruises – the boat companies will find you. **Royal Line** (☎ 020-711 8333; www.royalline.fi, 90-min cruise €18), **Sun Lines** (☎ 663 605; www.sunlines.fi; 90-min cruise €18) and **IHA Lines** (☎ 6874 5050; www.ihalines.fi; 90-min cruise €15) all have hourly departures in summer. Most cruises go past Suomenlinna and weave through other islands. Lunch and dinner cruises are also available for around €20 extra.

A visit to the Helsinki Zoo (p86) or Suomenlinna sea fortress (p87) is a good way to combine a scenic boat ride with other sightseeing (and they're both free with the Helsinki Card). There are also longer day cruises by ferry and steamer from Helsinki to the Finnish town of Porvoo; see p109.

FESTIVALS & EVENTS

Vappu (May Day) The student graduation festival is celebrated by gathering around the Havis Amanda statue, which receives a white 'student cap'.

World Village (www.maailmakylassa.fi) World music, dance and art take the town in mid-May.

Ice Hockey World Championships (www.ihwc.net) Televised on a big screen in Rautatientori in May, the atmosphere here is intense, especially if Finland makes the finals.

Helsinki Day (www.hel.fi/helsinkipaiva) Celebrating the city's anniversary brings many free events to Esplanade Park on 12 June.

Samba Carnival (www.samba.fi) The city goes to Rio for dancing and music for a weekend in early June.

Tuska Festival (www.tuska-festival.fi) A huge open-air metal festival in late June.

Ankkarock (www.ankkarock.fi) Rock festival held in Vantaa in early August.

Helsinki Festival (Helsingin Juhlaviikot; ☎ 6126 5100; www.helsinginjuhlaviikot.fi; Mannerheimintie 22-24; tickets €10-50) From late August to early September, this arts festival features chamber music, jazz, theatre, opera and more.

Flow Festival (www.flowfestival.com) An August weekend festival that sees hip hop, electronic and experimental music rock the outer suburb of Suvilahti.

Baltic Herring Market (www.portofhelsinki.fi) In the first week of October fisherfolk and chefs gather at Kauppatori to cook the time-honoured fish.

Lucia Parade This pre-Christmas parade takes over Senate Square on 13 December, with a procession of the Lucia maiden crowned with candles. A market is held the following day.

SLEEPING

There's a dearth of cheap accommodation in Helsinki, mainly due to the large business travel market, which means that higher-end places have proliferated. From mid-May to mid-August, bookings are advisable although July is often a quiet time for midrange and top-end hotels.

Budget

Rastila Camping (Map p107; ☎ 031-078 517; Karavaanikatu 4; tent sites €13-15, 2-person cabins €38-45, 4-person cabins €53-64, cottages with/without sauna €165/100; P 🖳) Set far from downtown Helsinki, this beach-side spot is a good option for families with several alternatives including powered sites for caravans and green wooden cabins with bunk beds and kitchenettes. There were building works when we visited so expect even more facilities, but at the time of research there were already two excellent private saunas on offer. The site is run by Helsinki city council, so high standards are maintained. To get here take the metro to Rastila station; the trip takes 20 minutes.

Hostel Stadion (Map pp80-1; ☎ 477 8480; www.stadionhostel.com; Pohjoinen Stadiontie 3; dm/s/d €19/38/47; 🕙 reception 7am-2am, 7am-3am in summer; P 🖳) A 10-minute tram ride from town, this HI hostel is actually part of the Olympic Stadium and has a slightly institutional feel. Dorms have a maximum of 12 beds, but they're quite roomy with small tables at the centre. There are good facilities such as free internet, luggage storage and a good cafe (breakfast €7).

Hostel Suomenlinna (off Map pp80-1; ☎ 684 7471; www.leirikoulut.com; Suomenlinna C9; dm €25, s/d/tr €50/50/75; 🕙 reception 8am-9pm; 🖳) This excellent alternative to staying in central Helsinki is an HI-affiliated hostel on the fortress island of Suomenlinna. The historic building was once a Russian primary school and later a barracks, which lends the place an institutional feel. Dormitories are high-ceilinged classrooms, while the private rooms upstairs have cosy sloping ceilings. There is a simple kitchen, as well as a laundry. It's very important to note that the warden doesn't live on the island, so you must check in during reception hours and remember to get the key code. The island has a supermarket and several restaurants.

Eurohostel (Map pp80-1; ☎ 622 0470; www.eurohostel.fi; Linnankatu 9; dm €22-24, s €38-44, d €43-55, tr €66-82; 🖳) Handy for an early ferry, this HI-affiliate offers both backpacker and hotel rooms. Hotel rooms are newer and with TVs, but both rooms share bathrooms and you can start the day with a sauna. The small cafe serves a breakfast buffet (€7) and other meals. The dock-side location can make for noisy neighbours, so the better soundproofing of a hotel room is advisable for light sleepers.

Hostel Erottajanpuisto (Map p86; ☎ 642 169; www.erottajanpuisto.com; Uudenmaankatu 9; dm €23.50, s/d/tr €49/68/81; 🖳) If you're looking for a place to drop your bags and head out to party, then you've found it. In the thick of the Punavuori area, it's a social spot with a large drawing room that doubles as a basic kitchen where free coffee is always brewing. Dorms are limited to eight bunks a room, though singles are a good chance to escape the party people.

Academica Summer Hostel (Map pp80-1; ☎ 1311 4334; www.hostelacademica.fi; Hietaniemenkatu 14; dm €23, standard s/tw up to €42/59, modern s/tw up to €55/69; 🕙 Jun-Aug; P 🖳 🏊) Definitely not a student share-house, this super-clean spot is packed with features (pool, sauna and wi-fi) and cheery staff with tips on exploring the city. Traditional rooms are older, but still have great additions like bar fridge and bathroom. Dorms are limited to four bunks a room, so even the cheapest rooms feel uncrowded. They're also environmentally aware with a carbon offset program and a WWF-certified green office.

Other recommendations:

Hostel Karavaani (off Map pp80-1; ☎ 031-071 441; www.hihostels.com; Karavaanikatu 4; dm €20, s/d €30/55, 2-person cabins €38-45, 4-person cabins €53-64, cottages with/without sauna €165/100; P ⏸) In summer this hostel operates near Rastila Camping (p93) with a good standard of backpacker accommodation. While it's managed separately to Rastila, you can use all the camping ground's facilities including the sauna.

Hostel Satakuntatalo (Map pp80-1; ☎ 6958 5233, fax 685 4245; www.sodexo.fi/satakunta; Lapinrinne 1A; dm €20, s €41, d €60; ☽ Jun-Aug; P ⏸) Handy for the bus station, this large place includes a good cafe that does a breakfast buffet. All rooms include desk, fridge and student dorm vibe.

Midrange

Omenahotelli Eerikinkatu (Map pp80-1; ☎ 060-018 018; www.omena.com; Eerikinkatu 24; r €90) Skip the concierge with this internet-bookable chain that's handy to Kamppi station and the city centre. As well as a double bed, there's a fold-out sofa that can sleep two more, plus there's a microwave and minifridge. You can add on zippy LAN internet (€16) and breakfast (€6), taken at a local Café Picnic. Omenahotelli Lönnrotinkatu (Map p86), at Lönnrotinkatu 13, was set to open at the time of research, offering similar rooms at the same rates.

Hotel Carlton (☎ 684 1320; www.carlton.fi; Kaisaniemenkatu 3; s/d €96/120; ⏸ ⚙) This competitive new place has wood-rich rooms in varying sizes with a modern feel that includes flatscreen TV and wi-fi. Business folks can be seen frantically using the photocopier and fax machines in the corridor before racing to the train station to catch a meeting in Espoo. There's a good share-kitchen but a continental breakfast is included in the price.

Hotel Arthur (Map p86; ☎ 173 441; www .hotelarthur.fi; Vuorikatu 19; s/d €104/124; P ⚙) This reliable spot close to the railway station and Kaisaniemi Park provides fine standard rooms with double doors and thick curtains to ensure a good night's rest before catching that early train. The restaurant and travel booking service mean you don't need to venture far if you want to take it easy in the centre.

Hotel Linna (Map p86; ☎ 010-344 4100; www.palace .fi; Lönnrotinkatu 29; s/d to €130/250; P ⏸ ⚙) Linna is Finnish for 'castle' and the turreted facade and courtly service give you the royal treatment. Built in 1903 as the student clubhouse for the technical university opposite, the castle decor never feels cheesy with rooms tastefully kitted out with extra-long beds, minibar and bathtubs in some rooms. There's a choice of three saunas and wi-fi is extra (€12 per day).

Stay At Parliament (Map pp80-1; ☎ 251 1050; www .accome.com; Museokatu 18; 2-/3-person apt from €137/155; ☽ reception 8am-8pm Mon-Fri; ⏸) These refurbished apartment-style rooms are located in the quiet district of Töölö, which is deceptively close to the centre. More affordable apartments have two modish bedrooms, a well-equipped kitchen and a laundry that makes these rooms perfect for a small family. Call ahead or check the web for regular specials.

Hotelli Helka (Map pp80-1; ☎ 613 580; www.helka .fi; Pohjoinen Rautatiekatu 23A; s/d €136/171, bike rental per day €15; P ⏸ ⚙) If you like Finnish design, you'll love Helka. A substantial renovation has made this a hip hotel with rooms decked out in chocolate browns and wheaty shades. Every room has a print of an autumn forest that hangs over it, and is backlit to give rooms a moody glow – daunting, but delicious. *Keittiö* (kitchen) is their restaurant, which serves a generous buffet breakfast.

Other recommendations:

Sokos Hotel Albert (Map pp80-1; ☎ 020-123 4638; www.sokoshotels.fi; Albertinkatu 30; r €80-95; ⏸) A boutique-style hotel from this hotel chain that's well-located for clubbing in Punavuori. Rooms are compact with flatscreen TVs and computers and there's a public sauna. Not to be confused with its big brother in the same street, the pricier Sokos Hotel Aleksanteri at Albertinkatu 34.

Hotel Anna (Map pp80-1; ☎ 616 621; www .hotelanna.fi; Annankatu 1; r from €130, ste from €205; ⏸ wi-fi) Owned by the Finnish Free Church, this reserved hotel is good for family or business visitors, and has meeting rooms, along with a family sauna.

Hotel Finnapartments Fenno (Map pp80-1; ☎ 774 980; www.hotelfenno.fi; Kaarlenkatu 7; economy s/tw/d €56/72/88; P ⏸) Offers basic self-contained rooms that include bathrooms, microwaves and flatscreen TVs. Other facilities include a laundry, a solarium and parking (€10). To get here catch bus 17 to Fleminginkatu.

Top End

Helsinki's luxury hotel scene has plenty of great options, thanks to that company credit card. The city is known both for design ho-

---

STAYING LONGER

Some locals call the city Hirentski, but if you're staying awhile you can economise by renting a short-term apartment. Options range from one-room studios with limited facilities, to expansive multiroom apartments that are like small homes. Often you'll get the use of an apartment building's sauna, parking area and other facilities. They're an ideal option for groups as you pay by the room, so the larger the group the cheaper the rate. Best of all, the longer you stay the cheaper rates get with deals for weekly and monthly stays.

We've listed their offices here so you can collect keys, but apartments are located throughout the city so you can find your own piece of Lowrentski.

Good agents for renting apartments include:

City Apartments (Map pp80-1; ☎ 612 6990; www.cityapartments.fi; Vourikatu 18, studios from €110, 2-room apt from €120)

Kotihotelli (Map pp80-1; ☎ 176 505; www.kotihotelli.fi; Uudenmaankatu 26; studios from €75, 1-bedroom apt from €105)

---

tels that are always easy on the eye, while monumental grand hotels offer another level of opulence.

our pick **Klaus K** (Map p86; ☎ 020-770 4700; www.klauskhotel.com; Bulevardi 2; s/d from €140/180; 🖳 wi-fi) Easily the slickest of the new generation of design hotels, this snazzy spot has Kalevala quotes woven into the gold walls of the lobby with the thread running a framed verse in every room. It's distinctly Finnish, from luxurious birch toiletries and space-conscious architecture to the corrugated sauna-style ceilings of the bathrooms. But there are also worldly comforts such as high-speed wi-fi and DVDs in all rooms, plus two good restaurants and a frostily cool bar.

Scandic Grand Marina (Map pp80-1; ☎ 16661; www.scandic-hotels.com; Katajanokanlaituri 7, Katajanokka; s/d from €142/181; 🅿 🖳 ♿) Katajanokka's great hotel is a superb conversion from an early-20th-century brick warehouse. The rather drab brick facade belies the sophisticated rooms within, which are coolly minimalist boasting wi-fi and ergonomic desks. Its location puts it seconds from the ferries, making it popular with visiting Swedes.

Hotel Cumulus Seurahuone (Map p86; ☎ 69141; www.cumulus.fi; Kaivokatu 12; s/d €175/195, ste €400; 🅿 🖳) Since 1914 this *seurahuone* (literally 'club room') has been a meeting place for high society, where visiting officers, gentlemen and ladies came to stay, and a venue for concerts and ballroom dances. The building remains a classic, with stately rooms in black and gold, and period fittings including the smoking cabinet and ballroom. Sadly there's no sauna, but Railway Square views provide succour.

Hotel Katajanokka (Map pp80-1; ☎ 686 450; www.bwkatajanokka.fi; Linnankuja 5; s/d €190/200; 🖳) Set in a refurbished prison, this characterful place offers so much more than proximity to the ferries. Double rooms stretch over two-and-a-half ex-cells, so they're anything but pokey and it's possible to buy handcuffs at the front desk to share with your cell mate. While they don't miss a chance to have cheeky nudges at the former penal complex, it's not at the expense of luxury with large flatscreen TVs and a sumptuous sauna. This jailhouse rocks.

Palace Hotel (Map p86; ☎ 1345 6660; www.palace.fi; Eteläranta 10; r with/without view €240/190; 🅿 🖳) This smaller hotel is one of the few that offers sea views in Helsinki. The views cost a little more but you can watch the progress of Baltic ferries from your room; otherwise you can dawdle in the intimate breakfast rooms that are on each floor, and serve up a good buffet. Rooms themselves are spacious and comfortable. The top-storey restaurant also affords good views and has a handy sauna.

Sokos Hotel Torni (Map p86; ☎ 020-123 4604; www.sokoshotels.fi; Yrjönkatu 26; s/d €220/250; 🖳) In 1931 this building became Finland's Empire State building and although no longer the country's tallest building, it still boasts excellent views, especially from Ateljee Bar (p100). Today, rooms have been stylishly renovated in keeping with the historic feel in art deco and nouveau styles, though modern rooms in rich red and black have hip decor. Each room has its own guestbook filled with glowing comments.

Glo (Map p86; ☎ 010-344 4400; www.palacekamp.fi; Kluuvikatu 4; d €170-330; 🖳 ♨ ♿) An offshoot of Hotel Kämp, this places promotes itself as a 'lifestyle hotel' offering exceptional extras including mini-gyms, laptops, painting supplies and musical instruments. Inside it's all bassy tunes and sexy curves, with in-room iPods and black toilet paper (as featured on Finnish *Big Brother*) adding to the sense of luxury. Best of all you have access to the three saunas and day spa of Hotel Kämp.

Hotel Kämp (Map p86; ☎ 576 111; www.hotelkamp.fi; Pohjoisesplanadi 29; r €430-475, ste €845-1470; P 🖳 ♿) If Helsinki is the daughter of the Baltic then this grand hotel is her most dashing suitor. It romances with a stately marble lobby that seduces you back to historic rooms furnished with antiques and then surprises in the marble bathrooms with their trademark rubber duck. In Finland's past the hotel has hosted Sibelius and Gallen-Kallela, along with the underground Kagaali movement during the Finnish Civil War. They probably came for the saunas (there are three including a eucalyptus inhalation), the plush day spa or the award-winning Japanese restaurant.

Also recommended:

Sokos Hotel Presidentti (Map pp80-1; ☎ 020-123 4608; www.sokoshotelpresidentti.fi; Eteläinen Rautatiekatu 4; s/d €165/185, ste €305-340; 🖳 🛒 ♿) Right near Kamppi metro station, this gargantuan revamped hotel sports close to 500 rooms including several large suites. It's one of the more affordable and central options.

Crowne Plaza (Map pp80-1; ☎ 2521 0000; www.crowneplaza-helsinki.fi; Mannerheimintie 50; s/d €199/229; P 🖳 wi-fi) From the grand lobby and lakeside locales you can expect a first-class hotel. There are good packages with the nearby Ooppera Talo, and also an excellent day spa.

Radisson SAS Royal (Map pp80-1; ☎ 020-123 4701; www.royal.helsinki.radissonsas.com; Runeberginkatu 2; s/d €165/255, ste €325-450; P 🖳 ♿) This striking modern pair of buildings is popular for business conferences, which makes rates more affordable on weekends. A good terrace and a breakfast buffet, with an array of options, are also good selling points.

Airport Hotels

There are fast transport connections from Helsinki-Vantaa airport (off Map pp80–1) to the city, but if you find yourself wanting to overnight here, there are some options.

Scandic Gateway (☎ 818 3600; www.scandic-hotels.fi; s/d from €176/209; P 🖳) The most convenient is this small hotel in the terminal itself. The rooms are Nordic and modern, although unfortunately they don't have windows, which

makes them a little claustrophobic and nips plane-spotting plans in the bud.

Hilton Helsinki-Vantaa Airport (☎ 73220; www.helsinki-vantaa-airport.hilton.com; Helsinki-Vantaa Airport, Lentäjänkuja 1; s/d from €97/132) Literally minutes from the airport, this big hotel has convenience and comfort on its side. Many rooms come with personal saunas and breakfast is available.

EATING

Helsinki has by far the best range of restaurants in Finland, be it for fast food, authentic Finnish cuisine or international dining. As well as great Russian restaurants, Helsinki has a fantastic selection of ethnic restaurants. Most restaurants offer multicourse set menus, which are often better value and may include wine. Unfortunately there's a dearth of budget eateries, though cafes (see p99) offer good lunch options and there are plenty of self-catering opportunities (see p99).

As Helsinki is famously the daughter of the Baltic, the city swims with seafood so look out for herring, juicy cuts of salmon and whole-roasted Arctic char. Check the Food & Drink chapter (p57) for more must-try dining experiences.

Restaurants
BUDGET

Koto (Map p86; ☎ 646 080; www.ravintola-koto.fi; Kalevankatu 21; mains €10-16, lunches €9-15; ✆ lunch & dinner Mon-Sat) It's blonde-wood Zen at this Japanese joint, which does sashimi, yakkitori and brilliant sushi. The takeaway packs fill the bellies of even the hungriest salarymen.

Zucchini (Map p86; ☎ 622 2907; Fabianinkatu 4; lunches €6-9; ✆ 11am-4pm Mon-Fri) One of the city's few vegetarian cafes, it makes up for it with friendliness and fresh baked quiches and piping-hot soups. The sunny terrace out the back is stunning in summer.

Namaskaar Bulevardi (Map p86; ☎ 6220 1155; Bulevardi 6; lunches €7.50-12, mains €12-18; ✆ lunch & dinner) There are several branches of this Indian buffet throughout the city, but this is the best with interesting decor and an excellent terrace.

Orchid Thai Restaurant (Map p86; ☎ 694 5491; Eerikinkatu 20; mains €9-15; ✆ 10.30am-10pm Mon-Fri, noon-10pm Sat, 2-10pm Sun) This cheap and cheerful little spot does tasty Thai, and some interesting interpretations, like stir-fried duck,

---

ISLAND DINING

There's no better way to appreciate Helsinki's seaside location than by heading out to the myriad of island restaurants. Most island restaurants are served by small boats ferrying to and from quays on the mainland opposite (return €4 to €6, every 10 to 15 minutes June to September). The most famous is the stylish, spired **Klippan** (Map pp80-1; ☎ 633 408; Ehrenströmintie, Luoto; mains €20-40; ☾ dinner May-Sep), which is set in a villa on Luoto island, and famous for society weddings and crayfish parties.

The most accessible restaurants are on Suomenlinna (off Map pp80–1). The gourmet restaurant **Walhalla** (☎ 668 552; www.restaurantwalhalla.com; Suomenlinna A10; mains €26-30, set menus €29-33; ☾ 6pm-midnight Mon-Sat May–mid-Sep) looks out onto the southwest side of Susisaari and serves Finnish classics like reindeer and Arctic char. The terrace bar is ideal for watching boats slide by, and a nearby pizzeria is good for the budget conscious.

If you like a beer then **Suomenlinna Panimoravintola** (☎ 228 5030; Suomenlinna; ☾ 3-10pm Mon-Fri, noon-10pm Sat, noon-6pm Sun, closed Mon & Tue Jan-Mar) brews several excellent beers including a hefty porter and offers good food to accompany it.

On the island of Liuskasaari, **Boathouse** (Map pp80-1; ☎ 6227 1070; Liuskasaari; mains €26-31; ☾ dinner Mon-Sat May-Sep) is a circular two-deck restaurant, with ferries from the jetty at Merisatamanranta. The restaurant does great seafood, which is best sampled with the seafood platter or a tuna steak. Instead of a guestbook, visitors pin notes to the lobby's chandelier.

Even if you're not dining at the restaurants, the islands can make a refreshing break and give a new perspective on the city. The boats are around €3 to €5 return for nondiners and run every 10 to 15 minutes during eating hours.

---

alongside typical dishes such as green curry and cashew-nut chicken.

Konstan Mölja (Map pp80-1; ☎ 694 7504; Hietalahdenkatu 14; lunch/dinner buffets €7.50/14; ☾ 11am-10pm Mon-Fri, 2-10pm Sat, dinner buffet from 4pm) You can almost smell the sea in the maritime interior of this old sailor's eatery. It's real working-man's food with a huge buffet that includes soup, salad, bread, meat (always reindeer) and vegetable dishes. If à la carte mains will break the budget, stick to the buffet – if you can resist Baltic herrings.

MIDRANGE

Demo (Map p86; ☎ 228 90840; www.restaurantdemo .fi; Uudenmaankatu 9-11; mains €19-25, set menus €48-52; ☾ 4-11pm Tue-Sat) A favourite with Helsinki's chefs, this fashionable spot does modern European food such as artichoke ravioli or roasted goose breast for a surprisingly good price. The location means it attracts bright young things who delight in their liquorice ice cream or rhubarb sorbets.

our pick **Tori** (Map pp80-1; ☎ 6874 3790; www.rav intolatori.fi; Punavuorenkatu 2; breakfasts €6-10, lunch specials €8-9, dinner mains €9-14; ☾ 10am-10pm Mon-Fri, noon-10pm Sat, 2-11pm Sun) Buzzing with a bohemian crowd and recognisable by the vinyl record on the door, this is the city's anytime favourite. The decor is snappily revamped in 1950s interior

kitsch, complete with period fittings, while the menu runs to beetroot-and-blue-cheese pasta, and a reinvention of meatballs with a brandy sauce. Breakfast is a build-your-own adventure or go for the porridge, while lunch sandwiches are good for the cash-strapped.

Juuri (Map p86; ☎ 635 732; www.juuri.fi; Korkeavuorenkatu 27; mains €23-26, sapas from €3.50; ☾ 3-11pm Mon-Fri, noon-11pm Sat, 4-10pm Sun) Who has time to sample every Finnish dish and risk having a plate of yuck to finish? Juuri's *sapas* (Suomi tapas) gives you a chance to sample the classic in tiny portions, such as lingonberry marinated salmon on slivers of maltbread, or cabbage leaves stuffed with crayfish. The mains aren't bad either and include grilled wild-boar ribs and raspberry-marinated Arctic char, which stay true to Finnish roots.

Bossa (Map p86; ☎ 278 5424; www.bosso.fi; Annankatu 21; ☾ lunch & dinner Mon-Fri) When winter is getting you down, this place with its lipstick-red interior, bright mosaic and mojitos can whisk you off to the warmer climes of Brazil. Film-maker Mika Kaurismäki brings some of his new home country back to his countrymen with dishes like a coconut-heavy fish stew and roasted lamb chops. Sunday boasts a 'sambalounas' with dancing added to the menu.

Elite (Map pp80-1; ☎ 434 220; Eteläinen Hesperiankatu 22; mains €15-24, set menus €35-42; ⚓ lunch & dinner Mon-Sat, dinner only Sun) This old-school place has a sun-beamed terrace in summer and dining cellar year-round where they serve up Finnish staples like *pyttipannu* (meat-and-potato hash) or Baltic herring. The range of set menus is good value for the indecisive.

Savotta (Map p86; ☎ 7425 5588; Aleksanterinkatu 22; mains €16-25; ⚓ 11am-11pm Mon-Fri, 1-11pm Sat & Sun) A little too themed for some tastes, this representation of a logger's mess hall does traditional Finnish working food. Waitresses in peasant tops bring *karjalanpiirakka* (rice-filled savoury pastry) starters before moving on to meaty fare such as elk, bear stew or the Forest Foreman's Plate, which is served in a skillet with much flourish. If you enter into the spirit of it, it's a good night out.

Kosmos (Map p86; ☎ 647 255; Kalevankatu 3; mains €15-25, set menus €40; ⚓ 11.30am-1am Mon-Fri, 4pm-1am Sat, closed Jul) Designed by Alvar Aalto, this place could qualify as an institution on that fact alone, but the Hellenic sculpture and artsy associations lift it to another level. The Finnish antipasto (including smoked reindeer and Baltic herring) is the ideal start before moving on to meaty mains such as Russian chicken breast served with roe and sauerkraut, and lamb kidneys with pilaf.

Sea Horse (Map pp80-1; ☎ 628 169; www.seahorse .fi; Kapteeninkatu 11; mains €12-21; ⚓ 10.30am-midnight) Established in the 1930s and largely unchanged since, Sea Horse is the lovable uncle of Helsinki's dining scene. Sometimes service may be hard of hearing, but they dish up real Fenno faves like cabbage rolls and reindeer fillet, in generous enough portions for you to forgive them their eccentricities.

Other recommendations:

Ateljé Finne (Map pp80-1; ☎ 493 110; Arkadiankatu 14; mains €16-22; ⚓ dinner Tue-Sat) A hipster spot with sculpture on the walls, great old coffee machine and fab fishcakes.

Lappi (Map p86; ☎ 645 550; Annankatu 22; mains €15-30; ⚓ noon-10.30pm Mon-Fri, 1-10.30pm Sat & Sun) One step closer to the Arctic Circle with faux-rustic decor and Lappish grub.

Belge (Map p86; ☎ 622 9620; Kluuvikatu 5; mains €12-22; ⚓ lunch & dinner Mon-Sat, dinner only Sun) A real treat for Tintin fans with menus in books, Belgian brews and fries, plus an after-work 'groovin library' where tunes are played in a large reading room.

Maithai (Map p86; ☎ 685 6850; Annankatu 31-33; mains €14-18, lunches €9; ⚓ 11am-11pm Mon-Fri, noon-11pm Sat, 2-11pm Sun) A good thing in a small package with flavoursome Thai that packs them in.

TOP END

Savoy (Map p86; ☎ 6128 5300; Eteläesplanadi 14; mains €36-58; ⚓ lunch & dinner Mon-Fri) Originally designed by Alvar and Aino Aalto, this is definitely a stand-out dining room with blonde wood and Artek furniture throughout. Dishes source the best in local ingredients with an eye on sustainability and conserving your food miles with highlights such as the roasted partridge with duck liver.

Chez Dominique (Map p86; ☎ 612 7393; www .chezdominique.fi; Rikhardinkatu 4; mains €45-50, set menus €99-139; ⚓ lunch & dinner Tue-Fri, dinner Sat, closed Jul) Helsinki's best French restaurant has moved to a larger location but has maintained its pair of Michelin stars. The menu sticks to French classics such as Dover sole and Anjou pigeon with Finnish flourishes including set menus (from four to nine courses) that include divine *pulla* (cardamom buns).

our pick **Olo** (Map p86; ☎ 665 565, www.olo-restaurant.com; Kasarmikatu 44; mains €22-79; ⚓ lunch Mon-Fri, dinner Tue-Sat) A relative newcomer on the fine-dining scene, Olo is refreshingly unpretentious with a dining room of muted greys and whites. The menu is playful with a saddle of lamb sauced with Madeira and forest mushrooms or tender piglet. All meals come with house-baked breads (try the fruity malt) and the wine list is broad enough to appeal to all palettes.

Nokka (Map pp80-1; ☎ 6128 5600; Kanavaranta 7, Katajanokka; mains €24-29, set menus €56-60; ⚓ dinner Mon-Sat, lunch Mon-Fri) Look out for the giant ship's propeller out the front of this distinctively Finnish place. Dishes use local cheeses and game, blended with berry wines to create Suomi sensations. Once a warehouse, the brickwork is warmed by rustic design and its wine cellar remains a highlight.

Also recommended:

Saslik (Map pp80-1; ☎ 7425 5500; Neitsytpolku 12; mains €25-70; ⚓ noon-midnight Mon-Sat, 4-11pm Sun) As close as you'll get to Russia without a visa, this atmospheric place does three kinds of bear, Russian caviar and blini aplenty; Cossack troubadours serenade at 10pm.

Ravintola George (Map p86; ☎ 010-270 1702; www.george.fi; Kalevankatu 17; mains €27-39; ⚓ lunch & diner Mon-Fri, dinner Sat) A Michelin-star restaurant that does excellent seafood in a quieter spot.

HELSINKI

Carma (Map p86; ☎ 673 236; Ludviginkatu 3-5; mains €28-32, set menus €49-69, lunches €28; ☺ lunch & dinner Mon-Fri, dinner Sat) Filling Chez Dominique's shoes, this stylish eatery does an innovative Nordic menu.

Cafes

Helsinki's famous love of coffee means there are always great places to grab a cup and maybe a *pulla*. Most also do meals and some even do *lounas* (lunch) specials.

Café Engel (Map p86; ☎ 652 776; Senaatintori; meals €10-18; ☺ 8am-10pm Mon-Fri, 9am-10pm Sat, 10am-10pm Sun) This heavenly spot in the Senaatintori hums with tourists and university students alike. There's always a good selection of cakes and enticing meals often of a vegetarian bent such as a beetroot lasagne. It's a cultural hub with films shown in the courtyard during summer, irregular piano recitals and a plump English-language magazine selection.

Café Lasipalatsi (Map p86; ☎ 020-7424 291; Mannerheimintie 22-24; sandwiches €3-4, mains €6-9, lunch specials from €7.50; ☺ 7.30am-10pm Mon-Fri, 9am-10pm Sat, 11am-10pm Sun) The warm interior is popular year-round with lunching city suits, while the terrace throngs during after-work drinks. The *ravintola* (restaurant) upstairs is plusher, but stick to the lower deck for the best value, including the popular lunch special that runs to pasta and soups with great breads.

Café Delicato (Map pp80-1 ☎ 694 0403; cnr Kalevankatu & Albertinkatu; rolls €6-10, slices €3-6; ☺ 8am-8pm Mon-Sat) At the cornerstone of Helsinki's Little Italy (OK, it's really just this place and a restaurant across the road), this deli makes an ideal ciabatta grab. You have to make the tough choices between fresh fillings like olives, gravadlax with spring onion and dill, or gutsy salami and Roma tomatoes, but otherwise there couldn't be a better Italian job in town. There's also authentic strong coffee plus a selection of slices.

Pos3 (Map p86 ☎ 663 300; Eteläesplanadi 8; 3-course lunches €29, desserts €8-10; ☺ 11.30am-2pm & 6pm-midnight Tue-Fri, 6pm-midnight Sun) Locals know to skip the mains (French, fusion and lunch menu that includes matched wines) and head straight for the desserts. The sumptuous dining room invites lingering coffee over sweet treats like the *tarte tatin* or an ever-changing roster of stunning cakes.

Café Ekberg (Map p86; ☎ 6811 8660; Bulevardi 9; buffet breakfasts & lunches €9; ☺ 7.30am-7pm Mon-Fri, 8.30am-5pm Sat, 10am-5pm Sun) There's been a cafe of this name in Helsinki since 1861 and today it continues to be a family-run place renowned for pastries like the Napoleon cake. The buffet breakfasts and lunches are also popular, plus there's fresh bread to takeaway.

Fazer (Map p86; ☎ 6159 2959; Kluuvikatu 3; sandwiches €7-8, pies €9-10; ☺ 7.30am-10pm Mon-Fri, 9am-10pm Sat) This classic cafe can feel a little cavernous, but it's the flagship for the mighty chocolate empire of the same name. The cupola famously reflects sound, so locals say it's a bad place to gossip. It is ideal, however, for buying Fazer confectionary or enjoying the towering sundaes or slabs of cake.

Also recommended:

Café Strindberg (Map p86; ☎ 681 2030; Pohjoisesplanadi 33; ☺ 9am-10pm Mon-Sat, 10am-10pm Sun) A well-trafficked spot on the Esplanadi that does a Swedish-style smorgasbord.

Café Krypta (Map p86; ☎ 709 2455; Kirkkokatu 18; coffees & pastries €2-4; ☺ 10am-5pm Mon-Sat, 11am-5pm Sun Jun-Aug only) In the crypt of the Lutheran cathedral, this place is best for a meditative coffee.

Café Java (Map p86; ☎ 640 065; Mannerheimintie 22-24; sandwiches €4-6, lunches €9; ☺ 8am-11pm Mon-Thu, 8am-1.30am Fri & Sat, 11am-11.30pm Sun) A pleasant lunch spot that's popular with female students meeting for salady lunches or using wi-fi.

Quick Eats & Self-Catering

Helsinki has no shortage of hamburger chains (Hesburger, Carrols and even McDonald's), pizza shops, kebab joints, hot-dog stands and grillis. There are also food courts in **Kamppi** (Map p86; ☺ noon-6pm Mon-Fri, 9am-6pm Sat, noon-6pm Sun) and **Forum** (Map p86; Mannerheimintie 20; ☺ 9am-9pm Mon-Fri, 9am-6pm Sat, noon-6pm Sun) shopping centres, which have chain stores and budget eats.

The **Kauppahalli** (covered market; Map p86; Eteläranta; ☺ 8am-6pm Mon-Fri, 8am-4pm Sat) was built in 1889 and remains one of the country's best with good snacks and produce. Touristy **Kauppatori** (Map p86) is good for grilled salmon, cheap snacks and fresh produce such as berries in summer. On summer afternoons, most food stalls set up plastic chairs and tables, which are besieged by seagulls.

Soppakeittiö (Map pp80-1; Hakaniemen Kauppahalli; soups €5-8; ☺ 10.30am-4pm Mon-Fri, 10.30am-3pm Sat) On the ground floor of the intriguing Hakaniemi market building north of the centre, this little soup kitchen is a great place to warm the cockles in winter. The delicious, generously portioned soups come with a bread and cheese spread; the bouillabaisse (€7) is a reader favourite.

S-Market (7am-9pm Mon-Sat, 7am-6pm Sat) is a well-stocked supermarket with several branches:

Kasarmitori (Map p86; Kasarmikatu)

Forum shopping centre (Map p86; Mannerheimintie 20)

Sokos (Map p86; Mannerheimintie 9) In the basement of the Sokos department store.

If you're after specialised supplies, **Ruohonjuuri** (445 465; www.ruohonjuuri.fi: Salomonkatu 5; 10am-9pm Mon-Fri, 10am-6pm Sat) stocks food that's ethically sound, organic and often catering to special dietary needs.

DRINKING

In case you haven't noticed, Finns don't mind a drink especially in summer when open-air beer terraces take advantage of the long daylight hours. Helsinki's biggest summer terrace is along Mikonkatu, though Lasipalatsi's courtyard is a strong contender for the title. The pedestrianised section of Iso Roobertinkatu is one of the more fashionable parts of Punavuori that boasts some hip bars.

To the northeast the Kallio district is infamous for its lower-priced beer and working-class character. The main street Helsinginkatu has several dive bars and brothels using the euphemism *Thai Hieronta* (Thai massage), but it's also home to some great little bars like Hola and Tokio.

our pick A21 Cocktail lounge (Map p86; 040-021 1921; www.a21.fi; Annankatu 21; 8pm-2am Tue-Sun) You'll need to ring the doorbell to get into this chic club but it's worth the intrigue to swing with Helsinki's arty set. The interior is sumptuous in gold, but the real lushness is in the cocktails, particularly the Finnish blends that toss *lakka* and rhubarb to create the city's most innovative tipples.

Tokio (Map pp80-1; 044-393 3801; www.tokiobar.com; Fleminginkatu 13; noon-1am Mon-Sun) This hole-in-the-wall distinguishes itself among the area's dives with a slick interior including funky art adorning the walls. The good sushi and lazy lounge music embody a bohemian feel that's everything that's good about Kallio. Look for the narrow bike parked out front.

Pub Tram Spårakoff (Map p86; 123 4800; tickets €8.50, beers €5; departs hourly 2-3pm & 5-8pm,Tue-Sat mid-May–mid-Aug) This bright red pub tram is the tipsy alternative to traditional tours stopping at the Opera House and Kauppatori. There are

cheaper places to drink but the trundle of the tram past Helsinki's major landmarks makes for an enjoyable evening. Departs Mikonkatu, east of the train station.

Zetor (Map p86; 010-766 4450; www.ravintolazetor.fi; Mannerheimintie 3-5; mains €10-22; 11am-4am Sat, 3pm-1am Sun & Mon, 3pm-3am Tue, 3pm-4am Wed & Thu) Ever wondered where the Leningrad Cowboys would park their pointy shoes? This whacky restaurant and pub has a kitschy Czech tractor theme from the mind of Finnish film-maker Aki Kaurismäki. Cabbage rolls, salmon soup and other traditional dishes complement the Finnish booze including *sahti* (traditional ale flavoured with juniper berries), but ease off if you're finishing the night with a tractor ride.

Hola (Map pp80-1; 694 8983; Helsinginkatu 13B; noon-2am;) The retro vibe with '70s tiles and comfy microcouches makes this place popular with university students. There's dancing potential in the front room and a small art exhibition – all of which mark this out as one of Kallio's better bars.

Aussie Bar (Map pp80-1; 737 373; www.aussiebar.net; Salomonkatu.5; from 6pm nightly) Run by descendants of convicts with plenty of 'G'days', this laid-back pub doesn't miss a cliché. Beneath the corrugated iron and faux colonial fittings it makes for a good watering hole that's popular with locals.

Arctic Icebar (Map p86; 278 1855; Yliopistonkatu 5; admission €10; 10pm-4am Wed-Sat) Not cold enough outside? Then try this bar that's literally carved out of ice including tables and bar. It's minus 5°C so you'll need the furry cape they loan you on entry and the complimentary warming drink included in the price. There's an age minimum of 24, and it's located above La Bodega.

Corona Bar & Kafe Moskova (Map p86; 611 200; Eerikinkatu 11-15; bar 11am-2am, cafe 6pm-2am) Those kooky film-making Kaurismäki brothers are up to their old tricks with this pair of conjoined drinking dens. Corona plays the relative straight man with 20 pool tables and cheap beer, while Moskova is back in the USSR with a bubbling samovar and Soviet vinyl. At closing they clear the place out by playing Brezhnev speeches. But wait there's more: Dubrovnik, in the same complex, does regular live jazz.

Ateljee Bar (Map p86; Sokos Hotel Torni, Yrjönkatu 26; 2pm-2am Mon-Thu, noon-2am Fri & Sat, 2pm-1am Sun) It's worth the climb up to this tiny perch on the roof of the Sokos Hotel Torni for the city panorama. Taking the lift to the 12th floor is the best option, then there's a narrow winding staircase to the top. Downstairs, the courtyard Tornin Piha is a cute little terrace with good wines by the glass.

Rymy Eetu (Map p86; ☎ 670 310; www.rymy-eetu .fi; Erottajankatu 15-17; ⊙ 11am-3am) Fancy a beer? Then you're after a 1L pint of a genuine German pilsener or one of the huge array of brews at this Bavarian beer hall. You can order some dumplings, or bread and sauer-kraut, to soak up the booze while tapping your foot to Finnish humppa (jazz-based music). The pub's namesake is, ironically, a modest, chubby Finnish cartoon character, who is known for his nonchalant resistance to the Nazis during WWII, and who you'll see throughout the bar's decor.

Bar Tapasta (Map p86; ☎ 640 724; Uudenmaankatu 13; tapas €3-5; ⊙ 11am-midnight Mon-Thu, 11am-2am Fri, 2pm-2am Sat) This tight spot has some tasty wines and deep jugs of sangria all in a relaxed 'early in the evening' decor. The menu has tapas meets pasta in some Med fusion that's worth hanging around for.

mbar (Map p86; ☎ 6124 5420; Mannerheimintie 22; internet per hr €5; ⊙ 9am-midnight, later on weekends) Not just a geek-bar with internet terminals and wi-fi, this cafe in the Lasipalatsi complex has a great terrace to soak up the sun, accompanied by DJs on weekends.

Cuba! Cafe (Map pp80-1; ☎ 050-505 0425; www .cubacafe.fi; Erottajankatu 4; ⊙ 5pm-2am Sun-Thu, 5pm-4am Fri & Sat) Certainly one of Helsinki's brighter bars, this place is done out in peach and mo-jito limes with a small stage that features a Havana-style taxi and DJs or salsa bands. Beers, cocktails and dancing are the order of the night in this party place.

Also recommended:

Roskapankki (Map pp80-1; ☎ 735 488; Helsinginkatu 20) A Kallio classic with cheap beer and ragged character.

Vltava (Map p86; ☎ 766 3650; Elielinaukio 2; bar meals €8-12; ⊙ 11am-3am or later) Right near the train station, this Czech pub has a sprawling terrace for meeting people.

Kappeli (Map p86; ☎ 681 244; Eteläesplanadi 1; ⊙ 10am-midnight Mon-Sat, 10am-11pm Sun) Aimed at the cruise-ship crowd, this pleasant outdoor terrace has occasional music in the nearby bandstand.

ENTERTAINMENT

As the nation's big smoke, Helsinki has the hottest culture and nightlife. Music is particu-larly big here, from metal clubs to opera. The latest events are publicised in *Helsinki This Week*. Tickets for big events can be purchased from **Lippupalvelu** (Map p86; ☎ 060-010 020; www.lip pupalvelu.fi), on Stockmann's 7th floor, **Lippupiste** (www.lippupiste.fi) and online through **LiveNation** (www.liven ation.fi).

Nightclubs

Helsinki has a dynamic club scene that's al-ways changing. Some club nights have age limits (often over 20) so check event details on websites before you arrive.

LUX (Map p86; ☎ 020-775 9350; www.luxnightclub.fi; Urho Kekkosenkatu 1A; door charge €5-10; ⊙ 10pm-4am Wed-Sat) Ascend into clubbing heaven at this super slick club with stellar lighting, Kamppi-top views and high-altitude cocktails. Music runs from sexy lounge to sweaty funk with local DJs and international visitors. Enter via Kamppi Square.

Redrum (Map p86; ☎ 045-635 5450; www.redrum .fi; Vuorikatu 2; DJ nights €3-10; ⊙ nightly from 8pm) The wood-panelled interior is drenched in red lighting and a murderous sound system that pushes out house, hip hop and even spacey disco. Sunday is a chill-down with reggae but most nights have good dancing.

Heavy Corner (Map pp80-1; ☎ 458 4309; www .heavycorner.com; Hietaniemenkatu 2; ⊙ 6pm-late Wed-Sat) Known as a pick-up joint, this metal club virtually has an all-black dress code to hear the rockingest tunes and often metal karaoke, featuring super-serious patrons who believe they are auditioning for Children of Bodom. Wait until you leave to start snickering.

Kuudes Linja (Map pp80-1; ☎ 045-111 1466; www .kuudeslinja.com; Hämeentie 13; admission €8-12; ⊙ 9pm-3am Sun & Tue-Thu, 10pm-4am Fri & Sat) A little fur-ther out than most, this is the place to find Helsinki's more experimental beats from top visiting DJs playing techno, industrial, post-rock and electro. There are also live gigs.

Lost & Found (Map p86; ☎ 680 1010; www.lostand found.fi; Annankatu 6; ⊙ to 4am) You can skip the bar upstairs and head down to the dark grotto-like dance floor downstairs that's decked out in lu-minescent designs. Still a gay venue (they style themselves as a 'hetero-friendly gay club'), the tunes are often chart-based, with a sign near the DJ booth 'Don't request. I'll play it eventually'. It's often the spot for after-parties for big gigs.

Teatteri (Map p86; ☎ 681 1130; Pohjoisesplanadi 2) In a stylish former Swedish theatre, this club has three floors of fun from the sophis-ticated Long bar with its modernist paintings and web-spun light fixtures to the summer-swelling terraces. It's got an older more relaxed crowd and can be packed on weekends.

Live Music
Major touring bands do gigs at **Hartwall Areena** (off Map pp80-1; ☎ 020-494 076; www.hartwall-areena .com) though **Kaapelitehdas** (Cable Factory; Map pp80-1; ☎ 4763 8305; www.kaapelitehdas.fi; Tallberginkatu 1C) is attracting big-name bands with its unique ambience.

Tavastia (Map pp80-1; ☎ 694 8511; www.tavastiak lubi.fi; Urho Kekkosenkatu 4; tickets from €10; ☺ 9pm-late) Helsinki's legendary rock venue attracts next-big-thing local acts and bigger international stars. Bands also play at the more intimate Semifinal, in the same building.

Storyville (Map pp80-1; ☎ 408 007; www.storyville.fi; Museokatu 8; ☺ 6pm-4am Mon-Sat) Always smoking with trad, swing or Dixieland, this late-opener is the place for jazz most nights of the week.

Juttutupa (Map pp80-1; ☎ 742 4240; Säästöpankinranta 6) West of Hakaniemi metro station is one of Helsinki's better music bars, focusing on contemporary jazz and rock fusion.

Other recommended venues:

Kuudes Linja (Map pp80-1; ☎ 045-111 1466; www .kuudeslinja.com; €8-12; ☺ 9pm-3am Sun & Tue-Thu, 10pm-4am Fri & Sat) Has regular indie and experimental gigs.

On the Rocks (Map p86; ☎ 612 2030; Mikonkatu 15; ☺ bar from noon in summer, 4pm winter, club from 9pm) Downstairs features rock bands and live comedy.

Opera, Theatre & Ballet
Helsinki This Week has the latest on concerts or you can inquire at the tourist office. The opera and concert season runs September to May with no indoor performances in summer. The Royal Symphony Orchestra (RSO) of the Finnish Broadcasting Corporation features popular concerts in **Finlandia Talo** (Map pp80-1; ☎ 402 4400; www.finlandiatalo.fi; Mannerheimintie 13). Call **Lippupiste** (☎ 060-090 0900; www.lippupiste.com) to book tickets.

Ooppera Talo (Opera House; Map pp80-1; ☎ 4030 2211; Helsinginkatu 58; tickets from €15) Opera, ballet and classical concerts are held here, though not during summer. Performances of the Finnish National Opera are subtitled in Finnish.

Kansallisteatteri (Map p86; ☎ 1733 1331; www .kansallisteatteri.fi, in Finnish; Läntinen Teatterikuja 1) The Finnish National Theatre occupies a beautiful building by the train station. Performances

(usually in Finnish) are always spectacular at this venue.

Cinemas
There are several cinemas in Helsinki, all of which show original-version films with Finnish and Swedish subtitles.

Kino Engel (Map p86; ☎ 020-155 801; www.cinema mondo.fi; Sofiakatu 4; tickets €9) As well as the *kesäkino* (summer cinema) in the courtyard of Café Engel (see p99) in the warmer months, this independent theatre shows art-house and Finnish indie films.

Orion Theatre (Map pp80-1; ☎ 6154 0201; www .sea.fi; Eerikinkatu 15; membership €4, tickets €4; ☺ screenings Tue-Sun) This classic cinema shows classics from the Finnish Film Archive. You need to purchase an annual membership as well as a ticket for the first entry.

FinnKino (☎ 0600 007 007; www.finnkino.fi; tickets €9) operates several Helsinki cinemas, which screen big-name films in English or with subtitles:

Maxim (Map p86; Kluuvikatu 1)

Tennispalatsi (Map pp80-1; Salomonkatu 15)

Sport
Helsinki has several great sporting events that are worth catching.

Hartwall Areena (off Map pp80-1; ☎ 060-010 800; www.hartwall-areena.com; tickets €15-35) Between September and April ice hockey reigns supreme and the best place to see top-level matches is at this arena, about 4km north of the city centre (take bus 23 or 69, or tram 7A or 7B). It's the home of local Super League side Jokerit Helsinki.

Helsingin Jäähalli (Map pp80-1; ☎ 477 7110; www .helsinginjaahalli.fi; Nordenskiöldinkatu 13) Ice-hockey matches are also played at this indoor arena in the Olympic Stadium complex.

Finnair Stadium (Map pp80-1; ☎ 0600 10800; www .lippupalvelu.fi; tickets €8-15) Next to the Olympic Stadium, this is the home ground of local footballers, HJK Helsinki. The team's the closest thing Finland has to a Real Madrid or a Manchester United, having won 21 Finnish league titles and even having made a foray into the group stages of the Champions League a few years back.

SHOPPING
Known for design and art, Helsinki is an epicentre of Nordic cool, from fashion to the latest furniture and homewares. The further you

wander from Pohjoisesplanadi, the main tourist street in town, the lower prices become. The hippest area is definitely Punavuori, which has several good boutiques and art galleries to explore.

Design

You can get some good pointers from **Design Forum Finland** (Map p86; ☎ 622 0810; www.designforum .fi; Erottajankatu 7; ☺ 10am-7pm Mon-Fri, 10am-6pm Sat, noon-6pm Sun), which operates a shop that hosts many designers' work. You're often better off price-wise to hunt down your own bargains though. You can look out for the black-and-white sticker of **Design District Helsinki** (www .designdistrict.fi), which can lead to innovative purchases, though oddly it can include hotels and bars – cheeky bars had started putting 'Drinking District Helsinki' stickers in their window when we visited.

Aarikka (Map p86; ☎ 652 277; www.aarikka.fi; Pohjoisesplanadi 27; ☺ 10am-7pm Mon-Fri, 10am-5pm Sat) Specialising in wood, Aarikka is known for its distinctly Finnish jewellery.

Artek (Map p86; ☎ 6132 5277; www.artek.fi; Eteläesplanadi 18) Originally founded by Alvar Aalto and his wife Aino, this homewares, glassware and furniture store maintains the simple design principle of its founders.

Arabia (Map p107; ☎ 020-439 3507; Hämeentie 135; ☺ 10am-8pm Mon-Fri, 10am-4pm Sat & Sun) The factory outlet of this legendary Finnish ceramics company is bleakly located but worthwhile. Take tram 6 to its terminus and walk a further 200m north.

Clothing

Marimekko (Map p86; ☎ 686 0240; www.marimekko.fi; Pohjoisesplanadi 31) Finland's most celebrated designer fabrics, including warm florals and hipper new designs, are available here as shirts, dresses, bags, sheets and almost every other possible application.

IvanaHelsinki (Map p86; ☎ 622 4422; www.ivana helsinki.fi; Uudenmaankatu 15; ☺ 11am-7pm Mon-Fri, 11am-4pm Sat) Currently the coolest label with its own Fennofolk style, it has to-die-for dresses and T-shirts that deftly play with Finnish icons.

Mental Wear (Map pp80-1; ☎ 050-303 6419; www .mentalwear.fi; Runeberginkatu 58; ☺ noon-6pm Mon-Fri, noon-4pm Sat) Wondering where everyone's getting those 'Lost in Helsinki' metro map threads? Or maybe you just need to tell the world 'I am a heterosexual and drive a Volvo' through the medium of cotton. With slogans in Finnish and English these are Helsinki's most sought-after T-shirts.

Other Shops

Fennica Records (Map pp80-1; ☎ 685 1433; www.fen nicakeskus.fi; Albertinkatu 36; ☺ 10am-6pm Mon-Fri, 9am-2pm Sat) This grungey store does a good range of second-hand and new CDs and vinyl from Suomi-pop to jazz.

Moomin Shop (Map p86; ☎ 622 2206; Kämp Galleria, Pohjoisesplanadi 33; ☺ 10am-8pm Mon-Fri, 10am-6pm Sat) Stock up on all things Moomin including books in English and Finnish.

Sauna Market (Map p86; ☎ 278 5051; Aleksanterinkatu 26-28; ☺ 10am-6pm daily) Gather sauna oils, backscrubbers, water ladles and hundreds of other accoutrements for your own sauna.

Stupido Records (Map pp80-1; ☎ 646 990; www .stupido.fi; Iso Roobertinkatu 23; ☺ 9am-8pm Mon-Fri, 10am-6pm Sat) Not so stupid when it comes to Finnish indie, rock and pop; they're even happy to play something to see how smart it would sound on your stereo.

Markets

FOOD MARKETS

An institution in most Finnish communities are the food markets, which are either outdoor (kauppatori) or in purpose-built halls (kauppahalli). Both sell the freshest produce, pastries and meats, with seasonal berries popular in summer.

Kauppatori (Map p86; ☺ 6.30am-2pm winter, longer hours summer) Famous market that's on the waterfront and often busy with tour groups; fishmongers still sell from boats moored at the quay, with local handicrafts and souvenirs at (sometimes) inflated prices. Nearby, the indoor kauppahalli teems with Finnish food stalls.

Hakaniemi kauppahalli (Map pp80-1; ☺ 8am-6pm Mon-Fri, 8am-4pm Sat) Includes an outdoor market at the metro stop which is less touristy than the Kauppatori (above).

Kauppahalli (Map p86; ☺ 10am-5pm Mon-Fri, 10am-3pm Sat) Renovated market at the Hietalahti flea market which includes mixture of craft and antique stalls; take tram 6.

FLEA MARKETS

These rambling open-air markets are a chance for Finns to do some spring cleaning by selling everything including clothes, furniture and other household items. You can often find bargains at:

Valtteri (Map pp80-1; Aleksis Kivenkatu 17; ☺ 9am-5pm) Indoor flea market in Kallio; trams 1 and 1A stop opposite.

Hietalahti flea market (Map pp80-1; 8am-3pm Mon-Sat, 8am-8pm daily Jun-Aug) Closest to central Helsinki, but it's pretty downmarket.

Department Stores

Stockmann (Map p86; ☎ 1211; Aleksanterinkatu 52) Helsinki's 'everything store' does a good line of Finnish souvenirs and Sámi handicrafts, as well as Finnish textiles, Kalevala Koru jewellery, Lapponia jewellery, Moomintroll souvenirs and lots more. It offers an export service.

Sokos (Map p86; ☎ 001-07650; www.sokos.fi; Mannerheimintie 9) Often cheaper than Stockmann, and with a good food selection.

GETTING THERE & AWAY
Air

There are flights to Helsinki from the USA, Europe and Asia on many airlines. See p358 for more information on reaching Finland by air. Finnair and its subsidiaries offer international as well as domestic services, with flights to 20 Finnish cities – generally at least once a day. Budget carriers **Blue1** (☎ 060-025 831; www.blue1.com) and **Finncomm** (☎ 4243 2003; www.fc.fi) have budget flights to some Finnish destinations. The **Finnair office** (Map p86; ☎ reservations 060-014 0140; www.finnair.fi; Asema-aukio 1; Mon-Sat) is in the train station complex. The airport is in Vantaa, 19km north of Helsinki.

The quickest way to Tallinn is by helicopter. **Copterline** (Map pp80-1; ☎ 020-018 181; www.copterline .com; Hernesaari helicopter terminal, Hernematalankatu 2B) flies hourly from Helsinki to Tallinn (one-way €98) in a zippy 18 minutes (7am to 8pm Monday to Friday, 9am to 5pm Saturday, 10am to 4pm Sunday). However, after research in late 2008, the company had gone into receivership. Please check the website for further details.

Boat

International ferries travel to Travemünde and Rostock in Germany, and Stockholm and Tallinn. There is also a regular catamaran and hydrofoil service to Tallinn. See p363 for more details on this.

Four of the five ferry terminals are just off Kauppatori: Kanava and Katajanokka terminals (Map pp80-1) are served by bus 13 and trams 2, 2V and 4, and Olympia (Map pp80-1) and Makasiini (Map p86) terminals by trams 3B and 3T. The last terminal, Länsiterminaali

(Map pp80-1; West Terminal), is served by bus 15.

Ferry tickets may be purchased at the terminal, from a ferry company's office (and often its website) or (in some cases) from the city tourist office. Book in advance during the high season (late June to mid-August).

Ferry company offices in Helsinki:

Eckerö Line (Map p86; ☎ 228 8544; www.eckeroline .fi; Mannerheimintie 10) Runs *Nordlandia* car ferry, which sails daily to Tallinn year-round (adult/car from €19/21, three to 3½ hours) from Länsiterminaali.

Linda Line (Map p86; ☎ 668 9700; www.lindaliini .ee; Makasiini terminal) Small passenger-only hydrofoil company ploughing the waters to Tallinn (from €19, 1½ hour) up to seven trips daily (when waters are ice-free).

Nordic Jet Line (Map pp80-1; ☎ 681 770; www.njl .info; Kanava terminal) Runs two catamarans, *Nordic Jet* and *Baltic Jet*, to Tallinn (adult/car from €28/35, 1¾ hours) sailing from May to September or later (depending on weather) with seven daily crossings.

Tallink (Map p86; ☎ 2282 1222; www.tallinksilja.com; Erottajankatu 19) Runs at least five services (one-way adult/vehicle from €23/20, two to 3½ hours), some on high-speed *Star* and *Superstar* or slower *Baltic Princess*, from Kanava terminal. It also runs services to Rostock (Germany) and Stockholm (Sweden).

Viking Line (Map p86; ☎ 123 577; www.vikingline.fi; Mannerheimintie 14) Operates car ferry *Rosella* (adult/car from €19/18, 2½ hours) from Katajanokka and Makasiini terminals.

In summer there are daily ferries between Helsinki and Porvoo, through the southeast archipelago. See p109 for details.

Bus

Purchase long-distance and express bus tickets at **Kamppi Bus Station** (Map pp80-1; Frederikinkatu; 7am-7pm Mon-Fri, 7am-5pm Sat, 9am-6pm Sun) or on the bus itself. There's a terminal for local buses to Espoo in one wing, while longer-distance buses also depart from here to all of Finland.

Destinations with several daily departures includes Jyväskylä (€43.90, four to six hours), Kuopio (€58.10, five to seven hours), Lappeenranta (€35.70, four hours), Oulu (€86, 11½ hours), Savonlinna (€52.60, five to six hours), Tampere (€31.70, 2½ hours) and Turku (€27.50, 2½ hours).

Train

The *rautatieasema* (train station) is in the city centre and is linked by pedestrian subway with Helsinki's metro. Helsinki is the terminus for three main railway lines, with regular trains from Turku (€32, two hours), Tampere (€26.90, 1½ hours) and Lahti (€19, one hour).

There is a separate ticket counter for international trains; see p362 for details. In 2010 a new high-speed train is scheduled to St Petersburg, but at the time of research no ticketing information was available.

GETTING AROUND
To/From the Airport

Bus 615 (€3.40, 30 to 50 minutes, 5am to midnight) shuttles between Helsinki-Vantaa airport and platform 5 at Rautatientori (Railway Square) next to the main train station. You'll need a regional ticket (see p106) and the bus also stops in Vantaa. Bus stops are marked with a blue sign featuring a plane.

Finnair buses (Map p86; ☎ 030-723 746) depart from the Finnair office at Asema-aukio (€5.90, 30 minutes, every 20 minutes, 5am to midnight). They make several stops en route, including most top-end hotels.

There are also door-to-door **airport taxis** (☎ 060-055 5555; www.airporttaxi.fi), which need to be booked the previous day before 6pm if you're leaving Helsinki (one to two people €25).

Bicycle

With a flat inner city and well-marked cycling paths, Helsinki is ideal for cycling. Get hold of a copy of the Helsinki cycling map at the tourist office.

The city of Helsinki provides 300 distinctive green 'City Bikes' at stands within a radius of 2km from Kauppatori. The bikes are free: you deposit a €2 coin into the stand that locks them, then reclaim it when you return it to any stand.

For something more sophisticated, **Greenbike** (Map pp80–1; ☎ 8502 2850; www.greenbike .fi; Fredrikinkatu 31; ☺ 10am-6pm Mon-Fri, 10am-3pm Sat, 10am-2pm Sun) rents out quality bikes (from €15/20/60 per day/24 hours/week) including 24-speed hybrid mountain bikes. Also **Ecobike** (Map pp80–1; ☎ 040-084 4358; www.ecobike .fi; Savilankatu 1B; ☺ noon-6pm, Mon-Thu) is a good option for bike rental (from €10 per day), opposite Finnair Stadium and near Hostel Stadion (see p93).

Car & Motorcycle

Parking in Helsinki is strictly regulated and can be a big headache. Metered areas in the city centre cost €3 per hour during the week, but are free on weekends. There are undercover car parks in Kamppii and Forum; for other locations consult the *Parking Guide for the Inner City of Helsinki*, a free map available at the city tourist office.

Car rental companies have offices in the city as well as at the airport:
Avis (Map pp80–1; ☎ 441 155; www.avis.fi; Hietaniemenkatu 6)
Budget (Map pp80–1; ☎ 686 6500; www.budget .com; Malminkatu 24)
Europcar (Map p86; ☎ 040-306 2444; www.europcar .fi; Railway & cnr Salomonkatu & Mannerheimintie)

TO ST PETERSBURG & BEYOND!

One of Russia's most beautiful cities feels tantalisingly close to Helsinki, but red tape has sprung up to replace the Iron Curtain. Applying in your home country for a Russian visa is key, and the process is constantly changing with differences based on your nationality.

At the time of research you require a tourist invite (also called visa support) and a confirmation of accommodation in Russia to qualify for a visa. Good travel agents (see p82) can organise this for you with at least two weeks to process your application, but there are several agencies that organise tourist invites over the internet, such as **Way To Russia** (www.waytorussia.net) or **Visa to Russia** (visatorussia.com). Anywhere that you book (including youth hostels) will issue you with confirmation of accommodation. The invite usually costs US$30 and accommodation will cost US$30 to US$50 depending on how urgently you need your request processed. Most accommodation will offer a combination of invite and accommodation confirmation.

Once you've got these two pieces of paperwork, you're ready to get the visa itself. You can pay more to get your visa processed faster, but at the time of research a single-entry visa for a US passport holder, for example, was US$131. Still want to go?

Thankfully, once you've got the paperwork sorted, it's easy enough to catch a train (see opposite). For information on ferry crossings to Russia see p167.

Hertz (Map pp80-1; ☎ 020-555 2300; www.hertz.fi; Mannerheimintie 44)

Lacara (Map pp80-1; ☎ 719 062; www.lacara.net; Hämeentie 12) A budget local option.

Sixt (☎ 872 4433; www.sixt.com; Helsinki-Vantaa airport)

Public Transport

Central Helsinki is easy to get around on foot or by bicycle and there's also a metro line and a reasonably comprehensive transport network. The city's public transport system, **Helsingin Kaupungin Liikennelaitos** (HKL; ☎ 310 1071; www.hkl .fi) operates buses, metro and local trains, trams and a ferry to Suomenlinna. A one-hour flat-fare ticket for any HKL transport costs €2.20 when purchased on board, €2 when purchased in advance. The ticket allows unlimited transfers but must be validated in the stamping machine on board when you first use it. A single tram ticket is €2 full fare. And because it's Nokialand you can order any of these tickets for the same prices using your mobile: send an SMS to ☎ 16355 texting A1 (for Finnish ticket) or A2 (for Swedish ticket).

Tourist tickets (€6/12/18 for one/three/five days) are the best option if you're in town for a short period of time. Alternatively, the Helsinki Card gives you free travel anywhere within Helsinki (see p78).

HKL also runs ferries from Kauppatori to Suomenlinna (see p87) and to the zoo (see p86). Departing from the passenger quay at Kauppatori in Helsinki, tickets (return €3.80, 15 minutes, three times hourly, 6.20am to 2.20am) are available at the pier. **JT-Lines** (☎ 534 806; www.jt-line.fi) runs an hourly waterbus (bus/ferry combination) from Kauppatori to Suomenlinna (return €5.50, 30 minutes, 8am to 7pm mid-May to August).

HKL offices (7.30am-7pm Mon-Thu, 7.30am-5pm Fri, 10am-3pm Sat) at the Kamppi bus station and the Rautatientori and Hakaniemi metro stations sell tickets and passes, as do many of the city's *R-kioskis*. Metro services run daily from about 6am to 11.30pm. The metro line extends to Ruoholahti in the western part of the city and northeast to Mellunmäki and Vuosaari.

The *Helsinki Route Map,* available at HKL offices and the city tourist office, is an easily understood map of the bus, metro and tram routes.

If you're heading to Vantaa or Espoo, you'll need a regional ticket (one/three/five days for €12/24/36) for travel by bus or train. These are available at bus and train stations, with timetables available from **Helsinki Metropolitan Area Council** (YTV; ☎ 156 11; www.yt v.fi).

Taxi

Vacant taxis are hard to come by during the morning and evening rush hours. You can hail cabs off the street or join a queue at one of the taxi stands located at the train station, bus station or Senaatintori. You can phone for a taxi on ☎ 010-00700.

AROUND HELSINKI

TUUSULAN RANTATIE

Just a 30-minute drive from Helsinki, the views from the narrow stretch of tar running along Tuusulanjärvi (Tuusula Lake) have inspired some of Finland's greatest artists. **Tuusulan Rantatie** (www.tuusulanrantatie.com; Tuusula Lake Rd) has hosted many heroes of the National Romantic movement including Sibelius, Nobel Prize–winning novelist FE Sillanpää and painter Pekka Halonen.

The road has several museums as tributes to its artists. One of the most significant is **Halosenniemi** (☎ 8718 3461; Halosenniementie 4-6; admission €5.50; 10am-7pm Tue-Sun May-Aug, noon-5pm Tue-Sun Sep-Apr), the Karelian-inspired log-built studio of Halonen, with a walking trail through his lakeside garden.

Another real highlight is **Syväranta Lotta Museum** (☎ 274 1077; www.lottamuseo.com; Rantatie 39; admission €4; 11am-6pm Tue-Sun May-Sep, Wed-Sun Oct-Apr), commemorating the Lotta Svärd women's voluntary defence force. Named for a character in a JL Runeberg poem, these unarmed women took on military service during WWII to become one of the world's largest auxiliaries. Look out for the blue-and-white swastika and rose medals, which many Lottas wore among the military paraphernalia.

The most popular stop is Sibelius' home **Ainola** (☎ 287 322; www.ainola.fi; adult €5.50; 10am-5pm Tue-Sun May-Sep), east of the lake just south of Järvenpää. The family home, designed by Lars Sonck and built on this forested site in 1904, contains original furniture, paintings, books and a piano on which Sibelius plotted out tunes until his death. The graves of Jean Sibelius and his wife Aino are in the garden.

Järvenpää, the main town in the area, is a modern service centre with numerous res-

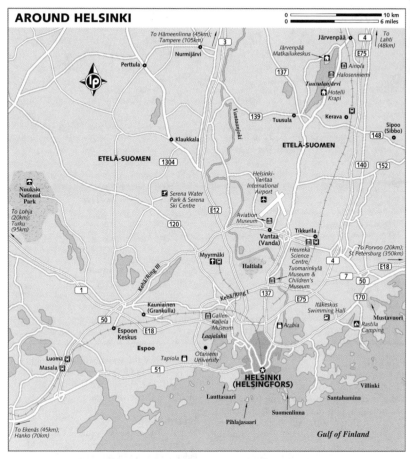

taurants and cafes but little to keep you there long. The **tourist information** (☎ 027-192718; www.jarvenpaa.fi; Hallintokatu 4, Järvenpää; ☺ 9am-3pm Mon-Wed, 9am-6pm Thu & 9am-1pm Fri) has maps of walking trails around the lake. The area also hosts **Puistoblues** (☎ 271 1305; www.puistoblues .fi), a laid-back event that moans and strums through a week in June with locals and a few international acts.

Sleeping & Eating
Järvenpään Matkailukeskus (☎ 7425 5200; www .matkailukeskus.com; Stålhanentie; tent sites €12-18, s €25, cabins €30-54; P) This camp site with a great lakeside location 2.5km from Järvenpää and good-value HI-hostel or cabin accommodation books out around Puistoblues.

Hotelli Krapi (☎ 274 841; www.krapi.info; Rantatie 2; s/d €128/154; P) Unfortunately named, this historic estate, south of Halosenniemi, features an excellent independent hotel in what was once a cowshed. It has great modern rooms, three restaurants, a traditional smoke sauna, summer theatre and, if you can believe it, its very own ghost. They also organise packages that can include cultural experiences like cooking classes, or activities such as cycling around the lake.

Getting There & Away
Tuusulanjärvi is about 40km north of Helsinki. Take a local train to Kerava or Järvenpää, or a bus to Hyrylä, and proceed from there by bicycle.

HELSINKI

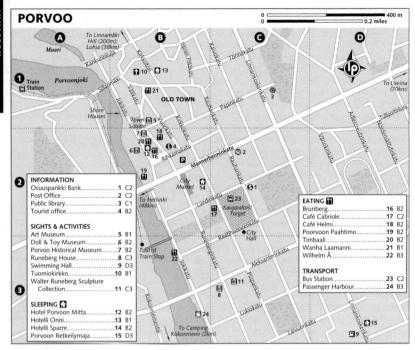

PORVOO

Train Station • Porvoonjoki

OLD TOWN

INFORMATION
Osuuspankki Bank.....................1 C2
Post Office...............................2 C2
Public library............................3 C1
Tourist office...........................4 B2

SIGHTS & ACTIVITIES
Art Museum.............................5 B1
Doll & Toy Museum...................6 B2
Porvoo Historical Museum..........7 B2
Runeberg House.......................8 C3
Swimming Hall.........................9 D3
Tuomiokirkko...........................10 B1
Walter Runeberg Sculpture
  Collection.............................11 C3

SLEEPING
Hotel Porvoon Mitta..................12 B2
Hotelli Onni.............................13 B1
Hotelli Sparre...........................14 B2
Porvoon Retkeilymaja...............15 D3

EATING
Brunberg.................................16 B2
Café Cabriole...........................17 C2
Café Helmi..............................18 B2
Poorvoon Paahtimo..................19 B2
Timbaali..................................20 B2
Wanha Laamanni......................21 B1
Wilhelm Å...............................22 B3

TRANSPORT
Bus Station..............................23 C2
Passenger Harbour...................24 B3

PORVOO

☎ 019 / pop 46,793

Finland's second-oldest town is an ever-popular day trip from Helsinki, but is also becoming a popular weekender. Porvoo (Swedish: Borgå) officially became a town in 1346, but even before that Porvoo was an important trading post.

The town is best known for the achingly beautiful brick-red former warehouses along the river that once stored goods bound for destinations across Europe. Today they're tipped to become a Unesco World Heritage Site and even newer developments across the river are in reds and yellows to suit the town's aesthetic.

Three distinct districts make up the city: the Old Town, the new town and the 19th-century Empire quarter, which was built under the rule of Tsar Nicholas I. The Old Town, with its tightly clustered wooden houses, cobbled streets and riverfront setting, is the most popular, but the Empire quarter has its charms including the home of Finland's national poet, JL Runeberg. During the day, Old Town craft shops are bustling

with visitors, but staying on a week night will mean you could have the place more or less to yourself. The old painted buildings are spectacular in the setting sun.

Information

North of the market square, Osuuspankki Bank has foreign exchange and an ATM.

Public library (☎ 520 2417; Papinkatu 20; ☷ 10am-8pm Mon-Fri, 10am-5pm Sat; ☐) Has free internet terminals, which can be booked.

Tourist office (☎ 520 2316; www.porvoo.fi; Rihka-makatu 4; ☷ 9am-6pm Mon-Fri, 10am-4pm Sat & Sun early Jun-Aug, 9.30am-4.30pm Mon-Fri, 10am-2pm Sat Sep-early Jun) Its free *Porvoo* booklet is a good resource.

Sights & Activities

OLD TOWN

Close your eyes in this tangle of cobbled alleys and wooden warehouses to hear the bustling market that the Old Town once was. The area north of Mannerheiminkatu was largely built after the Great Fire of 1760 but still throngs today with shoppers. Craft boutiques, art galleries, antique shops and souvenir stores jostle for attention on the main roads, Välikatu and

---

TRIPPING TO TALLINN

Taking the boat over to Tallinn is the original booze cruise for Finns. Boats heave with drinkers and Tallinn's pubs and clubs sometimes feel more like Kallio than another country. But Tallinn does boast a charming **Vanalinn** (Old Town) that's best enjoyed with an afternoon of ambling ,particularly around **Raekoja plats** (Town Hall Square) with a Gothic town hall complete with a minaretlike tower. Wander a little further to **Saiakang** (White Bread Passage) with the 14th-century **Püha Vaimu Kirik** (Holy Spirit Church) at one end.

But you've probably worked up an appetite by now. Take the opportunity to sample another national cuisine at **Eesti Maja** (☎ 645 5252; www.eestimaja.ee; Lauteri 1; mains 65-195Kr; ☺ 11am-11pm), which does great baked salmon and blood sausage for the adventurous diner; or try kookily named **Ö** (☎ 661 6150; www.restoran-o.ee; Mere puiestee 6e; mains 310-395Kr; ☺ noon-4pm & 6pm-midnight Mon-Fri, noon-midnight Sat, 1-10pm Sun), an ethereal dining room that highlights Estonian produce. There are plenty of good places to wet your whistle, such as the British-themed (right down to the 'bobby' waiters) **Scotland Yard** (☎ 653 5190; Mere puiestee 6e; ☺ 9am-midnight Sun-Wed, 9am-2am Thu-Fri, 9am-3am Sat), comfy purveyor of local brews **Hell Hunt** (☎ 681 8333; Pikk 39; ☺ noon-late) and super-slick cocktail lounge **Déjá Vu** (☎ 645 0044; www.dejavu.ee; Sauna 1; ☺ 5pm-5am Wed-Sat).

If you're looking to stay the night, check out **Tallinn Tourist Information Centre** (☎ 645 7777; www.tourism.tallinn.ee; cnr Kullassepa & Niguliste; ☺ 9am-5pm Mon-Fri, 10am-3pm Sat Oct-Apr, 9am-7pm Mon-Fri, 10am-5pm Sat & Sun May-Jun, 9am-8pm Mon-Fri, 10am-6pm Sat & Sun Jul & Aug, 9am-6pm Mon-Fri, 10am-5pm Sat & Sun Sep), which has a range of accommodation options. You'll need to change your Euros into Estonian Kroner (Kr) but visas are unnecessary as Estonia is part of the EU. See p357 for more information on Estonian entry requirements.

The easiest way to Tallinn is by ferry (see p104). If you're looking at staying in Estonia for a while, you might like to pick up a copy of Lonely Planet's *Estonia, Latvia & Lithuania*.

Kirkkokatu. The relatively less-touristed area is east of the cathedral; Itäinen Pitkäkatu is one of the nicest. The rows of **shore houses** along the Porvoonjoki and the river were first painted with red ochre to impress the visiting king of Sweden in the late 18th century. They were originally used to store goods traded with German ships from the Hanseatic League.

Dominating Old Town is the **Tuomiokirkko** (cathedral; ☎ 66111; ☺ 10am-6pm Mon-Fri, 10am-2pm Sat, 2-5pm Sun May-Sep, 10am-2pm Tue-Sat, 2-4pm Sun Oct-Apr), a stone cathedral where the first Diet of Finland assembled in 1809, convened by Tsar Alexander I, giving Finland religious freedom. It dates back to the 13th century, making its vandalism by fire in 2006 all the more shocking. At the time of research the wooden shingled roof had been replaced and visitors were just being allowed back in to view the vestiges of medieval frescoes and a hanging ship common in maritime communities.

Porvoo Historical Museum (☎ 574 7500; www .porvoonmuseo.fi; Vanha Raatihuoneentori; combined admission adult/child €5/1; ☺ 10am-4pm Mon-Sat, 11am-4pm Sun May-Aug, noon-4pm Wed-Sun Sep-Apr) is in two adjacent buildings on the beautiful cobbled Old Town Hall Square. The more interesting of the two is the **Art Museum** (Edelfelt-Vallgren Gallery), with paintings by Albert Edelfelt and sculptures by Ville Vallgren, two of Porvoo's celebrated artists. **Porvoo Historical Museum**, in the town hall building across the square, reproduces a 19th-century merchant's home.

Doll & Toy Museum (☎ 582 941; www.lelumuseo.com; Jokikatu 14; adult/child €2/1; ☺ 11am-3.30pm Mon-Thu & Sat, noon-3.30pm Sun Jun & Jul) houses over 800 dolls, tin toys and other childhood curiosities, making it Finland's largest toy museum.

RUNEBERG HOUSE

National poet Johan Ludvig Runeberg's former home has become a **museum** (☎ 581 330; Aleksanterinkatu 3; admission both museums €6; ☺ 10am-4pm Mon-Sat, 11am-5pm Sun May-Aug, closed Mon & Tue Sep-Apr), with a period interior including stuffed foxes and muskets portraying the poet's love of hunting. **Walter Runeberg Sculpture Collection** (Aleksanterinkatu 5) has 150 sculptures by Walter Runeberg, JL Runeberg's eldest son, who produced the town's sculpture of his father.

CRUISES

Several cruises depart from Porvoo to Helsinki, nearby Loviisa or through the archipelago in summer months. Departure times vary so check websites for the latest.

PORVOO'S POET

Born near Jakobstad in 1804, JL Runeberg came to Porvoo in his 30s as a lecturer at Porvoo Gymnasium (or college). A bit of an overachiever, Runeberg founded the town's newspaper, *Borgå Tidning*, and served as its editor for several years.

The two jobs barely kept Runeberg busy so he composed some of the epic poems of the period including *King Fjalar* and *The Songs of Ensign Stål*, the first part of which, *Vårt Land* (Our Land), became the Finnish national anthem. But all this couldn't keep Runeberg out of trouble as he had an affair with a pastor's daughter 20 years his junior.

The poet was a keen outdoorsman until a hunting accident in 1863 left him paralysed and he was unable to write during his final years.

Runeberg's work endured with the line 'Let not one devil cross the bridge!', which was used as a slogan in both the Finnish Civil War and WWII to inspire Finnish troops. His birthday is a national celebration on 5 February, but in Porvoo they make the cake that bears his name (see opposite) in his honour.

M/S Borgå departs from the passenger harbour (hourly 11am to 4pm, Tuesday to Sunday) and does a boat-based town tour (€6). With more time you can take on an archipelago cruise aboard **M/S Sandra** or **M/S Fredrika** (€12, four hours, Tuesday to Thursday, Saturday and Sunday), and stop off at islands en route.

M/S JL Runeberg (☎ 524 3331; www.msjlruneberg.fi), a former steamship, travels to Helsinki (adult/child return €33/15, daily except Thursday) or Loviisa (adult/child return €59/30, Thursdays in July) in summer and makes an excellent day trip that includes lunch. The trip takes four hours each way, so you may prefer to return by bus or, on Saturday only, on the vintage diesel train (adult/child combined ferry and train ticket €29/12).

M/S *Royal Cat* and M/S *Katarina*, both operated by **Royal Line** (☎ 020-711 8333; www.royal line.fi), are speedier alternatives. They travel from Porvoo (Tuesday to Saturday) zipping through the river and archipelago to Helsinki kauppatori with lunch possible (return with/without lunch €48/32).

Sleeping

Porvoo's accommodation has several mini-break options from Helsinki, though the popularity of day trips means places can be limited. The tourist office can recommend a couple of one-room-only options around town.

Hotel Porvoon Mitta (☎ 580 131; www.hotelpor voonmitta.fi; Jokikatu 43; d €130-205; 🐾) This plush place right in the heart of the Old Town combines modern luxury and heritage feel. Rooms named for former residents are tastefully decorated with three 2nd-floor

rooms boasting their own minisaunas and views over the courtyard. Look out for the clay pipes dug as part of archaeological excavations here.

Hotelli Onni (☎ 050-525 6446; www.hotelonni.fi; Kirkkotori 3; s/d €150/180, ste €250) Right opposite the cathedral, this gold-coloured wooden building couldn't be better placed. There's a real range here, from the four-poster bed and slick design of the Funk to the rustic single Peasant. Top of the line is the Honeymoon suite, a small self-contained apartment with bath and complimentary champagne. Breakfast is downstairs in the terraced cafe that serves as a popular coffee shop.

Porvoon Retkeilymaja (☎ 523 0012; http://personal .inet.fi/yritys/porvoohostel/; Linnankoskenkatu 1-3; dm/s/d €16/29/38; P) Far from the Old Town, this historic wooden house holds a well-kept hostel in a grassy garden. It caters for groups so you'll need to book ahead to ensure a spot and linen is extra, so be prepared. There's a great indoor pool and sauna complex over the road. Check-in is from 4pm to 7pm.

Hotelli Sparre (☎ 584 455; www.avainhotellit.fi; Piispankatu 34; s/d €75/90) It might never win any architectural beauty contests, but this serviceable hotel boasts friendly service, a business sauna and a restaurant. It's comfortable enough and well located for early bus departures.

Camping Kokonniemi (☎ 581 967; www.lomaliitto .fi/kokonniemi; tent sites €12, plus per person €4, 4-person cabins €67; ☀ Jun-Aug) On the western side of the river this well-equipped camping ground is just 2km south of Porvoo amid greenery. There are family-focused facilities such as saunas, bikes and a playground.

Eating

Brunberg (☎ 548 4235; Välikatu 4; ⏰ 10am-6pm Mon-Fri, 9am-4pm Sat) It's worth the trip from Helsinki just for Finland's most acclaimed sweet shop, makers of the *pusu* (kisses) or *riisi* (chocolate-coated rice). It's always crowded but mornings are best.

Wilhelm Å (☎ 580 155; mains €13-18; ⏰ lunch & dinner daily Jun & Jul) This is one of the slicker riverside spots doing a great European menu that runs to innovative pastas and salads. The terrace extends over the water, making for a pleasant afternoon-into-evening drinking spot.

Wanha Laamanni (☎ 523 0455; Vuorikatu 17; mains €20-26; ⏰ 10.30am-10pm) Top of the town in both geographic and culinary terms, this old Judges' Chambers serves up Finnish faves like reindeer and the unique tar-flavoured salmon. The building itself is a rambling late-18th-century conversion with a roaring fireplace and sprawling terrace that's ideal for people-watching.

Timbaali (☎ 523 1020; www.timbaali.com; Välikatu 8; mains €19-26, snails per half-dozen €10.50-13; ⏰ 11am-11pm Mon-Sat, also noon-6pm Sun Sep-Apr) Slow food doesn't get any slower than snails and they're best slurped up on a sunny day in the courtyard of this Porvoo legend. Try the escargots with duck-liver butter for a real treat, though they do nongastropod dishes including a reindeer pizza or wild boar fillet.

CAFES

Cafe culture is a Porvoo tradition that harks back to the market town days when locals would gather to gossip and share coffee and pastries. The local speciality is the Runeberg tart, a tower of almond and rum-flavoured pastry crowned with white icing and strawberry jam.

Porvoon Paahtimo (☎ 617 040; Mannerheiminkatu 2) The air is rich with caffeine in this coffeehouse, right by the river. The Tiramisu blend is a heady mix, but the cake selection is tempting too. There's a terrace and a boat, which come with blankets on cooler evenings, and you can enjoy a few beers here.

Café Helmi (☎ 524 5165; www.cafehelmi.net; Välikatu 7; ⏰ 10am-6pm Mon-Sat, 11am-6pm Sun, longer hours in summer) A kindly Russian grandmother would happily take tea from the distinctive lilac-and-white cups in the courtyard of this Tsarist teahouse. They do one of the best Runeberg tarts, but regular cakes and chocolates will also have you loosening your belt.

Café Cabriole (☎ 523 2800; Piispankatu 30; ⏰ 8.30am-6pm Mon-Sat) With white-lofted ceilings and chandeliers, this stylish old building on the market square remains an enduring place to sip tea or savour cakes and biscuits from a huge pastry cabinet.

Getting There & Away

BOAT

See p109 for information on one-way trips.

BUS

Buses depart for Porvoo from Helsinki Kamppi every 30 minutes or so (€10.30, one hour) and there are frequent buses to/from towns further east, including Kotka (€15.10) and Lappeenranta (€30.40).

TRAIN

The old diesel **Porvoo Museum Train** (☎ 752 3262) runs between Helsinki (departs 10.52am) and Porvoo (departs 4.30pm) on Saturday in July and August. The trip takes 1½ hours with tickets (one-way/return €15/25) at the Helsinki or Porvoo train station or on board the train. In Porvoo, the train runs to a final stop near the main bridge, about 1km past the old train station. The trip can also be combined with a cruise on the MS *JL Runeberg* (see opposite).

ESPOO

☎ 09 / pop 246,558

Officially the second-largest city in Finland, Espoo (Swedish: Esbo) is really part of greater Helsinki with many residents commuting daily to their larger neighbour for work. In 2008 it celebrated 550 years as a city, and the town has a bright future with Nokia's headquarters based here. The city is known for its 'campus feel' with plenty of green space and spread-out environs, such as five distinct centres and many suburbs, including seaside Westend, known for their exclusive residences.

Sights & Activities

The city's top sight is **Espoo Museum of Modern Art** (EMMA; ☎ 8165 7512; http://emma.museum; Ahertajantie 5, Tapiola; admission €10; ⏰ 11am-6pm Tue, 11am-8pm Wed-Thu, 11am-6pm Fri-Sun), which holds over 2000 works, ranging from the early 20th century to the present. It's definitely Finland's most significant private art collection and worth the trip from Helsinki. Sharing the same address and opening hours, and visitable with the same ticket, **Espoo City Museum** and **Finnish Toy Museum Leikkilinna** can round out a day trip. You can catch buses 106, 106T, 110, 110T or 110 TA from the Kamppi.

Part-castle, part-studio, the **Gallen-Kallela Museum** (Map p107; ☎ 541 3388; www.gallen-kallela .fi; Gallen-Kallelantie 27; admission €8; ◷ 10am-6pm mid-May–Aug, 10am-4pm Tue-Sat, 10am-5pm Sun Sep–mid-May) was the self-designed home of Akseli Gallen-Kallela, Finland's most significant artist. Many of his works are displayed here including his famed *Kalevala* illustrations. From Helsinki take tram 4 to Munkkiniemi, then walk 2km or take bus 33 (Monday to Friday only).

Aalto fans should visit **Otaniemi University** campus to see Aalto's main building and library, the Pietiläs' student building and Heikki Siren's chapel. **Tapiola** (Swedish: Hagalund) is a modern shopping centre that was hailed as a masterpiece of Finnish city planning.

Serena Water Park (Map p107; ☎ 8870 5555; Tornimäentie 10; water-park admission €20.50, lift pass per hr/day €16/26; ◷ 11am-8pm, closed 2 weeks in Sep) is the largest in the Nordic countries, with a cavalcade of pools, Jacuzzis and waterslides. There's also a ski centre here in winter that makes for a good day's skiing, close to Helsinki.

Espoo's April **jazz festival** (☎ 8165 7234; www .apriljazz.fi) draws big crowds with international artists and the Espoo Top 20 concert, which features audience favourites.

NUUKSIO NATIONAL PARK

No time to head into the wilderness? Nuuksio is on the doorstep of Espoo and close enough to Helsinki to be a half-day trip. As well as 29km of marked walking trails through valleys chiselled out by the Ice Age melt, there's excellent cross-country skiing and camping. The park is a habitat for elk and nocturnal flying squirrels, which you'll see on most walks.

There's an **information centre** (☎ 020-564 4790; ◷ 9am-5.30pm Mon-Fri, 10am-4pm Sat & Sun mid-Apr–Sep) at the main Haukkalampi entrance to the park and an unstaffed nature exhibition in another cabin. There are also several free camping sites. You can also book a variety of cottages and a smoke sauna through **Greenwindow** (☎ 040-750 6001; en.greenwindow.fi) or **Wild North** (☎ 020-344 122; www.villip ohjola.fi).

To get to Nuuksio, catch bus 85 from Espoo Centre. It drops you about 2km from the Haukkalampi centre. Helsinki Expert (see p82) also runs regular excursions out there in summer.

Getting There & Away

You can catch buses to various parts of Espoo from the dedicated Espoo wing in the bus terminal in Helsinki. Local trains from Helsinki will drop you off at several stations, including central Espoo.

VANTAA

☎ 09 / pop 192,552

Essentially Vantaa is a satellite suburb of Helsinki and best known as the location of the Helsinki-Vantaa international airport. However it's also home to **Heureka** (Map p107; ☎ 85799; www .heureka.fi; adult/child exhibitions only €14.50/9.50, with planetarium film €19/12.50; ◷ 10am-5pm Mon-Wed & Fri, 10am-6pm Sat & Sun, 10am-8pm Thu), a fantastic hands-on science centre, Imax theatre and planetarium, next to the Tikkurila train station.

In early August, Vantaa is the venue for **Ankkarock** (☎ 872 4446; www.ankkarock.fi; 2-day pass €75), one of Finland's bigger rock festivals.

There is frequent local train and bus service between Helsinki and Vantaa, 19km to the north; see p105.

For accommodation options see p96.

South Coast

Finland's southern coast stretches either side of Helsinki from a finger of land jutting into the Baltic to point at Sweden, to come up at the Russian border. And it is between these two great empires that the region has been squabbled over with harbours and fortresses to fend off the enemy.

The sea links the towns on this coast, both geographically and figuratively. They've used the sea to trade and fight, but as their fortunes have faded it's this common heritage that brings them together. Kotka's port remains a tough worker, while Hamina's glory days as a fortress town make it a reminiscing veteran with plenty of war stories to recount. Hanko, with its venerable villas and vibrant regatta scene, is a wealthy silver fox that still knows how to shake it. Inland, the lakeside retiree, Lohja, trades tales with the former smithies Fagervik, Ruotsinpyhtää and Fiskars, though the latter still hasn't quite hung up its apron. It's certainly an area that's rich in character.

The coast itself seems to have been sketched out by a drunken cartographer. Islands are liberally strewn to make for some yachting challenges or great island-hopping. The coast is also the Finnish section of the Kuninkaantie (King's Rd), a tourist route that could take you from Bergen, Norway, to St Petersburg.

HIGHLIGHTS

- Setting sail for the **Maritime Centre Vellamo** (p126), an epic-scale retelling of the area's love of the sea

- Balancing on the cutting edge of modern design and Finland's industrial heyday by exploring the ironworks at **Fiskars** (p120)

- Imagining you're in the stately luxury of a Chekhov play in one of Hanko's **Russian villas** (p123)

- Fly-fishing at the **Tsar's Imperial Fishing Lodge** (p129) at Langinkoski, near Kotka, or walking the surrounding nature reserve

- Boating around the islands of **Ekenäs Archipelago National Park** (p119) or its equivalent near Kotka, the **Eastern Gulf** of Finland National Park (p129)

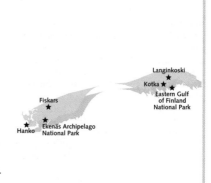

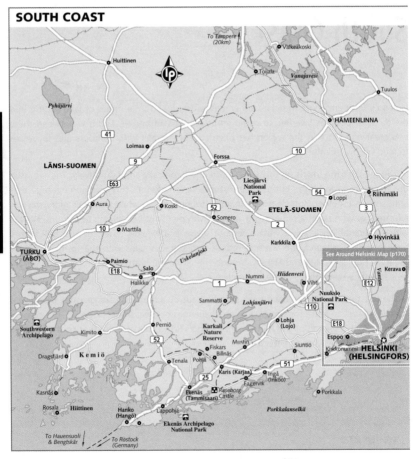

SOUTH COAST

History

In medieval times Sweden began asserting itself in southwestern Finland so the signing of the Peace of Pähkinäsaari with the rulers of Novgorod in 1323 established a border near St Petersburg. This allowed for centuries of peaceful coastal development.

Conflicts over the centuries with Russia and other Baltic powers saw the border yo-yo back and forth with fortifications created in many towns along the coast. Sweden lost part of the territory in the 18th century, regained it again, only to lose the whole of Finland to Russia in 1809. Hanko became *the* destination for the Russian aristocracy in summer while the tsar fished at Kotka. The Winter War and Continuation War broke this peace with brutal fighting across this region. See the boxed text, p36, for more details.

Activities

The south coast is a boaties' paradise, with numerous islets forming chains of archipelagos. Most towns offer summer cruises, guest harbour facilities and charter boats, so you can discover your own island. Alternatively, there's an afternoon messing about in a hired canoe or row boat; this can be done pretty much everywhere.

Fishing is popular here, and the Kymijoki just north of Kotka is known as being a great salmon water. The sizeable Lohjanjärvi, by the town of Lohja, is a good venue for ice-fishing in winter and lake sports in summer.

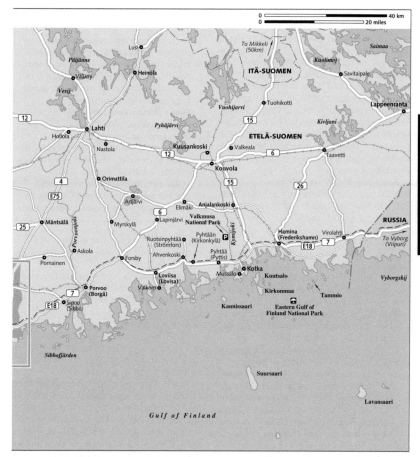

The region makes for brilliant cycling, with marked routes along the Kuninkaantie (tourist route from Bergen to St Petersburg) both west and east from Helsinki. There's also good horse riding to be had in the forests around Ingå.

WEST OF HELSINKI

LOHJA & AROUND
☎ 019 / pop 37,352

Lohjanjärvi is the biggest lake in this southern segment of Finland, and where most of Helsinki's residents seem to have a summer cottage. The woody environs were the stomping ground of Elias Lönnrot, compiler of the *Kalevala*. The town of Lohja (Swedish:

Lojo) keeps the lake houses in beer and supplies, but there are a few sights worth stopping for.

The **tourist office** (☎ 369 1309; www.lohja.fi; Karstuntie 4; ⏰ 9am-6pm Mon-Fri, 9.30am-2pm Sat Jun-Aug, 9am-3pm Mon-Fri Sep-May; 🖥) has information on cottages around the lake, as well as information on canoeing and fishing in summer, and ice-fishing and cross-country skiing in winter.

Lohja's church, **Pyhän Laurin Kirkko** (St Lawrence Church; ⏰ 9am-4pm May–mid-Aug, 10am-3pm mid-Aug–Apr) has a great wooden belltower and is renowned for its medieval murals. Rustic and naive in style, they depicted stories from both Testaments for the illiterate population of the early 16th century.

Lohja Museum (☎ 369 4204; Iso-Pappila; admission €3.50; ◷ noon-4pm Tue-Sun, noon-7pm Wed) recreates a schoolhouse, and a cowherd's cottage with an impressive range of horse-drawn carriages, including an old-style hearse. The main building is a former vicarage for the nearby church, and it has innovative special exhibitions in summer.

You can wet your whistle at **Opus K** (☎ 0500-476 632; Kauppakatu 6; ◷ 3pm-1am Tue-Thu, 4pm-2am Fri, noon-2am Sat), which is one of Finland's best pubs, lined floor to ceiling with books and always with a new discovery from an obscure Finnish microbrewery.

Buses run hourly from Helsinki to Lohja (€10.30, one hour). There are also buses from Lohja to Salo and Turku, and to Ekenäs and Hanko on the south coast.

Around Lohja

The limestone-rich soil around the lake is ideal for growing apples and you'll see orchards dotting the shores. The tourist office has a comprehensive booklet about orchards that produce their own ciders and wines. One of the largest is **Alitalo** (☎ 349 120; www.ciderberg.fi, in Finnish; Pietiläntie 138), on Lohjansaari, which has a cafe and gentle farm animals for younger children.

If you've got your own boat, or are passing through Virkkala (7km south of Lohja), the place for a summery drink is definitely **Kaljaasi** (☎ 040-522 6612; ◷ noon-11pm Sun-Thu, noon-midnight Fri & Sat May-mid-Aug). The bar floats on a platform in the middle of the lake and makes for a scenic watering hole as pleasure boats dock right before you and the lake surrounds. They'll collect you from Virkkala (€12 each way).

Twenty-three kilometres west of Lohja, and 5km north of the village of Sammatti, just off Rd 104, is **Paikkari Cottage** (☎ 356 659; admission €3; ◷ 11am-5pm mid-May–Aug), the birthplace of Elias Lönnrot, compiler of the *Kalevala* (see p44). It's an endearing cottage set amid summer-flowering meadows that would have motivated Lönnrot's Arcadian vision but today inspire picnics. Inside there's a small museum to the man that includes his *kantele* (Karelian stringed instrument).

INGÅ

☎ 019 / pop 5460

The demure seaside village of Ingå (Finnish: Inkoo) is a predominantly Swedish-speaking town with a little marina that holds a library and cafe, a pottery workshop, and not much

---

HORSING AROUND INGÅ

The thick woods around Ingå make for some excellent horseback riding and the stables around here have some interesting breeds. Prices start at €85 per day depending on your horse and need for lessons. Call ahead at any of the following stables:

Shetland Pony Rolle (☎ 045-651 5457, 050-651 5456; Södergårdsvägen 41, Solberg) Offers the chance to ride Shetlands with guides.

Taikatalli (☎ 044-9108217; www.taikatalli.fi, in Finnish; Ingarskilavägen 145, Täkter) Does activities on horses, or mules for beginners.

Violan talli (☎ 050-544 7018; www.violantalli .com, in Finnish; Västankvarnvägen 576) Has what the Finns call 'island horses' with lessons and guided rides.

---

else. It makes a good day trip but you'd be twiddling your thumbs if you stayed the night here.

St Nicholas Church (◷ 8am-4pm Mon-Fri year-round, 9am-6pm Sat & Sun May-Aug) was founded in the 13th century. There are beautiful frescoes over the altar, but most striking is the Dance of Death frieze opposite the entrance door. In this frieze, grinning Reapers escort various members of society to the afterlife; all are equal in death. Across the river is **Ingå Gammelgård**, the local museum.

About 8km west of Ingå, **Fagervik Ironworks** (☎ 295 151; Rd 105) was established in 1646 as a *bruk* (ironworks precinct) and makes a quieter alternative to Fiskars. The Russian army razed the area during the Great Northern War in the 1720s, but the factory was rebuilt forging iron blades and ploughs until finally closing in 1902. It's a pleasant stroll to the 18th-century wooden church located by a lake, and the nearby privately owned manor that includes the remnants of an orangery and a resident ghost, the enigmatic Blue Lady.

There are several cafes to choose from, though we like the harbourside **Delta Café** (☎ 298 0932; www.delta-cafe.com, in Finnish; Venesatama; ◷ 9am-6pm Mon-Thu, 9am-9pm Fri-Sun) and **Café Wilhelmsdahl** (☎ 595 188; Ola Westmans allé 1; ◷ lunch; ▯).

Ingå is southwest of Helsinki on Rd 51 with several daily bus connections.

EKENÄS

☎ 019 / pop 14,784

Seaside Ekenäs (Finnish: Tammisaari) is a dozy resort town, popular with holidaying

Finns and Swedes. The avenues of wooden buildings in its well-preserved Old Town are charming enough though less spectacular than those at Rauma (p234) or other towns settled by the Swedes along the west coast.

It's one of Finland's oldest towns – King Gustav Vasa conceived of it in 1546 as a trading port to rival Tallinn in Estonia. Its fortunes failed and many of its artisans were moved to Helsinki. Today it's a popular holiday destination (due to its proximity to both Helsinki and Turku) with a healthy fishing industry. It's the best base from which to explore the Ekenäs Archipelago National Park.

Information

Café Carl de Mumma (☎ 241 4640; Rådhustorget; internet per hr €5; 🕐 9am-5pm) Cafe and bakery with internet terminals.

Guest Harbour Café (☎ 241 1360; www.ekenasport .fi; Norra Strandgatan; bike rental per day €10; 🕐 8.30am-10pm Mon-Sat, 10am-10pm Sun) Has information and does bike rental. **Public library** (☎ 263 2700; Raseborgsvägen 6-8; 🕐 10am-7pm Mon-Fri, 10am-2pm Sat) Has free internet terminals.

Tourist office (☎ 263 2100; www.ekenas.fi; Rådhustorget; 🕐 8.30am-6pm Mon-Fri, 10am-2pm Sat summer, 8.30am-5pm Mon-Fri autumn-spring) Free internet terminal. Offers information for the entire southwest region.

Sights & Activities

Well-preserved **Gamla Stan** (Old Town) features wooden houses, which are from the late 18th century and were a result of the Swedish movement to create artisan centres for trade. So, narrow streets are named Hattmakaregatan (Hatter's Street), Linvävaregatan (Linen Weaver's Street) and after other types of artisans who worked in this precinct. Some buildings still contain artisans' shops, which are open in summer. The oldest buildings are on Linvävaregatan. The buildings themselves are named after types of fish, as this area was originally a small fishing village.

Gamla Stan's stone **church** (Stora Kyrkogatan; 🕐 10am-6pm May-Aug) has a tower that can be seen from anywhere in town. It was built between 1651 and 1680, damaged in the fire of 1821, and renovated in 1990.

The main building of the **Ekenäs Museum** (☎ 020-775 2240; www.ekenas.fi/museum; Gustav Wasasgatan

SOUTH COAST

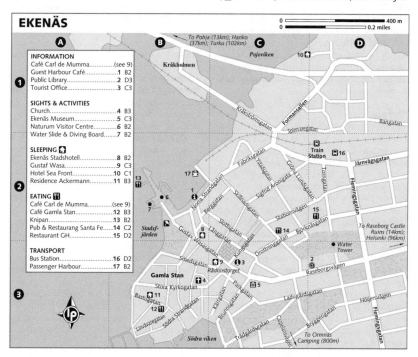

EKENÄS

0 ————————— 400 m
0 ——————— 0.2 miles

INFORMATION
Café Carl de Mumma.............(see 9)
Guest Harbour Café.................**1** B2
Public library...........................**2** D3
Tourist Office..........................**3** C3

SIGHTS & ACTIVITIES
Church....................................**4** B3
Ekenäs Museum.......................**5** C3
Naturum Visitor Centre............**6** B2
Water Slide & Diving Board.......**7** B2

SLEEPING
Ekenäs Stadshotell...................**8** B2
Gustaf Wasa............................**9** C3
Hotel Sea Front........................**10** C1
Residence Ackermann...............**11** B3

EATING
Café Carl de Mumma.............(see 9)
Café Gamla Stan......................**12** B3
Knipan....................................**13** B2
Pub & Restaurang Santa Fe.......**14** C2
Restaurant GH.........................**15** D2

TRANSPORT
Bus Station..............................**16** D2
Passenger Harbour...................**17** B2

To Pohja (13km); Hanko (37km); Turku (102km)
Pojoviken
Kråkholmen
Kråkströmsgatan
Formansallen
Spinnaregatan
Bångatan
Train Station
Järnvägsgatan
Fabriksgatan
Hagagatan
Gröna Lundsgatan
Torngatan
Flemingsgatan
Nora Strandgatan
Berggatan
Skillnadsgatan
Sigfrid Aroniigata
Stationsvägen
Björknäsgatan
To Raseborg Castle Ruins (14km); Helsinki (96km)
Stadsfjärden
Gustav Wasasgatan
Slottsgatan
Långgatan
Kungsgatan
Drottninggatan
Water Tower
Smedsgatan
Rådhustorget
Raseborgsvägen
Gamla Stan
Stora Kyrkogatan
Kungsgatan
Parkgatan
Ladugårdsgatan
Höljersvägen
Bastugatan
Brunnsgatan
Bryggargatan
Flemingsgatan
Linvävaregatan
Södra Strandgatan
Trädgårdsgatan
Capelansgatan
To Ormnäs Camping (800m)
Södra viken

11; admission €2; ⊙ 11am-5pm summer), built in 1802, features an exhibit on Ekenäs through the ages, tracing its history back to the Stone Age using realistic displays. Other buildings have temporary exhibitions of modern art and photography.

There's a small family beach with **water slide and diving board** where you swim just metres away from preening swans, plus there's a minigolf (€3 per game). Bicycles can be hired at the marina from the Guest Harbour Café (p117). You can also rent rowing boats and bikes at **Ormnäs Camping** (right).

Paddlingsfabriken (☎ 0400-411 992; www.paddlings fabriken.fi) offers kayak rental (€17 per day) and beginner's lessons (€30) and an awesome one-day safari (€57) from Raseborg Castle to Ekenäs. If you want to go it alone, they'll drop a kayak wherever you are for €20.

If you're thinking of heading out to the Ekenäs Archipelago, a visit to **Naturum Visitor Centre** (☎ 241 1198; ⊙ 10am-8pm May-Aug) is worthwhile for the eco-exhibits and information. They can give excellent advice on walking around town, and have events for kids.

Tours

Saariston Laivaristeilyt (☎ 241 1850; www.surfnet.fi /saaristoristeilyt) offers a huge range of archipelago cruises (€12/18/22 per two/three/four hours), which include one in the former steamship M/S *Sunnan II*, and all depart from the passenger harbour (Tuesday to Sunday July to mid-August).

Sleeping

The tourist office has details of weekly cottage rentals or overnight homestay accommodation in Ekenäs and around.

Hotel Sea Front (☎ 246 1500; www.hotelseafront.fi; Pojogatan 2; s/d €79/99) Set a little from the main harbour, this secluded spot feels like your own intimate yellow summer cottage with its own pier if you need to park your yacht. It's well kept and bayside rooms have great little balconies, while they all include a raft of extras like sauna, a serviceable restaurant and TVs.

Gustaf Wasa (☎ 241 3020; www.gustaf-wasa.nu; Rådhustorget; s/d from €68/86, 2-/4-person cottages €140/213) Set right in the market square, this 10-room guesthouse has several rooms that are comfortable if slightly chintzy (floral prints and pink abound). The separate cottage is best for a self-contained stay, though either option comes with a solid breakfast.

Ekenäs Stadshotell (☎ 241 3131; www.kaupungin hotelli.fi; Norra Strandgatan 1; s €85, d €95-125, ste €175-295; ⓟ ⓡ) Showing its age a little, this large hotel does well with families and functions and has views across the park to the water. Balcony rooms cost a little extra but you're never far from the town centre or the beach. The suites were recently refurbished to include a private sauna, DVD and bone-soaking bath.

our pick **Residence Ackermann** (☎ 040-050 3314; www.ilseackermann.com/residence; Bastugatan 4; per night/week €140/720) This lovingly restored stablehouse is one of the only brick buildings in the wooden old town and is peerless for self-contained accommodation. It includes its own yard, which spills into neighbours (as is the fashion in this small town), a kitchen and three bedrooms that sleep six. In summer they require a two-night minimum stay but there are discounts for a week or longer.

Ormnäs Camping (☎ 241 4434; www.ek-camping .com; tent sites €10 plus per person €4, 2-/4-person cottages €29/47, sauna per hr €10-18; ⊙ May-Sep, reception closes at 6pm) Within walking distance of town, this easy-going camping ground has its own slice of the beach and expertly caters to Finnish families, with bikes (€10 per day) and row boats (€10) for hire.

Eating

Hungry for the tourist euro, several good cafes and restaurants border the main square, Rådhustorget. Our favourite is **Café Carl de Mumma** (☎ 241 4640; Rådhustorget; ⊙ 9am-5pm), an ever-popular bakery that does pastries, rolls and coffee, but be warned their fabulous blueberry cheesecake sells out fast.

our pick **Knipan** (☎ 241 1169; www.knipan.fi, in Finnish; Strandallén; ⊙ 11am-midnight Mon-Fri, noon-midnight Sat & Sun May–mid-Sep) This revered restaurant turned 100 in 2008 though the pier building has been here since 1867. It affords the best views in town with a brief menu of Finnish favourites, particularly seafood. On weekend evenings it's a return to the grand old days of the Finnish foxtrot, so expect to cut some old-school rug.

Café Gamla Stan (☎ 241 5656; www.cafegamlastan.fi, in Swedish; Bastugatan 5; cakes €3-6, lunch €6-13; ⊙ 11am-6pm May, 11am-8pm Jun-Aug) This quaint garden cafe in the Old Town has limited seating in the greenery, so lunchtime can be frantic. It's family run and there's plenty of homebaking to sample plus a small craft shop and live music in summer.

Also recommended:
Pub & Restaurang Santa Fe (☎ 246 1173;
www.pubsantafe.com; Skillnadsgatan 14; mains €7-12;
⚇ 11am-3pm Mon-Sat, noon-10pm Sun) This joint
continues the Finnish affair with the taco and burrito,
also has live music of a rocking, folky stripe on Friday
nights.
Restaurant GH (☎ 241 3200; www.restaurantgh
.fi, in Finnish; Björknäsgatan 12; lunches €8.50, dinner
mains €10-16; ⚇ lunch Mon-Sat, dinner Wed-Sat) An
old-style Finnish lunchroom with the best-value lunch and
some hearty dinners.

Getting There & Around

Ekenäs is 96km southwest of Helsinki on Rd
25. There are five to seven buses a day from
Helsinki (€16.30, 1½ hours), Turku (with a
transfer in Salo; €16.30, two hours) or Hanko
(€7.20, 35 minutes).

Trains to Ekenäs coming from Helsinki
and Turku go via Karis (Finnish: Karjaa)
where a change is required. Seven to nine
daily trains run from Helsinki (€17.90, 1½
hours) and Turku (€20.30, 1½ hours), both
continuing on to Hanko (€4.50, 25 minutes).
Some connections from Ekenäs to Karis involve a railbus.

The town is reasonably spread-out and
hilly, so cycling will present a few small challenges. If you're puffed, get a **taxi** (☎ 241 1414)
from the market square.

AROUND EKENÄS
Ekenäs Archipelago National Park

Almost 90% of this 5200-hectare park is water,
so to explore the 1300 islands you'll need to
hire your own boat or find options in Ekenäs
harbour including tours (opposite). The best
place for information on where to stay is the
Naturum Visitor Centre.

The most popular island is **Älgö**, which
has a 2km nature trail that takes in the
island's observation tower. There's an old
fisherman's home that's been converted to
include a sauna and facilities for several
camp sites, which can be booked through
Naturum. There are also camping grounds
on the islands of **Fladalandet** and **Modermagan**,
but visits to many other islands are prohibited, particularly the ecologically fragile
outer islands.

Charter boats from Ekenäs:
M/S Johanna (☎ 040-0541 9480, 019-201350; www
.surfnet.fi/saaristoristeilyt) A small vessel that takes a
maximum of 12.

M/Y ALLI (☎ 040-041 2767; www.nic.fi/~ekl/, in Finnish) Has a good overnight boat that takes up to 32 people.
M/S Kennedy (☎ 040-047 0751; nevatek@dnainter
net.net) A smaller vessel that takes a maximum of 12.

Raseborg Castle

Dating from the late 14th century, Raseborg
Castle (Finnish: Raasepori) perches dramatically on a high rock overlooking a grassy
sward. The castle was strategically crucial
in the 15th century, when it protected the
trading town of Tuna. Karl Knutsson Bonde,
three times king of Sweden, was one of its
most prominent residents. By the mid-16th
century, Raseborg's importance had declined,
and it was deserted for more than 300 years.

The **castle** (☎ 019-234 015; www.raseborg.org; admission €1; ⚇ 10am-8pm) is 14km east of Ekenäs,
and about 2km west of the wonderfully
named village of Snappertuna. It's signposted
Slottsruiner/Linnanrauniot off the main
road; buy your tickets at the cafe. There's
not a lot of explanatory material in English,
but it's great to climb up and down the levels and patrol the ramparts. There are free
tours from mid-May to August weekends at
3pm. During July there are evening concerts
at Raseborg; contact the Ekenäs tourist office for details. There are occasional buses to
Snappertuna from Ekenäs or Karis.

Snappertuna

This fishy little burg makes for a good stay
away from it all. The small open-air folk
museum (☎ 019-234 033; admission €1; ☎ noon-5pm
Tue-Sun Jun-Aug) recreates the life of farmers
and fisherfolk in the village. There's a short
forest walk that leads to Raseborg Castle.

There are a few good overnight options
here that are quieter than in Ekenäs. HI-
affiliated **Snappertuna Youth Hostel** (☎ 019-234
180; Kyrkoväg 129; dm €20, cottages per person €15; P)
has basic dorms and a self-catering cottage
that sleeps two to four. For a slightly more
upmarket bed, **Norrby B&B** (☎ 040-531 7451; www
.norrbygard.fi, in Finnish; Norrbyvägen 277; per person €40;
P ⌨) has rudimentary double rooms in a
recently renovated building with shared bathrooms and a small sauna (€5).

FISKARS
☎ 019 / pop 200

This historic town is best known outside
Finland for the design company that produced

iconic orange-handled scissors in the 1960s. The scissors and the company both came from this small village known for its ironworks, which began in 1649 with a single furnace.

There are several small *bruk* villages in this area to visit. Fiskars itself is the most attractive with a river sidling between old brick buildings, many of which have been converted into shops, galleries, design studios and cafes. The *bruk* originally produced farming equipment, chiefly ploughs with more than a million horse-ploughs produced here in the 19th century.

In 1816 the mansion that housed the owner of the *bruk* was built, and this remains the village's centrepiece. You'll recognise the neoclassical flair of CL Engel in other buildings in the village. Although manufacturing operations have moved offshore, the Fiskars Company still produces those scissors and other metal pieces that make a practical souvenir from the village.

There's a **tourist information office** (☎ 277 7504; www.fiskarsvillage.fi; ☼ 10am-6pm Mon-Sat May-end Aug) located in the workers' tenement buildings, near the distinctive clock-tower building.

Sights

Fiskars is best explored on foot, starting from the western (Pohja) end, with the river on your right. The first building on the left is the **Assembly Hall**, built in 1896 as a public hall. Just beyond is the 1902 **Granary**, which now hosts various exhibitions and is approached from the top via a bridge. Behind it is the **Copper Forge** built in 1818 with more exhibition space, a glass studio and restaurant with a riverside terrace.

SHOPPING IN FISKARS

Fiskars is famous for its design shops. They open in summer from 11am to 6pm and at weekends during the rest of the year. These are some of our favourites:

Onoma (☎ 277 7500; www.onoma.org; Kellotornirakennus) A wide range of crafts and homewares.

Sassi Design (☎ 237 174; www.sassidesign.fi, in Finnish; Antskogintie 26 B) Specialising in high-end silver jewellery.

Takopaja (☎ 050-590 2797; www.takopaja.fi, in Finnish; Kuparivasarantie) A working forge that produces knives, axes and other metal pieces.

Continuing along the road, you pass the **Stenhuset** (stone house), the mansion originally occupied by factory owner John Julin and the old **mill**. The distinctive red-brick **clock-tower building** has characteristic CL Engel flourishes and now hosts houses, shops, galleries and a cafe. Where the road forks is the marketplace with stalls, a cafe and terrace in summer. Continuing along the unpaved road towards Degersjojärvi, you pass more **workers' housing** and what remains of **Fiskars ironworks**.

Near the lake is **Fiskars Museum** (☎ 237 013; admission €2.50; ☼ 11am-4pm May-Sep, 1-4pm Sat & Sun Oct-Mar), which details the ironworks evolution and the village that grew around it. Every season there is a different display of art and craft, with a special exhibition at Christmas.

Sleeping & Eating

Fiskars is best done as a day trip though there are B&Bs and other accommodation if you want to extend your visit.

Vanha Meijeri (☎ 044-594 1959; www.kahvilavanha meijeri.fi; Suutarinmäki 7; s/d €55/75) Upstairs in one of Fiskars' more popular cafes, this former maids' quarters has been converted into two great rooms decorated with period pieces and brass beds. Breakfast is a real highlight with breads made fresh every morning, and filling porridge.

Fiskars Wärdshus (☎ 276 6510; www.wardshus.fi; s/d from €110/130; ℗ ▣) This refined inn was built in 1836 and offers the best rooms in Fiskars. The neoclassical exterior is a disconnect from the swish Scandinavian chic of the rooms, but they use local timbers and include bathrooms and broadband. The restaurant serves up local game (mains €26 to €30) and does a great three-course lunch (€30) on the scenic terrace.

Restaurant Kuparipaja (☎ 237 045; www.kupari paja.fi; mains €12-20; ☼ lunch & dinner) In the old copper forge, this is an excellent setting for a long lunch in the à la carte restaurant (sample elk and mutton sausages, if you're feeling carnivorous). The cafe-bar does quick filled rolls, pasta dishes and salad buffet but it would be a shame not to enjoy the terrace overhanging the river.

In the clock-tower building, **Café Antique** (☎ 237 275; ☼ 11am-6pm May-Sep) has books and makes for a browsing brunch.

HANKO

☎ 019 / pop 9708

On a long sandy peninsula, Hanko (Swedish: Hangö) retains the past grandeur of a Chekhov play. It blossomed as a well-to-do Russian spa town in the late 19th century, when opulent seaside villas were built by wealthy summer visitors; they have become the town's star attraction. Locals refer to them as 'the old ladies', as many were named for Russian sweethearts (although newer ones have nautical names).

The population doubles in summer when Finns flock here for the sun and sand. While birdlife like the grey Canada goose summers here, and seals are regular visitors, the human guests arrive for the huge Hanko Regatta, which is as famous for its 'Spring Break' wildness as for its feats of sailing.

History

As the southernmost town in Finland, Hanko was a strategic anchorage well before the foundation of the town in 1874. The Russian Empire used it as a summer holiday destination, but Hanko was also a point of emigration from Finland. Between 1881 and 1931, about 250,000 Finns left for the USA and Canada via the Hanko docks, with many Finnish descendants tracing their families back to this port town.

At the end of the Winter War, the March 1940 peace treaty with Russia required the ceding of Hanko as a naval base. The Russians moved in with a garrison of 30,000 and constructed a huge network of fortifications. After several bloody naval engagements, Hanko was eventually abandoned in December 1941, having been isolated from the Russian front lines. The citizens of Hanko returned to see their damaged town the following spring (see boxed text. p122).

Orientation

The East Harbour is the centre of the town's activity in summer, the West Harbour handling only commercial traffic. Russian villas are on Appelgrenintie, east of East Harbour. The bus and train stations are a little way from the town centre and beachside villas.

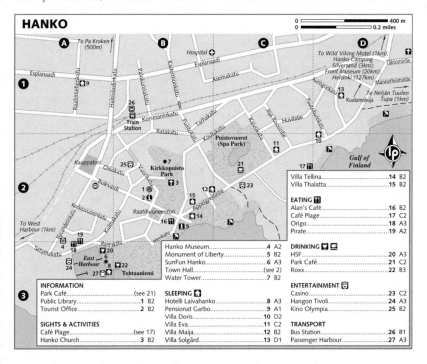

HANKO

0 — 400 m
0 — 0.2 miles

INFORMATION	
Park Café	(see 21)
Public Library	1 B2
Tourist Office	2 B2

SIGHTS & ACTIVITIES	
Café Plage	(see 17)
Hanko Church	3 B2
Hanko Museum	4 A2
Monument of Liberty	5 B2
SunFun Hanko	6 A3
Town Hall	(see 2)
Water Tower	7 B2

SLEEPING	
Hotelli Laivahanko	8 A3
Pensionat Garbo	9 A1
Villa Doris	10 D2
Villa Eva	11 C2
Villa Maija	12 B2
Villa Solgård	13 D1
Villa Tellina	14 B2
Villa Thalatta	15 B2

EATING	
Alan's Café	16 B2
Café Plage	17 C2
Origo	18 A3
Pirate	19 A2

DRINKING	
HSF	20 A3
Park Café	21 C2
Roxx	22 B3

ENTERTAINMENT	
Casino	23 C2
Hangon Tivoli	24 A3
Kino Olympia	25 B2

TRANSPORT	
Bus Station	26 B1
Passenger Harbour	27 A3

CHANGING LIBERTY?

Where Bulevardi meets the beach, the large obelisk-like **Monument of Liberty** marks an interesting passage in Hanko's history. The town was in Russian hands towards the end of WWI and when Germany took the town in 1918 they were seen as liberators. The townsfolk collected money to salute the Germans who 'assisted our country in the struggle for liberty'.

But when WWII came around Hanko was occupied again by the Russians who were none too impressed by the edifice that saluted their military defeat. When the Russians left they trashed the statue and it was taken down. After WWII it was difficult to see Germany as the bringers of liberty so the statue seemed to have become an anachronism. But civic pride prevailed and the statue was remade with an inscription that reads: 'This stone was defiled and destroyed by enemy hands.' Hardly stirring words of freedom.

Information

Park Café (☎ 248 6182; Appelgrenintie 11; ☼ May-Sep) Has a free internet terminal.

Public library (☎ 220 3380; Vuorikatu 3-5; ☼ 11am-7pm Mon-Thu, 9am-5pm Fri, also 9am-3pm Sat winter) Has several internet terminals.

Tourist office (☎ 220 3411; www.hanko.fi; Raatihuoneentori 5; ☼ 9am-4pm Mon-Fri Sep-May, 9am-5pm Mon-Fri, 10am-4pm Sat & Sun Jun & Jul)

Sights

Take the lift to the top of the 50m landmark **water tower** (admission €1; ☼ noon-6pm Jun & Jul, 1-3pm Aug) on Vartiovuori Hill for an excellent view across town and out to sea. The nearby neo-Gothic **Hanko Church** (☼ noon-6pm Jul-early Aug, 1-3pm rest of Aug), built in 1892, was damaged in WWII but has been thoroughly renovated. Photographers love the challenge of aligning the church spire with the town hall and water tower in a single panorama.

Hanko Museum (☎ 220 3228; Nycanderinkatu 4; adult/child €2/0.50; ☼ 11am-4pm Tue-Sun, 6-7pm Thu mid-May–Aug, shorter hours winter) is the town museum housed in the brick-and-stone building near East Harbour, with a smattering of local (especially military) history and changing exhibitions.

Hanko is quite an artistic community, and there are some half-a-dozen **art galleries** scattered around town, including changing exhibitions in the **town hall**. The tourist office has details of current exhibitions.

The **Monument of Liberty** is one of several impressive pieces of public art on the street, but it's significant for its historical reinvention (see boxed text, above).

EAST OF HANKO

On Little Pine Island, 1.5km east of the town centre, is **Neljän Tuulen Tupa** (House of the Four Winds; ☎ 248 1455; cakes €2-4; ☼ mid-May–mid-Aug), where locals snuck swigs of 'hard tea' (alcohol) during the Finnish prohibition (1919–32). Field Marshal CGE Mannerheim, who had his summer cottage on the neighbouring island, wouldn't stand for it. Disturbed by the merrymaking, he bought the whole joint in 1926, fired the chef, imported tea sets from France and personally ran the place until 1931. Little Pine Island is now connected to the mainland by a bridge and has a beautiful cafe and summer terrace perched over the water. Today the tea room itself is modest, but the view is free with granite tables carved from the surrounding rocks.

Nineteen kilometres northeast of Hanko, and just off the Ekenäs highway (Rd 25), the **Front Museum** (☎ 244 3068; www.frontmuseum.fi; Lappohja; adult/child €4/2; ☼ 11.30am-6.30pm May–mid-Sep) remembers Finland's WWII involvement at the site of some of the worst fighting. There are original trenches, bunkers, artillery guns and an extensive tent exhibition. This area was occupied by Russia during the war and the people of Hanko were evacuated for a year.

Activities

Hanko is a great place from which to explore the outdoors. There's some of Finland's best **surfing** with good breaks just west of the guest harbour. With over 30km of beaches around town, **swimming** and sunbathing draw the crowds. The stretch near Café Plage is the best, including some sweet changing boxes.

A bicycle is the best way to explore the parklands and Russian villas east of the town centre, though you can walk out to Neljän Tuulen Tupa on Little Pine Island easily in two hours. Bikes can be hired for €10 per day at **SunFun Hanko** (☎ 248 6699; www.sunfun.fi, in Finnish; East Harbour) or **Café Plage** (☎ 248 2776), which also offers blowkarting and several excellent tours.

Diving is popular around Hanko's troubled waters and many wrecks. You can get advice from dive shops such as **Hanko Diving** (☎ 040-562 4241; www.hankodiving.com; East Harbour).

Tours & Cruises

There are several excellent cruise companies operating out of East Harbour:

Marine Lines (☎ 040-053 6930; www.hk-service.fi) Runs a six-hour cruise (€46) out to the lighthouse island of Bengtskär (departs 10.30am in summer, also 2.30pm July), which includes lunch or dinner.

SunFun Charter (☎ 248 6699; www.sunfun.fi, in Finnish) Runs a variety of tours including a six-hour excursion to Bengtskär (€53), departing 10.30am mid-June to August, and a 2½-hour seal safari (€15) departing 3pm June to August.

The tourist office organises great little tours like the self-guided elk safari (€30), where they equip you with a map, bike and picnic basket to look for the area's wildlife. There are also guided wildlife tours (€70), though you'll need to book at least a week in advance. There are several good tours in or around Hanko:

Sightseeing Hanko (☎ 040-728 2000) Does two good historical walking tours: the cheaper one (€5) follows the coast; the other goes inland (€6) and is worth the extra euro.

Supervivo (☎ 050-564 3563; www.supervivo.net) Organises events that include survivalist courses and snowshoeing in the woods, plus 'fright nights' for tricky-to-please teens; rates by negotiation.

Festivals & Events

Hanko's massive marina hosts the **Hanko Regatta** (www.hrw.fi, in Finnish & Swedish) with more than 200 boats competing. The regatta takes place on the first weekend of July, attracting thousands of spectators with a real carnival atmosphere.

June brings **Hanko Theatre Days** (☎ 0400-419 537; www.hangoteatertraff.org), which is Finland's biggest festival of Swedish-language theatre and books out hotels throughout the town.

Sleeping

Accommodation can be tight in the summer months, so book ahead. Prices go up during the regatta. You can book private accommodation (sometimes in unused villas) through the tourist office, which has an extensive list.

A unique feature of Hanko is its selection of Empire-era Russian-style villas though many are showing their age and are more histori-

cal curiosities than accommodation options. Many share bathrooms as was the style of the period.

BUDGET

Hanko Camping Silversand (☎ 248 5500; www.silver sand.fi/camping; Hopeahietikko; tent sites €10 plus per person €4, 6-person cottages €68-88; ✆ Jun-Aug) About 3km northeast of the town centre, this camping ground is set on a long beach with good shade, plus sauna and other facilities. It's operated from the nondescript hotel and is pricier around Midsummer.

our pick **Wild Viking Motel** (☎ 040-758 4783; www .wildvikingmotel.fi; Lasitehtaankatu 6; d €50) OK, this Viking-themed place isn't going to be for everyone and the fact that it's owned by a bikie club might dissuade some, but if you grab it by the horns it's a whole mess of fun. There's a pioneer feel with raw wood and Viking ornaments, plus the redwood sauna gives off a pleasingly unique scent. The grounds include an expanding Viking-themed playground and grown-ups are included with a small amphitheatre that rocks out in summer.

Villa Solgärd (☎ 248 1481; Tähtikuja; d €64) Handy for the Spa Park and nearby beaches, this is a simple villa that makes a good family option with larger rooms available.

Pensionat Garbo (☎ 040-542 1732; fax 248 7897; Esplanaadi 84; s/d €45/65; **P**) This quirky guesthouse strains the celluloid connection with photocopied images tacked to the walls, but the rooms themselves are good value with raw wood and plenty of charm. There's a kitchen for self-caterers and the faded elegance of the breakfast saloon is almost worthy of Swedish-born Greta Lovisa Gustafsson herself.

MIDRANGE

Hotelli Laivahanko (☎ 050-061 0113; www.hotellilaiva hanko.fi; East Harbour, but moves seasonally; d €80-90, ste €150) Left your yacht in another harbour? This hotel boat gives you an ocean sleep with snug double rooms tricked out with flat-screen TVs and porthole views. It was purpose built with the suite featuring its own 'balcony' on the bow, and a large breakfast room.

Villa Maija (☎ 248 2900; www.villamaija.fi; Appelgrenintie 7; d with/without bathroom from €110/88; ✆ mid-Apr–mid-Oct; **P**) Built in 1888, this is the best of the villa options. They know renovation means more than a coat of paint with faultlessly restored rooms that feel like your own townhouse. Out the back is Villa Janne, a separate cottage that is as light-filled and pleasant as the main building, with the advantage of being self-contained. Breakfasts feel like a step back to the grandest days of the Russian Empire in a lovely setting with plenty of choices.

Villa Doris (☎ 248 1228; Appelgrenintie 23; d from €85; P) Done out in sky-blues and white, this charmer with blooming flower boxes in summer dates back to 1881. Rooms feature period furniture and a great breakfast is included.

Right by the beach, rambling **Villa Tellina** (☎ 248 6356; www.tellina.com, in Finnish; Appelgrenintie 2; s/d from €50/75, with bathroom from €60/90; ☼ Jun–mid-Aug; P) has basic rooms that can be a little tight. The same owners operate **Villa Eva** (☎ 248 6356; Kaivokatu 2) and **Villa Thalatta** (☎ 248 6356; Appelgrenintie 1), so they often have rooms during busy periods.

Eating

East Harbour has a row of red wooden buildings that host a school of gourmet fish restaurants with crowded terraces. In winter it's quieter with several places heading south. During crab season (August to September) the flavoursome crustacean scurries over most menus.

Alan's Café (☎ 248 7622; Raatihuoneentori 4; ☼ 11am-6pm Tue-Sun May-Jul) Set in a delightful villa with an appealing forecourt this place features treats (€1.50) hand baked by the jolly owner, plus there's a small (mostly Finnish) bookshop and gift shop attached. It's the ideal place for a post-seaside stroll and cuppa.

Café Plage (☎ 248 2776; ☼ Jun-Aug) This rudimentary cafe-bar right on the beach does for a simple meal while watching your kids play minigolf or run along one of the town's best stretches of sand.

Pirate (☎ 248 3006; www.pirate.fi, in Finnish & Swedish; Satamakatu 13; mains €8-18; ☼ 11am-1am Easter–mid-Sep) Plenty of other sea dogs know this is the spot to weigh anchor if you're after straight-up grub. Below decks on the ground level there's a restaurant that runs to burgers, pizzas and pastas, while up top there's a lively bar that plays the odd sea shanty (or other live music).

Henri'x (☎ 010-701 703; www.henrix.fi; Itäsatama; mains €15-21; ☼ lunch & dinner) You'll need to catch a free ferry out to this refined little island restaurant that feels a world away from the rugged granite island it perches on. The cane marine interior oozes comfort and the menu is hearty sailor fare including a rib-sticking potato and sausage stew. As it's in the port,

you can expect yacht rock and a boat-shoed crowd to match.

Origo (☎ 248 5023; www.restaurant-origo.com; Satamakatu 7; mains €16-24; ☼ 11am-10pm mid-Apr–mid-Oct) Another in the line-up of East Harbour eateries, this one distinguishes itself with quality seafood. The menu shows great care – blackened perch is a treat and even their crayfish soup comes with a croissant. It's a quality plate in this busy strip.

På Kroken (☎ 248 9101; www.pakroken.fi; Hangonkylä Harbour; mains €18-28; ☼ lunch & dinner) Think you've had good Finnish seafood? With its own smokehouse and boat-fresh shellfish (they sell to Helsinki's Hakaniemi market), this place will make you think again. The yacht-shaped buffet teems with tasty choices and service is cheerful but formal. Its location at the northern harbour makes for great views, and it's quieter than the bustle of Eastern Harbour.

Drinking & Entertainment

There are excellent summertime beer terraces in East Harbour, including **Roxx** (☎ 248 4393; saunas €6, snacks €4-6), which is a hang-out for Hanko's youth and has a good sauna, and the 2nd floor of **HSF** (☎ 248 2264; www.restauranthsf.fi, in Finnish).

Casino (☎ 248 2310; www.hangoncasino.fi; Appelgrenintie 10; ☼ May-Aug) The imposing green-and-white casino has long been a celebrated nightspot in Hanko and has regular live music, dancing, roulette and terrace drinking.

Hangon Tivoli (☎ 050-352 6950; www.hangontivoli .com, in Finnish; Satamakatu 4; ☼ 4pm-4am) This hip new spot has drinking and dancing in a deep-red building with a massive terrace and a party crowd in summer.

Park Café (☎ 248 6182; www.restaurangpark.fi, in Finnish & Swedish; Appelgrenintie 11; ☼ May-Sep; 🖥) Opposite the Casino in Spa Park, this converted rotunda makes for a brilliant evening's boozing where they'll bring you a rug when it gets too chilly. There's a good range of international beers including stout and it makes a good warm-up or come-down for the Casino.

Kino Olympia (☎ 248 1811; Vuorikatu 11; ☼ Thu-Sun) Has been an independent cinema showing Hollywood fare since 1919.

Getting There & Away
BUS

There are regular (two to six) daily express buses to/from Helsinki (€22.40, 2¼ hours) via Ekenäs (€7.20, 35 minutes).

TRAIN

Seven to nine trains travel daily from Helsinki (€21.10, 1¼ hours) and Turku (€24.30, two hours) via Karis (Finnish: Karjaa) where they are met by connecting trains or buses to Hanko (via Ekenäs).

AROUND HANKO

Pike's Gut

The narrow strait between Tullisaari and Kobben, called Hauensuoli (Pike's Gut), is a protected natural harbour where sailing ships from countries around the Baltic Sea once waited out storms. The sailors killed time by carving their initials or tales of bravery on the rocks, earning the area the nickname 'Guest Book of the Archipelago'. Some 600 rock carvings dating back to the 17th century remain. Hauensuoli can be reached by charter taxi boat or on a cruise from Hanko – see p123.

Bengtskär

This southernmost inhabited island of Finland is 25km from Hanko and famous for its **lighthouse** (☎ 02-4667 227; www.bengtskar .fi; 2-/4-person r €172/256). It was built in 1906 to protect ships from the dangerous waters of the archipelago and given the perilous nature of the waters it had to be 52m high, making it Scandinavia's tallest lighthouse. Damaged extensively during the Continuation War by the departing Red Army in 1941, it remains a stunning spectacle thanks to substantial refurbishment. Today it also takes guests in simple rooms that have quite a view. There are a few exhibits explaining the historical significance of the island, and a shop.

Day cruises to Bengtskär leave from Hanko in summer (see p123), or you can charter boats from Hanko or the village of Rosala on the island of Hiittinen. See also p219 for cruises to Bengtskär from Turku.

EAST OF HELSINKI

LOVIISA

☎ 019 / pop 7417

Named for Swedish Queen Lovisa Ulrika in 1752, Loviisa (Swedish: Lovisa) is a sleepy port that had its glory days as a Russian spa town in the 19th century. Like many of the coastal towns it was a pawn in Russo-Swede conflicts, most devastatingly in 1855 when much of it burnt down. Only a small vestige of the Old Town survives and today the town is very much a summer resort with little open out of season.

Information

Library (☎ 555 330; Kuningattarenkatu 24) Free internet access, just north of Mannerheiminkatu.

Tourist office (www.loviisa.fi) summer office (☎ 555 446; Brandensteininkatu 11B; ☷ 9am-5pm Mon-Fri, 10am-3pm Sat Jun-Aug); town hall (☎ 555 234; Mannerheiminkatu 4; ☷ 9am-4pm Mon-Fri Sep-May)

Sights

The tiny **Old Town**, just south of Mannerheiminkatu, is all that remains of Loviisa's heritage of wooden buildings. The narrow streets around **Degerby Gille** restaurant are charming and the restaurant was built in 1662, making it the oldest building around.

Dominating the market square is the red-brick neo-Gothic **Loviisa Church** (☷ 10am-6pm mid-May–mid-Aug), built in 1865. Summer guides give free tours.

About 200m north of the market square, **Loviisa Town Museum** (☎ 555 357; Puistokatu 2; admission €4; ☷ 11am-4pm Tue-Sun Jun-Aug, noon-4pm Sun Sep-May, extended hours during exhibitions) is set in an old manor house with three floors of interesting historical exhibits, particularly the exhibition on Jean Sibelius, who summered at Sibeliuksenkatu 10. Loviisa's biggest annual event is the **Sibelius Festival** (☎ 555 499; www.loviisa .fi; tickets €15-25) in early June, which features a weekend of Sibelius performances.

In summer most of the action is at **Laivasilta Marina**, 500m southeast of the centre. A cluster of old rust-coloured wooden storehouses now contains galleries, craft shops, cafes and a small maritime museum. Boats to Svartholma Sea Fortress depart from this marina.

The short trip to the **Svartholma Sea Fortress**, on an island 10km from the town centre, is a must when visiting Loviisa. Established in 1748 soon after Sweden lost eastern Finland, it was built as a defence against further Russian invasion. It lasted until the Crimean War in 1855 when the British destroyed it, but has been reconstructed. Several ferries (€10 return, 45 minutes, June to August) run each day from Laivasilta Marina. Guided walking tours (€5) of the fortress start from the small museum, which has a few free displays about the fort's history.

Sleeping & Eating

Hotel Degerby (☎ 50561; www.degerby.com; Brandensteininkatu 17; s/d €90/105, ste €133; P ᵭ ᵭ) Handy to the market and bus station, this hotel is the best the town's limited accommodation scene has to offer. Rooms are comfortable and include a solid buffet breakfast.

Gasthaus Loviisa (☎ 040-835 7997; www.majata loloviisa.fi; Sibeliuksenkatu 3; s/d €40/55; 🖵 wi-fi) With affordable rooms decorated in bold colours this guesthouse makes an option close to Sibelius' old house. There's share bathrooms but you get a small washbasin and there's wi-fi in all the rooms. At the time of research they were making some large renovations to include a pool.

Degerby Gille (☎ 50561; Sepänkuja 4; 🕑 by arrangement) In the town's oldest building, this enchanting restaurant opens for group bookings. It's worth inquiring, though, at the Hotel Degerby, as the restaurant is usually open for lunch once a week for the local Rotary Club, with the general public allowed as well. There are five separate and charmingly old-fashioned dining rooms.

Tamminiemi (☎ 530 244; www.tamminiemi.net; Kapteenintie 1; tent sites €12, s/d from €40/60; 🕑 camping early Jun-late Aug) Just 500m south of the marina, this green spot has plenty of excellent sites that suit boat owners. There are also rooms in two renovated wooden houses, most with bathrooms.

Getting There & Away

Loviisa is 90km east of Helsinki, reached by motorway E18 or Hwy 7. There are buses at least hourly to/from Helsinki (€10.30, 1½ to two hours), as well as a regular bus service to/from Kotka (€18, 1¼ hours) and Porvoo (€5.80, 15 minutes).

RUOTSINPYHTÄÄ
☎ 019 / pop 2895

The tiny village of Ruotsinpyhtää (Swedish: Strömfors) was split in two by the Swedish-Russian border that both warring nations defined in 1743. The border ran along the Kymijoki, whose waters powered the large ironworks that remain preserved today. The town wakes up for the annual hoedown of **Rootsinpyhtaa** (www.bluegrass.fi), held in early June.

The **information office** (☎ 618 474; 🕑 8am-4pm Mon-Fri) and **Forge Café** (🕑 8am-3pm Mon-Thu, 8am-2.30pm Fri May-Aug), which also does light meals, both stock plenty of brochures and offer information for visitors.

Most visitors make a beeline for the **Strömfors Ironworks** (🕑 10am-6pm Jun–mid-Aug), which dates back to 1695, making it one of Finland's oldest. Today it's an open-air museum of wooden farm and industrial buildings, nestled amid forest, rivers and bridges. The **Forge Museum** has two sections: an old smith's workshop and equipment and the working mill wheel. Forging demonstrations are common in summer and there are also **craft workshops** by potters, silversmiths, textile-makers and painters around the village. One ironworks building serves as an **art gallery** in summer.

The octagonal wooden **church** dates from 1771. Its Resurrection altarpiece was painted in 1898 by the young Helene Schjerfbeck who went on to become one of Finland's greatest painters.

The only buses to the village itself run from Loviisa (€4.60, 20 minutes, three daily in summer, many more on weekdays September to May).

KOTKA
☎ 05 / pop 54,759

Still an active industrial port, the fortunes of Kotka have long been tied to the sea. As well as being the junction of several roads it's also where the Kymijoki meets the sea, which was an important transport route for logging. The name means eagle in Finnish, but it's definitely as a sea eagle as this nuggety island has itself been swooped on by Russia and Sweden throughout its history.

Today the seafaring heritage is celebrated biannually with **Kotkan Meripäivät** (Kotka Maritime Festival; ☎ 234 4494; www.meripaivat.com), a festival in July with boat racing, concerts, markets and a huge wooden boat show. The completion of the Maritime Centre Vellamo in 2008 affirmed the town as a nautical destination.

Information
Public library (☎ 212 424; Kirkkokatu 24) Near Kotka Church with free short-term internet use.
Tourist office (☎ 234 4424; www.kotka.fi; Keskuskatu 6; 🕑 9am-5pm Mon-Fri Sep-May, 9am-6pm Mon-Fri, 10am-2pm Sat Jun-Aug) Has free internet access and includes a travel agent.

Sights

MARITIME CENTRE VELLAMO
Relocated here from Hylkysaari off Helsinki, this **maritime museum** (☎ 234 4433; www.merikeskus

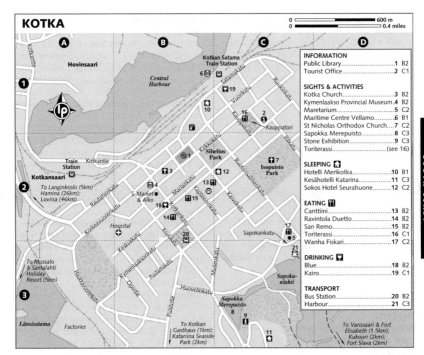

KOTKA

SOUTH COAST

vellamo.fi; Tornatorintie 99; adult €8, joint ticket with Maretarium €15; ⏱ 11am-6pm Tue & Thu-Sat, 11am-8pm Wed) is a spectacular new museum that fittingly recounts the maritime life of Finland. The tanker-sized building has a wavelike design with a mosaic facade of photographs that's coolly attractive. The star exhibit is the *Tarmo*, the world's oldest ice-breaker (1908) that determinedly ploughed Finnish waters until it was retired in 1970. There's a roster of changing exhibitions that showcase other sea-based memorabilia.

MARETARIUM

More than an aquarium, the impressive **Maretarium** (☎ 234 4030; www.maretarium.fi; Sapokankatu 2; adult/child €10/6.50, joint ticket with Maritime Centre Vellamo €15; ⏱ 10am-8pm mid-May–mid-Aug, 10am-5pm mid-Aug–mid-May, closed late Jan) has over 20 giant fish tanks representing various bodies of water. The Baltic tank, for example, is the largest, with local sea life fed regularly by a diver. The water is piped in from the sea to keep the natural life cycle of fish going, so salmon spawn in autumn and in winter the freakish eelpout give birth. It's an absorbing

insight with English signage, guided tours and a theaterette.

PARKS

South of Sapokka Harbour, **Sapokka Meripuisto** (Sapokka Water Park) is a verdant oasis in the city with bridges, walking trails and the **Rose Terrace** garden, which is stunningly illuminated every evening. Stone has been worked through the park and if you walk to the top of the cascade there's an exhibition of stonework that's disappointingly only explained in Finnish signage.

Katariina Seaside Park is a new reserve that has been built on an old oil harbour with much of the soil introduced since. The swimming beach makes for a handy dip, and there's a view across to Mussalo Deep Harbour. You can catch bus 14 to Mussalo to get here.

CHURCHES

Soaring **St Nicholas Orthodox Church** (☎ 212 490; ⏱ noon-3pm Mon-Fri, noon-6pm Sat & Sun Jun-Aug), in Isopuisto Park, was completed in 1801 and is Kotka's only building to survive the Crimean War (1853–56). It is believed to have been designed by architect Yakov Perrini, who also designed the St Petersburg Admiralty.

Kotka Church (☎ 225 9250; ⏰ noon-6pm Sun-Fri) is a neo-Gothic structure visible throughout town by its distinctive steeple. Inside there's artful woodcarving, a baroque-style organ that can belt out a holy volume and a beautiful altarpiece painted by Pekka Halonen.

Activities

A great way to get orientated around town and discover its history is to follow **Catherine's Path**, a self-guided walk with a brochure of the same name available from the tourist office. You can do it on a bike though the only place to hire bikes is from **Toriterassi** (☎ 044-055 7491; Kauppakatu 3; per day €15).

Archipelago cruises of all types depart from Sapokka Harbour in summer, along with scheduled ferries to the outlying islands (opposite); the tourist office has timetables and details.

For details on rafting and fishing the mighty Kymijoki see opposite.

Sleeping

Sokos Hotel Seurahuone (☎ 020-123 4666; www.sokos hotels.fi; Keskuskatu 21; d with/without sauna €123/103, ste from €200; [P] [💻]) This dignified link in the hotel chain has the best bed in a town of restricted quality accommodation. Elegant rooms are chilled with Nordic cool, featuring very Finnish birchwood headboards and furniture with a Sibelius score woven into the curtains. It's very central with a night-club and restaurant if you can't be bothered going out.

Kesähotelli Katerina (☎ 050-913 5763; www.kesa hotellikatarina.net, in Finnish; Lehmustie 4; s/tw €40/80; ⏰ Jun-Aug) This smart new place is university accommodation but it's so fresh it doesn't feel studenty at all. Rooms are clean and bright with a desk, and they connect with a shared kitchen, shower and TV room. The hilltop location, however, can be a tough walk with a lot of baggage.

Also recommended:

Santalahti Holiday Resort (☎ 260 5055; www.santa lahti.fi; tent sites €11, cottages from €62, r from €80; ⏰ May-late Sep) A sprawling resort on Mussalo, 5km from central Kotka with cottages, hotel rooms and camp sites.

Hotelli Merikotka (☎ 215 222; www.hotellimeriko tka.fi; Satamakatu 9; s/d/tr €55/77/95) Handy for the harbour and popular with sailors and oil workers, it has unusual hallways but a good standard of rooms.

Eating & Drinking

San Remo (☎ 212 114; Keskuskatu 29; pizza & pasta €8-10, other mains €11-16; ⏰ 11am-10pm Tue-Thu, 11am-11pm Fri & Sat, noon-10pm Sun) This refreshingly authentic Italian place in the middle of Finland does authentic risottos, pastas and pizzas that are best washed down with an espresso. Its up-stairs location makes for a pleasant balcony meal when it's warm.

Wanha Fiskari (☎ 218 6585; www.wanhafiskari.fi; Ruotsinsalmenkatu 1; mains €13-24; ⏰ lunch & dinner) Right by the Maretarium, this place special-ises in seafood, smoking its own salmon and pan-frying a mean Baltic herring. The nautical decor is laid on but the first-rate food means you might not even notice the model sail-boats and sea doggerel.

Ravintola Duetto (☎ 210 6400; www.sodexho.fi /konserttitalo, in Finnish; Konserttitalo, Keskuskatu 33; mains €12-18; ⏰ 10am-9pm Mon-Fri, 10am-4pm Sat) Set in the ground floor of the town's concert hall, this place is all blonde-wood sophistication with a menu of traditional Finnish.

Blue (☎ 217 335; Kotkankatu 9; ⏰ 6pm-2am Tue-Sun) The blue neon light might not be flattering for the 30-plus crowd, but this great little bar feels more comfy than cool. There are regular bands, and DJs usually with bluesy, R 'n' B beats, but it also just makes for a good place to shoot the breeze over a few wines.

Also recommended:

Canttiini (☎ 214 130; Kaivokatu 15; mains €9-16; ⏰ 10.30am-11pm Mon-Fri, noon-11pm Sat, noon-8pm Sun) A local favourite that dishes up pasta and Tex-Mex.

Toriterassi (☎ 044-055 7491; Kauppakatu 3; lunches €6-12; ⏰ lunch & dinner) A good central lunch spot that does light meals and hires out bikes.

Kairo (☎ 212 787; Satamakatu 7; ⏰ 11am-11pm Sun-Tue, until 1am or later Wed-Sat) A legendary old sailors boozer right down to the ships' flags and saucy paintings, with live music and a great terrace.

Getting There & Away

There are regular express buses from Helsinki (€25.20, 2¼ hours), via Porvoo, Loviisa and Pyhtää. Buses run roughly every half-hour to Hamina (€8.80, 35 minutes), 26km to the east.

There are between four and six local trains a day to Kouvola (€7.80, 45 minutes) from where you can catch connecting trains to all major Finnish cities. Trains stop both at Kotka Station, to the northwest of the city centre, and Kotkan Satama, at the main harbour which is handier for the centre.

AROUND KOTKA
Archipelago Islands

The islands around Kotka make good day trips during the summer months with daily boat connections from Sapokka Harbour.

Varissaari is famous for **Fort Elisabeth**, another Russian fortress built to defend the coast against the Swedes. A fierce naval battle was fought from here in 1789, and the fortress was abandoned in the late 19th century. Today it's a popular picnic spot with a good restaurant. Ferries make the 10-minute trip (adult/child return €6/3) from Kotka (hourly 9am to 9pm May to late August).

On **Kukouri** is **Fort Slava**, also called the Fortress of Honour, with a stunning round structure that you'll spot from the jetty. It was built by the Russians in 1794 as part of a chain of fortresses in the Gulf of Finland. Destroyed by the British in 1855, it was partially renovated in the 1990s. There are five daily ferries (adult/child return €7/2) from June to mid-August.

Kaunissaari has its own little community with a charming fishing village and a local museum, as well as a camping ground with cabins. There are one or two regular daily ferries (€7 one way) late May to late August. There are also evening cruises (€15), with singing and live music (departing 7pm Wednesday late May to late August).

On Kaunissaari is an information centre for the **Eastern Gulf of Finland National Park**, a 60km swathe of over a hundred islets beginning just to the south of Kaunissaari. It's an important breeding ground for seabirds and a habitat for grey and ringed seals. The park can only be explored with your own boat, but scheduled boats do run from Kotka and Hamina to Ulko-Tammio Island, which is part of the park. Here there's another information centre as well as a camp site and nature trail.

Langinkoski & Kymijoki

The **Langinkoski Imperial Fishing Lodge** (☎ 228 1050; www.langinkoskimuseo.com; Koskenniskantie 5C; admission €5; ☻ 10am-4pm daily May, 10am-6pm Jun-Aug, 10am-4pm Sat & Sun Sep-Oct), 5km north of Kotka on the salmon-heavy Kymijoki, is a surprisingly simple wooden lodge built in 1889 for Tsar Alexander III, who visited Langinkoski frequently. Most of the furniture is original and the rooms look much as they did at the end of the 19th century. There's a cafeteria here that does salmon in many forms. The riverside forest setting (now a 28-hectare na-ture reserve) is beautiful and there are several walking trails around the area.

Fly-fishing is still allowed at Langinkoski and the Kymijoki is one of Finland's best fishing rivers, but you need a permit from **Korkeakosken Kalastuskievari** (☎ 05-281 495; Kalakoski) or the tourist office in Kotka.

Reliable fishing and rafting guides include the following:

Erämys (☎ 228 1244; www.eramys.fi, in Finnish) Does guided group trips (three-hour/day €350/990) for groups of up to 15 people, with sauna and rafting options.

Keisarin Kosket (☎ 210 7400; www.keisarinkosket.fi) Organises one- and two-day fishing and rafting trips (from €390) with great meals from their restaurant.

The lodge is not well signposted – turn off Rd 15 at the signs (on the right if you're coming from Kotka) and drive about 1.5km to the road's end. You can get almost all the way to Langinkoski on bus 13 or 27. Alternatively, get off at the sign at the *pikavuoro* (express) bus stop and walk 1.2km.

HAMINA

☎ 05 / pop 21,737

Finnish ski-jumping champion and bad boy, Matti Nykänen, once quipped that 'Things are as mixed-up as the city of Hamina'. Given the strict octagonal street plan of this former fortress town, we assume he was being ironic. Hamina (Swedish: Fredrikshamn) has long been a military town, founded in 1653 as a Swedish outpost.

The town's incomplete fortifications that survive today were begun by panicky Swedes in 1722 after Vyborg fell to Russia. Their efforts were in vain though as the Russians marched in and captured Hamina. Today there's a modern military base in town and the whole town is on parade for the annual tattoo (see p131). The only invasion, however, is from shoppers and day-trippers coming across the Russian border, which is only 40km away.

Information

Monica Tours (☎ 344 0611; www.monicatours.fi; Raatihuoneentori 16; ☻ 9am-4pm Mon-Fri) Organises trips to St Petersburg as well as fishing excursions.

Post office (S-market, Isoympyräkatu)

Public library (Rautatienkatu 8; ☻ 1-7pm Mon-Fri, 10am-2pm Sat) Free internet terminals.

Tourist office (www.hamina.fi) main office (☎ 749 2641; Raatihuoneentori 16; ☻ 9am-5pm Mon-Fri, 10am-3pm Sat & Sun); summer office (☎ 749 2643; Lipputorni

SOUTH COAST

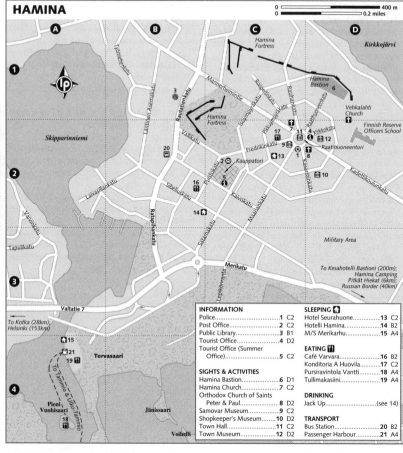

HAMINA

INFORMATION		SLEEPING
Police.........................**1** C2		Hotel Seurahuone............**13** C2
Post Office...................**2** C2		Hotelli Hamina................**14** B2
Public Library.................**3** B1		M/S Merikarhu.................**15** A4
Tourist Office.................**4** D2		
Tourist Office (Summer		EATING
Office)...................**5** C2		Café Varvara...................**16** B2
		Konditoria A Huovila...........**17** C2
SIGHTS & ACTIVITIES		Pursiravintola Vantti...........**18** A4
Hamina Bastion..............**6** D1		Tullimakasiini.................**19** A4
Hamina Church..............**7** C2		
Orthodox Church of Saints		DRINKING
Peter & Paul...............**8** D2		Jack Up....................(see **14**)
Samovar Museum............**9** C2		
Shopkeeper's Museum.......**10** D2		TRANSPORT
Town Hall..................**11** C2		Bus Station...................**20** B2
Town Museum...............**12** D2		Passenger Harbour............**21** A4

(Flagtower), Kauppatori; 9am-6pm Mon-Fri, 10am-3pm Sat & Sun Jun–mid-Aug)

Sights & Activities

Just wandering the restored 19th-century town with its octagonal-wheel street plan will take you past many of Hamina's sights. The spoke-like streets converge at the town centre, which is dominated by the 18th-century **town hall**.

Behind the town hall is the neoclassical **Hamina Church**, built in 1843 and designed by CL Engel, not to be confused with the 1837 **Orthodox Church of Saints Peter & Paul**. Its classic onion dome was designed by architect Louis Visconti, who designed Napoleon's mausoleum.

Housed in Hamina's oldest building, the recently refurbished **Town Museum** (Kaupunginmuseo; ☎ 749 4193; Kadettikoulunkatu 2; admission €2; 11am-3pm Wed-Sat, noon-5pm Sun Sep-May, 10am-4pm Tue-Sun Jun-Aug) is the museum of local history. King Gustav III of Sweden and Catherine II (the Great) of Russia held negotiations here in 1783.

If you're in the museum mood, the **Shopkeeper's Museum** (Kauppiaantalomuseo; ☎ 749 4196; Kasarminkatu 6; 11am-3pm Wed-Sat, noon-5pm Sun Sep-May, 10am-4pm Tue-Sun Jun-Aug) is a former merchant's store and residence, with staff dressing the part and serving customers. There's also the **Samovar Museum** (☎ 353 5005; Raatihuoneentori 8; 1-3pm Wed-Sun) that is a wonderful look at Russia's much-loved teapot.

Northwest of Old Hamina are the ruins of the 18th-century **Hamina Bastion**, including 3km of crumbling stone walls which would have made a star-shaped fortress. The bastion comes alive for the tattoo but you can get a deeper look by picking up a copy of *Walking in Old Hamina: The Rampart Route* from the tourist office.

From Tervasaari, **Meriset** (☎ 228 4648; www.meri set.com) does summer cruises to the fishing village on the island of Tammio (€15, three to four hours). Departures are five times a week and schedules vary significantly between mid-May and late August. It also goes to Ulko-Tammio (€18, five hours), an island further south but still within the boundaries of the national park (see p129), on weekends from mid-June to the end of July. The **information office** (☎ 040-594 4171; ⓨ 10am-4pm Mon-Fri, 10am-3pm Sat & Sun) at the harbour has timetables and sells tickets.

Festivals & Events

Every second (even) year in late July or early August, Hamina celebrates military music during the week-long **Hamina Tattoo** (☎ 749 2633; www.haminatattoo.com) featuring not only Finnish and Russian military marching bands, but rock, jazz and dance music.

Sleeping

The best option for accommodation around Hamina is the local B&B network. These rooms in private homes, some self-contained, others homestay, cost around €35 per person. The tourist office can arrange these.

Hotelli Hamina (☎ 353 5555; www.hotellihamina .fi; Sibeliuskatu 32; s/d €104/124, ste €165; P ⓧ ▣) If you're in town on business, chances are you'll be staying in this modern place with wi-fi (€8 extra) throughout with large suites (which are the same price year-round). It's well located between the bus station and old town.

Kesähotelli Bastioni (☎ 3500 263; www.hotelli bastioni.fi; Annankatu 1; s/d €43/79; ⓨ Jun-Aug) This is another excellent bargain place that you'll get at a cheap price while Finland's students are holidaying. It's a newer place so it feels less institutional and more like a swanky little boutique hotel with your own share kitchen, sauna and a basic breakfast.

Hamina Camping Pitkät Hiekat (☎ /fax 345 9183; tent sites €10, 4-/6-person cottages €40/65; ⓨ daily May-

late Aug, Sat & Sun winter) In Vilniemi, 6km east of Hamina, this quiet spot offers free row boats and a sauna and laundry. It's popular with visiting Russians.

Also recommended is **Hotel Seurahuone** (☎ 3500 263; Pikkuympyräkatu 5; r €74), an older place that's centrally located, and has a popular nightclub and restaurant.

Eating & Drinking

Some of the best places to eat are down at Tervasaari harbour.

OUR PICK **Pursiravintola Vantti** (☎ 354 1063; http:// vantti.fi; Pikku Vuohisaari; mains €15-30; ⓨ food 3-9pm Tue-Sat, noon-8pm Sun, bar closes later) On a small island, this yacht club has the best views in town. Dishes use local salmon and seafood, but also include traditional Finnish meatballs. Larger groups can book out the sauna. A ferry collects you from Tervasaari harbour with the press of the buzzer.

Tullimakasiini (☎ 344 7470; Tervasaari harbour; mains €15-30; ⓨ lunch & dinner May-Sep) This excellent restaurant is located in the old customs house, which gives it an historic atmosphere. The menu embraces Finnish fish and game dishes with flair, though lunches can be crowded by tour groups.

Café Varvara (☎ 231 1044; Puistokatu 2; ⓨ 7am-5pm Mon-Fri, 7.30am-2pm Sat) You'll know this sweet coffee spot by the cups and saucers stacked in the window. It does coffee and home-baked buns and cakes, and for a quick lunch there are rolls and quiches, which are made fresh.

Also recommended:

Jack Up (☎ 231 1110; Sibeliuskatu 32B) A big bar that's popular with the local military crowd.

Konditoria A Huovila (☎ 344 0930; Fredrikinkatu 1; ⓨ 8am-5pm Mon-Fri, 8am-1pm Sat) Another great coffee and cake place known for the berry pies, and handy to the town centre.

Getting There & Away

You can reach Hamina by hourly bus from Kotka (€8.80, 35 minutes). There are express buses from Helsinki (€27.50, 2¾ hours). Buses pass through Hamina on the way to Vyborg and St Petersburg in Russia and, if you have a visa (see p105), you can organise a tour with Monica Tours (p129).

SOUTH COAST

The Lakeland

Most of southern Finland could be dubbed lakeland, but this spectacular area takes it to extremes. It often seems that there's more water than land here, and what water it is: sublime, sparkling, and clean, reflecting sky and forests as clearly as a mirror. It's a land that leaves an indelible impression on every visitor.

It's an obvious place to get outdoors, whether you rent a cottage and try your hand at kindling the perfect blaze in the sauna stove, grab a canoe and paddle the family-friendly Squirrel Route or go in search of rare inland seals. Cruises on lake boats are another essential Finnish summer activity, but there are enough snow sports in the region to keep you entertained in winter as well.

The region's towns, too, have much to offer. Pretty Savonlinna hosts opera in the wonderful setting of its island castle. Jyväskylä's lively student feel and portfolio of Alvar Aalto buildings have obvious appeal, and Kuopio presents the chance to try a traditional Finnish smoke sauna and delicious creations made with *muikku* (vendace), a staple of the region.

The people of this area – the *savolaiset* – are among the most outspoken and friendly of Finns. They can laugh at themselves – nobody else could get away with holding a wife-carrying festival – and are often lampooned by other Finns due to their distinctive Savo dialect, accent and humour. But they have the last laugh thanks to the unparalleled beauty of their home region.

THE LAKELAND

HIGHLIGHTS

- Soaring on the wing of an aria in the memorable castle setting of the **Savonlinna Opera Festival** (p136)
- Relaxing in a typically Finnish way by renting an isolated cottage by one of the region's thousands of lakes, which include Finland's largest, **Lake Saimaa** (p145)
- Peering at the visionary buildings of Alvar Aalto in the lively university town of **Jyväskylä** (p149)
- Sweating it out in the **world's largest smoke sauna** (p154) in Kuopio
- Paddling your canoe around the Linnansaari and Kolovesi National Parks seeking a glimpse of the rare **Saimaa ringed seal** (p142)
- Entering a fantasy land at the seriously offbeat mechanical music museum in **Varkaus** (p146)
- Cruising the picturesque lakeland en route to a visit to the Orthodox monastery at **Valamo** (p147)

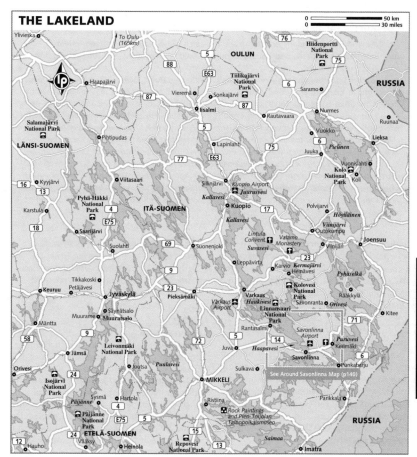

THE LAKELAND

History

The Savo people are a blend of the Finnic tribes that settled in the east of the country after the last Ice Age, and who pushed gradually northwards into Kainuu. Due to its location, the region has seen much historic conflict between Sweden and Russia: Olavinlinna Castle is testament to the constant shifts in the region's balance of power. Once Finland fell under Russian control, Savo became a favoured summering spot for the tsars and St Petersburg gentry.

Activities

With so many lakes, it's no wonder that the main summer activities involve getting out on them. One of the best ways to do so is to take a day-long lake cruise between Kuopio and Savonlinna; other cruises visit the Valamo Orthodox monastery.

The more active choice is to hire a canoe, whether for a short paddle or a longer trek. The Savonlinna area presents several choices, with two national parks offering great canoeing (p142), as well as the popular two-day 'Squirrel Route' from Juva to Sulkava (p144). Jyväskylä and Kuopio are the main snowskiing bases.

EASTERN LAKELAND

SAVONLINNA

☎ 015 / pop 26,775

One of Finland's prettiest towns, Savonlinna shimmers on a sunny day as the water

COTTAGES & FARMSTAYS

The Lakeland is a particularly enticing place to search out a waterside cottage retreat or cosy rural farmstay for a true Finnish holiday. Around 100,000 rental cabins and cottages are dotted around the myriad lakes.

A good first point of investigation is the nationwide operators (p349) – Lomarengas has heaps of options in this area and also has links to farmstays and rural B&Bs. A local operator with a decent portfolio is Saimaa Tours (www.saimaatours.fi). Local tourist offices and websites also have extensive lists of accommodation options. Mikkeli's tourism website, www.travel.mikkeli.fi, is a good example: you can choose by season and luxury levels. The Saimaa region site, www .visitsaimaa.com, and Savonlinna's travel website, www.savonlinna.travel, both link to farmstay and cottage-rental providers. Other local providers are mentioned throughout this chapter.

Cabins normally provide at least a row boat and wood-fired sauna, though you may need your own bedding; cottages come with fully equipped kitchens; and farmstays often offer all manner of summer and winter activities such as horse riding, fishing and snowmobiling. Despite the wilderness around, you may even be able to get online: south Savo is aiming for 99% wireless internet coverage by 2010.

ripples around its centre. Set on two islands between Haapavesi and Pihlajavesi lakes, it's a classic Lakeland settlement with a major attraction: perched on a rocky islet, one of Europe's most visually dramatic castles, Olavinlinna, lords it over the picturesque town centre. The castle also plays host to July's world-famous opera festival in a spectacular setting.

Even if you're no ariaholic, the buzz of the festival makes this the most rewarding time to visit, with animated post-show debriefs over dinner or bubbly going deep into the darkless night. But Savonlinna rewards a visit any time of year, and has other major drawcards like Kerimäki's church and the Retretti gallery within easy reach.

History

Savonlinna's slow growth began in 1475 with the building of Olavinlinna Castle, and in 1639 it received a municipal charter at the instigation of Count Per Brahe, the founder of many towns across Finland. Despite appearances, the castle didn't prove particularly defensible, and the Russians finally grabbed the town in 1743. It was returned to the Finnish grand duchy in 1812.

Information

Music library (Kirkkokatu 12; ☾ 1-7pm Mon-Thu, 10am-4pm Fri) CD collection and free internet in noble wooden building.

Public library (Tottinkatu 6; ☾ 11am-7pm Mon-Thu, 10am-4pm Fri) Free internet.

Savonlinna Travel (☎ 517 510; www.savonlinna .travel; Puistokatu 1; ☾ 9am-5pm Mon-Fri Aug-Jun, 9am-7pm daily Jul) Tourist information including accommodation reservations, farmstays, festival tickets and tours. Free internet.

Sights

OLAVINLINNA

Standing haughtily on a rock in the lake, this **castle** (☎ 531 164; www.olavinlinna.fi; adult/child €5/3.50; ☾ 10am-6pm daily Jun–mid-Aug, 10am-4pm Mon-Fri, 11am-4pm Sat & Sun mid-Aug–May, last tour leaves 1hr before close) is one of the most spectacular in northern Europe. As well as being an imposing fortification, it is also the spectacular venue for the month-long Savonlinna Opera Festival (p136), comfortably seating 2300 within its sturdy walls.

Founded in 1475 by Erik Axelsson Tott, then-governor of Vyborg and the Eastern Provinces, Olavinlinna was named after Olof, an 11th-century Norwegian king and saint. The castle was meant to protect the eastern border of the Swedish empire, however Russians occupied the castle from 1714 to 1721, and took control of it again from 1743 until Finnish independence in 1917. Two rooms have exhibits on its history plus displays of Orthodox treasures.

The castle has been heavily restored after fire damage, but is still seriously impressive, not least in the way it's built directly on the rock in the middle of the lake. To visit the interior, including original towers, bastions and chambers, you must join a guided tour (around 45 minutes). Tours are multilingual and depart on the hour. Guides are good at bringing the castle to life and furnish you with some interesting stories: the soldiers, for instance, were partly paid in beer – five litres a day and seven on Sundays, which makes the castle's frequent change-of-hands more understandable. During the opera festival, the last tour of each day includes a visit backstage.

PROVINCIAL MUSEUM & MUSEUM SHIPS

The **provincial museum** (☎ 571 4712; Riihisaari; adult/child €5/1; ☷ 11am-5pm Tue-Sun, 11am-6pm daily Jul-early Aug), in an old Russian warehouse near the castle, tells of local history and the importance of water transport to the area. There are plenty of old photographs and models and a changing art exhibition. Here also is **Nestori**, a national parks visitor and information centre for the Saimaa region.

Moored alongside are the historic **museum ships** of *Salama, Mikko, Ahkera* and *Savonlinna,* all with exhibitions open from May to September during the same hours as the provincial museum (and accessible by the same ticket). The museum won't take your breath away like the castle, but is worthwhile and several orders of magnitude less touristy.

Activities & Tours

Numerous operators run tours allowing you to explore some of this Lakeland area. The

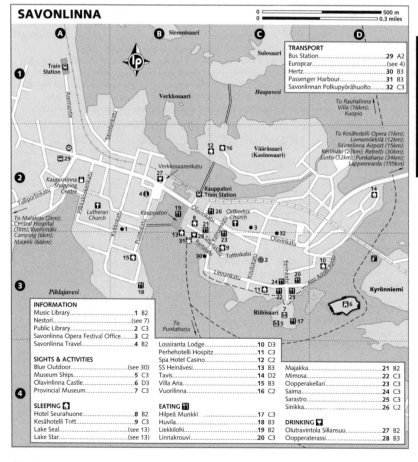

SAVONLINNA

0 _____ 500 m
0 _____ 0.3 miles

THE LAKELAND

JORMA HYNNINEN

Somehow this Savonlinna festival, this simple architecture, old architecture, is very special. You can't find a castle like this anywhere else. The atmosphere is unique, for the audience and the performers. We singers get something special out of it, and the acoustics are very good. It's easy to sing, easy to play. The only issue is that the stage is very wide, which adds some difficulties. But we have managed the problem.

Even getting to the castle, crossing the lake bridge, is unique. But when I first started my Savonlinna career as a choir singer, it was different. There was no bridge. Strong young men took the audience across the lake in row boats. It took much more time to arrive than nowadays. Though the audience was not so big as now, there were still over a thousand (people who were) rowed across to each performance!

The Savo region is quite unique, there's so much water, a lot of lakes, forests, the landscape is more rough than in the south and west of Finland. I was born here in Savo, and I live a third of each year here in my summer cottage. I feel this is the most valuable thing about the area, that in the nature here you can really get away from all the troubles of a normal life, a busy life. The peace of nature in Savo gives a lot. There are many animals, birds, seals, and places like Punkaharju with its 'national Finnish landscape'. Then there are many cultural places too: Retretti gallery (p141); at Kerimäki, the world's largest wooden church (p141); and, not so far north, around Heinävesi, there's the Valamo monastery (p147) and Lintula convent (p148). There are many ship routes in the region, from Savonlinna to Lappeenranta, or to Kuopio. Travelling on the Savo water in an old steamship, that's a very special experience.

People of Savo also have original character. When they are speaking with foreigners, they can be quite anxious, nervous, but they are also very interested in finding out about where people come from, about their lives. It can even be a little annoying sometimes! But they like to have contact, and are more communicative than other Finns.

Jorma Hynninen is a baritone and former artistic director of the Savonlinna Opera Festival.

tourist service runs many of them, from half-day to multi-day trips.

The Savonlinna area, with its quiet country lanes and gently sloping hills, is terrific for **bicycle touring**. Bikes can be carried on board lake-boats for a small fee. To rent **canoes and rowing boats**, visit Vuohimäki Camping (opposite).

Blue Outdoor (☎ 040-579 8315; www.blueoutdoor .fi; Matkustajasatama), by the harbour, organises water-based activities including canoeing trips, jet-ski jaunts and fishing. If you fancy lake views from the air in a flying boat, call **Lentotaksi** (☎ 040-067 0690).

LAKE CRUISES

From June to August, Savonlinna **passenger harbour** is buzzing with dozens of daily scenic cruises that last about an hour and cost between €11 and €13. Boats include the **Ieva** and **Elviira** (www.ieva.fi, in Finnish), the **Lake Star** and **Lake Seal** (www.lakestar.info, in Finnish), and the **Paul Wahl** and **Punkaharju** (www.vipcruise.info). The boats anchor alongside the kauppatori (market square) and you can soon see which is the next departure. There are also many boats available for charter.

The **SS Heinävesi** runs daily at 11am to Retretti art gallery (p141) in Punkaharju (adult/child one-way €22/9, return €9/14, two hours, mid-June to mid-August), giving you 2½ hours there.

For cruises to Lappeenranta and Kuopio see p139.

Festivals & Events

Savonlinna Opera Festival (☎ 476 750; www.opera festival.fi; Olavinkatu 27) is Finland's most famous festival, with an enviably dramatic setting: the covered courtyard of Olavinlinna Castle. It offers four weeks of top-class opera performances from early July to early August. The atmosphere in town during the festival is reason enough to come; it's buzzing, with restaurants serving post-show midnight feasts, and animated discussions and impromptu arias on all sides.

The first festival was held at Olavinlinna way back in 1912, the brainchild of Finnish soprano Aino Ackté. After a break of 39 years it was resurrected in 1967 and has grown in stature with each passing year. The festival's excellent website details the programme: the first three weeks have rotating performances of five operas by the Savonlinna company; the last week has a guest company performing.

The performances themselves are magical: the muscular castle walls are a magnificent backdrop to the set and add great atmosphere. There are tickets in various price bands. The top grades (€105 to €180) are fine, but the penultimate grade (€80 to €98) puts you in un-tiered seats, so it helps to be tall. The few cheap seats (€38 to €43) have a severely restricted view. Buy tickets up to a year in advance from **Lippupalvelu** (Ticketmaster; ☎ 060-010 800; www.lippupalvelu.fi, in Finnish) or from Savonlinna Travel.

When the opera's done, there's also an important **ballet festival** (☎ 044-500 2176; www.savonlinnaballet.net, in Finnish), which runs for four days in early August.

Less elegant, but keenly contested in late August, is the **Mobile Phone Throwing World Championships** (www.savonlinnafestivals.com). In 2008, this was held in Estonia, but should be back in 2009.

Sleeping

Prices rise sharply during the opera festival, when hotel beds are scarce. Fortunately, the students are out of town and their residences are converted to summer hotels and hostels. It goes without saying that you should book accommodation well in advance if you plan to visit during July. If you have a vehicle, staying in Punkaharju, Rantasalmi or Kerimäki is an option.

See also Huvila (p138) and Café Mimosa (p139) for accommodation.

BUDGET

Vuohimäki Camping (☎ 537 353; www.fontana.fi; tent sites €12 plus per person €4, 4-person r €58-68, 4-/6-person cabins €76/84; ☼ Jun-Aug; **P**) Located 7km southwest of town, this camping ground has good facilities but fills up quickly during July. You can hire canoes, bikes and row boats here. Prices for rooms and cabins are cheaper in June and August.

SS Heinävesi (☎ 533 120; cabins upper/lower deck per person €28/25) After the last cruise every afternoon/evening during summer, this steamer offers cramped but cute two-bunk cabins. There's a good chance of getting a bed here, even during the opera festival, and it's moored right in the centre of things. Nearby, the *Lake Star* and *Lake Seal* also offer **cabins** (☎ 040-020 0117; www.lakestar.info; d €40).

ourpick Vuorilinna (☎ 73950; www.spahotelcasino.fi; Kylpylaitoksentie; dm/s/d €28/60/74; **P**) Set in several buildings mostly used by students during term time, this friendly complex is run by the spa hotel (below) and is located in an appealing location across a beautiful footbridge from the town centre. Rooms are clean and comfortable; the cheaper ones share bathroom and kitchen between two. Dorm rates get you the same deal, and there's an HI discount. Reception is most helpful, and there are free laundry facilities. The spa hotel also runs Malakias, another summer lodging 2km west of town, with similar rooms and prices.

MIDRANGE & TOP END

Kesähotelli Opera (☎ 521 116; www.savocenter.fi; Kyrönniemenkuja 9; d €92; ☼ early Jun-early Aug; **P**) Operating as a summer hotel, this student residence is across the bridge from the main part of town, about 1.5km east of the centre. Some of the clean, spacious rooms share a bathroom and kitchen, while others have their own facilities.

Perhehotelli Hospitz (☎ 515 661; www.hospitz.com; Linnankatu 20; s/d €85/95; **P** **回** wi-fi) This cosy place near the castle is a Savonlinna classic, built in the 1930s and redolent of that period's elegance, with striped wallpaper and ornate public areas. The rooms are also stylish, although beds are narrow and bathrooms small; there are larger rooms available for families. A balcony costs a little extra. The hotel has a pleasant terrace and orchard-garden with access to a small beach. Opera festival atmosphere is great but rates rise accordingly (single/double €100/125), with midnight buffet laid on. Book eons in advance.

Kesähotelli Tott (☎ 573 673; www.savonlinnanseurahuone.fi; Satamakatu 1; s/d €85/100; ☼ Jun-late Aug; **P** **占**) Run by the same people as the Seurahuone (p138) and not far from the kauppatori, this is another university residence that'll have you envying the Finnish student. Spacious rooms feature couches, comfortable beds, minibar, and some have great views. Apartment-style rooms are larger, a little more downmarket – lino floors – but have a fully equipped kitchen. Rates rise during July.

Spa Hotel Casino (☎ 73950; www.spahotelcasino.fi; Kasinosaari; s/d/large d €89/111/132; **P** **回** **Ṣ** wi-fi) Charmingly situated on an island across a footbridge from the kauppatori, this is a good option. Nearly all rooms have a balcony; those that don't, have their own sauna. In the

THE LAKELAND

'small' rooms, the beds are arranged toe-to-toe. The rooms aren't luxurious for the price, but guests have unlimited access to the excellent spa facilities, and the location is fantastic. Nonguests can use the spa for €8. Room prices fall at weekends and during winter and rise substantially during the opera festival, when it's a real favourite.

Villa Aria (☎ 515 555; www.savocenter.fi; Puistokatu 15; s/d €137/155; ☼ early Jun-early Aug; **P**) By the water in a quiet but central part of town, this stylish wooden former hospital has spacious high-ceilinged rooms with tall windows, and runs as a summer hotel. The students who normally reside in it run reception in a haphazard manner, but it's still a fine, if expensive operatic base. It's a bargain in June and in the week after the opera festival (rooms €68).

our pick Lossiranta Lodge (☎ 511 2323; www.los siranta.net; Aino Acktén Puistotie; r €100-140; **P** ⓓ wi-fi) To get up close and personal with Olavinlinna Castle, this lakeside spot is the place to be: its impressive form looms just opposite. Offering five snug little nests in an outbuilding, this is one of Finland's most charming hotels. All are very different but decorated with love and style; they come with a small kitchen (yes, that's it in the cupboard) and numerous personal touches. The best has a wood sauna and Jacuzzi – a honeymoon special. Breakfast is brought to the room or served on the lawn if weather allows. It's like a summer retreat but in the middle of town; warm personal service seals the experience. Further along the lakeshore, Tavis is another building in a secluded end-of-the-road spot, and has summer art exhibitions as well as enticing rooms and suites with bright colours and an optimistic feel.

Hotel Seurahuone (☎ 5731; www.savonlinnanseu rahuone.fi; Kauppatori 4-6; s/d €103/123; **P** ⓓ ⓓ wi-fi) Towering over the kauppatori, this friendly hotel offers a bit of everything; its rooms have views, big flatscreen TVs, sofas, sober but recently renovated decor, and decent little bathrooms. The top-floor bar has great views and fries up *muikku* (vendace; tiny lake fish); however the restaurant has good service but disappointing food. There's also a nightclub onsite.

Eating & Drinking

The lively lakeside kauppatori is the place for casual snacking. A *lörtsy* (turnover) is typical and comes savoury with meat (*lihalörtsy*) or

sweet with apple (*omenalörtsy*) or cloudberry (*lakkalörtsy*). Savonlinna's also famous for fried *muikku*; try these at Kalastajan Koju on the kauppatori, or the Muikkubaari on the top floor of the Seurahuone hotel (left). Also near the kauppatori is Oopperaterassi, a flat wooden deck that's one of Savonlinna's most popular spots for a summertime drink. The opera festival peps up Savonlinna's nightlife, with restaurants open late and pubs overflowing with post-performance merriment.

Sinikka (☎ 534 150; Olavinkatu 35; lunches €6-8; ☼ 7am-6pm Mon-Fri, 9am-2pm Sat, noon-4pm Sun) Run with a motherly air, this reader-recommended cafe puts on a great breakfast buffet (between 7am and 11am Monday to Friday), and does salads, lunches, decent coffee and excellent cakes.

Hilpeä Munkki (☎ 515 330; Riihisaari; dishes €9-22; ☼ 2pm-1am mid-Jun–Aug) Alongside the museum in a delightfully ramshackle wooden building, this terraced restaurant gets back to basics in medieval style. Waiters dressed as monks bring out beer in tankards and meat on skewers. Views of the castle are superb.

our pick Majakka (☎ 206 2825; Satamakatu 11; mains €13-24; ☼ 11am-11.30pm Mon-Sat, noon-11.30pm Sun) This restaurant has a deck-like terrace which fits the nautical theme (the name means 'lighthouse'). Local meat and fish specialities are tasty, generously sized and fairly priced and the select-your-own appetiser plate is a nice touch. It's child-friendly too, and opens late during the opera festival when it buzzes with good cheer.

our pick Huvila (☎ 555 0555; www.panimoravin tolahuvila.fi; Puistokatu 4; mains €14-26; ☼ noon-midnight Jun-Aug, dinner Tue-Sat Sep-Dec & Mar-May) This noble wooden building was formerly a fever hospital then a mental asylum, but these days writes happier stories as an excellent microbrewery and smart restaurant just across the harbour from the town centre. The food focuses on fresh local ingredients, and one of the delicious beers will match your fare perfectly, whether it be fresh, hoppy Joutsen, traditional sweet *sahti*, or the deliciously rich dessert stout. The terrace is a wonderful place on a sunny afternoon; there are also two cosy, compact double attic rooms (€120 during opera festival, €65 at other times).

Liekkilohi (☎ 050-310 5850; Kauppatori; salmon €18; ☼ 11am-2am Jun-Aug) This bright red pontoon anchored just off the kauppatori specialises in 'flamed' salmon, a delicious late-night dish. It

---

LAND OF LAKES

As you'll appreciate by seeing it from the air or examining maps of the country, Finland is incredibly watery: some 10% of the country's surface is covered by lakes, the number of which depends on how you measure them: a figure around 188,000 is generally agreed on. Finns themselves differentiate between a *järvi* (big lake) and a *lampi* (pond or small lake).

Finnish lakes are shallow – only three are deeper than 100m. This means that their waters warm quickly in summer, freeze over in winter and are susceptible to pollution. They are important storehouses of carbon, and also traditionally used for recreation, industry, drinking water and transport: by boat in summer and snowmobile or car in winter.

---

also does tasty fried *muikku*. During the day they put on an excellent fish buffet (€34).

Oopperakellari (☎ 020-744 3445; www.savocenter.fi; Kalmarinkatu 10; dinners €54-56; ⏲ 4-7pm Aug-Jun, 10pm-4am Jul) This underground restaurant has lavish pre- and post-opera dinners, with music, arias from the staff, and perhaps even some of the stars answering questions or singing. Book in advance via Savo Center, based at Savonlinna Travel, or online.

Olutravintola Sillansuu (☎ 531 451; Verkkosaarenkatu 1; ⏲ 2pm-late) Savonlinna's best pub by a long shot is compact and cosy, offering an excellent variety of international bottled beers, a decent whisky selection and friendly service. There's a downstairs area with a pool table and during the festival amateur arias are sometimes sung as the beer kegs empty.

Several handsome Linnankatu cafe-bars compete for the pre- and post-opera crowd with mini bottles of fizz and traditional, if pricey, Finnish plates:

Sarastro (☎ 514 425; Linnankatu 10; mains €10-17; ⏲ 10am-8pm May–mid-Sep) Lovely verandah overlooking the garden.

Linnakrouvi (☎ 576 9124; Linnankatu 7; mains €16-24; ⏲ May-Sep) Tiered outdoor seating and tasty food.

Saima (☎ 515 340; Linnankatu 11; meals €7-17; ⏲ 10am-6pm Mon-Fri, 10am-4pm Sat & Sun, longer hours during festival) Cosy interior and open year-round.

Mimosa (☎ 532 257; Linnankatu 12; meals €8-14; ⏲ 9am-late May-Sep) Large shaded terrace. Salads, cakes and light meals. Also has 12 hotel rooms, some with lakeside balconies, available June to August (€90 to €100).

Getting There & Away

AIR

Finnair/Finncomm flies daily between Helsinki and Savonlinna in summer, and more seldom in winter. During the opera festival, a concert greets arriving passengers and night flights return punters to the capital after the show.

BOAT

From mid-June to mid-August, **MS Puijo** (www .mspuijo.fi, in Finnish) travels to Kuopio on Mondays, Wednesdays and Fridays at 9am (one-way €75, 10½ hours), returning on Tuesdays, Thursdays and Saturdays. The boat passes through scenic waterways, canals and locks, and stops en route at Oravi, Heinävesi, Karvio canal and Palokki, among others. Meals are available onboard. You can book a return from Savonlinna with overnight cabin accommodation for €160.

MS Kristina Brahe (www.kristinacruises.com) heads to/from Lappeenranta (€80, 8½ hours) once weekly during summer; the fare includes lunch and return bus transfer to Savonlinna.

Both these trips can be combined with others into a whole week's cruising extravaganza from Helsinki; see the website www.saimaa cruises.fi for ideas.

BUS

Savonlinna is not on major bus routes, but there are several express buses a day from Helsinki (€52.60, 4½ to 5½ hours), and buses run almost hourly from Mikkeli (€20.90, 1½ hours). There are also services to Joensuu (€28.70, three hours), Kuopio (€28.70, three hours) and Jyväskylä (€35.70, 3½ hours).

TRAIN

Trains from Helsinki (€49, five hours) and Joensuu (€24.60, 2½ hours) both require a change in Parikkala. For Kuopio, Jyväskylä and Tampere, railbuses run the two hours to Pieksämäki and connect with trains from there. The main train station is a walk from the centre of Savonlinna; board and alight at the Kauppatori station instead.

Getting Around

Savonlinna airport is 15km northeast of town. A **taxi shuttle** (☎ 040-536 9545; ⏲ 20 min trip one-way 2) meets arriving flights in July and August;

it picks up at hotels on demand and leaves from the taxi rank by the bus station one hour before the flight departs. A regular cab costs around €27.

Two car rental agencies have central offices: **Europcar** (☎ 040-306 2855; www.europcar.fi; Puistokatu 1), in the tourist office, and **Hertz** (☎ 555 2670; www.hertz.fi; Rantakatu 2). Others are based at the airport or will deliver. Rates are expensive and cars should be booked ahead.

Savonlinna Travel rents scooters (per three hours/day/weekend €25/50/100) and several places in town rent bikes, including **Savonlinnan Polkupyörähuolto** (☎ 533 977; Olavinkatu 19; ☺ 9am-5pm Mon-Fri), which charges €10 per day.

AROUND SAVONLINNA
Kerimäki
☎ 015 / pop 5789

Kerimäki is a small farming community, yet it's dominated by the world's largest wooden church (opposite), which towers over the village. It's a memorable sight, and close to Savonlinna.

The nearby protected island of **Hytermä** celebrates one of the weirdest human achieve-ments: it has a grandiose stone staircase and monument to Romu-Heikki (Junk Heikki), a man who built large structures with mill-stones. The island is also quite beautiful, and is easily visited by hiring a rowing boat at the **tourist office** (☎ 541 423; www.kerimaki.fi, in Finnish; Puruvedentie 59; ☺ 10am-5pm Mon-Fri, 10am-1pm Sat mid-Aug–late Jun, daily late Jun–mid-Aug) across from the church in a craft shop.

Hourly buses run Mondays to Fridays between Savonlinna and Kerimäki (€5.10, 30 minutes).

SLEEPING & EATING
Gasthaus Kerihovi (☎ 541 225; Puruvedentie 28; s/d €35/60; P) An attractive old wooden house not far from the church, this friendly guest-house has spotless, comfortable rooms, each with shared bathroom. Breakfast and sauna is included, and there's a popular restaurant-bar onsite. Discounted rates apply in winter.

Punkaharju
☎ 015 / pop 3992

Punkaharju, the famous pine-covered sand esker (sand or gravel ridge) is a popular

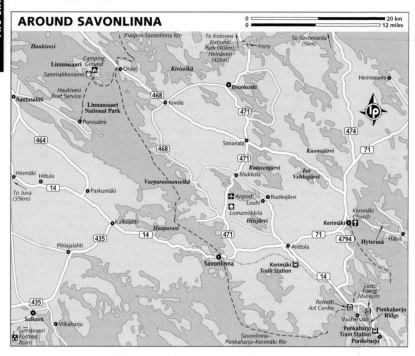

AROUND SAVONLINNA

KERIMÄKI CHURCH

Finland has many notable churches, but few impose like Kerimäki's – the largest **wooden church** (☎ 578 9111; ☺ 10am-6pm Jun & early–mid-Aug, to 7pm Jul, 10am-4pm late Aug) in the world. Built in 1847, it was designed to accommodate 5000 churchgoers.

The oversized church was no mistake, but was deliberately inflated from original plans by overexcited locals. At the time the church was built, the population of Kerimäki parish was around 12,000, and the reverend felt that half of the residents should be attending church on any given Sunday. Worshippers arrived by water, crossing the lakes in a *kirkkovene* (church longboat).

As stunning as the yellow-and-white church appears from outside (dominating the tiny township), the scale isn't apparent until you survey the massive interior – the height of the nave is 27m. Heating it was impossible: the original eight stoves weren't enough, and a smaller winter chapel was built at the rear. The main church is still used for services in summer. It's largely unadorned apart from an altarpiece by Aleksandra Såltin.

There's a cafe and gift shop in the separate bell tower in front of the church (proceeds go to the maintenance, an onerous burden for a small parish), and for €2 you can climb the tower on steep wooden steps for a better view.

summer destination and touted as 'Finland's national landscape'. It was first declared a protected area by Tsar Alexander way back in 1803. The ridge itself is very pretty, and great for walking or cycling; there's also an innovative gallery and a forestry museum. It's an easy day trip from Savonlinna on the train but also an appealing place to stay.

Punkaharju village has services, including a **tourist office** (☎ 734 1011; www.punkaharju .fi; Kauppatie 20), but there are also offices at the Lusto train station and at the petrol station by Retretti train station, the latter open long summer hours (9am to 8pm Monday to Friday, 10am to 8pm Saturday & Sunday).

SIGHTS
Punkaharju Ridge

During the Ice Age, formations similar to this 7km-long sand ridge were created all over the country. Because it crosses a large lake, it's always been an important travel route. Short sections of the original unsealed road along the ridge top remain – once part of a route to Russia connecting the Olavinlinna and Vyborg (Viipuri) castles. To stroll on the ridge, get off at the Retretti train station and walk east towards Punkaharju village. It is a spectacular walk, particularly on a sunny day, with water on both sides. Other labelled trails explore the forested areas from the Arboretum car park, which is located between Lusto and Retretti.

Boat cruises exploring the area leave from Retretti train station twice daily in summer (adult/child €15/7).

Retretti

our pick **Retretti** (☎ 775 2200; www.retretti.fi; adult/child €15/5, with Lusto €23/9; ☺ 10am-5pm Jun & Aug, 10am-6pm Jul; ⓖ) is one of the world's most unusual galleries. An innovative annual exhibition of contemporary art is displayed inside an enormous subterranean cavern complex, artificial but authentic in atmosphere. The intriguing combination of craggy walls, watery pools and semi-darkness allows for startling, elaborate installations. There's also a vast subterranean auditorium. More conventional exhibition spaces have high-profile annual exhibitions of more mainstream art; upstairs is a workshop, gallery for kids and a good cafe-restaurant. Entrance is steep, but it's unique, and the descent into the arty underworld is memorable.

Most reasonable children will allow you the gallery in exchange for the nearby **Kesämaa Water Park** (☎ 739 611; www.kesamaa.fi, in Finnish; admission €15; ☺ 10am-7pm mid-May–Aug), featuring waterslides, bouncy castles and pirate ships. It's cheaper after 4pm.

Lusto Forest Museum

Lusto (☎ 345 100; www.lusto.fi; adult/child €10/5, with Retretti €23/9; ☺ 10am-7pm Jun-Aug, 10am-5pm May & Sep, 10am-5pm Tue-Sun Oct-Apr) is dedicated to Finnish forests and forestry and is a good visit, with plenty of information in English. Displays cover hunting, cottage culture, and world global forest resources; a new section has a kid-pleasing range of machinery and chainsaws. More peaceable is the lakescape room from the Expo 2000 pavilion – a spot to relax for

THE LAKELAND

five minutes. The building itself is an interesting timber structure with the main display hall designed to represent the trunk of a tree, while the attractive cafe does a summer lunch buffet. There's a free internet terminal.

SLEEPING & EATING

Punkaharjun Lomakeskus Camping (☎ 020-752 9800; camping €12 plus per person €4, 2-/4-person cabins €49/70, self-contained cottages from €105; P) Very handy for Retretti, this enormous lakeside camp site has a whole town's worth of solid cabins and cottages, and a raft of facilities. It's a popular summer spot and good for the kids, who'll soon find a posse of Finnish playmates; there's also the popular waterpark (p141) next door.

Gasthaus Punkaharju/Naaranlahti (☎ 441 371; www.naaranlahti.com; Palomäentie 18; s/d €50/70; P 🐾) This guesthouse, in Punkaharju village 2km south of the bus station, has simple but comfortable rooms; there's a sauna and pool for an additional fee and you can also rent bikes, boats and snowmobiles. The owners run the farm-estate Naaranlahti, with good apartment rooms (singles/doubles €48/74) and cottages for rent by the week (for between €595 and €1150). There you can relax and take part in rural activities, including canoeing, fishing or gathering berries. It's 15km from Punkaharju but transport add to and from the town is provided from the guesthouse.

Punkaharjun Valtionhotelli (☎ 020-752 9800; Tuunaansaarentie 4; s/d €83/112; P) Right on the old walled ridge-road to Russia between Lusto and Retretti, this romantic wooden hotel dates from 1845, was once the gamekeeper's lodge for the royal Russian hunting estates, and includes a villa built for the tsarina. There's a variety of room types and prices, including cabins. It's wonderfully peaceful up here among the pines, and there's also a fine restaurant. Prices rise during the opera festival in Savonlinna.

Other accommodation options:

Kruunupuisto (☎ 775 091; www.kruunupuisto.fi; Vaahersalontie 44; s/d €96/116; P 🐾) Health and spa complex between Retretti and Punkaharju village. Excellent value for facilities on offer. Hires bikes and boats.

Mannila (☎ 644 265; www.maatilamatkailumannila .com; Koskelonniementie 127, Vaahersalo; s/d from €34/48; P) Peaceful wooden farmhouse accommodation or more modern rooms. Farm animals, pony riding, good breakfast and camping.

The best places to eat are the Valtionhotelli and the cafes at Retretti (p141; cafe open 9am to 7pm June to August, 8pm in July) and Lusto (p141; cafe open museum hours). Both put on a good buffet spread (€13 to €15) during busy periods so take your pick; we marginally prefer Lusto for its clean Nordic lines and less crowds.

GETTING THERE & AWAY

Trains between Savonlinna and Parikkala stop at Retretti, Lusto and Punkaharju train stations (€3.50 to €4.50, 35 minutes, five to six daily). You can also get here on less regular buses from Savonlinna or by boat (see p139).

The Seal Lakes

Linnansaari and Kolovesi, two primarily water-based national parks in the Savonlinna area, offer fabulous lakescapes dotted with islands, all best explored by hiring a canoe or rowing boat. Several outfitters offer these services, and free camping spots dot the lakes' shores.

This is the habitat of the Saimaa ringed seal. This endangered species *(Phoca hispida saimensis)* was separated from the Baltic ringed seal at the end of the last Ice Age, and is a lake-bound species. After being in imminent danger of extinction during the 20th century, due to hunting and human interference, its population levels have stabilised and are on the increase, although there remain only a precarious 300-odd of the noble greyish beasts.

Late May is the most likely time to see seals, as they are moulting and spend much time on rocks. As well as information points detailed below, the Nestori centre in the Savonlinna provincial museum (p135) is a good source of national park information.

LINNANSAARI NATIONAL PARK

This scenic park consists of Lake Haukivesi and hundreds of uninhabited islands; the main activity centres around the largest island, Linnansaari, which has marked hiking (5km to 7km) and nature trails (2km). As well as the seal population, which numbers between 60 and 80, rare birds, including ospreys, can also be seen.

The best way to experience the park is to pack camping gear and food, rent a rowing boat and spend a few days exploring. Boats, kayaks, canoes and camping equipment can be hired from the offices of **Saimaaholiday** (www.saimaaholiday.net; Oravi (☎ 647 290; Kiramontie 15);

Rantasalmi (☎ 020-729 1760; Porosalmentie 313). These guys can also organise tours, fishing, ice-fishing, lake-skating and snowshoe walks, as well as accommodation around the region.

Oskari (☎ 020-564 5916; ☼ 10am-6pm mid-Jun–mid-Aug, 10am-4pm mid-late Aug, 9am-4pm Mon-Fri Sep-Oct & mid-Feb–mid-Jun) in Rantasalmi is the visitor information centre for the park and also has environmental displays, slideshows and videos.

The island's **camping ground** (☎ 050-027 5458; tent sites free, huts €45) offers a wood sauna. In summer (late June to early August) you can buy simple provisions at a kiosk by the harbour, which fries up delicious *muikku* lakefish. Several smaller islands also have designated camping areas.

There are plenty of self-catering options around the park's access points, as well as **Hotel Oravi** (www.saimaaholiday.net), which hadn't yet opened at time of research. Apartment-style rooms will have small kitchens.

If you haven't rented your own, there are scheduled boat services to Linnansaari island from Oravi (adult/child €8.50/4, three daily mid-June to August, 15 minutes), and Porosalmi (adult/child €14/5, two daily, 30 minutes). If you miss a departure call a water taxi through Saimaaholiday (opposite); the one-way fare from Oravi is €15 per person, with a minimum cost of €30.

There are regular buses to Oravi and Rantasalmi (but not Porosalmi) from Savonlinna. From Rantasalmi, it's an extra 7km to Porosalmi; hitch, walk or taxi it. The Savonlinna–Kuopio ferry stops at Oravi.

KOLOVESI NATIONAL PARK

This great park northeast of Linnansaari covers several islands, which feature well-preserved pine forests. There are high hills, rocky cliffs and caves, and prehistoric rock paintings dating back 5000 years. Some 30 Saimaa seals, as well as otters and eagle owls, call Kolovesi home.

The park's a paradise for canoeing, the best way to explore the fantastic scenery. Motorboats are prohibited in the park. There are several restricted areas within the park, and the islands are out-of-bounds all winter to protect the seals, whose pups are born in February. Park information is at a small summer **cabin** (☎ 040-726 5587) in the village of Enonkoski, 15km south of the park; at Savonlinna; or at Savonranta (right). A free ferry north of Enonkoski crosses the narrows between two lakes on Rd 471.

Nahkiaissalo walking trail (3.3km) is in the south of the park and accessible without a boat. Mäntysalo, an island to the north, has another trail (3.9km). Just north of the park, **Vierunvuori hill** has prehistoric rock paintings depicting stick figures and elk.

Kolovesi Retkeily (☎ 040-558 9163; www.sealtrail .com) is the best and most experienced tour operator, specialising in canoe rental, outfitting and multiday journeys for all abilities. The office is located east of the park at Leipämäki, 15km west of Savonranta and 14km north of Enonkoski on Rd 471. The website www .norppateam.com lists other operators.

Inside the national park are eight simple camping grounds and a cabin on Mäntysalo. You can book this via Oskari (left) in Rantasalmi.

Kievari Enonhovi (☎ 479 431; raili.polonen@kievari -enonhovi.inet.fi; Urheilukentäntie 1; dm/s/d €25/35/60; ℗) is an HI-affiliated hostel and hotel-restaurant in Enonkoski village, close to the national park. It's a very pleasant place, with a terrace, parkland leading down to the river and occasional live music in summer. There are two grades of rooms, all simple and likeable. The better ones have their own shower and kitchenette.

SAVONRANTA

A handy base for Kolovesi National Park and a quiet, attractive stop on the way north from Savonlinna, this town is east of the park on mighty Orivesi lake.

Shoreside, **Noidankattila** (☎ 679 014; www .noidankattila.fi; Pirttimäentie 2; ☼ 9am-9pm daily, until midnight Fri & Sat May-Aug) serves as the information centre, and can organise fishing trips on the lake. It serves snacks, has a pleasant beer terrace and a simple waterside camp site.

our pick **Savonrannan Bed & Breakfast** (☎ 050-341 7204; http://personal.inet.fi/business/elina.gaynor; Yläsuluntie 5; r per person €40; ☼ Jun-Aug; ℗) is set in a charming converted bank alongside a splashing millstream and small lake. The comfortable rooms are thoughtfully and elegantly decorated, the shared bathrooms have great-power showers, and the hosts are most welcoming and lay on an excellent breakfast. In the garden is a genuine wood sauna and a barbecue, both free to use, and there's a balcony from which to view the spectacular sunsets.

There are two daily buses from Savonlinna to Savonranta (€10.30, 1¼ hours).

THE LAKELAND

THE LAKELAND

CANOEING THE SQUIRREL ROUTE

The 57km Juva to Sulkava canoeing route, known as **Oravareitti** (Squirrel Route; www.oravareitti.net) is a Lakeland highlight. The beginner- and family-friendly route starts on Jukajärvi (at Juva Camping; see below), and traverses lakes, rivers and gentle rapids on the way to Sulkava. It's normally done in two days. Information boards along the route identify some of the aquatic life.

Only one section is impassable – at Kuhakoski rapids, where canoes must be carried 50m past a broken dam. Otherwise the rapids are relatively simple. Water levels vary considerably; if it's been abnormally dry, there will be more portage required. Early summer normally sees the highest levels.

Juva Camping provides everything you need: it rents two-person Canadian canoes (per day €25) or single kayaks (per day €17), gives you a waterproof map, and can arrange to pick you up (or just the canoe) up at Sulkava. There are rest stops with fireplaces and toilets, as well as a camping area midway.

It's an easy 8km paddle across Jukajärvi to the first resting place and beginning of the river section, Polvijoki, where you must carry your canoe around the dam to the right. Passing through the small lakes Riemiö (where there's a resting place) and Souru, you come to the first rapids, gentle 200m Voikoski, followed by a rest area to the left of a small island. Continue along the canal, carrying the canoe across the road at the end, before negotiating the Karijoki.

There's a camping ground with tent sites and cottages, **Sulkavan Oravanpesät** (☎ 040-093 8076; www.oravanpesat.fi) on the 2km-long Kaitajärvi. This is more or less the halfway point so a logical spot to spend the night. Next comes a series of rapids including Kissakoski and the strong currents of the Kyrsyänjoki. You continue through the Rasakanjoki and Tikanjoki before coming to the large Halmejärvi, where there is another resting place at the end. The route continues on the western shore of Lohnajärvi to the Lohnankoski. From here it's a leisurely paddle down the Kuhajärvi, past a final set of rapids and into Sulkava, where you pull in at the Kulkemus Boat Centre on the right after the bridge. There's a camping ground and a cafe here.

Juva
☎ 015 / pop 7213

Just off the north–south highway between Mikkeli and Varkaus, and 60km west of Savonlinna, Juva has little to offer the passer-by but is the launch pad for the two-day Oravareitti canoeing trip (above).

Buses stop in the town centre; two blocks uphill is Juvantie, the main street, with the church, supermarkets, pizza, kebabs and a couple of pubs.

The hotel and camping ground, where the canoe trip starts, are another 3km west of here, near the highway. Nearly all bus services pass that way and will drop you off, where there's a supermarket too.

There are dozens of B&Bs around – contact Mikkeli tourist office (opposite) for information. **Juva Camping** (☎ 451 930; www.juvacamping.com; Hotellitie 68; tent pitch €17.50, 2-/4-person cabins €32/42; ⏱ late May-late Aug; **P**) is an excellent camping ground right beside Jukajärvi. There are various cabins available, including big ones with their own sauna (€95). They rent bikes, canoes and rowing boats. You can reach it by turning off the main road at low-slung **Hotelli Juva**

(☎ 020-798 0260; www.hotellijuva.fi, in Finnish; Hotellitie 3; s/d €55/75; **P**), which has spotless modern rooms. The rooms that haven't been refurbished yet are available a bit cheaper (singles/doubles €40/60). There's also a restaurant.

Several daily buses run between Savonlinna and Juva (€14.90, 45 minutes); buses running north and south between Mikkeli and Varkaus also call in.

Sulkava
☎ 015 / pop 3087

Scenic Sulkava, 39km southwest of Savonlinna, is quiet for most of the year but leaps into life in July when it hosts an enormous rowing festival that's an equally enormous party. Sulkava is the finishing point for the Oravareitti canoe route (above), which starts from Juva.

The **tourist kiosk** (☎ 739 1236; www.sulkava.fi, in Finnish; Alanteentie 36; ⏱ 9am-4pm Mon-Fri, 10am-2pm Sat Jul–mid-Aug) can provide details of the numerous rental cottages in the area.

Sulkavan Suursoudut (www.suursoudut.net) is a massive rowing festival that attracts big crowds and some 10,000 competitors over its four days, ending on the second Sunday in

July. Competitors row wooden boats around Partalansaari over a 70km two-day course or a 60km one-day course, then get thoroughly hammered. There are competitions for small boats, but the highlights are the races involving *kirkkoveneet*, 15-person longboats traditionally used to get to church across the lakes. There are competitions for all abilities, and you might be able to find an oar for yourself in one of the teams. Boat rentals and entry forms are available on the website.

Linnavuori is the most interesting sight in the Sulkava area. The ruins of a castle are spectacularly perched on a rocky wooded hill overlooking idyllic lakeland scenery. The site was originally a prehistoric settlement and some of the stonework dates back to the 12th century.

SLEEPING

Muikkukukko (☎ 471 651; www.muikkukukko.fi, in Finnish; Alanteentie 4; s/d €43/64; **P**) In the centre of town, this is a small motel attached to a popular pizza restaurant and Finnish dance spot. Its 10 double rooms are simply decorated and perfectly comfortable; there are also cabins available, popular with anglers.

Sulkavan Lomakeskus (☎ 471 223; www.lomaliitto .fi/sulkava; tent sites €13 plus per person €4, r €40-46, cottages €36-54; ☺ early Jun–mid-Aug) This place, in the Vilkaharju area 7km from Sulkava, is on a scenic headland across a pedestrian bridge (road access is possible). It's quite a village, with cottages, rooms and a dance restaurant.

Sulkava is served by buses from Mikkeli and Savonlinna. There are two buses from Sulkava to Juva each weekday, leaving at 7am and 12.25pm, respectively.

MIKKELI

☎ 015 / pop 48,720

Mikkeli is a sizeable provincial town on the shores of Saimaa, Finland's largest lake. It's an important transport hub and was the headquarters of the Finnish army during WWII; museums relating to those years are the main sights in town. It's still an important military base, and soldiers sometimes seem to outnumber civilians. It's a friendly place though, and although there's little to see, it often makes a convenient stopover between the northern and southern parts of the country.

Mikkeli **tourist office** (☎ 010-826 0246; www .travel.mikkeli.fi; Porrassalmenkatu 23; ☺ 9am-6pm Mon-Fri, 10am-3pm Sat) is near the large, lively kauppatori.

The office has free internet and can help find you a cottage to rent – there are hundreds around the area.

Päämajamuseo (Headquarters Museum; ☎ 194 2424; Päämajankatu 1-3; adult/child €5/free; ☺ 10am-5pm Fri-Sun Sep-Apr, 10am-5pm daily May-Aug) was Mannerheim's command centre during the war; and **Jalkaväkimuseo** (Infantry Museum; ☎ 369 666; www.jalkavakimuseo.fi; Jääkärinkatu 6-8; adult/child €5/2; ☺ 10am-5pm May-Aug, 11am-4pm Fri-Sun Sep-Apr) is one of the largest military museums in Finland. Mannerheim's wartime railway carriage is parked up at the station.

The Mikkeli area is excellent for **fishing** – the lakes teem with perch, salmon and trout, and ice-fishing is popular in winter. The tourist office can help with permits, guides and equipment rental.

Mikkeli Music Festival (www.mikkelimusic.net), held here in late June/early July, is a week-long classical music event featuring top Finnish and Russian conductors. Balancing it out is **Jurassic Rock** (www.jurassicrock.fi), a two-day festival in early August that features plenty of Finnish and Scandinavian bands.

Sleeping & Eating

Visulahti Camping (☎ 18281; www.visulahti.fi; Visulahdenkatu 1; tent sites €12 plus per person €4, cabins €55, cottages €90-140; ☺ late May-Aug) This camping ground, alongside an amusement park which features a wax museum, is the closest one to Mikkeli. It's about 5km east of the town centre and has lakeside tent sites and a wide range of cabins.

Hotelli Uusikuu (☎ 221 5420; www.uusikuu.fi; Raviradantie 13; r €59; **P**) This staffless hotel is quite a bargain. Rooms are clean and comfortable and decked-out in soft beige. They also have a fold-out bed and can sleep up to four, as well as a free internet jack. You must book online in advance; there's no lobby terminal, but the bus terminal and tourist office both have internet access. Turn right out of the train or bus station, then left on Savilahdenkatu; Raviradantie is on your right after 10 minutes walk or so.

Sokos Hotel Vaakuna (☎ 20201; www.sokoshotels .fi; Porrassalmenkatu 9; s/d from €83/93; **P** ☐ wi-fi) Mikkeli's most central hotel is just a block south of the kauppatori. It's been designed more with the business traveller in mind, but it's in a handy location and the rooms are attractive enough if a little short on space.

Café Sole (☎ 212 798; Porrassalmenkatu 19; lunch €6-12; ☻ 8.30am-6pm Mon-Fri, 10am-4pm Sat, 11am-4pm Sun) Facing the kauppatori, this is a good option for breakfast or lunch, when there are great salads as well as filling hot dishes. There's friendly service and a pretty terrace from which you can watch Mikkeli march by.

Kenkävero (☎ 162 230; www.kenkavero.fi; lunch €22; ☻ 10am-6pm Sun-Fri, 10am-4pm Sat) is a design shop and art centre picturesquely set in a lovely vicarage building 1km east of the centre. The cafe still feels like an elegant drawing room and you half expect the vicar himself to bring in tea and cucumber sandwiches. Instead there's a reader-praised lunch buffet that pulls out all the stops.

Getting There & Away

Mikkeli is a transport hub served by many trains and buses that run between Helsinki and the eastern Lakeland or Kuopio. Train and bus stations are adjacent, a block east (downhill) from the kauppatori.

Bus destinations include Helsinki (€38.40, 3½ hours), Kuopio (€28.70, 2½ to four hours) and Savonlinna (€20.90, 1½ hours). Trains run to Helsinki (€34.70, 2¾ hours), Kuopio (€20.80, 1½ hours) and further north around five times daily. For other cities, change at Pieksämäki or Kouvola.

AROUND MIKKELI

Twenty kilometres south of Mikkeli, **Ristiina** is one of the region's most historic villages, founded by Count Per Brahe in 1649 and named after his wife. Little remains of the village's glorious past, though it has a pleasant enough lakeside location.

The village stretches from the main Mikkeli–Lappeenranta road eastwards. Two kilometres in, there's a craft shop and gallery which doubles as the **tourist office** (☎ 661 750; www.ristiina.fi, in Finnish; Brahentie 53; ☻ 10am-3pm Mon-Fri, 10am-1pm Sat), the future of which was in doubt at time of research.

The scant but picturesque ruins of the castle built by Per Brahe occupy a forested headland a couple of kilometres beyond here; this is fertile ground for walking.

It's a further 19km (along Rd 4323 to Puumala) to the region's main attraction, the **rock paintings** of Astuvansalmi (Astuvansalmen Kalliomaalaukset). Estimated to be 5000 years old, they cover a 15m stretch of steep cliffs, and include elk, human and animal tracks. Amber artefacts have been found in the lake. From the car park, it's a 2.5km walk to the paintings.

Close by, the open-air **Pien-Toijolan Talonpoikaismuseo** (adult/child €5/free; ☻ 11am-6pm Tue-Fri, 10am-4pm Sat Jun-early Aug) is an estate dating from 1672, and consists of a series of historic wooden buildings, some of which have been brought here.

There's nowhere to stay in Ristiina itself, but **Tuukkalan Tila** (☎ 045-634 9299; www.tuukkalan tila.com; Mäntyharjuntie 61; r per person €35; P ☒ ☐) offers appealing farmhouse accommodation and fine facilities. From the Ristiina turn-off on the main road, head south a further 1.5km and turn right towards Mäntyharju. The farm is signposted off this road.

There are several simple cafes and bars in Ristiina. **Martan Baari** (☎ 661 102; 50 Brahentie; lunch buffet €7; ☻ 7.30am-9pm) does pizza, a lunch buffet and has a cute verandah terrace.

Several daily buses run between Mikkeli and Ristiina (€5.40, 20 minutes), and several more pick up and drop off on the main road at the entrance to the village. Boat cruises also run from Mikkeli in summer.

Hire bikes at Harju Sport, a red wooden building just off the main road in Ristiina (turn left at K-Market).

VARKAUS

☎ 017 / pop 23,405

Spread-out Varkaus is surrounded by water and covers several islands cut by canals. The location is appealing to the timber-pulp industry, whose looming factory complex is in the heart of the town. Varkaus is a road and rail hub, and you might find yourself changing buses here, especially to visit the monastery of Valamo. The town's name means 'theft' in Finnish.

our pick **Mekaanisen Musiikin Museo** (Museum of Mechanical Music; ☎ 558 0643; www.mekaanisenmusi ikinmuseo.fi; Pelimanninkatu 8; adult/child €12/6; ☻ 11am-6pm Tue-Sat, 11am-5pm Sun Mar–mid-Dec, 11am-6pm daily Jul) is Varkaus' stand-out attraction. 'You must understand', says the personable owner, 'it's not a normal museum; more a madhouse'. A truly astonishing collection of musical instruments ranging from a ghostly keyboard-tinkling Steinway piano to a robotic violinist to a full-scale orchestra emanating from a large cabinet. This is just the beginning; political cabaret in sev-

THE LAKELAND

eral languages and an overwhelming sense of good humour and imagination make it a cross between a Victorian theatre and Wonka's chocolate factory. Having a coffee outside under the steely gaze of sizeable macaws seems like a return to normality. The museum is signposted 1km west of the main north–south highway and also provides tourist information.

Varkaus has a few places to stay. Turn left out of the bus and train station, then left again across the bridge to reach **Hotelli Joutsenkulma** (☎ 366 9797; Käärmeniementie 20; s/d €59/79; P wi-fi). Reception is up the back of a low-key local drinking den, but the modern rooms have zippy silver sheets and a big comfy armchair as well as plenty of space.

Most eateries are around the kauppatori, 1km east of the station (head for the factory chimneys). The best is **Kaks Ruusua** (☎ 040-350 8420; Ahlströminkatu 25; mains €9-19; ☽ 7am-11pm Mon-Fri, 10am-11pm Sat, noon-6pm Sun) in a fine old building across the street from the monstrous pulp complex. It does all-day service as a popular cafe and offers a cheap lunch buffet before turning out tasty dinners in the evening.

Daily Finnair/Finncomm flights connect Helsinki with Varkaus. Keskusliikenneasema is the central station, which includes the train and bus terminals. Frequent trains run east to Joensuu (€15.20, 1½ hours), and west to Pieksämäki (€5.70, 30 minutes), where you can change for westbound, southbound or northbound services.

HEINÄVESI & AROUND
☎ 017 / pop 4152

Heinävesi village lies amid hills north of Kolovesi National Park and among some of the most scenic lakeland in Finland. The Savonlinna to Kuopio boat route passes through here and canals provide a means of local transport. The town itself isn't a beauty, but waterscapes and nearby monasteries are the drawcard.

A huge wooden **church** perches on a hill at the end of Kirkkokatu. It was built in 1890, seats 2000 people, and offers good views over Kermajärvi from the tower. Nearby is the local **museum** (☎ 578 1273; admission by donation; ☽ 11am-6pm Jul) in a former grain store.

On the northern side of Kermajärvi, 28km by road from Heinävesi, **Karvio** has scenic rapids that are good for fishing,

and a canal serving as a jetty for lake ferries. This is a stopover for the Savonlinna–Kuopio ferry and a jumping-off point for Valamo Monastery.

Sleeping
Gasthaus-Hotelli Heinävesi (☎ 562 411; Askeltie 2; s/d €60/80) Surprisingly full of character, this spot opposite the bus terminal draws you in right away with its cheery outdoor tables. With apologies to the church and petrol station, this is basically Heinävesi's focal point. Rooms are easy on the eye, and the restaurant does a good breakfast, lunch buffet (€9.50), and pizza and other choices by night.

Loma-Karvio (☎ 563 603; www.lomakarvio.com; Takunlahdentie 2; tent sites €10.50 plus per adult/child €3/1, cabins €55, cottages €80-98; ☽ May–mid-Sep) On the main Varkaus–Joensuu road in Karvio, and boasting a great location alongside the fast-flowing rapids (where you can fish to your heart's content), this camp site has a wide variety of accommodation in simple cottages and upmarket heated cottages, which are available all year. There's a pizza cafe and supermarket (with tourist information) nearby.

There's also accommodation at Valamo monastery (below) and Lintula convent (p148).

Getting There & Around
Heinävesi is easily reached by bus from Varkaus (€9.10, 45 minutes, up to four departures on weekdays); there are also services to Kuopio (€25.50, three hours). More buses pass through Karvio. Trains between Varkaus and Joensuu stop at Heinävesi station, but it's several kilometres south of the town.

In summer, the lakeboat MS *Puijo*, which runs between Kuopio and Savonlinna, calls at Karvio and the Heinävesi jetty just south of the village. Bikes can be hired at the Heinävesi harbour, and boats and canoes at Loma-Karvio (above).

VALAMO MONASTERY
Valamo (☎ 017-570 111; www.valamo.fi; Valamontie 42, Uusi-Valamo) – Finland's only Orthodox monastery – is one of Savo's most popular attractions and, although it's only been at this location for 70 years, has a long prior history on a Karelian island (which is now part of Russia).

One of the great, ancient Russian monasteries, old Valamo, set on an island in gigantic Lake Ladoga, survived the aftermath of the

Russian Revolution because it fell just within the territory of newly independent Finland, but was soon after under grave threat during the Winter War of 1939. Ladoga froze (a rare occurrence), allowing a hurried evacuation from Russia of monks, icons and treasures. Those men that survived the journey resettled here in a beautiful lakeside estate. Monks and novices, almost a thousand strong a century ago, now number just five, but the complex in general is thriving.

The first church was made by connecting two sheds; the rustic architecture contrasts curiously with the fine gilded icons. A painting of old Valamo just above the door of the recreated monk's cell gives some idea of its scale. The new church, completed in 1977, has an onion-shaped dome, is redolent with incense, and has icons including a Madonna from the similarly evacuated island monastery of Konevitse.

Visitors are free to roam and enter the churches; **services** take place at 6am and 6pm Monday to Saturday, and 9am and 6pm Sunday, with an extra one daily at 1pm from June to August. A **guided tour** (€4), which lasts an hour, is highly recommended for an insight into the monastery and Orthodox beliefs and symbolism; they are available in English and German. Take time to stroll to the peaceful **cemetery**, with a *tsasouna* (chapel) dedicated to Herman, a Valamo missionary monk who took Christianity to Alaska. The complex has a **museum** (admission €5) with changing exhibitions, and you could also walk to the Pilgrims' Cross or to Lintula convent, 18km away. There are also daily **boat cruises** (€12-19) from mid-June to early August.

Aware of the need to redefine a monastery's place in 21st-century Europe, the community openly encourages visitors, whether they just want a coffee, or to browse the icons and chant CDs in the shop. The monastery also offers visitors peace and relaxation in the beautiful surrounds, or the opportunity to engage further in Orthodox culture by attending a service or doing a course in theology, philosophy or icon-painting.

Whatever the case, Valamo makes an excellent place to stay, and is even more peaceful once evening descends. Two **guesthouses** (s/d €30/50; P &) in picturesque wooden buildings provide comfortable, no-frills sleeping with shared bathroom; the **hotel** (s/d/apt €70/100/130; P &) offers a higher standard of accommodation. The complex's eatery, **Trapesa**

(☺ 7am-9pm daily Jun-Aug, 7am-6pm Sun-Thu, 7am-8pm Fri, 7am-9pm Sat Sep-May) has high-quality buffet spreads (€12 to €15), Russian-style high tea (€7), and evening meals with not a hint of monastic frugality; try the monastery's own range of berry wines.

Getting There & Away

Valamo is clearly signposted 4km north of the main Varkaus–Joensuu road. A couple of daily buses run to Valamo from Joensuu and from Helsinki via Mikkeli and Varkaus. From Heinävesi change at Karvio.

The most pleasant way to get to Valamo (and Lintula, below) in summer is on a **Monastery Cruise** (☎ 015-250 250; www.mspuijo.fi, in Finnish; adult/child €65/30) from Kuopio. The cruise uses a combination of the regular Kuopio to Savonlinna ferry and car or bus transport. The ferry departs Kuopio at 9am Tuesday, Thursday and Saturday, then there's car transport from Palokki to Lintula and Valamo, then a bus back to Kuopio. On Mondays, Wednesdays, Fridays and Sundays, transport is reversed with a bus to Valamo at noon and a ferry back from Palokki.

LINTULA CONVENT

Finland's only Orthodox convent, **Lintula** (☎ 017-563 106; ☺ 9am-6pm Jun-Aug) is much quieter than popular Valamo. It's a serene contrast that is well worth the short detour, and it's only open to visitors outside of summer by appointment.

Lintula was founded in Karelia in 1895 and transferred to Savo and then Häme during WWII. A convent was founded at the present location in 1946; it's now at more or less full capacity, home to 15 nuns. A souvenir shop on the premises sells wool and candles handmade here (the nuns supply all the Orthodox churches in Finland with candles), and there's a pleasant coffee shop. The highlight is the lovely grounds, which are perfect for strolling. In the garden is a beautifully simple log chapel, whose icons glint in the candlelight.

Lintulan Vierasmaja (☎ 017-563 225; s/d €20/32; P) is a small red house at the back of the convent. There are simple but clean rooms, with separate bathrooms, and it's open to men and women.

Getting There & Away

For Lintula, daily buses from Kuopio stop in the nearby village of Palokki, but if you're coming from the south, be warned that the nearest bus stop is on the highway 9km away. The convent is an 18km walk from Valamo monastery. See Valamo (opposite) for details of cruises.

WESTERN LAKELAND

JYVÄSKYLÄ

☎ 014 / pop 85,402

Vivacious and young-at-heart, western Lakeland's main town has a wonderful water-side location and an optimistic feel that makes it a real drawcard. Jyväskylä (pronounced *yoo-vah-skoo-lah*) was founded in 1837 and, in the mid-19th century, was the site of the country's first Finnish-language school and teacher-training college. The city's reputation for scholarship was boosted with the 1966 inauguration of its university. Thanks to the work of Alvar Aalto, the city also has a global reputation for its architecture, and petrolheads know it as the legendary venue for the Finnish leg of the World Rally Championships.

The 16,000 students and lively academic and arts scenes give the town plenty of energy and nightlife. In summer you can't beat arriving by lakeboat from Lahti, while in winter there are plenty of winter sports on offer.

Information

Avatar (☎ 214 811; Puistokatu 1a; internet per hr €3; ✆ 10am-10pm) Good internet cafe.

Central hospital (☎ 269 1811; Keskussairaalantie 19)

Public library (☎ 624 440; Vapaudenkatu 39-41; ✆ 11am-8pm Mon-Fri, 11am-3pm Sat) Free internet.

Tourist office (☎ 624 903; www.jyvaskylaregion.fi, in Finnish; Asemakatu 6; ✆ 9am-6pm Mon-Fri, 10am-3pm Sat & Sun Jun–mid-Aug, 9am-5pm Mon-Fri, 10am-3pm Sat mid-Aug–May) Has comprehensive information on the whole of Finland, ticket sales and a free internet terminal.

Sights

Many people come to Jyväskylä for its modern architecture; at times the whole city centre is full of folk curiously pointing wide-angled lenses at every Aalto building. The best time to visit is from Tuesday to Friday, as many buildings are closed at weekends and the Aalto Museum is closed on Mondays.

Alvar Aalto (p46) was a giant of 20th-century architecture. He was schooled here, opened his first offices here and spent his summers in nearby Muuratsalo.

The city has dozens of Aalto buildings, but stop first at one of his last creations, the

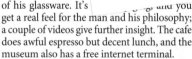

Alvar Aalto Museum (
Aallonkatu 7; adult/child €6,
Tue-Sun, from 10am Tue-Fri
sity to the west of th
his life and work, w
number of his majo
section on his furnit
of his glassware. It's ⸻ ⸻ ⸻, and you get a real feel for the man and his philosophy; a couple of videos give further insight. The cafe does awful espresso but decent lunch, and the museum also has a free internet terminal.

The museum sells the *Architectural Map Guide* (€2), which plots well over a hundred buildings in and around Jyväskylä, designed by Aalto and other notable figures. It also has simple bikes for hire (per day/two days €10/15) to help you explore them.

Aalto's list includes the university's main buildings and the **City Theatre** (Vapaudenkatu 36). On the corner of Kauppakatu and Väinönkatu is the old **Workers' Club Building** (1925), an early work with Renaissance-inspired features such as columns and a Palladian balcony; it's now a pub.

Also see Säynätsalo Town Hall (p153), where you can sleep in a room that the man himself slept in, and his experimental summer cottage at Muuratsalo (p153).

OTHER MUSEUMS

Jyväskylä's other museums are all free on Fridays and closed on Mondays.

Keski-Suomen Museo

The **Museum of Central Finland** (☎ 624 930; Alvar Aallonkatu 7; adult/child €5/free; ✆ 11am-6pm Tue-Sun; ♿) is adjacent to the Alvar Aalto Museum and designed by him, but sees a fraction of the visitors. A pity, for it's a well-presented display. The main exhibition is an attractive overview of rural life in central Finland from prehistoric times onwards. There's an ancient sledge-runner dated to 4000 BC, and displays on hunting, fishing and logging, with English translations. It gives a good feel for traditional Finnish life and finishes in a typical old grocery. Upstairs is a history of Jyväskylä itself, with great scale models; the top floor holds temporary art exhibitions, often associated with the arts festival.

Jyväskylän Taidemuseo

Opposite the church, **Jyväskylä Art Museum** (☎ 626 856; Kauppakatu 23; adult/child €4/free; ✆ 11am-

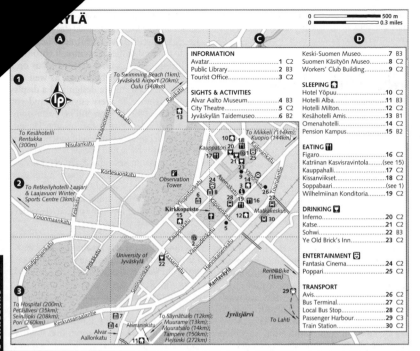

6pm Tue-Sun;) houses temporary exhibitions of modern art and sculpture, often arranged by the active local artists' association. This, the main gallery, is complemented by two other exhibition spaces nearby, all entered on the same ticket. Don't miss the astonishingly grand toilets.

Suomen Käsityön Museo
The **Craft Museum of Finland** (☎ 624 946; www.craftmuseum.fi; Kauppakatu 25; adult/child €5/free; 11am-6pm Tue-Sun) is all about Finnish handicrafts and their history, and incorporates the National Costume Centre, which displays regional dress from around Finland. The permanent collection is small, and most space is taken up with temporary exhibitions. It's an enjoyable insight into activities which, partly due to the long Finnish winters, have always been an important part of life here. There's also a good shop attached.

Activities
SKIING
Very handy for town, **Laajavuori Winter Sports Centre** (☎ 624 885; www.laajavuori.com, in Finnish;

Laajavuorentie) has five modest slopes plus a kids' run and 62km of cross-country trails, as well as a number of scary ski jumps. There's a good ski area for children and the resort is popular with families; there's a **hotel** (www.rantasipi.fi) here that offers packages as well as a hostel (opposite). It's 4km from the centre of Jyväskylä; catch bus 25.

LAKE CRUISES
There are numerous boating options – check www.jyvaskyla.fi for more choices.

Running north, Keitele canal **cruises** (☎ 263 447; www.paijanne-risteilythilden.fi, in Finnish) operate from June to late August. On Mondays, Tuesdays and Wednesdays there are trips to Kuusaan Sulku (Kuusaa Lock; single/return €18/27, seven hours round-trip); on Saturdays it ventures further along to Suolahti (single/return €25/37.50, five hours one-way); you can choose to go or return by bus (return €30, six hours).

Short cruises on Lake Päijänne are also available from early June to early August, with daily departures. Some of these are lunch cruises or evening affairs with dinner and dancing. Try to catch the SS *Suomi*, one of the oldest steamers still plying the Finnish lakes, which leaves Jyväskylä at noon Wednesday to Saturday (adult/child €17/8, three hours), and 7pm Tuesday to Saturday (adult/child €18/9, 3½ hours).

Get tickets from the tourist office or at the **passenger harbour** (☎ 218 024; Siltakatu 4). Take bus 18, 19 or 20 from the centre.

For the Jyväskylä to Lahti route see p152.

Festivals & Events

In mid-July, **Jyväskylän Kesä** (Jyväskylä Arts Festival; ☎ 624 378; www.jyvaskylankesa.fi) has an international program of concerts, exhibitions, theatre and dance. Over 50 years old, it has a strong liberal and radical tradition and is one of Finland's most important arts festivals.

In early August, Jyväskylä is the centre of what many Finns regard as the most important event of the summer calendar, the **Neste Rally Finland** (www.nesteoilrallyfinland.fi). Formerly called the Thousand Lakes, this is the Finnish leg of the World Rally Championship, which Finns follow closely and have traditionally been very successful at. The event goes for four days, with big concerts and parties on the Thursday, Friday and Saturday nights. Book tickets (€50) through **Jyväskylä Booking** (☎ 020-748 1830; www.jyvaskylabooking.fi; Piippukatu 7). They can also find you accommodation, which should be booked well in advance.

At time of research it looked like Finland might miss out on hosting this event in 2010.

Sleeping

As well as the following options, Sokos (www.sokoshotels.fi) and Scandic (www.scandichotels.com) have chain hotels right in the centre.

Retkeilyhotelli Laajari (☎ 624 885; www.laajavuori.com, in Finnish; Laajavuorentie 15; dm/s/d €26/36/58; P) Part of Laajavuori sports complex 4km from town, this hostel is often booked out in winter by ski groups. It's easily accessed by bus 25 (get off when you see the caravan park on your left) and has institutional rooms with whitewashed brick walls, OK beds, and shared bathrooms and kitchen. There's also a burger cafe. HI members get a discount.

Kesähotelli Rentukka (☎ 607 237; www.hotelrentukka.fi; Taitoniekantie 9; s/d/tr €42/54/66; mid-May–Aug; P) A half-hour walk from the centre (pleasant if you cut across parkland), or a short trip on bus 18, this student accommodation offers light, no-frills rooms which are particularly good for families, in a campus with restaurant, shops and a bar. Rooms have bathroom and kitchen facilities but no utensils. Breakfast is included.

ourpick Kesähotelli Amis (☎ 443 0100; www.hotelliamis.com; Sepänkatu 3; s/d/tr €48/60/72; June-early Aug; P 🖥) Five minutes uphill from the city centre, this excellent summer hotel has modern, light, spacious student rooms each with a kitchenette (no utensils, but there's an equipped kitchen downstairs) and good bathrooms. It's a real bargain, especially given that breakfast and an evening sauna are included.

Hotelli Milton (☎ 337 7900; www.hotellimilton.com; Hannikaisenkatu 29; s/d €75/100; P 🖥 wi-fi) Right in the thick of things, this family-run hotel has an old-fashioned dark foyer, but the modern rooms offer plenty of natural light, space and attractive wooden floors; most have a balcony. An evening sauna on weekdays is included and it's very handy for the bus and train stations.

Hotelli Alba (☎ 636 311; www.hotellialba.fi; Ahlmaninkatu 4; s/d €88/110; P 🖥 wi-fi) Within the university, and very handy for the Aalto museum, this hotel is right by the water, and the terrace of its restaurant and bar takes full advantage. The telescopic corridors lead onto mediocre rooms with narrow beds and parquet floors but the view from those facing the water compensates for this; you could fish out of the windows!

ourpick Hotel Yöpuu (☎ 333 900; www.hotelliyopuu.fi; Yliopistonkatu 23; s €99-115, d €146, ste €172-250; P 🖥 wi-fi) Among Finland's most enchanting boutique hotels, this exquisite spot has lavishly decorated rooms, all individually designed in markedly different styles (the Africa room is really something to behold). Service is warm and welcoming with an assured personal touch that makes for a delightful stay. Suites offer excellent value; the Pöllöwaari restaurant is one of the city's best, and there's a little flowery terrace to enjoy a glass of wine in peace.

Also recommended:

Pension Kampus (☎ 338 1400; pensionkampus@kolumbus.fi; Kauppakatu 11a; s/d €54/66; P) Central, spotless 3rd-floor option with kitchen facilities in rooms. Breakfast included.

Omenahotelli (☎ 020-771 6555; www.omena.com; Vapaudenkatu 57; r €45-65; P 🖥) Central receptionless hotel. One of the best, with comfortable beds and endless corridors. Book online or via the lobby terminal.

THE LAKELAND

Eating

Jyväskylä's kauppahalli isn't Finland's most intriguing, but it's still a place to go to grab fresh produce or a quick snack.

Wilhelmiinan Konditoria (☎ 010-397 1201; Asemakatu 3; snacks €3-7; 7am-8pm Mon-Fri, 9am-6pm Sat, 10am-6pm Sun) This sleek building diagonally opposite the tourist office is a good two-level cafe with mild coffee, tasty cakes and sandwiches, and a nice little terrace alongside. They also do crunchy takeaway bread and moreish meat-and-rice rolls.

Soppabaari (☎ 449 8001; Väinönkeskus; soup & pasta €6.50; 11am-10.30pm Mon-Fri, 1-11pm Sat) This cute wee spot is situated in a little arcade out the back of Ye Old Brick's Inn (right). They do three daily soups and pastas, either of which is €6.50 and pretty much guaranteed to be delicious.

Katriinan Kasvisravintola (☎ 449 8880; Kauppakatu 11; lunch €6-9; 11am-2.30pm Mon-Fri) A couple of blocks west of the pedestrian zone, this lunchtime vegetarian restaurant is an excellent bet. Six euros gets you soup and salad bar, seven buys a hot dish instead of the soup, and nine gets you the lot. The menu changes daily – you might get pasta, ratatouille or curry – but it's always tasty.

Kissanviikset (☎ 618 451; www.kissanviikset.fi, in Finnish; Puistokatu 3; mains €15-26; 11am-11pm Mon-Fri, 1-11.30pm Sat, 1-9.30pm Sun) Quiet, romantic and welcoming, the 'cat's whiskers' is an enticing choice. The genteel upstairs dining room is complemented by an atmospheric cellar space when busy. Dishes are thoughtfully prepared and feature delicious combinations of flavours such as salmon with baked fennel, or meat dishes with sinfully creamy wild mushroom sauces.

ourpick Figaro (☎ 212 255; www.figaro-restaurant.com; Asemakatu 4; mains €17-27; 10.30am-midnight Mon-Sat, noon-10pm Sun) With a warm drawing-room feel and cordial service, this backs up the atmosphere with really excellent food served in generous portions. A delicate pike carpaccio might be followed with aromatic and succulent salmon with coriander and ginger, sizeable steaks on a mountain of fried onion, or reindeer doused in creamy chanterelle sauce. There are good vegetarian mains too, and it's youngster-friendly.

Drinking & Entertainment

Jyväskylä's students ensure a lively nightlife when they're not on holidays.

Ye Old Brick's Inn (☎ 616 233; www.oldbricksinn.fi, in Finnish; Kauppakatu 41; 11am-2am or 3am) In the liveliest part of the pedestrian zone, this warm and welcoming pub has several excellent beers on tap, a cosy interior and an outdoor terrace screened by plastic plants – the place to be on a summer evening. It also has a bar menu (mains €13 to €20) until 11pm that looks ambiious but succeeds, with gourmet sandwiches, reindeer liver, roast pork with sweet potatoes, and further toothsome fare.

Sohwi (☎ 615 564; Vaasankatu 21; noon-late Mon-Sat, 2pm-midnight Sun) A short walk from the city centre is this excellent bar with a spacious wooden terrace, a good menu of snacks and soak-it-all-up bar meals, and plenty of lively student and academic discussion lubricated by a range of good bottled and draught beers. There's an internet terminal too. A great place.

Katse (☎ 667 459; Väinönkatu 26; 3pm-3am) This looks like a constricted dive from outside, but actually has an enormous, popular upstairs bar playing alternative and heavier music to Finns in their 20s and 30s.

Inferno (Yliopistonkatu 40; 8pm-4am Wed-Sun), You can kick on with the heavy stuff at this joint just up the street from Katse.

Poppari (☎ 621 398; www.jazz-bar.com, in Finnish; Puistonkatu 2; 3pm-late) This downstairs venue is the place for relaxing live music, with regular jazz slots and jam sessions, particularly on weekends (cover usually €2 to €5). There are long weekend happy hours and a small terrace.

Fantasia (Jyväskeskus Shopping Centre, Kauppakatu 29) This cinema is central, in the pedestrian zone, and shows major releases.

Getting There & Away

AIR

Finnair/Finncomm operates several flights from Helsinki to Jyväskylä each weekday and fewer on weekends. Jyväskylä airport is 21km north of the centre; shared taxis make the journey for €19, a normal cab is around €33. Both taxi types can be reserved on ☎ 106 900.

BOAT

There is a regular boat service on Lake Päijänne between Jyväskylä and Lahti, operated by **Päijänne Risteilyt Hildén** (☎ 783 2515; www.paijanne-risteilythilden.fi, in Finnish). Boats leave Lahti at 9am on Tuesdays from early June to early August and return from Jyväskylä on Wednesdays at 9am (one-way €50, 10½ hours) .

BUS
The bus terminal shares the Matkakeskus building with the train station and has many daily express buses connecting Jyväskylä to southern Finnish towns, including hourly departures to Helsinki (€43.90, 4½ hours). Some services require a change.

TRAIN
The train station is between the town and the harbour, in the Matkakeskus building. There are regular trains from Helsinki (€41.50, 5½ hours) via Tampere, and some quicker direct trains.

Getting Around
BICYCLE
Jyväskylä is a good spot to explore by bike, particularly if you plan on investigating some of the further-flung Aalto buildings. The tourist office also has maps of suggested circular routes in central Lakeland of three to five days. You can rent a bike at **Rent@Bike** (☎ 050-443 3820; Humppakuja 2; per day/week €15/50) and **Avis** (☎ 020-718 1700; www.avis.fi; Väinönkatu 8).

BUS
For reaching Aalto buildings or the ski centre, you'll find the network of local buses useful. Local buses all leave from Vapaudenkatu, near the tourist office. Tickets cost €2.90 to €5.90 depending on distance. A day-travel card (€7) can be bought at the tourist office and is cheaper than a return to Säynätsalo, for example.

AROUND JYVÄSKYLÄ
Säynätsalo
The large **Säynätsalo Town Hall** (Säynätsalon Kunnantalo; ☎ 623 801; admission weekdays by donation, weekends €4; ☯ 8.30am-3.30pm Mon-Fri year-round, also 1-4pm Sat & Sun mid-Jul–Aug) is on an island 10km southeast of Jyväskylä. It's one of Aalto's most famous works, the architect having won an international competition in 1949 to design it. The sturdy tower, brick steps and dim light of this 'fortress of democracy' recall a castle, but the grassy patio reflects a relationship with nature that is present in much of Aalto's work. Two **rooms** (r €45) are available here; they are furnished with Aalto chairs and stools and named after the man and his second wife, who

often slept here while supervising construction. They are singles (although extra beds can be put in), share a bathroom, and have simple kitchen facilities.

Säynätsalo can be reached from central Jyväskylä on bus 16 (€4.10, 30 minutes). A day ticket from the tourist office (€7) is cheaper than a return.

Muuratsalo
This peaceful wooded islet is connected to Säynätsalo by bridges and was Aalto's summer retreat from the early 1950s onwards. On Päijänne's shores he built **Koetalo** (☎ 624 809; www.alvaraalto.fi; adult/student/child €15/5/free; ☯ 1.30-3.30pm Mon, Wed & Fri Jun–mid-Sep), a must-see for Aalto lovers, but pricey if you're not. Entrance is by guided tour, and must be pre-arranged by phone or email (the Aalto Museum or tourist office in Jyväskylä can do this). You first see his beloved boat, *Nemo Propheta in Patria* ('nobody is a prophet in their own land') on dry land, never having been particularly seaworthy. Then it's the lakeside sauna and house itself. It's often called the 'experimental house', because Aalto used the charming patio to try out various types and patterns of bricks and tiles to see how they looked in different seasons and how they weathered.

The interior is surprisingly small; it's cool and colourful, but doesn't particularly evoke the man's spirit. A guest wing is perched on timber and stones (another playful experiment), but is deemed too precarious to enter.

The setting's very Finnish, and you can well imagine Aalto looking out over the beautiful lake and pondering his designs. It's a quiet, peaceful place (apart from the mosquitoes).

To get here, take bus 16 from central Jyväskylä and ride it to the end, where there's a small cafe. The house is 500m further along this road on the right. For the 1.30pm tour, get the bus at 12.15pm (€4.10, 40 minutes). A day ticket from the tourist office (€7) is cheaper than a return.

Petäjävesi
Thirty-five kilometres west of Jyväskylä, pause at Petäjävesi to see the wonderfully gnarled Unesco-listed wooden **church** (☎ 040-582 2461; Vanhankirkontie; admission €5; ☯ 10am-6pm Jun-Aug, call for winter visits). Finished in 1765, it's

THE LAKELAND

a marvellous example of 18th-century rustic Finnish architecture with crooked wooden pews and a fairytale shingle roof. Prior to its construction, there had been some debate about whether this village should get a church at all. Jaakko Leppänen started the job minus planning permission and properly drawn instructions. Burials took place under the floorboards, and there's also a spooky wine cellar under the nave – ask the guide to show you.

Buses from Jyväskylä to Keuruu stop in Petäjävesi. If coming by car, walk across a road bridge to the church from the car park.

NORTHERN LAKELAND

KUOPIO

☎ 017 / pop 91,320

Most things a reasonable person could desire from a summery lakeside town are in Kuopio, with pleasure cruises on the azure water, spruce forests to stroll in, wooden waterside pubs, and local fish specialities to taste. And what better than a traditional smoke sauna to give necessary impetus to jump into the chilly waters?

But Kuopio has year-round appeal, with its fistful of interesting museums, student-driven cultural scene and nightlife, and winter activities like ice-fishing and snowmobiling on offer.

Kuopio has good transport connections but there's no better way to arrive than by leisurely lakeboat from Savonlinna.

History

The first Savonian people entered the area at the end of the 15th century. In 1652 Count Per Brahe founded the 'church village' of Kuopio, which had little significance until 1775, when Gustav III of Sweden made it the provincial capital. Important figures of the National Romantic era lived here from the 1850s, but Kuopio's main growth was in the 20th century.

Information

Kuopio Tourist Service (☎ 182 585; www.kuopioinfo .fi; Haapaniemenkatu 17; ☺ 9.30am-4.30pm Mon-Fri Sep-May, to 5pm Jun-Aug, also 10am-3pm Sat Jul) By the kauppatori. Information on regional attractions and accommodation.

Public library (☎ 182 111; Maaherrankatu 12; ☺ 10am-7pm Mon-Fri, 10am-3pm Sat) Free internet.

Sights

PUIJO HILL

Even small hills have cachet in flat Finland, and Kuopio was so proud of Puijo that it was crowned with a TV tower. The views from the top of the 75m **Puijon Torni** (☎ 255 255; adult/child €4/2.50, free in winter; ☺ 9am-10pm) are very impressive; the vast perspectives of (yes, you guess correctly) lakes and forests represent a sort of idealised Finnish history. Atop the structure is a revolving restaurant, cafe and open-air viewing deck.

Surrounding it is one of the region's best-preserved **spruce forests**, popular for walks and picnics. Also here is a ski jump and chairlift. Even in summer you can see ski jumpers in training; the whoosh as they descend the ramp sounds like a small fighter plane. There are no public buses to Puijo, but it's a nice walk through the trees, or a short drive or cab ride.

JÄTKÄNKÄMPPÄ SMOKE SAUNA

There are different types of saunas, but the *savusauna* (smoke sauna) is the original and, some say, the best. This, the world's largest (few other countries have attempted the record), is a memorable and sociable experience that draws locals and visitors.

Jätkänkämppä Smoke Sauna (☎ 0306 0830; www .rauhalahti.com; adult/child €11/5.50; ☺ 4-10pm Tue, also Thu Jun-Aug) is by the lakeside near Rauhalahti resort (opposite) south of town. The 60-person, mixed sauna is heated 24 hours in advance with a large wood fire (ie there's no sauna stove). Guests are given towels to wear, but bring a swimsuit for a dip in the lake. Sweat it out for a while, cool off in the lake, then repeat the process several times – devoted sauna-goers do so even when the lake is covered with ice. Then buy a beer and relax, looking over the lake in Nordic peace.

There's a restaurant in the adjacent loggers' cabin serving traditional Finnish **dinners** (adult/child buffet plus hot plate €18/8.50; ☺ 4-8pm) when the sauna's on, with accordion entertainment and a lumberjack show. Bus 7 departs every half-hour from the kauppatori to the Rauhalahti hotel complex, from which it's a 600m walk to the sauna, or take the lakeboat from the passenger harbour in summer (see p157).

Always ring ahead to check the opening hours.

MUSEUMS

Kuopio has several worthwhile museums; if you're going to visit several, grab the Museum

Card, from the Kuopio Tourist Service or any museum, which gives discounted entry.

Kuopion Museo

The town **museum** (☎ 182 603; Kauppakatu 23; adult/child €5/3; ☽ 10am-5pm Tue, Thu & Fri, 10am-7pm Wed, 11am-5pm Sat & Sun) in a castlelike art-nouveau mansion has wide scope. The top two floors are devoted to cultural history, with household objects, a boat builder's workshop, coffee shop and a recreated wooden house among the attractions. But the real highlight is the natural history display, with a wide variety of beautifully presented Finnish wildlife, including a mammoth and an ostrich wearing snowboots. The ground floor is devoted to temporary exhibitions.

There's little information in English, but one of the staff members might give explanations. Tours in English are sometimes scheduled during summer.

Kuopion Korttelimuseo

This block of old **town houses** (☎ 182 625; Kirkkokatu 22; adult/child €3/free; ☽ 10am-5pm Tue-Sun mid-May–Aug, 10am-3pm Tue-Fri, 10am-4pm Sat & Sun Sep–mid-May) forms another of Kuopio's delightful museums. Several homes – all with period furniture and decor – are very detailed and thorough and the level of information (in English) is excellent. **Apteekkimuseo** in building 11 contains old pharmacy paraphernalia, while in another building it's fascinating to compare photos of Kuopio from different decades. There's also a cafe serving delicious *rahkapiirakka* (a local sweet pastry).

Kuopion Taidemuseo

The **art museum** (☎ 182 633; Kauppakatu 35; adult/child €3/free; ☽ 10am-5pm Tue, Thu & Fri, 10am-7pm Wed, 11am-5pm Sat & Sun) features mostly modern art in temporary exhibitions, but also displays permanent works. Look out for paintings by the local artist Juho Rissanen (1873–1950), whose realistic portraits of Finnish working people were a contrast to the prevalent Romanticism of the time.

Snellmaninkoti Museo

This **museum** (☎ 182 625; Snellmaninkatu 19; adult/child €2/free; ☽ 10am-5pm Wed & Sat mid-May–Aug) is a branch of Kuopion Museo (above). JV Snellman, an important cultural figure and a renowned thinker during the National Romantic era of the 19th century, used to live in this old house from 1843 to 1849.

Suomen Ortodoksinen Kirkkomuseo

A fascinating, well-presented display, the **Orthodox Church Museum** (☎ 020-610 0266; Karjalankatu 1; adult/child €5/1; ☽ 10am-4pm Tue & Thu-Sun, 10am-6pm Wed May-Aug, noon-3pm Mon-Fri, noon-5pm Sat & Sun Sep-Apr) holds collections brought here from monasteries, churches and *tsasounas* in occupied Karelia. Today it's the most notable collection of eastern Orthodox icons, textiles and religious objects outside Russia. The oldest artefacts date from the 10th century. There are summer exhibitions on particular aspects of Orthodox art or symbolism.

VB Valokuvakeskus

Excellent summer exhibitions grace the **Photographic Centre** (☎ 261 5599; Kuninkaankatu 14; admission summer/winter €5/3; ☽ 10am-7pm Mon-Fri, 11am-4pm Sat & Sun Jun-Aug, 11am-5pm Tue & Thu-Fri, 11am-7pm Wed, 11am-3pm Sat & Sun Sep-May), devoted to Victor Barsokevitsch, one of the pioneers of Finnish photography. His studio is now a gallery, but there are enough old cameras and photos to call this a museum. In the garden you can enjoy a coffee in summer and check out the camera obscura.

PIKKU-PIETARIN TORIKUJA

Just off Puistokatu, **Pikku-Pietarin Market Alley** (Pikku-Pietarin Kuja; ☽ 10am-5pm Mon-Fri, 10am-3pm Sat Jun-Aug) is an atmospheric narrow lane of renovated red wooden houses converted into quirky shops stocking jewellery, clothing, handicrafts and other items. Halfway along is an excellent **cafe** (☽ from 8am) with cosy upstairs seating and a great little back deck for the summer sun.

Activities

Rauhalahti (☎ 473 000; www.rauhalahti.com) is an estate converted into a year-round family park. The whole area is full of activities for families including boating, cycling, tennis and minigolf in summer, and skating, ice-fishing, snowmobile safaris and a snow castle in winter. You can rent bikes (per day from €10), rowing boats, canoes, in-line skates and even Icelandic ponies for gentle trail rides. Take bus 7 from the town centre or a ferry from the passenger harbour in summer (adult/child return €12/6, 30 minutes, five daily Monday to Saturday from early June to early August). There's also a variety of accommodation here (see p157).

Puijo Hill (p154) has mountain-bike and walking tracks; in winter there are cross-country ski trails and equipment rentals.

THE LAKELAND

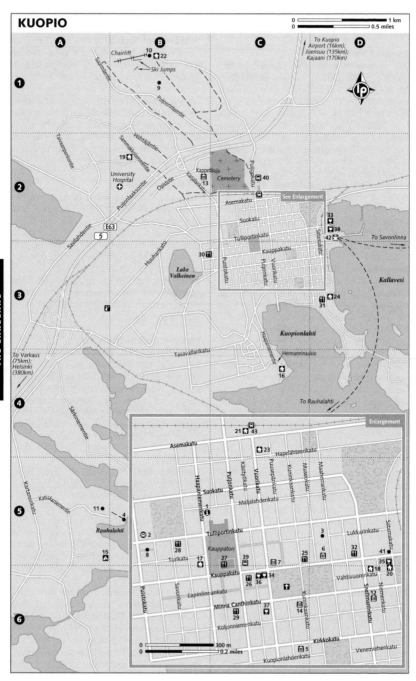

Tours

Several different **cruises** depart from the town's passenger harbour daily during summer. Ninety-minute jaunts from the harbour cost €11 (half price for children) and depart hourly from 11am to 6pm. There are also cruises to Rauhalahti tourist park (p155; €12 return) Monday to Saturday from early June to mid August; a good way to get to the smoke sauna (p154). Special theme cruises include dinner and dancing, wine tasting or a trip to a local berry farm. There are also canal cruises and a monastery cruise to Valamo (p147) and Lintula (p148), with return bus transport (adult/child €65/30).

Tickets for all cruises are available at the tourist office or at the booking office on Kauppakatu. Tickets for short cruises can be bought on the boat. Schedules are available at the harbour or from the tourist office.

A **tourist train** (adult/child €5.50/3.50) does the city circuit, with departures on the hour from the kauppatori. It has commentary in English.

Festivals & Events

Kuopion Tanssii ja Soi is the **Kuopio Dance Festival** (www.kuopiodancefestival.fi) in mid-June, the most international and the most interesting of Kuopio's annual events. There are open-air classical and modern dance performances, comedy and theatre gigs, and the town is generally buzzing at this time.

Kuopio Rock Cock (www.kuopiorock.fi, in Finnish) is a two-day rock festival in late July which features heaps of concerts by local acts and a couple of big-name headliners.

Sleeping

Camping Rauhalahti (☎ 473 000; www.rauhalahti .com; Kiviniementie; sites €12 plus per person €4, cabins €30-57, cottages €100; ☼ late May-Aug; ℗) Next to the Rauhalahti complex, this place has a great location, plenty of facilities and is well set up for families. Bus 7 or 16 will get you here.

Hostelli Hermanni (☎ 040-910 9083; www.hostel lihermanni.net; Hermanninaukio 3e; dm/s/d €20/40/50; ℗) Tucked away down the side of the Metsähallitus building in a quiet area 1.5km south of the kauppatori, this is a well-run little hostel with comfy wooden bunks and beds, high ceilings, Aalto furniture, and decent shared bathrooms and kitchen. It offers plenty of value; there are rooms suitable for families, and discounts if you stay three nights or more. Check-in is between 2pm and 9pm; if you'll arrive later, call ahead. Bus 30 from the centre makes occasional appearances nearby.

Matkustajakoti Rautatie (☎ 580 0569; www.kuopio nasemagrilli.com, in Finnish; Asemakatu 1 & Vuorikatu 35; s/d without bathroom €40/60, with bathroom €50/79; ℗) Let's get one thing straight: sleeping as close as you can to transport options isn't lazy, it's practical. True. This friendly place, operating out of the grilli (fast-food outlet) in the railway station, actually offers ensuite rooms in the building itself – very comfortable, exceedingly spacious and surprisingly peaceful. There are more rooms, with shared bathrooms, across the road on Vuorikatu.

ourpick Kesähotelli Lokki (☎ 261 4101; www .kesahotellilokki.fi; Satamakatu 26; s €39, studio s/d €49/70, apt for 2 €69/90; ☼ early Jun-early Aug; ℗) In a perfect harbourside location, this brand-new complex of buildings surrounding a courtyard again arouses envy of Finland's student population, some of whom normally reside here. The spotless industrial studios have heavy doors, bags of space, comfortable new beds and a kitchenette; the curtains are dotted with the gulls after which the place is named. Apartments have two rooms sharing bathroom and kitchen. It's great value though there's no breakfast.

Puijon Maja (☎ 255 5250; www.puijo.com, in Finnish; Puijontornintie; s/d/f €56/62/75; **P**) Right by the tower on top of Puijo Hill, this has neat little rooms, complete with fridges. Get one backing onto the forest if you can, so you can take advantage of the wide windows. Rates include breakfast, sauna and admission to the tower; there's also a lunch buffet (€11). HI members get a discount. It's popular with groups, including practising ski-jumpers, so book ahead. There's no public transport from the town centre.

Hotelli Savonia (☎ 255 5100; www.savonia.com; Sammakkolammentie 2; s/d/ste €100/120/175; **P** 🍴 🖳 🖭 wi-fi) Not far from Puijo Hill, this offers easy access from the main road and good value (for Finland). The spotless rooms are rather nice, with plenty of space and headroom; the new wing offers even better ones, including suites with huge comfy beds and a tiny Jacuzzi. There's a restaurant here, as well as a deli-cafe for lighter meals. Breakfast, sauna and swimming are included. Buses 5 and 14 stop outside.

Spa Hotel Rauhalahti (☎ 030-60830; www.rauhalahti .com; Katiskaniementie 8; s/d €99/130; **P** 🍴 🖳 🖭 wi-fi) This hotel at the Rauhalahti centre, 5km south of town, is a superb place to stay. In addition to the spa facilities, there's a restaurant, cafe and popular dance club. They offer some very attractive family packages on their website. In the same complex is the cheaper Hostelli Rauhalahti (single/doubles €72/84), with simple Nordic rooms and full use of the hotel's facilities, as well as Apartment Hotel Rauhalahti (2-/4- person apartment from €130/200) which has excellent modern pads with all the trimmings, including (for not much extra dough) a sauna. Take bus 7 from town.

Scandic Hotel Kuopio (☎ 195 111; www.scandic hotels.com; Satamakatu 1; s/d €138/158, summer from €72/79; **P** 🖳 🖭 ♿ wi-fi) Down from the busy part of the harbour, this unobtrusive but large hotel has an appealing, quiet lakeside location, professional service, and fine facilities that include a gym, sauna and Jacuzzi, as well as a couple of bikes able to be borrowed by guests. Rooms have plenty of natural light and crisscross parquet floors. The superior

rooms are worth the extra €10 to €15, as they have king-sized beds and balconies with lake views. The above rates are approximate, as supply-and-demand pricing operates.

Other recommendations:

Hotel Atlas (☎ 211 2111; www.hotelliatlas.com; Haapaniemenkatu 22; s/d €98/108; **P** 🖭 wi-fi) Ageing but comfortable, on the kauppatori. Popular €14 lunch buffet.

Hotelli Jahtihovi (☎ 264 4400; www.jahtihovi.fi; Snellmaninkatu 23; s/d €89/109; **P** 🖭 wi-fi) Pleasant and intimate with a good restaurant. Soft-coloured rooms with pine furnishings and small bathrooms.

Eating

Kauppahalli (Kauppatori; 🕑 8am-5pm Mon-Fri, 8am-3pm Sat) At the southern end of the kauppatori is a classic Finnish indoor market hall. Here, wrapped in foil, stalls sell local speciality *kalakukko*, a large rye loaf stuffed with whitefish and then baked. It's delicious hot or cold but you'll probably have to buy a whole one (around €20), enough for several picnics.

Kaneli (☎ 040-835 8187; Kauppakatu 22; pastries €2-3; 🕑 10am-7pm Mon-Fri, 10am-5pm Sat, 11am-4pm Sun) This cracking cafe just off the kauppatori evokes a bygone age with much of its decor. But it does offer modern comfort with its shiny espresso machine, as well as many other flavoured coffees to accompany your toothsome and sticky *pulla*.

Lounas-Salonki (☎ 281 1210; Kasarmikatu 12; lunches €6-9, mains €11-22, 🕑 9am-9pm Mon-Sat, noon-9pm Sun) This charming wooden building west of the city centre is warm and friendly, with little rooms sporting elegant imperial furniture. They do a salad buffet and daily hot lunch featuring traditional Finnish fare (on last visit sausage soup and liver 'n' onions) as well as coffee and à-la-carte options including vegetarian choices like crêpes filled with blue cheese and vegetables.

Vapaasatama Sampo (☎ 581 0458; Kauppakatu 13; muikku dishes €10-14; 🕑 11am-midnight Mon-Sat, noon-midnight Sun) Have it stewed, fried, smoked or in a soup, but it's all about *muikku* here. This is one of Finland's most famous spots to try the small lakefish that drive Savo stomachs. The 70-year-old restaurant is cosy, and classically Finnish.

Kreeta (☎ 282 8337; Tulliportinkatu 46; mains €11-17; 🕑 11am-10pm Mon-Thu, 11am-11pm Fri, noon-11pm Sat, noon-9pm Sun) This Cretan restaurant near the kauppatori is a good bet, with spacious interior and big windows. Meze for two (€49 to €59) gives you the chance to try a range of dishes, there's retsina and Greek coffee to wash it all down, and a play area for young kids.

Kummisetä (☎ 369 9880; Minna Canthinkatu 44; mains €12-19; ☺ 1-9.30pm Sun-Mon, 1-10.30pm Tue-Thu, 1-11pm Fri & Sat) The sober brown colours of the 'Godfather' restaurant give it a traditional and romantic feel that's replicated on the menu, with country pâté, pike-perch, chanterelle sauces and berries all making welcome appearances alongside chunky steaks. Food and service are both excellent. There's also a popular back terrace and an attractive bar that is open longer hours.

Isä Camillo (☎ 581 0450; Kauppakatu 25; mains €13-19; ☺ 11am-11pm Mon-Thu, 11am-midnight Fri & Sat) Set in a beautifully renovated former bank – look out for the old strongroom – this is an elegant but informal spot for a meal, offering fair prices for Finnish specialities. There's a good enclosed terrace at the side and a decent pub, Pannuhuone, downstairs.

Puijon Torni (☎ 255 5255; mains €19-25; ☺ 11am-10pm Mon-Sat May-Sep, noon-7pm Sun late Jun-early Aug) Revolving restaurants usually plunge on the culinary altimeter, but the food atop Puijo tower is pretty good – although the decor won't feature in *Finnish Design Monthly* anytime soon. Choices focus on Suomi specialities, including reindeer, Arctic char and pike-perch, and there are a couple of set menus (€32/38). The view is magnificent.

our pick **Musta Lammas** (☎ 581 0458; Satamakatu 4; mains €23-29, vegetarian/degustation set menu €32/48; ☺ 5pm-midnight Mon-Sat) One of Finland's best restaurants, the 'black sheep' has a golden fleece. Set in an enchantingly romantic brick-vaulted space, it offers delicious gourmet mains with Finnish ingredients and French flair. Roast reindeer with morel mushrooms was one of the highlights when we last visited, but the €32 vegetarian menu also caught our eye. The standard wine list is OK, but get the credit card out for some of the handwritten choices, which include some of the world's finest reds.

Drinking & Entertainment

Kuopio's nightlife is conveniently strung along Kauppakatu, running east from the market square to the harbour. Here, grungy but likeable **Ale Pupi** ('Sale Pub'; ☎ 262 5384; Kauppakatu 16; ☺ 9am-midnight or later) has a huge interior, surprisingly classy decor and big drawcards of cheap beer and karaoke, but there are many other options in this block, some with summer terraces.

Down by the harbour are two similar summer places in immense wooden buildings with imposing beamed interiors and traditional dance floors. **Wanha Satama** (☎ 197 304; mains €14-18; ☺ 11am-11pm Sun-Tue, 11am-4am Wed-Sat summer) is a noble light blue colour with an immense terrace, definitely the place to be on a sunny day if you're not on the water itself. They also serve up fairly pricey meals. **Albatrossi** (☎ 368 8000; ☺ 11am-midnight or later May-Sep), across the way, is another summer pub, set in old wooden warehouses.

Henry's Pub (☎ 262 2002; www.henryspub.net, in Finnish; Käsityökatu 17; ☺ 9pm-4am) One of Lakeland's best rock venues, this atmospheric place has bands playing several times a week, including big Finnish and international names, but it's a good spot for a drink even if there's nothing on.

K Klubi (☎ 262 5775; Vuorikatu 14; ☺ 6pm-late) Always interesting, this bar is friendly and bohemian, with a range of punters listening to alternative sounds. It's definitely not flash, but it's definitely one of Kuopio's best.

Helmi (☎ 261 1110; Kauppakatu 2; ☺ 11am-midnight or later) Located in a 19th-century stone building near the harbour, Helmi is a downmarket bar with an excellent terrace. It has no frills but does four things, and does them well: pizzas, panini, salads and seriously cheap beer.

Getting There & Away

AIR

Several daily flights by **Finnair/Finncomm** (☎ 580 7400; www.finnair.com) and **Blue1** (☎ 0600 025 831; www.blue1.com) link Helsinki and Kuopio. **Air Baltic** (www.airbaltic.com) flies to Riga in Latvia.

BOAT

From mid-June to mid-August, **MS Puijo** (www .mspuijo.fi, in Finnish) travels to Savonlinna (€75 one-way, 10½ hours) on Tuesdays, Thursdays and Saturdays at 9am, returning on Mondays, Wednesdays and Fridays. It passes through scenic waterways, canals and locks, stopping at Heinävesi and Karvio canal, among other places. You can book a return with overnight cabin accommodation for €160.

BUS

The busy bus station, just north of the train station, has regular departures to all major towns and villages in the vicinity. Express services to/from Kuopio include: Helsinki (€58.10, 6½ hours), Kajaani (€28.70, 2¾ hours), Jyväskylä (€26.20, 2¼ hours) and Savonlinna (€28.70, three hours).

THE LAKELAND

SHE AIN'T HEAVY, SHE'S MY WIFE

If the thought of grabbing your wife by the legs, hurling her over your shoulder and running for your life sounds appealing, make sure you're in Sonkajärvi, 18km northeast of Iisalmi, in early July, for the **Wife-Carrying World Championships** (www.sonkajarvi.fi, in Finnish). What began as a heathenish medieval habit of pillaging neighbouring villages in search of nubile women has become one of Finland's oddest – and most publicised – events.

The championship is a race over a 253.5m obstacle course, where competitors must carry their 'wives' through water traps and over hurdles to achieve the fastest time. Dropping your cargo means a 15-second penalty. The winner gets the wife's weight in beer and, of course, the prestigious title of World Wife-Carrying Champion. To enter, men need only €50 and a consenting female. Estonians are particularly proficient; teams from that nation had triumphed in 11 consecutive events to 2008. There's also a sprint and a team competition.

The championship is accompanied by a weekend of drinking, dancing and typical Finnish frivolity, with a big-name band on the Thursday night.

TRAIN

Five daily trains run to Kuopio from Helsinki (€50.40, 4½ to five hours). Trains run north to Kajaani (€22, 1¾ hours) and Oulu (€41.80, four hours). Change at Pieksämäki or Kouvola for other destinations.

Getting Around

TO/FROM THE AIRPORT

Kuopio airport is 14km north of town. **Buses** (☎ 020-141 5710) leave from the kauppatori by the Anttila department store 55 minutes before Finnair departures (one-way €5, 30 minutes). Airport **taxis** (☎ 106 400, one-way €18) must be booked two hours in advance. A boat service from the terminal to the centre is being planned.

BIKE & CAR HIRE

You can hire bikes for €15 a day at **Hertz** (☎ 020-555 2670; www.hertz.fi; Asemakatu 1) and **Asemagrilli** (☎ 580 0569; www.kuopionasemagrilli.com, in Finnish; Asemakatu 1), both in the railway station building. Both also hire cars.

IISALMI & AROUND

☎ 017 / pop 22,319

Iisalmi, 85km north of Kuopio and halfway to Kajaani, is a quiet place known as the home of **Olvi Brewery**, Finland's only remaining home-owned beer and, naturally, for its annual **beer festival** (www.oluset.fi, in Finnish) held over the second weekend in July. There's not a great deal to see, but enough to make it a decent stop on the way north or south. Plus there's the wife-carrying shenanigans (see boxed text, above) at nearby Sonkajärvi.

The **tourist office** (☎ 272 3223; www.iisalmi.fi; Kauppakatu 14; ☑ 9am-5pm Mon-Fri, 10am-2pm Sat) is in the kauppahalli, just near the bus terminal.

Evakkokeskus (Karelian Orthodox Cultural Centre; ☎ 816 441; Kyllikinkatu 8; adult/child €2.50/1.20; ☑ 10am-4pm Tue-Sat mid-Jun–mid-Aug, 10am-4pm Mon-Fri mid-Aug–mid-Jun) has pretty scale models of various Orthodox churches and *tsasouna* from Russian Karelia, traditional costumes, icons and murals. Opposite, the attractive **Orthodox Church** has beautiful illustrations which were painted in 1995. If it's not open, get the key from the cultural centre or hotel in the same building. The church faces the Lutheran one a few blocks away along the Kirkkopuisto gardens.

There's a hostel a couple of blocks north of the station as well as, a block west of it, the onion-domed **Hotel Artos** (☎ 812 244; www.hotel liartos.fi, in Finnish; Kyllikinkatu 8; s/d €67/89; ℗ wi-fi), the most appealing hotel in town. It's run by, and shares a building with, the Orthodox centre, and modern rooms offer plenty of value with polished wooden floors and loads of natural light; some have their own sauna (€99). The restaurant here has a cheap lunch buffet from Monday to Saturday.

Kuappi (☎ 192 6430; Satama; ☑ 1-7pm Mon-Sat Jun-Jul), by the harbourside square, bills itself as the world's smallest pub – it has one table, two seats, a bar, a toilet, and an entry in the *Guinness Book of Records*. The miniature bottles behind the bar fool you into thinking it's bigger than it is, but not for long.

Bus services include Kuopio (€18, 1½ hours) and Kajaani (€18, 1¼ hours), and surrounding towns and villages like Sonkajärvi (€5.40, 30 minutes).

Iisalmi is on the train line between Kuopio and Kajaani, with several trains a day either way. You can also get here by train from the west coast.

Karelia

Mythic in the Finnish imagination, Karelia inspires images of traditionally dressed peasants who strum the *kantele* (traditional Karelian stringed instrument), just as they did when Elias Lönnrot came here to gather tales for the *Kalevala* epic. Lönnrot's cultural adventures, along with works by Jean Sibelius and Pekka Halonen, have led many to call this area the soul of Finland. While a distinctive culture, language and cuisine survive, it's a region that has been contested through years of war and still bears the scars of the Winter and Continuation Wars against the Soviet Union.

Much of Karelia is actually part of Russia, with the Republic of Karelia across the border sharing culture and unique language. The territory was lost during WWII but for many Finns the 'Karelian Question' remains unanswered. Upon the collapse of the Soviet Union, there was even talk of the region being sold back to Finland by Boris Yeltsin, but today the region remains divided. With the area stretched between the two countries, you'll see a strong Russian influence throughout. You might also see the old spelling Carelia used, though both countries today refer to the region as Karelia. If you're lucky you might hear the language that borrows heavily from Russian and has only a passing resemblance to Finnish.

Most visits start at one of Karelia's two capitals: Lappeenranta in the south or Joensuu in the north. While you'll be able to sample the region's food, hear its music and see traditional dress, this is also a hard-working part of Finland with million-euro logging industries.

HIGHLIGHTS

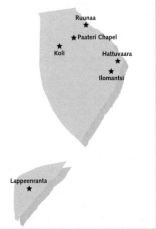

- Being wowed by the year's innovative sand architecture at Lappeenranta's **Hiekkalinna** (p164), which will have you throwing away your bucket and spade
- Seeing the view that inspired Finland's artists from the top of **Koli** (p183) before skiing down the country's highest slope
- **Cruising** (p167) to Vyborg or on to St Petersburg from Lappeenranta and imagining the Karelia that was
- Listening to a *kantele* performance at the **Parppeinvaara** (p174) in Ilomantsi
- Nudging the Russian border as you explore **Hattuvaara's WWII heritage** (p177)
- Realising why you failed woodwork as you admire **Paateri chapel** (p183), a building carved by a single artist
- Feeling the rubber raft crunch against rock as you shoot **Ruunaa's rapids** (p181)

expert.fi), which functions as a tourist information service for all North Karelia's towns and
organises everything from tent hire and tours
to fishing permits.

Self-Catering Accommodation

In North Karelia, Karelia Expert (left) organises cottage, cabin and apartment rental. For
South Karelia, **GoSaimaa** (www.gosaimaa.fi) has a
good selection of lakeside cottages around
Imatra (p168) and Lappeenranta (below).

SOUTH KARELIA

Beneath the waves of Russian and Swedish
empire building, South Karelia has almost
drowned as the border has risen and fallen
over the centuries. Today, just 10km separates
Lake Saimaa and the Russian border at the
narrowest point, near Imatra. The once-busy
South Karelian trade town of Vyborg (Finnish:
Viipuri) and the Karelian Isthmus reaching to
St Petersburg are now part of Russia. Wars
have haunted this troubled region, apparent
in the remains of Russian fortifications and a
common culture, particularly in the garrison
town of Lappeenranta.

LAPPEENRANTA

☎ 05 / pop 59,286

Sunning itself on the banks of Finland's largest lake, Lappeenranta has enjoyed halcyon
days both as a spa town and as a garrison for
Russians and Swedes. At the core of South
Karelia, it remains a popular destination for
Russians, particularly those with Karelian heritage, but also those just looking for luxury
goods. Much of the town was destroyed during the Winter and Continuation Wars but
its massive fortress and cavalrymen give it an
intriguing history.

The Saimaa Canal, cut through here in
1856, made it an important trading point, and
today Lappeenranta is still Finland's largest
inland port. The waterway from Lake Saimaa
to the Gulf of Finland is 43km long, incorporating eight lochs, and makes for a popular
day cruise to Vyborg. Vyborg, until WWII
Finland's second-largest city, is another piece
in the Karelian puzzle.

History

Established as a town by Count Per Brahe in
1649, Lappeenranta, then known by its Swedish
name of Villmanstrand (meaning 'Wild Man's

Activities

North Karelia is a favourite for lovers of the
outdoors. The whole area has over 1000km of
marked trekking routes, some through almost
untouched wilderness where you may be lucky
enough to spot elk, bears or even wolves.

Lieksa (p178) and Nurmes (p184) are the
best bases for more organised activities like
whitewater rafting at the exciting Ruunaa
rapids, canoeing and fishing in the remote
Nurmijärvi area or, in winter, thrilling dogsled
and snowmobile safaris. Located on the other
side of Lake Pielinen, Koli (p183) is a major
trekking trailhead and a winter ski centre.

Throughout North Karelia, the best first
point of contact for arranging activities and
trips is the excellent **Karelia Expert** (www.karelia

Shore'), was at the frontier of Sweden's empire and humming trade port. Nearby Vyborg businesses lobbied against their emerging rival and Lappeenranta lost its town status in 1683.

Russia took the town in 1741, destroying much of it during heavy fighting. The foundation of a spa in 1824 made it a playground for Russia's wealthy, and the development of railways and industry also saw rapid growth. The town was ceded to Finland when Russia's aristocracy was booted out in 1917.

Orientation

Kauppakatu and Valtakatu are Lappeenranta's main streets. The train and bus stations are located together, about 1km south of the town centre, but most intercity buses stop on Valtakatu in the middle of town. Lappeenkatu and Kirkkokatu run under the town with a large mall built over them. Bus 9 runs between the bus and train stations and the centre of town.

Information

Main post office (Pormestarinkatu 1)
Main tourist office (☎ 667 788; Kauppakatu 40d, Maakuntagalleria; ◷ 9am-5pm Mon-Fri Jun-Aug, 10am-4.30pm Mon-Fri Sep-May; 🖳) Difficult to find on the ground floor of this large shopping complex.

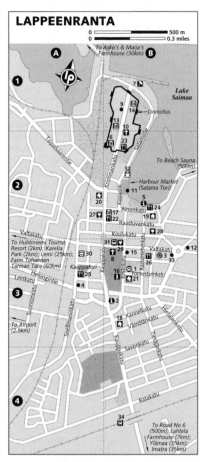

LAPPEENRANTA

KARELIA

Public library (☎ 616 2346; Valtakatu 47; ⏲ 10am-8pm Mon-Fri) Has free bookable internet terminals.

Summer tourist office (⏲ 9am-8pm Jun–mid-Aug, 9am-9pm Jul) In the wooden restaurant and theatre building in the harbour. There are other summer offices at Linnoitus (below) and at Hiekkalinna (below).

Sights

The home of a Russian family is lovingly preserved at **Wolkoff Home Museum** (Wolkoffin Talomuseo; ☎ 616 2258; Kauppakatu 26; adult/child €5/free; ⏲ 10am-6pm Mon-Fri, 11am-5pm Sat & Sun early Jun–mid-Aug). Built in 1826, the house was owned by the merchant clan Wolkoff from 1872 to 1986, and the 10 rooms have been maintained as they were. You have to join hourly guided tours (around 40 minutes; leaving quarter past the hour) to view them.

Lappee Church (⏲ 10am-6pm Jun-Aug) is an adorable wooden church built in 1794 to an unusual 'double cruciform' floor plan. It's barely on speaking terms with its bell tower, which is situated across the park and houses a cafe. South of the church stretches the graveyard, with an evocative **war memorial**, which features cubist and modernist sculptures commemorating Finns who died in the Winter and Continuation Wars. The most striking depicts a mother mourning her soldier son lost in battle, by Kauko Räsänen.

In summer, sand artists from all over Finland gather to build the **Hiekkalinna** (⏲ 10am-9pm Jun 15-Aug), a giant 'sandcastle' that uses around 3 million kilograms of sand. Previous incarnations of these huge art works have included themes such as a Wild West scene incorporating a gigantic steam train, and an outer space theme that brought together ET and Darth Vader. It's great for kids with a small selection of rides (many free).

LINNOITUS

This hulking fortification above the harbour was begun by the Swedes and finished by the Russians as a forward defence for St Petersburg in the late 18th century. Today it has a quaint village vibe with some fortress buildings transformed into galleries and craft workshops. Others have been turned into fascinating **museums** (☎ 616 226; www3.lappeenranta.fi/linnoitus; adult/child combined ticket €6/free; ⏲ 10am-6pm Mon-Fri, 11am-5pm Sat & Sun Jun-late Aug, 11am-5pm Tue-Sun Sep-May). Though wandering around the fort is half of the pleasure, there are also impressive views of the whole harbour from the fortress ramparts.

South Karelian Museum (Etelä-Karjalan Museo; admission €6) examines Karelia's prehistory with Celticlike artefacts – look out for the reconstruction of an elk hunted on ski (literally). There's a long look back at when Vyborg was part of Karelia with photos and oral histories from before 1939. It's a source of much wistful nostalgia for most Finns and some older Finns have been known to be moved to tears by how effectively this exhibit brings the town back to life.

South Karelia Art Museum (Etelä-Karjalan Taidemuseo; admission €8) has a permanent collection of paintings by Karelian and other Finnish artists. Most of the works are modern and a large part of the space is devoted to temporary exhibitions, which often feature local artists. Unless one of the temporary exhibits takes your fancy, you can probably skip this in favour of better studies of Finnish art in Helsinki.

The cavalry are honoured as Lappeenranta's greatest heroes, which may seem odd for a port town. The town's oldest building (erected in 1772) is the stately former garrison that houses the **Cavalry Museum** (Ratsuväkimuseo; admission €2.50; ⏲ 10am-6pm Mon-Fri, 11am-5pm Sat & Sun). The museum tells the story of how this band of red-trousered warriors began as the finest mounted forces in the Russian Empire and throughout the 1920s and '30s became Finland's national heroes. Exhibits of their trousers and skeleton jackets are a highlight along with their horseback armoury. Even today, dragoons are still garrisoned in Lappeenranta, and when they sweep down from the fort in regular parades throughout summer, you'll see how powerful this land-based force would have been against invasion.

The **Orthodox Church** (⏲ 10am-5pm Tue-Sun Jun–mid-Aug) is Finland's oldest, completed in 1785 by Russian soldiers. It features a glittering iconostasis and other saintly portraits.

There are daily **walking tours** (€4, one hour) of the fortress from late May to mid-September, leaving from the Pusupuisto kiosk. They last an hour and cost €2.50 for adults, with children free. To go your own way, grab a copy of the walking guide *The Fortress of Lappeenranta* (free), available from tourist offices.

Activities

The best way to explore this large town is to hire a bike from **Pyörä-Expert** (☎ 411 8710;

Valtakatu 64; 1-day hire €6-8) or **Toripyörä** (Kirkkokatu14a; 1-day hire €10).

There's a public **beach sauna** (admission €4.20) at Myllysaari, just east of the harbour area. Hours for women are 4pm to 8pm Wednesday and Friday, and 4pm to 8pm Tuesday and Thursday for men.

Tours & Cruises

Cruises on Lake Saimaa and the Saimaa Canal are popular and there are daily departures from late May to mid-September from the passenger quay at the harbour.

Saimaan Risteilyt (☎ 415 6955; www.saimaanristeilyt.fi; adult/child €14/7; ⏰ departs noon, 3pm & 6pm mid-May–Aug) offers two-hour cruises aboard the M/S *El Faro*, either around the archipelago or down the Saimaa Canal. **Karelia Lines** (☎ 453 0380; www.karelialines.fi; adult/child €14/7; ⏰ noon & 6pm Mon-Sat Jun–mid-Aug, plus noon, 3pm & 6pm Sat, 2pm Sun Jul) has two-hour cruises on Lake Saimaa and out to the archipelago aboard the spacious M/S *Camilla*. **Kristina Cruises** (☎ 21144; www.kristinacruises.com; 4hr cruise €53) does weekly cruises of the lake area; check their website for departure dates.

Many big hotels offer packages including a night's accommodation and a cruise, so check the websites or ask at the tourist office.

Festivals & Events

In early August **Lemi-Lappeenranta Musikkijuhlat** (www.lemi.fi/musiikki, in Finnish; tickets €20-30) is a festival of classical music that takes place mainly in churches throughout Lappeenranta, Imatra and Lemi.

Sleeping

BUDGET

This **Huhtiniemi Tourist Resort** (☎ 451 5555; www.huhtiniemi.com; Kuusimäenkatu 18; tent sites €10-12 plus per person €4.50, 2-/4-person cottages €35/45, apt €75; ⏰ mid-May–Sep) in a large complex has a bed for just about everyone. There's the expansive camping ground by the lake (mosquito repellent is a must in summer) as well as tidy cottages with bunks and fridges, and self-contained apartments. There are also two HI hostels at this location, with the same contact details: **Huhtiniemi Hostel** (dm €10; ⏰ Jun-Aug; P), with two simple six-bed dorms, and **Finnhostel Lappeenranta** (s/d €57/72; P 🕮) offering good hotel-style rooms with bathrooms and breakfast. The South Carelia Sports Centre is nearby, and hostel rooms include entrance to

the pool and sauna. Buses 1, 3 and 5 run past, but you might want to jump off an incoming intercity bus, as most pass by.

Karelia Park (☎ 453 0405; fax 452 8454; Korpraalinkuja 1; dm from €20, s/tw €45/70; ⏰ Jun-Aug; P) For most of the year this tidy hostel, 300m west of Huhtiniemi, is student accommodation. In summer it still has an institutional feel but rents out rooms to travellers. Each of the two-bed rooms has a shared kitchen and bathroom, and breakfast is included (€3 for dorm rooms).

ABCiti Motel (☎ 415 0800; Kannelkatu 1; s/d/tr €59/69/89; P wi-fi) A little way from the city centre, it might be a stretch to call this place a hotel as it has more of a hostel feel. Rooms are basic with TVs, shared bathrooms and kitchens though breakfast is included. Extras like wi-fi and sauna are worth a few euros more.

MIDRANGE

Lappeenrannan Kylpylä (☎ 616 7201; www.kylpyla.info; Ainonkatu 17; tw&d €116, tr €146; P 🖥 🕮) If you're after a healthy stay then this is your place. Rooms are decked out in appealing bronzes and golds, and some have great balconies that look across the park to the water. There are a couple of saunas, a gym, a pool and no tempting minibar. There are various excellent spa and wellness packages that include massages and crystal therapies. It's a popular spot with wealthier Russian tourists.

Scandic Hotel Patria (☎ 677 511; www.scandichotels.com; Kauppakatu 21; s/d €116/136; P 🖥 ♿) Definitely one of the better places to stay in Lappeenranta with a handy location for the harbour, and fortress excursions. The better doubles feature balconies with park views, but all the rooms are fitted out with minimalist Scandic chic and wi-fi throughout. Service is super-helpful especially the advice on sightseeing around town.

Sokos Hotel Lappee (☎ 67861; www.sokoshotels.fi; Brahenkatu 1; s/d €112/130; P 🖥 🕮 ♿) This place has been slickly refurbished with particular attention paid to the green-blue marina theme of the foyer. It's far from the water though and closer to the shopping malls, but it's a suave contemporary hotel with plenty to offer business travellers, and it also takes groups.

Eating

our pick **Kahvila Majurska** (☎ 453 0554; Kristiinankatu 1; pastries €2-5; ⏰ 10am-7pm) If you can't hop the border to a genuine Russian teahouse then

---

FARMHOUSES

The countryside around Lappeenranta has many farmhouses that offer B&B accommodation, which makes for a unique opportunity to meet locals and enjoy rural life. In some cases no English is spoken on these farms, so bookings or inquiries are best made through the tourist office at Lappeenranta.

Farm Tuhannen Tarinan Talo (☎ 332 704; Nikkarintie 137, 46530 Kannuskoski; per person from €35) With a name meaning 'house of a thousand tales', you'd expect the owners to be yarn spinners, and they don't disappoint. As well as recently renovated double rooms in the main farmhouse, there's an ambient former granary and a private apartment. They also have a smoke sauna for a unique and sooty experience. It's located on the way to Lappeenranta from Helsinki, 60km east near the village of Kannuskoski.

Lahtela Farmhouse (☎ 457 8034; http://matkailu.lahtela.info; Lahtelantie 120; d €60-70; P) Just 9km from Ylämaa, this is a dairy farm run by Hellevi and Lauri Lahtela, who speak a little English. Accommodation is in a smart Alpine-roofed villa, or simpler cottage with breakfast, sauna and use of a rowing boat on their small lake all thrown in. In winter you can rent showshoes to walk across the lake or through surrounding forests.

Asko's & Maija's Farmhouse (☎ /fax 454 4606; www.rantatupa.net; Suolahdentie 461; adult/child €33/16; ☺ mid-May–late Sep; P) This friendly dairy farm is 30km northwest of Lappeenranta in the village of Peltoi. Accommodation is in a traditional log cabin built in 1843, with breakfast and sauna included, as well as a barbecue for guests' use. There are also three cottages for daily (€65 to €90) or weekly (€410 to €485) rental.

---

this is as close as you'll get in Finland. A former officer's club (note the august portrait of Mannerheim and relic furniture), they still serve tea from the samovar and do a range of homemade pastries. The traditional serving maids outfits are a little too kinky.

Café Aleksandra (☎ 887 0113; Kauppakatu 28; snacks €3-7; ☺ 11am-5pm Mon-Fri, 10am-1pm Sat) This time-honoured favourite is another of the old-style Russian tearooms with antique furniture and snacks like meringues, quiches and sandwiches. Service gets a little brisk during busy lunchtimes but on a weekday afternoon you could easily plot a Dostoevsky novel here.

Café Wolkoff (☎ 415 0320; Kauppakatu 26; mains €16-25; ☺ 11am-11pm Mon-Fri, 4.30-11pm Sat) The bustling cafe arm of the Wolkoff Museum, this grand old restaurant specialises in Finnish cuisine such as reindeer, elk and cloudberry soup.

Kasino (☎ 040-716 8097; Ainonkatu 10; mains €16-26; ☺ 7am-3pm Mon-Fri, 8am-3pm Sat & Sun) Acclaimed as a favourite of Catherine the Great, this refurbished casino house has excellent Russian options like salmon blini and *zakuska* (light buffet), but also does more traditional European fare such as steaks and pork schnitzel.

Restaurant Olé (☎ 311 6961; www.ravintolaole.fi; Raatimiehenkatu 18; ☺ 11am-10pm Mon-Fri, 1-11pm Sat, 1-8pm Sun) This place does good Spanish fare, and even brings olives and bread with mains such as paella and hefty pastas. On weekends it has live music ranging from syrupy pan-European songs to flamenco guitar.

Drinking & Entertainment

Birra (Kauppakatu 19; ☺ 2pm-2am) This is one of the swankier bars in town with a shaded terrace and a great beer selection. On weekends it gets frantic but you can usually cosy up in a booth.

Old Park (Valtakatu 36; ☺ noon-1am Sun-Thu, noon-3am Fri & Sat) This is the best pick in a compact central complex that runs over two floors. It's a gently Irish-themed place (no shamrocks but plenty of hard rock) with a popular terrace.

Diva Nightclub (☎ 044-960 6290; www.nightclubdiva.com, in Finnish; Snellmaninkatu 10; admission €6; ☺ 6pm-2am Thu-Sat) This is the place for wild dancing in town, though there's a small bar attached that's good for a quiet Kilkenny when it all gets too much.

On the harbour in summer S/S *Suvi Saimaa* and *Prinsessa Armaada* both make for good booze boats, especially above decks on a sunny day.

Getting There & Away

AIR

There are daily flights between Helsinki and Lappeenranta with **Finnair** (☎ 020-314 0140). Bus 4 travels the 2.5km between the city centre and the airport.

BUS

All buses along Finland's eastern route, between Helsinki and Joensuu, stop in Lappeenranta. Bus and train tickets can be booked at the central office of Matkahuolto (see below), opposite the church park on Valtakatu, where many intercity buses stop. Regular services include: Joensuu (€38.40, 2½ hours), Helsinki (€35.70, 4¼ hours), Savonlinna (€25.50, four hours, via Parikkala), Mikkeli (€20.90, 1¼ hours) and Imatra (€10.10, 45 minutes).

Local connections run to smaller places in South Karelia, although some only run once on weekdays.

TRAIN

Seven to eight trains per day run via Lappeenranta on their way between Helsinki and Joensuu. There are also frequent direct trains to/from Helsinki (€43.20, 2¼ hours) and Savonlinna (€28.20, 2¼ hours, change at Parikkala).

AROUND LAPPEENRANTA
Ylämaa
☎ 05 / pop 1511

Ylämaa, 35km south of Lappeenranta, is a rural municipality best known for the gemstone spectrolite, a rare labradorite feldspar. Although also mined in Russia, Norway and Madagascar, the stone was first found here during excavations for WWII fortifications, and its dark colours glitter from red to blue.

Jewel Village, on the Lappeenranta–Vaalimaa road (Rd 387), is Ylämaa's main attraction, and has a helpful **tourist information office** (☎ 613 4200; www.ylamaa.fi; ◷ Jun–Aug). You'll

---

CRUISING TO RUSSIA

For Finns a boat cruise over the border to Vyborg (60km away, in Russia) along the Saimaa Canal is almost a spiritual journey to reunite Karelia. For the rest of us it can be a good chance to sample Russia or head further on to St Petersburg. You'll need a Russian visa, so this trip requires advance planning and can be very difficult for non-EU visitors (see p105).

There's an ever-changing range of cruises that set sail from Lappeenranta, from short shopping hops to Vyborg to in-depth history tours of St Petersburg. One of the better operators is **Saimaan Matkaverkko** (☎ 541 0100; fax 541 0140; www.saimaatravel.fi; Valtakatu 49), which runs cruises to both cities with boat/bus combinations to mix up your trip. They can also organise a 'cruise visa' for EU citizens (€35) if you can provide them with a copy of your passport at least a week before departure (booking significantly in advance is advisable, as these cruises are heavily subscribed).

Saimaan Matkaverkko also books a return cruise (including visa) aboard the M/S *Carelia* (from €79, 5½ hours, departs 8am three to four times weekly late May to mid-September) arriving in Vyborg with 3½ hours to sightsee and shop before returning to Lappeenranta by bus. It's also possible to stay overnight in Vyborg with prices varying by season and usually costing more on weekends. There are several options including a tour of a town and meals on board. It can also organise a package (from €450, departing July to August) to St Petersburg that includes the cruise to Vyborg and a bus on to St Petersburg, two days accommodation and tours of the Peterhof and Peter and Paul Fortress.

Of course if you want to travel independently (and you have a visa), the Sibelius and Repin trains pass through Lappeenranta on their way to St Petersburg (six to seven hours) and Vyborg (2½ to 4½ hours). Inquire with **VR** (Finnish Railways; ☎ 060-041 902; www.vr.fi) for price details. There are also various bus routes that can be researched at **Matkahuolto** (☎ 0200 4000; www.matkahuolto.fi; Valtakatu 36B; ◷ 9am-5pm Mon-Fri).

If you aren't an EU citizen and you haven't organised a Russian tourist visa before leaving your country of origin, then God help you. If you can endure a long wait and difficult bureaucracy then you could try the embassy in Helsinki (see p357) or the **Russian Consulate** (☎ 872 0700; Kievarrenkatu 1A; ◷ 9am-noon Mon, Wed & Fri) in Lappeenranta.

Two local agencies with good connections in Russia can help with applying for visas, though they may be wary of dealing with non-EU residents:

RTT (☎ 020-178 8130; www.rtt-matkapalvelut.fi; Kauppakatu 53)

Sojuz (☎ 453 0024; www.tourcentersojuz.fi, in Russian; Kauppakatu 53)

KARELIA

see stone grinderies, quarries, a goldsmith's workshop and a **gem museum** (☎ 020-495 9022; admission €2; ⏰ 10am-5pm) which has a collection of spectrolite and precious minerals and fossils, many in their raw, uncut state. Many of the gemstones are backlit to stunning effect, while others provide their own fluorescence. The **Gem Fair**, in early July, draws plenty of international rockheads.

Ylämaa Church (Koskentie; ⏰ summer) was built in 1931 and has an unusual facade made partially of spectrolite.

At the time of research, the town was kookily planning to build the world's most northerly **pyramid**, so look out for this large structure in the town centre in years to come.

Buses run from Lappeenranta (45 minutes) in the morning and afternoon, from Monday to Friday.

Lemi

Like Champagne and Burgundy, the tiny village of Lemi, 25km west of Lappeenranta, is more famous for its signature dish – *lemin särä* (roast mutton) – than any of its sights. Cooked in a birch trough, in order to add a sweet-woody flavour to the meat, it has been hailed as one of the seven wonders of Finland. As it takes nine hours to prepare, you'll need to book your meal at least two days in advance.

One of the more reliable restaurants serving the dish is **Säräpirtti Kippurasarvi** (☎ 414 6470; www.sarapirtti.fi; Rantatie 1; ⏰ dinner daily Jan-Nov, lunch daily Jun-Aug, Sat & Sun year-round), on the lakeshore. They serve it with thick rye bread and homemade *kalja* (beer).

IMATRA

☎ 05 / pop 29,155

Once the darling of Russian aristocracy, Imatra's waterfall was harnessed for hydroelectricity in 1929. During the summer it draws many new visitors from across the border. Aside from a historic hotel and the rapids, it's a brassy modern town with little to keep you beyond a weekend.

Orientation & Information

Although Imatra has four dispersed 'centres', separated by highways and shopping parks, the one of most interest to travellers is Imatrankoski at the rapids, where you'll also find the best restaurants and hotels. All incoming buses make a stop here, on the way to Olavinkatu. Three kilometres north,

Mansikkala has the bus and train station; bus 1 connects it with the centre (€2.50).

Post office (Pormestarinkatu 1)

Public library (☎ 020-617 6600; Virastokatu 1, Mansikkala; ⏰ 10am-7pm Mon-Thu, 10am-3pm Fri & Sat) In the Kaupungintalo near the bus and train stations. Has free internet access.

Tourist office (☎ 020-495 2500; www.travel.imatra.fi, in Finnish; Heikinkatu 1; ⏰ 9am-5pm Mon-Fri Jun–mid-Aug, 10am-4pm Sat mid-Jul–Aug, 9am-4.30pm Mon-Fri mid-Aug–May) Exceedingly helpful and friendly; extended opening hours for the Big Band Festival (opposite).

Sights & Activities

One of the first tourists to the area was Catherine the Great who, in 1772, gathered her entourage to view Imatra's thundering rapids. The building of the hydroelectric complex in 1929 dammed the river, but the watery wonder lives on with 20-minute **Rapids Shows** (⏰ 7pm May-Sep), when the dam is opened to light-classical warbling and a light show. It's still a spectacle with locals showing up half an hour early with beer and chips to make an evening of this artificial Niagara. Times vary according to sunlight hours so check the tourist office for exact times.

If your inner daredevil wants to get involved, **Imatra Express** (☎ 044-016 1096; basic/inverted €20/40) runs a flying fox over the gushing waters with an upside-down option to really make you lose your lunch. To work out the engineering of hydroelectricity make for the **Power Station Exhibition Room** (⏰ noon-6pm daily late Jun–mid-Aug), which has several slick displays on how the dam works.

Signposted as 'Ulkomuseo', **Karjalainen Kotitalo** (Pässiniemi; admission €2; ⏰ 11am-5pm Tue-Sun late Jun-Aug) is an open-air museum with a dozen traditional Karelian buildings moved here from other locations. The houses are typical of the region, with overlapping corner joints, overhanging eaves and a rustic log-cabin design.

Imatran Taidemuseo (Virastokatu 1; admission free; ⏰ 10am-7pm Mon-Thu, 10am-4pm Fri Jun-Aug, 11am-8pm Mon-Fri, 11am-3pm Sat Sep-May), in the same building as the library, is the town art gallery and has a strong collection of Finnish modernism including works by Wäinö Aaltonen. Temporary exhibitions take up much of the space, but it's worth seeking out the Gallen-Kallela water-colour of the rapids during their heyday in 1893, especially if you're visiting outside of the rapids show season.

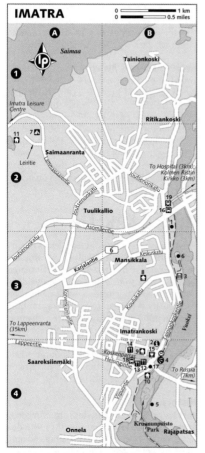

Ruokolahdentie 27; 9am-8pm Jun-Aug) was designed by Alvar Aalto, in 1957. For architecture fans it's a must, though there are better examples of his work in Finland. Take bus 1.

Festivals & Events
In late June to early July, **Imatra Big Band Festival** (020-747 9400; www.ibbf.fi; tickets €30-43) sees jazz, swing and even blues players blowing their own trumpets at several venues. On a different note, **Rock to the River** (040-500 3436; www.rocktothe river.com, in Finnish; tickets per day €35) in August brings heavier visitors including previous bands Uriah Heep, Lordi and… Anal Thunder.

Sleeping
Hostel Mansikkala (044-797 5452; www.hostelman sikkala.com, in Finnish; Pilvikuja 1; s/d €35/50, apt €100) It seems a little way from the action, but this summer hostel is like a pleasant stay in the country. It's excellent Finnish student accommodation with three spacious bedrooms, which share a well-equipped kitchen and bathroom. If you've got a group you can book out all three rooms at a special rate, creating your own apartment.

Imatran Valtionhotelli (625 2000; www.rantasipi .fi; Torkkelinkatu 2; castle s/d €134/159, congress centre

Vuoksen Kalastuspuisto (Vuoksen Fishing Park; 432 3123; www.vuoksenkalastuspuisto.com; Kotipolku 4; tent sites €13 plus per person €2, cottage €40; 9am-10pm May-Sep) is a stocked salmon pond on Varpasaari in Mansikkala. As well as the guaranteed catch of pike or salmon from the ponds, you can also purchase licences (per day/week €6/10) for the surrounding waters as fish suitable for smoking can be caught in the river here. They also rent bikes (per day €12), row boats and kayaks (per day 30), plus there's a good traditional sauna (per group €115). Accommodation is comfy camping for fisherfolk with basic tent sites and good-sized cabins.

As you approach you can tell by the clean white lines and soaring narrow tower that **Kolmen Ristin Kirkko** (Church of the Three Crosses;

KARELIA

s/d €119/144; (P □ ▣ ☺) With art-nouveau furnishings and flamboyant turrets, this is definitely the top of the town with some rooms even affording views of the rapids. The main hotel has long been a favourite with Russian aristocracy and now attracts their nouveau-riche equivalent with an opulent style that includes rich carpeting, carved doors and wi-fi throughout. The congress centre next door is a step down, going for bright modern rooms that represent value rather than views.

The best camping is at Vuoksen Kalastus-puisto (p169).

Also recommended:

Ukonlinna Hostel (☎ 432 1270; Leiritie 8; dm €20, f per person €25; P) A big family place that's a HI hostel with lake frontage and nearby leisure centre.

Hotel Cumulus Imatra (☎ 627 220; Koskenparras 3; s/d €106/131; ▣) A central option with good pub and swimming pool.

Eating & Drinking

Most of Imatra's eating is on the pedestrianised area of Imatrankoski.

Café Prego (☎ 050-491 4734; Napinkuja 2; snacks €3-8; ⊙ 9am-5pm Mon-Fri, 10am-4pm Sat) This excellent Italian coffee spot also does good salads, rolls and light meals, and has a lovely little terrace out the front. It's the best java in town, and has cakes and cookies that will have you lingering.

Buttenhoff (☎ 476 1433; www.buttenhoff.fi; Koskenparras 4; mains €14-26, set menu €46; ⊙ lunch & dinner Mon-Sat) Serving up Burgundy escargot and blini with caviar, this is definitely the best place in town. The menu wanders across the border with Russian favourites given a decidedly French treatment, such as the pan-fried *perch à la Russe*. Their three-course set menu is always a quality meal.

Café Julia (pastries €3-7, soup €5; ⊙ 8am-5pm Mon-Fri, 9am-3pm Sat Jun-Aug) Located below Buttenhoff, this is a more casual eatery with tempting cakes and espresso coffee.

Ravintola Vuoksenlahti (☎ 476 3468; Koskenparras 5; ⊙ lunch & dinner daily) This trusty boozer draws in locals with its basic pub grub and pool tables for after dinner. The terrace buzzes even on summer's more doubtful days, as it's the perfect place to watch the town pass by.

Woodoo (☎ 477 2710; http://woodoo.org; Jukankatu 50; ⊙ 9pm-2am Mon-Tue, 9am-3am, Wed-Sun) Running with the slogan 'Helping people get more sex since 2003', this larrikin place is the alternative hang-out in Imatra, attracting a younger

crowd to its terrace. The club out the back does hard beats, while the bar is a pleasant spot for a drink or game of pool. You can find your own dark corner in its large interior.

Getting There & Away

Imatra is served by trains (€47.70, 2¾ hours, seven daily) and buses (€38.40, five hours) from Helsinki, and bihourly buses from Lappeenranta (€10.10, 40 minutes). The central train station has lockers, but it's dead after 5.30pm. Buses also pick up and drop off in Imatrankoski (on Olavinkatu, a small lane between Helsingintie and the pedestrian zone), a handier option. Otherwise you'll need a **taxi** (☎ 020-016 464).

NORTH KARELIA

Even today Finland's wild frontier has many southerners imagining wolves and Russian border raids. True, the sparsely populated area does have some of Finland's best wildlife, but you'd be lucky to see a wolf or a bear on even the most rugged treks. There's stunning Russian influence in its Orthodox cathedrals and old towns, but today most of the Russians are cashed-up tourists.

Just beyond North Karelia, Kuhmo (p291) has a Karelian heritage though it's not strictly part of this province.

History

In 1227, a Russian crusade from Novgorod forcibly baptised Karelians into the Orthodox faith, sparking skirmishes that did not end until the Treaty of Nöteborg in 1323, which established Novgorod's suzerainty over the region.

In 1617, Sweden annexed much of Karelia, while North Karelia was constantly attacked by the Russians and religious intolerance forced Orthodox believers across the border into Russia. The Treaty of Uusikaupunki in 1721 divided the culture, with North Karelia remaining Swedish territory and South Karelia falling to Russian feudalism. In 1940 the Moscow Peace Treaty granted large chunks of Karelia to Russia with almost 400,000 people relocated within Finland.

Getting Around

In the North Karelia area a particularly useful service, given the scarcity of buses, is the *kimppakyyti* (shared taxi) system. They run several times daily along a variety of routes (such as Joensuu–Lieksa), and have a flat fare, which is about the same price as the bus. You need to book a day in advance. There's a different telephone number for each route; call ☎ 0100 9986 for Joensuu–Koli, ☎ 020-045 200 for Joensuu–Lieksa or ☎ 013-525 902 for general information. As English levels vary, it may be easier to ask the local tourist office or someone at the hotel to phone for you in Finnish.

JOENSUU

☎ 013 / pop 72,000

Capital of the province of North Karelia, Joensuu celebrated its 160th anniversary in 2008 by merging with the municipalities of Eno and Pyhäselkä to make it a super city. At the mouth of the Pielisjoki (Joensuu means 'river mouth' in Finnish), the town was founded by Tsar Nikolai I and grew to importance as a trading port with the completion of the Saimaa Canal in the 1850s.

Today it's a bubbly university town and the gateway to Karelia's wilderness area. On the surface the town is modern, but a little

exploration will bring out some interesting history and a lively market scene.

Orientation & Information

The Pielisjoki rapids divide Joensuu into two parts. The train and bus stations are in the east; the town centre, including the kauppatori (market square) and most accommodation, is in the west. Siltakatu and Kauppakatu are the two main streets.

Karelia Expert (☎ 248 5319; www.kareliaexpert.com, www.jns.fi; Koskikatu 5; ☺ 9am-5pm Mon-Fri, 11am-4pm Sat May-Sep, 11am-4pm Sun Jul; ☐) Located in the Carelicum, it handles tourism information and bookings for the region. Free internet access.

Post office (☎ 020-071 000; Rantakatu 26)

Public library (☎ 267 6201; Koskikatu 25) The library near the university campus has several free internet terminals.

Sights & Activities

If you want to know more about Karelian history or culture, the **Carelicum** (☎ 267 5222; Koskikatu 5; admission €4; ☺ 10am-5pm Mon-Fri, 11am-4pm Sat & Sun) should be your first stop. It's a conceptual museum with one main floor of

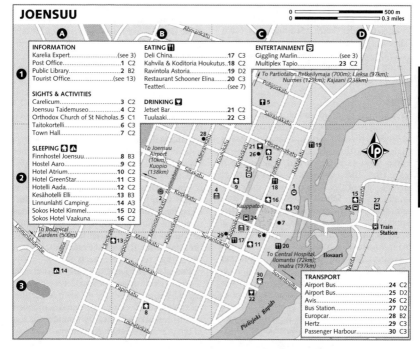

JOENSUU

0 _____ 500 m
0 _____ 0.3 miles

INFORMATION	
Karelia Expert	(see 3)
Post Office	**1** C2
Public Library	**2** B2
Tourist Office	(see 13)

SIGHTS & ACTIVITIES	
Carelicum	**3** C2
Joensuu Taidemuseo	**4** C2
Orthodox Church of St Nicholas	**5** C1
Taitokortelli	**6** C3
Town Hall	**7** C2

SLEEPING	
Finnhostel Joensuu	**8** B3
Hostel Aaro	**9** C2
Hotel Atrium	**10** C3
Hotel GreenStar	**11** C3
Hotelli Aada	**12** C2
Kesähotelli Elli	**13** B3
Linnunlahti Camping	**14** A3
Sokos Hotel Kimmel	**15** D2
Sokos Hotel Vaakuna	**16** C2

EATING	
Deli China	**17** C3
Kahvila & Koditoria Houkutus	**18** C2
Ravintola Astoria	**19** D2
Restaurant Schooner Elina	**20** C3
Teatteri	(see 7)

DRINKING	
Jetset Bar	**21** C2
Tuulaaki	**22** C3

ENTERTAINMENT	
Giggling Marlin	(see 3)
Multiplex Tapio	**23** C2

To Partiotalon Retkeilymaja (700m); Lieksa (97km); Nurmes (129km); Kajaani (238km)

To Joensuu Airport (10km); Kuopio (138km)

To Botanical Gardens (500m)

To Central Hospital; Ilomantsi (72km); Imatra (197km)

Ilosaari

Pielisjoki Rapids

Kauppatori

Train Station

TRANSPORT	
Airport Bus	**24** C2
Airport Bus	**25** D2
Avis	**26** C2
Bus Station	**27** D2
Europcar	**28** B2
Hertz	**29** C3
Passenger Harbour	**30** C3

KARELIA

photographic exhibits and static displays, an interactive area for kids modelled on part of old Joensuu, and a miniature model of the Karelian town of Sortavala (now in Russia), upstairs.

The art deco **town hall** (Rantakatu 20) dominates the town centre, between the kauppatori and river. It was designed by Eliel Saarinen, most famous for Helsinki's train station, and was built in 1914. It now houses the local theatre and Teatteri (opposite).

Near the kauppatori, **Joensuu Taidemuseo** (art museum; ☎ 267 5388; www.jns.fi; Kirkkokatu 23; admission €4.50; 🕐 11am-4pm Tue & Thu-Sun, 11am-8pm Wed Jun-Sep) boasts an impressive collection including Chinese pieces, examples of Finnish modernism and an intriguing selection of Orthodox icons swiped from the Soviets.

For more living art, **Taitokortteli** (Arts Quarter; ☎ 220 146; www.taitokortteli.fi; Koskikatu 1; 30min guided tour €25; 🕐 9am-5pm Mon-Fri, 9am-2pm Sat) is a pocket of local craftsfolk making clothing, toys and homewares. It's a chance to see weavers at work, browse contemporary art or secondhand books, and purchase local designers' work, plus there's a sweet cafe and gallery space. If you're coming from the park, look out for the monkey-baby sculpture perched on the balcony.

Joensuu's most intriguing church is the wooden **Orthodox Church of St Nicholas** (☎ 266 000; Kirkkokatu; 🕐 10am-4pm Mon-Fri mid-Jun–mid-Aug), built in 1887 with icons painted in St Petersburg during the late 1880s. There are services at 6pm on Saturday and 10am on Sunday.

Tours

In summer there are **scenic cruises** on the Pielisjoki, a centuries-old trading route. The M/S *Vinkeri II* has day and evening cruises (€15, 2½ to three hours) on Mondays to Fridays from early June to early August, which leave from the passenger harbour south of Suvantosilta bridge. You can book and check timetables with **Saimaa Ferries** (☎ 481 244; www.saimaaferries.fi) or the city tourist office. The **M/S Satumaa** (☎ 050-5660 815; www.satumaaristeilyt.fi, in Finnish; tours from €15) runs cruises on the Pielisjoki from June to mid-August.

To explore further afield, **Karelian Adventures** (☎ 040-027 3229; www.karelianadventures.com, in Finnish) does fishing tours (half-day from €45), boat trips (half-day from €20) and more, all bookable at Karelia Expert (p171).

From the park by the kauppatori you can take a carriage tour with **Ka' Vossikka** (☎ 050-351 3352; from €20) in a 19th-century Victorian buggy from mid-May to mid-August. In winter they switch to sled tours, which are also bookable through Karelia Expert.

For ferry cruises to Koli and Lieksa, see p174.

Festivals & Events

Over a weekend in mid-July **Ilosaari Rock Festival** (☎ 225 550; www.ilosaarirock.fi; tickets per day €10-20) attracts mostly Finnish acts to this massive annual event, which has received awards for its environmental record.

Sleeping

BUDGET

Kesähotel Elli (☎ 225 927; http//summerhotelelli.fi; Länsikatu 18; s/d/tr €44/60/78, apt €100; 🕐 mid-May–mid-Aug; 🅿) This student apartment building becomes a summer hotel in a spot that's pleasantly far from the centre of town. The facilities, including a sauna, laundry, and share kitchens and bathrooms (one for every two rooms), will make you think about enrolling in a Finnish university. The four-bed apartment is simple enough, but handy for families. There's also the Gaude pub which does pizzas and snacks.

Hostel Aaro (☎ 256 2200; www.hotelaada.fi; Kirkkokatu 20; s/d €39/52) This hostel offering of Hotelli Aada (opposite; collect keys from Aada) is an older place that was under renovation when we visited so expect a more modern place (and possibly updated prices to match). Rooms are small and private with tiny share kitchens and closet-sized bathrooms. It does come with the bonus of breakfast at the Hotelli Aada which is great value.

Finnhostel Joensuu (☎ 267 5076; www.islo.fi/accomodation; Kalevankatu 8; s/d from €41/57; 🅿) Another place that was being renovated when we visited, this smart HI-affiliated establishment is run by a sports institute and already had great rooms with plenty of space, TVs and mini-balconies. There are two separate buildings with gym and sauna as part of the institute so you can expect top-class facilities. Healthy breakfasts are included at Restaurant Sportti, which does serviceable meals.

Linnunlahti Camping (☎ 126 272; www.linnunlahticamping.fi; Linnunlahdentie 1; tent sites €12, 4-/6-person cabins €35/42) Relatively handy for the town centre, this pleasant lakeside camping ground is mobbed during the rock festival (above), but for the rest of the year you might have it to yourself.

MIDRANGE

Hotel GreenStar (☎ 010-423 9390; www.greenstar .fi; Torikatu 16; r €55) This brand-spanking new ('Opened last Thursday' the owner told us) hotel has all the usual hotel facilities without environmental guilt. Designed for low energy consumption, there's water heating rather than air-con blaring away and small communal areas to reduce heating. Rooms sleep up to three for the same price, with a pullout armchair for a snazzy third bed. The congenial breakfast room serves a light meal (€5), plus there's an automatic check-in at an ATM/Otto booth in the foyer, and internet booking.

Hotelli Aada (☎ 256 2200; www.hotelaada.fi; Kauppakatu 32; s/d €82/98) This pleasant little hotel was also renovating when we visited but it will continue to have spruce rooms in blue, red or yellow. Prices include breakfast and sauna, with the bonus of a popular nightclub onsite.

Hotel Atrium (☎ 225 888; www.hotelliatrium.fi; Siltakatu 4; s/d €74/107; **P**) One of the more characterful stays in town, this comfortable place has rooms with river views and a few with balconies or their own saunas. There are also quirky little embellishments like the wolf-whistling parrot and the inclusion of spare socks and chocolates on your pillow (awwwww!). Some rooms are showing signs of wear but it's still top of the town.

Sokos Hotel Vaakuna (☎ 020-123 4661; www.sokos hotels.fi; Torikatu 20; s/d €113/130; **▢** **&** wi-fi) The new Sokos on the block is a respectable and central addition to Joensuu's busy hotel scene. Rooms are slick and spacious with bathtubs in some and wi-fi throughout.

Also recommended:

Hotelli Karelia (☎ 252 6200; Kauppakatu 25; www .hotellikarelia.fi; s/d €79/105) Mature rooms are holding up well in a place that's popular for its cabaret-style shows on weekends.

Sokos Hotel Kimmel (☎ 020-123 4663; www.sokos hotels.fi; Itäranta 1; s/d €124/144; **P** **▢** **🐾** **&**) Joensuu's largest hotel; down by the river with amazing views and luxury rooms.

Eating

At the busy kauppatori, look for Karelian specialities such as the classic *karjalanpiirakka*, a rice-filled savoury pastry, and *kotiruoka* (homemade) soups. There are all sorts of food stalls set up here, along with cheap grillis (Finnish fast-food outlets). Joensuu's restaurant scene is overrun by fast-food chains but there are a couple of standouts.

Deli China (☎ 120 288; www.deli-china.fi; Koskikatu 5; mains €12-14; 🕑 lunch Mon-Fri, dinner Tue-Sat) Done out in bold reds and black this Chinese restaurant is a stylish spot with reliable noodle and rice dishes. Their takeaway prices are even more affordable if you want to eat in your hotel room.

Ravintola Astoria (☎ 229 766; Rantakatu 32; mains €11-26; 🕑 dinner Mon-Sun, lunch Sat & Sun, closed Sun Sep-Apr) Set in a former girls' school, this restaurant is a stylish affair with a Hungarian influence. Expect a menu with plenty of paprika and garlic in goulashes and hefty steaks. Hungarian wines complement the food and chilled *slivovitz* (plum brandy) makes a strong finisher.

Teatteri (☎ 256 6900; www.jns.fi/teatteriravintola, in Finnish; Rantakatu 20; lunch €8.50, mains €12-29; 🕑 9am-midnight Mon-Fri, 11.30am-midnight Sat year-round, noon-8pm Sun Jun-Aug) You'll have trouble keeping an eye on your plate amid the swanky surroundings of the town hall art deco building, which is decked out in Karelian maroons and blacks. The menu is representative of the region, with *muikku* (small whitefish) from nearby lakes and border-crossing borscht.

Also recommended:

Restaurant Schooner Elina (☎ 224 075; mains €14-22; 🕑 dinner Jun-Aug) A popular boat restaurant on the water that attracts a drinking crowd later.

Kahvila & Konditoria Houkutus (☎ 316 735; www .houkutus.fi; Torikatu 24; cakes €4-7; 🕑 7.30am-7pm Mon-Fri, 8.30am-5pm Sat) A smart bakery that does morning coffee with excellent cakes; the mint blackcurrant cake is a treat.

Drinking & Entertainment

The pedestrianised area of Kauppakatu has several late-night bars and nightclubs, which turn the volume to 11 on weekends.

Jetset Bar (☎ 123 009; Kauppakatu 35; 🕑 4pm-2am Mon-Thu, noon-3am Fri-Sun) This bar draws a blokey crowd with a good beer range and live rock on the weekends. It's very much a locals' hang-out.

Tuulaaki (☎ 227 170; Rantakatu 2; 🕑 11am-3am May-Aug) This summer terrace is sweetly placed right near the passenger quay and regularly features live rock. At other times it's often quieter, as it's away from the city centre.

Giggling Marlin (☎ 316 850; www.gigglingmarlin .fi, in Finnish; Koskikatu 5-7; 🕑 6pm-3am Thu-Sun) This large club plays very dance-friendly disco and Suomipop for Joensuu's younger crowd.

Multiplex Tapio (☎ 122 238; www.savonkinot.fi, in Finnish; Kauppakatu 27) This large cinema brings the big movies to town.

KARELIA

Getting There & Away

AIR

There are several flights a day between Helsinki and Joensuu. The airport is 11km west of town. Bus service one way is €5 and departs from Sokos Hotel Kimmel (50 minutes before departure) and a stop on Koskikatu (45 minutes before). A **taxi** (☎ 060-090 100) is €18.

BOAT

In summer the M/S *Vinkeri II* operates twice-weekly services from Joensuu to Koli (one way/return €30/45, 6½ hours), from which you can connect with another ferry to Lieksa, across Lake Pielinen. The ferry departs from Joensuu at 9am on Saturday, returning from Koli at 12.10pm on Sunday. You can also return the same evening from Koli to Joensuu on a bus. Book with **Saimaa Ferries** (☎ 481 244; www.saimaaferries.fi).

BUS

Joensuu is a transport hub for North Karelia so there are regular buses to all points, departing from the bus terminal east of the river. Services include Kuopio (€26.20, two hours), Oulu (€63.70, seven hours), Jyväskylä (€36.90, four hours), Helsinki (€63.70, 7¼ hours), Lappeenranta (€38.40, 2½ hours), Ilomantsi (€11.50, one to two hours) and Nurmes (€25.20, 1¾ hours). For Kuhmo, change at Nurmes or Sotkamo. Buses to Helsinki, Lappeenranta and Kotka depart from platform 6.

CAR

Joensuu is the best place to hire a car if you want to explore the region. Most big operators have offices at the airport with the following branches in town:

Avis (☎ 122 222; www.avis.fi; Kauppakatu 33)
Europcar (☎ 040-306 2852; www.europcar.com; Merimiehenkatu 37)
Hertz (☎ 123 597; www.hertz.fi, in Finnish; Kauppakatu 21)

SHARED TAXI

The *kimppakyyti* system is a good way to head on from Joensuu to the Lake Pielinen area, with departures to Koli and to Lieksa. See p170 for details.

TRAIN

Direct trains run frequently to/from Helsinki (€62.10, 4½ hours) and Jyväskylä (€39.60, 3½ hours), as well as north to Lieksa (€12, 1¼ hours) and Nurmes (€17.20, two hours, twice daily). From Savonlinna you have to change at Parikkala.

ILOMANTSI

☎ 013 / pop 6228

If the remains of Karelia had a capital, Ilomantsi would be a strong contender. It's closest to the border, has an Orthodox religion and even speaks its own dialect. Like Ålanders and Sámi in northern Lapland, Karelians see themselves as a distinct cultural group and you'll see that on the streets of this small town. The village refers to itself, not by the Finnish word *kylä*, instead borrowing the Russian *pogost*.

For many travellers it's a good base for the Karelian wilderness as the village itself has been razed by the Russians and left as a modern, relatively unattractive town. There are a few modest sights, but it's best to head out of town for hiking and cycling around the scenic area.

Information

Karelia Expert (☎ 248 5309; www.kareliaexpert.fi; Kalevalantie 13; 🕑 9am-4pm Mon-Fri Sep-May, 9am-5pm Mon-Fri Jun-Aug, 10am-3pm Sat Jul) Reservations and information.
Library (Mantsintie; 🕑 1-7pm Mon-Thu, 10am-3pm Fri) Free internet access.

Sights

PARPPEINVAARA

Few places bring Karelian traditions to life as vividly as the **Parppeinvaara Traditional Village** (☎ 881 248; adult/child €3/2; 🕑 10am-6pm Jun-Aug). The hill is named for Jaakko Parppei (1792–1885), a bard and *kantele* player, whose songs inspired the *Kalevala* epic. The folked-up harpsichordlike sounds of the *kantele* can be heard throughout the village and you can see this unique stringed instrument on display, along with various other Karelian cultural artefacts, in the small museum. The collection of Karelian buildings is a powerful evocation of history with informative guides wearing *feresi* (traditional Karelian work dress) and answering questions about the displays. The small **Orthodox Church** at the back of the village was actually built as a film set, but with genuine icons it makes a convincing stand-in. In summer there are theatre shows based on Karelian culture.

KARELIA

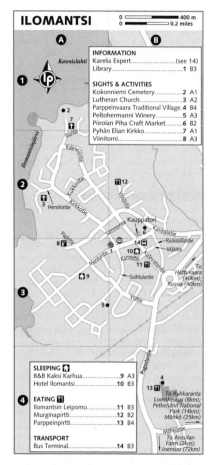

ILOMANTSI

0 ———————— 400 m
0 ———————— 0.2 miles

INFORMATION
Karelia Expert.....................(see 14)
Library.......................................**1** B3

SIGHTS & ACTIVITIES
Kokonniemi Cemetery...............**2** A1
Lutheran Church.......................**3** A2
Parppeinvaara Traditional Village.**4** B4
Peltohermanni Winery...............**5** A3
Piirolan Piha Craft Market..........**6** B2
Pyhän Elian Kirkko...................**7** A1
Viinitorni...................................**8** A3

SLEEPING 🏠
B&B Kaksi Karhua......................**9** A3
Hotel Ilomantsi........................**10** B3

EATING 🍴
Ilomantsin Leipomo.................**11** B3
Murginapirtti............................**12** B2
Parppeinpirtti...........................**13** B4

TRANSPORT
Bus Terminal............................**14** B3

PELTOHERMANNI WINE TOWER & WINERY

Finnish wine isn't necessarily an oxymoron. By blending blackcurrant, crowberry and white-currant there are some intriguing flavours to be sampled. And the local fields and bogs around Ilomantsi are perfect for collecting the raw ingredients. You can chat about the process at the cellar door of **Peltohermanni Winery** (☎ 882 281; www.peltohermanni.fi, in Finnish; Käymiskuja 1; ⏱ 9am-5pm), where you can also take part in a tasting. It's cheapest to buy liqueurs (from €10 a bottle) but you'll need to track down an Alko (liquor shop) if you want stronger stuff.

If you want to sample a little more than a swig, the former local water tower has become **Viinitorni** (wine tower; ⏱ noon-8pm Jun–late Aug) with wines sold here by the glass. The tower has a panoramic viewing deck, which is a great place to sit on a summer afternoon or evening.

CHURCHES

Ilomantsi features two fabulous churches. **Pyhän Elian Kirkko** (⏱ 11am-5.30pm mid-Jun–mid-Aug) is a beautiful wooden Orthodox church with an obvious Russian influence. Follow the *kalmisto* (graveyard) sign to the waterfront **Kokonniemi Cemetery**, where trees shade the graves of those lost in the many conflicts the town has endured.

When the Swedes took the area they sought to convert the Orthodox population by building the gigantic **Lutheran Church** (⏱ 11.30am-5.30pm Mon-Sat late Jun–mid-Aug) in 1796. It's also known as the Church of a Hundred Angels for its stunning paintings completed in 1832 by Samuel Elmgren, which with their vivid images of faith would have done much to sway illiterate locals to the Western faith.

Festivals & Events

As an Orthodox centre, Ilomantsi has several Praasniekka events. Originally these were strictly religious events, but these days they also attract tourists, with dancing afterwards. Ilomantsi village celebrates Petru Praasniekka on 28 and 29 June and Ilja Praasniekka on 19 and 20 July every year.

Sleeping

B&B Kaksi Karhua (☎ 040-561 0930; www.kaksikarhua .net, in Finnish; Mantsintie 26; s/tw €35/60) This beautiful new B&B is set among greenery and a few pecking chooks, giving it a relaxed country house vibe while also being very handy for the town centre and ski trails in winter. Rooms are freshly painted and smallish, but there's a cheerful welcome and hearty breakfast.

Anssilan Farm (☎ 040-088 1181; www.ilomantsi.com /anssila, in Finnish; Anssilantie; s/d €30/60, 4-person cottages €120; 🅿) Originally built in 1751, this former dairy farm is on a hill 4km south of the village and about 500m off the main road. It's family friendly with rides on horses and sleds for kids, and rooms available in a range of converted farmhouse buildings. Breakfast and linen are included. You can also camp in the garden here for a negotiable (but cheap) price. It's open year-round.

Hotel Ilomantsi (☎ 683 5300; www.hotelliilomantsi .com; Kalevalantie 12; s/d €69/89, small tw €66; 🅿) This is the town's only real hotel and the lack of competition shows in the older rooms, which

KARELIA

feature hellish heating but are reliable enough. There's also a quiet pub, passable restaurant and local disco.

Ruhkaranta Lomakeskus (☎ 045-138 9077; www .ruhkaranta.fi, in Finnish; Ruhkarannantie 21; tent sites €10 plus per person €3, cottages €34-85; ☽ Jun-Aug) Secluded in a thick pine forest 9km east of Ilomantsi, this camping ground has awesome lake views. There's a traditional smoke sauna here for groups and an electric sauna. Its reasonable restaurant is open only on weekends.

Eating & Drinking

Ilomantsin Leipomo (☎ 881 273; Kalevalantie 10; snacks €1-3; ☽ 6am-4pm Mon-Fri, 8.30am-2pm Sat) This little bakery is a local favourite for its top-notch *pulla* and preferred local breakfast of *karjalanpiirrakka* topped with scrambled egg. Most of the town grabs an early coffee on their way out here so it's a social hub on weekdays.

ourpick **Parppeinpirtti** (☎ 881 094; lunch €17; ☽ noon-3pm) This place in the Parppeinvaara village does the real-deal *pitopöytä* (Karelian buffet) in a traditional house complete with a *kantele* soundtrack. Here you can heap your plate high with *vatruskoita* (salmon-stuffed pastry), swill down the nonalcoholic *kotikalja* (which tastes like a home-brewed beer) and finish it with a berry soup that's like ladling jam.

Murginapirtti (☎ 881 250; Yhtiöntie; lunch buffet €6-8; ☽ 10am-3pm Mon-Fri) Up a dirt road away from the town centre, this old-style Finnish farmhouse restaurant does a hearty lunch buffet on weekdays. It's rustically Karelian right down to the icon in the corner.

The best place for a drink is the Viinitorni (p175) which does local and imported wines along with snacks.

PIIROLAN PIHA

At the top of the small hill in the centre of town the small **Piirolan Piha Craft Market** (☎ 220 150; Kauppatie 26; ☽ 9am-5pm Mon-Fri) not only sells authentic souvenirs, but also has a small workshop where you can see craftspeople at work on looms, spinning wheels and other traditional devices. You can buy linen, clothing, homewares and the *terva* (tar) soaps that Finns believe are good for skin problems. Outside there's a small flea market selling oddments and bric-a-brac.

Getting There & Away

Buses run frequently between Joensuu and Ilomantsi from Monday to Friday with fewer services on weekends (€11.50, one hour). During school term there are Monday to Friday buses from here to surrounding villages, but in summer you'll have to rely on taxi buses, which you may need to charter.

AROUND ILOMANTSI

From Ilomantsi, Rd 5004 heads east towards the Russian border, through a patchwork of lakes and into the wilderness trekking country.

Petkeljärvi National Park

The turn-off to one of Finland's smallest (6.3 sq km) national parks is about 14km east of the main highway. The main reason to visit Petkeljärvi is to walk the nature trails that cover birch and pine forest, eskers (gravel ridges) and ruined fortifications of the Continuation War. The marked 35km **Taitajan Taival** (Master's Trail) starts here and runs northeast to the village of Mekrijärvi, about 13km north of Ilomantsi. More than one-third of the park is water, with two sizeable lakes dominating.

Petkeljärvi Nature Centre (☎ 013-844 199; s/f tent sites €7/12, lodge s/d/q €36/46/76; ☽ May-Aug), in the heart of the park, is an excellent retreat. As well as tent and caravan sites, there's a modern lodge building with kitchen, a cafe, sauna, and boats and canoes for use on the lake. Park information, including maps, is also available here. The trailheads for two short walks – Harjupolku Nature Trail (3.5km) and Kuikan Kierros Nature Trail (6.5km) – also leave from here.

Möhkö

☎ 013

Only a few kilometres from the Russian border, Möhkö is a small village at the southern end of the Wolf's Trail (see p178).

This nondescript outpost was once a centre for heavy industry, after the establishment of an ironworks in 1849. At its peak the ironworks employed more than 2000 people and was one of Finland's largest ore-processing works. A canal was dug in 1872 to transport ore and timber out of the wilderness. The modest **ironworks museum** (☎ 844 111; www.mohkon ruukki.fi, in Finnish; admission €3.50; ☽ 10am-6pm May-Aug) showcases this glowing example of industry.

CYCLING THE VIINIJÄRVI LOOP

Roads around Viinijärvi are scenic, with beautiful churches and old houses. In August, you'll find blueberries in the nearby forests. If you have a bicycle (you can hire one in Joensuu or Ilomantsi), you can bring it to Viinijärvi by train or bus from Joensuu, Varkaus or Kuopio, and ride the 60km loop between Viinijärvi, Sotkuma, Polvijärvi and Outokumpu in a day. Another option is to take a bus from Joensuu to Polvijärvi, bypassing Sotkuma.

The tiny village of **Viinijärvi**, on the southern shore of the lake, has a pretty **Orthodox Church** to the west of the village centre. Its 19th-century icons are copies of those in Kyiv Cathedral.

The narrow 14km road from Viinijärvi north to **Sotkuma** is scenic. The small *tsasouna* (chapel), built in 1914, also has interesting icons inside. The traditional Praasniekka Festival is held here on 20 July each year.

A further 14km, **Polvijärvi** is a larger town with an interesting background. When a canal was being constructed at the southern end of Lake Höytiäinen in 1859, the embankment collapsed and the water level sank 10m, revealing fertile land. Polvijärvi was soon incorporated as a municipality and its population soared. The **Orthodox Church**, built in 1914, is not far from the village centre. Its icons are from St Petersburg and were probably painted in the early 20th century. The church holds its Praasniekka Festival on 24 June.

It's another 22km along Rd 504 to Outokumpu. There are several buses a day from Joensuu and a few others from Kuopio and Juuka. Buses from Outokumpu run on school days only.

You can break a journey here at **Möhkön Karhumajat** (☎ 844 180; rice.ekberg@kolumbus.fi; Jokivaarantie 4; tent sites €6 plus per person €3.50, 2-person cabins €32-37, cottages €70-130; May-Sep) a lakeside camping ground with cheerful cottages, a small beach, saunas and Finland's 'easternmost beer terrace'. Nearby is **Möhkön Manta** (☎ 040-861 6373; Möhköntie 210; May-Aug), a cafe in an old, grounded canal boat. Traditional Karelian pies, soups and sweets are dished up here.

HATTUVAARA

☎ 013

About 40km northeast of Ilomantsi, you'll know you're in the wilds by the dirt roads and logging trucks passing through this last outpost of eastern Finland. The village was famous for its poem-singers such as Arhippa Buruskainen who is thought to have inspired tales in the *Kalevala*. The *'runon ja rajan tie'* ('Poem and Border Rte') runs through Hattuvaara as a tribute, but don't try asking any of the Russian truck drivers if they're poets.

The main attraction here is the striking wooden **Taistelijan Talo** (Heroes' House; ☎ 830 111; www.taistelijantalo.fi; 11am-8pm daily Jun–mid-Aug, 11am-6pm Wed-Sun May & mid-Aug–Sep), designed by Joensuu architect Erkki Helasvuo to symbolise the meeting of East and West. The **WWII museum** (admission €4) downstairs shows a short film in several languages with multimedia, photo exhibitions and weaponry displays relating chiefly to the Winter and Continuation Wars fought along the nearby border. You'll see artillery and vehicles surrounding the building as well as a **Big Hat sculpture**, a nod to the translation of the town's name, literally Hat Mountain.

The Taistelijan Talo does an excellent all-day Karelian buffet (€12), which is heavy with meat, fish and *karjalanpiirakka* in the high-ceilinged wood cabin dining hall. You can also ask here about accommodation options in the village, the best of which is **Arhipanpirtti** (Arhippa´s Cottage; ☎ 830 111, 040-017 3607; www.arhipan pirtti.com; Hatunraitti 5b; s/d €25/43, cottage €75) with several rooms available and a four-person cottage. They also organise hunting trips into the surrounding wilds.

Hattuvaara has Finland's oldest **Orthodox tsasouna**, a sweet white wooden chapel by the side of the main road. Built in 1790, it has several original Russian icons and its small tower became a watchtower during WWII. Every 29 June, the colourful Praasniekka festival takes place here, complete with a *ristinsaatto,* or Orthodox procession.

EASTERNMOST POINT

With a vehicle you can journey east to the Finnish-Russian border crossing at **Virmajärvi**, the easternmost point of Finland. You need a permit from Taistelijan Talo (left) in Hattuvaara, issued free on the spot provided

KARELIAN TREKS

North Karelia's best trekking routes form the **Karjalan Kierros** (Karelian Circuit; www.karjalankierros .com), a loop of marked trails with a total length of over 1000km between Ilomantsi and Lake Pielinen. The best known are the Bear's Trail (not to be confused with the more famous Bear's Ring in Oulanka National Park) and Wolf's Trail, which link up in Patvinsuo National Park (see p180). You can walk in either direction, but we've described them here in a south-to-north direction. You'll need to arrange transport to the trailheads, including Patvinsuo National Park, in advance, although there is a bus service to/from Möhkö village.

There are wilderness huts and lean-to shelters along the way, but it's advisable to carry a tent. Hire of hiking equipment can be arranged at the Ilomantsi or Lieksa offices of Karelia Expert. Much of the Ilomantsi region is boggy marshland, so waterproof footwear is essential. For more information on these and other routes contact the Lieksa (below) or Ilomantsi (p174) offices of Karelia Expert, or **Metsähallitus** (☎ 020-564 5500; Urheilukatu 3a, Lieksa), the information office for the Forest & Park Service. You can book huts and cabins along the way with **Wild North** (☎ 020-344 122; www.villipohjola.fi).

See also the Great Outdoors chapter (p70) for general trekking tips.

Susitaival (Wolf's Trail)

The 90km Wolf's Trail is a marked three-day trek running north from Möhkö village to the marshlands of Patvinsuo National Park. The terrain consists mostly of dry heath, pine forest and swampy marshland which can be wet underfoot. This trail skirts the Russian border in places where many of the battles in the Winter and Continuation Wars were fought. Early in the trek, at Lake Sysmä, you'll see a memorial and antitank gun. There are wilderness cabins at Sarkkajärvi, Pitkäjärvi and Jorho, and farm or camping accommodation in the village of Naarva. In the Ilomantsi wilderness

you have your passport details with you. It's then a 15km drive down a fairly rough gravel road, signposted by blue 'EU' markers. There's not much to see and nothing to do at the end but it's a pilgrimage for Karelians to say they've been and you'll get a 'diploma' from Taistelijan Talo.

The actual border is marked by two posts on a small island in the lake. About 2km back is the **log house**, which contains nothing of interest but you can stay here overnight with permission from Taistelijan Talo, and along the way you'll pass several WWII *sotapaikka* (battle locations) and memorials.

LAKE PIELINEN REGION

At the heart of northern Karelia is Pielinen, Finland's sixth-largest lake, and with several tributaries there's plenty of watersports action. Finns flock to Koli National Park for epic views and winter skiing, while Lieksa and Nurmes equip intrepid travellers to head out into wilds such as Ruunaa for whitewater rafting. Bring your hiking boots, because this is a place to be active, with towns offering little apart from bases for getting into the great outdoors. A main road loops the lake while ferries cross it in several directions, and when it freezes solid during winter there's the thrilling short cut on snowmobiles or cross-country skis.

LIEKSA

☎ 013 / pop 13,260

Situated on the banks of Lake Pielinen, Lieksa is often used as a base for exploring Koli. It's known as a whitewater-rafting destination, and has several canoeing routes. Operators in Lieksa can kit you out for these activities or try the ever-helpful Karelia Expert (below) on the main street. It has good transport links, including lake ferries across to Koli, accommodation and all services.

Information

Karelia Expert (☎ 248 5312; kareliaexpert.lieksa@ kareliaexpert.fi; Pielisentie 2-6; ☯ 9am-5pm Mon-Fri, 9am-2pm Sat Jun-Aug, 8am-4pm Mon-Fri Sep-May) Books tours and accommodation.

Library (☎ 689 4125; Urheilukatu 4) Has free internet access.

Post office (☎ 020 4511; Pielisentie 34)

area there are about 100 bears and 50 wolves – chances of running into one are slim but not impossible.

Karhunpolku (Bear's Trail)

The Bear's Trail is a 133km marked trail of medium difficulty leading north from Patvinsuo National Park near Lieksa, through a string of national parks and nature reserves along the Russian border, including Ruunaa Recreation Area. Because of this accessibility, the trail can be walked in relatively short stages. The trail ends at Teljo, about 50km south of Kuhmo. You'll need to arrange transport from either end.

From Patvinsuo, the trail crosses heathland and boardwalks for 15km to the first wilderness hut at Kangas-Piilo, then another 14km to a hut and lean-to at Valkealampi. From here there's a short trail detouring to the WWII battleline of Kitsi. The trail then heads northwest to the Ruunaa Recreation Area, where there are several choices of accommodation, and opportunities for fishing, canoeing and rafting.

Beyond Ruunaa it's around 42km to Änäkäinen, another WWII battlefield. The trail follows the Jongunjoki on its final leg to the Ostroskoski wilderness hut, about 6km from Teljo.

Tapion Taival (Fighter's Trail)

The easternmost trekking route in Finland, Tapion Taival gives you the choice of a 13km wilderness track along the Koitajoki, or an 8km northern extension across the Koivusuo Nature Reserve, or yet another extension north of Koivusuo to Kivivaara. The Koitajoki section is certainly the highlight, a stunning walk through epic wilderness. The path is marked by orange paint on tree trunks. You'll need a car and good local map to reach the trekking area, or you can negotiate at Taistelijan Talo (p177) in Hattuvaara about transport.

Sights

The rambling complex of **Pielisen Museo** (☎ 689 4151; www.lieksa.fi/museo; Pappilantie 2; adult/child €4.50/1.50; ☺ 10am-6pm mid-May–mid-Sep) consists of more than 70 Karelian buildings and open-air exhibits, organised by century or trade (such as farming, milling, fire-fighting). There's an insight into the forestry industry, which was once crucial to the region, including an exhibit of a small logging camp and several floating machines used to harvest and transport.

The separate **indoor museum** (admission winter €3, summer adult/child €4.50/1.50; ☺ 10am-6pm mid-May–mid-Sep, 10am-3pm Tue-Fri mid-Sep–mid-May) features photographs and displays on Karelian folk history, which makes for an interesting look during the winter when the outdoor museum is closed.

Activities

Lieksa's watery locale means plenty of **whitewater rafting** in the Ruunaa Recreation Area (p181). Most operators will pick up from Lieksa and trips can also be booked through Karelia Expert (opposite).

Pony trekking on hardy Icelandic horses can be arranged through the tourist office. It normally costs from about €15 per hour.

Ratsastustalli Ahaa (☎ 040-525 7742; www.ahaatalli.com, in Finnish) does lessons and cross-country treks.

In winter, husky-dog, cross-country skiing, and snowmobile **expeditions** along the Russian border are popular – the tourist office has a list of tour operators. These trips can largely be tailored to your own needs, with up to four hours travel per day, and lasting up to a week. **Bear Hill Husky** (☎ 779 0898; www.bearhillhusky.com) is one of the best operators, based near Hattuvaara. Several of the rafting operators (p181) also offer snowmobile or cross-country skiing in winter. Looking to track down bear or other wildlife? **Erä Eero** (☎ 040-015 9452; www.eraeero.com; overnight trip per person €175) has an overnight cabin that is used as a base to go wildlife watching for bears, wolverines and even lynx.

Fishing is good in Lake Pielinen, Pudasjoki River and the Ruunaa and Änäkäinen recreational fishing areas. They each require separate permits, available from local sports shops or the Lieksa tourist office.

Festivals & Events

Lieksa Brass Week (☎ 045-132 4000; www.lieksabrass .com; Koski-Jaakonkatu 4; admission varies), during the last week of July, attracts a number of international musicians with a few free events.

KARELIA

Sleeping & Eating

There are a few places to stay in Lieksa, but it's also worth considering the surrounding options in Vuonislahti (p182), Koli (p184) and Ruunaa (opposite). Most places to eat and drink are on Lieksa's main street, Pielisentie.

Timitraniemi Camping (☎ 521 780; www.timitra .com; tent sites €12, cabins €32-90; ☺ mid-May–Sep) This no-fuss camping ground at the mouth of the river has log cabins, cottages of varying sizes, plenty of camp sites and facilities like lakeside cafe, saunas, and bikes and boats for hire. They're also great for organising additional activities like rafting and fishing.

Hotelli Puustelli (☎ 511 5500; www.finlandiaho tels.fi; Hovileirinkatu 3; s/d €85/110; P &) This lo-fi building by the riverside has good-sized (if a little musty) rooms with affordable rates that include breakfast and sauna. The restaurant also has a good lunch special (€10).

Timitran Linna (☎ 521 033; www.timitranlinna.fi, in Finnish; Timitrantie 3; dm €18, buffet lunch €7; ☺ cafe 8am-4pm) Once the offices of the border guard's commander, you may feel obliged to salute when you sample the generous lunch buffet at the coffee shop or stay in one of the hostel-style rooms. It's a little way from the main street but makes for a quieter stay.

Lieksan Leipomo (☎ 013-521 777; Pielisentie 31; lunch €5.50; ☺ 7am-5pm Mon-Fri, 9am-2pm Sat) This endearing weatherboard bakery is famous with locals for its homemade treats and filling soup lunches.

Tinatahti (☎ 521 914; Pielisentie 28; 💻) This lively pub serves straight-up meals and has internet access.

Getting There & Away

Buses from Joensuu are relatively frequent (€16.30, 1¾ hours), and shared taxis (see p174) even more so. There are daily trains to Lieksa from Helsinki (€64.50, 6½ hours), via Joensuu (€12, 1¼ hours). The more scenic mode of transport is by ferry from Joensuu, via Koli; see p174 for more information.

The car ferry **MF Pielinen** (☎ 481 244; www.saimaa ferries.fi; adult/child/car/bicycle €15/8/10/2) makes the 1¾-hour trip from Lieksa to Koli twice daily from early June to mid-August, departing from Lieksa at 9.30am and 3.30pm, and returning from Koli at 11.30am and 5.30pm. In winter, when the ice is thick enough, there is an ice road crossing the lake from Vuonislahti to Koli, a substantial short cut.

PATVINSUO NATIONAL PARK

This large marshland area between Lieksa and Ilomantsi is a habitat for swans, cranes and, if you're lucky, you might see some bears. Using the *pitkospuu* (boardwalk) network, you can easily hike around.

It's an easy 3.5km stroll to the southern shore of Suomunjärvi from the main road, where you'll find a **bird-watching tower** at Teretinniemi. The walk weaves through forests and wetlands, with bird sightings of waterfowl guaranteed if you're quiet.

There are three marked **nature trails** and several more-challenging **hiking routes** along the boardwalk path, which are mostly half-day walks. You can walk around Suomunjärvi or follow *pitkospuu* trails through the wetlands. In winter there's cross-country skiing on the unmaintained **Mäntypolku** and **Nämänpuro trails**, which both start from Suomu car park.

Suomu Information Hut (☎ 548 506; ☺ 11am-3pm) has a warden who can help with advice, fishing permits and free maps. They hire canoes and rowing boats here (per hour/day €5/20) and take bookings for cabins in the park including Lake Hopealampi's **loggers' cabin** (per night €115), which sleeps 30; or the smaller **Väälampi cabin** (per night €60), which sleeps four. Facilities are basic at both camps but include dry toilets, cooking facilities and, of course, saunas. They can also be booked via **Wild North** (☎ 020-344 122; www.villipohjola.fi). The Susitaival (Wolf's Trail) and Karhunpolku (Bear's Trail; see p178) trailheads begin here.

Getting There & Away

The only way to get to the national park is to drive. From Lieksa, head 18km east towards Hatunkylä, then turn right to Kontiovaara, along a narrow, very scenic road. When you reach a sealed road (Uimaharjuntie), turn left, drive a few hundred metres and turn right. If you drive along the eastern *runon ja rajan tie* route ('Poem and Border Rte'), turn west when you see the small 'Uimaharju' sign, just south of the Lieksa–Ilomantsi border. If you are trekking, the Karhunpolku and Susitaival both lead here – the park is where these trails meet.

RUUNAA RECREATION AREA
☎ 013

Ruunaa (www.ruunaa.fi), just 30km northeast of Lieksa, is an outdoorsy mecca east of Lake

Pielinen. It boasts 38km of waterways with six whitewater rapids, plus unpolluted wilderness, excellent trekking paths and good fishing. Designated camp sites (with fire rings) are also provided and maintained. Keep your eyes peeled as the area is home to otters, deer and, sometimes, bears.

There's an observation tower situated at Huuhkajavaara. Set atop a hill, it offers a magnificent panorama over Neitijärvi. **Ruunaa Nature Centre** (☎ 020-564 5757; ☼ 10am-5pm May, 9am-6pm Jun & Jul, 9am-5pm Aug) is near the bridge over the Naarajoki, where most boat trips start. There are exhibitions, maps, a library and a free English slideshow. It's a good place to research rafting operators and hiking trails.

Activities

Ruunaa is busy all year, hosting skiing and other snow sports in winter, while in summer the rapids are popular for rafting. Activities can be booked from Lieksa's Karelia Expert (p178).

BOATING, CANOEING & RAFTING

There are six rapids (class II-III), which you can shoot in wooden or rubber boats, the latter being more thrilling (and sometimes more spilling). There are several launches daily in summer from Naarajoki bridge (near the Nature Centre). Prices start at €23 for a three-hour trip and you can book at the Nature Centre or Karelia Expert in Lieksa (p178). Transport can also be arranged from Lieksa if you book a tour.

Most operators have a variety of packages that offer a choice of raft, and can also include camp meals and smoke saunas. Options include:

Erästely (☎ 040-027 1581; www.erastely.fi, in Finnish; 4hr €55) Organises canoeing expeditions from the Nature Centre with self-guided routes available.

Karjalan Kuohu (☎ 040-096 6428; www.saunalahti .fi/karkuohu) Offers rafting and snowmobile trips in winter.

Koski-Jaakko (☎ 050-036 6033; www.koski-jaakko.fi; 3hr trips from €23, 2-day trips €130) Shoot the rapids with good add-ons like a sauna and fire-cooked salmon.

Lieksan Koskikierros (☎ 521 645, 040-766 7148; www.lieksankoskikierros.fi; 4hr €30-46; ♿) Has wooden and electric-powered boats and skiing trips in winter.

Lieksan Matkakaverit (☎ 040-708 5726; www .lieksanmatkakaverit.fi; expeditions €30-52) Offers rafting and canoeing trips, as well as smoke sauna.

Ruunaan Matkailu (☎ 533 130, 040-035 2207; www .ruunaanmatkailu.fi; 4hr expeditions €38-45) Offers rafting

and organises cottages in the area, plus skiing, snowmobile safaris and ice-fishing in winter.

FISHING

Ruunaa is one of the most popular fishing spots in North Karelia. Trout and salmon fishing is exhilarating in the numerous rapids, with quieter spots accessible along a long wooden walkway. Two prized spots are Haapavitja and Siikakoski, where fly-fisher folk have long snagged bites.

One-week fishing permits cost €6 in summer and are available in Lieksa and at the Ruunaa Nature Centre (left). There is also a fishing-permit machine near the Neitijoki rapids. Fishing is allowed from June to early September and from mid-November to late December. There are several places to hire fishing equipment, including **Lieksan Retkiaitta** (☎ 526 420; Pielisentie 33, Lieksa).

TREKKING

The **Karhunpolku** (Bear's Trail) passes through Ruunaa. You can pick it up just 50m north of the Naarajoki bridge and the path is marked with round orange symbols on trees. See p179 for more details.

Around the river system, and over two beautiful suspension bridges, runs **Ruunaan koskikierros**, a marked 29km loop along good *pitkospuu* paths. If you have more time, there are another 20km of side trips you can take. Starting at the Naarajoki bridge, you will have to walk 5km along Karhunpolku to reach the Ruunaan koskikierros trail. Another 3.3km brings you to the **Ruunaa Hiking Centre**, where you'll find commercial services, road access and a car park.

Sleeping & Eating

There are at least 10 *laavu* (basic hiking shelters) and another 10 designated camp sites in the area. Camping and sleeping in a *laavu* is free of charge. You will need a lightweight mattress, sleeping bag and some mosquito repellent. You can book and browse National Park accommodation at **Wild North** (☎ 020-564 4333; www.villipohjola.fi). Grab a copy of the free *Ruunaa Government Hiking Area* map and guide for more accommodation information.

Ruunaan Matkailu (☎ /fax 533 130; www.ruunaan matkailu.fi; Siikakoskentie 47; d from €30, cabins €40-85; P) Five kilometres east of Naarajoki bridge, this place has self-contained cabins, as well as accommodation upstairs from their cafe. The

KARELIA

folks here also offer a traditional smoke sauna, rental boats and various snowmobile, rafting and boating tours.

Ruunaa Hiking Centre (☎ 533 170; www.ruunaa .fi; tent sites €12 plus per person €2, cabins/cottages €35/95) Near the Neitikoski rapids is this centre, which incorporates a large cafe, camping area, kitchen, sauna and luxurious four- to six-bed cottages as well as simpler cabins. There are mountain bikes, canoes and rowing boats for hire. The *pitkospuu* to the rapids starts near here.

Getting There & Away

Without your own car, you'll need to check with Karelia Expert about the infrequent minibuses that make the trip from Lieksa; otherwise you can join an organised rafting tour.

NURMIJÄRVI AREA
☎ 013

Known for its canoeing routes on the Jongunjoki, the Nurmijärvi area is wild and remote. **Nurmijärvi village** (www.nurmijarvi.fi) has enough services to get you to the Jongunjoki or Lieksajoki, or to the Änäkäinen area for fishing and trekking.

Activities
ÄNÄKÄINEN FISHING AREA

This government fishing area has the Karhunpolku running through it. The Forest and Park Service controls fish quantities in three lakes in the area including some stocking of the waters. Fishing is allowed year-round, except in the first three weeks of May. Jongunjoen Lomapirtti (right) has boats and fishing permits (per day/week in summer €10/35). Permits are also available in Lieksa.

CANOEING THE PANKASAARI ROUTE

This is a good circular route from Nurmijärvi village, where you can rent a canoe from **Erästely** (☎ 040-027 1581; www.erastely.fi, in Finnish; 4hr guided tour from €35). The paddle route starts across the road and can be easily done with a free route guide, which is available at Karelia Expert in the area. The route follows the Lieksajoki downstream to Pankajärvi then rounds Pankasaari, before returning to Nurmijärvi. There's almost no gradient on this route and it's suitable for beginners. Only the Käpykoski might present a challenge.

CANOEING THE JONGUNJOKI

This beautiful wilderness river has nearly 40 small rapids, none of them very tricky. Karelia Expert in Lieksa (p178) has a good guide to the route. You can start at either Jonkeri up north (in the municipality of Kuhmo), further south at Teljo bridge, at Aittokoski, or even at Lake Kaksinkantaja. Allow four days if you start at Jonkeri and one day from the last point. **Erästely** (☎ 040-027 1581; www.erastely.fi, in Finnish) can transport you to Jonkeri, Teljo or Kaksinkantaja, and also rents canoes.

Sleeping & Eating

Erästelyn Melontakeskus (☎ 040-027 1581; www .erastely.fi, in Finnish; Kivivaarantie 1, Nurmijärvi village; dm €18; **P** &) The main canoe rental company, Erästely, also offers beds at its headquarters, with decent dormitory accommodation and good facilities. There's a cafe and it's a good place to hire equipment.

Jongunjoen Lomapirtti (☎ /fax 546 531; Kivivaarantie 21, Jongunjoki; beds per person €25; **P**) This place is 2km from the main road towards Änäkäinen and the Russian border. There are two- to six-person rooms, cabins, camp sites and smoke saunas, and bicycles, canoes and boats for rent.

VUONISLAHTI
☎ 013

This rural lakeside village could be dismissed as just a train station in a field. An excellent hostel makes it a good place to break a trip. A **war memorial** on a small hill across the road from the train station commemorates where Finns halted a Russian advance in 1808.

The lakeside HI hostel, **Kestikievari Herranniemi** (☎ 542 110; www.herranniemi.com; Vuonislahdentie 185; dm €15; s/d €52/72; cabins €30-68, cottage €120; **P**) is about 2km south of the train station. It's a quaint 200-year-old farm with a restaurant and comfortable accommodation, including cheap dormitories in a newly refurbished cottage, two lakeside saunas and rowing boats. The owners even offer a range of treatment therapies such as herbal baths (€12) and *turvesauna* (a sauna-cum-mud bath; per hour €25). To get to Herranniemi, walk straight from the Vuonislahti train station to the main road, turn left and proceed 500m.

In Vuonislahti, **Hotelli Pielinen** (☎ 544 144; www.hotellipielinen.com; Läpikäytäväntie 54; hostel s/d €33/50, hotel s/d €53/78; **P**) is a modern hotel with hostel and hotel room styles, both of reasonable value. They have plenty of facilities and do year-round activities including trips to Russia, shooting Ruunaa rapids and snowmobile trips.

There are two daily trains to Vuonislahti from Joensuu (€10.20, one hour) and Lieksa (€3.60, 20 minutes). If you're driving, take Rd 5871 to get there.

Paateri

Set amid a pine forest near the village of Paateri on Vuonisjärvi is **Paateri church and gallery** (☎ 543 223; admission €4; ☉ 10am-6pm mid-May–mid-Sep), the studio-home of the late Eva Ryynänen (1915–2001), Finland's most respected wood sculptor. Here you'll find her greatest work, Paateri Wilderness Church, built in 1991 with walls and floor made of Russian pine and huge doors carved from Canadian cedar. Her home is also embellished with various sculptures from tiny carved bears on her spice rack, to horseshoe clovers on the doorstep. The free guided tour gives great extra insights and on the way out you can buy a birchwood postcard or stop for coffee and light meals at the cafe.

The trip across the lake makes for an adventure. In summer Herranniemi hostel rents out row boats (per day €30), which will take 1½ hours to cross the lake, and also does 20-minute motorboat trips (per person return €19). In winter **Koli Activ** (☎ 688 7250; www.koliactiv .fi) does cross-country skiing and snow-scooter trips across the frozen lake.

KOLI NATIONAL PARK

☎ 013

The magnificent sweep of islands strewn through Lake Pielinen is the landscape equivalent of the Finnish national park. Though relatively small, the 347m Koli inspired Finland's artistic National Romantic era (p53) with artists including Pekka Halonen and Eero Järnefelt setting up their easels here.

Accessible by ferry from Lieksa, Koli was dubbed Finland's first-ever tourist attraction and continues to draw holidaymakers year-round. It is a winter sports resort but boasts hiking, boating and, of course, that impressive scenery in summer. While the lake views are panoramic and nature trails are enjoyable leg-stretchers, without the Finnish cultural context it could just be a pleasant pine and birch-covered hill.

Koli was declared a national park in 1991 after hot debate between environmentalists and landowners, mainly about the placement of the hulking Hotel Koli on the hill. The area remains relatively pristine with over 90km of marked walking tracks.

The hill has road access with a short funicular (free) from the lower car park up to the hotel. From here it's a brief walk to **Ukko-Koli**, the highest point and 200m further is **Akka-Koli**, another peak. On the western slope of Akka-Koli is a 'Temple of Silence', an open space for contemplation, complete with a stone altar and wooden cross mounted in the rock. The solid rock peak nearby is called **Paha-Koli**. Further south is **Mäkrävaara**, a hill that offers the best views. For a slightly longer walk, it's 2.6km from Ukko to Koli village or a steep 1.9km walk to Satama.

Also at the car park, **Luontokeskus Ukko** (☎ 010-211 3200; www.outdoors.fi; adult/child €5/2; ☉ 9am-7pm late Jun-early Aug, 10am-5pm Sep-May) is a modern visitor centre with exhibitions on the history, nature and geology of the park, and information on hiking.

In Koli village, **Karelia Expert** (☎ 248 2315; kareliaexpert.koli@kareliaexpert.com; Kolintie 94; ☉ 10am-6pm Mon, 9am-7pm Tue-Fri, 11am-5pm Sat year-round, 11am-5pm Sun Jul) is the tourist office and has a comprehensive range of information and maps. The village also has a post office, supermarket and coin-operated internet, but the last stop for banks and fuel is Kolinporti.

Activities

As well as the walks mentioned above there are several great operators offering different ways of exploring Koli:

Koli Activ (☎ 688 7280; www.koliactiv.fi; half-day guided walks from €18) Do guided walks and snowmobile safaris with saunas and meals as optional extras.

Koli Husky (☎ 040-712 0366; www.kolihusky.com) Offer winter husky trips; rates vary.

Matkailutila Paimentupa (☎ 672 175; www .paimentupa.fi; Kotaniementie 1; 4hr rides €60, 1hr lesson from €20) Offers treks and lessons on Icelandic horses.

Piekoli (☎ 050-070 3611; www.piekoli.fi; half-day tour from €44) Takes guided walks around the park with sauna and meal included.

Winter brings out Koli's two **slalom ski centres** (Loma-Koli and Ukko-Koli with a total of nine lifts) and more than 60km of cross-country trails, including 24km of lit track. Short of Lapland, this is Finland's most accessible

KARELIA

ski resort. **Koli Ski Centre** (☎ 672 275, 673 141; www
.koliski.fi, in Finnish; snowboard hire per hr/day €16/24, lift
ticket per hr/day from €15/26) can kit you out with
lift tickets and equipment with prices highest
between mid-February and early April.

Sleeping & Eating

There are several basic huts (€9) in the national park which can be booked through the
heritage centre or Karelia Expert (p183). **Wild
North** (☎ 020-344 122; www.villipohjola.fi) can also
book cabins.

Koli Retkeilymaja (☎ 673 131; Niinilahdentie 47; dm/d
€12/24; P) The gravel road 9km from Koli
village will test your navigation skills, but for
this family-run find turn off at the statue of a
bear holding a spear. It's a basic hostel set in
the countryside, with good-sized twin rooms,
a kitchen and smoke sauna, plus a traditional
Sámi hut.

Loma-Koli Camping (☎ 673 212; tent sites €12, tent
rental €30, 2-/4-person cabins €30/40; ☿ late Jun–mid-Aug)
This simple camping ground is handy for the
Hiisi Hill slopes with family cottages and tent
sites. Rental tents sleeping three people are
available if you didn't pack your own.

Sokos Hotel Koli (☎ 020-123 4662; www.sokoshotels
.fi; Ylä-Kolintie 39; s/d €103/123; P ⬚) Yep, this is the
controversial place at the top of Koli Hill and
there's no doubt it has some of Finland's greatest views from the reliable Sokos rooms. It sells
out in winter when skiers pay higher rates for
the comfort of four saunas and a hot tub.

Art-Café Kolin Ryynänen (☎ 672 160; Kolintie
1c; meals €8-16) Opposite the supermarket
in Koli village, this pleasant cafe serves
as an exhibition space and even has
an artist-in-residence.

Getting There & Away

There are five to eight buses per day to
Koli *kylä* (village) from Joensuu (€10.70,
1½ hours), Juuka (€10.30, 45 minutes) and
Nurmes (€13.70, 1½ hours), including at least
one a day to the top of Koli Hill. In summer
the best way to arrive is by lake ferry from
Joensuu (p174) or Lieksa (p180). Buses to
the top of Koli Hill meet all arriving ferries.
If you're coming by car follow Rd 6 and turn
off at Rd 504.

JUUKA

☎ 013 / pop 6177

Juuka, just off the main highway about halfway between Nurmes and Koli, is known for

its soapstone mining and handicrafts. Many of
the wooden houses in its small **Puu-Juuka** (old
town) have been restored as shops, galleries
and homes. **Myllymuseo** (Mill Museum; ☎ 248 1300;
admission €2; ☿ 10am-4pm Mon-Fri, 10am-2pm Sat) is a
highlight of the old town as it's a working old
mill with a traditional smoke sauna nearby;
there's no signage so grab an English leaflet
inside the museum when you pay.

Thirteen kilometres south of Juuka, **Suomen
Kivikeskus** (Finnish Stone Centre; ☎ 681 1600; www.ki
vikeskus.com; Kuhnustantie 10; general admission €7, special exhibition €9, combined admission €14; ☿ 9am-7pm
daily Jun–mid-Aug, 9am-7pm Mon-Fri 10am-4pm Sat & Sun
mid-Aug–May) is an exhaustive look at Finnish
geology and the use of stone. It's almost compulsory to sneak a photo in the giant arm-
chairs of the sculpture garden.

Lolling on the banks of Lake Pielinen,
Lomakylä Piitteri (☎ 472 000; www.piitteri.fi; Piitterintie
144; tent sites €8-14, 2-/4-person cabins €32/42; ☿ early
Jun–mid-Aug) is a scenic camp site which has a
marina and swimming beach. There's a typical
Finnish *huvilava* (dancing stage), row boats
available for hire (per day €10) and tennis
courts for summer family fun.

PAALASMAA ISLAND

☎ 013

Noted for its scenery, this is the largest island
in Lake Pielinen and highest in Finland with
the tallest point 225m above sea level. The island is accessible from the mainland by a free
ferry that also wanders through several smaller
islands. The best view can be seen from the
wooden **observation tower** 3km from the camping ground via a marked trail. Following the
signs that read *'tornille'*, you'll see old houses
that tell the long history of Paalasmaa.

The ferry terminal is 15km east of the
main road and the turn-off is about 2km
north of Juuka. **Paalasmaan Lomamajat** (☎ 040-
592 4765; tent sites €10, cabins €25-40; ☿ Jun–mid-Aug) is
a camping ground at the eastern end of the
island with a nice lakeside spot.

NURMES

☎ 013 / pop 8900

With wide birched streets and a terraced
Puu-Nurmes (Old Town), the Russian heritage of this town, founded in 1876 by Tsar
Alexander II, is hard to miss. Its location at
the northwestern tip of Lake Pielinen makes
it an excellent base for winter activities such
as dog-sledding, snowmobiling, ice-fishing

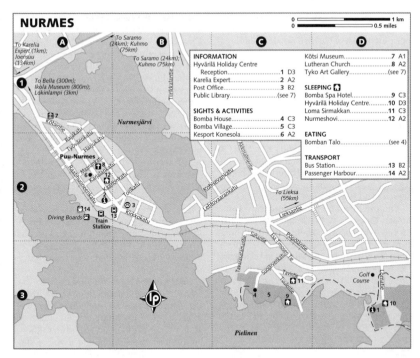

INFORMATION
Hyvärilä Holiday Centre
  Reception..........................**1** D3
Karelia Expert........................**2** A2
Post Office...........................**3** B2
Public Library....................(see 7)

SIGHTS & ACTIVITIES
Bomba House.........................**4** C3
Bomba Village.......................**5** C3
Kesport Konesola...................**6** A2

Kötsi Museum........................**7** A1
Lutheran Church....................**8** A2
Tyko Art Gallery................(see 7)

SLEEPING
Bomba Spa Hotel....................**9** C3
Hyvärilä Holiday Centre.......**10** D3
Loma Sirmakkan...................**11** C3
Nurmeshovi.........................**12** A2

EATING
Bomban Talo.....................(see 4)

TRANSPORT
Bus Station..........................**13** B2
Passenger Harbour...............**14** A2

and cross-country skiing tours, and canoeing and farmhouse tours in summer.

Orientation & Information

Kirkkokatu runs the length of the town with Puu-Nurmes at its northwestern end, while Bomba (a Karelian theme village) and the best places to stay are a few kilometres southeast of the centre.

Karelia Expert (☎ 050-336 0707; www.nurmes.fi, in Finnish; Raatihuoneenkatu 24; ⌚ 10am-6pm Mon, 9am-5pm Tue-Fri, 9am-2pm Sat Jun-Aug) Local information and bookings.

Post office (☎ 020-071 000; Torikatu 5) In Siwa supermarket.

Public library (☎ 689 5125; Kötsintie 2) Has free internet access, a reading room and a *Kalevala* collection in various languages.

Sights

Dating from 1896, the massive brick **Lutheran Church** (Kirkkokatu 17; ⌚ 10am-4pm Jun-Aug) is the largest in North Karelia, with around 2300 seats. You'll know it by its florid cross. Inside there are several models of Nurmes'

previous wooden churches that burnt down, hence earning this part of town the name Ash Village. **Puu-Nurmes** is on the esker above the train station. It's a pleasant if unexceptional neighbourhood with traditional wooden houses set among birch trees. The plan dates back to 1897.

Nurmes' biggest draw is **Bomba Village** (☎ 678 200; Suojärvenkatu), 2.5km southeast of the town centre. The imposing **Bomba House**, with its high roof and ornate wooden trim, is a replica of a typical Karelian family house, and was built in 1855 by Jegor Bombin, a farmer from Suojärvi (now in Russian Karelia). It now houses the Bomban Talo restaurant (p186) and eating there is the only way to see inside. The surrounding re-creation of a Karelian village makes for a pleasant browse among craft studios, especially when the summer market is on.

Kötsi Museum (☎ 689 5149; Kötsintie 2; admission €2; ⌚ 11am-5pm Mon-Fri), in the large Nurmes-talo Building, is the local museum of history, and has a variety of Stone Age artefacts on display. The same ticket lets you visit **Ikola Museum** (☎ 689 5152; Kotiniementie 2; ⌚ 9am-3pm Mon-Fri) an

KARELIA

agricultural museum in Tuupala, 1km north-east of Nurmes' town centre, which features an open-air exhibit of Karelian wooden buildings. Also at Nurmes-talo is **Tyko Art Gallery** (admission free; ⏱ 11am-5pm Mon-Fri, 10am-3pm Sat) with changing monthly exhibitions.

Activities
Nurmes offers a well-organised schedule of dog-sledding, snowmobiling, ice-fishing and cross-country skiing from January to the end of March, and canoeing, rapids-shooting (at Ruunaa) and farmhouse tours from June to the end of August. Karelia Expert takes bookings (at least 24 hours in advance) for most services and has the latest details.

You can hire a bike to explore town from **Kesport Konesola** (☎ 480 180; Kirkkokatu 16a; per hr/day €5/8), which can also help out with fishing permits for Pielinen and fishing tips. There's a good chance you'll hook salmon at **Lokinlampi** (☎ 461 206; www.lokinlampi.fi; Lokinvaarantie 3; 3hr licence €9, 3hr boat rental €8), a stocked pond north of town. If you want to head further out, Holiday Club Bomba hires out ATV (or quad bikes; per hour €35) and snowmobiles in winter (per hour €70).

Tours
Saimaa Ferries (☎ 481 244; www.saimaaferries.fi) has cruises (€14) on Lake Pielinen in summer, which depart from the passenger harbour near the train station. There are walking tours of the town organised by Karelia Expert (p185).

Sleeping & Eating
Hyvärilä Holiday Centre (☎ 687 2500; www.hyvarila .com; Lomatie 12; tent sites €13.50, cottages from €38, hostel dm/s €10.50/31, hotel rooms s €42-67, d €52-85, ste €125) This large complex is the first choice for accommodation in Nurmes, with a camping ground, two HI-affiliated hostels, a decent hotel and a restaurant. There's also a small swimming beach, tennis courts, golf, canoe and boat rentals and plenty of other activities. It's a short walk to Bomba Spa (1km) along marked walking routes. Not surprisingly, this is a very popular vacation destination for Finnish families and school groups. The camping area is spacious and the hostel is standard with the bonus of access to resort facilities. The better rooms are at Kartanohotelli, which has suites that come with their own sauna, while Pehtoori offers affordable standard rooms.

Holiday Club Bomba (☎ 687 200; www.bomba.fi; Suojärvenkatu 1; s/d €103/129, apt from €126; P ⛌ ⛉) Closer to a Karelian theme village, this huge place resembles an ocean liner complete with portholes and a landing dock between the buildings. It's actually an indulgent spa hotel complete with wellness centre, several saunas and chic rooms. The massive indoor pool is a feature of the breakfast lounge and other spa facilities can be used by nonguests (from €20). Set 200m from the main complex there's a group of Karelian-style cabins refurbished as apartments, several with their own saunas. There are packages available for all the accommodation, and various spa and massage treatments.

Loma Sirmakka (☎ 480 455; www.lomasirmakka.com, in Finnish, French, Russian & German; Tuulentie 5; apt from €97) Each furnished apartments in this cluster has a full kitchen and laundry and makes a great option for larger families. Rates are cheaper for longer stays.

Nurmeshovi (☎ 480 750; www.nurmeshovi.com, in Finnish & Russian; Kirkkokatu 21; s/d €45/70; P) In the centre of Puu-Nurmes this older hotel offers some of the cheapest rooms in town with a decent restaurant and sauna. Rooms are in need of a refresh, and if you're staying for a while you'll probably be wanting water views.

Bella (☎ 461 332; Porokylänkatu 14; mains €9-14) This Italian place in the commercial centre of Porokylä does pizza and pasta. Later it becomes a popular pub.

Bomban Talo (☎ 678 200; Bomba Village, Suojärvenkatu 1; lunch buffet €14.50, mains €12-25; ⏱ 10.30am-9pm or later, from 8am in summer) This mammoth wood cabin is the place to sample a Karelian buffet. Try the variety of *karjalanpiirakka* ingeniously designed to swab up *karjalanpaisti* (stew). The buffet is served throughout the day in summer, when the outdoor terrace is particularly tempting, but the à la carte options are just as authentic in winter.

Getting There & Away
Buses run regularly to/from Joensuu (€25.20, 1¾ hours), Kajaani (€23.70, 1¾ hours) and Lieksa (€10.30, 45 minutes). For Kuhmo, change at Sotkamo.

Trains go to Joensuu (€17.20, two hours, twice daily) via Lieksa (€7.80, 45 minutes).

Saimaa Ferries (☎ 481 244; www.saimaafer ries.fi; Kirkkokatu 16) operates on Lake Pielinen in summer.

AROUND NURMES
Saramo
☎ 013

This distant village 24km north of Nurmes is where the *Korpikylien tie* (Road of Wilderness Villages) begins. At the far end of the village, the **Kalastajatalo** (Fishers' House; ☎ 434 066; Saramontie 77; canoe rental per day €50, one-way transport to river €15; ☽ daily summer, Sat & Sun autumn & spring) serves as an information centre and restaurant, and can also book accommodation. It's also the best place for renting canoes if you're planning to paddle the Saramojoki. There's a shop and a post office in Saramo.

Saramo can be used as a base for the marked 75km **Saramo Jotos Trek**. Between Saramo and Peurajärvi there are two campfire sites in addition to Kourukoski. Between Peurajärvi and Rd 75, at Jalasjärvi, there's a *laavu*. Between Rd 75 and Mujejärvi, there are three *laavu* sites. South of Mujejärvi, there's a *laavu* at Markuskoski and cottages for rent at Paalikkavaara. Pick up maps from Karelia Expert in Nurmes (p185) or in Saramo.

KARELIA

Tampere & Häme

Modern cities and traditional settlements exist side by side in the historic Häme region, where you can explore Finland's rural past at ancient wooden churches, its unsettled history at Hämeenlinna's castle, and its industrial heritage at Tampere's textile factories. Lahti epitomises 21st-century Finland, which has a focus on technology.

The region saw much of the earliest Swedish settlement in Finland's interior. In 1249 Earl Birger, on a Catholic crusade, founded Tavastehus (Hämeenlinna). The Swedish settlers who followed established large estates – causing irritation among locals. Tampere's rise to prominence was in the 19th century, and its important workers' movement was bolstered by Lenin himself. Finland's Civil War erupted shortly after independence, and Tampere was the scene of the communist Reds' most decisive defeat at the hands of the progovernment Whites.

Tampere, Finland's second city, seduces visitors with two enormous lakes joined by the Tammerkoski channel, which churns through the town. Its imposing red-brick factories, left derelict in the hangover of industrial decline, now hold a spicy mixture of restaurants and museums, and the infectious energy of the people makes this many travellers' favourite Suomi stop.

Almost every town in the region sits on a magical stretch of water. Boats were once the main form of transport, and you can bring those slower-paced days back with a summer lake cruise. There are numerous shorter routes, but a whole day on the Poet's Way from Tampere or the run from Lahti to Jyväskylä, are really essential Finnish experiences.

HIGHLIGHTS

- Luxuriating in the acoustics of a Sibelius performance at **Lahti's magnificent Sibeliustalo** (p190), courtesy of the town's famous symphony orchestra
- Admiring the work of Finland's greatest sculptor, Emil Wickström, at peaceful **Visavuori** (p199)
- Cruising the **Poet's Way** (p205) from Tampere to Virrat, a memorable feast of Finnish lakescapes
- Getting your kicks on Finland's Route 66, staying in peaceful **Ruovesi** (p211), and walking through the nearby national park
- Feeling like a snooper as you go from room to room in **Palanderin Talo** (p197) in Hämeenlinna, one of Finland's most interesting house museums
- Perspiring like a racehorse in the soft steam of the traditional **public sauna in Tampere** (p204)

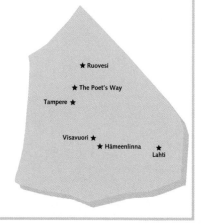

★ Ruovesi

★ The Poet's Way

Tampere ★

Visavuori ★

★ Hämeenlinna

★ Lahti

TAMPERE & HÄME

TAMPERE & HÄME REGION

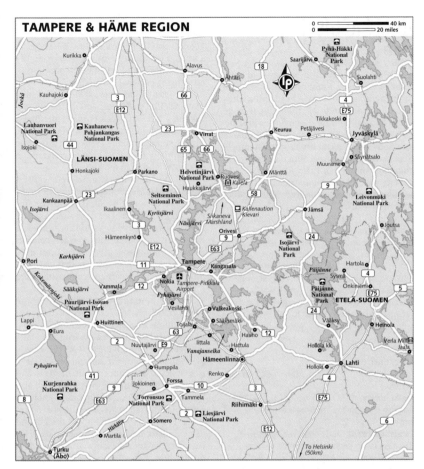

Activities

Connected waterways make for some fabulous boat trips between towns in this region, and there are several choices. Perhaps the most beautiful is the Poet's Way (p205), a romantic cruise from Tampere north to Ruovesi and Virrat. Lahti and Hämeenlinna are also aquatic launch pads.

Routes to explore by bike include the ancient trade route, the Härkätie (Ox Rd), which runs between Hämeenlinna and Turku.

The Tampere region is swimming with pike, zander, and salmon, and there are plenty of places where you can hire a rod, pay a small fee, and set about catching your next meal. Winter's no barrier either, as enthusiastic ice-fishers brave the cold with the help of thermos' of soup and hipflasks of something stronger.

Other winter activities are easily accessible: Lahti is a major winter sports centre, and has a comprehensive network of cross-country skiing trails.

Farmstays & Self-Catering Accommodation

As well as the nationwide operators mentioned in Directory (p348), there are several local options for seeking out that perfect cottage haven or warm and welcoming farmstay.

Check out:

Lahti Guide (www.lahtiguide.fi/en)

City of Tempere (www.tampere.fi/english/tourism/accommodation/index.html)

HÄME REGION

LAHTI

☎ 03 / pop 99,308

The region is steeped in history – indeed, some of Finland's oldest prehistoric sites are to be found not far away – but Lahti itself is basically a modern town, riding the wave of the technology boom and enjoying its proximity to Helsinki, 100km to the south. Its name is famous for winter sports – the frighteningly high ski jumps here have hosted several world championships – and classical music, with the city's symphony orchestra having gained worldwide recognition under former conductor Osmo Vänskä.

Lahti got its city charter in 1905 and lacks anything that could be called an old town: downtown consists of a series of linked shopping centres. However, architecture fans are amply provided for with the Aalto church and spectacular modern concert hall, and the city has a palpable energy, which was boosted after WWII with the arrival of thousands of refugees from occupied Karelia. Its lakeside location makes it a good activity base year-round.

Information

Lahti has free wi-fi through much of the centre.

Public library (☎ 812 511; Kirkkokatu 31; ☽ 10am-8pm Mon-Fri, 10am-3pm Sat) Several free internet terminals.

Tourist office (☎ 020-728 1750; www.lahtitravel.fi; Rautatienkatu 22; ☽ 9am-5pm Mon-Thu, 9am-4pm Fri, also 10am-2pm Sat Jun-Aug) Can book cruises and hotels. Free internet terminal. There's also a summer tourist booth at the harbour.

Sights

Lahti Historical Museum (☎ 814 4536; Lahdenkatu 4; adult/child €5/2; ☽ 10am-5pm Mon-Fri, 11am-5pm Sat & Sun) is in a beautiful old manor house by the bus station. The ground and top floors hold changing exhibitions on aspects of Lahti's history (a little English information is usually available), while the middle floor is mostly devoted to the collection of Klaus Holma, a 20th-century Finnish diplomat. It's a treasury of French and Italian religious art, rococo furniture and fine porcelain, and an excellent series of interactive computer screens allows you to access detailed information (also in English) on every piece.

Located in a modern office building, the **Art Museum & Poster Museum** (☎ 814 4547; Vesijärvenkatu 11a; adult/child €5/2; ☽ 10am-5pm Mon-Fri, 11am-5pm Sat & Sun) has temporary exhibitions of sculpture and paintings, and an offbeat collection of advertising posters from yesteryear.

The **Radio & TV Museum** (☎ 814 4512; Radiomäki; adult/child €5/2; ☽ 10am-5pm Mon-Fri, 11am-5pm Sat & Sun), on a hill just south of the centre, has a collection of old radios and a working broadcasting studio from the 1950s. You can create your own TV broadcast or radio program – a guaranteed hit with the kids.

Striking **Ristinkirkko** (Church of the Cross; ☎ 891 290; Kirkkokatu 4; ☽ 9.30am-6pm Mon-Fri, 10am-3pm Sat & Sun) was designed by Alvar Aalto and finished in 1978. The brick exterior and concrete steeple give little clue as to the interior, a white and airy space with wooden benches echoing the organ's pipes. Structural lines angle towards the simple wooden cross behind the altar or perhaps emanating from it like rays.

The art nouveau **Kaupungintalo** (town hall; ☎ 814 2224; Harjukatu 31) was designed by another famous Finnish architect, Eliel Saarinen. Phone ahead to arrange a guided tour.

Sibeliustalo (Sibelius Hall; ☎ 814 2811; www.sibeliustalo.fi; Ankkurikatu 7), by the harbour on Vesijärvi, is a spectacular concert hall in glass and wood and the home of the top-notch Lahti Symphony Orchestra, which is responsible for some of the best Sibelius recordings of recent years. The hall is wonderfully lit at night and has excellent acoustics. Guided tours (€10) run at 2pm on Tuesdays and Thursdays during July; phone to arrange tours at other times.

SPORTS CENTRE

At Lahti's **Sports Centre** (☎ 814 4570), a 10-minute walk west of town, things are dominated by three imposing ski jumps, the biggest standing 73m high and stretching 116m. You'll often see high-level jumpers training here in summer. There's a whole complex here, including the football stadium, a summer swimming pool, ski tracks and the delightful **Ski Museum** (☎ 814 4523; adult/child €5/2; ☽ 10am-5pm Mon-Fri, 11am-5pm Sat & Sun). A history of skis includes excavated examples from 2000 years ago, and Lahti's proud record as a winter sports centre is given plenty of treatment. The fun starts in the next room: frustrate yourself on the ski-jump simulator, then try the biathlon and skiing on Velcro before nailing five bulls-eyes with your rifle. A combined ticket (€7) includes the chairlift up to the observation terrace at the top of the ski jump; great if there's someone practising, and good for the views in any event.

Activities

There's plenty to do at the Sports Centre (opposite). In winter, there is an ice-skating hall and a total of 145km of cross-country ski tracks, 35km of which are illuminated. Skiing (per day €14) and skating gear (per day €8) can be rented in the main building. In summer the centre offers bike trails and a large outdoor **swimming pool**. FC Lahti also play their home games at the stadium here,

while the Pelicans, the local ice-hockey team, appear at the nearby Isku Areena.

The Lahti tourist office rents **bikes** (per day/weekend €15/25), and you can rent **canoes** (☎ 783 2005) at the island of Kahvisaari near the harbour at Mukkula, 5km from the centre. A good day trip could take you out to Enonsaari island and back.

CRUISES

As well as longer lake trips (see p193, in summer there are several daily 1½-hour return **cruises** from the passenger harbour, some including lunch (€15), as well as 3½-hour evening cruises to the Vääksy Canal and back on the **MS Suometar** (www.paijanne-risteilythilden.fi; adult/child return €15/9) or cruises to the Päijänne

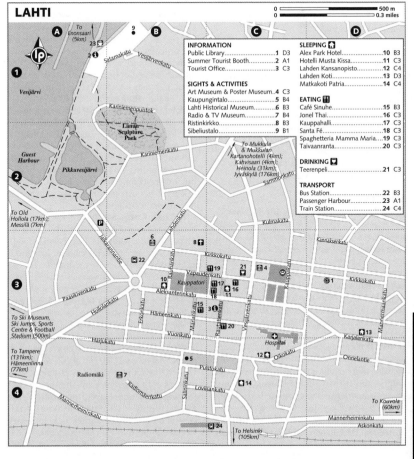

LAHTI

0   500 m
0   0.3 miles

INFORMATION
Public Library..............................1 D3
Summer Tourist Booth..............2 A1
Tourist Office.............................3 C3

SIGHTS & ACTIVITIES
Art Museum & Poster Museum..4 C3
Kaupungintalo...........................5 B4
Lahti Historical Museum............6 B3
Radio & TV Museum...................7 B4
Ristinkirkko.................................8 B3
Sibeliustalo................................9 B1

SLEEPING
Alex Park Hotel........................10 B3
Hotelli Musta Kissa..................11 C3
Lahden Kansanopisto...............12 C4
Lahden Koti..............................13 D3
Matkakoti Patria.......................14 C4

EATING
Café Sinuhe.............................15 B3
Jonel Thai................................16 C3
Kauppahalli..............................17 C3
Santa Fé...................................18 C3
Spaghetteria Mamma Maria.....19 C3
Taivaanranta............................20 C3

DRINKING
Teerenpeli...............................21 C3

TRANSPORT
Bus Station..............................22 B3
Passenger Harbour...................23 A1
Train Station............................24 C4

TAMPERE & HÄME

WE HAVE LIFT-OFF!

Finland takes the apparently suicidal sport of ski-jumping pretty seriously, and Lahti is one of its main centres. You'll see competitors practising even in summer, with the frightening whoosh as they descend the ramp sounding like a small fighter aircraft on manoeuvres.

Pioneered in Norway in the mid 19th century, the sport has progressed in bounds with various technical leaps that have added significant distance improvements; these days all ski-jumpers lean forwards and try to keep the skis in a 'V' as they sail towards, and hopefully beyond, the target line, usually set at 90m or 120m on competition pistes. Points are given for style as well as distance, so a slick, controlled flight and landing is preferable to risking life and limb in pursuit of extra distance. The 'extreme' version of ski-jumping is ski-flying, where special pistes produce extraordinary leaps of nearly 240m.

You can't really try it out as a visitor: you have to be a member of a local ski-jumping club, and start on gentle slopes before graduating to the serious jumps, but it's certainly worth watching these gravity-defying athletes perform.

National Park on the **MS Elbatar** (☎ 040-035 1959; www.epaijanne.net, in Finnish; adult/child €15/7) during July. Contact the tourist office for times and bookings.

Festivals & Events

Lahti hosts several annual winter sports events including the **Ski Games** (www.lahtiskigames.com) in early March. There are also some good summer music festivals such as **Jazztori/Rocktori** (www.jazztori.com, in Finnish), a week-long street festival in mid-August with jazz and rock performances in the kauppatori (market square), and the **Sibelius Festival** (www.sinfonialahti .fi) in mid-September, with performances by the Lahti Symphony Orchestra.

Sleeping

our pick **Lahden Kansanopisto** (☎ 87810; www.lah denkansanopisto.fi; Harjukatu 46; dm/s/d €22/30/50, s/d with bathroom €40/60; ☼ Jun–mid-Aug; **P** ☐ wi-fi) A standout budget option, the local folk college offers excellent summer accommodation in an enormous art nouveau building. The rooms feature comfortable beds, desks and bedside lamps, and there's a good kitchen on each floor. Shared facilities are good, and breakfast is included. There's a discount for YHA members.

Matkakoti Patria (☎ 782 3783; www.matkakotipatria .com; Vesijärvenkatu 3; s/d €30/45) Very handy for the railway, this curious guesthouse has compact singles and twins with washbasin, TV, and cheery aquamarine sheets on the beds. Some rooms have bunks; the front rooms are airier but the street's pretty noisy. There's free tea, coffee and chocolate biscuits, and a discount

for YHA members. Phone ahead on Sundays as reception isn't open.

Lahden Koti (☎ 752 2173; www.lahdenkoti.fi; Karjalankatu 6; s/d studio apt €75/85, 3-/4-person apt €111-155; **P**) A variety of attractive apartments are on offer in this building, and all come with tasteful furnishings and a well-equipped kitchen: a great option for families. Breakfast is left on a plate for you in your fridge, and you can use the sauna for an extra charge.

Hotelli Musta Kissa (☎ 544 9000; www.mustakissa .com; Rautatienkatu 21; s/d €82/92; **P** ☐ wi-fi) The 'Black Cat' is a discreet place in a larger building right in the heart of town, and offers excellent value for money. The commodious carpeted rooms look over the centre of Lahti but are pretty quiet and have low but comfy-enough beds. An evening sauna is available from Monday to Thursday.

Mukkulan Kartanohotelli (☎ 874 140; www.mukku lankartano.fi; Ritaniemenkatu 10; s/d €78/94; **P**) In the old manor house at Mukkula, 5km north of Lahti, this is a romantic spot; the lakeside location is superb and the price very reasonable. There's an outdoor Jacuzzi and sauna a hop, skip and plunge from the water, and friendly staff. There's also a **camp site** (☎ 753 5380; www .mukkulacamping.fi; tent sites €9 plus per car/adult/child €5/3/1; ☼ Jun-Aug, call ahead at other times) which has various upmarket cabins (per night €75 to €200).

Alex Park Hotel (☎ 52511; www.alexpark.fi; Aleksanterinkatu 6; s/d €105/125; **P** ☐ ☒ ☖ wi-fi) Despite the rather chaotic ground floor with posters of lugubrious Finnish musicians in the windows, and a circuitous route to the lifts via the breakfast buffet, the rooms in this central hotel are really rather nice, with dark wooden floors that your shoes squeak on and

– in some cases – views of the kauppatori. Facilities are good, with a restaurant, cafe and nightclub.

Eating & Drinking

Lahti's eating scene has taken off recently, with a variety of gastropubs and wine bars stretching their wings. The place to enjoy the summer sunshine is down at the harbour where, benevolently overlooked by the Sibeliustalo, a number of beer terraces, boat bars, cute cafes in wooden warehouses and the old station building, and an historic lake ship turned ice-cream kiosk draw the crowds.

The **kauppahalli** (8am-5pm Mon-Fri, 8am-2.30pm Sat) is a cosy spot for a coffee or snack; in fact it seems to have more cafes than stalls.

Café Sinuhe (☎ 751 1620; Mariankatu 21; light meals €5-9; 6.30am-8pm Mon-Fri, 8am-4pm Sat, 10am-6pm Sun) Half a block from the kauppatori, this is Lahti's best central cafe, with folk streaming in at all hours to sip mellow coffee, fork-up salads bursting with fresh things or buy a loaf of crusty bread.

Spaghetteria Mamma Maria (☎ 751 6716; Vapaudenkatu 10; mains €8-20; 11am-10pm Mon-Thu, 11am-11pm Fri, noon-11pm Sat, noon-9pm Sun) With a range of risottos, chicken, pastas and pizzas, this Italian eatery on the kauppatori is a firm Lahti favourite. Quantities are generous and the food's tasty enough, particularly the homemade gelati.

Sante Fé (☎ 781 8007; Aleksanterinkatu 10; mains €9-20; 11am-1am or 2am, kitchen to 11pm) The colourful terrace of this popular Tex-Mex bar occupies a corner of the kauppatori in summer and always seems to be full. The 1st-floor restaurant features nachos, fajitas, steaks and pastas.

Jonel Thai (☎ 734 2958; Vapaudenkatu 15; mains €10-16; 11am-8.30pm Mon-Thu, 11am-9.30pm Fri & Sat, noon-8.30pm Sun) Lahti has quite a few Thai restaurants and this is still the best. Friendly service complements the enticing aromas and satisfying flavours of the dishes. Takeaway prices are substantially cheaper, and the lunch special for €7.50 is a bargain.

Taivaanranta (☎ 042-492 5230; Rautatienkatu 13; mains €13-23; 11am-11pm Mon-Tue, 11am-midnight Wed-Fri, noon-midnight Sat) This place was closed for holidays when we visited, but our Lahti underworld informers rate it as one of the city's most interesting eating choices. A short but hearty menu includes a sausage pan with beer- and whisky-flavoured bangers, and wild mushroom risotto.

ourpick Teerenpeli (☎ 042-492 5220; Vapaudenkatu 20; noon-2am or 3am) A real Lahti success story, this popular pub sells its own tasty beers and ciders (try the blueberry one) and even distils a single-malt whisky. It's quite an upmarket interior these days, with white walls, plush stools, miniquiches and a tapas menu, and is always humming with chatter or live jazz. There's a summer branch at the harbour.

Getting There & Away

BOAT

From early June to mid-August **Päijänne Risteilyt Hildén Oy** (☎ 783 2515; www.paijanne-risteilythilden.fi) operates boats from Lahti's passenger harbour to Heinola at 10am (one-way/return €21/31.50, one-way 4½ hours, Monday to Saturday). The cruise goes via Vääksy and Kalkkinen Canals. It also has a weekly ferry to Jyväskylä at 9am on Tuesdays (€50, 10½ hours) from early June to early August, returning on Wednesdays.

BUS

There are regular buses along the motorway from Helsinki (€20.90, 1½ hours), and frequent services to/from Tampere (€23.70, two hours), Jyväskylä (€28.70, three hours) and Turku (€35.70, 3½ hours). There are also hourly buses to Helsinki airport.

TRAIN

There are at least 15 direct trains per day to/from Helsinki (€16.70, 1½ hours) and Riihimäki, where you can change for Tampere.

AROUND LAHTI
Hollola

☎ 03

Hollola (www.hollola.fi, in Finnish), west of Lahti, was the major settlement in the area until Lahti's rapid growth left the venerable parish as a pleasant rural backwater. These days there are two Hollolas – the modern town centre is on the highway 7km west of Lahti, but the old village and most of the attractions are 15km to 18km northwest of Lahti on the southern shores of Vesijärvi. To get there, you can either track north from the modern Hollola, or even better, take Rd 2956 from Lahti and follow Vesijärvi. It's also close enough for a leisurely bike tour.

Heading west along the lake from Lahti, the first place you'll reach is **Messilä**, a fine old estate with a golf course, craft shop, bakery, guest harbour and winter ski slopes (see also below). You can rent skis here for €16 per day, and there's also a ski school.

Pirunpesä (Devil's Nest) is a scenic rocky cleft near Messilä. A marked trail takes you there (it's 1km from the car park), or you can walk the entire 7km *luontopolku* (nature trail) that goes via a series of hills and offers some good views. **Tiirismaa** is a downhill-skiing resort in winter.

Continuing along the lake road towards old Hollola, you pass **Kutajärvi**, a resting place for migratory birds, on your left.

On the shores of Vesijärvi, the large **Hollola church** (☎ 788 1351; admission free; ☼ 10am-6pm Mon-Sat, 11am-4pm Sun May-Aug, 11am-4pm Sun Sep-Apr), 17km northwest of Lahti, was once the heart of this parish, before Lahti grew up. It's an elegant late-15th-century structure with steep gables; the belltower was designed by the indefatigable Carl Engel in the 19th century. Mounted above the double nave are fine polychrome wooden sculptures of saints; also noteworthy are the elaborate coats of arms, and the 14th-century baptismal font and Pietà that were from the earlier, wooden church. There are English-speaking guides in summer. The church is marked 'Hollola kk' on signs and bus timetables.

Nearby you'll find the local museum, **Hollolan Kotiseutumuseo** (☎ 041-440 5450; Rälssintie 6; adult/child €2/free; ☼ Tue-Sun noon-6pm Jun-Aug). The large red building not far from the church houses a collection of local paraphernalia, including a Stone Age axe, while a little further down the road, the open-air section features sturdy wooden buildings transferred from various locations in the area.

SLEEPING & EATING

Messilä Estate (☎ 86011; www.messila.fi; Messiläntie 208; s/d €98/115, 3-/4-person cottages €135/185; ⓟ ⓡ wi-fi) This place offers plenty of choices, with modern hotel rooms, character-laden accommodation in the 'old storehouse', plus a holiday village with self-contained cottages. The several restaurants here serve everything from gourmet cuisine to burgers and beers, and this is a popular summer venue for live music and dancing, and for après-ski socialising in winter.

Camping Messilä (☎ 753 7006; www.campingmessila .fi; tent sites €16 plus per adult/child €3/1, cabins/apt €55/85; ⓟ) This beautifully equipped holiday park

is next to the estate on Vesijärvi, 7km west of Lahti. There's a little swimming beach, a cafe with beer terrace, and a jetty, perfect for some light fishing. It's open year-round and offers a host of summer and winter activities. They even keep a hole open in the ice for a hardy post-sauna dip!

HEINOLA
☎ 03 / pop 20,612

Eighteenth-century Heinola is overshadowed these days by Lahti but has the Jyrängönkoski flowing through it and a scenic waterfront setting. It serves as a starting point for summer lake cruises. The **Kulttuuritoimisto** (☎ 849 3606; www.heinola.net, in Finnish; Maaherrankatu 1b; ☼ 9am-4pm Mon-Fri), just up from the passenger harbour, has tourist information and there's also a tourist office at a petrol station on the main north–south highway.

The yellow wooden **church** dignifies the centre of town; behind it, the Heinola ridge has a tower with views and the **Harjupaviljonki**, designed in 1900 to look like a Japanese temple – it holds art exhibitions in summer.

Right by the bus station, **Heinolan Lintutarhat** (☎ 715 2916; admission free; ☼ 10am-4pm Mon-Fri, 10am-2pm Sat & Sun) is a bird zoo with many Finnish species, all injured creatures rescued from the wild, as well as exotic varieties. The owls are particularly impressive, but some of the parrots look ragged to say the least. You can see some of the birds outside opening hours, a nice way to wait for your bus.

The **Sauna World Championships**, held at the summer theatre in mid-August, are an endurance test and a half, with plenty of beer consumed.

Camping Heinäsaari (☎ 050-049 1637; www.hei nasaari.com; camping €12 plus per adult/child €4/2, cabins €35-45, cottages €85-130; ☼ May–mid-Sep; ⓟ) is set on its own little island 1.5km west of the town centre. There's a simple cafe and plenty of charm; pitch your tent as far from the busy road bridge as you can though. The cabins are simple but comfy enough, and the cottages are very upmarket.

Halfway to the camping ground, **Kumpeli** (☎ 812 7100; www.kumpeli.fi; Muonamiehentie 3; s/d €106/128; ⓟ ⓟ ⓡ wi-fi) is a large modern hotel that offers smart rooms with balconies overlooking the water, a decent restaurant and sizeable swimming pool. They can organise snowmobiling in winter and quad-biking in summer.

Getting There & Away

There are buses roughly half-hourly from Lahti (€6.50, 20 to 40 minutes). Ferries from Lahti sail to Heinola in summer; see p193 for details.

HÄMEENLINNA

☎ 03 / pop 48,414

Dominated by its namesake, majestic Häme Castle, Hämeenlinna (Swedish: Tavastehus) is the oldest inland town in Finland, founded in 1649, though a trading post had already existed here since the 9th century. The Swedes built the castle in the 13th century, and Hämeenlinna developed into an administrative, educational and garrison town around it. The town is quiet but picturesque, and its wealth of museums will keep you busy for a day or two. It makes a good stop between Helsinki and Tampere, and you could head on to the latter by lake boat.

Information

Häme Tourist Service (☎ 010-617 2300; www .hameenmatkailu.fi, in Finnish; Viipurintie 4; �) 8am-4pm Mon-Fri) In the Verkatehdas complex. Sells tickets for lake cruises and books accommodation at hotels and cabins throughout the region.

Public library (Lukiokatu 2; �) Mon-Sat) Free internet terminals, but must be prebooked. Opens Sundays during winter.

Tourist office (☎ 621 3373; www.hameenlinna.fi; Raatihuoneenkatu 11; �) 9am-5pm Mon, 9am-7pm Tue-Fri, also 10am-2pm Sat May-Aug) Plenty of information and free internet.

Sights & Activities

Despite its small size, Hämeenlinna has a wealth of museums and other attractions.

HÄME CASTLE & MUSEUMS

Hämeenlinna means **Häme Castle** (☎ 675 6820; adult/child €5/3; ☒ 10am-6pm May–mid-Aug, 10am-4pm mid-Aug–Apr) so it's no surprise that this bulky twin-towered red-brick fortress is the town's pride and most significant attraction. Construction of the castle was begun by the Swedes during the 1260s, who wanted to establish a military redoubt against the power of Novgorod (p31). It was originally built on an island, but to the annoyance of the defenders, the lake receded and necessitated the building of new walls. It never saw serious military action and, after the Russian takeover of 1809 (p33), was converted into a jail. The last prisoners left in the 1980s and extensive renovations of the castle were finally completed in 1991.

The interior is a little disappointing, with a modern exhibition annexe displaying period costumes and furniture tacked on to the original building (whose bare rooms don't really evoke its past). Free tours in English and German are given hourly from June to August; if you don't read Finnish/Swedish, a tour or the €5 guidebook is recommended, as there's little other information.

By the castle are three worthwhile **museums** that can be visited with the castle on a combined ticket (adult/child €12/6).

Vankilamuseo

The old prison block near the castle has been converted into a **prison museum** (☎ 621 2977; adult/child €5/1; ☒ 11am-5pm) where you can visit a solitary confinement cell or admire the graffiti left by former inmates. The most interesting bit is the three cells, left more or less as they were when the inmates departed, along with a brief description of their occupants' crime and lifestyle. There's also a sauna, where prisoners would sometimes violently settle disputes. This particular building was last used as a prison in 1993.

Historiallinen Museo

Next to the prison museum, the unassuming **historical museum** (☎ 621 2979; adult/child €4/free;

VERLA MILL

A great day trip is a visit to the Verla Mill, a complex of beautiful brick buildings enchantingly set by a stream about 40km southeast of Heinola. Built in 1882, it operated as a ground wood and board mill until 1964 and is incredibly well preserved, so much so that Unesco has listed it. Entry to the **Verla Mill Museum** (☎ 020-415 2170; adult/child €6/2; ☒ 10am-5pm Tue-Sun May–mid-Sep) is by guided tour (English available), and you can bring a picnic to have in the gardens or by one of the nearby lakes. Otherwise, there's a cafe and restaurant here too. To get there, head just north of Heinola to the Kouvola turn-off, and follow that to Jaala, where there's a signposted left turn to Verla.

⊗ 11am-5pm) has displays labelled in English and covers the history of the town and the social history of the Häme region, with information on refugees from Karelia, the lynx, the town fire of 1831, and pop-culture memorabilia. While the reconstruction of a traditional savings bank might not get the pulse racing, it's the tangible respect for the everyday past that makes these Finnish museums lovable.

Tykistömuseo

There are numerous museums devoted to Finnish involvement in WWII, but this takes the cake. It's huge. The **artillery museum** (☎ 682 4600; adult/child €6/3; ⊗ 11am-5pm Oct-Mar, 10am-6pm Apr-Sep) consists of three floors packed with war memorabilia, and outside is a collection of phallic heavy artillery big enough to start a war on several fronts.

SIBELIUS MUSEUM

Johan Julius Christian (Jean) Sibelius (opposite) was born in Hämeenlinna in 1865 and went to school here, but surprisingly the town makes little fuss about this fact. His childhood home has been converted into a small **museum** (☎ 621 2755; Hallituskatu 11; adult/child €4/1; ⊗ 10am-4pm May-Aug, noon-4pm Sep-Apr) which contains photographs, letters, his upright piano and some family furniture. It's a likeable place, although uninformative about his life; a pianist often accompanies your visit with some of the man's music. There are also regular concert performances, free with an entry ticket.

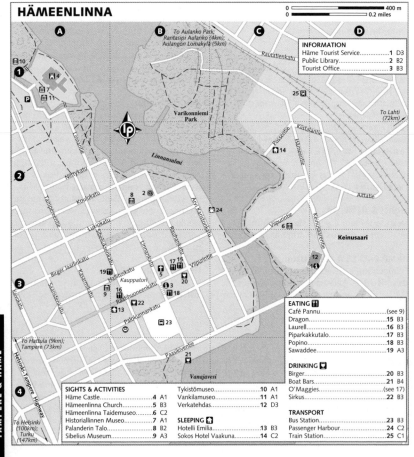

HÄMEENLINNA

0   400 m
0   0.2 miles

To Aulanko Park;
Rantasipi Aulanko (4km);
Aulangon Lomakylä (5km)

Rautatienkatu

To Lahti (72km)

Varikonniemi Park

Linnansalmi

Linnanranta

Niittykatu

Koulukatu

Tampereentie

Lukiokatu

Birger Jaarlinkatu

Kasarminkatu

Saaristenkatu

Hallituskatu

Kauppatori

Linnankatu

Arvi Karistonkatu

Raumankatu

Viipurintie

Possentie

Kustantie

Hämeentie

Aittatie

Keinusaari

Keinusaarentie

Kristalantie

Raatihuoneenkatu

Palokunnankatu

Paasikiventie

Vanajavesi

Helsinki-Tampere Highway

To Hattula (9km);
Tampere (73km)

To Helsinki (100km);
Turku (147km)

TAMPERE & HÄME

INFORMATION	
Häme Tourist Service	1 D3
Public Library	2 B2
Tourist Office	3 B3

SIGHTS & ACTIVITIES	
Häme Castle	4 A1
Hämeenlinna Church	5 B3
Hämeenlinna Taidemuseo	6 C2
Historiallinen Museo	7 A1
Palanderin Talo	8 B2
Sibelius Museum	9 A3
Tykistömuseo	10 A1
Vankilamuseo	11 A1
Verkatehdas	12 D3

SLEEPING	
Hotelli Emilia	13 B3
Sokos Hotel Vaakuna	14 C2

EATING	
Café Pannu	(see 9)
Dragon	15 B3
Laurell	16 B3
Piparkakkutalo	17 B3
Popino	18 B3
Sawaddee	19 A3

DRINKING	
Birger	20 B3
Boat Bars	21 B4
O'Maggies	(see 17)
Sirkus	22 B3

TRANSPORT	
Bus Station	23 B3
Passenger Harbour	24 C2
Train Station	25 C1

JEAN SIBELIUS

Leaving racing drivers out of the equation, good old Sibelius, born in 1865 in Hämeenlinna, probably still takes the garland of most famous Finn. Apart from his musical legacy, the role he played in the cultural flowering that inspired Finnish independence makes him a towering figure.

Like many artists of the time, Sibelius was fascinated by mythology and the forests at the heart of Finnishness. His first major works (*Kullervo, En Saga* and the *Karelia Suite*) were based on the *Kalevala* epic (p44), but his overtly political 1899 *Finlandia* symphony became a powerful symbol of the Finnish independence struggle and is still his best-known work.

Sibelius experimented with tonality and rejected the classical sonata form, building movements from a variety of short phrases that grow together as they develop. His work, particularly the early symphonies, is notable for its economical orchestration and melancholic mood.

Sibelius studied in Berlin and Vienna and visited the USA as an honorary doctor at Yale University. In later life he wrote incidental music for plays and a number of choral works and songs. He died in 1957, at the age of 92.

There are Sibelius connections all over Finland. A trail could lead from his monument in Helsinki (p91) to Ainola (p106), the country home where he lived with his wife Aino Järnefelt (sister of the painter Eero), and their six daughters. Then his birthplace in Hämeenlinna (opposite) and the excellent Sibelius Museum in Turku (p218), which frequently holds concerts. Festivals where you can hear his music include one in Loviisa (p125), where he had a summer home, and the Sibelius Festival in Lahti (p192), whose symphony orchestra is famed for its expertise in his works.

VERKATEHDAS

This attractive conversion of a former fabric mill looms large on the waterside across the bridge from the centre and has given Hämeenlinna a new **arts and functions complex** (☎ 621 6600; www.verkatehdas.fi; Paasikiventie 2), which includes a cinema, restaurant and theatre. Though it's not yet a hub of the community, it's worth a look if you're interested in urban renewal.

HÄMEENLINNAN TAIDEMUSEO

The town's pleasing **art museum** (☎ 621 2669; Viipurintie 2; admission €7; 🕙 11am-6pm Tue-Thu, 11am-5pm Fri-Sun) is housed in a former grain store designed by CL Engel and has an interesting collection of Finnish art from the 19th and 20th centuries. Notable is Gallen-Kallela's painting of the *Kalevala*'s final scene, with the shaman Väinämöinen leaving Finland, which demonstrates the arrival of Christianity. Other scenes from the epic are painted on the ceiling. There are a couple of Schjerfbecks, including a *Rigoletto* painted when she was just 19, and a beautiful wooden lynx and cubs by Jussi Mäntynen. The building opposite houses temporary exhibitions that are invariably excellent.

PALANDERIN TALO

Finland loves its house-museums and **our pick** **Palander House** (☎ 621 2967; Linnankatu 16; adult/child €4/1; 🕙 noon-3pm Jun-Aug, noon-3pm Sat & Sun Sep-May) is among the best, offering a wonderful insight into well-off 19th-century Finnish life, thanks to excellent English-speaking guided tours. There's splendid imperial and art nouveau furniture as well as delicate little touches like a double-sided mirror to spy on street fashion, and a set of authentic children's drawings from the period.

HÄMEENLINNA CHURCH

Dating from 1798 the town **church** (Linnankatu; 🕙 10am-6pm Jun-Aug, 11am-1pm Sep-May) was designed by Louis Jean Depréz, court painter for King Gustav III of Sweden. It is modelled on the Pantheon in Rome.

AULANKO PARK

This beautiful park, northeast of the town centre, was created early in the 20th century by Hugo Standertskjöld, who spent a fortune to create a central European–style park with ponds, swans, pavilions and exotic trees. Although the best way to explore it is on foot, the sealed one-way road loop is accessible by private car. An observation tower in a granite, fortress-style building is open daily in summer (free) and gives superb views. There's a nature trail in the park and a lakeside golf course.

Bus 2, 13 or 17 will take you to Aulanko from Hämeenlinna centre, but it's only 6km away (turn left on Aulangontie just east of the

TAMPERE & HÄME

railway tracks) and makes a pleasant bike ride. The park's **visitor centre** (☎ 621 3750; ☉ 10am-8pm Wed-Sun mid-Aug–May, daily Jun–mid-Aug) will supply you with a map.

Sleeping

Aulangon Lomakylä (☎ 675 9772; www.aulangonlomakyla .fi; Aulangonheikkiläntie 168; tent & caravan site €18, d/cabin/cottage €45/50/80; ☉ May-Sep; ⓟ wi-fi) Located beyond the main body of Aulanko Park on the shores of a lake, this excellent camping site offers cabins, cottages and simple bedrooms, as well as standard camping. It rents boats, bikes and fishing rods, and there's a restaurant and sauna.

Hotelli Emilia (☎ 612 2106; www.hotelliemilia.fi; Raatihuoneenkatu 23; s/d €94/114; ⓟ 🐕) Located on the pedestrian street, this privately owned hotel is a good deal. Sizeable modern rooms, some of which can be connected for families, offer large windows, crisp white sheets and air-conditioning. There's a bar with terrace seating, a sauna, weekend nightclub and worthwhile buffet breakfast. Summer specials drop room rates further than listed here.

Sokos Hotel Vaakuna (☎ 020-123 4636; www.sokos hotels.fi; Possentie 7; s/d €100/120; ⓟ 🖵 wi-fi) Across the river from the town centre and very near the train station, this attractive modern hotel has been designed to echo Häme Castle. Many of the rooms have great water views, as does the rounded restaurant, and the sunny bar terrace is particularly pleasant on a summer evening.

Rantasipi Aulanko (☎ 658 801; www.rantasipi.fi; d €134-184; ⓟ 🐕 🖵 🍴 wi-fi) This lakeside place in Aulanko Park is enormous, with a huge range of facilities including a popular spa complex, numerous saunas and restaurants, and an adjacent golf course. It's very family friendly, with heaps to keep the young entertained, and large multibed rooms. Various packages are available from travel agents or online that include features such as meals or golf.

Eating

Laurell (☎ 467 7722; Sibeliuksenkatu 7; pastries €2-3; ☉ 8.30am-6pm Mon-Fri, 8.30am-4pm Sat, 11am-5pm Sun) This spacious cafe on the kauppatori is a Hämeenlinna stalwart and popular meeting place. There's an appetising selection of squishy cakes, rolls, pastries and pasties, and another branch in the same building as the tourist office.

Café Pannu (☎ 612 2244; Hallituskatu 13; lunch €6-8; ☉ 9am-4pm Mon-Fri, 9am-3pm Sat) Tucked away behind Sibelius' birthplace, this typical Finnish lunching place has a Greek touch. Good-value soups, salads and hot dishes draw local workers daily, who take advantage of the outdoor seating on sunny days.

Popino (☎ 653 2555; Raatihuoneenkatu 11; pizzas €9-13, mains €13-25; ☉ 11am-10pm Mon-Sat, noon-8pm Sun) Just behind the tourist office, this fine pizza and pasta restaurant is well loved by locals. As well as pizza there are meat and fish dishes and lunch specials for €8 to €12. It's an informal, family friendly spot, with classic gingham tablecloths and a play area for young kids.

Piparkakkutalo (☎ 648 040; Kirkkorinne 2; most mains €13-19; ☉ 11am-11pm Mon-Thu, noon-midnight Fri & Sat, noon-8pm Sun) Pleasing for both eye and stomach, the 'gingerbread house' is set in an historic 1906 shingled house that was once home to artist Albert Edelfelt; the interior still has a warm, domestic feel. The food includes Finnish classics as well as more adventurous fare like quail in chocolate sauce; all are served in generous portions.

Also recommended:

Dragon (☎ 612 1858; Raatihuoneenkatu 8a; mains €10-18; ☉ 11am-9pm Tue-Fri, noon-9pm Sat & Sun) This Chinese restaurant is in a cellar on the town's main street; though not cheap, the portions are generous and the service good.

Sawaddee (☎ 044-073 7007; Sibeliuksenkatu 13; dishes €9-12; ☉ 11am-3pm Mon, 11am-8pm Tue-Thu, 11am-10pm Fri & Sat, noon-8pm Sun) Friendly Thai place with lunch for €7.80 and takeaway options.

Drinking & Entertainment

In summer two adjacent **boat bars** (Paasikiventie; ☉ from 11am) offer relaxed lakeside drinking on floating wooden decks. Though almost identical, Teemu is the earthier of the two, while Tyyne is more upmarket, with geranium boxes and beer served in glasses.

Birger (☎ 5709777; Raatihuoneenkatu 5; ☉ 4pm-midnight Sun-Thu, to 2am Fri-Sat) The dark candlelit interior of this relaxing pub resembles a ship's saloon with its low-hanging lamps and conspiratorial booth seating. They have an excellent range of bottled beer from around the world, plus interesting draught choices, and a few wines.

O'Maggie's (☎ 648 0450; Kirkkorinne 2; ☉ from 4pm Mon-Sat) Underneath the Piparkakkutalo restaurant (above), this cosy Irish pub is one for chilly nights, with a convivial hidden-away feel and occasional live Celtic music.

Sirkus (☎ 633 6391; Sibeliuksenkatu 2; admission €5-10; ☉ 10pm-4am Fri & Sat) Just down from the square, this place offers live music, both rock and softer sounds, every Friday night, and a 24-and-over nightclub on Saturdays that's more sophisticated and less rowdy than the town's other late choices on and around the square.

Getting There & Away

BOAT

Departing from Hämeenlinna's passenger harbour, **Suomen Hopealinja** (Finnish Silverline; ☎ 03-212 3889; www.hopealinja.fi) cruises to Visavuori (one-way/return €31/47, three hours) at 11.30am, Tuesday to Saturday between June and mid-August. From Wednesday to Saturday, you can continue to Tampere (one-way €41, 8½ hours).

BUS

Hourly buses between Helsinki (€20.90, 1½ hours) and Tampere (€16.40, one hour) stop in Hämeenlinna. From Turku, there are eight buses daily (€26.20, two hours).

TRAIN

The train station is 1km from the town centre, across the bridge. Hourly trains between Helsinki (€15.60, one hour) and Tampere (€13.20, 40 minutes) stop here. From Turku (€22, 1¾ hours), change in Toijala.

HÄMEENLINNA TO TAMPERE

Several interesting sights lie just off the main Tampere–Hämeenlinna highway.

Pyhän Ristin Kirkko (☎ 672 3383; admission €3; 🕙 11am-5pm Jun-Aug) in Hattula, only 9km north of Hämeenlinna, is one of Finland's oldest and most memorable churches. Dating from the early 1400s, the interior is filled with fabulous naive frescoes from the early 16th century. They tell the key stories of the Bible as you go around the nave; the Tree of Jesse in the sacristy is particularly fine. As this was the nearest that most of the parishioners of the time ever got to being able to read, it must have been an awe-inspiring place for them and it still is. Nearby, the **old grain store** houses the information office and sells handicrafts.

The church is easy to reach from Hämeenlinna by public transport; take bus 5, 6 or 16. Take something warm to wear if you plan a lengthy look at the interior.

Iittala

Little Iittala, 23km northwest of Hämeenlinna, is world-famous for the glass produced in its factory, and has been at the forefront of Finnish design for decades.

Behind the large **shop** (☎ 020-439 3512; 🕙 10am-6pm Sep-Apr, 9am-8pm May-Aug) and restaurant, a charming craft village includes chocolate shop, ceramics and gold studios, and the **Lasimuseo** (Glass Museum; ☎ 020-439 6230; admission €3; 🕙 10am-6pm daily May-Aug, 10am-5pm Sat & Sun Sep-Dec), whose two levels cover the history of the Iittala glassworks as well as the glass-making process, with pieces from most of the firm's famous ranges on display. Free tours of the nearby factory leave from here at noon from Monday to Friday; otherwise you can watch a glassblower at work in an adjacent shop. The main shop, though sizeable, doesn't offer more than similar Iittala/Arabia/Hackman shops elsewhere in Finland.

Four to six daily trains running between Hämeenlinna (13 minutes) and Tampere (€7.80, 45 minutes) stop at the station in the centre of town and five buses run here Monday to Friday from Hämeenlinna (€5.20, 30 minutes). Tampere–Hämeenlinna express buses stop on the highway 2km from town.

Sääksmäki

This historic and scenic area northwest of Hämeenlinna is one of the region's highlights.

Rapolan Linnavuori is the largest prehistoric fortress in Finland. There are fine views and you can follow a marked trail that will take you to 100 burial mounds on the western side of the hill. You can get to Rapola either following the signs from the main road, about 25km northwest of Hämeenlinna, or by taking the narrow road, Rapolankuja, that passes by the privately owned Rapola estate.

Once the studio of Emil Wickström (1864–1942), a sculptor from the National Romantic era, **Visavuori** (☎ 03-543 6528; adult/child €6/1; 🕙 10am-6pm daily Jun-Aug, 10am-4pm Tue-Sun Sep-Nov & Feb-May, 10am-4pm Tue-Fri Dec-Jan) is the best-known sight in the region. Stunningly situated on a ridge with water on both sides, it consists of three houses, the oldest of which was the home of Wickström, built in 1902 in Karelian and Finnish Romantic styles and containing fantastic art nouveau furniture; it really brings the man to life and is worth visiting first. Wickström was the curse of the local boatmen, who used to have to deliver huge slabs of marble. The beautiful studio next door, with dozens of models and sculptures, was built in

TAMPERE & HÄME

THE OX ROAD

The **Härkätie**, or Ox Rd, is one of the oldest trade conduits in Finland; it connected Turku and Hämeenlinna and was also an important pilgrimage route. Despite the name, most traffic was horse-drawn. There's good information in Hämeenlinna, in towns along the way, and at www .harkatie.net.

The first stop, **Renko**, is 15km southwest of Hämeenlinna: its church, Pyhän Jaakonkirkko, is a 15th-century structure with a curious octagonal shape. Next door is the erratically open local museum, a basic display of farming implements and clerical tools; upstairs are the carts and harnesses used for traditional transport.

Tammela village is on the shores of Pyhäjärvi, 11km north of Porras and the Ox Rd. It stretches along the lake and is a service centre for the summer cottages around. Its church, of prodigious length, originally dates from the early 16th century. North of the village, impressive **Mustiala Manor** (☎ 03-646 5519; ⏰ 10am-4pm Mon-Fri, also 11am-3pm Sat in summer) is a 16th-century estate which houses an agricultural school, a small museum devoted to farming tools, and a brewery and restaurant.

Four kilometres east of central Tammela, peaceful **Venesilta** (☎ 03-436 0077; Portaantie 225; tent sites €15 plus per person €1, cabins €40-50, cottages €90-120; P) camp site is lakeside and one of the best places to bed down in the area.

The Ox Rd town of **Somero** was founded in the 15th century. The *kivisakasti*, a stone building on the grounds of the old church, dates from that time. The church itself dates from 1859. **Someron torpparimuseo** (⏰ summer), the local museum north of the centre, includes a windmill and ancient peasants' houses.

Further on, Jokioinen's little **church** (1631), 1km past the granary, is the second-oldest wooden church in Finland but renovations hide the original architecture.

Near Jokioinen, **Forssa** is the largest town in the region. Originally built on the cotton-spinning industry, it's not a particularly enthralling place, but has plenty of accommodation options and a tourist office.

Regular buses link Hämeenlinna and Renko and the other towns mentioned. Local buses connect the rest of the towns, mainly coming from the large industrial town of Forssa. However, it's easiest to explore the Ox Rd by private car or bicycle.

1903; the pervasive smell of baking will force you to stop for a *pulla* (cardamon-flavoured bun) in the brick-vaulted cafe downstairs. Kari Paviljonki is dedicated to Kari Suomalainen, Emil Wickström's grandson. The best known of Finland's political cartoonists, his long career spanned several decades and he was drawing up to his death in 1999. His cartoons are excellent; the ones that can be, are translated well. Even more amusing is the award from the US National Cartoonist Society in 1959 for his daring cartoons 'exposing the deceit of communism'. Ferries from Hämeenlinna and Tampere stop at Visavuori in summer. Visavuori is 4km east of the Hämeenlinna–Tampere motorway, just off the road to Toijala.

TAMPERE

☎ 03 / pop 207,866

For many visitors, Tampere is Finland's number one city, and it's easy to see why. It combines Nordic sophistication with urban vitality and a scenic location between two vast lakes. Through its centre churn the Tammerkoski rapids, whose grassy banks contrast with the red brick of the imposing but picturesque fabric-mill chimneys that once gave the city the moniker 'Manchester of Finland'.

A popular weekend destination from Britain thanks to its budget flight connection, Tampere doesn't disappoint: its students ensure plenty of evening action, and its regenerated industrial buildings house quirky museums, enticing shops, pubs, cinemas and cafes. It's the launch pad for Finland's most romantic lake cruise, and a spot where there always seems to be something going on: its leap into the 21st century has given it an infectious energy.

HISTORY

In the Middle Ages, the area around Tampere was inhabited by the Pirkka tribe, a devil-may-care guild of hunters and trappers who collected taxes as far north as Lapland. Modern Tampere was founded in 1779 during the reign of Sweden's Gustav III.

During the 19th century, the Tammerkoski rapids, which today supply abundant hydroelectric power, were a magnet for textile industries. The busy town was inundated by both Finnish and foreign investors.

The Russian Revolution in 1917 increased interest in socialism among Tampere's large working-class population. It became the capital of the 'Reds' during the civil war that followed Finnish independence.

ORIENTATION
Tampere is set between Näsijärvi and Pyhäjärvi, which are connected by the Tammerkoski. Just about everything is conveniently arranged along one street, Hämeenkatu, with the train station at its eastern end.

INFORMATION
Bookshops
Akateeminen Kirjakauppa (☎ 248 0111; Hämeenkatu 6; 🕙 9am-9pm Mon-Fri, 9am-6pm Sat, noon-6pm Sun) Extensive selection of English-language books.

Emergency
Phone ☎ 112 in any emergency. To report a crime, phone ☎ 219 5111, or visit the police station at Sorinkatu 12.

Internet Access
In addition to the following, there are free terminals in the tourist office and at Vapriikki museum centre (p203).
Internet Café Madi (☎ 050-922 2346; Tuomiokirkonkatu 36; per hr €3; 🕙 10am-10pm Mon-Fri, 11am-10pm Sat & Sun) Free tea and coffee.
Log-In (☎ 040-770 6766; Hämeenkatu 30; per hr €3; 🕙 10am-10pm Mon-Fri, 11am-10pm Sat & Sun) Free coffee.
Tampere city library (Metso; ☎ 565 614; Pirkankatu 2; 🕙 10am-8pm Mon-Fri, 10am-4pm Sat, 11am-5pm Sun Sep-May, 10am-7pm Mon-Fri Jun-Aug) Named after the capercaillie because of its unusual architecture. Has several internet terminals, some first-come-first-served (15-minute time limit).

Laundry
Sol (☎ 042-457 6027; Aleksis Kivenkatu 10) Laundry service at €5.30 per kilogram.

Left Luggage
The train station has lockers for €3 to €4 per 24 hours, depending on size, as well as a left-luggage counter. Lockers at the bus station cost €2 for 24 hours.

Medical Services
Dial ☎ 10023 between 7am and 10pm to get an on-call doctor.
Hatanpää Hospital (☎ 565 713; Hatanpäänkatu 24) The main city hospital.

Money
Forex (☎ 020-751 2620; www.forex.fi; Hämeenkatu 4; 🕙 9am-9pm Mon-Fri, 9am-6pm Sat, noon-6pm Sun) Moneychangers in the Stockmann Building. There's another branch by the main square, open shorter hours.

Tourist Information
GoTampere Oy (tourist office; ☎ 5656 6800; www .gotampere.fi; Rautatienkatu 25; 🕙 9am-5pm Mon-Fri Jan-May, 9am-8pm Mon-Fri, 9.30am-5pm Sat & Sun Jun-Aug, 9am-5pm Mon-Fri, 9.30am-5pm Sat & Sun Sep, 9am-5pm Mon-Fri, 11am-3pm Sat & Sun Oct-Dec) The city's main tourist office, in the railway station. Has internet terminals and takes bookings for car hire, cruises, accommodation and city tours.

Travel Agencies
Kilroy Travels (☎ 020-354 5769; www.kilroytravels.fi, in Finnish, Swedish, Norwegian, Danish & Dutch; Tuomiokirkonkatu 34; 🕙 10am-6pm Mon-Fri) Deals in all travel including student and discount fares.

SIGHTS
Finlayson Centre
Tampere's era as an industrial city began with the arrival of Scot James Finlayson, who established a small workshop by the Tammerkoski in 1820. He later erected a huge cotton mill; the massive red-brick building was the first in the Nordic countries to have electric lighting, which started operating in 1882. It has now been sensitively converted into a mall of cafes and shops; you'll also find a cinema here, as well as a great brewery-pub and a couple of intriguing museums.

VAKOILUMUSEO
The offbeat **spy museum** (☎ 212 3007; www.vakoilumuseo.fi; Satakunnankatu 18; adult/child €7/5.50; 🕙 noon-6pm Mon-Sat, 11am-5pm Sun May-Aug, 11am-5pm daily Sep-Apr) under the Finlayson centre plays to the budding secret agent in all of us, with a

TAMPERE & HÄME

TAMPERE

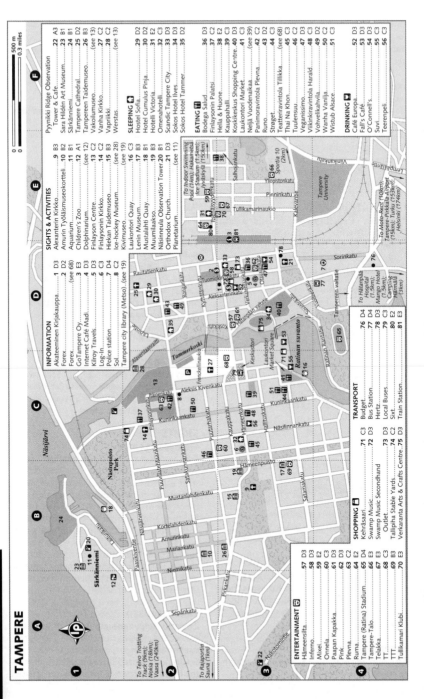

large and well-assembled display of devices of international espionage, mainly from the Cold War era. As well as histories of famous Finnish and foreign spies, it has numerous Bond-style gadgets and some interactive displays – write your name in invisible ink, tap a telephone call, intercept an email or measure the microwave emissions of your mobile. The folders with English translations are slightly unsatisfying though. For a little extra, the kids can take a suitability test for KGB cadet school.

WERSTAS

The **Labour Museum** (☎ 253 8800; www.tyoavaenmuseo .fi; Väinö Linnanaukio 8; adult/child €5/free; ⏰ 11am-6pm Tue-Sun) is dedicated to the history of working and of workers' movements, with a variety of changing exhibitions covering social history and labour industries. There's particularly good coverage of the steam engine, with the highlight one of the enormous wheels that powered up the Finlayson factory in the 19th century.

Other Museums

VAPRIIKKI

Tampere's premier exhibition space is **Vapriikki** (☎ 5656 6966; www.tampere.fi/vapriikki; Veturiaukio 4; adult/child from €5/1; ⏰ 10am-6pm Tue & Thu-Sun, 11am-8pm Wed), a bright, modern glass and steel gallery in the renovated Tampella textile mill. As well as regularly changing exhibitions on anything from bicycles to Buddhism, there's a permanent display on Tampere's history from prehistoric times to the present as well as a small but cluttered **ice-hockey museum**, with memorabilia of the players and teams that star in Finland's sporting passion. There's also a museum of shoes – Tampere was known for its footwear industry – and a pleasant cafe.

LENIN-MUSEO

Admirers of bearded revolutionaries won't want to miss the small **Lenin museum** (☎ 276 8100; www.lenin.fi; Hämeenpuisto 28; adult/child €5/2; ⏰ 9am-6pm Mon-Fri, 11am-4pm Sat & Sun), housed in the Workers' Hall where Lenin and Stalin first met at a conference in 1905 (see p34 for more on Lenin's time in Finland). His life is documented by way of photos and documents; it's a little dry but it's fascinating to see, for example, his old school report (a straight-A student) or a threadbare couch that the man slept on. One note, penned shortly before his death in 1924, recommends Comrade Stalin

to be ousted from his position as General Secretary. There's a crazy gift shop where you can buy Lenin pens, badges, T-shirts and other souvenirs of the Soviet era.

MUUMILAAKSO

Explore the creation of Tove Jansson's enduringly popular Moomins in the **Moomin Valley museum** (☎ 5656 6578; Hämeenpuisto 20; adult/child €4/1; ⏰ 9am-5pm Mon-Fri, 10am-6pm Sat & Sun, closed Mon Sep-May) in the basement of the public library building. It contains original drawings and elaborate models depicting stories from Moomin Valley (English explanations available), computer displays, toys and other memorabilia. Naturally, there's a gift shop.

KIVIMUSEO

Adjacent to the Moomin museum is the small **mineral museum** (☎ 5656 6046; Hämeenpuisto 20; adult/child €4/1; ⏰ 9am-5pm Mon-Fri, 10am-6pm Sat & Sun, closed Mon Sep-May), with a huge array of delicate, spectacular crystal formations and vivid colours, as well as fossils that include dinosaur eggs. Needless to say, although it has the same hours as Moomin Valley, it doesn't have the same crowds.

HIEKAN TAIDEMUSEO & TAMPEREEN TAIDEMUSEO

The collection of Kustaa Hiekka (1855–1937), a wealthy industrialist, is contained in the **Hiekka museum** (☎ 212 3973; Pirkankatu 6; adult/child €5/3; ⏰ 3-6pm Tue-Thu, noon-3pm Sun). There are paintings, furniture and fine old gold and silver items in the impressive building.

A block further west, **Tampereen Taidemuseo** (Tampere Art Museum; ☎ 5656 6577; www.tampere.fi/taide museo; Puutarhakatu 34) has good-quality changing exhibitions of mostly contemporary art.

AMURIN TYÖLÄISMUSEOKORTTELI

An entire block of 19th-century wooden houses, including 32 apartments, a bakery, a shoemaker, two general shops and a cafe is preserved in the **Amuri Museum of Workers' Housing** (☎ 5656 6690; Satakunnankatu 49; adult/child €5/1; ⏰ 10am-6pm Tue-Sun May–mid-Sep). It's one of the most realistic house-museums in Finland – many homes look as if the tenant has left just moments ago to go shopping.

Särkänniemi

On the northern edge of town, this promontory **amusement park** (☎ 020-713 0200; www.sarkan niemi.fi;

adult/child day pass up to €30/25; noon-7pm mid-May–Aug) is a large complex with several attractions, including a good art gallery and an aquarium. There's a bewildering system of entry tickets and opening times depending on what your interest is, and it is cheaper to book online. A day pass is valid for all sights and unlimited rides, while €8 will get you up the observation tower, and into the gallery and farm zoo. To get to Särkänniemi, take bus 4 from the train station.

Inside the amusement park are 30 **rides** including the 'Tornado super rollercoaster', plus cafes and restaurants. The **aquarium** (noon-7pm mid-May–Aug, plus 11am-9pm in winter) has limited information in English and isn't especially memorable, with the Finnish fish (including some rare sturgeon relatives) more interesting than the colourful hobby-tank favourites. The **planetarium**, with daily shows, is in the same complex, above which soars the 168m-high **Näsinneula Observation Tower** (11am-11.30pm). This is the tallest such tower in these northern lands and it alone is worth the visit, with spectacular views of the city and surrounding lakes. There's a revolving restaurant near the top.

Opposite, the **Dolphinarium** has five cheerful bottlenoses who put on a show one to five times per day in summer. At other times of the year you can watch them training. Nearby is the **children's zoo**, with gentle domestic animals.

On a different note, the complex also contains the **Sara Hildén art museum** (5654 3500; 11am-6pm Tue-Sun Sep–mid-May, noon-7pm daily mid-May–Aug), which has a collection of international and Finnish modern art and sculpture amassed by Sara Hildén, a local businessperson and art collector. The space is normally devoted to excellent exhibitions showcasing particular artists. There are good views from the cafe.

Churches

Intriguing **Tampere Cathedral** (Tuomiokirkonkatu 3; 9am-6pm May-Aug, 11am-3pm Sep-Apr) is one of the most notable examples of National Romantic architecture in Finland. It was designed by Lars Sonck and completed in 1907. The famous artist Hugo Simberg was responsible for the frescoes and stained glass; once you've seen them you'll appreciate that they were controversial at the time. A procession of ghostly childlike apostles holds the

'garland of life', the garden of death shows graves and plants tended by skeletal figures, while another image shows a wounded angel being stretchered off by two children. There's a solemn, almost mournful feel about it; the altarpiece, by Magnus Enckell, is a dreamlike Resurrection in similar style. The symbolist stonework and disturbing colours of the stained glass add to the haunting ambience.

The small, ornate, onion-domed **Orthodox Church** (Tuomiokirkonkatu 3; 11am-5pm Tue-Fri, noon-4pm Sun May-Aug), near the train station, is also worth a visit. During the Civil War, White troops besieged the church, which had been taken over by the Reds.

The landmark **Vanha Kirkko** (Keskustori; 10am-3pm May-Aug, 11am-1pm Sep-Apr) on the central square is a lovely old wooden building and has occasional gospel concerts on Saturday evenings.

Other notable churches include the beautiful **Alexanterin Kirkko** (Pirkankatu; 11am-3pm), with its red brick and green spires and which was named for the Tsar Alexander II, and the **Finlaysonin Kirkko** (Puuvillatehtaankatu 2; 10am-6pm), built for employees of the cotton mill and their families.

Pyynikki Ridge

Rising between Tampere's two lakes, this is a forested area of walking and cycling trails with fine views on both sides. It soars 85m above the shores of the lake – this is an Everest by Finnish standards – and claims to be the highest gravel ridge in the world. There's a stone **observation tower** (adult/child €1/0.50; 9am-8pm) on the ridge, and a cafe at the bottom serving Tampere's best doughnuts. You can easily walk to the tower, or take westbound bus 15 to its terminus and walk back from there along the ridge.

ACTIVITIES

Traditional **Rajaportin Sauna** (222 3823; Pispalan Valtatie 9; adult/child €5/1; 6-10pm Wed, 3-9pm Fri, 2-10pm Sat) is Finland's oldest operating public sauna. It's a great chance to experience the softer steam from a traditionally heated sauna rather than the harsher electric ones. It's a couple of kilometres west of the centre; buses 1, 13, 18, 19 and 26 head out there. There's a cafe onsite, and massages can be arranged. Take a towel or rent one there.

To **fish** in the Tammerkoski in the town centre, you will need a daily (€4.50) or weekly (€16) permit, available from the tourist office, among other places. The tourist office also has a list of operators who run guided fishing tours in the lakes and rivers in the area, which is known for pike and pike-perch. The website www.zanderland.fi has useful information about fishing in the Tampere area.

You can rent **rowing boats** and **canoes** from Camping Härmälä (p206) among other places. Bikes can be hired at **Sportia 10** (☎ 225 0000; Sammonkatu 60) or **Hertz** (☎ 020-555 2400; Rautatienkatu 28) and jet-skis, skis and kayaks from **Moto-Rent** (☎ 379 2778; www.kangasalan motorent.fi, in Finnish; Lentolantie 21, Kangasala), based in Kangasala, 10km southeast, but happy to deliver stuff to town.

Ten kilometres northwest of Tampere on Rd 3, **Teivo Trotting Track** (☎ 315 481; www.teivon ravit.fi, in Finnish) offers another popular, reader-recommended, Finnish experience. There are races nearly every Tuesday evening at 6pm, and entry is free, though you can bet as much as you like. Special buses from town run to the track on race evenings. In winter the horses race on compacted snow under floodlights.

The best-equipped **indoor swimming pool** (Tampereen Uintikeskus; ☎ 5656 4812; Joukahaisenkatu 7; adult/child €5/2.20; ⏱ 6am-7.45pm Mon-Fri, 10am-4.45pm Sat & Sun, closed Tue morning) lies about 1.5km east of the train station.

The town website www.tampere.fi has plenty more ideas for getting active in and around Tampere.

TOURS

You can get an overview of Tampere's attractions on a **bus tour** (adult/child €13/4; ⏱ 2pm mid-Jun–Aug). These depart from in front of the GoTampere Oy tourist office and cover the main sights, taking about two hours, with commentary in Finnish and English.

The tourist office can also book you a **walking tour** (90 min tour adult/child €5/2; ⏱ late Jun–mid-Aug) of the city. The Tampere in a Nutshell walk covers the major sights, while there's a variety of other themed walks. You can also book personal tours in taxis.

CRUISES

Trips on Tampere's two magnificent lakes are extremely popular in summer and there are plenty of options. Trips on Näsijärvi leave from Mustalahti Quay, while Laukontori Quay serves Pyhäjärvi. All cruises can be booked at the tourist office.

Suomen Hopealinja (Finnish Silverline; ☎ 212 4804; www.hopealinja.fi) runs a variety of cruises. From Laukontori Quay, short cruises run on Pyhäjärvi from June to August, as well as a shuttle service (adult/child return €8/2) to nearby **Viikinsaari**, a pleasant picnic island with a beach, barbecues and a good restaurant. At Laukontori Quay, the *Laiva* vessel does lunch (€20, Tuesday to Sunday May to September) and dinner (€27, Tuesday to Saturday May to August) jaunts with live entertainment.

From Mustalahti Quay, the glorious steamship **SS Tarjanne** (☎ 010-422 5600; www.runoilijantie.fi) does evening cruises on Näsijärvi with an optional dinner on Thursdays and some Saturdays in summer, but is best boarded for the **Poet's Way**, one of the finest lake cruises in Finland. A one-way ticket costs €36 to Ruovesi (4¾ hours) and €47 to Virrat (8¼ hours). For €30 per person, you can sleep in this old boat before or after your trip. Day use of a cabin is also €30. Bicycles can be taken on board for a small fee. You can book a day trip to Virrat (€62) or Ruovesi (€51), with one of the legs made by bus.

The same company also runs cruises between Tampere and Hämeenlinna; see p210.

FESTIVALS & EVENTS

There are events in Tampere almost year-round. Some of the best include:

Tampere Film Festival (www.tamperefilmfestival.fi) A respected international festival of short films usually held in early March.

Tampere Biennale (www.tampere.fi) A festival of new Finnish music, held in April of even-numbered years.

Pispala Schottische (www.sottiisi.net, in Finnish) An international folk-dance festival, which takes place in early June.

Tammerfest (www.tammerfest.fi, in Finnish) The city's premier rock-music festival, held over four days in mid-July with concerts at various stages around town.

Tampere International Theatre Festival (www.teatterikesa.fi) Held in early August, this is a showcase of international and Finnish theatre.

Off-Tampere (www.teatterikesa.fi) The city's fringe festival, held at the same time as the International Theatre Festival.

Tampere Jazz Happening (www.tampere.fi) An award-winning event featuring Finnish and international jazz musicians in October or early November.

Tampere Illuminations (www.tampere.fi) The city streets are brightened by 40,000 coloured lights between mid-October and early January.

TAMPERE & HÄME

SLEEPING
Budget
Camping Härmälä (☎ 265 1355; www.fontana.fi; Leirintäkatu 8; tent sites €12 plus per person €4, 2–5-person cabins €42-70; ☺ mid-May–Aug; **P**) Four kilometres south of the centre (take bus 1), this is a spacious site on the Pyhäjärvi lakeshore. There's a cafe, saunas and rowing boats, as well as an adjacent summer hotel (singles/doubles €40/54; open June to Aug), with self-contained rooms.

Hostel Sofia (☎ 254 4020; www.hostelsofia.fi; Tuomiokirkonkatu 12a; dm/s/d €25/45/65; **P** 🖳 wi-fi) Tampere's only hostel is right opposite the cathedral and fills up fast. A recent refit has left it looking very spruce, offering rooms with comfortable beds (no bunks), large windows and stepladder shelves, as well as good showers and a kitchenette on every colour-coded floor. YHA members save €2.50, and breakfast and laundry are available. If you're going to arrive late, they'll text you a door code.

Omenahotelli (☎ 020-771 6555; www.omenahotelli.fi; Hämeenkatu 28; r to €65; 🖳) At the western end of the main drag, this receptionless hotel offers the usual comfortable rooms with twin beds, microwave, kettle and a fold-out couch. Internet is expensive but the rooms are great value for a family of four or two couples. Breakfast is available downstairs for an extra €6.50. Book online or via the terminal at the entrance.

Mango Hotel (www.mangohotel.fi; Hatanpään puistokuja 36; s/d €59/79; **P** wi-fi) Unromantically set in a commercial district 20 minutes' walk south of the centre, this unstaffed hotel nevertheless represents value. The rooms – strange, with fake gilt baroque furnishings in pseudo-Asian style – are comfortable enough and share a bathroom between two. Wi-fi and simple breakfast are included, and there's free laundry. Book online or at the door. Buses 1, 3, 6, 7 and 21 get you there.

Midrange & Top End
Sokos Hotel Tammer (☎ 020-123 4632; www.sokoshotels.fi; Satakunnankatu 13; r €130; **P** 🖳 wi-fi) Constructed in 1929, this is one of Finland's oldest hotels and enjoys a fine rapids-side location. After the gloriously old-fashioned elegance of the public areas, the rooms, behind ornate doors, are a little disappointing, though they have the expected facilities and Nordic comfort levels. Parking is very limited; a good breakfast buffet and sauna are included.

Sokos Hotel Ilves (☎ 020-123 4631; www.sokoshotels.fi; Hatanpään valtatie 1; s/d €130/140; **P** 🔀 🖳 🐕 🚴 wi-fi) This huge tower hotel has over three hundred rooms, bright with turquoise paint and light wood, and offering excellent views over the heart of town or the Tammerkoski below. Superiors have bigger beds and extras like bathrobes and bottled water, and there's a variety of excellent suites. It's a busy centre, with several restaurants, a popular nightclub and good business facilities. As well as the saunas, there's an enticing Jacuzzi. As with all Sokos hotels, rates vary according to demand; above prices are a guide.

Hotelli Victoria (☎ 242 5111; www.hotellivictoria.fi; Itsenäisyydenkatu 1; s/d €109/14; **P** 🖳 🐕 wi-fi) Just on the other side of the railway station from the centre, this friendly hotel offers sound summer value with its spruce rooms, free internet and commendable breakfast spread including waffles, sausage omelette and berry pudding options. Rooms are light and quiet despite the busy road and there's a good sauna. It's closed most of December.

Hotel Cumulus Pinja (☎ 241 5111; www.cumulus.fi; Satakunnankatu 10; s/d €123/148; **P** 🖳 wi-fi) Around the corner from the cathedral, this elegant art nouveau choice features compact, recently renovated rooms and an intimate feel that's complemented by the quiet, appealing district and friendly, personal service. There are also suites with sauna and balcony.

our pick **Scandic Tampere City** (☎ 244 6111; www.scandic-hotels.com; Rautatienkatu 16; s/d €155/175; **P** 🔀 🖳 🐕 wi-fi) Right opposite the train station, this hotel has modern Nordic lines and a fistful of facilities including sauna, gym, various restaurants and a cocktail bar. The rooms are spacious and spotless with a clean wooden feel. Superiors are almost identical, but have coffee tray and a comfier chair. The hotel has a family friendly feel and you can borrow bikes or walking poles from reception.

EATING
Tampere's speciality, *mustamakkara*, is a mild sausage made with cow's blood, black-pudding style. It's normally eaten with lingonberry jam and is tastier than it sounds. You can get it at the kauppahalli (covered market) or a kiosk at Laukontori market.

Restaurants
BUDGET
Strøget (☎ 222 6490; Laukontori 10; sandwiches €5-8; ☺ 10.30am-5pm Mon-Fri, 11am-4pm Sat) A small bright spot at the quay, this place specialises

in spectacular Danish open sandwiches, huge things brimming with tasty fresh ingredients, as well as burgers and American-style tuna and club sandwiches. Outdoor seating lets you watch the marketplace and boating action.

our pick **Neljä Vuodenaikaa** (☎ 212 4712; Kauppahalli; dishes €7-15; 11am-4pm Mon-Fri, 11am-2.30pm Sat) Tucked into a corner of the kauppahalli, this recommended spot brings Gallic flair to the Finnish lunch hour with delicious plates like bouillabaisse and French country salad augmented by excellent daily specials and wines by the glass.

Thai Na Khon (☎ 212 1778; Hämeenkatu 29; lunch buffet €7.50, mains €12-18; 11am-9pm Mon-Fri, noon-10pm Sat, noon-9pm Sun) This Thai restaurant at the centre's western end is soothingly and tastefully decorated, with plush seats, varnished tables and a colonial-era feel. The mains are generously proportioned and come with rice; the menu has an English translation and spiciness key, as well as plenty of vegetarian choices.

Veganissimo (☎ 213 0323; Otavalankatu 10; mains €9-15; 11am-8pm Mon-Tue, 11am-10pm Wed-Thu, 11am-midnight Fri, 1pm-midnight Sat, 1-7pm Sun) A short stroll from the station brings you to this pleasing new vegan restaurant with smart contemporary decor and good vibes. Lunch (€7 to €9) is a bargain, with delicious salads; evenings offer a quieter ambience, with dishes like paella, seitan fillet and big burgers available, as well as various tapas-sized portions and organic wines.

Panimoravintola Plevna (☎ 260 1200; Itäinenkatu 8; mains €9-24; kitchen 11am-10pm) Inside the old Finlayson textile mill, this big barn of a place offers a wide range of delicious beer, cider and perry brewed on the premises, including an excellent strong stout. Meals are large and designed to soak it all up: massive sausage platters and enormous slabs of pork in classic beer-hall style as well as more Finnish fish and steak dishes. Vegetables here mean potatoes and onions, preferably fried, but it's all tasty, and service is fast.

Tuulensuu (☎ 214 1553; Hämeenpuisto 23; mains €13-20; kitchen 5pm-midnight Sun-Fri, noon-midnight Sat mid-Jun–Aug) The best of a range of gastropubs that have recently sprouted, this corner spot has a fine range of beers and wines, as well as a lengthy port and cigar menu. The food is lovingly prepared and features staples like liver and schnitzel as well as more elaborate plates like duck comfit. Even the bar snacks are gourmet: fresh-roasted almonds.

MIDRANGE & TOP END

Viikinkiravintola Harald (☎ 213 8380; Hämeenkatu 23; mains €13-24; 11am-midnight Mon-Thu, 11am-1am Fri, noon-1am Sat, 1-9pm Sun) With a dragon-ship salad bar, stuffed animals, costumed waiters and long-hall wooden tables, this Viking-theme restaurant isn't subtle but is plenty of fun. Dishes all bear Norse-sounding names and feature big steaks and game choices. Signature dishes are shared platters served on a shield, or enormous vegetable or meat kebabs speared on a sword.

Teatteriravintola Tillikka (☎ 010-767 2300; Hämeenkatu 14; lunch €7-9, mains €13-30; kitchen 11am-9pm Mon, 11am-11pm Tue-Thu, 11am-midnight Fri & Sat, noon-9pm Sun) In the Tampere Theatre (p209), this old-style restaurant has classically elegant decor and views over the Tammerkoski. The outdoor tables are popular for buffet lunches, while the evening choices include smoked moose on a tasty appetiser platter for two, and traditional Finnish mains. The building also has a bar-cafe with a great terrace on the main square, perfect for catching the evening sun.

Finlaysonin Palatsi (☎ 040-021 9530; Kuninkaankatu 1; mains €16-28; 11am-midnight Tue-Fri, noon-midnight Sat) This grand centenarian residence behind the Finlayson centre has gardens and grounds and houses a classy restaurant offering elaborate dishes with classically Finnish ingredients such as pike-perch with crayfish sauce. The relaxing terrace (open noon to 9pm Monday, 11am to midnight Tueday to Friday, noon to midnight Saturday, 2pm to 9pm Sunday) has some of the same meals plus a range of cheaper snacks.

Bodega Salud (☎ 233 4400; Tuomiokirkonkatu 19; mains €18-30; 11am-11pm Mon-Fri, noon-midnight Sat, 1-10pm Sun) Though no budget bargain, this Tampere favourite is enduringly popular for its cosy atmosphere and good salad, fruit and cheese bar (included with main courses). It styles itself as Spanish and certainly does a decent paella, but most dishes have a distinctly Finnish feel, with salmon, reindeer and creamy sauces all present and tasty. More adventurous are snails, gnu steak and Rocky Mountain oysters. You get a certificate if you eat the latter – shellfish are scarce in Colorado, but rams have been heard bleating in countertenor tones.

Wistub Alsace (☎ 212 0260; Laukontori 6b; mains €21-23; 4-10pm Tue-Thu, 3-10pm Fri & Sat) This small, authentic spot specialises in Alsatian cuisine and accomplishes it well. The seasonal menu offers a small selection of quality dishes, including an always-delicious fish of the day, as well as pizzalike *tartes flambées* (€14 to €16). Presentation is excellent; deliciously aromatic Alsatian white wines are available, as well as cheaper choices by the glass or jug. Desserts are original and scrumptious; a small terrace offers more casual dining.

Hella & Huone (☎ 253 2440; Salhojankatu 48; mains €24; ♥ 6-11pm Tue-Sat) This smart spot serves exquisite French-influenced gourmet creations off a short menu that features wild duck with lingonberries or roasted whitefish with white truffle foam. Fine cheeses and fresh Finnish berries round off a memorable meal, with wines matched to every course (per glass €11).

Cafes

Runo (☎ 213 3931; Ojakatu 3; sandwiches €3-5; ♥ 9am-8pm Mon-Sat, 10am-8pm Sun) With an arty crowd and bohemian feel, Runo ('poem') is an elegant, almost baroque cafe with books, paintings, decent coffee and huge windows that allow you to keep tabs on the weather. It's a top spot either for a light lunch or a spot of light contemplation.

Vohvelikahvila (☎ 214 4225; Ojakatu 2; waffles €3-6; ♥ 9am-8pm Mon-Sat, 10am-8pm Sun) This cosy and quaint little place does a range of sweet delights, but specialises in fresh waffles, which come laden with cream and chocolate.

Wanha Vanilja (☎ 214 7141; Kuninkaankatu 15; light meals €3-7; ♥ 10am-6pm Tue-Fri, 10am-5pm Sat) True to its name, this homelike cafe, a treasure-trove of timeworn furniture, is bursting with the aroma of vanilla, which they add to the coffee. A range of plump homemade cakes and pastries make the perfect accompaniment; sundaes, quiches and a lunchtime salad bar are also on offer.

Quick Eats & Self-Catering

our pick **Kauppahalli** (Hämeenkatu 19; ♥ 8am-6pm Mon-Fri, 8am-3pm Sat) This intriguing indoor market is one of Finland's best, with picturesque wooden stalls serving a dazzling array of wonderful meat, fruit, baked goodies and fish. There are good cafes, and, at No 50, Teivon Liha, the best place to try cheap *mustamakkara* with berry jam.

Laukontori Market (♥ 8am-2pm Mon-Sat) This is a produce and fish market at Laukontori, also called *alaranta* (lower lakeside).

Koskikeskus Shopping Centre (Hatanpään valtatie; ♥ 10am-7pm Mon-Fri, 10am-5pm Sat) By the river,

this centre is good for fast food – it has pizza, kebab, taco and hamburger outlets, as well as a supermarket.

DRINKING

In addition to the options below, Panimoravintola Plevna and Tuulensuu (p207) are also fine places for a beer or two.

our pick **Café Europa** (☎ 223 5526; Aleksanterinkatu 29; ♥ noon-1am Sun-Tue, to 2am Wed-Thu, to 3am Fri & Sat) This is easily Tampere's coolest bar. Furnished with 1930s-style horsehair couches and chairs, it is a romantic old-world European type of place complete with Belgian and German beers, board games, ornate mirrors and chandeliers, and an excellent summer terrace. Upstairs is a small weekend dance club.

O'Connell's (☎ 222 7032; Rautatienkatu 24; ♥ 4pm-2am) Popular with both Finns and expats, this rambling Irish pub is handy for the train station and has plenty of time-worn, comfortable seating and an air of bonhomie. Its best feature is the range of interesting beers on tap and carefully selected bottled imports. They also do hearty pub meals.

Teerenpeli (☎ 042-492 5210; Hämeenkatu 25; ♥ noon-2am) Another good pub with home-brewed beer and cider, this has a relaxing, candlelit interior and heaps of choice at the taps. They do some good fruit-flavoured brews and also have a terrace and a cavernous club downstairs.

Fall's Café (☎ 223 0061; Kehräsaari; ♥ noon-midnight Sun-Tue, to 3am Wed-Sat) Set among craft shops in a converted brick factory, this bar has a decent range of beers and ciders as well as perhaps Tampere's cutest terrace, a wedge-shaped balcony right by the water where you can watch crazy little fish jumping vertically in the evening light.

Suvi (☎ 211 0150; Laukontori; ♥ 10am-late) Moored alongside the Laukontori Quay, this is a typical Finnish boat bar offering no-nonsense deck-top drinking. Prepare a boarding party and lap up the afternoon sun.

ENTERTAINMENT
Nightclubs & Live Music

Tullikamari Klubi (☎ 343 9933; www.tullikamari.net; Tullikamarinaukio 2; ♥ 11am-10pm Mon-Tue, 11am-4am Wed-Fri, 3pm-4am Sat) This cavernous place near the train station is Tampere's main indoor live-music venue; there are usually several bands playing every week, and big Finnish names regularly swing by for concerts. DJs play classic rock on nights when there's no band. The cover charge varies from free to €15.

Telakka (☎ 225 0700; www.telakka.eu, in Finnish; Tullikamarinaukio 3) This is a bohemian bar-theatre-restaurant in another of Tampere's restored red-brick factories. There's live music regularly, theatre performances, art exhibitions and a brilliant summer terrace with colourful blocky wooden seats.

Hämeensilta (☎ 212 7207; Hämeenkatu 13; ⌚ Tue-Sat 9pm-late) A restaurant, bar and nightclub popular with middle-aged Finns, with wonderful views over the rapids and the city from the top floor. There's live crooner music and plenty of traditional dancing going on.

Mixei (☎ 222 0364; www.mixei.com; Itsenäisyydenkatu 7; ⌚ 8pm-late Tue-Sat) 'Why Not?', Tampere's premier gay venue, is a welcoming place that hosts regular club nights and themed parties and is a good place to meet Finns. There's a €3 cover at weekends.

Pink (☎ 214 3666; www.pinkclub.fi; Otavalankatu 9; ⌚ 10pm-4am) A popular weekend gay club is near the train station.

Onnela (☎ 020-775 9470; Puutarhakatu 21; ⌚ 10pm-4am Wed-Sun) This dark building looks like a library from outside but is the town's most popular nightspot, with several different sections playing rock, pop and electronica for a 20s and 30s crowd.

Also recommended:

Ruma (☎ 040-845 9888; Murtokatu 1; ⌚ 6pm-late) A cool spot with offbeat decor, quirky lighting, friendly staff, and a mixture of Finnish and European pop and alternative rock every day of the week.

Inferno (Tuomiokirkonkatu 17; ⌚ 9pm-4am Wed-Sun) Atmospheric bar and nightclub specialising in heavier and darker sounds. Sometimes has live music.

Paapan Kapakka (☎ 211 0037; Koskikatu 9; ⌚ noon-late) Live jazz and blues every day and a swinging terrace outside its zebra-chaired interior.

Classical Music, Theatre & Cinema

Tampere is a thriving performing-arts centre. There are several theatres and a program of what's on where is available from the tourist office.

Classical concerts are held in spectacular modern **Tampere-Talo** (Tampere Hall; ☎ 243 4111; www.tampere-talo.fi; Yliopistonkatu 55). Performances by the Tampere Philharmonic Orchestra (www.tampere.fi/filharmonia) are on Fridays from September to May. In addition to this it

also puts on regular chamber music concerts, and visiting opera and ballet performances.

The two main theatres, **TT** (Tampere Theatre; ☎ 216 0500; www.tampereenteatteri.fi, in Finnish; Keskustori 2) on the central square, and **TTT** (Tampere Workers' Theatre; ☎ 217 8222; www.ttt-teatteri.fi; Hämeenpuisto 28; ⌚) offer major Finnish and international shows, including musicals, with performances mostly in Finnish.

There are several cinemas in town, including one in the Koskikeskus centre, and **Plevna** (☎ 3138 3831; www.finnkino.fi; Itäinenkatu 4) in the Finlayson centre, the main venue for the film festival (p205). Films are in original language with subtitles.

Sport

Tampere has two ice-hockey teams – Ilves and Tappara – both of which are among the best in the country, and the city is generally regarded as the Finnish home of the sport.

Hakametsä Ice Stadium, about 2km east of the train station, is the venue for matches on Thursdays, Saturdays and Sundays from September to March. Buy tickets here, from the Stockmann or Sokos department stores in town, or from www.lippupalvelu.fi (for Tappara) or www.lippu.fi (for Ilves). It's off the Hervannan Valtaväylä fwy. Take eastbound bus 25 to get there.

Tampere United (☎ 255 4454; www.tampereunited .com, in Finnish) The local football team has been Finland's most successful in recent years. It plays games in summer at Tampere (Ratina) Stadium; tickets cost €10 to €20 and are marginally cheaper if you buy them online at www.lippupalvelu.fi.

SHOPPING

Verkaranta Arts & Crafts Centre (Verkatehtaankatu 2; admission €2.50; ⌚ 10am-6pm Mon-Fri, noon-5pm Sat & Sun) This small former factory building by the river features exhibits and sells extraordinary textiles and handicrafts.

Kehräsaari (⌚ 10am-6pm Mon-Fri, 10am-4pm Sat) Across the footbridge from Verkaranta, just east of Laukontori Market Square, this converted brick-factory building has many boutiques selling authentic Finnish glassware, handicrafts, knitted clothing and T-shirts.

Tallipiha Stable Yards (www.tallipiha.fi; Kuninkaankatu 4; ⌚ 10am-5pm daily Jun-Aug, 10am-4pm Tue-Sat, 11am-5pm Sun Apr-May & Sep-Oct, 11am-5pm Fri-Sun Nov-Mar) is a restored collection of 19th-century stable yards and staff cottages that house artists and craftworkers who make handicrafts, chocolates, ceramics and shoes.

Swamp Music (☎ 212 3087; www.swampmusic.com, in Finnish; Tuomiokirkonkatu 32) is a good place to pick up Finnish music, and they also have an online store. There's also a good-value **secondhand outlet** (Verkatehtaankatu 11) around the corner.

GETTING THERE & AWAY
Air
Finnair/Finncomm (☎ 383 5333) flies to Helsinki, though it's more convenient on the train. It also serves other major Finnish cities. **Wingo** (☎ 060-09 5020; www.wingo.fi) also flies to Turku and Oulu.

Ryanair (☎ 020-039 000; www.ryanair.com) has daily services from its dedicated terminal to London Stansted, 'Frankfurt' Hahn, Bremen, Dublin, Milan Orio al Serio and Riga. You can fly to Tampere direct from Stockholm with **Blue 1** (☎ 060-002 5831; www.blue1.com) and from Copenhagen with **SAS** (www.flysas.com). **Air Baltic** (www.airbaltic.com) flies to Riga.

Boat
Suomen Hopealinja (Finnish Silverline; ☎ 03-212 3889; www.hopealinja.fi) cruises to Visavuori (one-way/return €31/47, five hours) at 9.30am Wednesday to Saturday from June to mid-August, continuing to Hämeenlinna (one-way €41, 8½ hours). The Tarjanne cruises north to Virrat along the Poet's Way (see p205).

Bus
The **main bus station** (Hatanpään valtatie 7) is in the south of town. Regular express buses run from Helsinki (€31.70, 2½ hours) and Turku (€28.70, three hours) and most other major towns in Finland are served from here.

Train
The **train station** (www.vr.fi; Rautatienkatu 25) is in the city centre at the eastern end of Hämeenkatu. Express trains run hourly to/from Helsinki (€24.60, two hours). Intercity trains continue to Oulu (€53.10, five hours) and there are direct trains to Turku (€22, 1¾ hours), Pori, Jyväskylä, Vaasa and Joensuu.

GETTING AROUND
To/From the Airport
The Tampere-Pirkkala airport is 15km southwest of the city centre. Each arriving flight is met by a **bus** (☎ 010-029 400; www.paunu.fi; €2) which takes 40 minutes to the city centre.

Tokee (☎ 020-039 000; www.airpro.fi/ryanair; €6) serves Ryanair flights, leaving from the railway station forecourt three hours before take-off.

Shared **airport taxis** (☎ 10041; per person €15) carry up to eight passengers; these must be booked in advance from the city to the airport. A regular cab will cost between €25 and €30 between the airport and the centre.

Bus
The local bus service is extensive and a one-hour ticket costs €2; the Keskustori (central square) is a convenient place to catch most of them. A 24-hour traveller's ticket is €6. The tourist office has route maps; you can also check www.tampere.fi/tkl/english.html.

Car Hire
There are several car hire companies at the airport and in town. **Hertz** (☎ 020-555 2400; www.hertz.fi; Rautatienkatu 28), behind the Orthodox Church, also rents scooters (per day €45) and bikes (per day €12). **Budget** (☎ 020-746 6630; www.budget.fi; Hatanpään valtatie 24), **Sixt** (☎ 3141 9400; www.sixt.fi; Itsenäisyydenkatu 1) and **Netrent** (☎ 020-155 0000; www.netrent.fi; airport terminal 2) are among the cheaper operators.

Taxi
There are plenty of cab ranks in town; otherwise call ☎ 0100 4131. For a wheelchair-friendly taxi, call ☎ 0100 4531.

NORTH OF TAMPERE
ROUTE 66
☎ 03

Route 66, starting northeast of Tampere and winding 75km north to Virrat, is one of Finland's oldest roads. When the famous song, first performed by Nat King Cole, was translated into Finnish, the popular rock star Jussi Raittinen adapted the lyrics to this highway in his song 'Valtatie 66'. It's a good drive, through young pine forest and lakescapes. Cycling isn't such a great option, as the road is narrowish, and there are plenty of logging trucks hurtling by. Good hiking and fishing opportunities exist; Ruovesi is the best-equipped base.

Orivesi
Route 66 begins in Orivesi. There's nothing spectacular in the village itself, but it is at a

major crossroads. Its silo-like modern **church** (☺ Mon-Fri summer) was controversial when built, partly due to the Kain Tapper woodcarving in the altar. The old bell tower remains, with its *vaivaisukko* (pauper statue).

Kallenaution Kievari

This beautiful wooden **roadhouse** (☎ 335 8915; ☺ 10am-6pm) is the oldest building along Route 66, dating from 1757. Once very common, few of these historic spots now remain.

The complex has a beautiful cafe; sit at old long wooden tables and imagine winter travellers huddled around the blazing fire. There are handicraft exhibitions, including on the making of *päre*, thin wooden sheeting used for shingle roofs and also burned to provide light in houses. In times gone by this was often the cause of fires that destroyed entire towns.

Siikaneva Marshland

This large protected marshland accommodates some unusual bird species, including owls. It's a great place to walk, with duckboard paths across the peat bog alternating with stretches in peaceful pine forests. There are two loops; one of 3km, and one of about 10km. No camping is allowed, but there's a simple shelter and a couple of fireplaces. The entrance is on Route 66, 20km south of Ruovesi; you pass some sinister-looking military buildings on the way.

Kalela

The most celebrated artist of the National Romantic era, Akseli Gallen-Kallela painted most of his famous *Kalevala* works in this **studio** (☎ 476 0623; www.kalela.net; admission €8; ☺ 10am-5pm late Jun–mid-Aug), which he also designed and helped build. It's still owned by his family, who organise good exhibitions in summer. To get here, follow Route 66 5km south from the village of Ruovesi, then turn east 3km. The house is tucked away in the woods alongside a lake.

Ruovesi

pop 5195

Peaceful and pretty, Ruovesi's the main town on this stretch and the best place to stay along it. Apart from enjoying the nearby lakeside, there is not a huge amount to see or do in the village, but if you have a car it makes a good base for exploring the area's attractions.

There's **tourist information** (☎ 486 1388; www.ruovesi.fi; Honkalantie 12) at the bus station.

Ruoveden Kotiseutumuseo (☎ 044-526 2118; Museotie 2; adult/child €2/1; ☺ noon-6pm Jun–mid-Aug) is the local museum with a small history display and, more interestingly, a collection of 18th-century farm buildings including a picturesque wooden windmill.

The lakes around here are prime fishing country and teem with pike, perch, pike-perch (zander) and trout. Various fishing guides can take you out on trips in the area: www.ruovesi.fi has a list.

Haapasaari Lomakylä (☎ 044-080 0290; www.haapasaari.fi; Haapasaarentie 5; tents €13 plus per adult €4, cabins €38-60, 4-/8-person cottages €140/210; **P**) is a great place to stay on an islet north of the village, and is connected to town by a causeway. There's water all around, and fabulous self-contained cottages; they have a sauna, barbecue and fully equipped kitchen. The cabins are simpler, but also have simple cooking facilities. It's great for kids, with a large play area. They discount heavily when things are quiet.

Rustic organic **Ylä-Tuuhosen Maatila** (☎ 472 6426; www.yla-tuuhonen.fi; Tanhuantie 105; r per person €22-28; **P**) is a historic farm run by generous-hearted owners, who offer three pretty rooms (sharing two bathrooms) and use of an excellent kitchen and lounge. You can also sleep in one of the old log barns, converted to a cosy cottage. Breakfast and evening meals are available. To get there from Ruovesi, head 9km north on Route 66, then turn right onto Rd 3481 at Mustajärvi (signposted to Haapamäki). Continue for another 9km, and the farmhouse is 1km up a turn-off on the left.

Hotelli Liera (☎ 472 4600; www.liera.info, in Finnish; Ruovedentie 11; s/d €48/75; wi-fi) is one of two hotels in the centre of town. It looks like a dive from the front but is a friendly spot operated out of a bar. The rooms are, surprisingly, great, with heaps of space, a sofa, and peaceful pastoral views over the fields below to the lake, plus there's a long shared balcony divided by privacy screens. You get breakfast on a tray in the morning, and the pub does no-nonsense pizzas, fish and steaks until 10pm.

Several daily buses connect Ruovesi with Tampere and other places in the region. The SS *Tarjanne,* travelling along the Poet's Way between Tampere and Virrat, stops at Ruovesi; see p205 for more information.

see p205 for more information.

TAMPERE & HÄME

Helvetinjärvi National Park

This park's main attraction is narrow **Helvetinkolu Gorge**, gouged out by retreating glaciers at the end of the last Ice Age. There are numerous trails to follow, including a walk to **Haukanhieta**, a sandy beach and popular camping spot on the shores of Haukkajärvi. You can pitch a tent for the night at designated camp sites in the park and there's a free hut at Helvetinkolu, a couple of kilometres from the parking area, and signposted west off Route 66 just north of Ruovesi.

Virrat

pop 7693

The town of Virrat is the end point of the Poet's Way cruise (p205) from Tampere, though itself not an especially romantic place. There's a **tourist office** (☎ 485 1276; www .virrat.fi, in Finnish; Pääskyntie 6; ✆ 9am–6pm Mon–Fri) in the post office building, and information is also available in the bar by the boat dock, 1km from town.

The main sight is 5km northwest. **Virtain Perinnekylä** (☎ 472 8160; Herrasentie 16; admission €5; ✆ noon–6pm mid–Jun–mid–Aug) is a sprawling open-air museum with several buildings including loggers' cabins and a windmill, handicraft shops, and an elegant cafe-restaurant with a lavish buffet lunch.

There's little in the way of accommodation, but **Domus Virrat** (☎ 475 5600; www.domus virrat.fi; Sipiläntie 3; s/d €38/59; ✆ Jun–mid–Aug; **P**) is a reliable summer hotel not far up from the harbour. The smart rooms have kitchens (though no utensils) and plenty of space; there's also a tennis court, bookable sauna, and bikes to rent. Breakfast is available for a small extra charge.

Lakari (☎ 475 8639; Lakarintie; tent sites €12 plus per adult/child €2/1, cabins €39-58, cottages €95-120; ✆ May-Sep), 7km east of the town centre, is a beautifully situated camping ground between two lakes. It has tent sites, cabins and well-equipped cottages as well as a beach and plenty of trees.

Several daily buses head from Virrat to Tampere and other towns in the region.

KEURUU

☎ 014 / pop 10,919

Sweet Keuruu sits in a lovely location on the northern shore of Keurusselkä and, while it sees little nondomestic tourism, is definitely worth swinging by. Its major drawcard is its

fascinating **wooden church** (admission €1; ✆ 11am–5pm Jun-Aug, ask at museum at other times), built in 1758, which has superb portraits of Bible characters (although the artist didn't complete the set, due to a pay dispute), and dark clouds all across the ceiling depicting the firmament, peopled by scattered beasts, angels and devils. There are also photos of the mummified corpses buried below the chancel, and a set of stocks for miscreants.

Across the road (and the railway) from the church, **Kamana** (☎ 751 2523; www.keuruu.fi, in Finnish; Kangasmannilantie 4; ✆ 11am-6pm Tue-Sun Sep-May, 11am-5pm daily Jun-Aug) serves as local museum, exhibition centre and the tourist office. It's one of a clutch of historic buildings here, which house craft shops and the like. The museum has an excellent cafe serving various tasty lunches at the buffet.

There are lake cruises on the historic **MS Elias Lönnrot** (☎ 03-212 4804; www.eliaksenristeilyt.fi, in Finnish) Wednesdays to Sundays from May to August. It has a service to the town of Mänttä once weekly (one-way/return €15/22.50, 2¾ hours each way) and more frequent services to other destinations.

Another magnificent wooden church (p153) is only 28km east of here at Petäjävesi.

Keurusseuden Keskusvaraamo (☎ 754 6411; www .keurusseudunkeskusvaraamo.fi; Mäntymäentie 26) can book lakeside rental cottages around Keuruu. There are also a couple of nearby camp sites and the **Spahotel Keurusselkä** (☎ 751 0500; www .fontana.fi; Keurusseläntie 134; s/d €82/110; **P** 🖵 🐾 wi-fi), a family holiday complex with a lake beach, swimming pools, Jacuzzi and activities. As well as the comfortable hotel rooms, there are well-equipped cottages (€140) sleeping six, and cheaper rooms (singles/doubles €66/92) in a separate building near the lake. You can also hire bikes and boats.

Buses run to Keuruu from Tampere and Jyväskylä. Trains between Jyväskylä and Seinäjoki also stop here.

MÄNTTÄ

☎ 03 / pop 6413

Mänttä, set on a narrow isthmus between fast-flowing rapids, grew around its paper mill, founded in the mid-19th century by the Serlachius dynasty. Progressive in outlook, the family endeavoured to build a model industrial community around their factory and endowed the town with noble buildings and art. After a merger in the 1980s, the company,

Metsä-Serla, is now based in Espoo, but the paperworks still directly or indirectly employs much of the town.

The principal attraction was once the private home of Gösta Serlachius and is now the **Gösta Serlachiuksen Taidemuseo** (☎ 488 6802; www.serlachiusartmuseum.fi; adult/child €6/1, with Serlachius Museo €9/1; ☻ 11am-6pm Tue-Sun May-Aug, 2-8pm Wed, noon-5pm Thu-Sun Sep-Apr), one of the nation's premier galleries. Situated 2km east of the town centre in elegant grounds, it houses an excellent collection of Finnish art: all the names from the Golden Age are here, including seemingly dozens of Gallen-Kallelas, plenty of Edelfelts and Schjerfbecks, as well as Wickström sculptures. Look out for a mischievous painting of Gallen-Kallela getting pissed with his mate Sibelius, and Hugo Simberg's whimsical *Entrance to Hades*. There's also a sizeable European collection, including a fine Deposition by Van der Weyden.

In the town centre, an elegant white 1930s modernist mansion, formerly the company HQ, is now the **G.A. Serlachius Museo** (☎ 488 6800; www.gaserlachius.fi; Erik Serlachiuksenkatu 2; adult/child €6/1, with Göster Serlachiuksen Taidemuseo €9/1; ☻ 11am-6pm Tue-Sun May-Aug, 2-8pm Wed, noon-5pm Thu-Sun Sep-Apr;). There's a most comprehensive display on the history of the paperworks and old Gösta Serlachius himself, with audio exhibits on every conceivable aspect of the business – you'd be here a week if you listened to them all. Most information is in English. The attractive building also has two to three temporary exhibitions – of wonderful quality

at our last visit. It also functions as the town's tourist office.

Nearby, the art nouveau **church** (☎ 474 7497; ☻ 10am-4.30pm daily Jun-Aug, 10am-1pm Mon-Fri Sep-May) was, like most of the town, built (in 1928) by the company. It boasts elaborate woodcarvings around the altar and pulpit; the altarpiece by Alvar Cawén portrays the Madonna looking super-Nordic. The company crest adorns the front stained-glass window.

Honkahovi Taidekeskus (☎ 474 7005; www.honkahovi.fi; Johtokunnantie 11; ☻ early Jun-late Aug 11am-6pm) is another mansion belonging to the Serlachius family. It's a 1938 art deco building containing temporary art exhibitions. You can walk between Honkahovi and the Göster Serlachiuksen Taidemuseo via a trail along the lakeside.

Around the corner from the church, **Hotelli Alexander** (☎ 474 9232; www.hotellialexander.fi, in Finnish; Kauppakatu 23; s/d €54/72; ℗ wi-fi) has rather smart burgundy-walled rooms. The same people also run **Kesähotelli Mänttä** (☎ 488 6841; Koulukatu 6; dm/d €22/67; ☻ Jun–mid-Aug; ℗), a summer hostel in a student building; rooms have kitchen and bathroom. It's a short walk from the centre, crossing the main street.

Getting There & Away

In summer, you can catch the MS *Elias Lönnrot* from Keuruu. Otherwise, there are several weekday buses and a couple of weekends to Jyväskylä (€19.20, 1½ hours) via Keuruu, and Tampere (€18, 1½ to 1¾ hours).

Turku & the Southwest

Never heard of Turku? This area once ruled Finland when the Swedes established trading towns along the coast. They used their capital Turku to shine the light of Christianity across the country, with the odd forcible baptism for good measure. Venerable old towns like Uusikaupunki, Rauma and Pori have ports and historic buildings that are testaments to the success of local merchants and artisans. But the 19th century saw the rise of Russia, which wanted a Finnish capital it could keep an eye on at Helsinki, so Turku's fortunes changed.

The Swedish influence remains. Along with Pohjanmaa and Åland, this area is both geographically and culturally close to Sweden with plenty of summer visitors from the west. You'll hear Swedish spoken so often you'll wonder if you're in Stockholm – for language tips see boxed text, p264.

But the traffic runs both ways and the Archipelago Trail is a popular trip for Finns in summer, and a step closer to Sweden. As well as historic sights like the postcard-perfect old towns of Rauma or Naantali, there's the strong draw of Moomin trolls and Pori's hopping jazz festival. Turku itself is a strong challenger to Helsinki's cultural cred with galleries and museums that are turning heads in the EU.

HIGHLIGHTS

- Having a religious experience at the massive **Turku Cathedral** (p218), Finland's first church that's still divine

- Finding your inner child and outer troll at the delightful **Moominworld** (p225) in Naantali with characters leaping to life from the much-loved books

- Partying on the island festival **Ruisrock** (p220) or watching the city's artistic blaze with **Turku on Fire 2011** (p220)

- Listening out for the unique language that sailors brought back to Rauma as you sample odd-tasting **Puksprööt** (p237) on the terrace in **Vanha Rauma's kauppatori** (p234)

- Taking on the **Archipelago Trail** (p229), which meanders out to remote **Houtskär** (p230)

- Seeing Rauma's finest on display as they celebrate the lace festival, **Pitsiviikko** (p236), or award the kooky Herring Oscars at the **Blue Sea Film Festival** (p236)

- Cruising to Naantali aboard the **SS Ukkopekka** (p219), a traditional steamship that turns into a dinner dance in summer

TURKU & THE SOUTHWEST

Activities

The various archipelagos are much beloved of yachties in summer; even tiny islands have guest harbours that are well equipped; you can also arrange charters in Turku. The area is very well suited to exploration by bicycle, and can be combined into a circular route around the Archipelago Trail (p229) or heading out to Åland.

TURKU

☎ 02 / pop 175,286

The old Finnish joke that Turku brought culture to Finland but it never returned to the city is an obsolete gag probably borne from its joshing rivalry with Tampere. True, the historic castle and cathedral point to a rich cultural history when the city was capital but the future is bright for this 'second city'. There's a plethora of museums, and art galleries with experimental works, and there's a hectic festival calendar. There's a local TV station, Turku TV, and several of Finland's contemporary writers and artists call it home.

It's also the first Finnish city many visitors see as they get off ferries from Sweden and Åland. But don't just take our word for it: for 2011 Turku has been given the accolade of Capital of Culture by the EU. All this leads Turku's citizens to wipe a proud tear from their collective eye and shout 'In your face Tampere!'

HISTORY

A Catholic settlement began at Koroinen, near the present centre of Turku, in 1229. The consecration of a new church in 1300 and the construction of Turku Castle meant that Finland could be ruled from this administrative and spiritual base. At several points in history, Turku was the second-largest town in Sweden, though fire destroyed Turku on several occasions, including the Great Fire of 1827, which levelled much of the town.

Åbo was the original Swedish name because it's a settlement *(bo)* on a river *(å)*. Today, there's a slightly un-PC campaign for Turku's citizens to call themselves Åboriginals, including several T-shirts bearing the word. The Finnish name, Turku, is an archaic Russian word for 'marketplace'. The long Swedish connection led to the Russians' decision to swipe the capital title for Helsinki, allowing Turku to concentrate on its status as a merchant town.

ORIENTATION

Turku's centre is its kauppatori (market square), 3km northeast of the harbour, with a bus meeting each arriving ferry. The Aurajoki divides the city and locals have been known to ask visitors if they've crossed the river to Åbo yet, though (as this is the old name for Turku) they're really just fooling. Most of the city is within walking distance.

INFORMATION
Bookshops

Akateeminen Kirjakauppa (Hansa Shopping Arcade, Yliopistonkatu) Stocks maps, English-language books and foreign newspapers.

Internet Access

As well as the tourist office and Turku hostel you can also try:

CyberCafé (Hansa Shopping Arcade; per hr €2.40; ☼ 9am-9pm Mon-Fri, 10am-9pm Sat & Sun) Automated internet place with coin-operated computers.

Internet Resources

Turku (www.turku.fi) The city website, with links to many attractions and businesses.

Turku Touring (www.turkutouring.fi) The city's tourist board website.

Left Luggage

The train station offers a left-luggage counter and locker service, and there are more lockers (€2) located at the ferry terminal, and the Silja and Viking Line buildings.

Libraries

Public library (☎ 262 3611; Linnankatu 2; ☼ 11am-8pm Mon-Thu, 11am-6pm Fri, 11am-4pm Sat) Several free internet terminals (maximum 15 minutes) and plenty of English books.

Money

Several banks located on the market square have 24-hour ATMs.

Forex (☎ 751 2650; Eerikinkatu 23 & 12; ☼ 8am-7pm Mon-Fri, 9am-3pm Sat) Offering better rates than banks, these two locations are the best places to change cash and travellers cheques.

Post

Main post office (Humalistonkatu 1; ☼ 9am-8pm Mon-Fri) Situated two blocks west of the kauppatori.

Tourist Information

Turku City Tourist Office (☎ 262 7444; www.turkut ouring.fi; Aurakatu 4; internet per hr €5; ☼ 8.30am-6pm Mon-Fri, 9am-4pm Sat & Sun, 10am-3pm winter weekends) Busy, very helpful, information on entire region. Rents bikes (€15 per day); free internet access for short periods.

Travel Agencies

Citytours (☎ 251 0370; www.citytours.fi; Eerikinkatu 4) Finnair agent.

Kilroy Travels (☎ 273 7500; www.kilroytravels.com; Eerikinkatu 2; ☼ 10am-6pm Mon-Fri) Specialists in student and budget travel.

DISCOUNT CARDS

The **Turku Card** (adult 24-/48-hours €21/28, family €40) gives admission to most museums and attractions in the region, public transport and various other discounts for a set period. The family card (two adults and three kids) is good value but only valid for a day. The card is sold at the tourist office (and from its website) or from most participating attractions.

SIGHTS & ACTIVITIES

Turku Castle & Historical Museum

Mammoth **Turku Castle & Historical Museum** (Turun Linna; ☎ 262 0300; www.turunlinna.fi; admission €7, guided tours €2; ☼ 10am-6pm daily mid-Apr–mid-Sep, 10am-3pm Tue-Sun mid-Sep–mid-Apr, English tours 12.10pm Jun), near the ferry terminals, is easily Finland's largest and possibly one of the biggest in Scandinavia. Founded in 1280 at the mouth of the Aurajoki, the castle has been growing ever since. Swedish Count Per Brahe ruled Finland from here in the 17th century, while Sweden's deposed King Eric XIV was imprisoned in the castle's Round Tower in the late 16th century. He was moved to several prisons including Åland's Kastelholms Slott (see p252) to prevent his discovery by rebels.

The castle's highlights include two dungeons and sumptuous banqueting halls, as well as a fascinating historical museum of medieval Turku in the castle's Old Bailey. Models in the castle show its growth from a simple island fortress to medieval castle. Most Finns recognise the castle's distinctive architecture as the logo for Turun Sinappi (Turku Mustard).

Guided tours in English are conducted daily in June, but by arrangement at other times.

Luostarinmäki Handicrafts Museum

If you only see one museum in Finland, make it this **handicrafts museum** (☎ 262 0350; admission €5; ☼ 10am-6pm daily mid-Apr–mid-Sep, 10am-3pm Tue-Sun mid-Sep–mid-Apr). Forget the stuffy exhibits, this is a genuinely historic portion of town that has survived the near-destruction of Turku including the savage Great Fire of 1827. All of the buildings are in their original locations, unlike other open-air museums where the buildings are relocated or recreated. The area consists of artisans' and workers' homes with a very real sense of their lives, thanks to in-period staff.

Since 1940 it's been a national treasure with 30 furnished and often functioning workshops, including a printing press, silversmith, watchmaker, bakery and cigar shop. In summer, artisans in traditional garb practise their trades inside the wooden workshops while musicians stroll the streets. Guided tours in English are given roughly hourly from

TURKU

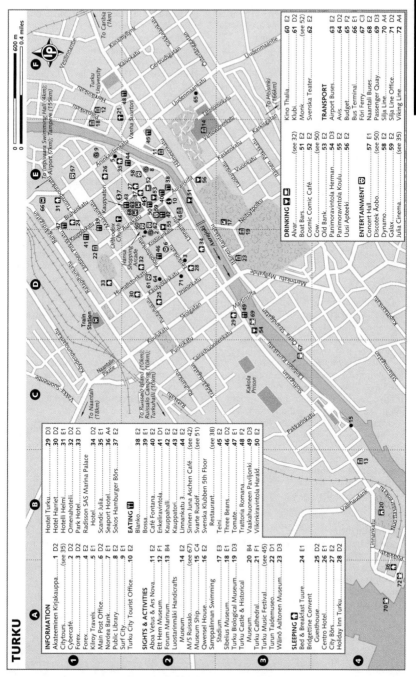

INFORMATION
Akateeminen Kirjakauppa.....................1 D2
Citytours.....................................(see 35)
Cybercafé..2 D2
Forex..3 D2
Forex..4 E2
Kilroy Travels.......................................5 E2
Main Post Office...................................6 D2
Nordea Bank...7 E1
Public Library..8 E2
Surf City...9 E1
Turku City Tourist Office.....................10 E2

SIGHTS & ACTIVITIES
Aboa Vetus & Ars Nova.......................11 E2
Ett Hem Museum.................................12 F1
Forum Marinum....................................13 B4
Luostarinmäki Handicrafts
  Museum..14 E2
M/S Ruissalo.......................................(see 67)
Museum Ship..15 C4
Qwensel House....................................16 E2
Samppalinnan Swimming
  Stadium...17 E3
Sibelius Museum..................................18 E1
Turku Biological Museum.....................19 D3
Turku Castle & Historical
  Museum..20 B4
Turku Cathedral...................................21 F1
Turku Music Festival..........................(see 45)
Turun Taidemuseo................................22 D1
Wäinö Aaltonen Museum.....................23 D3

SLEEPING
Bed & Breakfast Tuure........................24 E1
Bridgettine Convent
  Guesthouse..25 D2
Centro Hotel..26 E1
City Börs..27 E2
Holiday Inn Turku................................28 D2

Hostel Turku..29 D3
Hotel Harriet..30 D2
Hotelli Helmi..31 E1
Omenahotelli..32 D2
Park Hotel..33 D1
Radisson SAS Marina Palace
  Hotel...34 D2
Scandic Julia..35 D2
Seaport Hotel......................................36 A4
Sokos Hamburger Börs........................37 E2

EATING
Blanko..38 E2
Bossa...39 E1
Café Fontana..40 D1
Enkeliravintola......................................41 E2
Kauppahalli..42 E2
Kauppatori...43 E2
Linnankatu 3..44 E2
Sininen Juna Aschen Café..................(see 42)
Svarte Rudolf.......................................45 E2
Svenska Klubben 5th Floor
  Restaurant.......................................(see 38)
Teini...45 E2
Three Beans...46 D2
Tomate...47 E1
Trattoria Romana.................................48 F2
Vaakahuoneen Paviljonki....................49 D3
Viikinkiravintola Harald.......................50 E2

DRINKING
Alvar...(see 32)
Boat Bars..51 E2
Cosmic Comic Café...............................52 E2
Cow..(see 50)
Old Bank..53 E2
Panimoravintola Herman......................54 D3
Panimoravintola Koulu.........................55 E2
Uusi Apteeki..56 E2

ENTERTAINMENT
Concert Hall...57 E1
Discotek Aobo..................................(see 50)
Dynamo..58 E2
Galax..59 E2
Julia Cinema......................................(see 35)

Kino Thalia...60 E2
Klubi...61 D2
Monk..(see 52)
Svenska Teater.....................................62 E2

TRANSPORT
Airport Buses.......................................63 E2
Avis...64 D2
Budget..65 F2
Bus Terminal...66 E1
Föri Ferry..67 C3
Naantali Buses......................................68 D3
Passenger Quay....................................69 A4
Silja Line..70 A4
Silja Line Office....................................71 D3
Viking Line..72 A4

10.30am to 4.30pm in the height of summer. The gift shop, selling goods produced in the museum's workshops, is a real treat.

Turku Cathedral

Called the 'mother church' of Finland's Lutheran faith, **Turku Cathedral** (cathedral & museum 9am-7pm mid-Sep–mid-Apr, 9am-8pm mid-Apr–mid-Sep) towers over the town in a spacious square that makes even approaching it feel divine. Consecrated in 1300, the building has been rebuilt over the centuries after fire damage.

The towering interior features a retable and pulpit, which were designed by the famous German architect CL Engel (who in the spirit of bipartisanship also built the Orthodox church on the market square). The walls are decorated with Romantic frescoes by RW Ekman, depicting the baptism of Finland's first bishop and Gustav Wasa presenting the nation with the first Finnish New Testament. The side chapels hold tombs of Finnish and Swedish war heroes, including Catherine Månsdotter, Queen of Sweden, and wife of the unfortunate Erik XIV.

The **cathedral museum** (admission €2) has models showing stages of the cathedral's construction from the 14th century, as well as medieval sculptures and religious paraphernalia.

Most Tuesday evenings the cathedral offers live music, and English-language services are held at 4pm every Sunday. If you can't get to a concert, listen out for the cathedral's distinctive hourly bell which chimes across the country at noon via the radio station YLE1.

Opposite the cathedral, the **Vanha Suurtori** was once the main town square. It's surrounded by elegant buildings, including trading mansions and the town hall, from where there's an annual Christmas address across the country. A cobbled courtyard holds a bookshop cafe that makes a peaceful spot on a sunny day.

Forum Marinum

Set back from the river, this excellent **maritime museum** (282 9511; www.forum-marinum.fi; Linnankatu 72; admission €7, with museum ships €12; 11am-7pm daily May-Sep, 10am-6pm Tue-Sun Oct-Apr) has a permanent exhibition in an old granary. It's a comprehensive look at different aspects of ships and shipping, from scale models to full-size vessels. Kid-friendly highlights include the hydrocopter, WWII torpedoes and multimedia displays. The newer building opposite has regular exhibitions, as well as several ves-

sels and a cabin from a luxury cruise-liner, as many were built in Turku.

Outside, anchored in the river, is a small fleet of **museum ships** (per ship €5, all ships & museum €12; 11am-7pm Jun-Aug), which you can climb aboard. The mine-layer *Keihässalmi* and the corvette *Karjala* take you back to WWII, while the beautiful three-masted barque *Sigyn* was originally launched from Göteborg in 1887 and has well-preserved cabins. There's the *Daphne,* a cute little motor and sail boat that was home to author Göran Schild, and the rescue vessel *Anna Gadd* – both boats were built in Ruissalo's once-thriving shipyards.

Aboa Vetus & Ars Nova

This pair of **museums** (250 0552; www.aboa vetusarsnova.fi; Itäinen Rantakatu 4-6; admission €8; 11am-7pm, closed Mon mid-Sep–Mar, English-language tours 11.30am daily Jul & Aug) under one roof unite art and archaeology. Digging continues in the museum and along the Aurajoki, and excavations of the Convent Quarter have created an engaging display of 15th-century artefacts in the Aboa Vetus. Back in the present, Ars Nova showcases the best of contemporary art with temporary exhibitions, which peak around the Turku Biennaali, a themed show in summer in odd years. The new *Oma Tila* (Our Own S) is accumulating work from local artists and craftspeople, especially work produced as part of their own projects. Free guided tours offer insights into both museums.

Turun Taidemuseo

The excellent **Turku Art Museum** (262 7100; Aurakatu 26; adult/child €6/free; 11am-7pm Tue-Fri, 11am-5pm Sat & Sun;) is a striking granite building with elaborately carved pilasters and conical turrets. Much of the art is modern, though the Victor Westerholm offers Finnish landscapes and Akseli Gallen-Kallela's depictions of the *Kalevala* are always jaw-dropping. Gunnar Berndtson's *Kesä* (Summer) is an idyllic depiction of sunny Suomi while RW Ekman's *The Muses* is transcendent Romantic.

Sibelius Museum

Near the cathedral, **Sibelius Museum** (215 4494; Piispankatu 17; admission €3; 11am-4pm Tue-Sun, 11am-4pm & 6-8pm Wed) displays some 350 musical instruments from across Finland and memorabilia of the famous Finnish composer

THE FLYING FINN

When Finnish champion runner Paavo Nurmi saw a sculpture of him by Wäinö Aaltonen unveiled on Itäinen Rantakatu, he laconically remarked 'I don't run naked'. It was typical of Finland's greatest athlete who had humbly won a total of 12 track and field medals for middle- and long-distance running during the 1920s. The press hailed him as the Flying Finn and there was much speculation about how saunas aided his phenomenal speed. He broke 22 world records and always ran with a stopwatch, which he was known to throw away when he knew he had enough of a lead.

His career was ended by bureaucracy when he was disallowed from competing at the 1932 Olympics as his paid-running appearances and tours of the US were deemed to make him a professional athlete. He left the spotlight and quietly opened a haberdashery store in Helsinki. When he reappeared to light the flame at the 1952 Olympics in Helsinki, he was met with a very Finnish silence that burst into the sound of the 70,000-strong crowd cheering its champion.

Jean Sibelius. It is the most extensive musical museum in Finland. You can listen to Sibelius' music on scratchy record or, better still, attend a Wednesday evening concert (from September to May, less often in summer) which showcases jazz, folk, rock and classical performers from around the country. For more information on Sibelius, see boxed text, p197.

Other Museums

In a beautiful building, the **Turku Biological Museum** (☎ 262 0340; Neitsytpolku 1; admission €4; ☷ 10am-6pm mid-Apr–mid-Sep, 10am-3pm Tue-Sun mid-Sep–mid-Apr) features much of Finland's wildlife represented in realistic dioramas.

On the riverfront, **Qwensel House** is Turku's oldest, built around 1700. It houses the small **Pharmacy Museum** (☎ 262 0280; Läntinen Rantakatu 13; admission €4; ☷ 10am-6pm daily mid-Apr–mid-Sep, 10am-3pm Tue-Sun mid-Sep–mid-Apr) with an old laboratorium featuring medicinal herbs, 18th-century 'Gustavian' (Swedish) furnishings and an exhibition of bottles and other pharmacy supplies.

Ett Hem Museum (☎ 215 4279; Piispankatu 14; admission €3; ☷ noon-3pm Tue-Sun May-Sep) preserves a wealthy turn-of-the-20th-century home designed by CL Engel, with furniture of various styles, and works by famous painters Albert Edelfelt and Helene Schjerfbeck.

Wäinö Aaltonen Museum (WAM; ☎ 262 0850; www .wam.fi; Itäinen Rantakatu 38; admission €7; ☷ 11am-7pm Tue-Sun) displays sculptures by the famous artist, with temporary exhibitions of contemporary and experimental art.

Cruises

Archipelago cruises are a popular activity in summer. Most departures are from the quay at Martinsilta bridge.

The historic steamship **SS Ukkopekka** (☎ 515 3300; www.ukkopekka.fi) cruises to Naantali (one-way/return €20/25, 9.30am and 2pm early June to late August). The trip takes 1¾ hours, and there's a cafe on board. To make a night of it, there's an evening dinner-dance cruise (€41 to €48, departs 7pm), with meals served on the island of Loistokari.

Less atmospheric, but affordable, **M/S Rudolfina** (☎ 250 2995; www.rudolfina.fi) runs 90-minute lunch (€21 to €24) and dinner cruises (€28), including a buffet meal (1pm and 3pm daily, 7pm Monday to Saturday June to August).

Rosita (☎ 469 2500; www.rosita.fi) does a one-hour cruise out to Vepsä island (€10) three times daily from mid-June to mid-August and four-hour cruises out to Maisaari (€15) on Friday and Sunday evening. In May and September, cruises are on Friday to Sunday only. They do a tour to Bengtskär (€45), on scheduled Saturdays in May, June and August, which is a day-long adventure that includes a guide to help you explore this lighthouse island.

Cycling

The city tourist office hires bikes, can suggest cycling routes, and publishes an excellent free *pyörätiekartta* (bike route map) of the city and surrounding towns. You can rent bikes from it per day/week for €15/75; Hostel Turku (p220) also offers hire services.

Swimming & Sauna

At the **Samppalinnan Swimming Stadium** (☎ 262 3590; Samppalinnanvuori; admission €4; ☷ 6am-8pm Mon-Thu, 6am-7pm Fri, 10am-7pm Sat & Sun May-late Aug), the entry fee includes a sauna and use of the 50m pool, which has diving boards. In winter, go to the indoor **Impivaara swimming hall** (☎ 262 3588; Uimahallinpolku 4; admission €4; 10am-5pm) for swimming and a sauna, north of the city centre (take bus 13 to Impivaara).

There are also good beaches at **Maisaari** and **Vepsä**.

FESTIVALS & EVENTS

Turku Jazz (☎ 250 2376; www.turkujazz.fi; tickets €70) Has been warming the cockles in March with hot bee-bop and smoking sax for more than 30 years.

Turku Music Festival (☎ 262 0814; www.tmj.fi; tickets €12-35) During the second week of August a feast of classical and contemporary music and opera with amazing venues including Turku Castle and cathedral.

Medieval Market (☎ 262 0900; www.turku.fi/kult tuurikeskus) Held over a variable weekend in summer, this event brings a Middle Ages market back to Vanha Suurtori with jousting at Turku Castle; the city tourist office has program details and tickets.

Paavo Nurmi Marathon (www.paavonurmisports.com) Named for the legendary distance runner, this big run in late June/early July attracts an international field and runs from the town centre to Ruissalo island.

Ruisrock (☎ 09-872 4446; www.ruisrock.fi; 1-day ticket €50-62, 30-day €100) Finland's oldest and largest annual rock festival, held since 1969. The festival takes place over three days in July at the recreational park on Ruissalo island.

Down by the Laituri (DBTL; ☎ 040-086 0446; www .dbtl.fi) By the river, this annual rock festival in August attracts local and a few international bands.

Turku on Fire 2011 (☎ 262 7186; www.turku2011.fi) A year-long salute to the city's cultural life as it takes on the mantle of European City of Culture with art, performance and music taking over the town.

SLEEPING

Because of Turku's proximity of Muumimaailma (p225), there's an emphasis on family accommodation with some motels offering family packages that head out to the park as well. This emphasis on family options means that top-end accommodation is rare.

Budget

Hostel Turku (☎ 262 7680; www.turku.fi/hostelturku; Linnankatu 39; dm/s/tw/q €16/36/42/65; reception 6-10am & 3pm-midnight;) Between the ferry and the city, this HI hostel is well placed for coming and going. It's a neat place with good lockers, spacious dorms (no more than four bunks) and a mini-fridge in each room. There's also bike hire (€10/50 per day/week) and a speedy internet cafe.

Ruissalo Camping (☎ 262 5100; tent sites €10 plus per person €4, 2-/4-person r €35/60; Jun-Aug) On idyllic Ruissalo island, 10km west of the city centre, this camping ground has lots of room for tents and a few cabins along with saunas, a cafeteria and nice beaches – including a nude option. It's the bunkhouse for the Ruisrock festival so expect it to be booked out then and at Midsummer. Bus 8 runs from the kauppatori to the camping ground.

Omenahotelli (www.omenahotelli.fi; Humalistonkatu 7; r €55;) This larger hotel in this chain, which takes internet bookings, was actually designed by Alvar Aalto, but the plainness suggests that AA phoned it in. Still, it represents the usual excellent value of the 'apple hotels' with spaces that can sleep up to four, with lower digit room numbers closer to the lifts in a warren of rooms. Options like internet and breakfast are add-ons.

Hotel Harriet (☎ 250 0265; www.hotelharriet.fi; cnr Käsityöläiskatu & Puutarhakatu; s/d €55/80) There have been a few cosmetic changes at this place, though rooms remain comfortable, if unexceptional, and it's still handy for the trains. It's tough to find because it's set above shops but look for an entrance on Käsityöläiskatu.

Bed & Breakfast Tuure (☎ 233 0230; www.netti .fi/~tuure2; Tuureporinkatu 17C; s/d €37/50;) Upstairs in a homely building, this affordable option is good for independent travellers who want a little more, including a microwave and fridge in each room. The owners are friendly and have good tips on the local area.

Midrange

our pick Centro Hotel (☎ 469 0469; www.centrohotel .com; Yliopistonkatu 12; s/d €96/106;) Central but far enough from the raucous kauppatori to still be quiet, Centro has a good balance here. Attentive service always feels friendly, and blonde-wood rooms are a good compromise between size and price, with superior ones that have a more designer feel. The breakfast buffet has fresh pastries and a varied spread that's worth getting out of bed for.

Seaport Hotel (☎ 283 3000; www.hotelseaport.fi; Matkustajasatama; s/d €93/113; wi-fi) Perfectly placed for an early ferry (it's right next to the Viking Line and Silja Line terminals), this restored warehouse makes for an easy stay. There's a restaurant and sauna so it can be a good night in with simple rooms that include wireless internet access and a minibar. Bus 1 shuttles to the city.

Bridgettine Convent Guesthouse (☎ 250 1910; birgitta.turku@kolumbus.fi; Ursininkatu 15A; s/d incl breakfast €45/65; P) You'll see the habited nuns of this guesthouse around town because there are so few Catholics in Finland. Their guesthouse is simple but spacious. Silence is expected in the public areas after 10pm so it's generally a quieter place, but represents good value and is handy for the train.

Scandic Julia (☎ 336 000; www.scandic-hotels.fi; Eerikinkatu 4; s/d €104/114; P 🖵 ♿) Set in a massive cinema complex, this place was slated for renovation in 2009 so we're expecting rooms will be spruced-up but still have excellent views of the city and cathedral, particularly from the 6th-floor sauna. At the time of research rooms came with great extras such as recycling bins and a fruit platter, so expect the great service to continue.

Park Hotel (☎ 273 2555; www.parkhotelturku .fi; Rauhankatu 1; s/d €120/150, ste €240; P 🖵) Ever wanted your own cosmopolitan eccentric aunt? This art nouveau house is a genuine character right down to Jaakko, the parrot that squawks a welcome when you check in. Rooms themselves are lavishly decorated in individual styles, and the other facilities like a pool table, a fireplace-warmed drawing room and breakfast make for a great stay. Shame the sauna (€10) isn't complimentary.

Sokos Hamburger Börs (☎ 337 381; www.sokos hotels.fi; Kauppiaskatu 6; City Börs s/d €89/104, main hotel s/d €106/146; P 🖵 🖵 ♿) Towering over the market square, this is the town's biggest hotel, and has Sokos' reliability. The City Börs option is across the road and has simpler rooms that are more affordable. The main hotel (where you check in for both options) comes with the lot: free sauna, flatscreen TVs and tastefully decorated rooms with solid doors that could take a battering ram (and will keep out the noise). The included breakfast is extensive, and includes a Japanese option.

Also recommended:

Hotelli Helmi (☎ 786 2770; www.hotellihelmi.fi; Tuureporinkatu 11; s/d €73/83; P ♿ wi-fi) Brand-spanking new, this small hotel boasts inexpensive rooms that include wi-fi and minifridges, plus a great breakfast buffet.

Holiday Inn Turku (☎ 338 211; www.holiday-inn.com; Eerikinkatu 28; bikes per day €10, s/d €109/124; 🖵) Good central place that caters to a family crowd.

Top End

Radisson SAS Marina Palace Hotel (☎ 020-123 4710; http://sas.radisson.com; Linnankatu 32; d €140, ste from €215;

P 🖵) Reconditioned in 2006, this modern affair is Turku's top of the town with service laid on for busy executives. As well as wi-fi throughout and several meeting rooms, there's the grab-and-run breakfast (coffee and a power bar as you jog out the door) and a choice of three saunas. Dark-wood rooms are nondescript but serviceable while suites are roomier and have luxuries like in-room espresso machines – so you can enjoy that caffeine hit.

EATING

Turku's dining scene is fairly sophisticated with international options and some good chances to try Finnish food. The historic **kauppahalli** (covered market; Eerikinkatu; ⏰ 7am-5.30pm Mon-Fri, 7am-3pm Sat) is ideal for groceries and quick eats, and its brilliant cafe, Sininen Juna (below). The **kauppatori** (⏰ 8am-4pm Mon-Sat May-Sep) hosts a fruit and vegetable market, but there's no shortage of grilli (fast food) and kebab shops here. If you were ever going to try a Hesburger, Finland's answer to McDonald's, Turku is the hometown of the ubiquitous chain.

Budget

Cafe Fontana (cnr Aurakatu & Linnankatu; pastries €3-6; ⏰ 9am-8pm Mon-Sat, noon-6pm Sun) Close to the city's heart, this art nouveau cafe serves up delicious pastries and pies. Inside it's classic Nordic pine tables but the outdoor terrace is the beating heart of the city.

Sininen Juna Aschan Café (kauppahalli; pastries €3-6) With a name meaning 'blue train', you'd expect to be able to sit in a converted carriage in the middle of the market, right? But this coffee institution is currently run by the Turku bakery chain, which supplies delicious buns and cakes, so it's a tasty destination.

Three Beans (☎ 250 5573; Humalistonkatu 3; pastries & sandwiches €3-8) Serious caffeine freaks converge on this little shop for their java hits, because of the fresh-ground beans and espresso machine. They also do take-home beans and light lunches and pastries.

Cosmic Comic Café (☎ 250 4942; www.cosmic.fi; Kauppiaskatu 4; snacks €4-9; ⏰ noon-2am Mon-Thu, noon-3am Fri & Sat, 4pm-midnight Sun) Sipping coffee in the sea of comics (both papered to the walls and available to browse) at this late-night haunt is a fanboy's dream but there are also some good cakes on offer.

Vaakahuoneen Paviljonki (☎ 515 3324; Linnankatu 38; mains €8-18; fish buffet €9; ⏰ food served 11am-10pm

May-Aug) Set a little way from town, this restaurant is worth tripping out to find. As well as an à la carte menu of snacks, pasta, pizzas and steak, there are daily buffets in summer, which include a variety of fish and several Asian options. The river-front locale can be enjoyed in spring and summer when live jazz accompanies the sunshine.

Svarte Rudolf (☎ 250 4567; Leirikatu 7; mains €10-18; lunch & dinner) The best of the floating restaurants moored on the south side of the Aurajoki, this place does Italian with a leaning towards seafood. While long summer evenings invite top-deck drinking, the downstairs dining room is an elegant alternative.

Trattoria Romana (☎ 233 8290; Hämeenkatu 9; mains €10-15; 11am-10pm Tue-Fri, 1-10pm Sat, 1-9pm Sun) Food surrounds you in this Mediterranean favourite, from the pots and pans decorating the walls and ceiling to rich flavours wafting from the kitchen. The menu has classic lasagne and a tasty chicken with goat's cheese, but blackboard specials always bring a bit of experimentation to the intimate tables.

Midrange & Top End

Tomate (☎ 4885 5511; Brahenkatu 20; tapas €6.50, mains €12-18; 11am-11pm Mon-Fri, noon-midnight Sat, 1-9pm Sun) An ebullient Spanish restaurant washes down its meals with plenty of Iberian wine. Meals-wise they pull off classics like gazpacho and shrimp-rich paella, but make a few concessions to Finnish palates (there are simple fish dishes). The selection of three tapas dishes is best with a few *cervezas* (beers) on the terrace.

Bossa (☎ 251 5880; www.restaurantebossa.fi; Kauppiaskatu 12; mains €12-19, 4-10pm Mon-Fri, noon-11pm Sat, 2-9pm Sun) First-rate Brazilian food is the order of the day at this vibrant eatery, from heart steaks to black-bean soups. Tuesday night features live music that jazzes up the joint.

Teini (☎ 223 0203; Uudenmaankatu 1; lunch €8.70, mains €13-24; lunch & dinner) Something of an institution with city workers for its lunch specials, this traditional grill house does great fish, lamb and steaks in an atmospheric little dining room. Dinner is a little pricey.

Enkeliravintola (☎ 231 8088; Kauppiaskatu 16; mains €15-26; dinner Tue-Fri, lunch & dinner Sat & Sun) This heavenly eatery features several rooms brightly decorated with their namesake angels (*enkeli* means angel) in a tasteful fashion. It's tough to escape the winged wonders with so

many of the dishes named for them. Mains, all served with house-baked bread and pesto, run to roast duck and a classic roast reindeer with lingonberry sauce.

Svenska Klubben 5th Floor Restaurant (☎ 04-691 670; www.svensaklubben.net; Aurakatu1B; lunches €20, mains €15-30, set menus €30-50; lunch & dinner Mon-Fri) It's often tough to spot the menu that's at street level and points the way up to this excellent Scandinavian (yes, we know it's not technically Finnish) eatery. If you can, get a 'cabinet' (small room for groups) that is decked out in Nordic minimalism. You can nosh down on the likes of whitefish with pickled lime, or roasted duck breast sweetened with cognac cream. Three-course lunches are consistently delicious and set menus have several choices.

our pick Linnankatu 3 (☎ 233 9279; www.linnankatu3.fi; Linnankatu 3; mains €16-30; 11am-midnight Mon-Fri, 5pm-midnight Sat) This fashionable spot is the best of a small knot of restaurants. It does a modern twist on Finnish staples like reindeer fillet with cranberry butter and potato pancakes, or crayfish tails swimming in a soup of Bloody Mary.

Viikinkiravintola Harald (☎ 276 5050; www.ravintolaharald.fi; Aurakatu 3; set menus €27-45, mains €10-22; lunch & dinner) Dust off your feasting horned helmet for this Viking restaurant where subtlety is run through with a berserker's broadsword. Food fits the theme, and while set menus (or Voyages as they're called here) are filling three-course samplers, picking and mixing means you can indulge in barbarian ribs on a plank or tar ice cream with cognac. It's not exactly gourmet, but it is great fun.

Blanko (☎ 233 3966; www.blanko.net; Aurakatu 1; dishes €11-25; bar until midnight Sun-Thu, 3am Fri & Sat, kitchen lunch & dinner daily) Look for the Scrabble-tile signage to double-word score on a hip eatery. Inside it's all Scandic chic with periodic DJs, but the dining area is discrete enough for you to enjoy the global menu of pastas, curries and a worthwhile lunch special.

DRINKING

Summer reawakens Turku's drinking crowds, who splash out along the river. Evenings kick-off on one of the booze boats lining the south bank of the river. While some serve food, they are primarily floating beer terraces. Young kids drink on the grassy riverbank nearby. Popular boats on the south side of the river include the upmarket *Donna*, and the down-to-earth *Papa Joe* and *Cindy*.

Alvar (☎ 231 4370; cnr Puutarhakatu & Humalistonkatu; ⏰ 2pm-midnight Sun-Thu, 4pm-2am Fri & Sat) In this building that Aalto designed on a deadline, the low-key pub has a towering beer list that's a magnet for local students and ale-fetishists alike. Artek-esque furniture is a nod to the designer of the building and free wi-fi makes it a lounge rather than a party.

Panimoravintola Koulu (☎ 274 5757; www.panimoravintolakoulu.fi; Eerikinkatu 18) This is the town's greatest brewery pub in the town centre if not all of Finland. Set in a former school, the pub's owners have done their homework on good brews with more than nine of their own beers plus a cheeky cider. As well as inkwells and school desks, there's a row boat on the roof, which is disorientating after a few drinks. The restaurant upstairs is solid, but you won't be able to leave the downstairs pub.

Cow (☎ 276 5053; www.lehmaravintolat.fi; Aurakatu 3; ⏰ 4pm-2am Mon-Thu, 4pm-3am Fri & Sat, 8pm-2am Sun) If you were going to hold a hen's night in Turku, the Cow would be the place. They keep the cocktails flowing and have a good wine selection, but the atmosphere never gets too barnyard, with friendly staff and relaxed couches.

Uusi Apteekki (☎ 250 2595; Kaskenkatu 1; ⏰ 10am-3am) South of the river, this bar is a converted old pharmacy where medication has been dispensed from over a hundred spent beer bottles. It attracts an older local crowd and is ideal for the quiet drink.

Panimoravintola Herman (☎ 230 3333; Läntinen Rantakatu 37; mains €16-24, lunches €8-12) Another brewery pub-restaurant with river frontage that would be a star attraction were it not for Koulu. Its stained glass and large dockside terrace makes for an excellent watering hole, and the food is worth visiting for, especially the lunch buffet.

Old Bank (☎ 274 5700; www.oldbank.fi; Aurakatu 3; ⏰ until 1am, later at weekends) This former bank remains a grand monument, with the trappings of an Irish pub and a formidable roster of beers. The crowd is usually male and older, often enjoying a post-work drink or watching the hockey.

ENTERTAINMENT
Nightclubs & Live Music
Klubi (☎ 231 2155; www.klubi.net; Humalistonkatu 8A) This massive complex has several speeds from the casual drinking of Kolo ('cave') to the DJ-fuelled nightclub of Ilta, plus regular big Finnish bands at Live. It's part-owned by a local record label, which means it snares its fair share of local Finnish bands and visiting international acts.

Galax (☎ 284 3300; www.galax.fi; Aurakatu 6; ⏰ 9pm-3am or 4am) This monster venue holds the Kooma nightclub, known for its disco ambience, and Taivas Music Bar, which attracts some of the biggest bands and the occasional stand-up. Galax itself has regular DJs who spin danceable grooves.

Monk (☎ 251 2444; www.monk.fi; Humalistonkatu 3; admission €8-12; ⏰ 8.30pm-1am Wed-Sat, 8.30pm-4am Mon) Turku's best (OK only) jazz club in town plays live jazz, funk and Latin, with DJs on weekends.

Also recommended:

Åbo Discotek (☎ 276 5700; www.sokeriklubi.com; Aurakatu 3; ⏰ 10pm-4am Thu-Sat) A good place for dancing to chart music.

Dynamo (☎ 250 4904; www.dynamoklubi.com; Linnankatu 7; ⏰ 8pm-4am Wed-Sat) Eclectic sounds with local DJs duelling national bands for places on this busy bill.

Cinema
Julia (☎ 060-000 7007; Eerikinkatu 4) Central cinema in the same building as the hotel of the same name.
Kino Thalia (☎ 237 9400; Hansa Shopping Arcade) Shows more off-beat films and art-house releases.

Classical Music & Theatre
Concert Hall (☎ 262 0800; Aninkaistenkatu 9; tickets €7-16) Founded in the 1790s, the Turku Philharmonic Orchestra is one of the oldest in Europe; it performs here.

Svenska Teater (☎ 277 7377; Eerikinkatu 13) Next to the Hansa Shopping Arcade, this is one of the oldest theatres in Finland and it hosts well-known musicals with performances in Swedish.

GETTING THERE & AWAY
Air
Finnair (☎ 415 4909; www.finnair.fi) flies to Turku from a number of Finnish cities daily along with several European capitals, including Stockholm. Business airline **Turku Air** (☎ 02-276 4966; www.turkuair.fi) flies to Mariehamn on weekdays.

Boat
Turku is a major gateway to Finland from Sweden and Åland, and smaller boats ply the waters up and down the coast.

SWEDEN & ÅLAND
The harbour, southwest of the centre, has terminals for **Silja Line** (☎ 060-015 700; www.tallinksilja.com)

and **Viking Line** (☎ 333 1331; www.vikingline .fi). Both companies sail to Stockholm (11 hours) and Mariehamn (six hours). Prices vary widely according to season and class, with deck class one-way tickets ranging from €14 to €35. **Finnlink** (☎ 010-436 7676; http://passenger .finnlines.com) offers a faster but pricier service from nearby Naantali.

Tickets are available at the harbour, from Viking Line in the Hansa Shopping Arcade, or Silja Lines on Käsityöläiskatu. It's advisable to book ahead during the high season, if you plan to take a car or if you're travelling on a weekend (or Friday night). Connecting trains and buses from other cities may stop at the harbour itself.

See p363 for more details about international ferry travel.

It's also possible to travel using the archipelago ferries to and from mainland Finland via Korpo (southern route, from Galtby passenger harbour) or Kustavi (northern route, from Osnäs passenger harbour), though it's cheaper to break your outward journey in the archipelago (see p258).

Bus

From the bus terminal at Aninkaistentulli there are hourly express buses to Helsinki (€27.50, 2½ hours), and frequent services to Tampere (€28.70, three hours), Rauma (€19.20, 1½ hours), Pori (€25.10, 2½ hours) and other points in southern Finland. Regional buses depart from the kauppatori.

Train

Turku is the terminus for the southeastern railway line. The train station is a short walk northwest of the centre; trains also stop at the ferry harbour and at Kupittaa train station east of the centre. Bus 32 shuttles between the centre and the main train station. Express trains run frequently to and from Helsinki (€32, two hours), Tampere (€22, 1¾ hours), Oulu (€72, six to nine hours), Rovaniemi (€77.70, 9½ to 14 hours). For Oulu and Rovaniemi there's usually a change in Tampere.

GETTING AROUND
To/From the Airport

Bus 1 runs between the kauppatori and the airport, about 8km north of the city, every 15 minutes from 5am to midnight Monday to Friday, from 5.30am to 9.30pm Saturday and from 7am to midnight Sunday (€2.50, 25

minutes). This same bus also goes from the kauppatori to the harbour.

Bus

City and regional buses are frequent and you pay €2.50 for a two-hour ticket or €5.50 for a 24-hour ticket. The Turku Card (p216) allows for free bus transport. Important city bus routes include bus 1 (harbour–kauppatori–bus station–airport) and buses 32 and 42 (train station–kauppatori).

Car Hire

There are several car rental offices, among them **Avis** (☎ 231 1333; Käsityöläiskatu 7B) and **Budget** (☎ 233 4040; Sirkkalankatu 15).

Ferry

There's a small **Föri ferry** (◷ 6.15am-9pm, until 11pm May-Jun) that's free and crosses the river a few blocks downstream from the last bridge. It's the last crossing point.

M/S Ruissalo (☎ 040-052 4151; www.ruissalolautta.fi) departs from the same spot as Föri to go to the island of Ruissalo (one-way €10).

AROUND TURKU

NAANTALI
☎ 02 / pop 14,081

For many Finns Naantali (Swedish: Nådendal) means Moomins. Many skip the quaint old town to get to the theme park dedicated to the children's storybook characters, but it's worth a wander. Most visitors are day trippers from Turku, which is only 18km away, but some come from Sweden for the day out. Even the president spends her time off here, leading many to call it the summer capital of Finland.

Out of season the town is quiet and the big attractions close their gates, lending the old town the melancholic air of an abandoned film set.

History

Naantali grew around the Catholic Convent of the Order of Saint Birgitta, which was founded in 1443. After Finland became Protestant in 1527, the convent was dissolved and Naantali struggled not only spiritually but economically. In the 19th century the town grew to prominence again as a spa town that was handy for Turku's wealthy. Industry returned in the 1950s and far from the old town is

MOOMINMANIA

When Tove Jansson's uncle tried to scare her from midnight snacking in the kitchen, he told her that Moomintroll lived there. It only heightened the young Finn's appetite for fiction as she began imagining what Moomins looked like. Her first Moomin drawing appeared as a signature character for Jansson's political cartoons, but she wrote her first book, *Smätrollen och den stora översvämningen* (The Moomins and the Great Flood), to cheer herself up during WWII.

The characters are the real delight of the books. The large white hippopotamus-like family consist of the parents – a top-hatted Moomimpappa and Moominmamma – and their child Moomin, who manages to get into all sorts of strife. They're based on Jansson's own bohemian family, who were known for their love of difference and nature-loving ways. Many readers believe that the Groke, a gloomy blob that freezes the ground and kills with a touch, is a representation of Nordic winter depression.

Jansson wrote nine books and drew several cartoon books based on her characters, but later adaptations included a Japanese cartoon series, a film and an album, and Moomin even appeared on Finnair planes. Although translated into English, books can be difficult to come by, though at the time of research Canadian comic publisher **Drawn & Quarterly** (www.drawnandquarterly.com) was re-releasing comic strips that originally appeared for 15 years in London's *Evening News*. Moomin merchandise seems to be everywhere in Finland but the real deal is at the Moomin Shop (p103), which was set up by Jansson's heirs. Of course if you want to get even closer then there's Tampere's Moomin Valley Museum (p203) or Muumimaailma (below).

Finland's third most-trafficked port, an oil refinery and an electricity power plant.

Orientation

Naantali sprawls on both sides of the channel Naantalinsalmi. The island of Luonnonmaa is on the southwest side of the channel, accessible only by bridge, and the mainland, with the town centre, is on the northeast side. The old town of Naantali surrounds the harbour, 1km west of the bus terminal.

Information

Library (Tullikatu 11; ☉ noon-7pm Mon-Thu, noon-4pm Fri) Free internet access on the 2nd floor of the post office building.

Tourist service (Naantalin Matkailu; ☎ 435 9800; www.naantalinmatkailu.fi; Kaivotori 2; internet €2, bikes €10; ☉ 9am-6pm Mon-Fri, 10am-3pm Sat & Sun mid-Jun–mid-Aug, 9am-4.30pm Mon-Fri mid-Aug–mid-Jun) By the harbour. Internet access and bike hire.

Sights

MUUMIMAAILMA (MOOMINWORLD)

Crossing the bridge takes you into the down-right delightful world of the Moomin, one of Finland's most popular characters. Even if you've never read the books, seen the TV series or film, there's still something wonderful about these characters (see boxed text, above). **Muumimaailma** (☎ 511 1111; www.muumi maailma.fi; 1-/2-day pass 3yr & over €19/28; ☉ 10am-6pm

early Jun-late Aug) is based on Kailo Island, and has costumed characters wandering through Moominhouse, Snork's Workshop (where kids help with inventions) and a host of places that leap to life from the books.

Bring your swimsuit as there's a swimming beach, plus there's a theatre that retells a different Moomin tale every year. It stops just short of being tacky by having limited merchandise and a focus on participating with the character rather than taking rides. It's busiest in July so visiting in June and August is advised.

Older adventure-seekers will prefer **Väski** (☎ 511 1111; www.vaski.fi; over/under 6yr €15/7, with Moominworld entry discount €1; ☉ 11am-7pm early Jun–mid-Aug), the nearby pirate island that features rock climbing and tracking down buccaneer relics.

OLD TOWN

Naantali's Old Town is a living museum with many townspeople living and working in the historic buildings. The town grew around the convent, without any town plan, and new buildings were always built on the sites of older ones. The photogenic district is best explored by wandering through old narrow cobbled streets with their wooden houses – many of which now house handicraft shops, art galleries, antiques shops and cafes. The main thoroughfare is Mannerheiminkatu

TURKU & THE SOUTHWEST

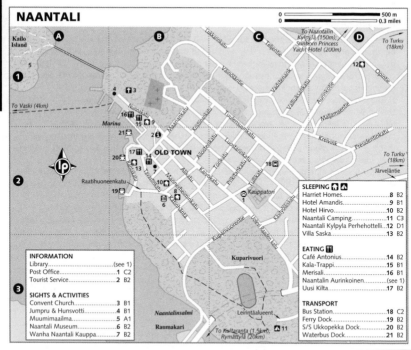

NAANTALI

INFORMATION	
Library.................................(see 1)	
Post Office................................1 C2	
Tourist Service.........................2 B2	

SIGHTS & ACTIVITIES	
Convent Church.........................3 B1	
Jumpru & Hunsvotti....................4 B1	
Muumimaailma...........................5 A1	
Naantali Museum........................6 B2	
Wanha Naantali Kauppa..............7 B2	

SLEEPING	
Harriet Homes................................8 B2	
Hotel Amandis.................................9 B1	
Hotel Hirvo...................................10 B2	
Naantali Camping...........................11 C3	
Naantali Kylpyla Perhehottelli......12 D1	
Villa Saska...................................13 B2	

EATING	
Café Antonius...............................14 B2	
Kala-Trappi..................................15 B1	
Merisali......................................16 B1	
Naantalin Aurinkoinen...............(see 1)	
Uusi Kilta.....................................17 B2	

TRANSPORT	
Bus Station...................................18 C2	
Ferry Dock....................................19 B2	
S/S Ukkopekka Dock....................20 B2	
Waterbus Dock.............................21 B2	

and **Wanha Naantali Kauppa** (☎ 040-545 4467; Mannerheiminkatu 13; ⏰ 11am-5pm daily, to 4pm Jun-Aug) is a popular shop selling old-fashioned Finnish sweets (brace yourself for liquorice and tar drops), bottled soft drinks, postcards and souvenirs – it's a slightly pricey nostalgia trip.

Housed in three old wooden buildings dating from the 18th century, **Naantali Museum** (☎ 434 5321; Katinhäntä 1; admission €2.50; ⏰ noon-7pm Tue-Sun mid-May–Aug) casts a light on disappearing trades such as needlemaking and goldsmithing, as well as looking at how the town prospered from sock knitting.

CONVENT CHURCH
The only building remaining from the Convent of the Order of Saint Birgitta is the massive **Convent Church** (⏰ 10am-6pm daily May, 10am-8pm daily Jun-Aug, 11am-3pm Sun, noon-2pm Wed Sep-Apr), which towers above the harbour. The church was completed in 1462 though its baroque stone tower dates from 1797. The interior is surprisingly wide, with elegant vaulting and a very handsome 17th-century pulpit depicting the apostles and evangelists

in a blaze of colour. Also noteworthy is the carved 15th-century polychrome wood triptych behind the altar and an evocative wooden head of Christ below it. Recent archaeological digs around the church revealed more than 2000 pieces of jewellery, coins and other relics that appear in the museum.

During summer there's a program of organ music; the tourist office can provide a schedule. At 8pm on summer evenings you'll hear the 'vespers' (evensong) played by a trumpeter from the belfry of the church.

KULTARANTA
The president of Finland's summer residence is an elaborate stone castle on Luonnonmaa island, with the flamboyant tower visible from Naantali harbour. The castle, designed by Lars Sonck, was built in 1916 and is surrounded by beautiful, extensive rose gardens.

Kultaranta grounds (☎ 435 9800; tour from gate/ Naantali €8/12; ⏰ Tue-Sun late Jun–mid-Aug) can only be visited by guided tours, which leave from the front gate (at 2pm and 3pm) or with a bus trip from Naantali tourist office (1.55pm). Book at the tourist office.

Activities

Naantali's spa traditions date from 1723, when people took health-giving waters from a spring in Viluluoto. **Naantalin Kylpylä** (☎ 445 5100; www .naantalispa.fi; spa per 2hr €15, day spa packages €83-141), the town's top-class spa hotel, allows non-guests to use its fantastic facilities – including several pools and a Turkish bath – during the day. The huge range of spa, massage and beauty treatments are popular with mothers who don't want to go to Muumimaailma so book ahead in summer.

You can rent bicycles at **Jumpru & Hunsvotti** (☎ 533 2242; per day €10), a small marine shop at the harbour near the bridge to Moominworld.

Gold Coast Cruises (☎ 045-129 2279; www.gcc.fi) does a one-hour cruise (€12) in a zippy inflatable that will take you around the bay.

Festivals & Events

For over 30 years, **Naantali Music Festival** (☎ 434 5363; www.naantalimusic.com; tickets €10-40) has been held over two weeks from early June featuring first-rate classical music. Events in the Convent Church are a real highlight and performers come from around the globe.

Naantali celebrates the unusual Finnish festival of **Sleepyhead Day** (27 July), by electing a 'Sleepyhead of the Year' who is woken early by being tossed into the sea. A carnival with music, dancing and games ensues.

Sleeping

Harriet Homes (☎ 040-910 4444; www.harriethomes .com; Katinhäntä 3; per person €40) This collection of mini-houses are all named after family members (Vincent or Rebecca?) and make for an extremely central family stay. It's close enough to walk to Muumimaailma or the harbour. The buildings all gather around a central courtyard and the rooms themselves are roomy enough for even larger families.

Naantali Camping (☎ 435 0855; Kuparivuori; tent sites €13 plus per adult €4, 2-person cottages €40, 4-person €50-110) About 400m south of the harbour is this exceptional camping ground that's always popular with holidaying Finns. It's open all year and has great management and good facilities, including a beachside sauna. Cottages have been recently refreshed and four-person cabins have a huge range from basic to their own sauna, bathrooms and kitchens.

Naantalin Kylpylä Perhehotelli (☎ 445 5100; Opintie 3; 1-/2-/3-room apt €56/112/168; [P]) Despite its institutional appearance, this family hotel is an affordable option. Apartments, which include kitchens, are popular with families and mean you can also use the neighbouring spa facilities (swimming €10).

Naantalin Kylpylä (Spa Hotel; ☎ 44550; www.naan talispa.fi; Matkailijantie 2; s/d €129/156; [P] [□] [🛋] [&]) Uberindulgence is the call of the day at this upmarket spa hotel. It's large but stylish with treatment rooms (massage and beauty) and pools downstairs. Rooms are spacious enough to almost be suites, with a lounge area and balcony or verandah; the sofa folds out to make a family room. The spa also owns the Sunborn Princess Yacht Hotel (singles/doubles €149/176), a stationary cruise ship with comfortable rooms (called minisuites), though they're no larger than the main complex's doubles.

Villa Saksa (☎ 040-761 8384; www.villasaksa.doldrums .fi; Rantakatu 6; apt Jun/Jan €135/75) With views across to the president's summer palace, this dignified old wooden villa is one of the real finds in Naantali. The apartment is richly decorated in antique pieces with a small kitchen. Prices vary wildly by season (we've provided two months as examples) and availability, so booking ahead could snag a bargain.

Other recommendations:

Hotel Hirvo (☎ 435 1619; Mannerheiminkatu 19; d €65) Well placed in the Old Town, friendly staff, quiet garden; guests can use the kitchen.

Hotel Amandis (☎ 430 8774; www.hotelamandis .com; Nunnakatu 5; d €120; [P]) Close to the harbour, there are six snug little mini-cabins that include breakfast by the water.

Eating

Naantali has a cluster of eating options around the harbour and you'll also find bites to eat at Muumimaailma.

Cafe Antonius (Mannerheiminkatu 9; cakes & pastries €3-6; 🕙 10am-6pm Mon-Sat, 11am-5pm Sun) Well-placed for snack attacks ('If you're quiet until we get to Muumimaailma, Ulli, then you can have a gingerbread'), this cafe does pastries, sweets and other 'quieteners' for little ones. The convenience isn't cheap though.

Merisali (☎ 435 2451; Nunnakatu 1; buffet lunch/dinner €9.70/11.50, Sun breakfast €7.30, lunch €12, dinner €16.50; 🕙 breakfast, lunch & dinner) This favourite spot is a restored spa pavilion that offers buffets that are the best in town. The pierside terrace is the perfect place to enjoy your selection from the large salad bar as well as fish and often a roast.

Kala-Trappi (☎ 435 2477; www.kalatrappi.fi; Nunnakatu 3; mains €11-23; ☺ lunch & dinner) This more gourmet option in a fine wooden building, is perfect for a refined meal. The menu is based on Finnish specialities with roast goose in an apple and seabuckthorn sauce and several options for whitefish, but also has seafood or reindeer pastas and simpler steaks. Save room for the expertly chosen cheeses including deep-fried camembert with *lakka* (cloudberries).

Also recommended:

Naantalin Aurinkoinen (☎ 075-325 7303; www .aurinkoinen.fi, in Finnish; Tullikatu 11; sandwiches & pastries €4-6; ☺ 8.30am-6.30pm Mon-Fri, 8.30am-2.30pm Sat) By the kauppatori, this refreshingly local place is packed with pastries and other bakery favourites, along with good coffee, magazines and internet.

Uusi Kilta (☎ 435 1066; Mannerheiminkatu 1; meals €10-18) Another harbourside restaurant with an international menu and top terrace.

Getting There & Away

Buses to Naantali (routes 11 and 110) run every 15 minutes from the market square (opposite Hansa Shopping Arcade) in Turku (€4.50, 20 minutes).

SS *Ukkopekka* sails between Turku and Naantali in summer, arriving at the passenger quay on the south side of the harbour. For more information see p219.

Finnlink (☎ 010-436 7676; http://passenger.finnlines .com) ferries go to Kapellskär (€30 plus car €90, 7½ hours), near Stockholm in Sweden, four times daily. The ferry includes two meals, and berths are available.

LOUHISAARI MANOR

The village of Askainen, 30km northwest of Turku, has stunning **Louhisaari Manor** (☎ 02-31 2515; admission €5; ☺ 11am-5pm mid-May–Aug). This lavishly decorated home was once owned by the Dutch Fleming family before being purchased by the Mannerheim family. It's the birthplace of Finland's greatest military leader and president, Marshal CGE Mannerheim, so it attracts a lot of interested Finns. The manor was built in 1655 in the Dutch Renaissance style and is surrounded by an English landscaped park that makes for a good picnic. Tours are disappointingly only in Finnish.

The village and manor are located just off Rd 193. There are three to four buses daily from Turku to Askainen.

NOUSIAINEN

Nousiainen, 25km north of Turku, makes a good day trip for the **Nousiainen church** (☺ noon-6pm Tue-Sun). It's a noteworthy medieval church because it's the first resting place of St Henry, an Englishman and Swedish-consecrated bishop who was the first to bring Christianity to the Finns (with a little accompanying light war) in the mid 12th century. His bones were taken to Turku Cathedral in the 13th century. The current church post-dates this, having been largely built in the 14th century and restored in the 1960s.

Hourly buses from Turku to Mynämäki stop at Nousiainen.

TURKU ARCHIPELAGO

☎ 02

The tightly clustered islands that stretch west of Pargas out to Houtskär are known as the Turku Archipelago. Ferry-hopping between islands and islets is the best way to see the area including the wealth of birdlife that calls these islands home in summer. You can also just pop out for day trips to Kustavi or Nagu.

Information

Archipelago Booking (☎ 02-465 1000; www.archipel agobooking.com) There's plenty of accommodation on the islands, but this place is particularly useful for booking cottages.

Turku City Tourist Office (☎ 02-262 7444; www .turkutouring.fi) Also has useful information on the archipelago.

Turun Saaristo (☎ 02-458 5942; www.saaristo.org) The best source of information on the archipelago, including brochures and accommodation options.

Getting There & Away

Out as far as Houtskär, the islands almost join, making it easy enough to explore with public transport (including ferries) but the Archipelago Trail is easiest for cyclists and motorists. Want more? It's possible to island-hop all the way over to Åland and then Sweden by heading even further west then skipping from Galtby in Korpo out to Kökar (p260) and on to Mariehamn. This trip is sometimes confusingly called the Archipelago Route.

There are two types of ferries in the area: the white public-transport ferries and the rubber duck–like yellow ferries that run less

---

ARCHIPELAGO TRAIL

The **Archipelago Trail** (www.saaristo.org) is a popular itinerary that heads out through Pargas, Nagu and then Korpo then loops out to Houtskär before heading back via Inniö to Kustavi. It can be done counter-clockwise and mostly uses public transport with the exception of the Houtskär-Iniö ferry (p230).

The whole route is roughly 250km and very doable over a week of easy cycling and taking your time to see the islands.

---

frequently and cost nothing. The white ferries between Pargas, Nagu, Korpo and Houtskä run continually but you may need to book if you're bringing your car. For details of all ferries and timetables see **Ferryportal** (www.lautat.fi).

KUSTAVI

The island village of Kustavi (Swedish: Gustavs) offers scenic seascapes and a jumping-off point for the Åland islands. Ferries depart to the island of Brändö (p258) from the port of Osnäs (Finnish: Vuosnainen) on the western tip of the island.

Kustavi's wooden **church** (May–mid-Aug), built in 1783, features the cruciform shape and votive miniature ships common in coastal churches. You can find out more about Kustavi at the **tourist office** (☎ 842 6620; www.kustavi.fi; 8.30am-4pm Mon-Fri) as well as book accommodation. A great place to eat is **Laura Peterzéns Studio** (☎ 877 696; www.laurapstudio.com; Kustavi; noon-10pm Jun-Aug), with outdoor tables on a picturesque wooden deck.

Getting There & Away

At least seven buses run each day to Turku (€13.50, two hours). A free ferry connects Kustavi with Inniö. There are regular passenger ferries to Långö on northern Brändö, with details from **Ålandstrafiken** (☎ 018-525 100; www.alandstrafiken.ax).

PARGAS

Hard-working Pargas (Finnish: Parainen) is the de facto 'capital' of the archipelago. It was once a port for the Hansa League on the way to Turku, and continues to be a major port with limestone mining nearby. There's a **tourist office** (☎ 458 5942; www.parainen.fi; Runeberinkatu 6; 9am-4pm Mon-Fri).

Sights & Activities

The attractive old town of **wooden houses** (☎ 050-596 2112; by appointment) is behind the **Greystone Church** (☎ 454 7757; Kyrkoesplanaden 4), which was built in the 14th century and includes the chapel of Finland's first archbishop, completed much later in the 19th century.

When Lenin was on the lamb from Russia to Stockholm in 1907 he stayed in Pargas under the pseudonym Mr Mueller and you can see his room at **Pargas Local History Museum** (☎ 458 1452; Storgärdsgatan 13; admission €2; 11am-4pm Tue-Sun Jun-Aug) along with a seaman's croft and restored schoolhouse. For more on Lenin in Finland, see boxed text, p34.

Just 10km on the Nagu–Pargas road, **Sattmark** (☎ 050-596 2112; admission €2; 11am-4pm Tue-Sun) is a charming 18th-century red wooden crofter's cottage with a cafe and rustic handicrafts, plus a few nature trails and ski tracks.

If you're wanting to explore the islands, **Pelago** (☎ 548 5700; www.pelago.fi; Kauppiaskatu 18) rents bikes (€16 per day) and can organise accommodation and ferry packages (two days €85) to take you all the way to Åland.

Sleeping & Eating

Solliden Camping (☎ 485 5955; www.solliden.fi; Norrby; tent sites €10 plus per person €4, 4-/8-person cottages €40/120; May-Sep) Pargas' seaside camping ground, 1.5km north of the centre, with camping, a range of cottages that sleep up to eight, saunas and a laundry.

Axo (☎ 454 4422; Kauppiaskatu 13; pastries €2-5; 8am-5pm Mon-Fri, 9am-2pm Sat) The iconic coffee shop draws a local crowd with its array of cakes and pies.

Getting There & Away

At least two buses run to Turku (€5.40, 40 minutes) each day. If you want to explore some of the more obscure islands, **Rosita** (☎ 469 2500; www.rosita.fi) island-hops out to Nötö Aspö and Utö.

NAGU

Nagu (Finnish: Nauvo) is an idyllic island strung between Pargas and Korpo. Its guest harbour attracts yachties and cruise ships, so a lot of the action centres there.

Nagu church (Jun-late Aug) dates from the 14th century and contains the oldest Bible in Finland. You can explore much of the island on foot by getting a copy of *Walkways of*

Nagu (www.nagu.fi/vandraren), which details the network of paths in the surrounding area including Avivon oma Polku, a short stroll designed just for kids. You can also hit the water with **Nagu Kayak** (☎ 050-354 1616; per 2hr/1-day €15/30).

Sleeping & Eating

Hotel & Hostel Gammelgård (☎ 040-511 2800; www .nagugammelgard.fi; Norrstrandsvägen 22-1; dm €16, s/d €54/80) is an atmospheric former village set in the middle of the forest, and includes a barn, chapel and restored bakery that's a brilliant summer pizzeria (pizzas €9). Rooms range from basic dorms to B&B-style cottages, plus there's a minigolf, a sauna and a few walking trails. It's about 2.5km out of town.

Hotel Stranbo (☎ 460 6200; Strandvägen 3; s/d €100/138; ⏰ 11.30am-2pm; 🖳) This is the sophisticated option at the guest harbour with quality rooms in a stately seafront building, and a good restaurant offering a great lunch buffet and autumn à la carte.

KORPO

Korpo (Finnish: Korppoo) is the perfect place to ship out to the Åland archipelago but is remote enough to be an intriguing destination in its own right. The **tourist information centre** (☎ 463 1100; www.korpo.fi) has some information in English. A highlight is the medieval **Korpo church** (⏰ summer) built in the late 13th century and featuring naïve paintings on the ceiling and a statue of St George fighting a dragon. The main harbour is Galtby, which connects to Kökar (p260).

Sleeping & Eating

Korpo has plenty of B&Bs and cottages; a list can be provided by tourist information.

Faffas B&B (☎ 464 6106; www.korpo.fi/faffas; s/d €45/70; 🅿) is an upmarket year-round guesthouse about 4km east of the Galtby harbour in Österretais. As well as rooms there are some more affordable 'sheds' (really cabins).

Buffalo Ravintola (☎ 463 1610; www.restraurangbuf falo.com; Verkan; ⏰ 9am-midnight Mon-Thu, 9am-2.30am Fri & Sat, 10am-10pm Sun) unsurprisingly, given its name, specialises in steaks. Its pierside location also means that it does excellent fish, all on a sun-drenched terrace.

Getting There & Away

Regular buses go to Turku (€13.50, two hours). There's an hourly ferry from Galtby

to Houtskär. The trip from Galtby to Kökar takes 2¼ hours. It's free for passengers and bicycles, and €20 for cars.

Passenger ferries (€3) leave from nearby Verkan to outlying islands like Bergham, Lillpensar, Storpensar, Kälderso and Elvsö.

HOUTSKÄR & INIÖ

Houtskär and its tiny neighbour Iniö represent the final pieces of the Archipelago Trail puzzle and are delightfully tranquil, if a little short of sights. Both islands have Swedish-speaking populations.

Houtskä's two ports are **Mossala** in the north and **Kittius**, in the south, with Nasby between them. You can pitch camp or rent a cabin at Mossala's **Skagardens Fritidcenter** (☎ 463 3322; www.saaristo.com; tent sites €6 plus per person €4, cabins from €50), which also has a restaurant and rents boats.

A small **tourist information point** (☎ 07-5325 8869; www.houtskar.fi; ⏰ 10am-5pm Mon-Fri early-mid Jun, 10am-3pm Sat, noon-5pm Sun Jun-Aug) operates in Nasby, which also has a modest **museum** (admission €2; ⏰ noon-4pm Mon, 1-7pm Tue-Fri, noon-4pm Sat & Sun Jun-early Aug) that includes a small windmill, restored dairy shed and period home.

Iniö boasts a sweet stone **church of Sofia Wilhelmina**, built in the 18th century. You may also be lucky enough to see **Midsummer poles** (see p248), if you're visiting in summer, but mostly the area is a good place for nature strolls with the aid of maps from the **tourist office** (☎ 040-773 0210; www.inio.fi; ⏰ 10am-5pm Mon-Fri early-mid-Jun, 10am-3pm Sat, noon-5pm Sun Jun-Aug).

The ferry between Houtskär and Iniö (adult €5, bicycle €2, car €20, one hour) is one of the few privately operated routes and it's run by **Finstaship** (☎ 030-620 7000; www.finstaship.fi). It's also possible to go from Kannvik on Iniö to Torsholma on Brändö (p258) on **M/S Carolina** (☎ 040-717 3455) daily.

KIMITO & ARCHIPELAGO NATIONAL PARK
☎ 02

Kimito is the jumping-off point for the Archipelago National Park, a scattering of islands that stretches south of Korpo and west of Kasnäs. Kasnäs, the harbour on the southern extreme of Kimito Island, is the best place to explore the park from though it's worth breaking a journey at either Dragsfjärd or the township of Kimito. Swedish is the prominent language in this area and you'll hear it more if you journey into the islands of the archipelago such as Hittis or Bengtskär.

Information

Tourist office (☎ 423 572; Arkadiantie 13, Kimito)
Visitor Centre Blåmussian (☎ 466 6290; Kasnäs; ✆ 10am-6pm summer) Has good information on exploring the national park.

Sights & Activities

Dragsfjärd, in the southwest of Kimito Island, is a quiet, rural village with a gold-coloured **church** dating back to 1755. The manor house of **Söderlångvik** (☎ 424 662; www.soderlangvik.fi; Amos Andersonvägen 2, Dragsfjärd; adult/child €3.50/free; ✆ 11am-6pm summer) belonged to local newspaper magnate and art collector Amos Anderson. There are paintings, furniture and special exhibitions in this beautiful manor, as well as an extensive garden and a cafe.

Near Kimito village, **Sagalund Museum** (☎ 421 738; www.sagalund.fi; adult/child €4/free; ✆ 11am-6pm daily Jun-Aug, 9am-3pm Mon-Fri Sep-May) is an open-air museum with more than 20 old buildings including a traditional sauna and blacksmith. There are guided tours every hour.

If you're looking at exploring the national park, make for the **Visitor Centre Blåmussian** (☎ 466 6290; Kasnäs; ✆ 10am-6pm summer) for further information. The centre organises tours to some islands in June, July and August, depending on demand, and offers tips on nature trails in the area. There are also several films in English (most around 10 minutes long). It's on a small dirt road just away from the pier.

Kasnäs Water Sports (☎ 040-769 6405, 045-638 475; Hotel Kasnäs) rents out bikes (€15 per day) and kayaks (€20), but also offers surf lessons (€40) and an exhilarating jet-boat ride (€185 for a minimum of 12 people), plus cruises to Bengtskar (€50 per person) for half-day trips.

Ferries M/S *Rosala II* and M/S *Aura* run to nearby islands, including Hitis (Hiittinen), daily in summer. Even if you don't want to visit the islands, they make a pleasant day cruise. **M/S Rosala** (☎ 040-032 0092) goes eight times daily (25 minutes) to Hitis (Hiitinen), which is known for its wooden church. There's also a good one-day round trip (€53) that goes to **Bengtskär's lighthouse** (☎ 466 7227; www.bengtskar.fi; admission €7), Scandinavia's tallest lighthouse, which runs as a museum now,

and **Rosala Viking Centre** (☎ 466 7227; www.rosala .fi), which looks at Viking ships and daily life. The trip includes lunch at the centre.

Sleeping

Backas Gård (☎ 466 6112; www.backasgard.fi; Kasnäs; cabins per person €30-35) Handy for the harbour is this collection of spruce cottages, each with a shower and kitchen. There's a good restaurant and sauna, if you're prepared to pay a little extra.

Hostel Panget (☎ 424 553; www.panget.fi; Kulla; s/d €55/70, cottages €110; ✆ May-Sep) At the turn-off to Dragsfjärd, Hostel Panget is a pleasant spot. Rooms are comfortable and there are several common areas, including a pub downstairs and a well-stocked kitchen. The seaside cottage is a good getaway with its own sauna and capacity to sleep six.

Hotel Kasnäs (☎ 521 0100; www.kasnas.com; Kasnäs; d €124, ste €210; **P** 🖳 🖳) At the end of the road this sprawling hotel complex is perfect for pampering before heading further out. Facilities are laid on, and include a water-sports hire kiosk and a modern spa complex with a 25m pool. Rooms are spread over several buildings and there's an excellent restaurant and a terrace.

Getting There & Around

There are one or two daily bus-and-ferry connections from Dragsfjärd (Taalintehdas) to Turku (€15.10, 1¾ hours) and Helsinki (€25.50, three to four hours). To get here by car, turn off onto Rd 1835 from Salo, which will take you to Kimito village.

For information on ferries to nearby islands see left.

NORTH OF TURKU

UUSIKAUPUNKI

☎ 02 / pop 16,260

Sweet Uusikaupunki (*oo-see-cow*-poonki) has a name that means 'New Town', which is ironic for a town founded way back in 1617. It's famous for the treaty of 1721 which quelled hostilities between Russia and Sweden after the gruelling Great Northern War.

Built either side of an inlet, the town's port has been honey to the buzzing yachty crowd, but has also made it a smuggling destination

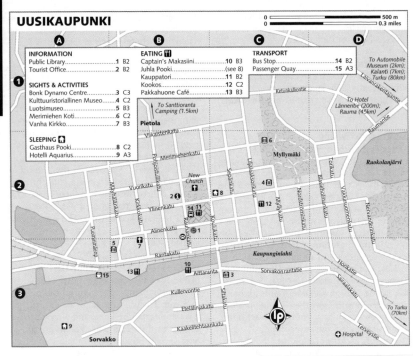

until the customs house was built in 1760. The local car-manufacturing industry today draws as many suited visitors as the port.

Information

Public library (☎ 8451 5382; Alinenkatu 34; ✆ 11am-7pm Mon-Fri, 11am-5pm Sat & Sun) Free internet access.

Tourist office (☎ 8451 5443; http://uusikaupunki.fi; Rauhankatu 10; ✆ 9am-5pm Mon-Fri, 9am-3pm Sat late Jun-early Aug, 8.30am-4pm Mon-Fri rest of year) Has free internet terminal and rents bikes (€2/10 per hour/day).

Sights

One of Finland's kookiest, **Bonk Dynamo Centre** (☎ 841 8404; www.bonkcentre.fi; Siltakatu 2; admission €5; ✆ 10am-6pm mid-May–late Aug, 10am-4pm late Aug–mid-May) is part museum, part art installation and all joke. It creates the believable story of the Bonk dynasty which began by shipping giant Peruvian anchovies to the Baltic, and went on to produce 'fully dysfunctional machinery applications'. The creation of local artist Alvar Gullichsen, this is a classic display of the oddball dry Finnish sense of humour. Kids are included as they can construct their own Bonk machines in the workshop.

Three museums concentrate on the region's seafaring history and can be visited on a combined ticket (€3). **Kulttuurihistoriallinen Museo** (Museum of Cultural History; ☎ 8451 5447; Ylinenkatu 11; admission €2; ✆ 10am-5pm Mon-Fri, noon-3pm Sat & Sun early Jun-early Sep, noon-5pm Tue-Fri rest of year) is set in a delightful house built by a business magnate. Rooms are furnished in wealthy 19th-century style and exhibit seafaring memorabilia, though the charming grounds are worth exploring too.

Merimiehen Koti (Seaman's Home; ☎ 8451 5413; Myllykatu 18; admission €1; ✆ 11am-3pm Tue-Fri, noon-3pm Sat & Sun early Jun–mid-Aug, weekends only in late Aug) was once home to a local sailor, and evokes family life in the early 20th century. **Luotsimuseo** (Pilot Museum; ☎ 8451 5450; Vallimäki; admission €1; ✆ 11am-3pm Tue-Fri, noon-3pm Sat & Sun early Jun–mid-Aug, weekends only in late Aug) is a small house devoted to maritime navigation.

Vanha Kirkko (Old Church; Kirkkokatu 2; ✆ 11am-3.30pm Mon-Sat, noon-4pm Sun Jun–mid-Aug) is one of the town's oldest buildings, and was completed in 1629. Its ornate barrel-vaulted roof alludes to a ship's hull while outside there are the graves of Finns who were lost during the

Winter War. The New Church was built when architects suspected the original was unstable, but they kept with the Gothic style although it was completed in 1863. The stunning altarpieces were completed by RW Ekman, who was born in Uusikaupunki.

Northeast of the centre, **Myllymäki** (Windmill Hill) is a hilltop park with four windmills – reflecting different ages of the technology that once surrounded the town. They're in sharp contrast to the modern wind-power generators to the west of town.

The village of **Kalanti**, about 7km to the east of Uusikaupunki on Rd 43, is where the first sizeable party of Swedes, led by King Erik, arrived on a crusade in 1155. Among the party was Henry, an Englishman who was the bishop of Uppsala. He began the process of Christianising Finland; this incursion also marks the beginning of our knowledge of Swedish influence and rule over Finland. **Kalanti Church** dates from the late 14th century and its interior paintings depict Bishop Henry meeting a pagan on the Finnish coast. There are buses roughly hourly from Uusikaupunki to Kalanti (10 minutes); they are marked Laitila.

Activities

There are plenty of charter boats and water taxis available for archipelago cruises from the harbour in Uusikaupunki. **M/S Marival II** (☎ 050-66698; www.marival.fi; ☾ Thu & Sun late Jun–mid-Aug) runs to the **Isokari Lighthouse** on Thursday and Sunday, and on Saturday to **Katanpää Fort Island** (€35, both 6½ hours). The cost of this full-day cruise includes lunch and a guided walk. On Fridays the boat heads to Kustavi (€15), from where you can head out on a ferry to the nearby Åland. There are various other trips available on this boat. Cruises just to the lighthouse and back (adult/child €5/2) are also arranged in summer and it can be booked through the tourist office.

Archipelago Cruises (☎ 9451 5443) does a half-day cruise (€20) to nearby Isokari (11am Friday and Sunday) that includes lunch and a guided tour.

Sleeping

Santtioranta Camping (☎ 842 3862; Kalalokkikuja 14; tent sites €10 plus per person €3, 2-/4-person cabins €33/45; ☾ mid-May–mid-Sep) This picturesque seaside camping ground is 1.5km northwest of the town centre, which is within walking distance.

Alternatively, you can rent bikes or row boats to get around. There's a small kiosk, and cabins have kitchens.

Hotel Lännentie (☎ 845 6100; www.hotelli-lannentie .fi; Levysepänkatu 1; s/d from €55/65; P ☺) East of the centre, on the road to Rauma, is a hotel-motel with plain but serviceable rooms. There are plenty of facilities including a sauna, croquet and a small pool table, plus golf and ski packages.

Gasthaus Pooki (☎ 847 7100; pooki@uusikaupunki .fi; Ylinenkatu 21; s/d €75/100; P) A good thing in a small package, this endearing granite building has only four rooms that feel more like an old-fashioned inn and include a great breakfast. Rooms have a nautical theme in clean ocean blues with the danger of drowning in the well-stocked minibar. The twin is plainer and more businesslike, but still winning.

Hotelli Aquarius (☎ 841 3123; www.hotelliaquarius .fi; Kullervontie 11; s/d €99/119, ste €175; P ☐ ☺) This large hotel caters for the 'big end of town' business travellers but represents great value on weekends. It's set away from town in a parklike setting with tennis courts and a pool, with breakfast and sauna included.

Eating & Drinking

The **kauppatori** (☾ 10am-6pm Mon-Fri May-Sep) is good for snacks and produce.

Pakkahuone Café (☎ 842 4822; snacks €4-9; ☾ 8.30am-8pm Mon-Sat, 9am-8pm Sun) This place does a roaring trade with visiting boaties who come for a quick coffee or leisurely beer on the quayside terrace. It also operates as a quasi-information centre with a good stock of brochures.

our pick **Kookos** (☎ 040-414 1409; Liljalaaksonkatu 7; mains €6-10; ☾ 8.30am-7pm Mon-Fri, 10am-4pm Sat) This small snazzy coconut (*kookos* in Finnish) is decked out in muted nutty browns and does delicious homemade cakes, sandwiches and salads, plus they have local Laitilan soft drinks. As well as a small but intriguing gallery there is a dedicated play room for kids.

Juhla Pooki (☎ 847 7100; Ylinenkatu 21; buffet lunches €14, bar meals €6-10, mains €10-16; ☾ buffet noon-6pm Jun-Aug, other areas lunch & dinner daily) Attached to the guesthouse, this multilevel courtyard and indoor dining room has something for everyone. There's terrace drinking, casual burgers outside and an à la carte menu. The attractive wooden building next door is called Juhla and it does the best lunch buffet, which offers plenty of choice. They've been given Slow Food Awards but the service is anything but snail-like.

Captain's Makasiini (☎ 841 3600; Aittaranta 12; pizzas €6-8, steaks €15-16; ☒ from 5pm weekdays, from 2pm weekends) This makes a good place to sit back with a beer or 20 when the sun is out. They do passable bar food here but you wouldn't come here for that. At the time of research this was the best of the converted riverside shophouses though new ones are popping up all the time so wander along the river to see what takes your fancy.

Getting There & Away

Uusikaupunki is 70km north of Turku and 50km south of Rauma, off the main north–south road (Rd 8) – take Rd 43 west to reach Uusikaupunki.

Buses to Turku (€12, 1¼ hours) run from behind the kauppatori in the centre of town once or twice per hour on weekdays, less frequently on weekends. There are five to eight buses per day from Rauma (€8.20, 1½ hours). Buses from Helsinki run via Turku.

RAUMA

☎ 02 / pop 36,783

Founded in 1442, Rauma (Swedish: Raumo) was one of the few artisan towns to ignore the order from King Gustav Wasa to move to Helsinki to make the capital a trade centre. The move paid off, and by the 18th century Rauma was a trade centre thanks mostly to its handmade lace that decorated Europe's finest bonnets. Locals still turn out the delicate material, and celebrate their heritage of lacemaking with an annual festival.

Rauma's Vanha Rauma (Old Town) district is the big draw to the town with day trippers from Turku visiting during the day. The old town is the largest wooden town preserved in the Nordic countries and swarms with visitors by day, but at night you'll have its cobbled streets to yourself. You might hear snatches of Rauman giäl, the local dialect that mixes English, Estonian, German and other languages that worked their way into the lingo from its intrepid sailors.

The town doesn't just live off past glories; Rauma remains an important shipping centre that transports Finnish paper round the world. Two of Finland's nuclear power plants are located nearby, and there are plans for a third.

Information

Public library (☎ 834 4531; Ankkurikatu 1; ☒ 10am-4pm Mon-Fri, 10am-2pm Sat) Has free internet terminals.
Tourist office (☎ 8378 7731; www.rauma.fi; Valtakatu 2; ☒ 8am-6pm Mon-Fri, 10am-3pm Sat, 11am-2pm Sun Jun-Aug, 8am-4pm Mon-Fri Sep-May) Publishes the helpful *A Walking Tour In The Old Town* (free).

Sights
VANHA RAUMA

The World Heritage–listed **Old Town** (☎ 834 4750; www.oldrauma.fi) in the heart of modern Rauma remains a living centre, with low-key cafes, hardware shops, residences and a few artisans and lacemakers working in small studios.

The wooden buildings were built in the 18th and 19th centuries, and each introduces itself by name – look for the small oval nameplate near the door. There are over 600 old buildings to meet as you wander the cobbled streets popping into museums and shops along the way. The main streets of Kuninkaankatu and Kauppakatu have many of the major sights and there's good shopping on both, but meander away from them and you'll find several serendipitous spots. It makes for an enchanting day trip from Turku especially if you pick up a copy of *A Walking Tour In The Old Town* from the tourist office.

As with much of Finland, the **kauppatori** is the heart of old Rauma. Although there was recently a controversy about creating a covered area of the market, it remains a lively market square where you're still likely to hear Rauma's unique dialect. To the south is Rauma's most impressive building, Vanha Raatihuone (Old Town Hall), built in 1776. It now houses the **Rauma Museum** (☎ 834 3532; Kauppakatu 13; combined entry to 4 museums €6, single entry €3; ☒ noon-5pm Tue-Fri, 10am-2pm Sat, 11am-5pm Sun Sep-May, 10am-7pm Tue-Sun Jun-Aug), exhibiting maritime heritage and a few choice lace pieces.

Marela (☎ 834 3532; Kauppakatu 24; combined entry to 4 museums €6, single entry €3; ☒ noon-5pm Tue-Fri, 10am-2pm Sat, 11am-5pm Sun Sep-May, 10am-7pm Tue-Sun Jun-Aug) is the most interesting of Rauma's museums and one of its most elaborate buildings. The preserved home of a wealthy 19th-century merchant family is furnished with antiques, wall paintings and Swedish ceramic stoves.

Kirsti (☎ 834 3532; Pohjankatu 3; combined entry to 4 museums €6, single entry €3; ☒ noon-5pm Tue-Fri, 10am-2pm Sat, 11am-5pm Sun Sep-May, 10am-7pm Tue-Sun Jun-Aug) is another lovable collection of buildings

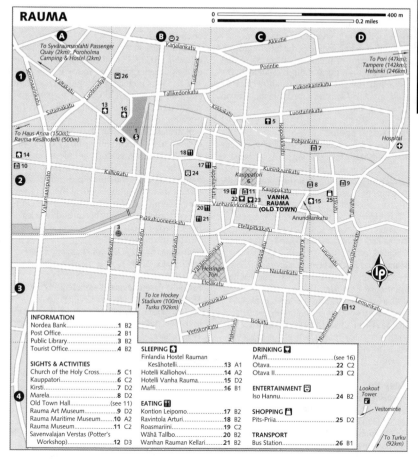

RAUMA

with a yard that's circled by a stable, granary and barn. Inside, rooms represent different periods of the home's life right through to the 1970s.

Located outside of Old Town, due to the fire risk, **Savenvalajan Verstas** (Potter's Workshop; ☎ 834 3532; Nummenkatu 2; combined entry to 4 museums €6, single entry €3; ⏰ noon-5pm Tue-Fri, 10am-2pm Sat, 11am-5pm Sun Sep-May, 10am-7pm Tue-Sun Jun-Aug) is a small museum that once made distinctive stove tiles. It provides an insight into this fascinating trade, and you can have a go yourself.

North of the kauppatori is the bold stone **Church of the Holy Cross** (Pyhän Ristin Kirkko; Luostarinkatu 1; ⏰ May-Sep), a 15th-century Franciscan monastery church set by the Raumanjoki. It has early-16th-century frescoes and several beautiful painted panels, a fine Prussian triptych from the 15th century and an ornate pulpit. On the north wall is Finland's oldest votive painting, an image of Margareta, a former mayor's daughter.

Rauma Art Museum (☎ 822 4346; www.raumantaide museo.fi; Kuninkaankatu 37; admission €5; ⏰ 10am-6pm Tue-Thu, 10am-4pm Fri, 11am-4pm Sat & Sun), in the heart of Vanha Rauma, features changing exhibitions of traditional and modern art. The Old Town well is in the courtyard.

OTHER SIGHTS

Wandering around the Old Town, it's easy to forget that Rauma is a port, so the **Rauma Maritime Museum** (☎ 822 4911; www .rmm.fi; Kalliokatu 34; admission €7; ⏰ noon-4pm Sun) is a good reminder of the town's seafaring livelihood. As well as old photos and displays, there's a thrilling navigation simulator.

Another port survivor is the lookout tower, a wooden copy of the observation point that gave weather reports and shipping news to the town until the 1940s. It's a visual spectacle in itself but it also affords a fresh perspective on the archipelago.

Festivals & Events

Rauma's biggest event is **Pitsiviikko** (Rauma Lace Week; www.pitsiviikko.fi), beginning in the last week in July, and celebrating the town's lacemaking history. From the turning of the first bobbin to the crowning of Miss Lace the whole town comes to life, particularly for Black Lace Night.

The town has several other interesting festivals:

Rauma Rock (www.raumarock.fi) June's predominantly Finnish rock festival.

Rauma Blues Festival (www.raumablues.com) Draws in Finland's best bluesmen and a few international visitors for a weekend in mid-July.

Festivo (www.raumanfestivo.fi) A week of classical and choral music at various venues held in early August.

Blue Sea Film Festival (☎ 822 5054; www.blue seafilmfestival.com) A Finnish film festival in August that includes the presentation of Herring Oscars for short-film winners.

Sleeping

Poroholma Camping & Hostel (☎ 8388 2500; fax 8388 2502; Poroholmantie; tent sites €10 plus per person €4, dm €14, s/d €30/45, cottages €44-54; mid-May–late Aug) On Otanlahti bay, 2km northwest of the city, this pleasing waterside HI hostel and camping ground has basic dorms and a more upmarket villa that's a cheap hotel and cafe. The sauna, laundry and kitchen are available to all visitors.

Maffi (☎ 533 0857; www.hotelliravintolamaffi.fi; Valtakatu 3; s/d €55/80) Don't be dissuaded by the sports bar downstairs, the rooms here are private and double-glazed so you won't hear even the most raucous hockey game. Rooms include a small bar fridge, toilet (but shared shower) and wi-fi. The basic breakfast is an extra €6 and is set out for you in the communal kitchen.

Hotelli Vanha Rauma (☎ 8376 2200; www.hotel va nharauma.fi; Vanhankirkonkatu 26; s/d €115/140;) Set in an old fish market, there's nothing on the nose about this slickly refurbished hotel on the edge of the old town. Rooms embrace

modern Scandinavian cool with leatherette chairs, flatscreen TVs and views onto the park or courtyard.

Hotel Raumanlinna (☎ 83221; www.raumanlinna.fi; Valtakatu 5; s/d €120/145, ste €175;) This is one of the larger hotels in town with first-rate facilities including a popular restaurant and bar. Rooms are done out in navy and sandy tones, with LAN and small desks for business travellers.

Hotelli Kalliohovi (☎ 83881; Kalliokatu 25; s/d €140/147; wi-fi) This modern hotel does well with the business visitors. Simple rooms are furnished in dark woods, and have wi-fi, bathrooms and well-stocked minibars. The restaurant has a subtle nautical theme (given the proximity of Maritime Museum) including portholes and plenty of seafood. The hotel has a Hertz office.

Also recommended:

Haus Anna (☎ 822 8223; www.hausanna.fi; Satama-katu 7; s/d €55/70;) A modern family-run B&B with rooms that include their own bathroom and TV.

Finlandia Hostel Rauman Kesähotelli (☎ 824 0130; Satamakatu 20; s/d/tr €40/52/72; Jun-Aug;) Ten minutes' walk from the bus station, this summer hostel offers student-style rooms with their own bathroom, TV and kitchen.

Eating

Kontion Leipomo (Kuninkaankatu 9; pastries €4-8, mains €8-14; 7.30am-5.30pm Mon-Fri, 8am-3pm Sat, 11am-4pm Sun) This cute old-school place has been doing such good cakes and pastries that it has released its own cookbook. The working man's grub of stew and mash is a lunch favourite, though the teddy bears dining on nearby tables hit new levels of twee.

Rosmariini (☎ 822 0550; www.rosmariini.fi; Kauppa-katu 11; lunch €8, mains €10-14; 7.30am-7pm Mon-Thu, 7.30am-9pm Fri & Sat, 11am-7pm Sun) This winning lunchroom is decked out in traditional woods and throws on good old-fashioned belly-busting buffets that include salads, sweet-grandmotherly pastries, house-baked breads and fruity pot roasts. The terrace out the back is relaxed given its closeness to the bustling kauppatori.

Ravintola Arturi (☎ 824 0531; Kauppakatu 16; mains €10-15; lunch & dinner) This popular spot has snug booths inside but it's hard not to keep drinking in the sunny kauppatori seats. Food isn't particularly Finnish but does good-sized mains with crispy fries and affordable pizzas, plus a varied salad bar.

Wanhan Rauman Kellari (☎ 866 6700; Anundilankatu 8; mains €12-18; ⏰ 11am-11pm Mon-Thu, 11am-midnight Fri & Sat, 1-11pm Sun) Looking for atmospheric dining? Serving easily the best meals in Vanha Rauma, this ever-busy cellar restaurant has a sun-drenched rooftop terrace in summer. Meals run to top-notch salads and French food, with seafood and chicken prevailing. If you can, snaffle a booth, because historic leather slingback chairs prove to be crippling for longer meals.

Wähä Tallbo (☎ 822 6610; Vanhankirkonkatu 3; lunch €7-9, mains €11-20; ⏰ 10.30am-7pm Mon-Fri, 11am-4pm Sat) This sophisticated Old Town eatery maintains many of its original fittings. Food is unspectacular but affordable – particularly the lunch special – but the ambience is the real appeal.

Drinking & Entertainment

Rauma's nightlife is limited by day trippers who leave with the sun. They miss Rauma's signature drink, Puksprööt, a juniper-rowan liqueur mixed with white wine and served with tar-infused rope.

Otava (Isoraastuvankatu; ⏰ 9pm-3am Fri & Sat) This likeable Finnish dance club is the place for tango and humppa (Finnish jazz) music. Otava II, just around the corner, is more of a drinking pub that attracts serious barflies.

Maffi (☎ 533 0857; Valikatu) This laid-back sports bar runs across a couple of levels, with a small outdoor terrace and pool tables.

Iso Hannu (☎ 822 5054; www.iso-hannu.fi; Savilankatu 4) This delightful independent cinema shows films on the edge of Old Town.

Shopping

The venerable lacemaking workshop, **Pits-Priia** (Kauppakatu 29; ⏰ 11am-3pm Mon-Fri, 10am-1pm Sat), is the place to buy the town's distinctive bobbin lace. You can also watch it being made.

Getting There & Away

Between Rauma and Pori (€10.30, 50 minutes), there are buses every hour or so. From the south, Turku and Uusikaupunki (€8.20, 1½ hours) are connected by buses every two hours or so. There are also direct services to Helsinki and Tampere.

Get off the Tampere-to-Pori train at the Kokemäki train station, and transfer to a connecting bus. Your train pass will be valid on the bus.

AROUND RAUMA
Lappi

The small village of Lappi (Finnish for Lapland) has the Lapinjoki running through it, and makes a great base for those who wish to visit a couple of very significant prehistoric sites. In the village an old stone bridge survives, and nearby is a **church** dating from 1760. It has medieval sculpture and a separate bell tower.

Sammallahdenmäki is a Bronze Age burial complex that probably dates back more than 3000 years. Spread over a 1km radius are a number of stone burial cairns of different shapes and sizes. The main attraction near the car park is **Kirkonlattia** (Church Floor), a monumental flat stone tableau that continues to baffle archaeologists. The **Huilun pitkä raunio** (Long Cairn of Huilu) is an enigmatic find, a burial cairn that's wall-shaped and then surrounded by a stone wall.

To get here turn off Hwy 12 towards Lappi then follow Rd 2070, which is well signposted. Buses to Lappi from Rauma (10 a day, 15 minutes) drop you off at the turn-off.

PUURIJÄRVI-ISOSUO NATIONAL PARK

Puurijärvi, 65km due east of Rauma, is one of the best **bird-watching** lakes in Western Finland. The lake and surrounding marshlands have been protected since 1993 and are a favourite nesting site for migrating waterfowl of many varieties, totalling about 500 pairs in season. The lake itself can be reached by an 800m nature trail from the main road. A boardwalk makes a loop of the open marshland, where there's an observation tower. The *näköalapaikka* (viewing cliff) also offers a good general view. Visitors are required to stay on marked paths during breeding season, and camping is not allowed in the park at any time.

PORI
☎ 02 / pop 76,205

There's more to Pori (Swedish: Björneborg) than the annual jazz festival, which has the streets scatting for a week in July. Domestically it's one of the most important deep-water harbours in Finland at the estuary of the Kokemäenjoki, which also makes for some good beaches and scenic hiking.

The town has an industrial heart, known across Finland for the Porin Olut brewery, which produces the Karhu (bear) brand. The

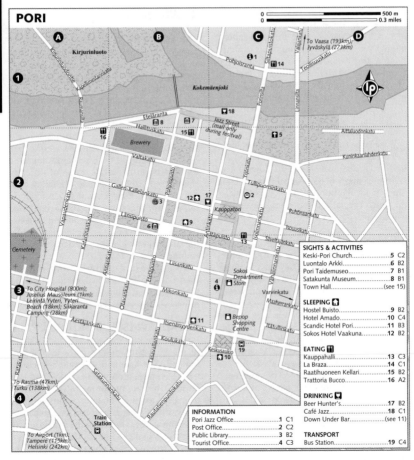

PORI

INFORMATION	
Pori Jazz Office	1 C1
Post Office	2 C2
Public Library	3 B2
Tourist Office	4 C3

SIGHTS & ACTIVITIES	
Keski-Pori Church	5 C2
Luontalo Arkki	6 B2
Pori Taidemuseo	7 B1
Satakunta Museum	8 B1
Town Hall	(see 15)

SLEEPING	
Hostel Buisto	9 B2
Hotel Amado	10 C4
Scandic Hotel Pori	11 B3
Sokos Hotel Vaakuna	12 B2

EATING	
Kauppahalli	13 C3
La Braza	14 C1
Raatihuoneen Kellari	15 B2
Trattoria Bucco	16 A2

DRINKING	
Beer Hunter's	17 B2
Café Jazz	18 C1
Down Under Bar	(see 11)

TRANSPORT	
Bus Station	19 C4

bear is at the cornerstone of Pori, making an appearance on the town seal, but also in the old Swedish name, which is derived from Bear Castle. Despite the bears, Duke Juhana, who governed Finland, established this trading town on the eastern coast of the Gulf of Bothnia in 1558.

Information

There are 24-hour luggage lockers at the train and bus stations.

Public library (☎ 621 5800; www.pori.fi/kirjasto; Gallen-Kallelankatu 12; ☼ 10am-7pm Mon-Fri, 10am-3pm Sat) Has several free internet terminals.

Tourist office (☎ 621 1273; www.pori.fi; Yrjönkatu 17; ☼ 9am-6pm Mon-Fri, 10am-3pm Sat Jun-Aug, 9am-4.30pm Mon-Fri) Has internet access here.

Sights & Activities

Despite being one of Finland's oldest towns, Pori has limited historic buildings and other attractions.

Satakunta Museum (☎ 621 1063; Hallituskatu 11; admission €4; ☼ 11am-5pm Tue-Sun, 11am-8pm Wed) is a stimulating museum of regional history and archaeology – the theme is water and how the river and sea have affected life in the town over the centuries.

Luontotalo Arkki (☎ 621 1176; Pohjoispuisto 7; admission €3; ☼ 11am-5pm Tue-Sun) makes for an absorbing look at the wetlands surrounding Pori, particularly with regard to the osprey and other wildlife, which are captured on film.

Pori Taidemuseo (Pori Art Museum; ☎ 621 1080; www.poriartmuseum.fi; Eteläranta; admission €3; ☼ 11am-

---

PORI JAZZ FESTIVAL

Running over a week in mid-July, **Pori Jazz Festival** (☎ 626 2200; www.porijazz.fi; Pohjoisranta 11D; tickets €50-60, 4-day passes €190; ⏲ 8.30am-4.30pm Mon-Fri, during festival 8.30am-10pm daily) is one of Finland's biggest summer events. Even if you don't attend any of the major concerts, the free jam sessions are always fun. The festival began in 1966 when local jazzsters ran a two-day event, with an audience of only 1000 people. These days the jazz festival has more than 100 concerts held in tents, outdoors, clubs or old warehouses. Performers – and thousands of visitors – pour in from around the globe, and hotels are fully booked up to a year in advance. Even the local football team is now called FC Jazz.

Although the emphasis is on jazz, other musical styles are included, so previous line-ups have included Carlos Santana, James Brown, Sting, Bob Geldof and Sharon Jones. There are more than 10 venues, but the main arena is Kirjurinluoto Concert Park, on the north side of the river, where an open-air stage is set up for an audience of up to 25,000. Jazz Street, the closed-off section of Eteläranta along the riverfront, is where a lot of the action happens, with stalls, free concerts, makeshift bars and street dancing.

6pm Tue-Sun, 11am-8pm Wed) combines a modern art museum with a regional gallery. The stronger collection is the modern art gathered by Maire Gullichsen, who was something of a Nordic Peggy Guggenheim, gathering interesting works, particularly abstract pieces, up till the 1980s.

Keski-Pori Church (Yrjönkatu) is a uniquely Finnish example of neo-Gothic with a cast-iron steeple and stained-glass windows. Over 400 Finns who died during WWII are buried in the grounds, with other memorials to WWI, and Finns who were 'lost' to Karelia.

Very much a family affair, **Juselius Mausoleum** (Käppänä Cemetery; ☎ 623 8746; Maantiekatu; admission free; ⏲ noon-3pm summer) was built by FA Juselius, a wealthy businessman, as a memorial to his daughter who died of tuberculosis at the age of 11. The original frescoes were painted in 1898 by Finnish artist Akseli Gallen-Kallela (who had just lost his own daughter). The present ones were painted by Akseli's son, Jorma Gallen-Kallela, after his father's death.

As well as Pori's excellent beach (see p240), there are some good walking trails around the town, including an architectural tour following the tourist map, *Architectural Map of Pori,* available at the tourist office. Further afield the **Reitti Satakunta-Pirkanmaa trail** (☎ 621 6995; www.reitti.org) is a multiday hike that runs from Pori to Tampere.

Sleeping

During the Jazz Festival accommodation books out up to a year in advance, particularly for the final weekend, and hoteliers send rates higher than the church steeple and just as sharp. The tourist office has a list of festival-only accommodation. Check the Yyteri beach options, which are not far from town.

Hostel Buisto (☎ 633 0646, 044-333 0646; www.hostel buisto.net; Itäpuisto 13; s/d €34/48; **P**) Once one of the best beds in town, this place has been neglected and is starting to show its age. It's still a quality place, with bright rooms that include washbasins, and a modern kitchen.

Hotel Amado (☎ 631 0100; www.amado.fi; Keskusaukio 2; s €70-80, d €80-98; **P**) Well placed for an early bus, this independently owned hotel is a good option. The building feels a little 1970s, but there's a sauna and no-fuss à la carte restaurant.

Sokos Hotel Vaakuna (☎ 020-123 4626; www .sokoshotels.fi; Gallen-Kallelankatu 7; standard s/d €81/101, superior s/d €91/111; **P** 💻) The town's grandest hotel is well placed, with reliable rooms from this always-chic chain. Superior rooms have a few extras like bathrobes, and tea-and-coffee facilities. The restaurant and club make this place a centre for local nightlife.

Scandic Hotel Pori (☎ 624 900; www.scandic-hotels .com; Itsenäisyydenkatu 41; s/d €89/124, ste from €175; **P** 💻) Within walking distance of both the bus and train stations, this place has older-style rooms that are well kept and a casual feel. The 'Down Under' bar is an hilarious attempt at the Outback of Australia in the Arctic Circle, but otherwise this place is tastefully decorated.

Eating & Drinking

Pori has few good dining options but plenty of bad ones – grillis and the usual fast-food suspects crowd out the kauppatori.

Kauppahalli (Isolinnankatu; ☺ 9am-5pm Mon-Fri, 8am-2pm Sat) This is a good source of pastries and picnic victuals. Look out for the local speciality, smoked river lamprey, an eel-like fish that killed England's Henry I when he gorged too many.

Raatihuoneen Kellari (☎ 633 4804; Hallituskatu 9; entrees €8-10, mains €15-23, lunches from €9; ☺ 11am-11pm Mon-Thu, 11am-midnight Fri, noon-midnight Sat) One of the top plates in town, this swanky cellar spot is in the town hall, designed by CL Engel. The weekday buffet luncheon impresses but Finnish cuisine is the speciality in the evenings, when meals include salmon tournedos with morel mushroom sauce, or roast reindeer with sea buckthorn.

La Braza (☎ 633 3228; www.labraza.fi; Siltapuistokatu 1; mains €12-18; ☺ 11am-11pm Mon-Fri, 1pm-midnight Sat, 1-6pm Sun) This hip little spot is on the other side of the river, and has a decor that recovers a raw brick cellar to marvellous effect. The menu is wide ranging, from a hearty borscht to escargot in a Roquefort sauce, before bringing it home with grilled Arctic char with goat's cheese.

Trattoria Bucco (☎ 622 6185; www.bucco.fi; Hallituskatu 22; mains €18-25; ☺ lunch & dinner Tue-Fri, dinner only Sat) You won't find any overalls in this dashing Italian place, once an old brewery workers' canteen. While it's decidedly Mediterranean there's good use of local specialities like grilled whitefish served on risotto with a snap of pear.

Café Jazz (☎ 641 1344; Eteläranta; ☺ 11am-midnight Mon-Thu, 11am-2am Fri & Sat, noon-midnight Sun) One of Jazz Street's more lively year-round venues, this riverside spot features regular jazz slots and jam sessions. The food here is unimaginative but affordable.

Beer Hunter's (cnr Gallen-Kallelankatu & Antinkatu; ☺ 11am-2am) An ale-lovers' paradise, this microbrewery specialises in its own beers, though it also does a pretty good cider, and meals are available.

Getting There & Away

AIR

There are two to four daily Finnair flights between Pori and Helsinki (€150 to €180, 45 minutes). The airport is a couple of kilometres southeast of the centre.

BUS

There are frequent daily buses between Pori and Helsinki (€34.70, four hours), Rauma (€10.30, 50 minutes), Turku (€25.10, 2½ hours) and Tampere (€18, 1¾ hours). Some Tampere-bound buses require a change at Huittinen and take considerably longer, so avoid those. There are also direct connections with Vaasa, Oulu and Jyväskylä.

TRAIN

All trains to Pori go via Tampere, where you usually have to change. There are frequent daily trains (regional and Intercity) between Tampere and Pori (€15.20, 1½ hours), all of which have good connections with trains from Helsinki (€33.50, three to four hours).

Getting Around

Local buses run from the kauppatori; route maps are available from the tourist office. These are handy for reaching the attractions just beyond the city (see below) but won't be necessary within the town, which is compact. If you're cycling, the excellent *Pori Pyöräilykartta* (Pori Cycling Map) gives details of bike paths around town.

AROUND PORI
☎ 02
Yteri Beach

Yteri beach, 18km northwest of Pori town centre, is a classic Finnish beach resort town and very accessible from town. It's the nation's best beach for windsurfing with hire equipment available in summer, plus there are good family beaches for swimming.

Beyond Yteri, **Reposaari**, linked by a causeway to the mainland, has a pretty, wooden harbour village, which is a great place to wander around or enjoy a drink.

SLEEPING

The tourist office in Pori has privately owned villas that can be rented for short periods.

Yterin Kylpylähotelli (☎ 628 5300; www.yyter inkylpyla.fi; Sipintie 1, Yteri; s/d €83/108; P ⊠) Situated on Yteri beach, this is a good-value spa hotel with several good packages on offer.

Siikaranta Camping (☎ 638 4120; www.siikaranta camping.fi; tent sites €10, 2-person cabins €35, 4-person €40-45; ☺ Jun–mid-Aug) This peaceful camp site is on Reposaari, just northwest of Yteri beach. There are good facilities including a sauna and bicycle hire (€10 per day). The island is linked to the mainland by a bridge. Take bus 30 or 40 from the centre.

Leineperi

This venerable village was first developed in 1771 by the Swedish as a *bruk* (ironworks precinct) for making household items, and was in operation for about a century. Today it is a lively place, particularly on summer weekends. Attractions along the scenic Kullaanjoki riverside include **Masuuni ironworks**, now renovated, a blacksmith's shop and some **artisans' workshops**. There's also **Museo Kangasniemi** (☎ 559 1551; Pitkäjärventie 8; admission €2; ⏰ 10am-4pm Tue-Sun), which is devoted to Kaarlo Kangasniemi, the 1968 Olympic Finnish weightlifting champion, and has a scale model of the ironworks. Free town maps are available at most attractions.

Leineperi is on an unpaved road that runs parallel to the Tampere–Pori Rd 11. Buses between Pori and Kullaa stop at Leineperi; there are usually two daily.

Åland

This sweeping archipelago remains a kooky geopolitical entity that will have you shaking your head and saying 'Only in Finland!' The islands belong to Finland, speak Swedish and are closer culturally to their western neighbour, but have their own parliament, fly their own blue-gold-and-red flag from every pole, issue their own stamps and have their own web suffix: 'dot ax'. And then there's the 'special relationship' with the EU that means they can sell duty free and make their own gambling laws.

Over 6000 islands comprise Åland, but most are granite chunks rising centimetres above sea level. The main island is actually called Fasta Åland, but most people just refer to it as the mainland. The islands are broken up into various municipalities, each with its own fascinating coat of arms, representative of its history.

Because the islands are flat and compact, cycling is generally the preferred way of exploring. A lattice of bridges and free cable ferries connect most of the central islands, while the archipelago islands require a little more planning. Taking the ferry from Sweden to Finland (or vice versa) will give you a taste for the remote beaches of Jurmo as well as the ferry crowds of Mariehamn and Eckerö.

Åland has a very defined holiday season. From Midsummer until the end of July, the islands are full of Swedes and Finns enjoying the sun, cycling and camping. Outside these months few places are open, but if you visit in May or September you'll have the islands to yourself.

HIGHLIGHTS

- Imagining the vain empire that would construct the majestically over-the-top post office at **Post och Tullhuset** (p256)
- Slaking your thirst with a brew at **Stallhagen Brewery** (p252) in Godby or a more genteel drop at **Tjudö Vingård** (p255) in Tjudö
- Choosing your favourite church: is it the art nouveau glory of **Sankt Göran's Kyrka** (p246) or perhaps the quaint charm of **Sankta Maria Magdalena Kyrka** (p260)?
- See history come to life with jousting and feasting at **Kastelholms Slott** (p252) on Gustav Wasa Day
- Running the ramparts and finding your own piece of the ruins at **Bomarsund** (p253)
- Cycling around the fantastically flat archipelago by renting a bike in **Eckerö** (p256)

History

More than a hundred Bronze and Iron Age *fornminne* (burial sites) have been discovered on Åland, attesting to more than 6000 years of human habitation. Though all clearly signposted, most are in fairly nondescript fields. Åland was an important harbour and trading centre during the Viking era, with more than six fortress ruins discovered.

During the Great Northern War of 1700–21 (nicknamed the 'Great Wrath'), most Ålanders fled to Sweden to escape the Russians. During the 1740s the Russians returned during what was called the Lesser Wrath. Another incursion took place in 1809.

When Finland gained independence in 1917, Ålanders feared occupation by Russian Bolsheviks. Many Ålanders lobbied to be incorporated into Sweden, but Finland refused to give up the island. The dispute concluded in 1921, when Åland was given its status as an autonomous, demilitarised and neutral province within Finland by a decision of the League of Nations.

Åland joined the EU in 1995, but was granted a number of exemptions, including duty-free tax laws that allow ferry services to mainland Finland and Sweden to operate profitably.

Information

Åland shares Finland's time zone, an hour ahead of Sweden. While the euro is the currency, most places accept the Swedish krona.

Finnish telephone cards can be used on Åland, but local cards are also available. Åland uses the Finnish mobile phone network but most mobile networks can be sketchy, especially in the outer islands. Mail sent in Åland must have Åland postage stamps.

The website www.visitaland.com is very helpful, while www.alandsresor.fi lets you book accommodation online. The general EU-wide emergency number is ☎112; for the police call ☎10022, for medical services ☎10023.

Activities

Åland is hugely popular as a cycling destination (p245) with plenty of bike rental places and great facilities.

Sailing boats from all around the Baltic pull in at the archipelago's secluded islands in summer. You can do anything from charter-

---

ÅLAND MUSEUM CARD

The **Åland Museum Card** (€9) allows visits to four museums in Åland and is available at the tourist office and in most museums. Unless you're a real history buff the best value is to be had by using it in Mariehamn's museums (p246), though smaller museums in Foglö and Brändö have a certain charm.

---

ing a luxury yacht to renting a kayak. Fishing is popular, both from boats and the shore. In winter, Åland is many Swedes' destination of choice for ice-fishing.

Self-Catering Accommodation

There are a wealth of cottages for rent on Åland. Both Eckerö and Viking ferry lines (see p251) have a comprehensive list of bookable places, as does **Destination Åland** (☎ 040-300 8001; www.destinationaland.com; Elverksgatan 5, Mariehamn).

Getting There & Away

AIR

Åland's airport is 4km northwest of Mariehamn, with a bus into the city centre. A taxi to the centre costs about €18. Since 2005 the main airline to fly here has been **Air Åland** (☎ 17110; www.airaland.com), which does at least two flights daily to/from Helsinki and Stockholm, with occasional bargains as cheap as €50. Business airline **Turku Air** (☎ 02-276 4966; www.turkuair.fi) flies to Turku for €379 return.

BOAT

Several ferries head to Åland and have car-carrying facilities (at extra charge). Prices vary with season and web specials are common, but these prices are all based on a one-way adult fare, with cars costing extra:

Birka Line (☎ 27027; www.birkaline.com; Östra Esplanadgatan 7, Mariehamn) Runs luxury cruises to Mariehamn (€175, 22 hours) from Stockholm, including meals.

Eckerö Linjen (☎ 28000; www.eckerolinjen.fi; Torggatan 2, Mariehamn) Sails from Eckerö to Grisslehamn, Sweden (€8.90, three hours).

Tallink & Silja Lines (☎ 060-015 700; www.tallinksilja .com; Torggatan 14, Mariehamn) Runs direct services to Mariehamn from Turku (€17, 4½ hours), Helsinki (€39, 11½ hours) and Stockholm (through Silja Lines; €29, 5½ hours).

Viking Line (☎ 26211; www.vikingline.fi; Storagatan 2, Mariehamn) Runs to Helsinki (€34, 11 hours) and Stockholm (€36, ninr hours).

ÅLAND

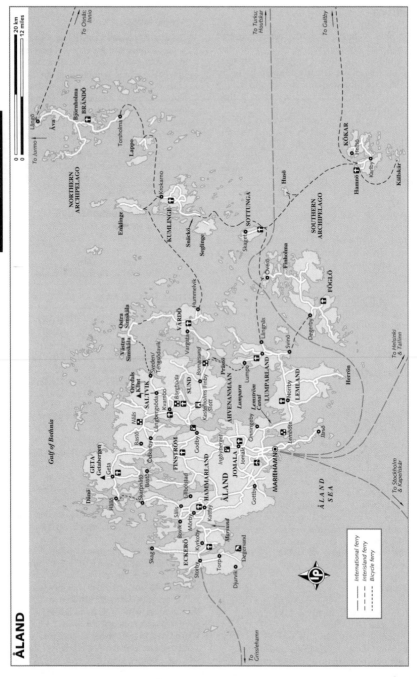

ÅLAND

| 0 | 20 km |
| 0 | 12 miles |

To Orrdás; Innio
To Turku; Houtskär
To Galtby

Långö

NORTHERN ARCHIPELAGO

Björnholma
BRÄNDÖ

Áva

Torsholma

To Jurmo

Lappo

KÖKAR
Helsö

Krokarno

Enklinge

KUMLINGE

Snäckö

Seglinge

Hamnö
Kárlby

Kállskär

SÖTTUNGA

Skaget

Husö

SOUTHERN ARCHIPELAGO

Överö
Finholma

To Helsinki & Tallinn

FÖGLÖ

Östra Simskäla
VÅRDÖ

Hummelvik

Västra Simskäla

Vargata

Bomarsund

Långnäs

Degerby

Prästö

Tengsödavik

SALTVIK

Orrdals Klint

Sveden

Borgboda

SUND

Långnäs

Svinö

Kvarnbo

Kastelholms Slott
Finby

AHVENANMAAN

Lumparn

LUMPARLAND

Herrön

Näs

Långbergsöda

Norrby

LEMLAND

Bastö

Ödkarby

Godby

Lumparn

Lemström Canal

Lembote

FINSTRÖM

ÅLAND

Ingebyberget

Onningeby

Järsö

GETA
Getabergen

Geta

Dånö

Hällö

Skarpnåto

Bastö

JOMALA

Jomala

MARIEHAMN

Ulfsby

Jomala

HAMMARLAND

ÅLAND SEA

Böville

Mörby

Salis

Kattby

Gottby

To Stockholm & Kapellskär

ECKERÖ

Kyrkoby

Marsund

Skag

Storby

Torp

Djurvik

Degersand

To Grisslehamn

	International ferry
	Interisland ferry
	Bicycle ferry

It's also possible to travel using the archipelago ferries to and from mainland Finland via Korpo (southern route, from Galtby passenger harbour) or Kustavi (northern route, from Osnäs passenger harbour), though it's cheaper to break your outward journey in the archipelago (see p258).

Getting Around

BICYCLE

Cycling is a great way to tour these flat, rural islands. Ro-No Rent has bicycles available at Mariehamn and Eckerö harbours. Green-white signs trace the excellent routes through the islands. Bicycle routes generally follow smaller, less busy roads, but special bicycle paths run parallel to main roads.

BUS

Five main bus lines depart from Mariehamn's regional bus terminal on Torggatan, in front of the library. Rte 1 goes to Hammarland and Eckerö; rte 2 to Godby and Geta; rte 3 to Godby and Saltvik; rte 4 to Godby, Sund and Vårdö (Hummelvik); and rte 5 to Lemland and Lumparland (Långnäs). Rte 6 runs from Godby from Monday to Friday, servicing other destinations in Finström. The one-way fare from Mariehamn to Storby (in Eckerö) is €4.90; from Mariehamn to Långnäs it is €4.70. Bicycles can be carried on buses (space permitting) for €4.

FERRY

There are three kinds of interisland ferry. For short trips, free vehicle ferries sail nonstop. For longer routes, ferries run to a schedule, taking cars, bicycles and pedestrians. There are also three private bicycle ferries in summer, from Hammarland–Geta, Lumparland–Sund and Vårdö–Saltvik. A ride is €7 to €9 per bicycle.

Timetables for all interisland ferries are available at the main tourist office in Mariehamn and online at www.alandstrafiken.ax.

MARIEHAMN

☎ 018 / pop 10,902

Two out of every five Ålanders live in Mariehamn and, with the *lagting* (parliament) and the *landskapsstyrelse* (Åland's government) both located here, it's the biggest smoke in the islands. But you wouldn't know it.

The town was named for Empress Maria by Alexander II, and the broad tree-lined streets such as Storagatan are indicative of its Russian heritage. The streets also give the town its nickname: town of a thousand Linden trees.

The peninsula location of Mariehamn has given it a unique strategic importance with the ports on either side traditionally used for ship-building and repairs. Today the ports mean Mariehamn regularly plays host to ferries from both Finland and Sweden, whose residents take advantage of Åland's extra-EU status to buy duty-free goods. In 2009, the huge **Alandica** (www.alandica.ax) is due to open as a conference space, bringing a new generation of visitors to the town.

Orientation

Most visitors to Mariehamn arrive via its two harbours: Västerhamn (West Harbour) and Österhamn (East Harbour). Ferries from Sweden and mainland Finland dock at Västerhamn, but just about everything else, including the guest harbour for small boats, is at Österhamn, a stone's throw from the city centre. Torggatan is the colourful partially pedestrian street, while the long, broad, tree-lined Storagatan is the main thoroughfare which connects the two harbours. The airport is 4km northwest of the centre.

Information

You can store luggage in the lockers (€2) at the ferry terminal for up to 24 hours.

Ålands Turistinformation (☎ 24000; www.visit aland.com; Storagatan 8; ☼ 9am-5pm Mon-Fri, 9am-4pm Sat & Sun Jun-Aug, 9am-4pm Mon-Fri, 10am-4pm Apr-May & Sep, 9am-4pm Mon-Fri Oct-Mar; 🖳) Has useful information on Åland and books tours. Internet costs €1 for 15 minutes. It also runs a booth at **Västerhamn ferry terminal** (☎ 531 214; ☼ daily Jul, Mon-Sat Jun & Aug).

Ålandsresor (☎ 28040; www.alandsresor.fi; Torggatan 2; ☼ 8.30am-5pm Mon-Fri year-round, 9am-2pm Sat Jun & Jul) Eckerö Linjen's travel-agent arm handles hotel, guesthouse and cottage bookings for the entire island. Viking Line offers a similar service.

Ålandstrafiken (☎ 25155; www.alandstrafiken .ax; Strandgatan 25; ☼ 9am-5pm Mon-Fri year-round, 9am-3pm Sat Jun & Jul) Has information on buses and ferries around the islands and will store backpacks for longer periods.

Cycle Info (☼ 11am-6pm Jun-Aug) Two-wheeled tourist information units during summer: just flag them down and ask a question.

ÅLAND

Main hospital (☎ 5355; Norragatan 17)

Main post office (☎ 6360; Torggatan 4; ✦ Mon-Sat)
Sells the uber-collectable Åland stamps, required to send
mail from Åland.

Mariehamn library (☎ 531 441; Strandgatan 8;
✦ 10am-8pm Mon-Fri, 11am-4pm Sat, noon-4pm Sun)
Several free internet terminals, available for a maximum of
20 minutes at a time if you don't book ahead.

Telebutiken (☎ 27448; Storagatan 6) Rents mobiles
and has one of the few coin-operated payphones in town.

Sights
MUSEUMS

In the centre of town, the **Ålands Museum &
Ålands Konstmuseum** (Åland Museum & Art Museum;
☎ 25426; Stadhusparken; admission €3; ✦ 10am-4pm Wed-
Mon, 10am-7pm Tue Jun & Aug, 10am-7pm daily Jul, 10am-
4pm Wed-Sun, 10am-8pm Tue Sep-May; ♿) are housed
in the same large building. Permanent exhibits
offer an insight into the complete history of
the islands including a replica of a Stone Age
boat made of sealskin, a reconstructed traditional pharmacy and a large illustration of
Bomarsund (p253) in all its glory. The panels
don't have information in English, so take a
leaflet on entry.

The gallery has changing exhibitions as well
as a handful of paintings by local artists. The
most interesting among them are the canvases
of Joel Pettersson (1892–1937), which capture
the elemental forces at work behind the Åland
treescapes. Perhaps the best known of Åland's
paintings is Karl Emanuel Jansson's *Åland
Peasant Bride* depicting a woman wearing
an outfit that makes her look a little like a
Midsummer pole.

Åland marine heritage is explored at
the **Sjöfartsmuseum** (Maritime Museum; ☎ 19930;
Hamngatan 2; admission €5, combined ticket with Pommern
€8; ✦ 9am-5pm May-Aug, 9am-7pm Jul, 10am-4pm Sep-
Apr), a traditional museum that's designed
to look like a ship's prow cutting into the
land. Preserved boats make up most of the
exhibitions, particularly glorious ship's fig-
ureheads such as a rare male carving that
once graced the *California*. It's a great place
to discover your inner pirate with plenty of
ships in bottles, sea chests and nautical accoutrements. The central part of the museum
is a re-creation of a ship with mast, saloon,
galley and cabins.

To see the real thing, the **Museum Ship
Pommern** (☎ 531 423; admission €5, combined ticket
with Sjöfartsmuseum €8; ✦ 9am-5pm May-Aug, 9am-7pm
Jul, 10am-4pm Sep & Oct) is anchored just behind the
Sjöfartsmuseum. It's a beautifully preserved
four-masted merchant barque and a symbol
of Mariehamn. Built in 1903 in Glasgow,
Scotland, the ship once carried tonnes of
cargo and a 26-man crew on the trade route
between Australia and England. Its record
run was a speedy 110 days. An audio guide
(available in English; €3.50) brings the creaking timbers back to life.

At the northern end of Österhamn,
Sjökvarteret (Maritime Quarter; ☎ 16033; www.sjokvar
teret.com) has long been devoted to boat-building
and you can see various traditional schooners
moored here and possibly even boats like the
traditional *öka* (rowing boat) under construction. The **museum** (adult/child €4/free; ✦ 9am-5pm
Mon-Fri, 10am-6pm Sat mid-Jun–mid-Aug, 9-11am Mon-Fri mid-
Aug–mid-Jun), with exhibitions on ship-building,
is located in a small boatshed that still has the
whiff of timber and sea salt. The quarter also
has a good cafe, Café Bönan (p250), and several
artisan galleries and shops (p250).

OTHER ATTRACTIONS

The copper-roofed **Sankt Göran's Kyrka** (✦ 10am-
3pm Mon-Fri), built in 1927, is one of the few
modern churches on the islands. Its art nouveau style was conceived by Lars Sonck, who
grew up in Åland. The glittering mosaic altarpiece is a real highlight.

It may seen like a local council building,
but **Sjalvstyrelsegården** (Self-Government Building;
☎ 25000; cnr Österleden & Storagatan; ✦ tours 10am Fri
Jun–mid-Aug) is actually the home of the Åland
parliament. The free guided tours (available
in English) explain the autonomous nature
of Åland and the election of the Lantråd, the
premier of Åland, and end with a slide show
about the area.

South of Österhamn is **Tullarns Äng**, a small
park prized for its spring wildflowers. **Lilla
Holmen** island, connected to Tullarns Äng by
a bridge, has a summer cafe, a decent swimming beach and peacocks strolling through
the grounds.

The **Järsö** recreational area, 12km south of
Mariehamn at the tip of the peninsula, is a
good place for short bicycle and walking excursions. The area is at its most beautiful in
spring and early summer, when wildflowers
cover the ground.

Activities

Ro-No Rent (☎ 12820; bicycles per day/week €8/40,
mopeds per day/week €65/210, small boat hire per 4hrs/day

MARIEHAMN

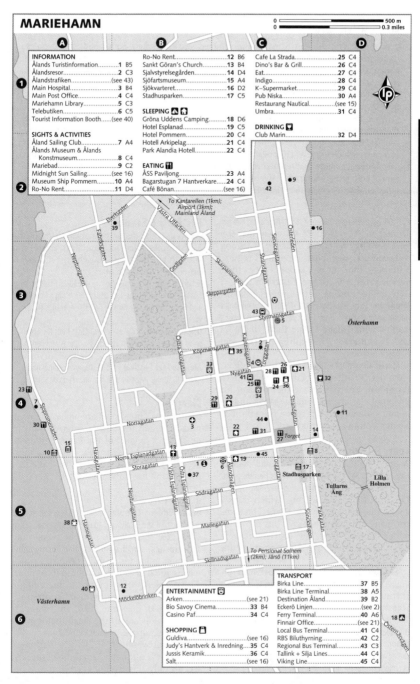

0 —————— 500 m
0 —————— 0.3 miles

INFORMATION
Åland's Turistinformation............1 B5
Ålandsresor.........................2 C3
Ålandstrafiken....................(see 43)
Main Hospital........................3 B4
Main Post Office.....................4 C4
Mariehamn Library....................5 C3
Telebutiken..........................6 C5
Tourist Information Booth.......(see 40)

SIGHTS & ACTIVITIES
Åland Sailing Club...................7 A4
Ålands Museum & Ålands
 Konstmuseum........................8 C4
Mariebad.............................9 C2
Midnight Sun Sailing.............(see 16)
Museum Ship Pommern................10 A4
Ro-No Rent........................11 D4

Ro-No Rent........................12 B6
Sankt Göran's Church..............13 B4
Sjalvstyrelsegården...............14 D4
Sjöfartsmuseum....................15 A4
Sjökvarteret......................16 D2
Stadhusparken.....................17 C5

SLEEPING 🏠 🏡
Gröna Uddens Camping..............18 D6
Hotel Espland.....................19 C5
Hotel Pommern.....................20 C4
Hotell Arkipelag..................21 C4
Park Alandia Hotell...............22 C4

EATING 🍴
ÅSS Paviljong.....................23 A4
Bagarstugan 7 Hantverkare.........24 C4
Café Bönan......................(see 16)

Cafe La Strada....................25 C4
Dino's Bar & Grill................26 C4
Eat...............................27 C4
Indigo............................28 C4
K–Supermarket.....................29 C4
Pub Niska.........................30 A4
Restaurang Nautical.............(see 15)
Umbra.............................31 C4

DRINKING 🍷
Club Marin........................32 D4

Eckerögatan
Vastra Utfarten
To Kantarellen (1km);
Airport (3km);
Mainland Åland
Fabriksgatan
Neptunigatan
Cecilgatan
Skarmansvagen
Österleden
Servicegatan
Strandgatan
Skeppargatan
Ostra Skolgatan
Kopmansgatan
Kalmarstan
Styrmansgatan
Nygatan
Österhamn
Sloppmenaden
Hagsgatan
Norra Esplanadgatan
Norragatan
Storagatan
Vastra Esplanadgatan
Ostra Esplanadgatan
Alandsvagen
Södragatan
Torget
Strandgatan
Torggatan
Parkgatan
Stadhusparken
Tullarns Äng
Lilla Holmen
Mariegatan
Hamngatan
To Pensionat Solhem
(2km); Järsö (11km)
Skillnadsgatan
Sodclastrom
Möckelobrinken
Västerhamn
Österbovagen

ENTERTAINMENT 🎭
Arken...........................(see 21)
Bio Savoy Cinema..................33 B4
Casino Paf........................34 C4

SHOPPING 🛍
Guldiva.........................(see 16)
Judy's Hantverk & Inredning.....35 C4
Jussis Keramik....................36 C4
Salt............................(see 16)

TRANSPORT
Birka Line........................37 B5
Birka Line Terminal...............38 A5
Destination Åland.................39 B2
Eckerö Linjen....................(see 2)
Ferry Terminal....................40 A6
Finnair Office..................(see 21)
Local Bus Terminal................41 C4
RBS Biluthyrning..................42 C2
Regional Bus Terminal.............43 C3
Tallink + Silja Lines.............44 C4
Viking Line.......................45 C4

ÅLAND

MIDSUMMER POLES

If you're passing through Åland during summer, you'll definitely notice Midsummer poles. Undecorated, they could be telegraph poles, but when they're done up they're a cross between a mast and totem pole. The long poles are decorated with leaves, miniature flags, small boats and other trinkets, the nature and symbolism of which varies from village to village. Each village usually has one or more poles, decorated in a public gathering the day before Midsummer. The pole then stands until the next Midsummer.

When the Midsummer pole came to Åland remains something of a mystery. Although some theorists believe that the pole is a manifestation of an ancient fertility rite, its origins on Åland itself are probably more recent. Others point to the resemblance to ships' masts, with cross-spars and cords, which suggests an appeal to a higher power for safe seas. Atop the poles there is the Fäktargubbe, a figure that represents toil and diligence. Other motifs may include sailing boats, ears of corn representing the harvest, a wreath symbolising love, a sun symbol facing east and other symbols of community togetherness.

€50/100; kayak hire per 4hr/day €25/50, fishing rod hire per day/week €7/15; ☺ 10-11am & 4-5pm May, 10am-6pm mid-Jun–end Aug) rents out a variety of fishing rods, kayaks, small boats (that don't require a licence), bicycles and mopeds from their outlets at Österhamn and Västerhamn.

If you're wanting to try out larger boats, **Midnight Sun Sailing** (☎ 57500; www.midnight sunsailing.fi; charters from €500 per week) charters yachts while **Åland Sailing Club** (☎ 040-724 5797; Västra Hamnen) runs sailing courses and private lessons.

Mariebad (☎ 531650; www.mariebad.net; Österleden; adult/child €7.30/4.40) is one of those fun northern European waterparks that are excellent for the whole family, with slides, sauna and an indoor-outdoor pool where you swim through a gateway into an external park.

Tours & Cruises

A good sightseeing option is **Londonbussen** (☎ 0457-548 3554; www.rodeorm.ax, in Finnish; tickets €7; ☺ departs 11am Mon-Fri mid-Jun–mid-Aug), a red London double-decker bus which does a 45-minute return tour to Järsö. The same company also offers a longer bus trip (€10) which departs from the tourist office at 1pm Monday to Friday between mid-June and mid-August.

Setting sail from Sjökvarteret between July and August, several cruises take in the waters surrounding Mariehamn:

Schooner Linden (☎ 0242 1280; www.linden.aland .fi; cruise incl meal from €55; ☺ lunch & dinner Fri-Sat) Offers lunch and dinner cruises in a genuine sail boat.

Schooner Nordboen (☎ 040-721 3808; www.apalmer sailing.aland.fi; half-day from €90) Specialises in day and overnight cruises for groups in a 1933 schooner.

Festivals & Events

As well as the decorating and raising of the Midsummer poles (see boxed text, above) and subsequent dancing, Mariehamn has a few other interesting events:

Rockoff (☎ 13713; per day/week €30/75) This rocking festival kicks off in late July usually with big Swedish and Finnish groups; it runs during the evenings for a week.

Organ Festival (www.alfest.org) Cleans out the organ pipes of some of the best churches on the island with Mariehamn as its centre.

Alandia Jazz Festival (☎ 16508; www.alandiajazz .aland.fi) Brings jazz greats to play at waterside venues.

Sleeping

Mariehamn's hotel rates are highest between mid-June and the end of August, but can be cheaper outside of the summer season. Booking ahead is definitely a good idea especially when large ferries arrive. Note that Mariehamn has no youth hostels.

BUDGET

Gröna Uddens Camping (☎ 21151; www.gronaud den.com; tent site €6 plus per adult €6, 2-/4-person cabins €60/85, r €60; ☺ mid-May–Aug) By the seaside and 15 minutes' stroll south of the centre, this camping ground is a family favourite, which means you'll need to book ahead in summer. There's plenty of outdoor fun including a safe swimming beach, minigolf course (admission €4), bike hire (€10) and sauna. If the tent plots are a little small then opt for the fully equipped spruce red cabins.

Pensionat Solhem (☎ 16322; fax 16350; Lökskärsvägen; s/d €45/65; P) Although 3km south of the centre, it's only 2km from the ferries to this delightful seaside spot, which can feel like your very own villa. Rooms are basic with share bathrooms, but cheerful staff keep the place running like clockwork. Guests also have use of the rowing boats and sauna. The local bus (routes B and D) stops nearby.

Hotell Esplanad (☎ 16444; Storagatan 5; s/d €55/64) This hotel close to the centre of town is an older-style place with tight rooms but it is one of Mariehamn's most affordable. There's also the bonus of a breakfast buffet that includes Swedish *kaviar* and other continental items.

MIDRANGE

our pick Hotell Arkipelag (☎ 24020; www.hotellarkipelag.com; Strandgatan 31; s/d €118/148, ste from €220; P ☐ ☐ wi-fi) One of the best hotels on the island and scheduled to have the Ålandica (p245) as a neighbour, this is a high-class spot that caters well to business visitors, though water views from the balconies are tempting for anyone. As well as wi-fi there's a small business centre and a spacious sauna. Rooms are large with tasteful minimalist decoration, but with an outdoor pool and the Arken nightclub onsite you won't be spending long in them.

Hotell Pommern (☎ 15555; www.hotellpommern.aland.fi; Norragatan 8-10; s/d €95/110; ☐) This family-owned hotel has pleasant, older-style rooms that include minibars, TVs and space-saving fold-out shavers that are a marvel. It's handy for the town centre but a hike from the ferry.

Park Alandia Hotelli (☎ 14130; www.vikingline.fi/parkalandiahotel, in Finnish; Norra Esplanadgatan 3; s/d €87/106; P ☐ ☐) This sophisticated spot is on the main boulevard and has good deals with Viking Lines. The spacious rooms are popular, though Sunday nights are cheaper. On sunny days its public terrace packs in the crowds.

Eating

Mariehamn's many cafes serve the local speciality, *Ålandspannkaka* (Åland pancakes), but look out for the real deal – a fluffy square pudding made with semolina and served with stewed prunes (not strawberry jam as the cheaper places often serve them). Look out in local markets for the tasty local speciality, *Ålands svartbröd* (Åland dark bread), a malt-fruity loaf that takes four days to make and complements *sill* (pickled herring) or light local cheeses.

RESTAURANTS

our pick Umbra (☎ 51550; www.umbra.ax, in Swedish; Norra Esplanadgatan 2; mains €1-16; ☺ lunch Mon-Fri, dinner daily) Modern Mediterranean has hit Åland. You can expect first-rate house-made tortellini and an expansive antipasto selection in a rustic setting that runs to bronzed fireplaces. Staff are swift and informed but remarkably down-to-earth for fine dining. Lunch is a choice of two great specials that are filling and tasty.

Pub Niska (☎ 19141; Vasterhamn; lunch €13, mains €19-25; ☺ lunch & dinner May-Aug) This offshoot of ÅSS Paviljong is a remarkably cosy little boozer decked out to look like the inside of a ship, complete with portholes and sailors' newspapers. It also does a good *plåtbröd*, an Åland-style pizza.

Indigo (☎ 16550; www.indigo.ax; Nygatan 1; mains €19-29; ☺ restaurant 11am-3pm & 5-11pm, bar until 3am Fri & Sat) This slick spot mixes a warm interior of historic raw brickwork and a hip courtyard for summer. The menu is contemporary with some innovative takes on fish, such as grilled swordfish on roast sweet potato, though there's a bar menu of burgers and desserts for lighter meals.

ÅSS Paviljong (☎ 19141; Västerhamn; lunch buffet €13, mains €19-25; ☺ lunch & dinner May-Aug) The positioning could not be better for this yachty favourite. The kitchen serves up a great seafood pappardelle or white fish carpaccio, but the lunch buffet is a good sampler for the budget conscious. Oh, and they've heard all the jokes about the name so leave them behind.

Restaurang Nautical (☎ 19931; Hamngatan 2; mains €21-32; ☺ lunch & dinner Mon-Fri, dinner Sat) Upstairs from the maritime museum, this swanky dining room presides over the western harbour and down into the *Pommern*. There are maritime references in the decor (ship's wheel, the odd model ship) while much of the menu is local. Try the seabuckthorn-glazed duck or fish soup that includes local scallop and deep-fried cheeses.

CAFES

There are several reasonable cafes and takeaway joints along the pedestrianised section of Torggatan and in the Galleria shopping arcade just off this street.

Bagarstugan 7 Hantverkare (☎ 19881; Ekonomiegatan 2; light meals €3-8; ☺ 10am-5pm Tue-Fri, 10am-3pm Sat) In the midst of the bustling market, this cafe is the

ÅLAND

place for bargain hunters to pause for a coffee, homemade soup or cake.

Café Bönan (☎ 21735; Sjökvarteret; lunch buffet €8; 🕙 10.30am-2pm) Something of an oasis in a desert of meat and fish, this vegetarian place does healthy salad buffets such as fresh beans with couscous, to be washed down with an organic elderflower drink. Plus it's sourced from ethical producers so it's total guilt-free dining. The evenings sometimes feature laid-back DJ sets. It also hosts the occasional Indian Night, with good curry options.

Eat (☎ 19999; Torget; meals €5-12; 🕙 11am-6pm Mon-Fri, 11.30am-3.30pm Sat) Located in the market square, the large terrace is always packed with drinkers and diners, particularly Åland's parliamentarians. The menu is ideal for light meals – some good salads, sandwiches and a good range of pastries to enjoy with coffee.

Dino's Bar & Grill (☎ 13939; www.dinosbar.net, in Swedish; Strandgatan 12; mains €13-25; 🕙 lunch Mon-Sat, dinner daily) Popular as a meeting spot, this bar serves thick burgers, creative pastas and steaks on a panoramic outdoor deck. It's a good place to hang around for a few beers, especially when the house band is playing.

Café La Strada (☎ 13270; Torggatan 6; meals €7-10; 🕙 10am-6pm Mon-Fri, 10am-4pm Sat) One of Torggatan's sweeter spots, this little cafe does quality pizza and pasta, often with a fish of the day special that's good value. You should save room for dessert – they do great *Ålandspannkaka* and have a good ice cream selection for strolling.

SELF-CATERING

If you're heading further out, Mariehamn may be your best chance to stock up as some islands have limited general stores. There are several minimarkets around town, but the most central supermarket is **K-Supermarket** (☎ 22122; cnr Ålandsvägen & Norragatan; 🕙 9am-7pm Mon-Fri, 9am-4pm Sat, 11am-4pm Sun). If you can't find what you're after here, try **Kantarellen** (☎ 32840; Nya Godbyvägen; 🕙 9am-9pm Mon-Fri, 9am-6pm Sat, 10am-6pm Sun), about 2km north of town on the road to Godby.

Drinking

The holidaying crowd in Mariehamn means that the city has the most varied nightlife in Åland, from older bars to nightclubs (see right). The hotel bars at Hotell Arkipelag and Park Alandia (see p249) are also both good options.

Club Marin (Österhamn; 🕙 11am-1am May-Jul, lunch & dinner Aug-Apr) One of the best waterside options, this upmarket harbour pavilion is ideal for a beer or wine as the sun sets, or a meal. It's evening dancing for an older crowd, who enjoy the live bands.

Entertainment

Bio Savoy Cinema (☎ 19647; cnr Nygatan & Ålandsvägen) This refurbished cinema, west of the centre, shows films in English with Swedish subtitles. At the time of research the cinema had just changed hands and no website existed, so check with the tourist office for latest screenings.

Arken (see p249; admission €5-10; 🕙 10pm-3am Mon-Sat) is a hotel nightclub with chart-conscious DJs; admission is cheaper earlier on.

Dino's Bar & Grill (see left) also has regular live music on weekends and is known for a versatile Thai cover band.

Because of its autonomous status Åland has been able to make its own rules about gambling. **Casino Paf** (☎ 24231; www.casinopaf.com; Torggatan 14; 🕙 10am-midnight) gives punters a chance to bet the house on poker, slots and more.

Shopping

Mariehamn serves as a place where Åland's many artists can sell their work to visitors and the tourist office has maps of craft shops and artisans in Mariehamn and around mainland Åland. There are a few good craft markets at Sjökvarteret (p246), which makes it a great place for quality mementos.

Salt (☎ 21505; www.salt.ax; Sjökvarteret; 🕙 10am-5pm Mon-Fri, 10am-2pm Sat) Features local artists and craftspeople selling textiles, ceramics, silverware and other jewellery. They also sell, well, salt.

Jussis Keramik (☎ 13606; www.jussiskeramik.fi, in Finnish; Nygatan 1) This outlet sells a large range of ceramics and glassware in a wide variety of bright colours.

Guldviva (☎ 22130; www.guldviva.com; Sjökvarteret; 🕙 10am-5pm Mon-Fri, 10am-2pm Sat) Broaches, cufflinks and necklaces from this goldsmith make top-notch gifts or souvenirs of Mariehamn.

Bagarstugan 7 Hantverkare (☎ 19881; Ekonomiegatan 2; 🕙 10am-5pm Tue-Fri, 10am-3pm Sat) This craft collective represents nearly a dozen artists with a lovely cafe of the same name (p249).

Judy's Hantverk & Inredning (☎ 19988; www.visit aland.com/judys; Köpmansgatan 11; ☺ 9am-7pm Mon-Fri, 10am-4pm Sat) This backstreet find does hand-painted ceramics and if you're lucky you'll see them being painted and fired. They also stock the bold textiles of local designers Korpi and Gordon.

Getting There & Away

See p243 for information on travelling to and from Mariehamn by plane or ferry.

Viking and Tallink/Silja ferries depart from the ferry terminal at Västerhamn. Just north of it is a smaller terminal used only by Birka Line.

All ferry lines have offices in Mariehamn:

Birka Line (☎ 27027; www.birkaline.com; Östra Esplanadgatan 7)

Eckerö Linjen (☎ 28000; www.eckerolinjen.fi; Torggatan 2)

Tallink & Silja Lines (☎ 040-300 8000; www.tallink silja.com; Torggatan 14)

Viking Line (☎ 26211; www.vikingline.fi; Storagatan 2)

Regional buses depart from the terminal in front of the library; for route and fare information see p245, or get a timetable from the tourist office.

Getting Around

Four local bus routes run two circular routes around town: A and C serve the northern parts of town, while B and D serve the south. They run half-hourly in winter and hourly in summer and are free. For a more direct route, **Rode Orm** (☎ 0457-548 3554; www .rodeorm.ax, in Swedish; tickets €2; ☺ 11.30am-6.30pm) is a car with carriages that runs a circuit of the major tourist attractions, including Sjöfartsmuseum and Sjövarteret.

Hiring a car is a good way to see Åland. The best place is the friendly **RBS Biluthyrning** (☎ 535 505; www.rundbergs.com; Strandgatan 1) at the St1 garage petrol station opposite Mariebad. Rates for small cars start at around €70 per day, but there's often a 24-hour special for €60, plus they deliver free within Mariehamn.

Ro-No Rent hires out bicycles, mopeds and other recreation gear (see p246). Alternatively, call a taxi on ☎ 26000.

MAINLAND ÅLAND & AROUND

The archipelago has several large islands that form the core of Åland and are the most popular with travellers to the province. Some of Finland's oldest historical landmarks are in this region, particularly around Saltvik and Sund. Eckerö in the west is a much-loved Swedish family destination as it is the closest part of Fasta Åland to that country and is serviced by regular ferries to/from Grisslehamn.

Bicycle tours around this part of Åland are very popular in summer as there are marked paths, comfortable distances, and bridges or ferries connect the various islands and make up an area large enough for an interesting week of touring.

JOMALA
☎ 018 / pop 3774

Wherever you are in the Jomala region you'll see its coat of arms, which features an enthroned St Olaf, Åland's patron saint. Jomala has two main centres: Kyrkby, with a range of facilities, and the smaller Gottby.

In 1886 the famous landscape painter Victor Westerholm invited some of his artist friends to his summer house in Önningeby, a tiny village in eastern Jomala. For almost 30 years artists gathered here, with the house earning the name of the Önningeby Colony. There's an interesting **museum** (☎ 33710; admission €3; ☺ noon-3pm Sun May-Aug, 10am-4pm Tue-Sun late Jun-early Aug), which showcases the work of these artists alongside historical memorabilia from the era. The art collection and exhibitions include works by many of the artists influenced by the Önningeby School, but none by Westerholm himself. Other exhibits follow the work of contemporary artists.

Jomala's **Sankt Olaf's Kyrka** (☺ Mon-Fri May-Sep) dates back to the 12th century, having had several repairs and patch-ups in the meantime. It's still possible to make out a lion's jaw with a human head inside in the worn stonework, which was originally worked by Italian stonemasons.

Two kilometres west of Gottby and 4km off the main road, the peaceful hamlet of Djurvik overlooks a gentle bay. Right by the water, **Djurviks Gästgård** (☎ 32433; www.djurvik.ax; s €29-40, d €35-45, 2-person cabins €42-45, 4-person €53-64; P) offers a choice of apartment with a kitchen,

ÅLAND

several cabins or simple rooms, and also has an endearing garden. Prices go up from mid-July to August though this is usually a quiet spot for a break.

From Mariehamn, catch bus 5 to near Önningeby or bus 1 to Gottby. From Tuesday to Thursday in July, a special taxi leaves for the Önningeby museum from Mariehamn, allowing a couple of hours at the museum. A return ticket including museum entry is €6 – cheaper than the bus.

FINSTRÖM

☎ 018 / pop 2399

Finström is the central municipality in Åland, with Godby the island's second-biggest town. It has a **tourist office** (☎ 41890; ◷ 10am-8pm Mon-Fri, 10am-4pm Sat, noon-4pm Sun mid-Jun–mid-Aug) in the main shopping centre.

In a small village just 5km north of Godby, **Sankt Mikael Kyrka** (◷ Mon-Fri May-Sep) features a well-preserved interior including a wealth of medieval frescoes and sculptures.

At the bridge across to Sund, the 30m-high **observation tower** (admission €1.50) at Café Uffe på Berget (below) affords superb views of the archipelago and is a popular photo stop. Across the road is **Godby Arboretum**, a small nature park with native and exotic trees along a short, marked nature trail.

Sleeping & Eating

Bastö Hotell & Stugby (☎ 42382; www.basto.aland.fi; s/d €68/88, cabins per week from €415; ◷ May-Sep; [P] [ ]) They do everything right at this large holiday complex 12km northwest of Godby. There's the choice of short-term basic hotel rooms including ensuites and kitchenettes, or longer stays in your own waterside cabin. There are also loads of family-friendly facilities including saunas, minigolf, a restaurant and a massage clinic. They do good packages that can include hiring a fishing boat and licence.

Café Uffe på Berget (☎ 41190; ◷ 10am-8pm Mon-Sat, 11am-8pm Sun May-Aug) Just outside Godby, this cafe lords it over the bridge on the Mariehamn-Sund Rd. The espresso machine is busy, the pancakes are good and if you can't afford the observation tower, the views from the cafe are pretty impressive.

our pick **Stallhagen Brewery** (☎ 48500; www.stall hagen.com; Getavägen 196, Godby; admission €12; ◷ tours 2pm Wed-Sun Jul & Aug or by appointment with group of 10) You'll see Stallhagen's brews being downed throughout Åland, but here's a chance to get

it fresh and take a tour to see it being made (don't worry, it definitely includes a sample and snacks at the end!).

Getting There & Away

Rd 2 from Mariehamn takes you to Godby. Buses 2, 3 and 4 from Mariehamn all go via Godby (€3), while bus 6 services other parts of Finström, leaving Godby three times a day, Monday to Friday.

SUND

☎ 018 / pop 1052

Sund, just east of the main island group and connected to Saltvik by bridge, is Åland's very own action hero. As well as having a muscular medieval castle and the big guns of the open-air museum, it's got its battle scars in the ruins of a Russian stronghold.

Sund is just 30km from Mariehamn, which makes it an easy half-day trip by car or, if you're cycling, an excellent place to overnight. Finby is the largest town, with all services.

Sights & Activities

One of Åland's premier sights, **Kastelholms Slott** (☎ 432 156; admission €5; ◷ 10am-5pm Mon-Fri May, 10am-5pm daily Jun & Aug, 10am-6pm daily Jul, 10am-4pm Mon-Fri early–mid-Sep, English tours 2pm daily late Jun-early Aug) is a breathtaking castle picturesquely set alongside a little inlet. Construction began in the 14th century but several extensions have been made since, most notably by Gustav Wasa before he became king of Sweden. The keep towers are 15m high in parts with walls 3m thick and you can see how this castle would once have ruled over all of Åland.

Gustav's son Eric XIV was imprisoned here after he was deposed; his cell is particularly small given that he was once monarch of Sweden and Estonia. The hall, a later construction, ended up being used as a grain storehouse and has an exhibition of items unearthed by archaeologists. Entry is by regular guided tour; while English tours are rare, there are plenty of information panels. The castle is just off the main road, Rd 2, clearly signposted and visible to the right (when heading east), after passing Kastelholm village.

The best time to visit is on **Gustav Vasa Dagarna** (Gustav Wasa Day; www.gustavvasadagarna.aland .fi; admission €10), actually a weekend in early July when the castle travels back in time with medieval dancing, feasting and jousting.

Handily located next to the castle, **Jan Karlsgårdens Friluftsmuseum** (admission free; ☺ 10am-4pm daily May, 10am-5pm daily Jun-Aug, 10am-4pm Mon-Fri early Sep) is a sprawling open-air museum. You can stroll around traditional Ålandic buildings, including windmills and a smoke sauna. The guidebook (€1) from the Vita Björn museum is essential to get the background on each building. At the centre of the village is, of course, a Midsummer pole which makes an impressive spectacle when erected before or during the Midsummer festival.

By the entrance to the Jan Karlsgården Museum is **Fängelsemuseet Vita Björn** (☎ 432 156; admission €2; ☺ 10am-5pm May-Aug, 10am-4pm Mon-Fri early Sep), a small prison museum. The building was a jail until 1975 and demonstrates how cells and conditions evolved over the two centuries it was in use. Although it looks like a cottage, the walls and floor are of thick stone, so there was no tunnelling out.

Also near Kastelholm is **Alandia Escargots** (☎ 43964; admission €9; ☺ 2-3 tours daily Jul, 2 tours Tue-Fri late Jun & Aug), which runs a snail safari. This one-hour tour scampers around the snail farm looking at how the gastropods are carefully raised and fattened until they're gourmet. You'll get to taste one of the little critters done in garlic butter, but for the squeamish it's best washed down by a glass of strong cider.

North of Kastelholm, **Sankt Johannes Kyrka** (☺ May-Aug) is the biggest church in Åland. It is 800 years old and was twice destroyed by fire. The altarpiece is decorated with a dazzling triptych and a stone cross with the text 'Wenni E'. According to researchers, it was erected in memory of the Hamburg bishop Wenni, who died here while on a crusade in 936.

To the east of Sund are the distinctive octagonal blocks of the ruined Russian fortress **Bomarsund**. Following the war of 1808–09, Russia began to build Bomarsund as a defence against the Swedes. The epic project would take decades, bringing craftsmen and soldiers from across the Russian Empire. By 1854 the Crimean War occurred while construction was still under way and, in the last battle fought in Åland, a French-British naval force bombarded it heavily from the sea. After two days the Russians surrendered. Only three of the 14 planned defence towers were completed and today they make the most impressive ruins along with the lines of crumbled walls.

Ruins can be seen on both sides of the main road at the eastern end of Sund, by the bridge leading across a beautiful sound to the island of Prästö. There are several graveyards – Greek Orthodox, Jewish, Muslim and Christian – clearly marked on Prästö, attesting to the reach of this massive project. On the other side of the water is the small **Bomarsund museum** (☎ 44032; admission by donation; ☺ 10am-4pm Mon-Fri Jun–mid-Aug, Sat & Sun Jul), which has more information and displays bits and pieces excavated from the site of the fortress ruins.

Sleeping & Eating

Östergårds Bed & Breakfast (☎ 43927, http://home .aland.net/m02400; Östergård; s/d €60/90) This one-cottage wonder is set on a peaceful dairy farm just outside the village of Östergård (Gästerby in Finnish) which is just north of Kastelholm. It's well equipped with a full kitchen, though the room price includes a hearty breakfast.

Puttes Camping (☎ 44040, 0457-313 4177; puttes .camping@aland.net; tent sites per person €2.50 plus per tent or vehicle €2, cabins from €29; ☺ May-Aug; **P** &) Right on the doorstep of Bomarsund, this cheerful place has plenty of grassy camp sites and well-priced simple four-bed cabins. The beach sauna, nearby golf course, rowboats and a canoe jetty attract an outdoorsy crowd. Linen is an extra €6, so pack a sleepsheet. Its cafe does good pancakes.

The cafe at Jan Karlsgården Friluftsmuseum serves light snacks and sandwiches that make it a good lunch stop.

Getting There & Away

Rd 2 and bus 4 from Mariehamn to Vårdö will take you to Sund. The bus goes via Kastelholm (€3.60, 20 minutes), Bomarsund and Prästö (€4.90, 30 to 45 minutes).

A **bicycle ferry** (☎ 040-553 3256; ☺ departs Prästö 12.30pm & returns from Lumpo noon Mon-Sat Jun–mid-Aug) runs between Prästö and Lumpo, Lumparland with just one departure on selected days, though it means your route can skip the outer islands.

It's also possible to request a **bicycle ferry** (☎ 040-078 3086; per bicycle €9; ☺ late Jun–mid-Aug) from Bomarsund to Västra Simskäla although you'll need to call ahead and see if they're available.

ÅLAND

VÅRDÖ
☎ 018 / pop 425

Vårdö is often skipped by tourists in favour of the more remote, outer islands. But the cluster of isles, connected by bridges and ferries, stretches up to the two remote islands of Simskäla (Västra and Östra; West and East, respectively) with plenty of remote beaches to discover. It's been a refuge for Finnish and Swedish writers who have come for its rippling bays, rustling silver birches, and views over the numerous islets of the archipelago. Mountain-top bonfires were once lit by the people of Vårdö to warn the rest of Åland's inhabitants of dangerous approaches. The bonfires can still be seen today on the municipality's coat of arms.

Ferries to outer islands leave from Hummelvik, but Vargata is also a key settlement, with a bank (but no ATM), a shop and a post office. The **library** (☎ 47970; ☽ 2-4.30pm & 6-9pm Tue & Thu) has free internet access.

Beyond here, the island's **church** (☽ 10am-6pm Jun-Aug) is recognisable by its curiously bulbous tower. Parts of the church date back to the 15th century though much of the structure is spruce 18th-century work.

On the main road between Vargata and Lövö, **Seffers Hembygdsgård** (Seffers Homestead; ☎ 040 0777; admission free; ☽ noon-3pm Tue, Thu & Sat mid-Jun–Jul) is an 18th-century farmhouse that makes an easy if not essential break. It has a windmill, farm equipment and a Midsummer pole on display.

Sandösunds Camping (below) provides plenty of chance to explore the outdoors with basic kayak lessons (€30, three hours) or guided paddles (€40) around the northern parts of the island.

If you're pressed for time but want a quick excursion, then there's a **cruise** (☎ 040-078 3086; Västerövägen 176; adult €30; ☽ departs 6pm Tue Jul) that leaves from Västra Simskäla's port.

Sleeping
Sandösunds Camping (☎ 47750; www.sandocamping.aland.fi; tent sites per person €4 plus tent or vehicle €3, 2-/4-person cabin from €37/46) This well-positioned camping ground can be remarkably peaceful and offers several quiet camping plots. The beachside cabins are well kept, but the facilities here are the real bonus, and include kayak lessons and the unique 'floating sauna' that lets you hop straight into the water on the picture-perfect sound. It's open from May to

August, but you won't be turned away if you ring ahead out of season.

Bomans Gästhem (☎ 47821; www.visitaland.com /bomansgasthem; Vårdöby; dm €22, d €60-70; ☽ May-Sep; **P**) This hostel is signposted 500m off the road between Vargata and Lövö. As well as dorms, there are slick rooms in little bungalows and simpler cabins. There are all sorts of facilities and activities; guests have use of a kitchen and sauna, and can rent bikes. There's even a driving range in the field out the front. Breakfast and linen are all part of the deal.

Stormsärs Konferens & Värdhus (☎ 47560; www .stormskar.ax; Västerövägen 176, Västra Simskäla; d from €80) Set on the island of Väster Simskäla, this family-run place has excellent rooms in a traditional home that also has broadband sockets in every room. Bathrooms are shared but the house is small enough for it not to be an issue. They also run the bicycle ferry to the island.

Getting There & Away
Vårdö is connected to the island of Prästö by a network of ferries. Bus 4 will take you to Vårdö from Mariehamn (€5.60, 40 to 55 minutes), crossing on the short, free car ferry from Prästö.

Ferries on the northern archipelago route depart from the village of Hummelvik on Vårdö; the bus meets them. For more details see p259. For information on the bicycle ferry between Saltvik and Vårdö, see opposite.

SALTVIK
☎ 018 / pop 1731

Vikings have been sharpening their horned helmets here for centuries and many of their relics have been unearthed around Saltvik, though few signs of longhouses remain. The best chance to see Viking heritage is at Saltvik's annual **Viking Market** (☎ 0457-342 7500; www.aland-vikingar.com; admission €10), a three-day festival of eating, drinking and costumed merrymaking in July.

Southeast of Kvarnbo, the central village of Saltvik, is the Iron Age fortress of **Borgboda**. On the main Saltvik bicycle route, it is thought to have been built in the mid-to-late 1st millennium. Some stone outcroppings remain but the only structure is Ida's Stuga (Ida's Cottage), the home of folk singer Ida Jansson in the 20th century.

Kvarnbo also has the red-granite **Sankta Maria Kyrka** that dates from the 12th century and is thought to be the oldest church in

Finland. Wall paintings (though retouched throughout the centuries) and sculptures date back to the 13th century, as well as a fine baptismal font. Other paintings are from the Lutheran era in the 1500s. Around the church, it's possible to discern ruins of Vikings' homes.

At 129m above sea level, Åland's highest 'mountain' is really no more than a big hill, but it makes an easy hike. Two short, well-marked walking tracks (1km and 2.5km long, respectively) lead to the top, where there's a viewing tower and a simple four-bed camp hut.

On the road to Orrdals Klint near Långbergsöda is a Stone Age walking trail starting from a clearly marked car park. It's more of a stroll than a hike, taking you past two excavated settlements and then to a fully reconstructed **Stone Age Village** (11am-6pm late Jun–mid-Aug), with sealskin-covered huts. In summer there are plenty of Neolithic skills to try your hand at; there are even people living Stone Age-like lives there. There is no public transport; you'll have to make your own way from Kvarnbo.

Sleeping

Kvarnbo Gästhem (44015; www.kvarnbogasthem.com; Kvarnbo; d €80) This neat little spot has several top-notch rooms and does brilliant food – understandable, as one of the owners is Swedish TV chef Ella Grüssner Cromwell-Morgan. They do great cooking courses and wine tastings that are worth a little extra.

Getting There & Away

Bus 3 runs from Mariehamn to Kvarnbo (€3.60, 35 minutes) and also to other villages in Saltvik.

A private bicycle ferry **Kajo** (040-078 3086; €9; departs Tengsödavik 11am & Västra 11.30am late Jun–early Aug by request) runs between Tengsödavik and Västra Simskäla in Vårdö with only one daily departure each way. You'll need to call ahead to confirm.

GETA

 018 / pop 443

The quiet northern municipality of Geta is known as the apple basket of Åland. The main attraction is **Getabergen**, a formidable peak of 98m. One nature trail here is aimed at kids (2km), while a longer trail (5.5km) leads to Djupviksgrottan, a spacious natural grotto that is one of several striking geological features hereabouts.

Tjudö Vingård (0457-072 1192; Tjudö; tours €17, with lunch/dinner €27/52.20; 11am & 2pm late Jun–mid-Aug) distils spirits from cherries, apples and other berries that make an intriguing taste for any visitor. The whole tour runs for just under four hours and is best combined with lunch or dinner after, which includes crayfish or ostrich from the quirky farm. You can also call ahead and organise a tour, which is a particularly good idea for groups.

Bus 2 runs from Marienhamn to Geta (€5.40, 50 minutes) via Godby.

The bicycle ferry **Silvana** (040-022 9149; Jun–mid-Aug) travels between Hällö in Geta, and Skarpnåtö in Hammarland. There is one departure daily in early June (leaving Skarpnåtö at noon and arriving at Hällö at 12.30pm) and two daily departures from mid-June to late August (the second leaves Skarpnåtö at 4.30pm and and arrives at Hällö at 5pm). The one-way trip costs €7.

HAMMARLAND

 018 / pop 1409

The northwestern mainland of Åland is known as Hammarland and has one of the largest populations of Swedish speakers in Finland. It's also one of the oldest inhabited areas in Åland with over 40 burial mounds having been discovered. Although it's pleasant enough, there are few real sights, which make it an ideal place to put your feet up. Kattby is the main village, with all facilities.

Sankta Catharina Kyrka (summer) in Kattby was built in the 13th century though a fire in the beginning of the 15th century led it to be rebuilt with fresh wall paintings. There's an **Iron Age burial site** to the west of the church, with more than 30 burial sites.

Sleeping & Eating

Kattnäs Camping (37687; tent sites €7, cabins €35-40; May–mid-Sep) This well-equipped camping ground is delightfully distant from the touristy Eckerö but still waterside. Cabins are comfy and there's a TV lounge and cafe in case you're missing civilisation. To get here turn off the Eckerö–Mariehamn Rd and head 3km south to Kattby; the camping ground is to the west.

Kvarnhagens Stugor (/fax 37212; 2-/3-/4- person cottages €45/50/55; May-Sep) This reliable spot near Skarpnåtö has six sturdy timber cottages

ÅLAND

that come with fridges and kitchenettes. There are some handy communal facilities including a sauna, a laundry, and a smoke hut in case you catch any fish!

Getting There & Away

Bus 1 from Mariehamn to Eckerö runs through Hammarland. For information on the bicycle ferry between Hammarland and Geta, see p255.

ECKERÖ

☎ 018 / pop 923

Let's face it: Eckerö is basically Sweden. This tiny island is a two-hour ferry ride from mainland Sweden and vacationing Swedes have been outnumbering locals since Gustav Wasa decreed that an inn be built near Eckerö for his hunting pleasure. Even the red Viking longboat on the municipality's coat of arms seems to be setting sail for the west, possibly towing this little island back as a souvenir.

And you can see why. It's a picturesque spot with sandy beaches, rusty red boatsheds and granite rocks looming from the water. Storby (Big Village), at the ferry terminal, is the main centre, with a **tourist office** (☎ 38095; www.eckero.ax), petrol station and bank.

Sights & Activities

Storby's **Post och Tullhuset** (Post & Customs House; ☎ 38689) was designed by German architect CL Engel, famous for his classic architectural work in central Helsinki. It was completed in 1828, during the era of Tsar Alexander I of Russia, and has the hallmarks of that grand epoch. As Åland was the westernmost extremity of the Russian Empire, the building was built as a show of might to Sweden, which explains why this small town has such a majestic post office. It was also a crucial point in the Mail Rd that ran from Sweden to Finland.

The building has become a hub for local artists and craftspeople. There's a popular **cafe** (snacks €3-5) and chocolate shop as well as a small unattended **museum** (♡ 10am-6pm) of postcards and stamps. Upstairs there are changing exhibits by local artists (♡ 10am-3pm Jun–mid-Aug). There's also the small **mailboat museum** (☎ 39000; admission €1.70; ♡ 10am-3pm Jun–mid-Aug, 10am-4pm mid-Jun–Jul) which tells the story of the dedicated people who worked on the Mail Rd by boat. The building is open daily in summer, and Monday to Friday only in winter.

Also in Storby, **Labbas Homestead & Bank Museum** (☎ 38507; admission €2; ♡ noon-4pm Wed Jul–mid-Aug) shows off the typical archipelago house of sailor Johan Ekblom, with a section devoted to banking history. The museum is known for limited opening hours so call ahead to check.

Just north of Storby is the attractive **Käringsund harbour**. On summer evenings this peaceful little cove with its rustic old wooden boathouses reflecting on the water is so scenic it's almost unreal. There's a nature trail and small beach here and canoes and rowing boats can be hired from a kiosk nearby.

At Käringsund harbour is **Ålands Jakt och Fiskemuseum** (Åland Hunting & Fishing Museum; ☎ 38299; admission €3.40; ♡ 10am-5pm May–mid-Sep, 10am-6pm mid-Jun–mid-Aug), which gets a little ghoulish after so many stuffed animals and gun-toting photographs, though the pearl-digging displays might kill some time while you're waiting for a ferry.

Departing from the museum is a 45-minute tour of **Viltsafari** (☎ 38000; tour €8; ♡ departs noon, 1pm, 2pm & 3pm mid-Jun–mid-Aug), a fenced-in nature park where you can get up close to Finnish fauna like red and fallow deer, swans and wild boar, plus the odd ostrich.

The village of Kyrkoby, about 5km east of Storby on the road to Mariehamn, was named for the 13th-century **Sankt Lars Kyrka** (admission by donation; ♡ 10am-6pm May-Sep). It's an attractive church with a 14th-century Madonna sculpture and rustic murals. The altar painting is a 19th-century work depicting a Magdalene penitent.

Degersand, about 9km south of Storby beyond the village of Torp, has a good **beach** for swimming and sunning.

There are several good places that offer activities:

Käringsund (opposite; adults €58; ♡ departs 4pm Tue Jun-Aug) Offers a three-hour seal safari out through the neighbouring islands.

Nimix (☎ 0506 6716; www.nimix.ax; per 2hr/day hire €15/30) Rents out canoes and delivers to locations outside of Eckerö for a fee (€25 to €80).

Ro-No Rent Has an office near the harbour with bicycles, scooters and canoes for the same prices as those in Mariehamn (see p246 for contact details and prices).

Sleeping

Eckerö has more cabin and cottage rentals than any other Åland province – contact Ålandsresor (p245) for details.

Käringsund (☎ 38300; www.karingsund.ax; tent sites €6-9, cabins €55-80, bungalows €90-110; ⓨ mid-May–Aug) It's hard to put a finger on what this place is – its cushy bungalows and bonus activities like a seal safari or bicycle borrowing all make you feel like you're at a resort. Then there are more basic cabins or you can unfurl your tent in the green expanses near the cafe, which does great pizzas and calzones. Set near a family beach and in green fields, perhaps the best word is heavenly.

Österängens Hotell (☎ 38268; osterangen@aland .net; s/d €70/83; ⓨ Mar-Sep; Ⓟ Ⓡ) There are just over 20 cabins in this place, but all of them look out onto the quiet beach of Torp. With a sweet little restaurant, an indoor pool, two saunas and fishing equipment it's hard to find a reason to leave.

Degersands (☎ 38004; www.degersand.nu; tent sites €5, cabins €90-110) This spot south of Storby reckons they specialise in 'Qamping' – quality camping. With five well-kitted out cottages with generous balconies that include their own barbecues, they make a convincing argument. They also hire out kayaks and fishing gear.

Hotel Elvira (☎ 38200; www.visitaland.com/hotelelvira; Eckerö; s/d/tr €80/100/140; wi-fi) This modern place is good for holidaying Swedish lads, with an onsite pub with large-screen satellite TV and GameCube. Rooms are individually decorated with ensuites and wireless throughout. The included breakfast is hearty enough to power a long day's cycling.

Eckerö Hotell & Restaurang (☎ 38447; www.eckero hotell.aland.fi; Eckerö; d €90-100; wi-fi) Famous (some might say notorious) for its summer Elvis shows, this hotel is like the King – big but hard not to like. The rooms might not be Graceland but they're serviceable with wi-fi and a good breakfast thrown in. For the record, Presley pretender Ronald Karlsson might not have the look (he has a moustache) but sounds bang-on.

Eating

Café Lugn & Ro (☎ 38420; Post & Customs House; snacks €5-9; ⓨ 10am-4pm May-Sep, 10am-6pm Jul–mid-Aug) This friendly place serves sandwiches, hamburgers and delicious pastries with a Venezuelan touch. There's also accommodation available in the historic complex from mid-January to December (singles/doubles €60/68).

Jannes Bodega (☎ 38530; Käringsund Harbour; meals €9-13; ⓨ lunch & dinner Jun-Aug) Set right on the pier, this atmospheric place is perfect for downing a few beers and watching the sun set over the red creaking boathouses. The menu runs to pasta and some good snacks fill the hole between drinks.

Koriander Wok & Grill (☎ 38429; Storby; mains €17-23; ⓨ lunch daily Jun-Aug, dinner Tue-Fri Jun-Aug) This restaurant, by the side of the road just out of Storby, has a refreshing Asian bent with peppy stir-fries and strong curries. They also do burgers and simpler meals for kids.

Getting There & Away

Rd 2 runs from Mariehamn to Eckerö. Alternatively, you can take bus 1 (€4.90, 40 minutes). For information on ferries between Eckerö and Grisslehamn in Sweden, see p243.

The distance from Mariehamn to Storby (40km) makes this a suitable day trip by bicycle.

LEMLAND
☎ 018 / pop 1773

When the occupying Russians needed a shipping route in the late 19th century, their prisoners of war dug the Lemström Canal. Today it remains one of Lemland's defining sights. Lemland lies between Lumparland and the canal, 5km east of Mariehamn on Rd 3 (take bus 5) with Norrby village at its centre.

In Norrby, **Sankta Birgitta Kyrka** (ⓨ Mon-Fri May-Aug) has 13th- and 14th-century wall paintings that tell the story of St Nicholas, the patron saint of seafarers. At Lemböte, on the western side of the island, is a restored 13th-century church and several ancient burial mounds. Near the crossing to Lumparland, **Skeppargården Pellas** (☎ 34001; adult/child €2.50/free; ⓨ 11am-4pm late Jun-Aug) is the homestead museum of a local shipmaster.

LUMPARLAND
☎ 018 / pop 387

Most travellers go straight to Lumparland's two ferry harbours, Svinö and Långnäs, but there are a few reasons to day trip here.

Sankt Andreas Kyrka (ⓨ Jun-Aug) was built in 1720 making it a relative youngster, but it is Åland's oldest surviving wooden church which lends it a certain charm. The curious cross is actually a weathervane that was once attached to the steeple. The large altarpiece was painted by Victor Westerholm of the Önningeby colony (p251).

ÅLAND

ÅLAND

VIA THE ARCHIPELAGO FERRIES

If travelling by car between the main part of Åland and the Finnish mainland it's cheaper to spend a night en route: reservations will not be accepted on through ferries without a stopover. The ferries cost €77 if you want to rush it, but are only €20 if you stopover in the southern or northern archipelago.

Lumparland is a good place to explore the wilderness. **Get Out Adventures** (www.get outadventures.ax, 4hr kayak tour €60, 4hr nature hike €50) does excellent guided kayak expeditions and hikes. If you're keen to do it yourself, there's a well-marked **Lumparlandsleden trail** from Svinö that takes four hours through easy terrain and a few little villages.

From Mariehamn take bus 5 to Svinö and Långnäs (€4.50, 45 minutes); it meets the ferries from Sweden. For information on the bicycle ferry to Prästö see p253.

NORTHERN ARCHIPELAGO

Kumlinge and Brändö are municipalities of the scattered islands that make up the northern archipelago. They're less travelled than the southern group and you may find yourself the only traveller on some islands. Coming to Åland from Kustavi on the Finnish mainland via Osnäs, you'll arrive at Långö in the north of the Brändö island group. You can also depart from here, but confirm ferry times in advance to avoid getting stuck.

KUMLINGE
☎ 018 / pop 366
About 1¼ hours by ferry from Vårdö, this municipality consists of the main island, **Kumlinge** (www.kumlinge.info), flanked by **Enklinge** to the north and **Seglinge** to the south. Most services can be found on Kumlinge, and there is a bank on Enklinge. Seglinge only has a shop in the main village.

The ferry to Seglinge departs from the island of **Snäckö**, 8km from Kumlinge village, while a 7km walking path goes from Remmarina to Sankta Anna Kyrka. Local ferries from the main island to Enklinge depart from the village of **Krokarno**. A marked **cycling** route runs from Snäckö north to Krokarno, with bridges between the islands.

Sankta Anna Kyrka (☎ 040-031 1805; ☷ noon-5pm Mon-Fri summer) is an attractive church 2km north of Kumlinge village with 500-year-old Franciscan-style paintings.

On Enklinge the open-air **Hermas Farm Museum** (☎ 55334; admission €2; ☷ 11am-5pm Mon-Fri Jun-Aug, 10am-7pm Jul), 3.5km from the pier, has 20 original buildings and a myriad of farm tools.

Sleeping & Eating
Hasslebo Gästhem (☎ 55418; www.hasslebo.com; bike hire €9; tent sites €7, dm €20, s/d €50/70; ☐ wi-fi) Just 3km down a dirt road outside Kumlinge village, this spot has a green emphasis including bio toilet, wood-fired sauna with scented oils and wireless throughout. As well as making their own soaps and jams, the folks here complete the eco-farm with a donkey that offers rides only to well-behaved kids.

Ledholms Camping (☎ /fax 55647; tent sites per person €2.50; ☷ Jun-Aug) This camping ground is on the island of Snäckö near the ferry pier. It also has cheap cabins and a small grocery store.

Remmarina Stugor (☎ 040-052 9199; www.rem marina.com; 2-/3-/4-person cottages €55/65/70; ⓟ) At the guest harbour 2km south of Kumlinge village, there are 12 clean, reasonably priced cottages on a small hill here.

The same people also operate **Restaurang Kastören** (mains €19-25; ☷ lunch & dinner Jun-Aug) that offers reliable meals priced for their yacht crowd.

Getting There & Away
Ferries on the route between Hummelvik and Torsholma (on Brändö) stop at both Enklinge (one hour) and Krokarno on Kumlinge island (70 minutes). One or two ferries a day go from Långnäs in Lumparland to Snäckö in Kumlinge, via Överö in the Föglö island group (1¾ hours).

BRÄNDÖ
☎ 018 / pop 510
There are over 1180 islands in this municipality, but the core group of Brändö, Torsholma, Åva and Jurmo are connected by free ferries and bridges. Further to the south most travellers stay on the ferry and skip the island of Lappo, so it is quiet if a little uninteresting. Services are on the main island and in the villages of **Lappo** and **Torsholma** on smaller islands.

The peculiar shape of the Brändös' main island means you're never far from the sea and a signposted **bike route** runs from Torsholma harbour north across the main island to **Långö** harbour on Åva.

Sankt Jakobs Kyrka (noon-5pm late Jun-early Aug), the wooden place of worship on Brändö island, dates from 1893 and is an example of the whitewashed style. On Lappo, **Skärgårdsmuseet** (56689; adult/child €3.50/free; 10am-noon & 2-4pm mid-Jun–mid-Aug) has exhibits of local history, boats and nature as well as a photography exhibition.

In addition to admiring Jurmo's hallmark long-haired cattle, you can ride Icelandic horses at **Talli Perla** (040-562 0488; www.talliperla .com, in Finnish; 2-day package €185), which does a two-day ride and accommodation package on the northern island.

Sleeping & Eating

Brändö Tourism (040-080 7444; www.brandotur ism.aland.fi) can book cottages throughout the municipality.

Hotell Gullvivan (56350; www.gullvivan.aland .fi, in Swedish & Finnish; s/d €61/68, cabins €84; P) Set near the pier in idyllic wilderness, this comfortable hotel sits on Björnholma island not far from the central services, with a restaurant, sauna and minigolf as well as hire boats and fishing gear. The four-person huts are modern with microwaves, fridges and other cooking facilities.

Brändö Stugby (56221; http://come.to/brando .stugby; May–mid-Oct) This camping ground on Brändö has log cabins, a basic shop, barbecues and rowing boats for hire.

Jurmo Vandrarhem (040-506 4777; www.jurmo .ax, in Swedish; Jurmo; dm €12) On the far northern extreme of Brändö, this youth hostel opens year-round in a secluded spot.

Pellas Gästhem (040-832 4333; www.pellas.aland .fi; Lappo; cabins from €61, 2-person apt from €99; late Mar-early Dec; P) Formerly a school, this accommodation option is on Lappo with good cabins and roomy apartments which include kitchens and bathrooms.

Getting There & Away

There are three ferry connections a day from Vårdö to Lappo and Torsholma via Kumlinge. The trip from Hummelvik to Torsholma takes about 2½ hours. It's free for passengers and bicycles, and €20 for cars. It's possible to go from Torsholma to Roslax (Houskär) and Kannvik (Innio) on **M/S Carolina** (040-717 3455) daily.

From Turku on mainland Finland, take a bus to Kustavi, and on to Vartsala Island to reach the harbour of Osnäs (Finnish: Vuosnainen). There are five to seven connections a day from Osnäs to Långö on the northern Brändö island of Åva. This journey is free for passengers and bicycles, and €20 for cars.

SOUTHERN ARCHIPELAGO

Your first glimpses will probably be from a boat – silver birches clinging to low-lying granite islands that invite exploration. Åland's southern islands are strewn with tiny islets but the major municipalities are Föglö, tiny Sottunga and remote Kökar. Kökar has the most appeal as the arrival point for archipelago ferries from Galtby harbour on Korpo, on the Finnish mainland (see p260). It's possible to explore this area as a day trip from Mariehamn, or complete the loop of islands by heading north, which requires an overnight stay (opposite).

FÖGLÖ
 018 / pop 582

The **Föglö** island group was first mentioned in historical records in 1241 by a Danish bishop, who landed here en route to Tallinn. The main town is **Degerby** and a signposted bike route runs from here to **Överö**, with archipelago ferries departing from both these destinations.

Degerby has a bank, post office and grocery, as well as a summer **tourist information kiosk** (045-7342 7274; www.foglo.ax/turism; 10am-7pm Mon-Fri, 10am-5.30pm Sat, 10am-4pm Sun mid-Jun–mid-Aug). Degerby is notable for its unusual architecture as historically, many Föglöites were civil servants rather than farmers, and chose to build in art nouveau or Empire styles instead of the traditional archipelago style.

At the harbour you'll find the local **museum** (50348; admission €2; 10am-5pm Tue-Sun mid-Jun–mid-Aug) which has historical and artistic exhibits – a good time-waster while waiting for the ferry. Another good diversion from the harbour is the 14th-century

ÅLAND

Sankta Maria Magdalena Kyrka (🕙 Mon-Fri summer), on an island south from Degerby, connected by a bridge and a scenic road.

Degerby's harbour is a good place from which to explore other islands, though you'll need to charter a boat. **Coja Fishing** (☎ 040-094 7502; www.coja.nu; tours €30; 🕙 departs 1pm Wed & Sat Jun-Aug) conducts a four-hour tour to the wilderness island of **Björkör** including a well-preserved 18th-century archipelago home.

Sleeping & Eating

Enighetens Gästhem (☎ 50310; s/d €48/68; 🕙 May-Sep; **P**) This rustic former courthouse once hosted Finnish President Tarja Halonen and the series of grand red buildings is suitably impressive. The cafe makes for a good bite as well as solid breakfasts.

C & C Camping (☎ 51445; tent sites €2 plus per person €3, 2-/3-/4-person cabins €30/35/39, sauna €11, meals €4-10; 🕙 Jun-Aug; 🚿) This place is on the Degerby-Överö cycle route with a variety of cabins with good facilities including grills, fish smokers, a sauna and a cafe that does good pancakes. Look out for the giant creepy ogre statue by the side of the road.

Degerby Mat & Café (☎ 50002; www.visitaland .com/degerbymat, in Swedish; s/d €50/75, meals €5-9; 🖳) This year-round cafe and guesthouse does good snack meals and has rooms that include sauna, bikes and internet usage. They also have good storage for bikes.

Getting There & Away

From Mariehamn, bus 5 goes to the Svinö and Långnäs ferry harbours, both in Lumparland. A dozen or so ferries a day make the one-hour trip between Svinö and Degerby. There are six to seven ferries a day from Långnäs to Överö, some going on to Kumlinge, and others to Kökar.

SOTTUNGA
☎ 018 / pop 116

Only three of the of several islands in this municipality are actually inhabited – Husö, Finnö and Storsottunga (usually just called Sottunga) make up Åland's least-populated municipality. Only Sottunga island is really worth visiting and is best equipped for tourists with its own bank, shop, school, health-care centre, library and church.

Sankta Maria Magdalena Kyrka was rebuilt in 1728 and is an endearing wooden church. A short **nature trail** starts at the fishing harbour,

and a marked **cycling route** runs north from the harbour to the village of Skaget.

If you need to stay here **Strandhuggets Stugor** (☎ 55255; d €35; 🕙 Jun-Aug; **P**), right next to the harbour, has six pine-shaded cottages, as well as a cafe and sauna.

Ferries on the southern archipelago route from Lumparland or Föglö, as well as occasional ferries from Kumlinge, will take you to Sottunga.

KÖKAR
☎ 018 / pop 284

The barren landscape of this island group means that many travellers use them as a stepping stone to mainland Finland, with ferries departing from here to Korpo and Galtby. It was once an outpost for seal hunters, and had a Franciscan monastery built in the 14th century on the site of the contemporary church.

Today most of the inhabitants live in and around the quaint little town of Karlby, which has a bank, post office and grocery store.

Sights & Activities

Historic **Hamnö Island** is connected to the main island of Kökar by a bridge. It was once a crucial stop on the Hanseatic trade route between Germany and Turku. The **Sankta Anne Kyrka** (🕙 daily May-Sep) dates back to 1784 and features a model ship for penitent sailors to pray to.

Kökar Homestead Museum (☎ 55816; admission €2; 🕙 noon-5pm mid-Jun–mid-Aug) is a modest collection of local history on the east side of the main island in the village of Hellsö. A short **nature trail** starts near Hellsö.

Sleeping & Eating

Hotell Brudhäll (☎ 55955; Karlby; s/d €96/114, ste €200; **P**) This cute red place right on the little harbour has a great restaurant with a terrace to sun and sip on. Rooms are stylish and suites have their own minisauna. This is one of the archipelago's best hotels.

Sandvik Camping (☎ 55911; tent €12; 🕙 May-Sep) This low-key camping ground is 3.5km southwest of Karlby. You can hike here via the coast (to your right as you exit the ferry). There are kitchen facilities, sauna and a grilli (June to August), as well as a good swimming beach.

Getting There & Away

Ferries depart for Kökar once or twice daily from the harbour of Galtby on Korpo Island, 75km from Turku and connected by bus. The trip from Galtby to Kökar takes 2¼ hours. It's free for passengers and bicycles, and €20 for cars.

To get to Kökar from mainland Åland, there are three to five ferry connections a day from Långnäs (take bus 5 from Mariehamn) via Föglö and Sottunga. Ferries also stop at the tiny island of Husö. Travel time is 2½ hours from Långnäs. It's free for passengers and bicycles and €20 for cars.

See the boxed text, p258, for important information about this ferry route.

Pohjanmaa

Better known as Ostrobothnia (Swedish: Österbotten), as it is the coast to the east of the Gulf of Bothnia, Pohjanmaa shares more with neighbouring Sweden than Suomi. Newstands are packed with Swedish gossip magazines, Stockholm's radio and TV fills the airwaves, and you'll hear Svenska spoken almost everywhere.

Swedes began coming here in the 17th century to strip the forests for tar. After the 'other black gold' dried up, many Swedes remained as farmers and fisherfolk. Today they continue to treat this region as a holiday spot calling it *Parallelsverige,* which means 'Parallel Sweden'. You'll hear Swedish spoken more commonly than Finnish.

Stretching along the coast from Pori in the south to Kalajoki in the north, you should take locals' suggestions that this is the 'Finnish Mediterranean' with a dose of *salmiakki* (salty liquorice). Sure, the north boasts some expansive beaches with cottages dotting the nearby woods that are ideal for family holidays, but Ibiza it ain't.

Comparisons aside, there's plenty to charm in the region. The unofficial capital is seaside Vaasa, known for its arty feel, but it's worth venturing to the beautiful wooden old towns of Kokkola and Jakobstad and some of Finland's best music festivals.

POHJANMAA

HIGHLIGHTS

- Seeing a city as a symphony with Alvar Aalto's masterful town centre in **Seinäjoki** (p271)
- Exploring the **Kvarken Archipelago** (p268) by cycling out to Replot or canoeing further
- Exploring the modern art of Vaasa's **Kuntsi museum** (p264)
- Pitching a tent for the **Kaustinen Folk Music Festival** (p273) in July; Finland's answer to Woodstock
- Wandering the picturesque **Skata** (p274), in the old town of Jakobstad
- Visiting the excellent art collection in Vaasa's **Pohjanmaan Museo** (p264)

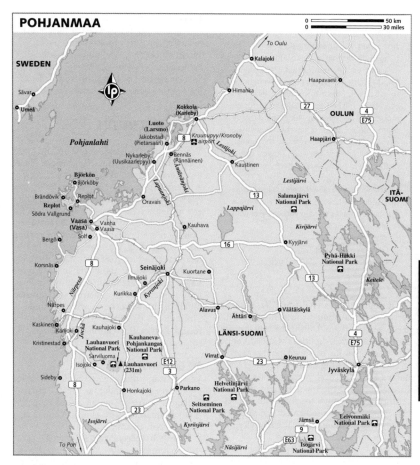

POHJANMAA

Activities

Pohjanmaa is two-wheeled heaven with rolling fields, unchallenging hills, evenly spaced towns and beautiful coastal scenery making for leisurely cycling. The water is a big drawcard with boating, fishing and swimming (in summer, though ice swimming is not out of the question) all popular and quite easily accessible. You can explore further afield with the help of Travel Ostrobothnia (www.matkailupohjanmaa.fi) which has have tips on accommodation and tours.

Self-Catering Accommodation

Local tourist offices have details of cottages in the area. **Lomarengas** (☎ 03-0650 2502; www.lomarengas.fi; Eteläesplanadi 22 C, FI-00130 Helsinki; cottages per week from €200) is a reputable agency that can arrange cottage rental. See p349 for more information on self-catering accommodation.

VAASA

☎ 06 / pop 57,998

Just 45 nautical miles from Sweden, Vaasa (Swedish: Vasa) embraces the culture of the country that's visible across the Gulf of Bothnia, according to locals. A quarter of the population here speaks Swedish as a first language and you'll hear conversations in restaurants and bars switching deftly between Finnish and Swedish, often in the same sentence.

FINNISH OR SWEDISH?

Just when you thought you'd gotten the hang of the double vowels of Finnish, you're in a part of the country that often prefers Swedish. Often? Yep, that's right sometimes they'll speak Swedish in Ostobothnia, but sometimes it'll be Finnish. Jakobstad, for example, will be called by this Swedish name often but if you look on the VR website (www.vr.fi) you'll have to know the Finnish name, Pietarsaari. We suggest you know both names particularly when you're asking for tickets.

And when you're in the area, a few words of Swedish will come in handy. Here are a few basic phrases to help you connect with locals:

Yes	Ja
No	Nej
Please	Snälla/Vänligen
Thank you	Tack

During Finland's civil war, Vaasa briefly served as capital, though the town began with very Swedish origins. During the 14th century a village called Korsholm (now called Vanha Vaasa; see opposite) occupied the area nearby. In 1606 Swedish King Charles IX created Vasa, named after the royal Swedish Wasa family. Russia occupied the town early in the 19th century. The original town, like all respectable Finnish wooden settlements, was burned down in Vaasa's Great Fire; the new city was begun in the mid-19th century.

We're beyond the 63rd parallel here so southern Finns distance Vaasa as 'The North'. But the city has three universities, a thriving art scene and has long been a popular family destination so it's anything but a one-reindeer town.

ORIENTATION

Vaasanpuistikko is the main street through the centre of Vaasa. Vaskiluoto to the west and Palosaari to the north are two islands connected to central Vaasa by bridges.

INFORMATION

Art City Passport (www.artcityvaasa.com; 4-day pass €6) Available from the tourist office, this pass includes entry to most galleries and museums.

Main post office (Hovioikeudenpuistikko 23A; ☯ 10am-6pm Mon-Fri) Opposite the train station.

Public library (☎ 325 3533; Kirjastonkatu 13; ☯ 10am-8pm Mon-Thu, 10am-6pm Fri, 10am-3pm Sat, closed Sun) Several free internet terminals.

Tourist office (☎ 325 1145; matkailu.vaasa.fi; Raastuvankatu 30; ☯ 9am-6pm Mon-Fri, 10am-6pm Sat & Sun Jun-Aug, 9am-4pm Mon-Fri Sep-May; ⌨) In the town hall building; books accommodation and rents bikes.

SIGHTS & ACTIVITIES
Museums

Vaasa has two museum in one building with very different focuses. **Pohjanmaan Museo** (Ostrobothnian Museum; ☎ 325 3800; http://museo.vaasa .fi; Museokatu 3; admission €4; ☯ 10am-5pm Tue-Fri, 10am-8pm Wed, noon-5pm Sat & Sun) is a dynamic modern museum with plenty of opportunity for interaction. Downstairs in the **Terranova** section there's a brilliant evocation of natural history including information on the nearby Kvarken area (see p268). Upstairs there are exhibitions about daily life in yesteryear Vaasa and the Hedman collection (named for the museum's great patron who donated much of this collection), which includes a Tintoretto, a pair of Luca Giordanos, and a round Botticelli Madonna. There are also coins and ceramics.

Art Galleries

Vaasa has a thriving art scene. Look out for public art as you wander the streets especially Finland's 'Statue of Liberty' in the kauppatori (market square) by Yrjö Liipola (1938), a man holding aloft an arm.

Tikanoja Art Gallery (☎ 325 3916; www.tikanojantaid ekoti.fi; Hovioikeudenpuistikko 4; admission €5; ☯ 11am-4pm Tue-Sat, noon-5pm Sun) features a strong international collection, including work by artists such as Degas, Gauguin, Matisse and Picasso.

For a modern take, **Kuntsi** (☎ 325 3920; www .kuntsi.fi; Sisäsatama; admission €6; ☯ 11am-5pm Tue, Wed & Fri-Sun, 11am-8pm Thu, closed Mon) covers pop art, kinetic art, surrealism and postmodernism. The collection opened in the former customs house during 2007, and was based on the collection of local collector Simo Kuntsi who had over 1000 pieces. It's especially good on modern Finnish works – don't miss the burning sauna or the Elovena girl hanging herself. If you're after something even more cutting edge, check out **Platform** (www.platform.fi; Hovioikeudenpuistikko 3; ☯ 2-6pm Wed & Sun, 2-8pm Thu), an artists' space that displays local works.

Vanha Vaasa

Vaasa's Old Town developed around the harbour, about 30 minutes' walk southeast of the modern centre, but was abandoned after the fire in 1852 as the harbour had become unsuitable for large vessels. Ruins of a **medieval church** have been restored, but the most interesting sight is the **Korsholm Church** (☺9am-4pm Mon-Fri Jun-Aug). Built in 1776, this grand structure was once the Court of Appeal, but began serving as a church after the Great Fire of 1852. **Köpmanshuset Wasasferne** (☎356 7578; Kauppiaankatu 10; admission €2; ☺11am-5pm Thu-Sun mid-May–mid-Aug) is a museum of local history with reconstructions of a 19th-century post office and some furniture salvaged from the blaze.

Buses 7, 9, 12A and 12B travel between Vanha Vaasa and the town centre.

Churches

The most impressive church in town is the neo-Gothic **Vaasa Church** (Kirkkopuistikko; ☺10am-6pm Tue-Fri Jun–mid-Aug, 1-3pm Tue-Fri rest of year), made of local red bricks. The **Orthodox Church** (☎317 2620; Barracks Sq; ☺11am–4pm Mon-Fri late Jun-Jul) features some old icons brought from St Petersburg. Korsholm Church (see left) in Vanha Vaasa is also worth visiting.

Vaskiluoto

The island of Vaskiluoto is a big holiday destination for Finnish families, with beaches, boating, a popular camping ground and

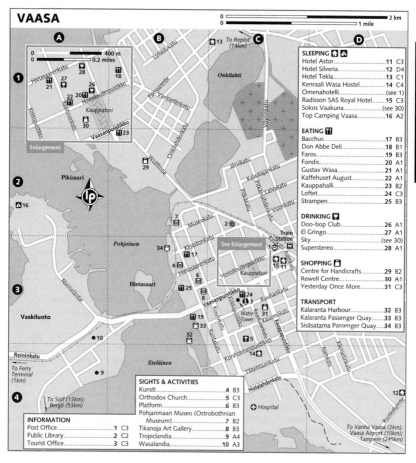

VAASA

POHJANMAA

SLEEPING
Hotel Astor...................................11 C3
Hotel Silveria.................................12 D4
Hotel Tekla....................................13 C1
Kenraali Wasa Hostel......................14 C4
Omenahotelli..............................(see 1)
Radisson SAS Royal Hotel.................15 C3
Sokos Vaakuna............................(see 30)
Top Camping Vaasa........................16 A2

EATING
Bacchus.......................................17 B3
Don Abbe Deli................................18 B1
Faros...19 B3
Fondis..20 A1
Gustav Wasa..................................21 A1
Kaffehuset August...........................22 A1
Kauppahalli...................................23 B2
Loftet..24 C3
Strampen......................................25 B3

DRINKING
Doo-bop Club.................................26 A1
El Gringo......................................27 A1
Sky...(see 30)
Superstereo....................................28 A1

SHOPPING
Centre for Handicrafts.......................29 B2
Rewell Centre..................................30 A1
Yesterday Once More.........................31 C3

TRANSPORT
Kalaranta Harbour...........................32 B3
Kalaranta Passenger Quay..................33 B3
Sisäsatama Passenger Quay................34 B3

SIGHTS & ACTIVITIES
Kunsti...4 B3
Orthodox Church..............................5 C3
Platform...6 B3
Pohjanmaan Museo (Ostrobothnian
  Museum).......................................7 B2
Tikanoja Art Gallery............................8 B3
Tropiclandia.....................................9 A4
Wasalandia....................................10 A3

INFORMATION
Post Office.......................................1 C3
Public Library....................................2 C2
Tourist Office....................................3 C3

POHJANMAA

THE MULTICULTURAL WEST

As you wander around Western Finland, you'll notice that Swedish isn't the only influence. Other cultures have made this area their home as Finland has welcomed refugees from Chile, Vietnam and Somalia. Latest census stats put non-Finnish-born Finns at around 2.5% of the population, but you'll notice them more among the blonde-haired Finns. Many choose to settle in the west, because Swedish is easier to learn than Finnish.

Nine years ago Wafa came from Syria to Vaasa where she's studying engineering, volunteering at Kuntsi (p264) and practising belly dancing. In between this busy schedule, she has learned both Swedish and Finnish. 'I had many Finnish friends who helped me,' Wafa says 'They'd use their hands and make gestures, but never used English so I had to learn. It took nine months in language school.'

During the 1990s increased refugee numbers created tensions – probably because their arrival coincided with Finland's economic slowdown. But for Wafa, these problems have only ever appeared in headlines. 'I love Finnish people but they are shy, not close-minded. It's rare to find people who don't welcome you. People shout out "Hola, señora!" to me because they think I'm from Spain.'

Wasalandia Amusement Park (☎ 211 1200; www .wasalandia.fi; adult/child day pass €19/15; ⊙ from 11am mid-May–mid-Aug, closing varies 4-7pm), a great amusement park for pre-teens.

Nearby is the waterpark, **Tropiclandia** (☎ 211 1300; www.tropiclandia.fi; adult/child €16/12; ⊙ 7am-9pm Mon-Fri, 10am-9pm Sat, 10am-8pm Sun, closed most of Sep), with plenty of water slides, Jacuzzis and health spas to keep both kids and adults happy.

TOURS

M/S Tiira (☎ 315 4057; www.jannensaluuna.com; tickets €13; ⊙ departs 11am & 2pm Jun–mid-Aug) cruises the Vaasa archipelago to Kuusisaari departing from Kalaranta passenger quay. The cruise lasts about 3½ hours, with a lunch stop (food not included) at **Janne's Saloon** (meals €14-23), a restaurant owned by the same outfit. In winter it's possible to take a sleigh trip around the restaurant (€80).

FESTIVALS & EVENTS

Vaasa's shoreline reverberates to **Rockperry** (www.rockperry.fi; 3-day pass €70-75), a summer music festival on Vaskiluoto held in mid-July and attracting mostly Finnish bands plus a few international acts.

Korsholm Music Festival (☎ 322 2390; www.kor sholmmusicfestival.fi), an international chamber music festival, is held in late June. **Vaasa Choirfestival** (☎ 325 3745; www1.vaasa.fi/choirfestival) showcases Finland's best choirs in atmospheric venues for a week in May.

SLEEPING

Vaasa doesn't have many accommodation options, with many families opting for packages with Wasalandia Amusement Park (see left).

Top Camping Vaasa (☎ 211 1255; www.topcamp ing.fi/vaasa; Niemeläntie; tent sites per person €11, 4-person cabins €65; ⊙ late Jun–mid-Aug) This good family getaway is 2km from town on the green edge of Vaskiluoto. They rent bicycles and boats, with packages that include discount coupons for the Tropiclandia spa and free admission to Wasalandia Amusement Park.

Kenraali Wasa Hostel (☎ 040-066 8521; www .kenraaliwasahostel.com; Korsholmanpuistikko 6-8; s/d/tr €40/50/55; P) This former military base is guarded by quirky rusted statues to let you know you're in the right place. The khaki history is treated with playful decoration, but otherwise this hostel is well appointed, with several cabins surrounding a pleasant courtyard. Plus there's bike hire, which makes the city centre all the more accessible.

Omenahotelli (020-771 6555; www.omenahotelli.fi; Hovioikeudenpuistikko 23; r €55) With only 34 rooms this is one of the smaller hotels in this chain that takes internet bookings (you can also book using the terminal in the foyer). Rooms are newish, with a twin bed and fold-out couch that can accommodate a couple for the same price. Internet access and breakfast at a nearby cafe are optional extras.

Hotel Tekla (☎ 327 6411; www.hoteltekla.net; Palosaarentie 58; s €50-55, d €70-72, tr €89; P 🖵) Not much to look at on the outside, this affordable place has an institutional feel but packs on facilities including a gym, a small cafe, a sauna and badminton. Rooms have well-used beds and desks, and some include a bar fridge. It's on Palosaari so take bus 1, 3 or 4 from the centre.

ourpick Hotel Astor (☎ 326 9111; www.astorvaasa.com; Asemakatu 4; s €78-99, d €98-119; P ⌨) The best independent hotel in town has a personal feel, from the fresh-baked cakes at breakfast to the cheery staff offering sightseeing directions. It's one of the older-style hotels with an historic interior, and rooms in the older wing feature polished floors and dark-wood interiors. The better rooms have their own microsauna and are worth a little more.

Radisson SAS Royal Hotel (☎ 020-123 4720; www.radissonsas.com; Hovioikeudenpuistikko 18; r €120, ste €1300; P ⌨ ⌨ ⌨) The biggest and boldest hotel in Vaasa traverses the road between with an underground tunnel in a complex that includes an Irish pub, restaurants and nightclub. Rooms definitely have everything you could want, and if you don't like to share, suites come with their own cosy saunas and coffee machines. This is the first choice for business travellers.

Hotel Silveria (☎ 326 7611; www.hotelsilveria.com; Ruutikellarintie 4; s €98, d & tw €120; P ⌨ ⌨ ⌨) A spacey silver exterior makes it easy to find this place, which is out of the town centre (take bus 4). Rooms include a small couch and LAN connection with a vaguely '70s decor.

Sokos Vaakuna (☎ 020-123 4671; Rewell Centre; s/d €120/135; P ⌨) Centrally located, this place has slick, well-appointed rooms with clever Scandinavian design that makes for spacious rooms right in the middle of the action. The excellent rooftop bar, Sky (p268), and attached restaurants make a good metro minibreak.

EATING

Vaasa has a great dining scene thanks to its migrant population (see opposite). Cheap grillis (fast-food outlets), pizzerias, ice-cream stands and hamburger joints encircle the kauppatori and Rewell Shopping Centre, with quick snacks at the **kauppahalli** (Kauppapuistikko; ⌨ 8am-5pm Mon-Fri, 9am-4pm Sat), the covered market where stalls sell fresh pastries and market goodies.

Don Abbe Deli (☎ 312 3323; Pitkäkatu 34; lunches €5-7; ⌨ 10am-3pm Mon-Fri) This likeable little Mediterranean lunch spot does good paella, salads and lasagne. Look out for their panini and salad deal (€6.50), a healthy alternative to the grillis and pizzerias.

ourpick Loftet (☎ 318 5314; www.loftet.fi; Raastuvankatu 28; cakes €3-6, lunches €6-12; ⌨ 10am-5pm Mon-Fri, 10am-3pm Sat) This cafe-cum-craft shop does great cakes and coffee. It's a relaxed lunch spot that does good vegetarian-friendly soups and salads, which makes a change from heaving plates of meat. Aim to snag a room in the wood-panelled room out back then browse the adjoining craft shop that has good jewellery and linen.

Kaffehuset August (☎ 320 0555; www.kaffehuset august.fi; Hovioikeudenpuistikko 13; mains €10-20; ⌨ 9am-11pm Mon-Fri, 11am-11pm Sat) This wonderfully central spot attracts an older crowd with Swedish pastries and sandwiches for lunch then more substantial dinners such as plank-grilled salmon on a bed of horseradish and mussels. It's ideal if you like your coffee served with a side of people-watching.

Fondis (☎ 280 0400; Hovioikeudenpuistikko 15; mains €14-20; ⌨ 11am-11pm Mon-Thu, 11am-midnight Fri & Sat, noon-9pm Sun) This restaurant-bar does a meaty menu that runs from burgers to liver in a lingonberry sauce. It's a large joint with an always popular bar.

Strampen (☎ 320 0355; Rantakatu 6, Sisäsatama; mains €14-23, lunch buffets €9-10; ⌨ lunch & dinner May-Aug) This waterfront favourite manages to do top-end meals inside and affordable burgers and pastas for drinkers on its harbourside terrace. Somehow both clientele are happy and the unassailably perky staff keep the outdoor bar pumping until late.

Faros (☎ 312 6411; Kalaranta; snacks €9-12, mains €14-23) This boat restaurant is moored in Kalaranta Harbour south of the bridge and makes for an atmospheric bite, especially its salmon soup with a dollop of mousse. They also do great steak and reindeer tournedos. Don't miss the bathrooms with portholes (making them 'portaloos').

Bacchus (☎ 317 3484; www.bacchus.fi; Rantakatu 4; mains €26-29; ⌨ 3pm-1am Mon-Sat, noon-10pm Sun) This golden wooden building not far from the water has a well-chosen menu that could include slow-baked hare with potato terrine. The rustic brickwork interior is warmed by animal skins, though the Wineroom section is minimalism chic. As you'd expect from a place named for the Greek god of boozing, the wine cellar is exceptional.

Gustav Wasa (☎ 326 9200; Raastuvankatu 24; mains €21-34; ⌨ dinner Mon-Sat) This underground restaurant is one of Finland's best with a concise gourmet menu that blends classic Finnish

POHJANMAA

with modern cuisine such as reindeer on tangy risotto. Once a coal cellar, the transformation to suave restaurant is achieved through low lighting and attentive service. For business meetings there's a sauna to put the heat on clients.

DRINKING

Superstereo (☎ 361 0557; www.superstereo.fi; Hietasaarenkatu 14; ☺ Munkhaus 10pm-4am Wed, Fri & Sat, terrace 5pm-4am Mon-Sat Jun-Aug) One of the best bars in town, this university student hang-out has a pop culture–pastiche interior (check out their mural of the Vaasa skyline) and a summer-popular terrace. But wait there's more! The clubby Munkhaus bar opens later with a pumping sound system playing electronica and danceable indie. Or chillax by ringing ahead to book the sauna for a sound-drenched soak.

Sky (☎ 212 4115; Sokos Hotel Vaakuna, Rewell Centre; ☺ 4pm-late) Great views of the city are a big part of this popular bar's appeal. Friday and Saturday feature DJs (€7 to €10) and the terraces are always relaxing. Don't drink too much though as the zippy lift could leave your stomach on the 9th floor.

Doo-bop Club (☎ 353 9044; www.doobop.fi; Kauppapuistikko 12; ☺ 9pm-2am Fri & Sat) This joint swings with live jazz, funk and soul in a suitably dark bar that attracts a 30-plus crowd. Periodic jam sessions are not unheard of – if you've packed your clarinet – or can just click your fingers to the beats to look like a jazz-cat.

El Gringo (☎ 280 0415; Raastuvankatu; ☺ nightly from 7pm) Around the corner from Fondis this basement faux–Tex Mex saloon bar does guitar-based music and booze so cheap (€2.50 for beer or cider) you'll forget the cheesy number plates and cardboard cowpokes. Head upstairs to Fontana Club for two dance floors and a summer terrace.

SHOPPING

There are a few good bargains to be snaffled up in Vaasa. As well as the craft shop at Loftet (see p267), there's also **Vaasa Centre for Handicrafts** (☎ 317 0802; Wolffintie 36, Palosaari; ☺ 9am-6pm), both of which are excellent spots to find locally made gifts. If you're looking for fashion, wander Kauppapuistikko for boutiques like **Yesterday Once More** (☎ 050-511 0454; www.yesterdayoncemore.fi; Kauppapuistikko 31; ☺ 10am-5pm Tue-Fri), which recycles vintage styles into new takes.

GETTING THERE & AWAY
Air
Finnair offers daily flights from Vaasa to Helsinki, Kokkola and Stockholm. **SAS** (www.flysas.com) flies to Stockholm and Helsinki as does the budget operator **Blue1** (www.blue1.com). **Finncomm** (www.fc.fi) does the cheapest flights to Helsinki.

Boat
From late June to early August there are at least daily (more in summer) ferries (adult/car €60/65, four hours) between Vaasa and the Swedish town of Umeå (Finnish: Uumaja) with **RG Lines** (☎ 320 0300; www.rgline.com). Check the website for departure times. The ferry terminal is on the western side of Vaskiluoto (take bus 10).

Bus & Train
From 2009 the bus and train stations will be combined in the same location. There are several express buses a day from Helsinki (€43.90, seven hours) and normal buses from Turku (€52.60, 5½ hours), both via Pori (€33.40, three hours). Buses run up and down the west coast pretty much hourly from Monday to Friday.

Vaasa trains connect via Seinäjoki (€9.50, 50 minutes, up to eight daily) to main-line destinations such as Tampere (€32.50, 2½ hours) and Helsinki (€50.20, four to five hours).

GETTING AROUND
The airport is situated 12km southeast of the centre; airport buses depart from the city bus station (one way €4).

Local buses from the kauppatori come in handy if you want to reach areas outside the centre. Take bus 5 or 10 to Vaskiluoto and bus 1 or 2 to the hostel on Palosaari. The fare is €2.40. The Lilliputti city train runs between the kauppatori and Wasalandia (€3) daily in summer. You can also call a **taksi** (☎ 100 411).

Avis (☎ 315 8313; www.avis.fi) and **SixT** (☎ 305 8053; www.sixt.fi) both offer car rental at the train station and airport. Bicycles can be rented at the tourist office or **Top Camping Vaasa** (☎ 211 1255; www.topcamping.fr/vaasa) for around €4 for two hours.

AROUND VAASA
KVARKEN ARCHIPELAGO
Listed as a Unesco World Heritage site in 2006, **Kvarken** (www.kvarken.fi) stretches across

POHJANMAA

to the Umeå region of Sweden and includes the sea and islands between the two countries. Kvarken is unique for the way in which the land is actually rising at a surprising rate, so islands are appearing and joining each other. The best place to learn more is **Terranova** (see p264), which has details of the nature trails and hiking huts in the area. There's also good canoeing around many of the islands.

Thanks to Finland's longest bridge, Kvarken's most accessible point is **Replot** (Finnish: Raippaluoto), a large island just off the Vaasa coast. It's a great cycle out here with bridges linking smaller islands. **Södra Vallgrund** is a small village on the island's southwest, some 10km from the main village which is also called Replot. **Klobbskat** village, at the western end of the island, is in a barren, Lappish-like setting. **Björkön** (Swedish: Björköby) is a fishing village on a smaller, northern island, accessible from Replot by bridge.

Further afield smaller islands like **Rönnskären** are good for intrepid explorers with their own boats. You can even explore across to Swedish islands such as **Holmöarna**, which is known for hiking, camping and bird-watching.

STUNDARS HANDICRAFT VILLAGE

In the attractive village of Solf (Finnish: Sulva), **Stundars Handicraft Village** (☎ 344 2200; www.stundars.fi; adult/child €5/2; ☯ 11am-5pm Jul–mid-Aug) is an open-air museum and crafts centre boasting 60 traditional wooden buildings that were moved here from surrounding villages. Look out for windmills, which once dotted the countryside around this area. The whole place hums with activity in summer, when artisans demonstrate lost crafts such as wool dyeing and woodcarving. The entrance fee includes a guided tour.

Regional buses from Vaasa make the 15km trip south to Solf, with six daily Monday to Friday, but only one on Saturday, and a late one on Sunday (€4.20, 15 minutes).

SOUTH OF VAASA

KRISTINESTAD

☎ 06 / pop 7389

Named for Queen Kristina of Sweden, this seaside town (Finnish: Kristiinankaupunki) is dominated by Swedish speakers and was founded in the mid-17th century by the maverick count Per Brahe. The town has led many lives as a ship-building centre and

as a port for shipping tar and timber out of Pohjanmaa, but these days it's a sleepy little spot in virtual retirement.

Information

Tourist office (☎ 221 2311; www.krs.fi; Sjögatan 47; ☯ 8.30am-4pm Mon-Fri, 10am-2pm Sat Aug-Jun, 9am-5pm Mon-Fri, 10am-2pm Sun Jul) Plenty of information and free internet access.

Sights

The town itself is the biggest attraction, with rows of colourful, old wooden houses. In its heyday as a key port, travellers had to pay customs duty, collected at the **Old Customs House** (Staketgatan), a smallish rust-wood building dating from 1720, just along from the imposing town hall.

Behind the customs house is the striking red-wood **Old Church** (Ulrika Eleonora Kyrkan; ☯ Tue-Sat mid-May–late Aug), from 1698 and retaining much of its original detail. The red-brick **New Church** (Nya Kirka; Parmansgatan; ☯ 9am-4pm Mon-Fri, 9am-2pm Sat, 9am-1pm Sun) has a high wooden ceiling and an archetypal church-ship dedicated by mariners.

Sjöfartsmuseum (Maritime Museum; ☎ 221 2859; Salutorget 1; admission €3.50; ☯ noon-4pm Tue-Sun May–mid-Aug) was originally built in 1837 as a merchant's home to dominate the market square. Today it showcases Kristinestad's maritime heritage, especially ship-building, with reconstructions of a captain's cabin and a ship's helm.

Another affluent merchant built **Lebell House** (Lebellska Köpmansgården; ☎ 221 2159; Strandgatan 51; admission €4; ☯ 11am-5pm Mon-Fri, 11am-2pm Sat & Sun May-Aug), a block south of the market square. Dating from the mid-19th century, the museum gives an insight into upper-class life including a baroque-styled salon with original linen wallpaper.

About 5km north of town, the summer villa of yet another cashed-up merchant has become **Carlsro Museum** (☎ 221 6343; Carlsrovägen 181; admission €4.50; ☯ 11am-6pm Tue-Sun Jun-late Aug). If the collection of over 11,000 toys, bric-a-brac and other items from around the area doesn't impress, then there's always a wander in the idyllic gardens from the Tsarist era.

Heading east on Rd 663, you'll find **Susiluola** (Wolf Cave; ☎ 040-508 0405; www.susiluola .fi; ☯ 11am-5.30pm daily Jun & Jul) just before the village of Karijoki. This small cave is one of the most significant archaeological finds in

POHJANMAA

Finland with evidence to suggest that humans occupied this area more than 120,000 years ago, before the ice age. As well as walking up the 500m trail to the cave itself, you can view some of the tools and artefacts found here in the visitors centre.

Sleeping & Eating

Bockholmens Camping (☎ 221 1484; Salavägen 32; tent sites €12, cabins €27-65; ☷ late May-early Sep) Just 1.5km southwest of the town centre, this small camping ground boasts its own beach and has bikes for rent. Cabins (shared bathrooms and limited linen) vary based on location and extras but all have kitchenettes.

Houneistomajoitus Krepelin (☎ 040-066 1434; www.huoneistomajoituskrepelin.fi/krepelineng.htm; Östra Långgatan 47; d €60-80; P ☷) This former sailor's residence does refurbished double rooms that include kitchenette, wi-fi and cable TV. They're comfortable, and there's a higher rate to include sheets and breakfast.

Café & Hotel Alma (☎ 221 3455; www.hotelalma .info; Sjögatan; s/d €79.60/99.20, hostel s/d €35/55; ☷ 7am-9pm Mon-Tue, 7am-11pm Wed-Thu, 7am-2am Fri, 9am-2am Sat, 9am-7pm Sun; P) In a waterfront building, this place offers elegant rooms with canopied beds and period furniture. They also operate a summer hostel, across the river about 2km east of the centre, which does basic rooms. The cafe is spectacular with a scale replica of a ship dominating the dining room, which serves an excellent lunch buffet (€8.50; €9.50 on Sunday) and à la carte dinner.

Crazy Cat (☎ 221 3100; Östralånggatan 53-55; lunches €7.50, mains €7-9.50; ☷ 11am-9pm Mon-Fri, noon-9pm Sat & Sun) This frisky feline is a cut above the town's many pizzerias, adding filling pastas and a generous lunch spread to make you feel like the cat who got the cream.

Getting There & Away

Kristinestad is on Rd 662 off Hwy 8, 100km south of Vaasa. Buses between Pori (€19.20, one hour 20 minutes) and Vaasa (€20.90, 1½ hours) stop at Kristinestad.

KASKINEN

☎ 06 / pop 1485

Built on a strict grid system, Kaskinen (Swedish: Kaskö) is technically Finland's smallest town, so it's hard to get lost on this small island connected by two bridges. It's also the westernmost town on the Finnish coast, with a large pulp factory and fish-processing plant to keep the town's economy going. The excellent brochure *Town Walk through Squares and Parks of Kaskinen* takes in most of this sweet town's sites and is available from most shops and guesthouses. The brochure is available at the **tourist office** (☎ 220 7310; www.kaskinen.fi; ☷ Jun–mid-Aug) and most hotels or guesthouses in town.

One of the town's highlights is 18th-century **Bladh House** (☎ 220 7211; cnr Cneiffinpolku & Satamakatu; ☷ by appointment), a restored burgher house that was one of the first in Kaskinen. It's a solid, impressive sight with its trapezoid roof, characteristic of the period. The **local museum** (☎ 220 7711; Raatihuoneenkatu 48; admission €2; ☷ Jun-Aug or by appointment) recreates a wealthy Finnish home from the 19th century, as well as a fisherman's cottage.

At the northern end of the island, near Kalaranta boat dock, is a small **fishing museum** (☎ 220 7711; Sjöbobacken; admission €2; ☷ Jun-Aug or by appointment), which includes smokers and other gear used to snag herring, whitefish and salmon in the surrounding waters. A well-preserved **windmill** is nearby and **Mariestrand Beach** makes for good swimming.

Recently **Kaskinen Music Summer** (☎ 2207 212; www.kaskistenmusiikkikesa.com; whole event tickets €45; ☷ Jun & Jul) has been drawing in visitors over two weekends in June and July, with concerts at Blanh House and other venues.

Sleeping & Eating

Marianranta Camping (☎ 220 7311; tent sites €12, cabins from €25; ☷ Jun-Aug) Set on the tranquil northern part of the island, this small camping ground is right by Mariestrand Beach. There are a few well-maintained cottages as well as good plots to pitch a tent.

Björntrå Vandrarhem (☎ /fax 222 7007; Raatihuoneenkatu 22; r per person €18-23; ☷ Jun–mid-Aug) This chirpy hostel has six rooms almost of hotel standard in a low wooden building that includes a kitchen and TV room. There's an extra charge for sheets (€5).

Hotelli Kaske (☎ 222 7771; www.hotelkaske.com; Raatihuoneenkatu 41; s/d €76/90; P) The village's only hotel is reasonably comfy with rooms that have large recessed windows. The restaurant bar is a focal point for drinking and the menu is simple European food.

our pick Rivendell Guesthouse (☎ 222 7151; www.rivendellguesthouse.fi; Rådhusgatan 31; s/d €25/60, tw/tr €80/80) Run by an English couple who are crazy about *Lord of the Rings,* this place is loaded with Tolkien references. Rooms have recently beeen refitted in Nordic pine and, for a romantic getaway worthy of Aragorn and Arwen, there's an annexe out the back that is self-catering. Best of all the owners are keeping it green by limiting laundry and recycling. They also have a modest cafe (snacks €4 to €8; try the pumpkin soup) and offer professional massages (from €30).

NÄRPES
☎ 06 / pop 9515

Known as the tomato capital of Finland, Närpes (Finnish: Närpiö) is worth stopping at for the impressive church stables as well as sampling the 'red gold' grown in local greenhouses. It has one of the highest populations of Swedish speakers in the country (93% Swedophone), with a local accent that has evolved into a peculiar dialect that wouldn't be understood in Sweden.

Built in the 15th century with several additions, the main reason to stop here is the more than 150 *kyrkstallar* (church stables). Parishioners rode in from the surrounding area to worship at the medieval **Närpes Church**, a well-preserved wooden building with an atmospheric graveyard filled with Swedish names. Just 100m on the same road, **Öjskogparken** (☎ 040-077 3347; www.ojskogparken.fi; Kyrkvägen 23; lunches €9; ☀ Jun-Aug) is a collection of historic buildings, the marooned locomotive Kasköbässin and an outdoor revolving theatre, which gives performances in the local dialect. The buffet lunch boasts an excellent salad selection.

CENTRAL POHJANMAA
SEINÄJOKI
☎ 06 / pop 37,336

Recently Seinäjoki (Swedish: Östermyra) has garnered fame as the birthplace of madcap pranksters the Dudesons (see p42) and the home of speed skater Pekka Koskela, and it's easy to see why this commercial hub would inspire risk-taking to liven the place up. Three huge events, the Tango Fair, Provinssirock and Vauhtiajot, bring in thousands and the town centre designed by Alvar Aalto appeals to more than just architects, but Seinäjoki is often overlooked by visitors hugging the coast.

Information

Café Frame (☎ 417 7200; Kalevankatu 16; ☀ 10am-10pm Tue-Thu, 11am-1pm Fri & Sat, 2-11pm Sun) Free internet with your order.

Public library (☎ 416 2318; Koulukatu 21; ☀ 10am-7pm Mon-Fri, 11am-3pm Sat, closed Sat Jun-Aug) The library has three internet terminals.

Tourist office (☎ 420 9090; matkailu@epmatkailu .fi; ☀ 9am-5pm Mon-Fri) In the bus and train station complex; book accommodation here in private homes during the festivals.

Sights & Activities
AALTO CENTRE

Not far from the great architect's birthplace in the small town of Kuortane, Alvar Aalto (see p46) was given the town centre to experiment with his distinctive architectural style. Several buildings make up the Aalto Centre (1960), a collection of icy white structures that exemplify his modernist style. You'll need to walk around the buildings to appreciate the space, balance and different aspects Aalto created. Wander into the **public library** to understand the multilevel approach, and nearby the blue-tiled town hall curves like a wave

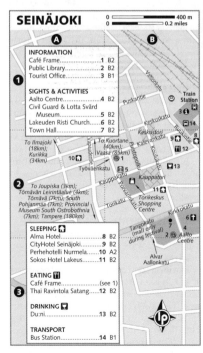

SEINÄJOKI

0 — 400 m
0 — 0.2 miles

INFORMATION
Café Frame.....................1 B2
Public Library..................2 B2
Tourist Office..................3 B1

SIGHTS & ACTIVITIES
Aalto Centre....................4 B2
Civil Guard & Lotta Svärd
    Museum.....................5 B2
Lakeuden Risti Church......6 B2
Town Hall......................7 B2

SLEEPING
Alma Hotel.....................8 B2
CityHotel Seinäjoki...........9 B2
Perhehotelli Nurmela.......10 A2
Sokos Hotel Lakeus.........11 B2

EATING
Café Frame..................(see 1)
Thai Ravintola Satang......12 B2

DRINKING
Du;ni...........................13 B2

TRANSPORT
Bus Station...................14 B1

POHJANMAA

('aalto' means wave so it was almost a signature for the architect) from the courtyard. It almost flows over the road to the crowning achievement, **Lakeuden Risti church** (noon-6pm), recognisable by its oddly secular steeple-clock tower. You'll get a great perspective of the whole project by taking the lift (€1) to the top of the tower.

MUSEUMS

Designed by Alvar Aalto, the **Civil Guard & Lotta Svärd Museum** (416 2734; Kauppakatu 17; admission free; noon-6pm Wed, noon-4pm Thu, Fri & Sun, ring for other times) houses a collection around the Lotta Svärd women's voluntary defence force. Named for a fictional character in a JL Runeberg poem, these unarmed women took on military service during WWII and became one of the world's largest auxiliaries.

Seven kilometres south of town in the leafy suburb of Törnävä, the **Provincial Museum South Ostrobothnia** (416 2642; Törnäväntie 23; admission €2; noon-6pm Wed, noon-4pm Thu, Fri & Sun, ring for other times) is an open-air museum based around the mansion of the wealthy Wasastjerna family. On your right from the town centre is the **Agriculture Museum** and **Mill Museum**. On your left in the old yellow building is the **Gunpowder Museum**. Behind is a smoke house and a smith's house from the 17th century. Local bus 1 runs from Seinäjoki bus station to Törnävä.

JOUPISKA

This modest **ski field** (429 6310; www.joupiska.fi; Jouppilanvuorentie 1) isn't going to wow serious skiers as it's a flat area, but there are some reasonable runs and cross-country skiers find enough snow to strap the boots on.

Jouppilanvuori is a nearby hilly nature area with 4.5km of trails and a chance to take a dip in the reservoir in the warmest weather.

Festivals & Events

Seinäjoki has major summer festivals that pull huge crowds, so book accommodation in advance.

Provinssirock (421 2700; www.provinssirock.fi; 1-/3-day pass €60/95) is an open-air international rock concert held 4km south of town, near Törnävä, over three days in mid-June. International acts duel guitars with top Finnish bands, from across the musical spectrum (David Bowie and the Black Eyed Peas

---

> ### TANGO
>
> Seinäjoki is the undisputed tango capital of a country that is certifiably tango-mad. In the rest of the world the tango craze was swept away by Elvis, but in Finland it never died.
>
> Argentinean musicians and dancers brought tango to Europe around 1910. A Finnish version of tango developed soon after, championed by the composer Unto Mononen and Olavi Virta, the Finnish king of tango dancing.
>
> No other music could better epitomise the melancholic Finn. If Finns lack the electrifying tension that Latin Americans bring to the tango, they lack none of the enthusiasm. Finnish tango music is usually performed with a live band and the lyrics deal with loneliness, unrequited love and desperation. It's fair to say that it's not as popular with the younger generations.

---

have held the same stage as HIM and The Rasmus). There are five stages and connecting buses both from Seinäjoki and Helsinki.

An older crowd turns out in their finery for **Tangomarkkinat** (420 1123; www.tangomarkkinat.fi; Torikatu) but it attracts the biggest numbers of Finland's busy festival calendar. Held in early July, the first heels are kicked up at a huge open-air dance and party in 'Tango Street'. It continues over four days with dance competitions, tango classes and other festivities, culminating with the awarding of the 'Tango King & Queen', the best singers of the festival.

Bringing together revheads and rockers, **Vauhtiajot** (487 2800; www.vauhtiajot.fi) features street racing and two rocking stages in mid-July. Recent bands have included Iggy and the Stooges, and Thin Lizzy.

Sleeping

Seinäjoki's bunks book out around festivals but any other time of the year it's easy to get a bed here.

Törnävän Leirintäalue (412 0784, 414 6585; Törnäväntie 29; tent sites €10, cabins €35-50; Jun-Aug) South of the city centre, this camping ground is one of the most affordable. There are also temporary camping areas set up near the festival during Provinssirock, which cost €15 per person for the weekend or €7 for one night.

Perhehotelli Nurmela (☎ 414 1771; www.netikka
.net/hotellinurmela; Kalevankatu 29; s/d from €50/55; P)
This good-value family-run hotel won't blow
you away with its small sauna and modest
rooms, but with breakfast included, it won't
blow the budget either.

CityHotel Seinäjoki (☎ 215 9111; www.sdr.fi;
Kalevankatu 2; s/d €90/110; P 🖳 🖭) Right opposite
the train and bus stations, this reliable spot
has some tight rooms that are favoured by
people overnighting and getting early trains.
There are plenty of add-ons such as the good
bar and grill, a pool and wi-fi.

Alma Hotel (☎ 421 5300; www.hotelalma.info;
Ruukintie 4; s €78-98, d €88-120, ste €120-150; P 🖳) This
well-appointed boutique spot has traditional
wood decor and generously spaced rooms
with plenty of luxuries. It's popular with visiting business folks who enjoy the restaurant
and terrace area for a post-deal tipple.

Also recommended is **Sokos Hotel Lakeus**
(☎ 419 3111; www.sokoshotels.fi; Torikatu 2; s/d €99/119;
P 🖳 🖭), which is not just another link in
the chain, with its stunning views across to
Aalto Centre.

Eating & Drinking

Aside from the pizzerias and kebab shops
along Kauppakatu and Kalevankatu, Seinäjoki
has limited dining options. Hotel restaurants
are reliable, while there are fast-food places in
shopping centres like Torikeskus.

Thai Ravintola Satang (☎ 414 2144; Maamiehenkatu;
mains €9-13; 🕑 lunch & dinner daily) Look out for the
flower-filled window of this side-street place
for a very meat-based (this is Finnish Thai
after all) menu that includes favourites such
as green chicken curry and fried pork with
bamboo. This place is a spicy antidote to the
winter blues.

Café Frame (☎ 417 7200; Kalevankatu 16; lunches
€3-7; 🕑 10am-10pm Tue-Fri, 11am-1pm Sat, 2-11pm
Sun) This corner cafe does well-priced rolls,
wraps and some kicking coffee for a quick
fix. The terrace outside is a good place for a
warm-afternoon beer.

Du:ni (☎ 417 8666; cnr Kauppakatu & Koulukatu;
🕑 4pm-late daily) This is the unofficial bar for
Provinssirock and it's busy year-round with
a great summer terrace, free internet access
and a popular club downstairs.

Getting There & Away

The bus station and train station are adjacent and very central. There are buses

to towns and villages throughout Western
Finland.

Seinäjoki is a rail hub and has the fastest
intercity trains from Helsinki (€44.20, three
hours), with connections to Vaasa (€9.50, 50
minutes), Jyväskylä (€27.80, 1½ hours) and
cities further north.

There are commuter flights Thursday,
Friday and Sunday to/from Helsinki to
Seinäjoki (return from €143 to €329) by
subsidiaries of Finnair.

KAUSTINEN
☎ 06 / pop 4298

In the Finnish translation of the *Peanuts*
cartoon, the character of Woodstock is
called Kaustinen (Swedish: Kaustby), which
indicates how closely this town is tied to
its traditional musical roots. The population of this tiny village just 47km southeast of Kokkola explodes in July to host
the Nordic country's biggest folk music
festival. Outside of the festival, there's little to see here.

Kaustinen Folk Music Festival (☎ 020-72911;
www.kaustinen.net; Jyväskyläntie 3; daily/weekly pass
€30/170) kicks off in the third week of July
and is Finland's most beloved summer
festival. More than 300 Finnish bands and
international acts perform, with a theme
country chosen to showcase its music and
dance. And dance they will, at official
concerts, bar gigs and endless impromptu
jam sessions.

Sleeping

The festival has an **accommodation office** (☎ 020-729 1206; majoitus@kaustinen.fi) that
does camping, homestays and summer
hotel beds.

Koskelan Lomatalo (☎ 861 1338; www.koskel
anlomatalo.kaustinen.fi; Känsäläntie 123; per person €30)
About 5km north of Kaustinen, this farm-
based place has plenty of animals to feed as
well as facilities like a kitchen, sauna and
cafe. It's a good refuge if the festival gets
too much.

Getting There & Away

There are several buses daily from Kokkola
(€11.70, 50 minutes), which has a railway
station. There are express buses from other
cities during the festival season; check the
festival website.

NORTHERN POHJANMAA

JAKOBSTAD

☎ 06 / pop 19,467

There's a distinctly Swedish feel to Jakobstad (Finnish: Pietarsaari) with over half the population speaking Swedish, making it the unofficial capital of *Parallelsverige*. The well-preserved historic Skata is filled with 18th- and 19th-century wooden houses, as the whole area was built up after Russia sacked the town in 1714. The warships and Weapons Museum are a tribute to how the town came to defend itself and become Finland's leading shipping town.

The town's name comes from Swedish war hero Jacob de la Gardie, whose widow Ebba Braha founded Jakobstad in 1652, naming it in her husband's memory. The surrounding region, Pedersöre, gave the town its Finnish name, which, despite translating as Peter's Island, has been part of the mainland for years.

Information

After Eight (Storgatan; ☽ 10am-3pm Mon-Fri) Free internet terminals at this cafe and cultural centre.

Public library (☎ 785 1272; Runebergsgatan 12; ☽ 11am-7pm Mon-Thu, 11am-4pm Fri summer, 11am-8pm Mon-Fri autumn-spring) Has a couple of internet terminals; maximum 15 minutes without booking.

Tourist office (☎ 723 1796; www.jakobstad.fi; Köpmansgatan 12; ☽ 8am-6pm Mon-Fri, 9am-3pm Sat Jun-Aug, 8am-5pm Mon-Fri Sep-May)

Sights

SKATA

Stretching for several blocks to the north of the new town, Skata, the old town of Jakobstad, has around 300 **wooden houses** that are some of the best preserved in Finland. Most were built in the 19th century and were originally occupied by sailors, but later working-class people moved into the area. While the 18th-century houses along **Hamngatan** are the oldest in town, the prettiest street is **Norrmalmsgatan**. You enter through an ornamental entranceway, with a stunning clock tower bridging the street. Remarkably, most of the town remains residential so it feels refreshingly untouristy.

GAMLA HAMN

The old harbour (Gamla Hamn) holds the pride of Jakobstad, **Jacobstads Wapen** (admission

€1.60; ☽ mid-May–late Aug), modelled after a 17th-century galleon. There's a small museum explaining the history of the ship and the building of the replica. There are public sailings a few times a year; inquire at the tourist office. Also by arrangement with the tourist office, it's possible to visit the **Vega** (admission €3; ☽ mid-May–Aug), a training schooner that was originally built in Turku but served in Estonia.

FantaSea (☎ 785 1625; www.fantasp.fi; admission €3; ☽ 11am-6pm Jun-Aug) is a small amusement park in the harbour with waterslides, pools and a swimming beach.

MUSEUMS

Jakobstad has an eclectic collection of small private museums.

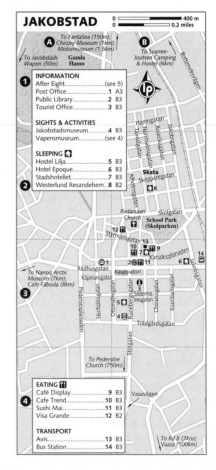

JAKOBSTAD

0 — 400 m
0 — 0.2 miles

To FantaSea (150m);
Chicory Museum (1km);
Motormuseum (1.5km)

To Jakobstads   Gamla
Wapen (50m)   Hamn

To Svanen-
Joutsen Camping
& Hostel (6km)

INFORMATION
After Eight......................(see 5)
Post Office.....................1 A3
Public Library..................2 B3
Tourist Office..................3 B3

SIGHTS & ACTIVITIES
Jakobstadsmuseum............4 B3
Vapensmuseum.............(see 4)

SLEEPING 🏠
Hostel Lilja....................5 B3
Hotel Epoque...................6 B3
Stadshotellet..................7 B3
Westerlund Resandehem...8 B2

To Jacobstads
Wapen (50m)

Skata
Skepparegatan

Pietarsaari
Church

Skolgatan

School Park
(Skolparken)

To Nanoq Arctic
Museum (7km);
Cafe Fåboda (8km)

Rådhusgatan

Kauppatori

Söderma-
lmsgatan

Trädgårdsgatan

To Pedersöre
Church (750m)

EATING 🍴
Café Display....................9 B3
Cafe Trend.....................10 B3
Sushi Mai.......................11 B3
Visa Grande....................12 B2

Vasavägen

TRANSPORT
Avis............................13 B3
Bus Station.....................14 B3

To Rd 8 (7km);
Vaasa (100km)

Jakobstads Museum (☎ 758 1111; Storgatan 2; admission €2; ☻ noon-4pm) includes the old main building (Malmska Gården; dating back to 1904) with local-history displays on the shipping industry and the town itself, as well as the tobacco minimuseum and several historic houses scattered around the town centre.

Next door is the **Vapenmuseum** (Weapons Museum; ☎ 723 2974; Storgatan 2; admission €4; ☻ noon-5pm Tue-Sun Jun & Jul), a small private collection of Jakobstad gun-nut Bengt Ena, including hunting rifles, machine guns and military pistols dating back to the 1740s.

The **Motormuseum** (☎ 724 4500; Alholmsvägen 71; admission €5; ☻ noon-5pm Mon-Fri, noon-4pm Sat & Sun mid-May–mid-Aug), to the north of town and by the harbour, is a private museum with a fascinating collection of over 120 motorcycles – from old Harley Davidsons and Nortons to homemade, motor-powered bicycles.

Nearby, the **Chicory Museum** (☎ 020-416 1113; Alholmen; admission free; ☻ noon-5pm Tue-Sat Jun-Aug, noon-6pm Jul) is housed in the old chicory factory, founded in 1883 and recognisable for its large oven pipe that was used to bake the herb. The factory was built by local entrepreneur Wilhelm Schauman who made his fortune processing chicory, a popular coffee additive or substitute. As well as talking you through chicory processing, guides can chat about the contemporary art exhibited here.

PEDERSÖRE CHURCH

Beautiful **Pedersöre Church** (☎ 040-310 0477; Vasavägen 118; ☻ 9am-4pm daily mid-May–mid-Aug, by appointment other times) dates back to the 1400s, making it one of the oldest churches in Pohjanmaa. The oldest bell is marked 1488AD though the bell tower itself was replaced in the 18th century. King Gustav III of Sweden personally signed off on the plans to expand the church into the cruciform, though builders ignored his instruction to demolish the towering spire, which was later destroyed by fire, then restored in its dazzling original form.

Sleeping

Svanen-Joutsen Camping (☎ 723 0660; www.multi .fi/svanen; Larsmovägen 50; tent sites €14.50, 2-person cabins €22-28, 4-person €38-65; ☻ Jun-Aug) Definitely aiming for the family market, this camping ground includes minigolf, plus canoe and bike hire. Rates are cheaper by the week. Cabins are comfy and self-catering is easy enough if you bring your own food – it's located 6km

north of town in Nissasörn. Without a car, you can take the Larsmo–Kokkola bus from the city bus station.

Westerlund Resandehem (☎ 723 0440; Norrmalmsgatan 8; s/d/tr €27/41/54; P) You'll forgive this charming spot – in need of a coat of paint when we visited – anything for its location in the heart of Skata. Rooms share a bathroom and the owners are strictly Swedish speaking, but it feels secluded.

Hostel Lilja (☎ 781 6500, 050-516 7301; www.after eight.fi/hostellilja/; Storgatan 6; s/d/tr €40/50/60, ste €80, breakfast extra €5; ☻ 9am-4pm Mon-Fri; P 🖳) This thoroughly restored spot ranges through several buildings including the old stable, though you'd never know it for all the Nordic chic on show. It's boutique that keeps to a budget, even in the honeymoon suite, which includes a small bathroom. Extras like cheap bike rental (€5 per day), a sauna and the excellent After Eight cafe all add up to a great stay.

Stadshotellet (☎ 788 8111; www.stadshotellet .multi.fi; Kanalesplanaden 13; d €84-110; P 🖳) Well placed on the main pedestrian boulevard, Jakobstad's top hotel offers comfortable rooms, two restaurants and a nightclub. The characterful building is popular with visiting Finn executives for its conference facilities and first-rate sauna.

Hotel Epoque (☎ 788 7149; www.hotelepoque.fi; Jakobsgatan 10; s €102-122, d €97-117; 🖳 ♿) This restored Customs House has the feel of a sophisticated restaurant with well-appointed rooms in a navy-and-gold colour scheme. From the extreme close-up mirrors to the blondewood floors, every aspect of this hotel has been well thought out. The open restaurant downstairs does a blend of Finnish and modern European that will have you dining in.

Eating & Drinking

Café Display (☎ 040-847 2612; www.cafedisplay.com; Styrmansgatan 4; lunches €5-9; ☻ 9am-5pm Mon-Fri, 10am-3pm Sat) This likeable spot features moonunit chairs, and a large painting of Audrey Hepburn. And their coffee is the best in town and comes with snack sandwiches and cakes. The adjoining design shop is worth a quick browse.

Café Trend (☎ 723 1265; Storgatan 13; lunch buffets €8, cakes €3-6; ☻ 9am-11pm Mon-Thu, 9am-1am Fri & Sat, noon-11pm Sun) Young beautiful people crowd into this central cafe for the indulgent cakes and well-priced lunches. The terrace is undeniable when the sun's shining and the beer's flowing.

POHJANMAA

Sushi Mai (☎ 050-574 1835; www.sushimai.fi; Passagen btwn Kauppatori & Kanalesplanaden; sushi from €7, meals €12-14; ☺ lunch & dinner Tue-Fri, dinner Sat) Zen minimalist signage makes this place tough to spot (look for the gnarled tree bough as a door handle) down a side alley, but it's worth seeking out for the sushi, yakitori and 'world food' including olives and tortilla. Benches out front are brilliant in summer.

Visa Grande (☎ 723 4150; Storgatan 20; pizza & pasta buffets €7-9, mains €12-22; ☺ food 10.30am-10pm Mon-Sat, bar 10.30am-2am Mon-Sat, 8pm-2am Sun; ▣) Handily placed for a post-Skata drink, this pub does a good trade with locals and manages some solid meals ranging from the pizza and pasta lunch buffet to steak dinners. It's also one of the late-opening watering holes but after a few too many the underfloor fish tank can make you a little nauseous.

Getting There & Away

There are regular buses to Jakobstad from Vaasa (from €19.20, 1½ to 2½ hours), Kokkola (€7.40, 40 minutes) and other towns along the west coast.

Bennäs (Finnish: Pännäinen), 11km away, is the closest railway station to Jakobstad. A shuttle bus (€4, 10 minutes) meets arriving trains.

Kruunupyy/Kronoby airport (see p278) is 30km from Jakobstad and buses (€5) meet arriving flights.

Avis (☎ 309 4586; www.avis.fi; Styrmansgatan 4) has an office that's handy for exploring further afield.

AROUND JAKOBSTAD
Fäboda

About 8km west of Jakobstad, Fäboda is a recreational area on the Gulf of Bothnia. Small sandy beaches make for top swimming, sunbathing, surfing and windsurfing while rocky inlets and thick forests are favoured for walking and mountain biking. Cycling to Fäboda is easy on a narrow country road.

While not strictly accurate (the Arctic Circle is, after all, several hundred kilometres to the north), **Nanoq Arctic Museum** (☎ 729 3679; Pörkenäsvägen 60; admission €6; ☺ noon-6pm Jun-Aug) is a surprisingly good little museum that's worth a detour. Housed in a model of a Greenlandic peat house, the collection is the private achievement of Pentti Kronqvist, who has made several expeditions to the Arctic. There are Inuit tools, fossils, authentic Arctic

huts from Greenland and elsewhere, and various other Arctic souvenirs.

Café Fäboda (☎ 729 3510; Lillsandvägen; mains €13-21; ☺ 10am-11pm May-Aug), near the beach, has a generous lunch buffet and international menu for dinner. On summer evenings the terrace throbs with live music.

Mässkar

Northwest of Jakobstad about 10km as the crow flies, this island is becoming a popular day trip, especially for day hikers who can easily tackle the 1km trail. There's also secluded swimming and cycling. There's a **nature information station** (☎ 729 4092; www.masskar.fi; ☺ May-Aug), which has a cafe and sauna, and can provide maps of trails and camping spots.

It's a popular mooring for boats, but if you haven't got your own vessel you'll need to head for the fishing village of Ädo and call the nature information station for a ferry across.

Nykarleby
☎ 06 / pop 7399

Founded in 1620, in Nykarleby (Finnish: Uusikaarlepyy), 20km south of Jakobstad, most people speak Swedish. Although the riverside town was founded on the same day as Karleby (Kokkola), it was given the name Nykarleby meaning 'new Kokkola'.

The yellow **Nykarleby Church** (☺ 9am-6pm summer) on the riverside was built in 1708 and is famous for its beautiful 18th-century paintings on the ceiling. **Nykarleby Museum** (☎ 722 1403; Itäpuistikko 35; ☺ 10am-4pm Mon-Fri Jun & Jul, noon-5pm Sat & by appointment) features local bric-a-brac, old costumes and furniture.

Finns know Nykarleby as the birthplace of Zacharias Topelius, author of much-loved children's poetry. His home, **Kuddnäs** (☎ 785 6111; 22 Jakobstadsvägen; admission €3; ☺ May-Aug), is a beautiful old house but doesn't really evoke the man himself.

Juthbacka Hotel och Restaurant (☎ 722 0677; www.juthbacka.multi.fi; Jutasvägen 34; s/d €50/65; ☺ lunch) Makes for an atmospheric stay near a manor house, plus their restaurant is an ideal place for a pasta lunch buffet (€7) or possibly to sample the famous local *våfflor* (waffles) with cream and strawberry jam.

Daily buses connect Nykarleby with Jakobstad (€8.30, 20 minutes) and Vaasa (€16.40, 1½ hours).

KOKKOLA

☎ 06 / pop 36,966

The biggest draw in Kokkola (Swedish: Karleby) is its charming old town or Neristan (Lower Town), which was once the home of the town's fisherfolk. Until the 1960s locals reckon fishing boats used to be able to sail up the coffee-coloured river to sell fish in the kauppatori, but you wouldn't believe it to look at the shallow water today. Contrary to global warming, the land around Kokkola is rising, which means Kokkola is chasing its port as the sea gets further from the town.

Orientation & Information

The compact town centre makes it an easy walk north from the train and bus station, while the kauppatori is at the intersection of Rantakatu and Torikatu.

Public library (☎ 828 9560; Isokatu 3; ⏱ 10am-8pm Mon-Thu, 11am-6pm Fri, 11am-5pm Sat Sep-May, Mon-Thu 10am-7pm, 10am-5pm Fri Jun-Aug) Free internet at this spectacular modern building, one block north of the train station.

Tourist office (☎ 828 9402; www.kokkola.fi; kauppatori; guided walks from 1hr €42; ⏱ 8am-5pm Mon-Fri, 9am-1pm Sat Jun-Aug, 8am-4pm Mon-Fri Sep-May) Extremely helpful near Krunni (see p278); grab a copy of *Old Kalle's Town Walk* (free) for a walk around the town, including Neristan. They also offer great one-hour guided walks with locals.

Sights & Activities

NERISTAN

Once the working-class area of Kokkola (Neristan means 'Lower Town') where the sailors and fishermen lived, this collection of **wooden houses** (www.neristan.fi) makes for a pleasant afternoon's wander. Strolling along the struggling river from the kauppatori will take you past the Baltija Fountain, a female figure that was a gift from the Lithuanian twin town Marijampole. One of the first buildings you'll spot is the well-preserved gold-coloured **Rantakatu 27**, the childhood home of Finnish statesman, JV Snellman. At the other end of the economic scale are **Läntinen kirkkokatu 57 and 59**, two tiny sailors' cottages. On the same street there's the **Home of Anna and Fredrik Drake** (Läntinen kirkkokatu 20), originally built in the 1830s and one of the few that's open to the public. To explore further, pick up the *Neristan Step by Step* brochure at the tourist office.

If you follow the Suntti stream beyond Neristan, you'll come to **Halkokari**, the beach that was once another retreating harbour. A British attack was repelled here during the Crimean War and the captured gunboats at the English Park just north of Neristan is one of few trophies ever taken from the mighty British navy. The event is commemorated on **Kahakka Day** (7 June), when townspeople dress-up 1854-style for a theatrical re-enactment.

MUSEUMS

Pitkänsillankatu near the town centre is the **museum quarter** (☎ 828 9474; 1 museum €2, all museums €4; ⏱ noon-3pm Tue-Fri, noon-5pm Sat & Sun Sep-May, noon-5pm Tue-Sun Jun-Aug, free Thu in winter) where the museums share opening hours and ticketing.

The **Mineraalikokoelma** (mineral collection; Pitkänsillankatu 28) will surprise with an amazing assembly of natural beauty. Resident geologists have been known to give emphatic tours through the exhibits, which include stunning but fragile crystals and meteorite fragments. In the same building, the **Luontomuseo** (natural history collection) has a collection of stuffed mammals and birds, plus traps and other hunting devices.

Across the courtyard, the **Historiallinen Museo** (Historical Museum) is housed in the old school, which dates from 1696, making it the country's oldest secular building in a town. After 200 years of education, it currently houses a collection depicting Kokkola's maritime heritage including model ships and navigational gadgets. Nearby **Lassander House** is preserved as an 18th-century house. There's also a small cafe here that specialises in waffles.

A block up the street, **KH Renlund Museo** (Pitkänsillankatu 39) is in a large 19th-century merchant's mansion. It contains the collection of Karl Herman Renlund, a shopkeeper who left his art collection for the benefit of 'students and the working class'. The collection is unexceptional, but for a Victor Westerholm canvas depicting a raging torrent of the Voikkaa rapids.

TANKAR ISLAND

This **lighthouse island** (www.tankar.fi, in Finnish & Swedish) once offered safe passage through the tangled waters surrounding it but has become a popular day trip (adult/child €17/7) for nature walks and a leisurely lunch at the pierside **Café Tankar** (☎ 044-780 9139; meals €8-14; ⏱ lunch &

POHJANMAA

dinner May-Aug). **Kokko Line** (☎ 828 9716) departs from the camping ground in summer (4½ hours, noon and 8am June and August, noon and 6pm July).

WATER SPORTS

It's not exactly Bondi or Venice Beach, but there are several good family beaches including around the camping ground (see below), the paddling water around **Elba** and **Laajalahti**, where volleyball is popular in summer. In winter or if you need a sauna, the newly remodelled **Vesi Veijari swimming centre** (☎ 822 2532; www.kokkola.fi; Kaarlelankatu 57; admission €4.70; ⏲ 8am-8pm daily) has waterslides, Jacuzzi and three different kinds of sauna (infrared was a little too weird for us).

Sleeping

Camping Suntinsuu (☎ 831 4006; www.kokkolacamping .com; Pikiruukki; camping per person €5.20, cottages €35-65, boat r from €35; ⏲ late Jun-late Aug; **P**) This riverside camping ground is 2km northwest of the centre, following the river from the kauppatori. At the time of research cabins were being refitted, but they remain a good self-contained option. Camping spots are popular and there are some bunks aboard the Lighthouse Hotel, actually a moored boat that is cheaper for longer stays and larger groups.

Hotel Seurahuone (☎ 865 3111; www.seurahuone .com; Torikatu 24; s €70-99, d €79-115; **P** **✕**) One of Finland's oldest continuous hotels (since 1894), this place is hardly showing its age thanks to a recent refit that's created well-appointed rooms and an atmospheric restaurant. Most rooms have views onto the square and include tubs in the tight bathrooms.

Kaupunkikartano Lumitähti (☎ 050-016 2302; www.citymansion.net; s/d €80/120; **P**) Set in the heart of Neristan, this endearing spot features small cottages behind the 19th-century house. Each cottage includes a full kitchen, which includes homemade jam and biscuits on arrival, though breakfast is extra (€2). Bikes are available for loan to guests.

Eating & Drinking

Vanhankaupingin Ravintola (☎ 834 9030; www.vkr .kpnet.com; Isokatu 28; mains €13-22; ⏲ lunch & dinner Tue-Sat) Set in a Neristan townhouse, this elegant spot does great Finnish cuisine. Try the reindeer entrée that's set off with Lappish cheese or sample local seafood Arctic char with scallops.

Wanha Lyhty & Kellari (☎ 868 0188; www.kpnet .com/wanhalyhty; Pitkänsillankatu 24; mains €12-24; ⏲ lunch & dinner Mon-Sat, dinner only Sun) This cellar restaurant is a testament to the nautical history, bedecked with model ships and ropes, but the traditional Finnish food is first rate. Upstairs the more casual bar does irregular live music.

Krunni (☎ 040-516 2311; kauppatori; ⏲ May-Sep) The best spot for a drink in town is the deck of this old Danish fishing boat around and dominating the market square. There's also a terrace and indoor seating where snacks are served.

Old English Pub (☎ 831 9969; www.englishpub.fi; Kaarlelankatu 43; ⏲ daily) Thirsting for the British Isles? This boozer slakes with UK beers that have made it a hit with a local cross-section of young and old, suits and Goths.

Also recommended:

Bailiff's House (☎ 050-594 9655; Kaarlelankatu 43; lunch €8-10; ⏲ lunch Jun-Aug) Magnificent grounds that make for a good place for coffee and cake.

Mustakari (☎ 831 2414; www.hotelkaarle.fi/musta kari.html; Mustakarintie; lunch specials €7-10; ⏲ lunch & dinner Jun-Sep) One of Finland's oldest yacht clubs that's celebrated for seafood.

Kokkolinna (☎ 825 2025; Isokatu 1; lunches €6-8; ⏲ lunch Mon-Sat) An art nouveau cafe with an excellent salad selection and staffed by an adjoining restaurant school.

Getting There & Around

The Kruunupyy/Kronoby airport is 22km southeast of Kokkola and served by a regional bus service to Kokkola (€7) and Jakobstad (€6). There are several flights a day to/from Helsinki, run by Finnair subsidiaries.

Regular buses run to/from all coastal towns, especially Vaasa (€25.20, three hours) and Jakobstad (€7.40, 40 minutes). The bus station is one block northwest of the train station.

Kokkola's train station is a main westernline stop. The daytime journey from Helsinki (€51.40, seven daily) takes less than five hours, with several night trains.

If you're driving to or from Jakobstad, a scenic (and quicker) alternative to the main highway is to take Rd 749, which crosses the island of Luoto.

You can hail a **taxi** (☎ 010-085 111) around the kauppatori.

KALAJOKI

☎ 08 / pop 9421

Red-brown holiday houses snuggling into white sand dunes – it's easy to see why Finnish families come here for their summer holidays. Cosy rather than stunning, there's swimming for beginners with sandbars to catch your breath on, and golf for executive stress relief. The tourist industry here has survived the advent of budget international flights and attracts winter visitors with cross-country skiing.

Kalajoki village is just off the highway, with most of the facilities (bus terminal, banks, post office and travel agency), but the resort area, with the beach, airfield and most of the accommodation, is 6km south of the village along Hwy 8 in Hiekkasärkät.

The **tourist office** (☎ 469 4449; www.kalajoki.fi; Jukupolku 5; ☯ 9am-5pm Mon-Fri Sep-May, 9am-8pm Mon-Fri, 11am-8pm Sat & Sun Jun-Aug) is on the highway at the turn-off to the beach. Both the office and the website have a list of all the rental cottages hereabouts. They also run the **Beach Bus** (☯ May-Sep), which connects the village and Hiekkasärkät.

Sights & Activities

Hiekkasärkät is one of the country's most popular holiday beaches. **JukuPark** (☎ 469 2308; www .hiekkasarkat.fi/en/jukupark-en/; Hiekkasärkät; admission €14-20; ☯ 11am-6pm early Jun-early Aug) has reopened with family fun including water slides, racing tracks and pirate ship. The 18-hole **golf course** (☎ 466 666; www.kalajokilaaksongolf.fi; Hiekkasärkät; green fees €42; ☯ year-round, snow permitting) wanders pleasantly between the forest and beach.

Sleeping & Eating

Hiekkasärkät is ideal for beachside accommodation with dozens of summer cottages and some resortlike options. Nearly all are also available by the day. The best place to book is through the tourist office, which has deals that include amusement park entry or a round of golf.

Hostel Retkeilijä (☎ 050-051 0303; Opintie 2, Kalajoki; dm €17, s/d €25/34) Handy for the bus station in Kalajoki village, this new place has basic though spacious rooms and includes a sauna and a self-catering kitchen.

Tapion Tupa (☎ 466 622; www.tapiontupa.com; Hiekkasärkät; r €40, apt €110; ℗ ☯) Just off the main road (the bus can drop you here) and close to the beach, this rambling complex has red cottages set in the forest. There's a range of options, from basic log cabins to self-contained holiday apartments, though some require you to book for at least three nights.

Fontana Hotelli Rantakalla (☎ 466 642; Matkailutie 150; s/d Jun-Aug €85/117, cottages from €79; ℗ ☯) This is one of the best hotels on the beach, with top-notch facilities such as minigolf, saunas and occasional bands. Their cottages are reliable options year-round if you want to escape the crowds.

Ravintola Lokkilinna (☎ 469 6700; lunch buffets €11; ☯ lunch & dinner) This well-positioned yet secluded spot overlooks the dunes, making for an excellent summer terrace for a beer or filling lunch buffet. A new development promises to make this area busier so enjoy it before it gets too crowded.

Getting There & Away

Several daily buses running between Oulu (€25, 2½ hours) and Kokkola (€14.90, 40 minutes express) stop at Kalajoki and the beach.

AROUND KALAJOKI
Maakalla & Ulkokalla Islets

An isolated islet that has only existed since the 15th century, Maakalla has managed to retain a genuine fishing-village feel. There are no roads, shops or electricity – in fact, there are no permanent humans – but you will find an interesting wooden **church**, abundant plant and birdlife and some old **fishing huts**. The owners of the huts hold regular meetings and vote to keep the islet exactly as it is.

You can stay at **Ulkokalla Lighthouse** (☎ 040-569 0896; www.fememare.fi; full board €50), a renovated lighthouse keeper's house on the rocky islet of Ulkokalla that offers accommodation and board. There's no power, but fresh water for the sauna stove is brought from the mainland.

In summer (mid-June to early August) there are three-hour **cruises** (www.kallanmatkailu .fi) to Maakalla (return €15) from the pier at Kalajoki with a minimum of 10 passengers.

Oulu, Kainuu & Koillismaa

Stretching across Finland's waist from the Gulf of Bothnia to the long Russian border, this broad swathe of territory takes in the boffins of Oulu's booming technology sector and the brown bears raising their shaggy heads as they patrol the eastern forests. It offers some of the nation's most memorable outdoor experiences, from bird-watching and beachcombing in the west to skiing, canoeing and trekking in the east, but also enough to keep you indoors, with a cracking chamber music festival and some great museums for all ages.

The region's geography reflects its tar-producing history. In the 19th century the remote Kainuu and Koillismaa areas began producing tar from the numerous pines, and sent it on the precarious journey downriver to Oulu, whence it was shipped to the boat-building nations of Europe. The merchants prospered, and Oulu still has a sleek, cosmopolitan feel compared to the backwoodsy feel of the rest of its province. A vibrant and exciting place to be in summer, it now makes its euros on the back of its flourishing IT industry. With wonderful cycle paths, weird festivals, handsome kauppatori and plenty to discover nearby, it's a real drawcard.

The further you get from Oulu, the more remote things become. Kainuu is a heavily forested wilderness and important animal habitat traversed by the famed UKK trekking route close to the border with Russia. Koillismaa, near the Russian border, is the transitional region between the south and Lapland, and includes the rugged Kuusamo area and Oulanka National Park – one of Finland's natural highlights. It is an area of tumbling rivers, isolated lakes and dense forests. The opportunities for activities are limitless, with a bewildering array of choices in both summer and winter.

HIGHLIGHTS

- Canoeing the varying river routes or trekking the Karhunkierros in **Oulanka National Park** (p299), through some of the best wilderness scenery in Finland

- Creeping into the evening forests to spot brown bears near **Kuusamo** (p295)

- Chilling out in the evening sunshine that kisses the kauppatori in **Oulu** (opposite), or getting involved in one of the city's weird festivals

- Getting back to Finland's stone age at the informative **Kierikki** (p288) museum

- Braving the Bothnian waters on relaxing **Hailuoto Island** (p288)

- Letting the young musicians string you along at Kuhmo's excellent **Chamber Music Festival** (p294)

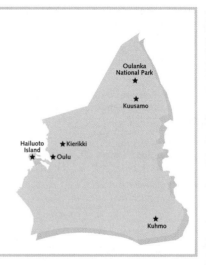

Activities

This large province covers a wide swathe of Finnish territory, from the coast to the Russian border, so it's no surprise that the scope for activities is almost endless.

In the east, the Karhunkierros (Bear's Ring) is one of Finland's most rewarding and popular trekking routes, with a good network of huts and variety of scenery. The longer UKK route is another memorable hike.

On the waterways, fishing and canoeing are popular, with the Oulankajoki and Kitkajoki particularly suitable for the latter, while the Limanganlahti wetlands are great for bird-watching.

The city of Oulu and surrounds is a paradise for cyclists, who'll seldom see a more comprehensive network of cycle paths. Some hardy Finns cycle in winter, but you might prefer to try skiing; the province has the high-profile resort of Ruka, and the more family-oriented Syöte.

OULU REGION

OULU

☎ 08 / pop 131,585

Prosperous Oulu (Swedish: Uleåborg) is one of Finland's most enjoyable cities to visit. In summer, the angled sun bathes the kauppatori (market square) in light and all seems well with the world. Locals, who appreciate daylight when they get it, crowd the terraces, and stalls groan under the weight of Arctic berries.

The centre is spread across several islands, elegantly connected by pedestrian bridges, and water never seems far away. This layout has made it very convenient for cycling, and Oulu's network of bike paths is one of Europe's best.

Oulu's the largest city north of Tampere and the sixth biggest in Finland; it's also one of the world's foremost technology cities; the university turns out top-notch IT graduates and the corporate science and technology parks on the city's outskirts employ people from all over the globe. The town centre has a free wireless network, so you can check your email from the terrace of the local pub.

But never fear, it's not all laptops and cycle lanes; this is Finland after all, and there's a good dollop of weirdness, particularly in the summer season, when the World Air Guitar Championships come to town.

History

Oulu was founded by King Karl IX of Sweden in 1605. It wasn't long before industrious and hard-working Swedish pioneers descended upon the Kainuu forests to make tar, which was floated in barrels to Oulu – the sticky stuff was essential to the building of unsinkable wooden ships. By the late 19th century Oulu boasted Finland's largest fleet.

In 1822 Oulu burned to the ground and was rebuilt, although few old buildings now remain.

Information

Wireless internet is available throughout the city centre on the PanOulu network.

Akateeminen Kirjakauppa (☎ 317 9411; Kirkkokatu 14) Third-floor bookshop with decent English selection.

Forex (☎ 020-751 2680; www.forex.fi; Kauppurienkatu 13) Currency exchange.

Public library (☎ 558 410; Kaarlenväylä; ☷ 10am-8pm Mon-Fri, 10am-3pm Sat, noon-4pm Sun) On the waterfront opposite the Oulu Theatre. Several internet terminals.

Sol (☎ 042-457 6050; Hallituskatu 26; ☷ Mon-Sat) Will do laundry for €5.30 per kilohgram.

Tourist office (☎ 5584 1330; www.visitoulu.fi; Torikatu 10; ☷ 9am-4pm Mon-Fri) Publishes the useful guide *Look at Oulu*. Should be back at this address by 2009, hopefully with longer hours.

Sights

KAUPPATORI

Oulu has the liveliest market square of all Finnish towns, and its position at the waterfront makes it all the more appealing. The square is bordered by several old wooden storehouses now serving as restaurants, bars and craft shops. The squat *Toripolliisi* statue, a humorous representation of the local police, is a local landmark. On the square is the **kauppahalli** (covered market, ☷ 8am-6pm Mon-Fri, 8am-3pm Sat), with freshly filleted salmon glistening in the market stalls and plenty of spots to snack on anything from cloudberries to sushi.

OULU CATHEDRAL

Oulu's imposing **cathedral** (Kirkkokatu 36; ☷ 11am-8pm Jun & Aug, 11am-9pm Jul, noon-1pm Sep-May) was built in 1777 but then came the great fire of 1822, which severely damaged the structure. Tireless architect CL Engel rebuilt it in Empire style, adding dome and renaissance-style vaulting, which impart a powerful airiness to the fairly unadorned interior. It got promoted

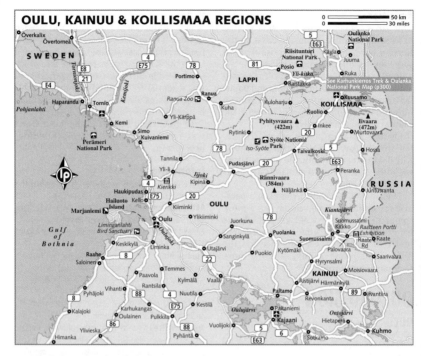

OULU, KAINUU & KOILLISMAA REGIONS

to cathedral in 1900 when the bishopric moved here from Kuopio; notable artworks include a fine altarpiece of the Ascension, a very Finnish Crucifixion in the transept, Finland's oldest portrait (1611) above the door to the vestry and, typically, a hanging boat, for the protection of the sailors of this most maritime city.

TIETOMAA

This mammoth **science centre** (☎ 5584 1340; www.tietomaa.com; Nahkatehtaankatu 6; adult/child €13/10; ☯ 10am-6pm mid-Feb–Aug, 10am-8pm Jul, 10am-4pm Mon-Fri, 10am-6pm Sat & Sun Sep–mid-Feb), in an old factory building, is Scandinavia's oldest and largest science museum and one of those places you can poke around in for half a day. It's most child-friendly, and in term-time gets very full with school groups. The excellent interactive exhibits range from UFOs to dinosaurs, and there's always one mega-exhibition as the highlight. If you need some breathing space, head up the tower for the views.

POHJOIS POHJANMAAN MUSEO

This park **museum** (Museum of Northern Ostrobothnia; ☎ 5584 7150; Ainolanpuisto; adult/child €3/free, free Fri; ☯ 10am-6pm Tue & Thu-Fri, 10am-7pm Wed, 11am-6pm Sat & Sun) merits exploration but has almost too much information to take in at first bite. It covers the earliest habitation of the region through to the 20th century, including plenty of information on the tar trade. Cameras allow you to zoom in on the impressive scale model of 1938 Oulu; a traditional pharmacy, paintings of the great fire, and a schoolroom are included in the wide-ranging display. A series of reconstructed rooms from different periods of history range from formal 19th-century salons to a student's 1960s bedroom with Che poster, typewriter and hair-curlers.

TAIDEMUSEO

Oulu's **art museum** (☎ 5584 7450; Kasarmintie 7; adult/ child €3/1, free Fri; ☯ 10am-5pm Tue-Sun) is a bright gallery opposite Tietomaa. It has excellent temporary exhibitions of both international and Finnish contemporary art, and a good permanent collection. The cafe is an exhibit in its own right. The gallery was closed at last visit for extensive renovation, but is due to open again in spring 2009.

MERIMIEHEN KOTIMUSEO

The **Sailor's Home Museum** (☎ 044-703 7188; Pikisaarentie 6; adult/child €3/1; ⏰ 10am-4pm Wed-Sun Jun–mid-Aug) on Pikisaari belonged to a local sailor. Built in 1737, it is the oldest house in Oulu and was transferred here from the town centre in 1983. The wallpaper and extendable bed are typical of 19th-century Finnish homes. Entrance is free with entry to the Pohjois Pohjanmaan Museo.

OULUNLINNA

There's not much left of Oulu Castle, although you can clearly see the remaining fortlike structure dominating the small park near the bridge. The observation tower, which was rebuilt in 1873, now houses a weekend cafe, and the cellar below has a small interpretative display. The original castle was built in 1590 as a base for the Swedish army moving east towards Russia, but was heavily damaged by Russian troops during the Great Wrath in the early 18th century. What remained of the castle blew up in 1793, when a lightning strike hit a powder magazine.

PARKS & GARDENS

Oulu University Botanical Gardens (☎ 553 1570; Kaitoväylä 5; ⏰ 8am-8pm, greenhouses 8am-3pm Tue-Fri, noon-3pm Sat & Sun), in Lineman, north of the centre, are pleasantly landscaped with thousands of exotic plants – including hardy 5m-tall cacti. A pair of greenhouses, named Romeo and Juliet, house tropical species.

Just north of the town centre and connected by small bridges, **Hupisaaret Park** has bike paths, greenhouses and a summer cafe, as well as a fishway built so that salmon can bypass the hydroelectric dam to get to the spawning grounds. A control room collects data on the fish, whose progress you can watch through a window.

Activities

One of Oulu's best features is the extensive network of **bicycle paths**. Nowhere is the Finns' love of two-wheeled transport more obvious than here in summer. Paths cross bridges, waterways and islands all the way out to surrounding villages. A good short ride is from the kauppatori, across the bridge to Pikisaari and across another bridge to Nallikari where there's a beach facing the Gulf of Bothnia.

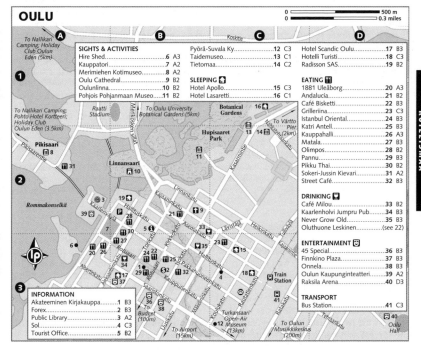

OULU

0 ————— 500 m
0 ————— 0.3 miles

OULU, KAINUU & KOILLISMAA

LET IT ALL OUT

As if an air-guitar festival wasn't enough, Oulu is also home to one of Finland's most unusual musical ensembles, Mieskuoro Huutajat. The name, which translates to 'Shouters Male Choir', says, or rather yells, it all.

Under the steely gaze of conductor and composer Petri Sirtiö, 30-odd men, dressed in smart black suits with rubber ties, shout various complex arrangements of well-known songs and anthems. It's actually more musical than it sounds, with softly melodic barks building to stunning crescendos of red-faced bellowing. Some shouters have long cardboard tubes to add an orchestral tone to proceedings. It's a memorable display, added to by their traditionally silent, expressionless entrance and exit.

At times, the shouters have courted controversy, particularly with national anthems; the Finnish embassy in Paris tried, in vain, to prevent them shouting 'La Marseillaise'. A documentary film, *Screaming Men*, was even made about their tour to Japan.

Throughout, Sirtiö has trodden a very Finnish line between the totally serious and the absurdly comic. Critics have raved about the primal forces at play, but be assured the Huutajat do everything with a large dose of irony. Check their website, www.huutajat.org, for upcoming dates.

Bikes (€2/15 per hour/day), scooters (€10/25/35 for hour/half/full day) and canoes (€30/40 for half/full day) can be hired from Kiikeli **hire shed** (☎ 044-055 2 808; ⌚ 9am-6pm) near the kauppatori, and from Nallikari Camping. The tourist office has a free cycle-route map. Other bike hire places include **Pyörä-Suvala Ky** (☎ 375 467; Saaristonkatu 27).

Tours

From Midsummer to mid-August, free bus (1pm Saturdays, two hours) and walking (6pm Wednesdays, two hours) tours leave from the town hall.

The 'Potnapekka' – a tourist train – travels around from June to mid-August, from Rotuaari pedestrian street to Hupisaaret island or Nallikari beach. The fare is €5/2.50 per adult/child to either destination; departures are from Rotuaari on the hour from 11am to 5pm.

Unique Adventures (☎ 040-764 8923; www .uniqueadventures.fi) can get you out to places like Turkansaari (€35), Hailuoto (€63) or Kierikki (€52) on day trips.

Festivals & Events

In a country that wrote the book on oddball festivals, Oulu hosts more than its fair share. Take the **World Air Guitar Championships** (www .airguitarworldchampionships.com), which is part of the **Oulu Music Video Festival** (www.omvf.net) in late August. Contestants from all over the world take the stage to show what they can do with their imaginary instruments.

There are two unusual winter events, both the largest of their kind anywhere in the world. The **Oulu Tar Ski Race** (www.oulunhiihtoseura .fi), held in early March, is a 70km skiing race (40km for women) that is entering its 113th year. The **Ice-Angling Marathon** (www.oulutourism .fi) is a 48-hour contest held on the open sea in late March (the ice is still thick) and draws more than 400 participants.

Pack the breath-mints for the **Garlic Festival** (www.oulunliikekeskus.fi) held over a weekend in mid-July. Eats on offer include everything from garlic potatoes, pizzas and bread to garlic-flavoured beer and ice cream – all enhanced by festivities and live entertainment. **Elojazz & Blues** (www.elojazz.com) is a two-day music festival in early August, while **Qstock** (www.qstock.org) is a high-profile rock festival in late July.

Sleeping

There's precious little budget accommodation in Oulu.

Nallikari Camping (☎ 5586 1350; www.nallikari.fi; Hietasaari; tent sites €10-17 plus €4/1 per adult/child, cabins €35-40, cottages €80-135; P 🖳 ☒ wi-fi) This excellent camping ground offers all sorts of options in a location close to the beach on Hietasaari, a 40-minute walk to town via pedestrian bridges. Both summer and winter activities are on offer, plus a large variety of cabins and cottages, substantially cheaper outside of peak season. It's very child-friendly, and there are minding services available if you want to get away for a bit. Bus 17 gets you there from the kauppatori (€2.80), as does the tourist train.

Hotelli Turisti (☎ 563 6100; www.hotellituristi.fi; Rautatienkatu 9; s/d €80/95, weekends & summer €55/65;

OULU, KAINUU & KOILLISMAA

P 🔧) You can't beat this spot for convenience: it's bang opposite the train station. It's a no-nonsense affair with reception doubling as a convenience kiosk, but offers value, with bright modern rooms that have plenty of space. There are rooms sleeping up to five; rates include sauna and breakfast.

Pohto Hotel Kortteeri (☎ 550 9700; www.pohto.fi; Vellamontie 12; r/f €68/100; 🕑 daily mid-Jun–mid-Aug, Mon-Fri rest of year; **P** 🖥 🔧 wi-fi) Near the camp site, this congress complex consists of low brick buildings tranquilly set among mature pines. Facilities are good for this price, and there's a kitchen and common room for guests to use, as well as a 12m pool. It's basically a summer hotel, but rooms are available during the week at other times if it's not booked out for a conference. Family rooms are decent value, putting your kids in easy reach of the beach and the fun facilities of the spa hotel.

Hotel Apollo (☎ 52211; www.hotelapollo.fi; Asemakatu 31; s/d €84/105, weekends €67/82; **P** 🖥 wi-fi) Handy for the station, this spot boasts warm and efficient service and three types of room. Standards are compact, with ultra-compact bathrooms, but comfortable enough; the top-floor rooms have sloping ceiling windows and more space, while the sauna rooms are classier, with dark furniture and flatscreen TVs. There's also a restaurant and karaoke bar open late. Check for good-value packages on their website.

ourpick Hotel Lasaretti (☎ 020-757 4700; www.lasaretti.com; Kasarmintie 13; s/d €115/132, summer €69/79; **P** 🖥 🔧 🔧 wi-fi) Bright, modern and optimistic, this inviting hotel sits in a group of renovated brick buildings, once a hospital. It's close to town but the parkside location by the bubbling-bright stream makes it feel rural. The artistically modern rooms have floorboards and flatscreen TVs; some have fold-out sofa-bed for families. Facilities and staff are excellent and there's also a busy restaurant with sun-kissed terrace.

Radisson SAS (☎ 887 7666; www.radisson.com/oulufi; Hallituskatu 1; s/d €130/150, weekends & summer €90/100; **P** 🖥 🔧 🔧 wi-fi) This business hotel is ideally located near the waterfront and kauppatori. Standard rooms are spacious and airy, with good bathrooms; superior and business rooms add extras and views, and there's a tempting suite with magnificent perspectives.

Holiday Club Oulun Eden (☎ 884 2000; www.holidayclub.fi; Nallikari; s/d €130/150, superior €150/170; **P** 🔧 🖥 🔧 🔧 wi-fi) This excellent spa hotel by the beach on Hietasaari offers great watery facilities – slides, intricate indoor pools, saunas – and massage treatments. Superior rooms on the new side of the building are bigger and have air-conditioning (handier than you may think) as well as a sea-view balcony. There's a big effort made with kids: nonguests can use the bouncy castle and ball-pit for a small fee. You can also use the whole spa facilities for the day for a pretty reasonable €15 (€9 for kids). You can nearly always get a cheaper room online.

Hotel Scandic Oulu (☎ 543 1000; www.scandic-hotels.com; Saaristonkatu 4; s/d €138/158, summer €79/89; **P** 🔧 🖥 🔧 wi-fi) This sleek, recently opened hotel occupies half a city block right in the middle and added much-needed rooms to the Oulu hotel scene. From the space-opera lights in its spacious foyer to the high-ceilinged rooms with clean Nordic decor and flatscreen TV, it's a temple to efficiency, hygiene and modern design (art, individuality, look elsewhere). Superior rooms add a little space plus coffee tray, bathrobes and upmarket toiletries, and there are bikes and ski-poles for guests to borrow.

Eating

Snacks and local specialities can be found in the kauppatori and kauppahalli. In summer stalls sell salmon, paella and Oulu specialities, such as *rieska* (flat bread), *leipäjuusto* (cheese bread) and *lohikeitto* (salmon soup).

CAFES & QUICK EATS

Oulu's hungry student population means there are plenty of cheap kebab and pizza places.

ourpick Café Bisketti (☎ 375 768; Kirkkokatu 8; lunch €6-8; 🕑 8am-10pm Mon-Thu, 8am-1am Fri & Sat, noon-10pm Sun) This top double-sided spot transforms itself throughout the day. Think twice before getting that pastry with your morning coffee; they're enormous, and might not leave room for lunch, when soup, salad, coffee and a pastry are €6.30, and only €7.80 with a tasty hot dish. In the evenings, the terrace is a decent spot for a people-watching beer.

Katri Antell (☎ 311 2182; Kirkkokatu 17; pastries €2-4; 🕑 7am-7pm Mon-Fri, 9am-4pm Sat) An Oulu institution, this competes with Bisketti opposite for the classic-cafe garland but definitely takes the venerability award; the first Katri was founded in 1880. The elegant chairs and hook-shaped couch make comfortable seats to enjoy a *munkki* (doughnut) and coffee, though all you can usually see from the terrace is a forest of bikes.

Andalucía (☎ 050-338 6175; Kirkkokatu 2; tapas €3-8; ☯ 3-11pm Mon-Thu, 3pm-midnight Fri, 1pm-midnight Sat) By the cathedral, this new tapas bar has quickly attracted a loyal local following. Tasty snacks plus various wines by the glass are on offer, and there's an atmospheric cellar bar in this characterful 1829 building.

Street Café (☎ 040-769 0840; Isokatu 23; lunches €6-8; ☯ 10am-6pm Mon-Fri, 10am-4pm Sat) Squirreled away in a little corner on the ground floor of the Galleria shopping centre, this has a good fresh salad bar and various lunch deals that offer pretty good value.

Grilleriina (☎ 370 927; Asemakatu 29; snacks €2-6; ☯ 6pm-5am) There are grillis (fast-food outlets), and then there's this, a class above and a step beyond the standard. While it boasts the usual all-possible-permutations menu, it's far tastier than most, and has a spacious, Marimekko-furnished dining room to enjoy the abundant portions at any hour of the night.

RESTAURANTS

Pannu (☎ 020-792 8200; Kauppurienkatu 12; mains €12-29; ☯ 10.30am-10pm Mon-Thu, 10.30am-11pm Fri & Sat, noon-9pm Sun) Secreted away in a brick cellar underneath Stockmann's department store, this spot is famous for its deep-pan pizzas but also does a decent line in salads, steaks, grilled reindeer, and Italian-style foccacia and garlic breads.

Sokeri-Jussin Kievari (☎ 376 628; Pikisaarentie 2; mains €13-30; ☯ kitchen 11am-10pm) An Oulu classic, this timbered local on Pikisaari was once a sugar warehouse and has outdoor tables that have good views of the centre. Although the renovated interior has lost a bit of the original character, it's still an attractive spot to eat, with no-frills traditional dishes, including reindeer.

Istanbul Oriental (☎ 311 2922; Kauppurienkatu 11; mains €20-32; ☯ noon-midnight Mon-Fri, 1pm-midnight Sat) This stylishly decorated place in the heart of things is a rather good Turkish restaurant with plenty of vegetarian options and succulent chargrilled meat. Service is excellent, though the food's somewhat overpriced.

our pick **Matala** (☎ 333 013; www.matala.fi; Rantakatu 6; mains €19-33; ☯ 4-11pm Mon-Sat) One of a clutch of upmarket restaurants around the kauppatori, this consistently delivers on food, service and, of course, location; outside seating puts you in the middle of things but the awning

affords you a little privacy. There are various degustation menus (€48 to €83) using typical northern Finnish ingredients; delicious Arctic char, or veal sweetbreads with globe artichoke are examples from the regularly overhauled à la carte menu.

1881 Uleåborg (☎ 881 1188; www.uleaborg.fi; Aittatori 4; set menus €54-58; ☯ 5-11pm Mon-Thu, 5pm-midnight Fri, 3pm-midnight Sat, 3-10pm Sun) In an old warehouse near the kauppatori, this classy spot combines chic Finnish style with a traditional setting. The dishes subtly purr 'Suomi' to your palate, with Baltic herrings accompanied with crayfish sauce and new potatoes with dill and sour cream, or vendace terrine with whitefish and fennel salad, as well as a mouth-cleanser of traditional strawberry milk.

Other recommendations:

Olimpos (☎ 311 3941; Pakkahuoneenkatu 7; mains €12-24; ☯ 11am-10pm Mon-Thu, 11am-11pm Fri & Sat, noon-9pm Sun) Serving uncomplicated fare from Greece and the Mediterranean, offers massive portions and decent lunches.

Pikku Thai (☎ 370 889; Pakkahuoneenkatu 8; mains €11-16; ☯ 10.30am-10pm Mon-Fri, noon-11pm Sat, noon-9pm Sun) Cosy Thai restaurant with better food than exterior decor, and a €7.90 lunch.

Drinking

There's plenty going on in Oulu at night. The kauppatori is the spot to start in summer: the terraces lick up every last drop of the evening sun. Keltainen Aitta and Makasiini are the main ones, set in traditional wooden warehouses.

Oluthuone Leskinen (☎ 311 7993; Kirkkokatu 10; ☯ noon-2am) This bar on the central pedestrian zone has a popular terrace that complements the dark, cosy interior with its wide range of Finnish and international beers, as well as malt whiskies. There's notably friendly service and a good atmosphere.

Never Grow Old (☎ 311 3936; Hallituskatu 17; ☯ 2pm-2am Mon-Fri, 2pm-3am Sat & Sun) This enduringly popular bar hits its stride after 10pm, with plenty of dancing, DJs and revelry in the tightly packed interior. The goofy decor includes some seriously comfortable and extremely uncomfortable places to sit, and a log-palisade bar that seems designed to get you to wear your drink. On the same block are convivial St Michaels, an Irish bar with decent Guinness and whisky selection, and Sarkka, an oldtime Finnish bar that charges a €1.50 entrance fee at night but is worth it for the downbeat traditional atmosphere and heroic 9am to 3am opening hours.

Cafe Milou (☎ 554 4181; Asemakatu 21; ◷ 2pm-late) Don something black and head down to this casual bar named after Tin Tin's hound to while away some time with Oulu's streetwise rock and metal crowd. Bookshelves filled with comics, a Friday poker tournament, and small terrace add appeal.

Kaarlenholvi Jumpru Pub (☎ 562 4500; Kauppurienkatu 6; ◷ 11am-2am Mon-Tue, 11am-4am Wed-Sat, noon-2am Sun) This Oulu institution is a great place for meeting locals and its enclosed outdoor area always seems to be humming with cheerfully sauced-up folk. There's a warren of cosy rooms inside, as well as a nightclub opening from 10pm Wednesday to Saturday.

Entertainment
NIGHTCLUBS
45 Special (☎ 881 1845; Saaristonkatu 12; ◷ 8pm-4am) This grungy club is Oulu's best rock venue, with wall-to-wall patrons. There's a €5 cover at weekends and regular live gigs.

Onnela (☎ 020-775 9410; Isokatu 35; ◷ 10am-4pm Wed-Sun) A huge club with several separate areas with different styles of music ranging from Suomipop to electronica and rock and metal.

CINEMA
Finnkino Plaza (☎ 060-000 7007; www.finnkino.fi; Torikatu 32) An enormous new central cinema complex, with eight screens.

CLASSICAL MUSIC & THEATRE
Oulun Musiikkikeskus (☎ 044-703 7221; www .ouka.fi; Lintulammentie 1-3) The Oulu Symphony Orchestra holds regular concerts here.

Oulun Kaupunginteatteri (☎ 5584 7000; Kaarlenväylä 2) The city theatre has classical music, and contemporary and classic theatre, almost all in Finnish.

SPORT
Oulu loves its ice-hockey team, the Kärpät (Stoats), who had won four Finnish titles out of five up to 2008. They play at **Raksila Arena** (☎ club 815 5700, ticketline 060-010 800; www.oulunkarpat .fi; tickets €10.50-26) east of town.

Getting There & Away
AIR
There are several daily direct flights from Helsinki, operated by Finnair/Finncomm, which has occasional summer flights to Rovaniemi. Blue1 services Helsinki, **Air Baltic** (www.airbaltic.com)

links Oulu with Riga, while **Wingo** (☎ 060-095 020; www.wingo.fi) flies to Tampere and Turku.

BUS
The bus station, near the train station, has services connecting Oulu with all the main centres. These include Rovaniemi (€38.40, 3½ hours), Tornio (€22, 2½ hours), Kajaani (€31.70, 2½ hours) and Helsinki (€86, 10 to 11 hours). For nearby villages, catch a local bus from the centre.

TRAIN
The station's just east of the centre. Six to 10 trains a day (€63.50, seven to nine hours) run from Helsinki to Oulu; the Pendolino service takes only 6 ¼ hours (€72). There are also trains via Kajaani and trains north to Rovaniemi.

Getting Around
Bus 19 runs between the centre and the airport (€2.80, 25 minutes, every 20 minutes). Shared **airport taxis** (☎ 060-030 084; www.airport taxioulu.fi) cost €14.

There's a good network of local buses (www.koskilinjat.fi). Each ride costs €2.80; check route maps online and at bus stops.

The various car-hire operators in town, including **Sixt** (☎ 050-049 8875; www.sixt.fi) at the airport and **Budget** (☎ 020-746 6640; www.budget.fi; Kirkkokatu 55), do cheap weekend deals.

Call ☎ 060-030 081 for a cab.

AROUND OULU
The zoo at Ranua (p314) is an easy day trip from Oulu.

Turkansaari
Set across two river islands on the scenic Oulujoki, this **open-air museum** (☎ 044-703 7154; Turkansaarentie 165; adult/child €3/1; ◷ 10am-8pm late May–mid-Aug, 10am-4pm mid-Aug–mid-Sep) is a collection of wooden buildings of various traditional types, from loggers' cabins to stables, and includes a handsome traditional farmhouse. The 1694 church is an original from this former trading settlement; look for the faded date carved above the inside doorway. A working tar-pit at the far end of the complex comes to the fore during Tar-Burning Week, a festival in late June.

Turkansaari is 14km east of Oulu off Rd 22; catch bus 3 or 4. You can also get there by boat from town in summer: the tourist office has the timetable. Entry is free with the Pohjois Pohjanmaan Museo ticket.

Hailuoto Island

☎ 08 / pop 987

A favourite Oulu beach escape, Hailuoto is a sizeable island of traditional red farmhouses, venerable wooden windmills, modern wind-farms, and Scotch pines growing tall from the sandy soil. It's only been around for a couple of thousand years: it rose from the sea with the land's 'bounceback' (isostasis) after the last Ice Age. Named after the herring, it's long been a base for fishermen; the grey lichen growing abundantly here is also harvested for reindeer food.

A free car ferry crosses the 7km from the mainland, dropping you at Hailuoto's eastern-most point, from where the road winds 30km to the beach at Marjaniemi at the opposite end of the island. There's **tourist information** (☎ 044-497 3500; www.hailuoto.fi) at the cafes at both ferry docks, in Marjaniemi, and in the middle of the island at Hailuoto village, which has shops, a bank and a striking A-frame church. Here also is **Kniivilä** (☎ 044-497 3565; Marjaniementie 20; admission €2; ◷ 11am-5pm Wed-Sun mid-Jun–mid-Aug), an open-air museum of old wooden buildings.

At Marjaniemi, there's a shallow-water beach perfect for kids, looked over by a **light-house** (☎ 040-556 2572; adult/child €5/3; ◷ noon-2pm Sat & Sun early Jun-Aug). At the base of the lighthouse is Luototalo, which contains a free **nature exhibition** (◷ 9am-6pm daily) on the dune ecosystem, a wooden-tabled restaurant/cafe with lunch buffet and great sea views.

ourpick Luotsi Hotelli (☎ 772 5500; www.luotokeskus.fi; Marjaniementie 783; s/d/ste €60/85/100; ◷ Mar-Nov; P 🖳) is an excellent modern facility with spacious rooms airily kitted out in light wood and a vague nautical feel. It's worth upgrading to the suites: wonderful spaces with curving picture-windows. Excellent rates are available for longer stays.

The **RantaSumppu camp site** (tent site €20, small/large cabin €65/85; P 🖳) is a 10-minute walk down the beach, with cabins within striking distance of the sea and good facilities including a cafe/lunch restaurant. Reception is open here in summer until 8pm, otherwise check in at the hotel.

Bus 66 travels two to three times daily from Oulu, crossing on the ferry and running the length of the island to Marjaniemi. Free **ferries** (☎ 040-028 2791) run half-hourly at busy

times, and hourly at other times. Rides are 30 minutes. The ferry is 28km southwest of Oulu via Rd 816.

Limanganlahti Bird Sanctuary

The bird sanctuary at Liminka Bay, near the attractive old farming village of Liminka, attracts numerous avian species, with several rare waders nesting here during summer, and many species of waterfowl and birds of prey also visible. Prominent species include the yellow-breasted bunting, black-tailed god-wit, Ural owl, bittern, marsh harrier and tern. There are several observation towers, board-walks and a couple of designated camp sites.

Head first for **Limanganlahden Luontokeskus** (☎ 562 0000; www.limanganlahti.net; Rantakurvi 6; ◷ 11am-6pm Apr-Jun, noon-8pm Wed-Sun Jul-early Aug), a nature centre 6km west of Liminka village. As well as the display explaining the birdlife, migrations and flora, there's an observation tower, cafe and information desk. A guide is in attendance and you can rent binoculars (€2) to use at one of the many watchtowers in the area – the nearest is just 400m away.

The centre also has an accommodation wing, with comfortable, modern rooms sleeping two to six, a sauna and kitchen. The rooms range from €40 to €60. Call ☎ 040-038 3600 outside of centre opening hours.

Several daily Raahe-bound buses make the 30km trip from Oulu to Liminka and on to Lumijoki, and will stop at the turn-off to the nature centre.

Haukipudas

☎ 08 / pop 18,113

Haukipudas, 21km north of Oulu at a scenic spot along the Kiiminkijoki, is known for its beige **church** (admission free; ◷ 10am-6pm Mon-Fri early Jun-late Aug), one of Finland's most notable 'picture churches'. The interior is decorated with striking naïve scenes painted in the 18th century and depicting biblical events, including a scary Day of Judgement. Outside, by the separate belfry, stands a wooden mous-tachioed *vaivaisukko* (pauper statue).

From Oulu town centre, bus 15 or 20 runs to Haukipudas.

Kierikki

This excellent **museum** (☎ 08-817 0492; www.kierikki.fi; adult/child €7/4; ◷ 10am-6pm Jun-early Aug, 10am-4pm rest of Aug) is set by the Iijoki, whose banks are riddled with Stone Age settlements that have provided archaeologists with valuable information about this period in the Nordic lands. The communities made a comfortable living fishing and sealing, using surplus production for trade. Settlements in the Kierikki area date from about 4000 BC to 2000 BC and were coastal, moving gradually west as the land rose.

The display is most informative, and sensibly only includes a handful of artefacts, including fortunately preserved wooden fences to trap fish. A somewhat ponderous video gives excavation histories, and there's a cafe-restaurant. A short boardwalk takes you down to the picturesque riverbank, where they've re-created some buildings from the period, including the intriguing 'terrace', several houses joined together to form one long structure. You can take pot-shots at a deer using a primitive bow and arrow, or send the kids out for a paddle in a Stone Age canoe.

There's also a **hotel** (s/d €65/90; ☽ all year; **P**) here, consisting of wooden buildings surrounding a little pond; the attractive, spacious rooms have balconies over it. Rates include museum entry.

Kierikki is 5km south of Yli-Ii, itself 27km east of Ii, on the main road north of Oulu. Buses run from Oulu on school days only and you have to change in Ii.

KAINUU REGION

KAJAANI
☎ 08 / pop 38,089

Essentially a one-street town, Kajaani is nevertheless the major settlement in these parts. Apart from its pretty riverside and fabulous rural church nearby, there's little to keep you, though it makes a handy stopover between Lakeland and the north.

Kajaani was long an important station on the Kainuu tar transportation route – until the 19th century this region produced more tar than anywhere else in the world. Other claims to fame are that Elias Lönnrot, creator of the *Kalevala* (see p44), worked here for a period, using it as a base for his travels, and long-reigning president Urho Kekkonen lived here as a student (at Kalliokatu 7).

Information
Kajaani Info (☎ 6155 2555; www.kajaani.fi; Kauppakatu 21; ☽ 9am-5.30pm Mon-Fri, 9am-2pm Sat Jun-Aug, 9am-4.30pm Mon-Fri Sep-May) Tourist information and free internet.
Public library (☎ 6155 2422; Kauppakatu 35; ☽ 10am-8pm Mon-Fri, 10am-3pm Sat) Free internet.

Sights & Activities
The beautiful wooden **church** (Pohjolankatu; ☽ 10am-6pm early Jun-late Aug) from 1896 is a fine example of Finnish neo-Gothic. It's typically Karelian, with lots of ornate wooden trim and a delicate, slender, bell tower. The Orthodox church is nearby. See p291 for Paltaniemi church.

Picturesquely set on a river island in the town centre, **Kajaani Castle** ruins show all the signs of thorough damage by war, time and more recent mischief. It's a fine spot to bask on the grass on a sunny day, but there isn't much more to it than what you can see.

Near the castle there's a **tar-boat channel** with a lock built in 1846 to enable the boats laden with tar barrels to pass the Ämmäkoski rapids. The replica boat moored by the lock features in demonstrations at 11am on Saturday in July.

Kainuun Museo (Kainuu Museum; ☎ 6155 2409; Asemakatu 4; adult/child €2/free; ☽ noon-4pm Fri-Tue, noon-7pm Wed-Thu) was revamping its permanent collection at last visit. It puts on temporary exhibitions upstairs, and downstairs has information on the tar industry, the *Kalevala* and its author, Elias Lönnrot, and other local history.

Facing the small *raatihuoneentori* (town square) is the old **town hall**, designed by Engel. Behind it is the former police station, which now serves as the **Kajaanin Taidemuseo** (Kajaani Art Museum; ☎ 6155 2599; Linnankatu 14; adult/child €2/free; ☽ 10am-5pm Sun-Fri, to 8pm Wed). It hosts changing exhibitions of mostly contemporary art from the region.

Festivals & Events
Kainuun Jazzkevät (www.jazzkevat.fi) in late May is a festival of international jazz, blues and rock. There was no event in 2008 but it was due to restart in 2009. Other festivals include a dance celebration, **Kajaani Tanssii** (www.kajaanidance.fi), warming things up in early February, and **Kajaanin Runoviikko**, a poetry week in early July. The tourist office can sort out tickets.

Sleeping
Kainuunportti (☎ 613 3000; Mainuantie 350; tent site €9.50, s/d €50/60; ☽ camping May-Oct; **P**) The

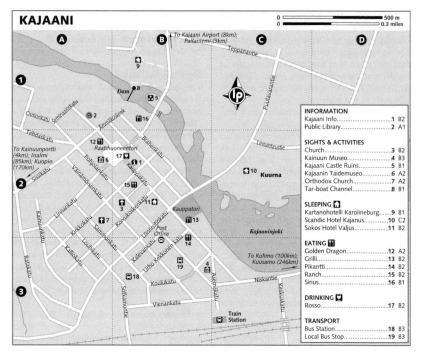

KAJAANI

cheapest accommodation choice is this hotel and camp site by a service station 4km from town down the Iisalmi road. It's not a romantic location, but the rooms are decent value and include sauna and breakfast.

our pick **Kartanohotelli Karolineburg** (☎ 613 1291; www.karolineburg.com; Karoliinantie 4; s/d from €70/80, d with sauna €110, ste €120-250; P) Set in a wooden manor house and various outbuildings across the river from town, this makes an intriguing place to stay; a refreshing change from sterile business hotels. Run somewhat airily by a friendly family, it offers a wide range of chambers, from suites with their own sauna and terrace to simpler modern rooms. Elegant furnishings, bosky grounds and classy restaurant fare make it a romantic choice. Prices drop a little in summer.

Sokos Hotel Valjus (☎ 615 0200; www.sokoshotels .fi; Kauppakatu 20; s/d €105/125, weekends & summer from €65/85; P wi-fi) Right in the centre of town on the main street, this is one of two Sokos hotels almost opposite each other. There's a mixture of rooms in its labyrinthine interior; some have a staircase down from the door, while superiors have their own balcony with garden furniture. Service is good, and there's a restaurant as well as a bar-cafe and nightclub.

Scandic Hotel Kajanus (☎ 61641; www.scandichotels .com; Koskikatu 3; s/d €120/125, weekends & summer around €81/91; P wi-fi) Across the river from the centre, this place is enormous and has three grades of rooms, which differ in size and a few extra conveniences; there's also a gym, squash court, large sauna complex, bar and good restaurant. The hotel has bikes for guests to borrow.

Eating & Drinking

The kauppatori has stalls selling smoked fish and other goodies and a cheap grilli. As you head north, Finland's restaurant scene starts to worsen somewhere around Kajaani.

Sirius (☎ 612 2087; Brahenkatu 5; lunch €6.50-26; 10.30am-1.30pm Mon-Fri) Located above the rapids, this restaurant is set in a characterful 1940s villa built as a residence for the local paper company. Choices range from salad table to a full buffet, and there are also delicious, classy daily fish or meat specials. There's a great terrace out the back. It opens in the evenings for group bookings only.

OULU, KAINUU & KOILLISMAA

Pikantti (☎ 628 870; Kauppakatu 10; lunch €6.90-10.90; ⏱ 10am-4pm Mon-Fri, 10am-3pm Sat) This attractive spot has a stylish interior with white wooden fittings and lamps off-setting the lack of natural light. It offers an excellent lunchtime salad buffet, with options to include daily soup or hot dish specials. Dessert and coffee are included, and there's pleasant outdoor seating.

Ranch (☎ 636 696; Kauppakatu 26; mains €13-25; ⏱ 10.30am-8pm Mon & Tue, 10.30am-10pm Wed & Thu, 10.30am-11pm Fri, noon-11pm Sat) In an alley off the main street, the painted windows here defy casual stickybeaking but conceal a pleasant interior. The food's for meat-eating people with an appetite; big burgers and choose-your-weight steaks fried and served in the pan with crunchy vegetables and a mountain of potato. Good service and free corn chips add points.

Also recommended:

Golden Dragon (☎ 627 776; Kauppakatu 38; lunch €7-8, mains €8-14; ⏱ 10.30am-7pm Mon-Thu, to 8pm Fri, noon-8pm Sat, noon-6pm Sun) Tasty Chinese serving Cantonese and Sichuan cuisine. Lunch buffet is €8.

Rosso (☎ 615 0341; Kauppakatu 21; ⏱ 11am-10pm, later at weekends) This branch of the Rosso chain is also the town's most popular public bar, with a large terrace on the town hall square.

Getting There & Away

Finnair flies daily from Helsinki. The airport is 8km northwest; a **bus** (☎ 044-294 0920; ticket €4) runs from the kauppatori via the Kajanus hotel to coincide with flights; bus 4 also runs twice daily from Pohjolankatu. It's about €20 in a cab.

Kajaani is Kainuu's travel hub. There are up to eight daily departures for Kuhmo (€17.70, 1¾ hours) and other towns in the region during the week, but few departures on weekends. There are four daily trains from Helsinki (€62.30, seven hours), via Kuopio, and services on to Oulu.

AROUND KAJAANI
Paltaniemi

Paltaniemi village is 9km northwest of Kajaani and has its own distinctive history as a separate and significant parish. Its enchantingly weathered wooden **church** (☎ 687 5334; Paltaniementie 851; admission free; ⏱ 10am-6pm mid-May–mid-Aug) was built in 1726, and has some of Finland's most interesting church paintings; rustic 18th-century works full of life and colour that enliven the roof and walls. Above the entrance, symbolically representing the dangers of life outside the church's protective

bosom, is a vivid scene of hell, complete with a queen riding a scary beast and numerous serpents and tormented souls. It was covered for many years to avoid offending parish sensibilities. There's someone on hand to explain or answer any questions.

Alongside the church, what looks like a woodshed is the **Keisarintalli**, an old stable that was actually used as a boarding house for Tsar Alexander I when he toured Finland in 1819. This simple building (moved from Vuolijoki) was the best available.

Nearby, the **Eino Leino-Talo** (Sutelantie 28; admission free; ⏱ 10am-6pm Sun-Fri mid-Jun–mid-Aug) is a re-creation of the place where Leino, one of Finland's foremost independence-era poets, was born in 1878. It's a lovely lakeside spot, with a cafe as well as photos and memorabilia. You can rent bikes here to explore the area.

Take local bus 4 from Pohjolankatu in Kajaani to Paltaniemi. There are hourly departures on weekdays only, otherwise it's 9km or a €20 cab.

KUHMO
☎ 08 / pop 9943

Kuhmo, once a major tar producer, is a good launch pad for the wilderness; it makes a natural base for hiking the UKK route, Finland's longest marked trek. The vast taiga runs from here right across Siberia and harbours 'respect' animals like wolves, bears and lynx; you can learn about these creatures in the nature centre.

It's also the unofficial capital of Vienan Karjala, the Karelian heartland that is now in Russia. This was the region that artists explored in the Karelian movement, such a crucial part of the development of Finnish national identity (see p41). Most of their expeditions set off from Kuhmo, as did one of Elias Lönnrot's, when he headed into 'Songland' to record the verses of bards that he later wove into the *Kalevala* epic. There's a fine Kalevala resource centre in town, as well as a theme park.

This likeable little town also has a great chamber music festival in July, when there's a real buzz about the place, and quality concerts at accessible prices.

Information

Petola Luontokeskus (☎ 205-646 380; petola@metsa .fi; Lentiirantie 342; ⏱ 10am-5pm Jun-Aug, 10am-4pm Mon-Fri Sep-Dec) National park and hiking information.

OULU, KAINUU & KOILLISMAA

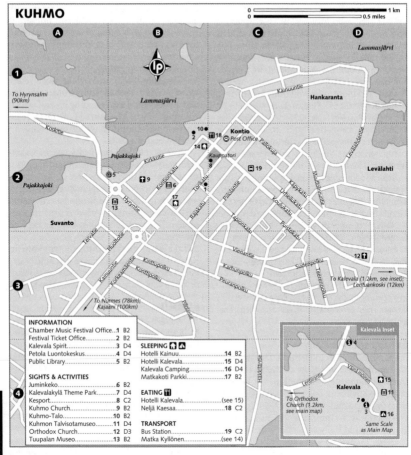

KUHMO

INFORMATION	
Chamber Music Festival Office..**1**	B2
Festival Ticket Office.................**2**	B2
Kalevala Spirit........................**3**	D4
Petola Luontokeskus................**4**	D4
Public Library.........................**5**	B2

SIGHTS & ACTIVITIES	
Juminkeko.............................**6**	B2
Kalevalakylä Theme Park.........**7**	D4
Kesport.................................**8**	C2
Kuhmo Church.......................**9**	B2
Kuhmo-Talo..........................**10**	B2
Kuhmon Talvisotamuseo..........**11**	D4
Orthodox Church....................**12**	D3
Tuupalan Museo.....................**13**	B2

SLEEPING 🏠 🛏	
Hotelli Kainuu.......................**14**	B2
Hotelli Kalevala.....................**15**	D4
Kalevala Camping...................**16**	D4
Matkakoti Parkki....................**17**	B2

EATING 🍴	
Hotelli Kalevala.....................(see 15)	
Neljä Kaesaa.........................**18**	C2

TRANSPORT	
Bus Station...........................**19**	C2
Matka Kyllönen......................(see 14)	

Kalevala Spirit (☎ 044-075 5 500; www.kalevalaspirit .fi; Väinämöinen; ⏲ 8am-10pm Jun-Aug, 8am-5pm Mon-Fri Sep-May) Pending renovation of the town hall building, this, at the entrance to the Kalevala Village, is the tourist office.

Public library (☎ 6155 5390; Pajakkakatu 2; ⏲ 10am-7pm Mon-Wed & Fri, 2-7pm Thu, plus 9am-3pm Sat Sep-May) Free internet.

Sights

JUMINKEKO

If you are interested in the *Kalevala* or Karelian culture, pay a visit to the excellent **Juminkeko** (☎ 653 0670; www.juminkeko.fi; Kontionkatu 25; adult/child €4/free; ⏲ noon-6pm Sun-Thu, daily in Jul), a beautiful building made using traditional methods and modern styling. The fantastic staff can tell

you anything you wish to know; there are also three to four detailed exhibitions here yearly. The auditorium, walls hand-worked by adze, has three worthwhile audiovisuals in English; also on display is a collection of *Kalevala* books translated into over 50 languages. With the multimedia program you can view pictures, and read and listen to extracts from the epic in anything from Japanese to Swahili.

TUUPALAN MUSEO

This charming **museum** (☎ 6155 5394; Tervatie 1; adult/child €3/2; ⏲ 10am-4pm Mon-Fri, 11am-4pm Sat & Sun Jun&Jul, by request May & Aug) is one of a complex of traditional Karelian red-painted wooden farm buildings that has been, in past lives, a general store, pharmacy, inn, post office and home to the town's police chief. It has now been refurbished to show what life at the turn of the 20th century in a wealthy Kuhmo home was like, with dignified furnishings and fittings.

CHURCHES

The muscular mustard-yellow wooden **Kuhmo Church** (☎ 653 0235; Kirkkotie 11; ☷ noon–6pm midsummer–early Aug) was built in 1816 but had its dome added later. The interior is fairly unadorned but features a striking modern organ built in nearby Sotkamo. It's a picturesque venue for concerts during the festival.

On the road to the theme park, the tiny **Orthodox Church** (☎ 622 695; Koulukatu 47) is modern but contains several 18th-century icons that were painted in the Valamo Monastery before it was annexed by the Soviet Union, plus a 300-year-old altarpiece. It's open on request only.

KALEVALAKYLÄ

Four kilometres from the centre, **Kalevala Village** is a theme park that's actually less about the *Kalevala* epic than traditional Karelian life. Part of the village, by the camp site, is free to enter. It has a number of Karelian wooden buildings with characteristic overlapping corners, including a sauna, craft shops and Pohjolantalo, a large hall that functions as cafe, restaurant and gallery.

The rest of the area is accessed on the **Kalevala Spirit Experience** (adult/child €20/10; ☷ noon & 2pm mid-Jun–mid-Aug), a two-hour tour in Finnish or English that tests your inherent Finnishness with costumed guides, sauna, tar-making, fishing, woodcarving and so on. It's fun for families; there's also a tour for smaller kids at 1pm. From mid-December to mid-January, the site opens as a Christmas village.

Opposite, **Kuhmon Talvisotamuseo** (☎ 6155 5395; adult/child €3/2; ☷ 9am-6pm Mon-Fri, 11am-4pm Sat & Sun Jun–mid-Aug) displays various artefacts, mementos and photographs from the bitter Winter War, much of the worst fighting of which was done near here. A diorama depicts one of the key turning points, and an armoured cannon-carriage, models of Russian planes and an anti-tank gun take pride of place.

PETOLA LUONTOKESKUS

This **visitor centre** (☎ 020-564 6380; petola@metsa.fi; Lentiirantie 342; ☷ 10am-5pm Jun-Aug, 10am-4pm Mon-Fri Sep-Dec) is near Kalevalakylä and has an excellent exhibition in various languages on Finland's quartet of large carnivores, known hereabouts as *karhu* (bear), *ilves* (lynx), *ahma* (wolverine) and *susi* (wolf), as well as wild reindeer, present in the region in small numbers, and the golden eagle. There are various audiovisuals, as well as a cafe serving vanilla coffee, comprehensive information sheets on most of Finland's national parks and a cute gift shop.

Activities

Hiking's the big drawcard in Kuhmo, but there are plenty of other ways to get active; the tourist office can help organise things like whitewater rafting, while Petola visitor centre has more walking information and can arrange fishing permits.

There are bears, flying squirrels, beavers, wolverines and wild reindeer in the Kuhmo region: safaris and bear-viewing from hides are organised by **Wild Brown Bear** (☎ 040-546 9008; www.wildbrownbear.fi) and **Taiga Spirit** (☎ 040-746 8243; www.taigaspirit.com) for €130 to €160 a time.

Ultima Taiga (☎ 040-557 1977; www.ultimataiga.fi) can sort you out with canoeing and trips to Russian Karelia in summer, as well as husky-sledding in winter.

OULU, KAINUU & KOILLISMAA

DIY: TREKKING THE UKK

Pockets of the now-rare Finnish wilderness still exist – in pristine condition – along the eastern border of Finland. They are best seen and experienced on a trek along the Urho K Kekkonen (UKK) route. This 240km trail is the nation's longest and greatest trekking route, starting at Koli (p183) in Karelia, and ending in Syöte (p303).

There are numerous possible access points, and alternative branches of the route, but the Kuhmo area offers some excellent portions of it: the Kuhmo to Hiidenportti leg and the Kuhmo to Lentiira leg. The trek east from Kuhmo to Lentiira village via Iso-Palonen park takes at least four days and offers superb scenery. It's well marked and has *laavu* shelters at regular intervals: these have an established campfire place, firewood and pit toilet. Carry a sleeping bag and *plenty* of repellent, and pick up route maps at the Petola Luontokeskus in Kuhmo.

Bicycles can be hired from **Kesport** (Kainuuntie 85; ☺ 9am-6pm Mon-Fri, 9am-2pm Sat) on the kauppatori for €15 per day.

Festivals & Events

our pick **Kuhmo Chamber Music Festival** (☎ 652 0936; www.kuhmofestival.fi; Torikatu 39) This festival is two weeks in late July and has a full program of about 80 top-quality concerts performed by a variety of Finnish and international musicians: well over 100 participate. Most concerts, usually five or six short pieces bound by a tenuous theme, are held in the Kuhmo-Talo, a beautiful hall that looks like one of those hobby models made out of matchsticks. There's loads of legroom, and tickets are a steal at around €14 for most events. Other concerts are in the adjacent school and in Kuhmo Church, and there's a shop with a few good Finnish recordings on sale. Ask about late-night informal events not in the schedule. Get tickets via the festival office or, once in Kuhmo, the ticket office in the school.

Sleeping

Book well ahead during the festival, when prices are up a little.

Kalevala Camping (☎ 044-075 5500; www.kalevalaspirit.fi; Väinämöinen 13; tent sites €10, 2-/4-person cabins €35/42, cottages €72/92; ☺ Jun-Aug) Four kilometres from town, this has a most attractive lakeside location among tall pines. Facilities aren't wonderful, but there are saunas, boats and different cabins, some with their own bathroom. Reception is at adjacent Kalevalakylä.

Matkakoti Parkki (☎ 655 0271; matkakoti.parkki@ elisanet.fi; Vienantie 3; s/d/tr €30/50/60; P) Run in a motherly manner, this quiet and handsome little guesthouse offers excellent value near the centre of town. Rooms are spotless and need to be booked ahead during the festival. It rents bikes at €3 per hour.

Hotelli Kainuu (☎ 655 1711; www.hotellikainuu.com; Kainuuntie 84; s/d €61/78; P ▯) Right in the slow-beating heart of Kuhmo, this family-run hotel offers the kauppatori and Kuhmo-Talo concerts within metres. Rooms are comfortable without being flashy, there's gym and sauna, a bar with a terrace, and a restaurant, Eskobar, serving uninspiring food. It's cheaper at weekends; a little extra cash gets you a room with private sauna.

our pick **Hotelli Kalevala** (☎ 655 4100; www.hotellikalevala.fi; Väinämöinen 9; s/d €82/110; P ▯ ▣ wi-fi) Four kilometres away, by the Kalevala Village, this striking building of wood and concrete is a great place to stay. The pretty rooms in yellow colours mostly have tantalising lake views with sounds of the lapping water. It's the facilities that win you over here, though, with rentals of boats, snowmobiles and more; a gym and spa complex, peat sauna and various tailored trips on foot or skis, or to land a fish or two. It's about €10 from the centre in a cab.

Eating

Try a *rönttönen* in the kauppatori; this open pastry with potato and lingonberry mixes sweet and savoury tastes.

Neljä Kaesaa (☎ 652 1573; Koulukatu 3; lunch €7-8; ☺ 8am-5pm Mon-Fri, 8am-1pm Sat) The best central option is only open at lunchtime, when it doles out portions of warming and traditional Finnish comfort food like stews (sometimes with elk), or fried *muikku* (vendace). It opens extended hours during the festival.

Hotelli Kalevala (☎ 655 4100; Väinämöinen 9; mains €12-19; ☺ 11am-10pm, to 11pm Jul) The only proper restaurant in Kuhmo is out at this hotel, but it's a good one. The short menu has fish or reindeer soup, and succulent pike-perch and pork with sauces made from berries and wild mushrooms. Lunch is also a rewarding time to visit, with the €12 daily special invariably delicious.

A worthwhile cafe can be found at Petola visitor centre; it does a lunchtime buffet at busy times. The cafe in Kuhmo-Talo is good for festival-time drinks and snacks, while Pohjolantalo, a wooden hall in the Kalevalakylä, functions as a cafe and also, according to demand, as a restaurant serving traditional Karelian food. Check with Kalevala Spirit for opening times.

Getting There & Away

Numerous daily buses head to/from Kajaani (€17.70, 1¾ hours), and two Monday to Saturday to Nurmes, changing at Sotkamo. For other destinations, you'll have to go via Kajaani. There's a direct connection between Kajaani's airport and Kuhmo.

Buses run east on Monday and Friday to the Russian Karelian town of Kostamus – they're run by **Matka Kyllönen** (☎ 652 0771; Kainuuntie 84), behind Hotelli Kainuu.

KOILLISMAA REGION

KUUSAMO

☎ 08 / pop 16,899

An excellent base for the active, though neither handsome nor seductive in itself, Kuusamo already feels like Lapland, with reindeer roaming the tarmac hereabouts and a frontier feel to the spread-out settlement. Russia's just down the road, and the recently opened border crossing is creating increasing tourism both ways. Wonderful canoeing, hiking and wildlife watching is available in the surrounding area; nearby Ruka also draws the winter crowds.

During WWII, the village was a command centre for German troops, who supervised the construction of the 'Death Railway' that operated for 242 days. When the Soviet army marched into Kuusamo on 15 September 1944, the Germans burned the town and blew up the railway. The Soviets retreated, after occupying Kuusamo for about two months, and the inhabitants returned to their shattered town.

Information

Karhuntassu (☎ 030-650 2540; www.kuusamo .fi; Torangintaival 2; ☼ 9am-8pm Mon-Fri, 10am-6pm Sat & Sun late Jun-Jul, 9am-6pm Mon-Fri, 10am-4pm Sat & Sun early Aug, 9am-5pm Mon-Fri mid-Aug–late Jun) This large visitor centre is at the highway junction, 2km from the centre. There's comprehensive tourist information, free internet, a FinFun desk for booking rental cottages, and a cafe-shop. The national parks service has an information desk here too, as well as an excellent exhibition of wildlife photography.

Public library (☎ 040-860 8900; Kaiterantie 22; ☼ Mon-Fri year-round, also Sat Sep-May) Free internet.

Sights & Activites

Kuusamo is short on sights, but you're here for the outdoors. The **wildlife photography exhibition** (adult/child €4/2; ☼ 10am-6pm Mon-Fri, 10am-2pm Sat, noon-4pm Sun) in the tourist office centre is well worth the price of admission.

On a lake near the centre is **Kuusamon Ulkomuseo** (☎ 040-860 8717; Kitronintie 6; adult/child €2.10/free; ☼ noon-6pm mid-Jun–mid-Aug, 9am-3pm Mon-Fri mid-Aug) the local open-air museum, which brings together a selection of venerable farm buildings from the region.

A sleek, elegant, Finnish creation designed by Arto Sipinen, **Kuusamotalo** (☎ 850 6550; Kaarlo Hännisentie 2), a concert hall and cultural centre,

is the pride of Kuusamo. Check with the tourist office for performances and exhibitions.

The modern **water tower** (Joukamontie 32; ☼ 10am-6pm Tue-Sat Jun-early Aug) has an observation platform with a good view, as well as a cafe.

Bjarmia (☎ 853 869; www.bjarmia.fi; Vienantie 1; ☼ 9am-6pm Mon-Fri, 9am-3pm Sat) is a ceramics factory and studio right in the centre of Kuusamo. It has a good range of high-quality pieces and can arrange overseas delivery. Upstairs is a cafe and Marimekko outlet.

Kuusamon Uistin (☎ 860 3450; www.kuusamonuistin.fi; Kemijärventie 44; ☼ 9am-7pm Mon-Fri, 10am-6pm Sat & Sun late Jun–mid-Aug, 10am-6pm Mon-Fri, 10am-3pm Sat mid-Aug–late Jun), north of the centre on the main road (Rd 5) to Ruka, sells its beautifully crafted world-famous fishing lures and sheath knives from its factory.

Thirty-three kilometres south of Kuusamo, on the Kajaani road, **Kuusamon Suurpetokeskus** (☎ 861 713; Keronrannantie 31; adult/child €6/3; ☼ 10am-5pm Apr-Sep) is a bear zoo originally set up as a rescue centre; there are also foxes, lynx and a wolverine, as well as reindeer. Entry is by guided tour.

For a range of activities on offer, see Tours (below).

Tours

There are many tour operators based in Kuusamo and Ruka, offering a full range of winter and summer activities. The Ruka webpage, www.ruka.fi, is a good place to look for active ideas.

Operators include:

Arctic Safaris (☎ 020-786 8760; www.arcticsafaris.fi; Rukanriutta 11, Ruka) On the main road at Ruka turn-off. Big and reliable Lapland operator with full range of winter and summer activities.

Green Line Safaris (☎ 852 3041; www.greenlinesafaris.fi; Kitkantie 38-40, Kuusamo) Specialises in fishing and ice-fishing, as well as offering canoeing and sledding.

Karhu-Kuusamo (☎ 040-021 0681; www.karhukuusamo.com) Recommended bear-watching trips (€115). Leaving at 6pm, you head to a comfortable hide overlooking a meadow where bears regularly stop by for a feed: most of the summer, you have a 60% to 90% chance of seeing a honeypaw. You get back to town around midnight. The guide Tuomo is very knowledgeable and can also arrange bird-watching.

NorthTrek (☎ 040-418 2832; www.northtrek.net; Erkkorannantie 1, Ruka) Offers family-friendly rafting, canoeing and hiking trips. In winter it's snowshoeing, cross-country skiing, huskies and snow ponies.

EXPLORING NORTHERN KAINUU

Kainuu is a sizeable swathe of largely unvisited territory; as you venture further north rivers and lakes become steelier, you'll see traditional haystacks and farmsteads in the middle of nowhere and might spot your first reindeer, or hear the howling of sled-dogs impatient for snow.

Suomussalmi & Around

Suomussalmi is northern Kainuu's hub. In recent years the town has throbbed with pride for local boy and Formula One driver Heikki Kovalainen. At the heart of the settlement, a replica racecar crowns the entrance to brick **Scandic Kiannon Kouhut** (☎ 08-710 770; www.scandichotels.fi; Jalonkatu 1; s/d €83/103; P 💻 ♿ wi-fi), the best hotel in the area, with an adjacent spa complex. Nearby, on the shore of scenic Kiantajärvi is the **tourist office** (☎ 08-6155 5545; www.suomussalmi .fi; Jalonkaarre 5).

Near Suomussalmi was some of the bitterest fighting of the Winter War, along the Raate Rd. Rusted bits of ordnance commemorate it, as does **Raatteen Portti exhibition** (☎ 08-6155 5545; adult/child €7/4; ☻ daily mid-May–Sep) 20km east of town. Near it, the moving **Avara Syli** monument is endowed with 105 bells, one for each day of the war, and surrounded by a field of stones, one for each dead soldier.

Thirty kilometres north of Suomussalmi, by the main road to Kuusamo, another unearthly field confronts travellers; a thousand scarecrowlike figures with heads of peat and straw stand like mute witnesses to the triumphs and failures of humanity and also, inevitably, recall the war dead. A creation of local choreographer Reijo Kela, they are given a biannual change of look by locals donating clothes.

Hossa

From Suomussalmi Kirkko, 9km northeast of the main settlement, a **minibus** (☎ 040-015 3184) leaves at 3.10pm Monday to Friday (connecting with the 1.10pm bus from Kajaani) to Hossa (€16.30, 1½ hours). This remote, strung-out settlement is wonderfully set-up for fishing, hiking, snowmobiling and cross-country skiing: there are many marked trails and numerous lakes. A **reindeer park** (Poropuisto; ☎ 040-755 9834; www.hossa.fi/poropuisto; ☻ 9am-9pm mid-Jun–Sep) offers the opportunity to get to know these gentle antlered beasts.

The settlement's centre is the **Luontokeskus** (☎ 020-564 6041; hossa@metsa.fi; Jatkonsalmentie 6; ☻ daily mid-Feb–Oct), a lakeside nature centre arranging fishing permits (there's a machine outside too) and hiring equipment including tackle, boats and skis. It also deals with bookings for the network of trail huts scattered around the area and runs the adjacent **Karhunkainalo** (tent site €14 plus per person €4; ☻ mid-Feb–Oct), which has tent pitches and cottages.

Four kilometres south, **Hossan Lomakeskus** (☎ 08-732322; www.hossanlomakeskus.com; Hossantie 278; s/d/cabin €48/59/60; P) has lake frontage and a selection of cabins, as well as a long hotel, whose rooms have decent bathrooms and exterior doors. Sauna and breakfast are included, and there's a bar and mediocre restaurant. Adjacent **Erä-Hossa** (☎ 050-016 6377; www.era-hossa.fi; Hossantie 278; tent site €13, plus per person €1, cabins €30-70; P) has cabins, a shop, and tent and caravan sites.

From Hossa, a morning **minibus** (☎ 040 089 0084) runs the 75km north to Kuusamo (€13.50, 1½ hours) Monday to Friday in summer.

Ruka Safaris (☎ 852 1610; www.rukasafaris.fi; Ruka-rinteentie 1, Ruka) At the hairpin on the way up to Ruka fell. Wide range of summer and winter activities including reindeer safaris, fishing, canoeing, and have their own accommodation and restaurant.

Rukapalvelu (☎ 860 8600; www.rukapalvelu.fi; Ruka-tunturintie 18, Ruka) Comprehensive range from husky and snowmobile safaris to winter and summer fishing, canoeing, and rapids-floating. It also arranges trips to Russia to see breathtakingly pretty Karelian villages (visa required).

Sleeping

Numerous holiday cottages dot the area. Contact the tourist office, **FinFun** (☎ 020-370 021; www.finfun.fi), which has a portfolio of hundreds, or **ProLoma** (☎ 020-792 9700; www.prol oma.fi).

ourpick Kuusamon Kansanopisto (☎ 050-444 1157; kuusamon.kansanopisto@koillismaa.fi; Kitkantie 35; s/d €30/50, with shared shower €25/42; P) Around the corner from the bus station, this folk high school of-fers great budget accommodation in comfort-

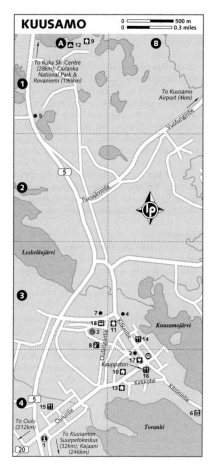

Holiday Club Kuusamon Tropiikki (☎ 020-123 4906; www.holidayclub.fi; Kylpyläntie; s/d €107/117; P 💻 🐾 wi-fi) Six clicks north of Kuusamo centre is a modern hotel and spa complex in a forest setting. Rooms are comfortable (superiors have a lot more space and a couple of extras); and the spa is a plastic tropical wonderland with a 45m water slide and numerous facilities: nonguests can use it for a small fee. The hotel also has holiday cottages and a camp site, Rantatropiiki Camping, and rents mountain bikes to guests.

Sokos Hotel Kuusamo (☎ 020-123 4693; www .sokoshotels.fi; Kirkkotie 23; s/d €103/123, summer r €93; P 💻 🐾 wi-fi) Large and central, this low-slung hotel backs on to parkland running down to the lake. The rooms are very standard, with no-nonsense Finnish wood floors and white sheets. The restaurant has a wide selection of steaks and tapas, and a €7.90 lunch.

Eating & Drinking
Choices are limited, but there's always the kauppatori's grilli or cheap Chinese, kebabs or pizza (locals reckon Ampan Pizza Bar is the best) along Kitkantie.

Martina (☎ 852 2051; Ouluntie 3; pizzas €9-14, grills €15-26; 🕙 11am-10pm Mon-Thu, 11am-midnight Fri & Sat, noon-10pm Sun) Warm and welcoming, this chain

able spacious rooms with ensuites (some share shower facilities) in a variety of buildings. There are kitchen and laundry facilities; the bad news is that you have to arrive during office hours (8am to 3.45pm Monday to Friday). There's still some availability during term-time.

Hotelli Kuusanka (☎ 852 2240; hotellikuusanka .kuusamo@co.inet.fi; Ouluntie 2; s/d €59/77; P ♿) A cordial welcome is guaranteed at this sweet main-street hotel, whose blue-shaded rooms are so clean you can smell it. They vary widely in size and sleep up to four; some have tables, chairs and a sofa, so if it's not busy ask for one with extra space. Good breakfast is included and there's a little gym, but the sauna costs extra. It also has big, well-equipped cottages 6km up the Ruka road.

place has a huge menu for the whole family, with a range of pizzas and pastas as well as fish, salad buffet, and grilled chicken, meat and vegetables. You can create your own dish: main course, accompaniment and sauce, a happy thing if you've tired of the same old combinations. In the same place is Wanha Mestari, the reliable town boozer.

Baari Martai (☎ 851 4199; Airotie; lunch €7-9; ☽ 10am-3pm Mon-Fri) In an unattractive industrial area not far from the tourist office, this place keeps lunching workers happy with excellent, very authentic hot dishes. Sautéed reindeer and fried vendace were the choices the day we last dropped in; there's also a plate for kids.

Herkkusuu (☎ 852 1424; Ouluntie 3; ☽ 7am-6pm Mon-Fri, 8am-3pm Sat) This early opening cafe next to the kauppatori has tasty breads and pastries, and tempts people later in the day with a lunchtime salad bar and an ice-cream parlour.

Near the tourist office are several giant supermarkets where you can stock up on trekking supplies.

Kuukettu (Kitkantie 1; ☽ 6pm-late Wed-Sun) is one of a couple of central nightclubs, kicks on late, and has the liveliest dance floor in town.

Getting There & Away

Finnair hits Kuusamo airport, 6km northeast of the town centre, from Helsinki. Buses meet flights (€7 to Kuusamo, €10 to Ruka), leaving Kuusamo bus station just over an hour before departure. Call ☎ 010-084 200 for taxis.

Buses run daily from Kajaani (€38.10, 3½ hours), Oulu (€35.70, three hours) and Rovaniemi (€30.20, three hours). Several daily services run to Ruka (€5.90, 30 minutes).

RUKA
☎ 08

Ruka is one of Finland's major ski centres and a useful base for hiking the Karhunkierros. The centre buzzes during the winter, but has plenty to offer in summer, with enough services open and people about that it doesn't feel spooky. There's good bird-watching here, and numerous other opportunities for activities at any time of year. In summer you can nab excellent accommodation deals too.

Orientation & Information

The Ruka turn-off is 26km north of Kuusamo. Two kilometres down this road,

you can turn right to the small centre of Itä Ruka (another 3km), or continue up the hill to the main centre of the resort, where most facilities are.

Ruka Info (☎ 860 0200; www.ruka.fi; ☽ 10am-6pm, to 8pm late Jun-Sep & during ski season) is in the Kumpare building in the main village square and offers tourist information and accommodation booking. In the same building is pricey internet access (€1 per 10 minutes), a national parks information point, childcare, pool table, ski rental shops, a supermarket, a gym and more.

If you stay in Ruka in summer, you get a 'Summer Wristband', which gets you plenty of decent discounts on meals and activities in the area. If you're not staying, it costs €5.

Activities

See p295 for details of tour operators in Ruka and Kuusamo. You can rent canoes, mountain bikes and fishing equipment at RukaPalvelu (p296), among other places.

SKIING

Busy **Ruka fell** (www.ruka.fi) boasts 31 downhill ski slopes, dedicated snowboard areas, a vertical drop of 201m and a longest run of 1300m, as well as the bonus of well over 200 skiable days per year: the season normally runs from mid-October to early June. Ruka also boasts cross-country trails totalling an impressive 500km.

A single/day/week lift pass costs €5/33/165; rates are slightly lower in the shoulder seasons. All types of rental and instruction are available.

Sleeping

Ruka's very busy in winter and it can be difficult to find a reasonably priced bed. In summer, rooms are great value.

There are numerous apartments available in Ruka itself, and cottages in the surrounding area. See p296 for agencies. For apartments and chalets also try **Ruka-ko** (☎ 866 0088; www.ruka-ko.fi; Postibaari) at the resort. There are links for cabin and cottage bookings on www.ruka.fi.

There are places for caravans in Itä Ruka, with power points and toilets. It's run by **Rukakeskus** (☎ 860 0200; ☽ May-Sep).

Viipus Camping (☎ 868 1213; Kemijärventie; tent site €12, 2–4-person cabins €27-57; ☽ Jun–mid-Sep) This is a very small rustic camping ground at

Viipusjärvi, several kilometres north of Ruka. It's a good spot in summer, with camp sites, a few cabins, a shop, sauna, boats for hire and salmon fishing.

Willi's West (☎ 868 1712; www.williswest.com; Rukanriutta 13; apt summer €49, winter €59-89; **P**) At the Ruka turn-off on the main road is this friendly motel-style set-up offering good value. Rooms are small apartments sleeping up to five, and have spacious bathroom and a small, equipped kitchen. There's not a lot of privacy, but it's a steal at the price. The owner will take groups of walkers to the Karhunkierros trailheads.

RukaSuites (☎ 860 0225; www.ski-inn.fi; apt weekend/weeknight May-Aug €75/55, Sep-Oct €85/75, apt Nov-Apr €100-450; **P**) On the main Ruka square, these apartments offer top summer value. They sleep four, and have full facilities including equipped kitchen, sauna and laundry. A few larger apartments sleep an extra two. Winter bookings must be for two nights or more; in summer you pay an extra €20 if you stay only one night. Save a €12 'service fee' by booking online.

Hotel Rantasipi Rukahovi (☎ 85910; www.restel.fi; Rukatunturientie 16; r €104-172, summer r €83; **P** **▯** wi-fi) Right by the major slopes in the centre of town, this huge complex aims to please everyone from conferencing execs to snowball-lobbing families, and largely succeeds, thanks to plenty of facilities and a wide variety of rooms, from standard Nordic pads to more upmarket beds in the new extension, and capacious duplex apartments. Its restaurant, bars and nightclub are well patronised in the cold season.

ourpick Royal Hotel Ruka (☎ 868 6000; www.royal ruka.fi; s/d €170/190, r Aug-Oct €80; ☻ Aug-Apr; **P**) Down at the foot of the fell at the turn-off to Rukajärvi, this small and intimate hotel looks like a children's fort to be populated with toy soldiers. It's the most luxurious accommodation choice in the Kuusamo area; service is excellent here, and the classy restaurant offers delicacies like roast hare. It's closed in early summer, and even in August you should call ahead to book.

Eating & Drinking

Piste (☎ 860 0360; mains €12-27; ☻ 11am-midnight) At the base of the lifts on Ruka's main square, this cavernous wooden hall has several attractive dining areas and good service. There's a pleasing range of dishes, all generously por-

tioned, ranging from burgers and fried fish to weightier mixed grills and more delicate offerings such as arctic char cooked on hot stones with barley risotto, or house snails.

Riipisen Riistaravintola (☎ 868 1219; most mains €14-40; ☻ 1-9pm Tue-Sat) At the Kelo ski-lift area, a five-minute walk from Ruka square, this friendly spot specialises in game dishes, and you'll find Rudolf, Bullwinkle and, yes, poor Yogi (€60) on the menu here in various guises, depending on availability and season. Ptarmigan and capercaillie in cream sauce will get bird-lovers twitching too.

Kalakeidas (☎ 868 1800; Rukatunturintie 2; mains €15-30; ☻ 5-11pm Sep-Apr) In a kota-style building nearby, this aquatic-oriented restaurant does a great fish soup and other temptations like pike fillet with blue cheese. There are various shared fish platters that should be ordered the day before. All the fish is locally caught, and they can take you out on fishing trips too.

Zone (☎ 860 8600; ☻ noon-4am) This central bar's big glassed-in terrace packs out at night in the ski season and has its own fast-food kiosk. There's karaoke nightly, regular live music, and a general vibe of pissed-up goodwill.

Getting There & Away

Ruka is 30km north of Kuusamo on Rd 5 and served by bus a few times daily (€5.90, 30 minutes). Buses run between Kuusamo airport and Ruka, and during the ski season there's a shuttle bus between Ruka and Kuusamo, stopping at major hotels.

KARHUNKIERROS TREK & OULANKA NATIONAL PARK

The 80km Karhunkierros (Bear's Ring), one of the oldest and best-established trekking routes in Finland, offers up some of the country's most breathtaking scenery. It is extremely popular during the *ruska* period (during autumn), but it can be walked practically anytime between late May and October.

Despite the name, it's not a circuit, rather a point-to-point walk. A summer bus runs from Kuusamo and Ruka to the main northern trailheads. There are four possible starting points: the northern access point is from Hautajärvi visitor centre on the road to Salla; further south on Rd 950 is the Ristikallio parking area; in the south you can start the walk at Ruka ski resort; or further northeast at Juuma village. The best section of the trail runs from Ristikallio to Juuma. Also at Juuma there's a short but demanding marked loop trail, the 12km Little Bear's Ring (p303).

Most people choose to walk north to south for transport connection reasons.

Information

The 1:50,000 *Rukatunturi-Oulanka* map is useful for treks of any length. It costs €19

and is sold at both park visitor centres and the Kuusamo and Ruka tourist offices. That said, the trail is so well signposted that you can easily make do with the free map.

If you need gear, RukaPalvelu in Ruka rent tents, packs, and other hiking equipment.

Hautajärvi Visitor Centre (☎ 020-564 6870; www .outdoors.fi; ⏰ 10am-4pm Mar-Jun, 9am-5pm Jun–

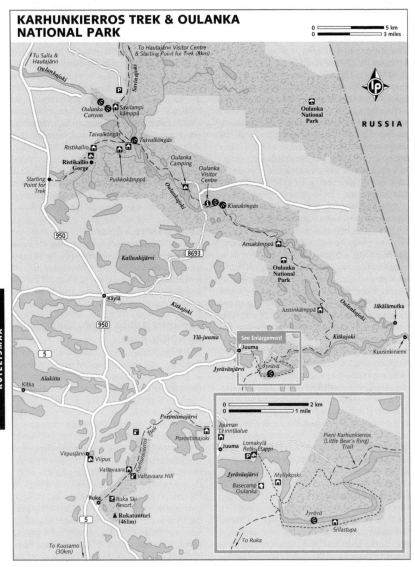

KARHUNKIERROS TREK & OULANKA NATIONAL PARK

mid-Aug, 10am-5pm mid-Aug–Sep, 10am-4pm Mon-Fri Oct) Helpful, at the northern trailhead, right on the Arctic Circle on the Kuusamo to Salla road 1km north of Hautajärvi village. There's a cafe and wildlife exhibition.

Oulanka Visitor Centre (☎ 020-564 6850; www .outdoors.fi; Liikasenvaarantie 132; ✆ 10am-4pm Oct-Apr, 10am-6pm May-Sep) In the middle of Oulanka National Park, accessible along a partly sealed road from Käylä on Rd 950. Nature exhibits, cafe, slide show, trekking supplies, maps and fishing licences. Easy walking trails take you along the Oulankajoki to the Kiutaköngäs rapids.

Trekking

The track's well marked. If you're just on a day trip, you could do it in light shoes on dry summer days, but for the full route, you'll need proper hiking boots, particularly for the Juuma to Ruka section. Prior to mid-June the ground is too soggy to make hiking enjoyable. Even if you don't intend to walk the whole route, a day walk can take you from Ristikallio to Oulanka Canyon and back, for example. It's also possible to drive to within 1km of Oulanka Canyon along a signposted dirt road about 12km north of Ristikallio.

The following description is divided into easy days, but many people do the route to Juuma in two.

DAY ONE

Start at the parking area at Ristikallio; you'll soon enter the national park. There's a wilderness hut (of use if you're coming the other way) at Ristikallio. Less than an hour further gets you to Puikkokämppä hut at a small lake. Continue another kilometre and a bit past the lake to Taivalköngäs (near the wilderness hut of the same name), with two sets of rapids and three suspension bridges.

Another starting point is frther north at the Hautajärvi visitor centre – this adds an extra 9km to the hike. The landscape is unimpressive until the path reaches the Savinajoki. The deep Oulanka Canyon is a highlight of this part of the trek. A wilderness hut is at the Oulanka riverfront near Savilampi, a lake 15km south of Hautajärvi. The distance from Savilampi to Taivalköngäs – where you'll join the Ristikallio trail – is 4km.

DAY TWO

The first leg is an 8km trek from Taivalköngäs through typical forest scenery enlivened by beautiful lakes. After 4.2km, you can camp at Lake Runsulampi; there's dry wood available. About 4km further east, there's Oulanka Camping; another 1.5km brings you to the Oulanka Visitor Centre and its welcome cafe. The rugged cliffs and muscular waters of the Kiutaköngäs rapids are a short way further on. Then on to Ansakämppä cabin by early evening, or even Jussinkämppä wilderness hut on Kulmakkajärvi.

DAY THREE

Tougher than the preceding days. A hike through ridges and forests takes you to the Kitkajoki in another deep gorge. After following the river, choose between several routes, either walking directly to Juuma or crossing the river at Myllykoski to see the mighty Jyrävä waterfall (3km from Juuma) with an elevation of 12m. There's the Siilastupa hut at Jyrävä, and Basecamp lodge on the trail just outside Juuma.

Ruka Extension

Juuma is a convenient end to the trek, but you can also walk 24km further to Ruka, which has a big choice of accommodation and better road connections to Kuusamo. This is much more strenuous than the previous three days, with many ascents and descents. There is one wilderness hut, Porontimajoki (often full), and several lean-to shelters.

Sleeping

WILDERNESS HUTS

There is a good network of huts along the Karhunkierros. All are pretty similar and tend to be crowded in high season. Although tradition says there's always room for the last-to-arrive, a tent's handy, as someone often ends up sleeping outside. Dry firewood is generally available, and there's a gas cooker in most, but carry a lightweight mattress. From north to south, your options are as follows:

Savilampi On the Hautajärvi route, about 15km in, this hut sleeps 10.

Ristikallio 5km east of the main road, has a nice lakeside location. Accommodates 10 and has dry firewood.

Puikkokämppä 2.5km further east, a basic lakeside hut sleeping 10 people.

Taivalköngäs 1.3km further east, accommodates 15 on two floors.

Ansakämppä 6.5km east from the visitor centre, sleeps 20. **Jussinkämppä** 9km further on, sleeps 20.

Siilastupa 4km from Juuma opposite the Jyrävä waterfall, sleeps 12. Often full. Once a fishing lodge for a Finnish general.

Porontimajoki 8km south of Juuma, accommodates eight in two huts. Popular last- or first-night stop, and often full.

CAMPING

Oulanka Camping (☎ 020-564 6855; www.outdoors.fi; Liikasenvaarantie 137; 1/extra person tent €5/10, 4-person cabins €40; ☻ Jun-Aug) The trail runs right through this place, 1.5km from the visitor centre. It rents canoes and rowing boats to use on the Oulankajoki, and has a kiosk and sauna.

There are a few camping grounds in Juuma; see opposite.

LODGE

Basecamp Oulanka (☎ 040-050 9741; www.basecamp oulanka.fi; Myllykoskentie 30; s/d/tw €89/105/115, summer €55/80/90; **P**) This excellent wilderness lodge is just the place to rest your weary legs, right on the trail itself near Myllykoski, about 1km from Juuma (but 4.5km by car). The snug rustic rooms smell of pine, have a roof-space that can sleep extra bodies, and a charming balcony looking over the forest. There's a convivial bar and restaurant (lunch always on, dinner by arrangement), a sauna and even a Jacuzzi. Friendly staff organise all sorts of daily activities; rafting, fishing, husky-sledding and snowshoe-walking among others. Off-season, it's worth asking about discounted rates.

Getting There & Away

From June to early August, an early morning bus runs from Kuusamo to Ruka, Juuma, Ristikallio and Hautajärvi to Salla from Monday to Friday, and returns, arriving back in Kuusamo at 2pm. There's a connection from Käylä to the Oulanka Visitor Centre. Outside these dates, the bus runs a little later, doesn't go to Juuma, but still passes Ristikallio and Hautajärvi. There are no buses at weekends.

A **taxi** (☎ 868 1222) from Ruka can be a good option if shared between three or four people; it costs €35 to Juuma, and about €60 to Hautajärvi.

RIVER ROUTES AROUND KUUSAMO

The Oulankajoki and Kitkajoki, that meet almost at the Russian border, offer wonderful canoeing opportunities in protected wilderness areas. You can do these trips as organised adventures, or hire canoes or kayaks from operators, who can also arrange transport at either end. Most operators are based in

Kuusamo or Ruka (p295). Juuma-based operators include:

Basecamp Oulanka (☎ 040-050 9741; www.base campoulanka.fi) Trips on the Kitkajoki for varying levels of expertise. Their Wild Route (€50) lasts two hours and is for 18s and over, as is their weekly 10-hour trip from Käylä to the border zone (€110). Routes for the whole family include the top (€45, five hours) or bottom (€28, three hours) sections. Conservation fee included.

Kitkan Safarit (☎ 040-028 0569; www.kitkansafarit.fi; Juumantie 134) Near the car park, arranges whitewater rafting along the Kitkajoki and Oulankajoki, and rents canoes and kayaks. A short 'family' paddle costs €25 per person, the two-hour 'wild route' is €50, the four-hour complete route is €70, and canoeing on the Oulankajoki is €40.

The Oulankajoki

Shadowing the Karhunkierros much of the way, the Oulankajoki gives you a chance to see mighty canyons from a canoe or kayak. You *must* carry your canoe at least four times. Take a river map.

The first leg, a 20km trip, starts from Rd 950, north of Ristikallio. The first 7km or so is relatively calm paddling, until you reach the impressive Oulanka Canyon. The safe section extends for about 1km, after which you should pull aside and carry your canoe twice past dangerous rapids. You can overnight at Savilampi hut, which is also a popular spot to start.

Some 3km after Savilampi are the Taivalköngäs rapids (carry your canoe) where there's a wilderness hut. The next 8km are quiet and pass a couple of camping grounds before reaching the **Oulanka Visitor Centre** (☎ 020-564 6850; www.outdoors.fi; Liikasenvaarantie 132; ☻ 10am-4pm Oct-Apr, 10am-6pm May-Sep) which has a cafe.

Not far below here are the Kiutaköngäs rapids, where you'll need to carry your canoe again. Below them starts the Lower Oulankajoki stretch, 25km of easy paddling, suitable for beginners. You end up at the Jäkälämutka parking area just short of the Russian border.

The Kitkajoki

The rugged Kitkajoki offers some of the most challenging canoeing and kayaking in Finland. There are plenty of tricky rapids, including the class IV, 900m Aallokkokoski.

The village of **Käylä**, on the Kuusamo to Salla road, is a starting point for both canoeing and whitewater rafting. There's a shop, petrol station and post office. You can also start from Juuma, where it's about a 20km trip to the exit point near the Russian border.

KÄYLÄ TO JUUMA

The first 14km leg of the journey is definitely the easier of the two, suitable for families with children, and does not involve any carrying at all. You start at the Käylänkoski, continue 3km to the easy Kiehtäjänniva, and a further kilometre to the Vähä-Käylänkoski. These are both class I rapids. After a bit more than 1km, there are three class II rapids spaced every 400m or so. A kilometre further, there's the trickiest one, the class III Harjakoski, which is 300m long. The rest of the journey, almost 7km, is mostly lakes. The road bridge between the lakes Ylä and Ala-Juumajärvi marks the end of the trip. It is 1km to Juuma from the bridge.

JUUMA TO THE RUSSIAN BORDER

This 20km journey is one of Finland's most challenging river routes: you should be an expert paddler, and you *must* carry your canoe at least once – around the 12m, class VI Jyrävä waterfall. Inspect the tricky rapids before you let go and ask for local advice. There's a minimum age of 18 to canoe this route.

The thrill starts just 300m after Juuma, with the class II Niskakoski. From here on, there is only 1km of quiet water. Myllykoski, with a water-mill, is a tricky class IV waterfall. Right after Myllykoski, the 900m Aallokkokoski rapids mean quick paddling for quite some time. The Jyrävä waterfall comes right after this long section. Pull aside before Jyrävä, and carry your canoe. You might want to carry it from Myllykoski to well beyond the Jyrävä waterfall, skipping the Aallokkokoski rapids.

After Jyrävä things cool down considerably, although there are some class III rapids. After about 6km, there is a wilderness hut, the Päähkänäkallio. When you meet the Oulankajoki, 7km further downriver, paddle upriver to Jäkälämutka or downriver to Kuusinkiniemi, 100m from the Russian border. At either spot you can access a forest road that'll take you back to civilisation. You must arrange return transport from this point in advance, as traffic is nonexistent.

JUUMA
☎ 08

The village of Juuma is a popular base for Karhunkierros treks and canoeing on the Kitkajoki. It's a convenient place to stock up on supplies

If you have a little time for trekking, take the Pieni Karhunkierros, or **Little Bear's Ring**, a fairly strenuous 12km loop trail, to Myllykoski rapids and Jyrävänjärvi. The trail (leaving from by the Lomakylä cafe) crosses varying terrain, and has several interesting sights, including the 12m Jyrävä waterfall. The walk can be done in five to six hours and takes in some of the best of the entire Bear's Ring. There's a wilderness hut on this trail – Siilastupa (see p301) – and a day hut at Myllykoski. It's well signposted, and busy.

See opposite for details of getting to Juuma.

Sleeping & Eating

Juuma has several summer accommodation choices. Best is Basecamp lodge (see opposite). Cottages can be rented year-round; see Kuusamo (p296) for details.

Lomakylä Retki-Etappi (☎ 863 218; www.retkietappi .fi; Juumantie 134; tent sites €10; cabins from €30; Jun-Sep; P) This place, on the Karhunkierros trail and at the start of the Little Bear's Ring, is a convenient spot to stay. There are several cabins, a couple of them available in winter, and a cafe serving snacks and meals. There's also a sauna and boats and bikes to rent.

Juuman Leirintäalue (☎ 863 212; Riekamontie 1; tent sites €13, cabins €30, cottage €60; P) This place has a lakeside location, sauna, laundry and a cafe that can do evening meals if you book the day before. It also arranges fishing licences and rents boats. It's just north of the centre of Juuma, on the Käylä road.

SYÖTE
☎ 08

Syöte, the southernmost fell in Finland, is a popular winter sports escape from Oulu, with two downhill areas, substantial tracks for cross-country skiing and snowmobiling, and plenty of cabin and cottage accommodation dotted around the area. The Syöte National Park covers several discrete areas of old-growth spruce forest north and east of the ski slopes and is great for skiing or hiking treks, with plenty of wilderness huts and simple shelters. Despite this, it's pretty empty in summer, with many services closed.

Syöte Visitor Centre (☎ 020-564 6550; syote@metsa .fi; Erätie 1; 10am-4pm, until 5pm Jun-Oct, closed Sun Nov-Feb), 2km from Iso-Syöte skiing area, has excellent information on the wildlife and settlement history of the region, with short audiovisual presentations in various languages, as well as information on paths and huts in the national park. Many trails actually start from here, including the short 3.7km Trapper's Trail, with examples of various traps historically used to snare foxes, elk and game birds. The centre also has a cafe open for lunch.

Activities

The fell's twin peaks, Iso-Syöte and Pikku-Syöte ('big' and 'little'), have decent downhill slopes; the network of trails and plentiful huts and shelters among the spruce forest makes the area great for cross-country skiing and, in summer, hiking, with relatively few people on the paths. Much of the track is part of the UKK trail (p293), but there are other circular routes.

Sleeping & Eating

Most of Syöte's cabin and cottage accommodation is managed by **Pudasjärven Matkailu** (☎ 823 400; www.syote.net; Kauppatie 3, Pudasjärvi; ☼ 9am-5pm Mon-Fri), based in Pudasjärvi between Syöte and Oulu. This is a little inconvenient, especially if you're reading this in Syöte, but you can book via the website. The cottages are a bargain in summer.

Hotelli Iso-Syöte (☎ 020-147 6400; www.isosyote.fi; r summer €69, winter €102-138; **P** ▣ & wi-fi) Right atop Iso-Syöte hill, this welcoming hotel has simply staggering views over rolling spruce forests way below. The rooms, too, are spruce and offer great summer value, while the friendly bar-restaurant takes full advantage of the panorama. Opposite are upmarket log cottages (€75 to €120 summer, €123 to €200 winter).

Syötekeskus (☎ 815 4440; www.syotekeskus.fi; s/d €80/110, summer €60/85; ☼ early Aug-early Jun; **P** ▣ & wi-fi) Based on Pikku-Syöte hill, this hotel and activity centre has smart new rooms at a very fair price; €15 extra gets you your own sauna. It also runs cheap cabins by the Kunto Syöte (Syöte Market) on the main road. These have toilet, camp stove, microwave and fridge. You can book them at the supermarket next door but be warned, in summer they operate on a 'leave it clean for the next person' basis, and are often filthy.

Getting There & Away

There's a bus service from Oulu to Syöte (€23, 2¼ hours) leaving once daily Monday to Friday. Another option is to change in Pudasjärvi.

Lapland & Sápmi

Lapland casts a powerful spell, and has an irresistible romance to it that haunts the imagination and memory. While you won't see polar bears or rocky fjords, there is something intangible here that makes it magic.

The midnight sun, the Sámi peoples, the aurora borealis and the wandering reindeer are all components of this, as is good old ho-ho-ho himself, who 'officially' resides here. Another part of the spell is in the awesome latitudes – at Nuorgam, the northernmost point, we have passed Iceland and nearly all of Canada and Alaska.

Lapland has awesome wilderness and is *the* place in Finland to get active; the sense of space, pure air and big skies is what is memorable here, more than the towns.

It's important to pick your time here carefully. In the far north there's no sun for 50 days of the year, and no night for 70 days. June is very muddy, and in July insects can be hard to deal with. If you're here to walk, August is great and in September the autumnal *ruska* colours can be seen. There's thick snow from mid-October to May; December draws charter flights looking for Santa, real reindeer and guaranteed snow, but the best time for skiing and husky safaris is March and April, when you get at least some daylight, and less extreme temperatures.

Lapland's far north is known as Sápmi, home of the Sámi people. Their main communities are around Inari, Utsjoki and Hetta. Rovaniemi is the most popular gateway to the north.

HIGHLIGHTS

- Trekking the lonely wildernesses of **Saariselkä** (p336)
- Dashing through the snow in a sled pulled by a team of huskies in **Muonio** (p323)
- Lapping up the wonderful winter experiences on offer in **Kemi** (p315), where you can sail on an ice-breaker, swim in the frozen-over sea, then spend the night in the ethereally beautiful snow castle
- Discovering the culture of the displaced Skolt Sámi in remote **Sevettijärvi** (p346)
- Panning for gold by the beautiful **Lemmenjoki** and walking in the national park (p343)
- Picnicking with an awesome view at the top of Saana Fell in far northwestern **Kilpisjärvi** (p328)
- Learning about the northern environments at Rovaniemi's superb **Arktikum museum** (p308) and the Sámi at **Siida** (p340) in Inari, their Finnish capital

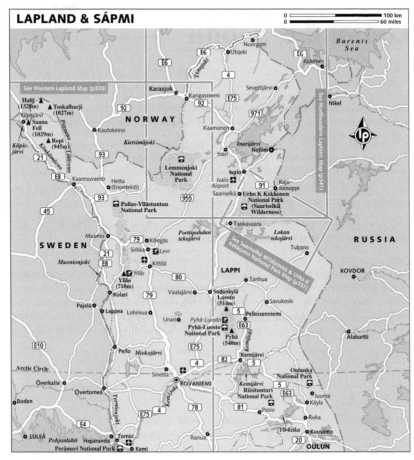

LAPLAND & SÁPMI

History

For information on Sámi and the history of Finland, see the History chapter, p30. See p326 for more detailed information on the Sámi and their culture. Sámi settlements were spread throughout the vast region but during the 1600s, Swedes increased their presence and in 1670 various cult sites and religious objects were destroyed by the Lutheran Church's Gabriel Tuderus (1638–1703). Churches were built throughout Lapland: Sodankylä's is one of the oldest left.

In the following centuries, more Finns filtered into the vast province, adopted reindeer-herding and were assimilated into Sámi communities (or vice versa), especially in southern Lapland.

The Petsamo area, northeast of Inari, was annexed to Finland in 1920 by the Treaty of Tartu; a nickel mine opened in 1937. The Soviet Union attacked the mineral-rich area during the Winter War (1939–40), annexed it in 1944, and has kept it ever since. The Skolt Sámi from Petsamo were resettled in Sevettijärvi, Nellim and Virtaniemi.

The German army's retreat in 1944–45 was a scorched-earth affair; they burned all buildings in their path to hold off pursuit. Only a few churches, villages and houses in Lapland date from the period before WWII.

Activities

Lapland's joy is the outdoors and range of exciting things to do year-round. There's good downhill skiing for almost six months of the year at several spots; Levi (p321) is Finland's most popular resort, while smaller Pyhä-Luosto and Ylläs are more family- than party-oriented. All these spots also have extensive cross-country trails.

Most memorable are sleigh safaris. Pulled by a team of huskies or reindeer, you cross the snowy wilderness, overnighting in log cabins with a relaxing wood sauna and eating meals cooked over a fire. You can organise trips of up to a week or more, or just head out for a jaunt of a couple of hours. Similar trips can be arranged on snowmobiles; Muonio and Saariselkä are particularly good places for these excursions.

Once the snow melts, there are some fabulous multiday treks and shorter walks. The national parks network offers everything from wheelchair-accessible nature trails to demanding wilderness routes for experienced hikers, but there are good walks almost everywhere, including around Kilpisjärvi, in the far northwest, and Sevettijärvi, in the remote northeast.

Walking in Lapland is good from July until mid-October – there's snow cover from November to mid-May, and the ground is mushy from the thaw until late June. It's great in August, when most of the biting insects have disappeared, and beautiful in September, when *ruska* colours paint the landscape in an incredible array of hues.

Lapland's rivers are frisky, and there are several excellent canoeing routes and spots for whitewater rafting. The Ounasjoki (p321) offers perhaps the best paddling. Fishing is popular year-round: ice-fishing is a memorable and sociable experience, and the beautiful Teno Valley (p345) offers superb salmon-fishing.

Major settlements have plenty of tour operators offering all these activities. Rovaniemi, Lapland's capital, is a popular base, but Saariselkä, Levi and Muonio are equally good and are closer to genuine wilderness.

National Parks

Lapland has six national parks, three of which – the country's largest – offer particularly rewarding trekking.

In the northeast, Urho K Kekkonen National Park (p336) covers a huge wilderness area and is one of the country's most popular hiking destinations. Even larger is Lemmenjoki National Park (p343) near Inari, while the

Pallas-Yllästunturi National Park (p325) offers a particularly pleasing forest trek. As they are throughout Finland, Lapland's national parks are administered by Metsähallitus, whose excellent website www.outdoors.fi is full of useful information. Also see the Great Outdoors chapter (p68) for more information on national parks.

Self-Catering Accommodation

There is a huge quantity of self-catering apartments, cottages and cabins throughout the region. Out of season, ski resorts are particularly fertile ground; fully furnished places with their own sauna can be great value in summer.

Local tourist offices often double as booking agents for these accommodation options; see the Information sections of the relevant towns. **Villi Pohjola/Wild North** (☎ 020-564 7647; www.villipohjola.fi), an arm of the Forest and Park Service, has a large selection of cabins available throughout the region.

Language

Three Sámi languages are spoken in the region, and signs in Sámi areas are bilingual. See p327 for more on Sámi languages.

Dangers & Annoyances

From mid-June to early August, Lapland is home to millions of biting insects: at times there are quite literally clouds of them, and during this räkkä season, you'll need heavy-duty repellent. By early August, most squadrons have dispersed.

Parts of Lapland are real wildernesses; always speak to staff at national park centres before attempting unmarked routes.

Driving in Lapland calls for particular caution due to the reindeer (see p65).

Getting Around

Considering the remoteness, bus connections are good, although there may only be one service a day, and none on Sundays. The two main bus operators are **Goldline** (www .goldline.fi) and **Eskelisen Lapinlinjat** (www.eskelisen -lapinlinjat.com); pocket a copy of their timetable leaflets. Buses often double as postal vans; some drivers are experts at lobbing the daily paper into roadside letterboxes from their seat. Remote villages are accessed by shared taxi-bus or not at all. Hitching is possible but slow: patience and insect repellent are the keys.

Hiring a car is a good option, with plenty of choice in Rovaniemi, Kittilä/Levi, and Saariselkä/Ivalo. Petrol stations are sparsely spread, and some are automatic: carry cash.

ROVANIEMI

☎ 016 / pop 58,825

Expanding rapidly on the back of a tourism boom, the 'official' terrestrial residence of Santa Claus is the capital of Finnish Lapland and a more-or-less obligatory northern stop. Its wonderful Arktikum museum is the perfect introduction to the mysteries of these latitudes, and Rovaniemi is a good place to organise activities from. It's also a transport hub, a convenient spot to hire a car, and has some of Lapland's best accommodation.

Thoroughly destroyed by the retreating Wehrmacht in 1944, the town was rebuilt to a plan by Alvar Aalto, with the major streets in the shape of reindeer antlers (no, we couldn't either). Its unattractive buildings are compensated for by its marvellous location on the fast-flowing Kemijoki, spanned by a bridge dubbed the 'Lumberjack's Candle' for its light-topped pylons. More recently, the central square has been named after Lordi, whose triumph in the 2006 Eurovision contest put a smile on Rovaniemi faces.

Though the museum is by far the most impressive sight, the tour buses roll north of town, where everyone's favourite beardie-weirdie has an impressive grotto among an array of tourist shops that straddle the Arctic Circle marker. It's free to visit, if not to photograph, the personable chap.

Information

There are lockers (€2) at both train and bus stations, and a storage counter at the train station.

Etiäinen (☎ 020-564 7820; etiainen@metsa.fi; Koskikatu 44; 8am-4pm Mon-Fri) Information centre for the national parks, with information on hiking and fishing in Lapland. The office sells maps and fishing permits, and books cottages.

Public library (☎ 322 2463; Hallituskatu 9; 11am-7pm Mon-Fri, 11am-5pm Sat) Aalto-designed; has free internet.

Rovaniemen Kem & Valkopesu (☎ 312 340; Valtakatu 26; 9am-5pm Mon-Fri) Laundry, charging per item.

Suomalainen Kirjakauppa (☎ 420 1400; Koskikatu 27) In the Revontuli centre. Sells English-language paperbacks and maps of Lapland.

LAPLAND & SÁPMI

PLANNING AHEAD

Lapland is the coldest part of Finland; winter temperatures regularly fall to -30ºC, and sometimes much lower. Even in summer, bad weather can descend rapidly, so be prepared for all conditions when hiking. Whether you've got the trekking boots or cross-country skis on, it's always a good idea to let someone know where you're going and when you plan to be back.

Tourist Information (☎ 346 270; www.visitrovaniemi.fi; Maakuntakatu 29; 8am-5pm Mon-Fri Sep-May, 8am-6pm Mon-Fri, 10am-4pm Sat & Sun Jun-Aug, also opens some weekends in Sep & Dec) On the square in the middle of town. Source of information for all of Lapland. Free internet.

Sights

ARKTIKUM

With its beautifully designed glass tunnel stretching out to the Ounasjoki, **Arktikum** (☎ 322 3260; www.arktikum.fi; Pohjoisranta 4; adult/student/child/family €12/8/5/25; 9am-7pm mid-Jun–mid-Aug, 10am-6pm daily early Jun, late Aug & Dec, 10am-6pm Tue-Sun Sep-Nov, 10am-6pm Tue-Sun Jan-May) is one of Finland's best museums and well worth the admission fee if you are interested in the north. There are two main exhibitions; one side deals with Lapland, with some information on Sámi culture, including both traditional and modern music, and a variety of costumes. There's a display of canoes, dwellings and fishing materials, as well as a room devoted to the history of Rovaniemi itself. A scale model shows the destruction wrought by the German retreat in 1944.

The highlight, though, is the other side, with a wide-ranging display on the Arctic itself, with superb static and interactive displays focusing on Arctic flora and fauna, as well as on the peoples of Arctic Europe, Asia and North America. The level of information impresses without overwhelming, and the photography is stunning. The museum stresses the importance of a combined response from the Arctic countries to the challenges of global warming and preservation of indigenous culture. There's a research library here if you want to learn more, as well as a good restaurant. There are three daily auditorium shows; it's basically a pretty slide show, so don't stress should you miss it.

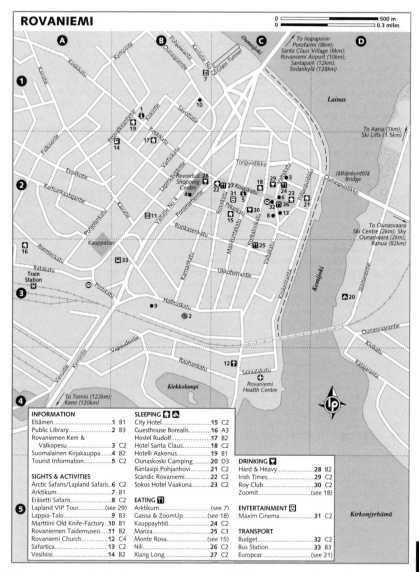

ROVANIEMI

INFORMATION
Etiäinen.....................................**1** B1
Public Library.........................**2** B3
Rovaniemen Kem &
   Valkopesu...........................**3** C2
Suomalainen Kirjakauppa.....**4** B2
Tourist Information................**5** C2

SIGHTS & ACTIVITIES
Arctic Safaris/Lapland Safaris..**6** C2
Arktikum.................................**7** B1
Eräsetti Safaris.......................**8** C2
Lapland VIP Tour..............(see 29)
Lappia-Talo............................**9** B3
Marttiini Old Knife-Factory...**10** B1
Rovaniemen Taidemuseo.....**11** B2
Rovaniemi Church.................**12** C4
Safartica................................**13** C2
Vesihiisi.................................**14** B2

SLEEPING
City Hotel..............................**15** C2
Guesthouse Borealis.............**16** A3
Hostel Rudolf.......................**17** B2
Hotel Santa Claus.................**18** C2
Hotelli Aakenus....................**19** B1
Ounaskoski Camping............**20** D3
Rantasipi Pohjanhovi............**21** C2
Scandic Rovaniemi................**22** C2
Sokos Hotel Vaakuna............**23** C2

EATING
Arktikum.............................(see 7)
Gaissa & ZoomUp............(see 18)
Kauppayhtiö..........................**24** C2
Mariza....................................**25** C3
Monte Rosa......................(see 15)
Nili..**26** C2
Xiang Long............................**27** C2

DRINKING
Hard & Heavy........................**28** B2
Irish Times............................**29** C2
Roy Club...............................**30** C2
ZoomIt.............................(see 18)

ENTERTAINMENT
Maxim Cinema......................**31** C2

TRANSPORT
Budget..................................**32** C2
Bus Station...........................**33** B3
Europcar..........................(see 21)

LAPPIA-TALO

Rovaniemi's **concert hall** (☎ 322 2495; Hallituskatu 11) is one of several buildings in Rovaniemi designed by architect Alvar Aalto (others include the adjacent library and town hall). The hall is used by the local theatre company and the Chamber Orchestra of Lapland for performances.

ROVANIEMEN TAIDEMUSEO

This **gallery** (☎ 322 2822; Lapinkävijäntie 4; adult/child €4/free; ☼ noon-5pm Tue-Sun) has a wide collection of contemporary Finnish art that it rotates in its clean white exhibition space. It's closely affiliated with the University of Lapland and often shows works by young Finnish artists. Admission's free on Saturday.

SANTA CLAUS

My name in Finnish, Joulupukki, actually means 'Christmas goat'. Many old European stories tell of goats, which were sometimes considered holy. A couple of centuries ago I used to wear goat horns, but eventually I changed to the floppy red hat.

I've travelled rather a lot in my time and have seen gorgeous places all over the world. If I recommend one thing about Lapland, it's the wilderness. Get out of the towns, off the roads, and go to the lakeside, the forests, the fells. Just try to listen and smell how it is without a built environment and experience the sounds of pure nature.

What can I say about reindeer? You know Rudi, of course, the guy with the red nose and big horns. No snow, no work is his principle and he heads up the reindeer union – a bit like the EU but global and more powerful. Local people have traditionally eaten reindeer up here. But I have to admit I prefer my reindeer alive.

Are children as good as they used to be? A very good question. I think that basically all children are good. Being good is more of a problem for us grown-ups. Throughout my life I've looked out for three things, the welfare of children, the behaviour of grown-ups, and third, the environment. My own opinion is that the best present to give the coming generation is the environment. It's a big issue up here; a solution to global warming isn't something we're going to get as a present, it's something we have to find as a present for our children. We are not the objects here but the subjects.

What do I want for Christmas? Nice of you to ask! A lot of smiles. Through happy faces I get energy for next Christmas and those to come. Dreams are very important too. One girl asked me 'Will you die one day?' I promised I'd continue as long as children have their dreams. I could also do with a new pair of socks. I'm an old man and need things to keep me warm…

Related to Andy Symington

ROVANIEMI CHURCH

Completed in 1950, this **church** (☎ 335 511; Rauhankatu 79; ⊙ 9am-9pm mid-May–Aug) replaced the one destroyed during WWII. The impressively large fresco behind the altar depicts a Christ figure emerging from Lappish scenery. A work of Lennart Segerstråle, it has two sides, one populated by the faithful, the other by brawling drunkards and ravening wolves.

MARTTIINI OLD KNIFE-FACTORY

This former **factory** (☎ 040-311 0604; www.martiini.fi; Vartiokatu 32; ⊙ 10am-6pm Mon-Fri, 10am-2pm Sat, also noon-4pm Sun mid-Jun–Aug) of Finland's famous knife manufacturer is now a shop open to visitors with a small knife exhibition, and cheaper prices than you can get elsewhere. It's near the Arktikum. They've another shop at Napapiiri.

OUNASVAARA

This long fell across the river to the east of town is a place to get active. In winter, there's a **ski centre** (☎ 369 045; www.ounasvaara.fi), with six main downhill runs, a kids' run, a half-pipe, and a metal toboggan run. There are also three ski-jumps here, plus more than 100km of cross-country tracks around the hill and further afield. You can rent skis here, and there's a ski school. At the top of the ski-lifts is the Sky Ounasvaara hotel.

In summer, one ski-lift and the **toboggan run** (1/3/5 rounds €6/15/20; ⊙ 11am-7pm mid-Jun–mid-Aug) are working if it's not raining. Walkers can take advantage of the cross-country tracks, which are well signposted. You can walk to Napapiiri (12km) as well as other places.

Bus 9 gets you to the bottom of the ski slope from town.

Activities & Tours

Rovaniemi is Lapland's most popular base for winter and summer activities. Though the wilderness you'll explore isn't really remote these days, it offers the convenience of frequent departures and professional, well-oiled trips with multilingual guides.

In summer, things offered by most operators include guided walks and Nordic walks, mountain biking of various difficulties (€54 to €60), river cruises (€22), visits to a reindeer farm (€50 to €60) or huskies (€80), easy whitewater rafting (€72), quad-bike trips (€77), midnight-sun excursions (€95) and trips to Pyhä-Luosto or Santa's grotto. Lapland VIP offers its 'Finnish for a day' trip (€138), which includes woodchopping, firing up the sauna, fishing and more; Safartica offers canoeing on the Ounasjoki estuary (€56) or Lapp wilderness cooking (€94), while Eräsetti, Arctic and Lapland Safaris (see below), which club together in the summer, have a Sámi mythology excursion (€49).

Winter activities are snowmobiling (€90 to €115 for a two- to three-hour trip), snowshoe-walking (€70), reindeer-sledding (€100 to €120), husky-sledding (€120 to €180), cross-country skiing (€50 to €60), or a combination. These can include ice-fishing, a sauna, a shot at seeing the aurora borealis, or an overnight trip to a wilderness cottage (€350 to €450). Longer safaris might take you to the Arctic Ocean or across central Lapland (€300 to €500 per day). All prices are based on two people sharing a snowmobile/sled; you always pay up to 50% more if you want one all to yourself. You need a driving licence to operate a snowmobile.

All trips can be reserved via the tourist office, most hotels or the operators themselves. Recommended operators:

Arctic Safaris/Lapland Safaris (☎ 340 0400, 020-786 8700; www.arcticsafaris.fi, www.laplandsafaris.fi; Koskikatu 6) Recent merger of two of the most reliable and well-established outfits.

Eräsetti Safaris (☎ 362 811; www.erasetti.fi; Valtakatu 31) Experienced operator with another office at Santa's village.

Lapland VIP Tour (☎ 040-054 2868; www.laplandviptour.fi; Valtakatu 33)

Safartica (☎ 311 484; www.safartica.com; Valtakatu 20) Also offers various hunting and fly-fishing trips.

Places to visit animals include **Napapiirin Porofarmi** (☎ 384 150; www.porofarmi.fi; Tamsintie 76), a reindeer farm 8km north of town. **Huskypoint** (☎ 367 7231; www.huskypoint.fi) at Sinettä offers guided kennel visits for €10/5 per adult/child, more if you need transport from Rovaniemi. You can go hiking with huskies in summer and sledding in winter. **Napapiirin Huskypuisto** (☎ 040-824 7503; www.polarspeed.fi) is near Santa's grotto and allows you to meet dogs.

A city **tourist train**, Nätti-Jussi, runs daily on the hour (11am to 5pm June to August) from opposite the City Hotel on a 45-minute jaunt around town. Tickets are €6/4 per adult/child.

Bicycles can be rented from **Arctic Safaris** (Koskikatu 6) and from **Europcar** (Pohjanpuistikko 2) for €20 a day.

Vesihiisi (☎ 322 2592; Nuortenkatu 11; admission €5.50) has an outdoor and indoor pool as well as saunas, with separate times and sections for men and women. It's cheaper in summer.

Festivals & Events

With the Arctic Circle – and Santa Claus – close by, Christmas is a big time of the year and there are plenty of festive activities in December. In March, Rovaniemi hosts the **Ounasvaara Winter Games**, with skiing and ski-jumping competitions. **Jutajaiset** (www.jutajaiset.fi), in late June, is a celebration of Lapland folklore by various youth ensembles.

Sleeping

Several self-catering options lie around the Ounasvaara hill, some only open in winter. Check www.santasport.fi, www.oh.fi (in Finnish) and www.ounasvaaranlakituvat.fi for details.

BUDGET

Ounaskoski Camping (☎ 345 304; Jäämerentie 1; tent sites €14 plus per adult/child €4.50/2.50; ☯ late May–mid-Sep) Just across the elegant bridge from the town centre, this camp site is perfectly situated on the riverbank. There are no cabins, but plenty of grassy tent and van sites, with great perspectives over the Ounaskoski.

Guesthouse Borealis (☎ 342 0130; www.guesthouseborealis.com; Asemieskatu 1; s/d/tr €45/56/77; P ⌨ wi-fi) Cordial hospitality and its proximity to the train station make this family-run spot a winner. The rooms have no frills but are bright and clean; some have a balcony. The airy dining room is the venue for breakfast, which features Finnish porridge; there's also a sauna for a small extra charge. A downstairs apartment (€189) sleeps up to seven. Prices given here are for April to mid-November and rise over winter.

Hostel Rudolf (☎ 321 321; www.rudolf.fi; Koskikatu 41; dm/s/d €44/60/88; P ⌖) Run by Hotel Santa Claus, where you inconveniently have to go to check in, this staffless hostel is Rovaniemi's only one and can fill up fast. Dorms are comfortable, and the private rooms excellent for the price, with spotless bathrooms, solid desks and bedside lamps; there's also a kitchen available. There's a discount for HI members.

Also recommended is **Aaria** (☎ 040-023 8235; www.bbaaria.com; Rannamukka 6; r per person Jan-Nov €40, Dec €60), a red wooden house in a quiet suburban cul-de-sac, and a homelike B&B very handy for the ski-lift. Breakfast is €5 extra.

MIDRANGE & TOP END

Hotelli Aakenus (☎ 342 2051; www.hotelliaakenus.net; Koskikatu 47; s/d €70/80; P 🖳 wi-fi) Offering excellent summer value right from mid-May to the end of August, this friendly, efficient little hotel is a short distance west of the centre and a short stroll from the Arktikum. The bright comfortable rooms vary in furnishing and size, but are all spacious and comfortable. A sauna (with big time-window) and buffet breakfast are included.

City Hotel (☎ 330 0111; www.cityhotel.fi; Pekankatu 9; s/d €103/128; P 🖳 wi-fi) There's something pleasing about this place, cheerfully tucked between the convivial ambience of its own restaurant and bar. Although sizeable, it retains an intimate feel, and the stripy sheets, flatscreen TVs and dark panelled furniture add a classy touch to the decent rooms. Get one streetside in summer: the noise is a fair trade for the cooler temperatures.

Rantasipi Pohjanhovi (☎ 33711; www.rantasipi .fi; Pohjanpuistikko 2; s/d €120/140; P 🖳 🐾 ⬤ wi-fi) Right by the river, this is the historic hotel of Rovaniemi, dating to before the war, though much had to be rebuilt after it. There are two grades of room (as well as lovely suites); the standards are gradually being renovated but have plenty of space and colour, though they can be a little stuffy. The superior rooms, which don't cost too much more, are classier, with dark floorboards, Lapp shaman motifs and flatscreen TV. Summer prices represent real value. The restaurant has live music on Friday and Saturday of the Finnish golden-oldie type: a good chance to see the local dance scene in action.

Scandic Rovaniemi (☎ 460 6000; www.scandichotels .com; Koskikatu 23; s/d €130/145; P 🖳 ⬤ wi-fi) The clean lines, no-nonsense parquet floors and reassuring fabrics make this a solid choice in the centre of Rovaniemi. The helpful service and little extras like free bikes to borrow, and that weird lobby shop selling apples and starched business shirts, add value.

Hotel Santa Claus (☎ 321 321; www.hotelsanta claus.fi; Korkalonkatu 29; s/d €135/162; P 🖳 ⬤ wi-fi) Thankfully this excellent hotel is devoid of sleighbells and 'ho-ho-ho' kitsch. It's right in the heart of town and very upbeat and busy, with helpful staff and a great bar and restaurant. The rooms have all the trimmings and are spacious, with a sofa and good-sized beds; a small supplement gets you a superior room, which is slightly bigger. The bathrooms are stylishly black-marbled. There are also suites with their own sauna and a couple of apartments available.

Sky Ounasvaara (☎ 323 400; www.laplandhotels .com; Ounasvaarantie; r Nov & Jan-Apr €118-150, Dec €174; P 🖳 ⬤ wi-fi) Atop the Ounasvaara fell by the ski runs, this offers great summer value, when just €5 extra gets you a room with a sauna. The rooms have huge windows and are very spacious with a Nordic feel; ask for one with views down the hill. There's also a good restaurant here with fine perspectives.

Also recommended is **Sokos Hotel Vaakuna** (☎ 020-123 4695; www.sokoshotels.fi; Koskikatu 4; r €132-152; P 🖳 wi-fi) with its elegant rooms, big breakfast and free sauna. It can feel empty in summer, but rates are good at this time.

Eating

Mariza (☎ 319 616; Ruokasenkatu 2; lunches €6.20-7.20; 🕙 9.30am-3pm Mon-Fri) A couple of blocks from the centre in untouristed territory, this simple lunch place is a real find, and offers a great buffet of home-cooked Finnish food, including changing-daily hot dishes, soup and salad. Authentic and excellent.

our pick Kauppayhtiö (☎ 342 2422; Valtakatu 24; light meals €5-9; 🕙 10.30am-8pm Mon-Thu, 10.30am-2am Fri & Sat) Rovaniemi's most personable cafe, this is an oddball collection of retro curios with a coffee and gasoline theme and colourful plastic tables. All the knick-knacks are purportedly for sale here, but it's the espresso machine, outdoor seating, salads, sundaes and bohemian Lapland crowd that keep the place ticking. The coffee is bottomless.

Xiang Long (☎ 319 331; Koskikatu 21; mains €11-17; 🕙 11am-10pm Mon-Fri, noon-10pm Sat & Sun) This main-street Chinese is family-run and a level above your typical Finnish example of the genre. Friendly service, tasty steamed prawn dim sum, a salad bar and several reindeer dishes, including one served on a sizzling platter, are the highlights, and the lunch buffet (€8.40, Monday to Friday) is great value.

Monte Rosa (☎ 330 0111; Pekankatu 9; most mains €12-20; 🕙 food 11am-10.30pm Mon-Fri, 1-10.30pm Sat & Sun) Attached to the City Hotel, this goes for the romance vote with a low candlelit interior and chummy booth seating. Most of the dishes are Finnish, with a pinch of oregano or sprinkling of pine nuts as a nod to Italy, and very tasty they are too. The house salad comes with a slab of salmon and sliced smoked reindeer, while main courses are aromatic and generously sized. They also do fajitas and pizzas.

Arktikum (☎ 322 3263; Pohjoisranta 4; mains €14-20; ☺ 10am-4pm, to 6pm mid-Jun–mid-Aug) The Arktikum museum's pleasant restaurant is a fine place for a decent lunch to break your visit. The short à la carte menu has tasty local dishes, while the lunch (€8.50, 11am to 1pm Monday to Friday) gives you tasty soup and a cold buffet, with an optional hot dish for a little extra.

Nili (☎ 040-036 9669; www.nili.fi; Valtakatu 20; mains €15-26; ☺ 5-10.30pm Mon-Sat) Evoking a Lapland atmosphere with reindeer skins, Sámi music and cosy wooden cladding, this main-street restaurant has no problem pulling in the tourist crowd. Reindeer features heavily on the menu, but whitefish, char and salmon argue a fishy case too. The dishes are well presented and the service good, but the quality isn't quite there to make it a classic, and the portions aren't quite big enough for it to be a local favourite. Nevertheless, a sound option.

Gaissa (☎ 321 321; mains €19-26; ☺ 5.30-11pm Mon-Sat, also Sun Dec & Jan) The upstairs restaurant of the Hotel Santa Claus is split into two attractive areas. Elegant Gaissa has a short menu aimed at visitors and served from a semi-open kitchen. Service is willing but error-strewn; the dishes are petite and reindeer-heavy but feature some great creations, such as spot-on reindeer rillettes and slow-roasted lamb that falls off the bone. Adjoining it is ZoomUp, a bar with salads, pastas, steaks, ribs (€13 to €19) and snacks like potato wedges, in a more casual atmosphere aimed at pulling a local crowd.

Drinking & Entertainment

Excluding ski resorts, Rovaniemi is the only place north of Oulu with a half-decent nightlife. There's often a winter bar built as part of the Christmas festivities, in recent years an igloo made of river ice.

ZoomIt (☎ 321 321; Koskikatu; ☺ 11am-11pm, later at weekends) Large, light, modern ZoomIt is a popular, buzzy central bar and cafe, a good place for a drink or coffee while you scope out Rovaniemi. Right in the heart of town, its terrace is the spot to be on a sunny afternoon and its spacious interior gives room to stretch out with a book if it's raining.

Irish Times (☎ 319 925; Valtakatu 33; ☺ 2pm-3am or later) A convivial Irish bar with a distinctly Finnish flavour, this is a fine choice for an animated night of pubbing. It has an excellent heated terrace at the back, and regular live music and karaoke, while the downstairs bar has pool tables. There's a snug, friendly feel about the whole set-up. There's a cover charge at weekends, when it's at its best.

Hard & Heavy (☎ 050-447 3543; Koskikatu 25; ☺ 6pm-2am) The band Lordi cashed in on their Eurovision success by opening a 'horror-rock-taurant'. The food's pretty dire, but it's worth visiting the downstairs bar for its extravagant bat-and-belfry decor and heavy tunes on the sound system.

Roy Club (☎ 313 705; Maakuntakatu 24; ☺ 9pm-4am) This friendly bar has a sedate, comfortable top half with relaxing vine stencils, cosy seating, a very cheap happy hour until 1am nightly, and well-attended Monday karaoke. There's also a downstairs nightclub that gets cheerily boisterous with students and goes late.

Maxim (☎ 060-000 7007; www.finnkino.fi; Koskikatu 17) Rovaniemi's twin-screen cinema is in the Sampokeskus shopping centre.

Shopping

Sámi handicrafts made from reindeer skin and horn, or birch, are popular souvenirs; colourful Sámi hats, mittens and shoes are also top sellers.

The widest selection of souvenirs can be found in shops at Napapiiri (p314), where you'll also find branches of Marttiini knife shop, Marimekko and Taigakoru, a Lapland jeweller.

Getting There & Away
AIR

Rovaniemi's airport is a major winter destination for charter flights from all over Europe and it's the 'official airport of Santa Claus' – does he hangar his sleigh here? Finnair flies daily from Helsinki and Oulu. The budget carrier Blue1 also flies to Helsinki.

BUS

Rovaniemi is Lapland's main transport hub. Frequent express buses go south to Kemi (€19.20, two hours) and Oulu (€38.40, 3½ hours), and there are night buses to Helsinki (€113.80, 12½ hours). Daily connections serve just about everywhere else in Lapland: see under each town for details. Some buses head on north into Norway.

LAPLAND & SÁPMI

TRAIN

The train between Helsinki and Rovaniemi (€70 to €75, 10 to 12 hours) is quicker, cheaper and more commodious than the bus. There are three daily direct services (via Oulu), including overnight services (high-season total prices from €92 in a berth, up to €179 in a smart modern cabin with bathroom) with car transport and other connection possibilities. There's one train daily to Kemijärvi, further northeast (€13.80, 1½ hours).

Getting Around

Rovaniemi airport is 10km northeast of the town centre. Buses meet each arriving flight (€5, 15 minutes). Airport buses leave the bus station an hour before departures, picking up at hotels in the centre. Shared airport taxis cost €9: book them on ☎ 362 222 a day before departure.

In Rovaniemi, call ☎ 106 410 for a cab. A trip on a local bus costs €2.70.

Major car-rental agencies have offices in the centre and at the airport. Helpful **Budget** (☎ 020-746 6620; www.budget.fi; Koskikatu 9) is beside the post office, and **Europcar** (☎ 040-306 2870; www.europcar.fi; Pohjanpuistikko 2) at the Rantasipi Pohjanhovi hotel.

AROUND ROVANIEMI
Napapiiri & Santa Claus Village

The southernmost line at which the sun doesn't set at least one day a year, the Arctic Circle, is called **Napapiiri** in Finland and crosses the Sodankylä road about 8km north of Rovaniemi (although the Arctic Circle can actually shift several metres daily). Though the Arctic Circle can be crossed by road at several points in Lapland, the **Arctic Circle marker** is here, conveniently painted on the roadside – and built right on top of it is the 'official' **Santa Claus Village** (www.santaclausvillage.info; admission free; ☼ 10am-5pm Sep-May, 9am-6pm early Jun & late Aug, 9am-7pm mid-Jun–mid-Aug). There's a mixture of humdrum souvenir stands and classier shops, and it's just about the best spot to buy Sámi handicrafts if you're not heading further north. Tour groups have great fun crossing the line painted on the asphalt in order to be awarded their Arctic Circle certificates (€4.20).

Here too is **Santa Claus Post Office** (☎ 020-452 3120; www.santaclaus.posti.fi; FIN-96930 Arctic Circle), which receives nearly three-quarters of a million letters each year from children all over the world (with kids from the UK, Italy, Poland, Finland

and France the biggest correspondents). Your postcard sent from here will bear an official Santa stamp, and you can arrange to have it delivered at Christmastime. For €6, you can get Santa to send a Christmas card to you.

But the big attraction is, of course, **Santa** himself, who sees visitors year-round in a rather impressive new **grotto** (☎ 020-799 999; www.santaclauslive.com; admission free; ☼ 9am-6pm Jun-Aug, 10am-5pm Sep-May), where a huge clock mechanism (it slows the earth's rotation so that Santa can visit the whole world's children on Christmas night) eerily surrounds those queuing for an audience. The portly saint is quite a linguist, and an old hand at chatting with kids and adults alike. A private chat with the man is absolutely free, but you can't photograph the moment…and official photos of your visit start at an outrageous €25.

Other things at the complex are Santamus, the 'Arctic Circle Experience', a 20-minute immersion (€7) into Lapp 'culture' with a tepee interior, nature sounds and a hot berry juice; a husky park and varying Christmassy exhibitions in the Christmas House. There's also a cafe serving salmon smoked over a traditional fire and an office of Eräsetti Safaris.

Napapiiri is 8km north of Rovaniemi on the Sodankylä road. Bus 8 heads there from the train station, passing through the centre (adult/child €6.40/3.60 return).

Santapark

This Christmas-theme **amusement park** (016-333 0000; www.santapark.com; adult/child €25/20; ☼ 10am-6pm Tue-Sun late Nov–mid-Jan, 10am-4pm Easter holidays & Tue-Sat Midsummer–mid-Aug) is built inside a cavern in the mountain and features an army of elves baking gingerbread, a magic sleigh ride, a Christmas carousel, an ice-bar, a theatre, a restaurant and, of course, Santa Claus himself. The most intriguing section is the gallery of ice sculpture, though it costs an extra €10 per person. It's great fun for kids in winter but lacks a bit of atmosphere in the summer season.

Bus 8 heads on from Napapiiri to here (same fare from town, adult/child €2.90/1.50 to go from one to the other).

RANUA
☎ 016 / pop 4512

This small town is 82km south of Rovaniemi on Rd 78 and famous for its excellent **zoo** (Ranuan Eläinpuisto; ☎ 355 1921; www.ranuawildlife.com;

adult/child €12.50/9.50; ⏰ 9am-7pm Jun-Aug, 10am-4pm Sep-May; ♿), which focuses almost entirely on Finnish animals, although there are also polar bears and musk oxen from further north. A boardwalk takes you on a 2.5km circuit past all the creatures, which include minks and stoats, impressive owls and eagles, wild reindeer, elk, a big bear paddock (they hibernate from November to March), lynx and wolverines. Apart from the animals, there's plenty to do for kids, with horse rides, a minikart circuit, pettable domestic animals and little assault courses. Ice-cream stops dot the route, and there's a cafe and lunch restaurant.

In Ranua itself, 3km south of the zoo, **Hotelli Ilveslinna** (☎ 355 1201; www.hotelliilveslinna.fi; Keskustie 10; s/d/f €66/79/130; P wi-fi) makes a good place to hole up, with light, clean rooms that are gradually being renovated. There are interconnecting rooms so you can keep an eye on the kids, and they offer various packages including meals and zoo entry for families. The simple hostel out the back was due to be demolished and replaced by two-person cabins by mid-2009. The closest camp site is 2km south of town.

There are four to six daily buses from Rovaniemi to Ranua (€14.20, 1¼ hours) as well as connections from Kajaani and Oulu.

WESTERN LAPLAND

KEMI
☎ 016 / pop 22,669
Kemi is an industrial town and important deepwater harbour. Although not hugely appealing (in summer only the gem museum and wide waterfront have any sort of siren song), Kemi's home to two of Finland's blockbuster winter attractions: the Arctic ice-breaker *Sampo*, and the Lumilinna (snow castle), complete with ice hotel.

Off the Kemi/Tornio coast, the Perämeri National Park is an archipelago of small islands that's an important conservation area for seals and a richly populated bird habitat. You need a boat (or snowmobile) to explore, but there may be boat trips running out there by the time you read this: ask at the tourist office.

Information
Kemin Matkailu (☎ 259 690; www.kemi.fi; Kauppakatu 16; ⏰ 9am-5pm Mon-Fri) The tourist office. The gemstone gallery also has tourist information.

Public library (☎ 258 207; Marina Takalonkatu 3; ⏰ 11am-8pm Mon-Thu, 11am-6pm Fri, 10am-4pm Sat) At the kauppatori (market square), has free internet access.

Sights
ICE-BREAKER SAMPO
Kemi comes into its own in winter; *Sampo*, a retired ice-breaker built in 1960, runs memorable, though overpriced, excursions. The four-hour cruise includes lunch and ice-swimming in special drysuits – a remarkable experience. The *Sampo* sails at noon on Thursday, Friday and Saturday from late December to mid-April, with several Wednesday departures during busy periods, and costs €225 per person. If you choose to approach and leave the good ship on snowmobiles (with a reindeer visit included), the price is €365. The best time to go is when the ice is thickest, usually in March. Contact **Sampo Tours** (☎ 256 548; www.sampotours.com; Kauppakatu 16), in the same office as tourist information, to book.

Departures are from Ajos Harbour, 11km south of Kemi. The *Sampo* is out to pasture here in summer and open as a **restaurant** (☎ 040-039 7045; mains €11-15; ⏰ 10am-6pm early Jun–mid-Aug) serving OK sandwiches, soups, salads and a lunch buffet in the rather dark interior. You're free to clamber over the decks and explore the ship, but it's not that interesting without the eerie crunching of ice.

LUMILINNA
Of all the marvels under the big sky, few things conjure the fairy-tale romance of a **snow castle** (☎ 259 502; www.snowcastle.net; adult/child €7/3.50; ⏰ 10am-7pm end Jan–mid-Apr), and few can compete with Kemi's. First built in 1996 as a Unicef project, the castle is now one of Lapland's winter highlights and a favoured destination for weddings, honeymoons, or just general marvelling at the weird light and sumptuously realised decoration of the multistoreyed interior.

The castle's constructed over a four-week period, opening at the end of January until mid-April. The design changes every year but always includes an ethereally beautiful chapel (here's hoping the vows last longer than those ice wedding rings), a **snow hotel** (s/d/ste €165/260/310) and a **restaurant** (3-course menus €34-45). Overnighting in the hotel is memorable: the interior temperature is 5°C below, but a woolly sheepskin and sturdy sleeping bag keep you warm(ish) atop the ice bed. Sleep

LAPLAND & SÁPMI

on top of your clothes or your jeans might snap when you put them on the next day. In the morning you can thaw out in the sauna of a nearby hotel.

JALOKIVIGALLERIA

The **Gemstone Gallery** (☎ 259 690; Kauppakatu 29; adult/child €5/2.50; ⏱ 9am-5pm), in an old seaside customs house, has an internationally notable collection of over 3000 beautiful, rare stones and jewellery, including a replica crown based on a design that was meant for the short-lived king of Finland. Sheets in various languages guide you in an offbeat manner around the exhibits, which include replicas of famous diamonds, and a solid dose of Finnish humour.

Festivals & Events

Every May, Kemi hosts **Arctic Comics**, an international comic festival. Check www.kemi .fi/sarjis for details.

Sleeping & Eating

Lumilinna (p315) is the most interesting place to sleep or eat until it melts. Apart from it, there are three hotels in the centre, and a hotel-camp site 4km south.

Hotelli Palomestari (☎ 257 117; www.hotellipalom estari.com; Valtakatu 12; s/d €82/110; P ⏝ wi-fi) This likeable family place is a block south and one west of the train and bus stations, and offers friendly service and decent rooms with trademark Finnish furniture including a desk and sofa. There's also a convivial bar downstairs with outside seating.

Orkidean Kukka (☎ 257 750; Valtakatu 7; mains €8-13; ⏱ 10.30am-8pm Mon-Thu, 10.30am-9pm Fri, 11am-9pm Sat, noon-8pm Sun) The best year-round eating spot in a town not overburdened with options is this attractive Vietnamese, which puts on a lunch buffet as well as tasty and good-value fish, chicken and beef dishes served with a smile.

Drinking

In summer, two lively and picturesque spots for a drink are **Rantamakasiini** (☎ 458 0100), an old wooden building by the water and, opposite, **Katariina** (☎ 040-039 2925), a beer terrace and boat bar. Otherwise, it's the bar at the Palomestari, or **Hemingway's** (⏱ 2pm-late), a popular chain spot whose terrace overlooks, er, the supermarket car park.

If you like your morning coffee with a stunning view, and aren't superstitious by nature, **Näköala Kahvio** (☎ 259 363; Valtakatu 26; ⏱ 9am-3pm

Mon-Fri), a cafe on the 13th floor of the town hall, is the place to be.

Getting There & Away

Kemi-Tornio airport is 6km north, and Finnair/Finncomm has regular Helsinki flights. A trip in a shared airport taxi costs €10.

Buses run to Tornio (€5.90, 45 minutes) more than hourly (fewer at weekends), Rovaniemi (€19.20, two hours) and Oulu (€13.50, 1¾ hours), among other places.

There are trains from Helsinki (€70.50, nine hours), Oulu (€15.60, 1¼ hours) and Rovaniemi (€16.70, 1½ hours).

TORNIO
☎ 016 / pop 22,373

Right on the impressive Tornionjoki, the longest free-flowing river in northern Europe, Tornio is joined to its Swedish counterpart Haparanda (Finnish: Haaparanta) by short bridges. Modest trade exchange flourishes across the border: Ikea lures Finns across, and Marimekko pulls Swedes in the other direction. Tornio smells not of paper mills but of malt, as the Lapin Kulta brewery drifts its aromas across town. Don't forget that Finland is an hour ahead of Sweden.

History

In medieval times this region was the centre for Pirkka tax collectors (working for the king of Sweden). Tornio was founded in 1621, and the entire Tornionjoki valley was administered by Sweden until 1809, when it was incorporated into Finland, under Russian suzerainty. In 1821, Haparanda was founded as a Swedish trading town to replace the loss of Tornio.

Information

Green Line Centre (☎ 432 733; www.visithaparanda tornio.com; ⏱ 8am-8pm Mon-Fri, 10am-6pm Sat & Sun Jun–mid-Aug, 10am-6pm Mon-Fri mid-Aug–May) Acts as the tourist office for both towns. Free internet terminal.
Public library (☎ 432 433; Torikatu 2; ⏱ 11am-6pm Tue-Thu, 11am-3pm Fri-Sun) Free internet.

Sights

Tornio church (☎ 480 042; ⏱ 9am-7pm Mon-Fri, 1.30-7pm Sat & Sun Jun & Jul, 9am-5pm Wed-Fri, 1.30-6pm Sat & Sun Aug) was completed in 1686 and is one of the most beautiful wooden churches in Finland. The unusual and petite 19th-century oniondomed **Orthodox church** (☎ 432 733; ⏱ 10am-6pm

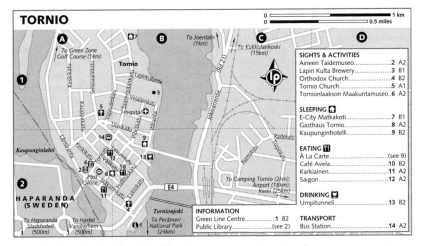

TORNIO

SIGHTS & ACTIVITIES
Aineen Taidemuseo	2 A2
Lapin Kulta Brewery	3 B1
Orthodox Church	4 B2
Tornio Church	5 A1
Tornionlaakson Maakuntamuseo	6 A2

SLEEPING
E-City Matkakoti	7 B1
Gasthaus Tornio	8 A2
Kaupunginhotelli	9 B2

EATING
À La Carte	(see 9)
Café Avela	10 B2
Karkiainen	11 A2
Saigon	12 A2

DRINKING
| Umpitunneli | 13 B2 |

INFORMATION
| Green Line Centre | 1 B2 |
| Public Library | (see 2) |

TRANSPORT
| Bus Station | 14 A2 |

Tue-Sat Jun-Aug), opposite the tourist office, was built by order of Tsar Alexander I of Russia.

Attractive modern **Aineen Taidemuseo** (☎ 432 438; Torikatu 2; adult/child €4/free; ☑ 11am-6pm Tue-Thu, 11am-3pm Fri-Sun) gallery features a private collection of Veli Aine, a local business tycoon. It features Finnish art from the 19th and 20th centuries as well as decent temporary exhibitions, and has a good cafe.

Tornionlaakson Maakuntamuseo (☎ 432 451; Keskikatu 22; adult/child €4/2; ☑ noon-5pm Tue-Fri, 11am-3pm Sat & Sun), the local historical museum, has a collection of interesting old artefacts and costumes, although all displays are labelled in Finnish.

Lapin Kulta Brewery (☎ 020-717 5671; Lapinkullantie 1), founded in 1873, was the original home of the ubiquitous Lappish lager and still produces some. Hour-long free tours of the brewery begin at the front gate at 1pm on Tuesday and Thursday from late June to late August.

Across the border in Haparanda, the main sight is the huge brick water tower built in 1919 and visible for miles around.

Activities

River-rafting is popular in summer on the Kukkolankoski (p318). Trips are run by **Lapland Connection** (☎ 253 405; www.laplandconnection.com) and **Pohjolan Safarit/Nordic Safaris** (☎ 040-755 1858; www.nordicsafaris.com; Koskitie 130, Kukkola) from around €45 to €75 per person, using inflatable rubber rafts or traditional wooden boats. Safaris Unlimited also has kayaking trips, and both companies offer winter excursions such as

snowmobile, reindeer and husky safaris. **Arctic Iceroad Production** (☎ 040-555 8529; www.arctic-iceroad .com) organises fishing, canoeing and winter adventures including ice-driving in rally cars.

The tourist office can make bookings for all trips and handles **fishing** permits; there are several excellent spots along the Tornio River.

There's a famous **golf course** (☎ 431 711; Näräntie) here straddling Finland and Sweden, allowing you to fire shots into a different country and time zone. You'll need a Green Card or handicap certificate to play. There's also a driving range and pitch 'n' putt course here.

Sleeping

Hostel Vandrarhem (☎ 046-9226 1171; www.haparan davandrarhem.se; Strandgatan 26; dm/s/d/f €20/36/52/63, s without bathroom €28; ☐ ☐ ☐) The cheapest accommodation in the twin cities is this hostel just across the bridge in Sweden. There's a variety of clean rooms, a riverside location and a cafe-restaurant. The kitchen and common lounge are excellent, and there are high-standard disabled facilities. Linen costs an extra €5.50.

Joentalo (☎ 040-744 5260; www.ppopisto.fi; Kivirannantie 13; s/d €50/58; ☑ reception 8am-4pm; ☐ ☐ ☐) Two kilometres north of the bridge on the other side of the river from town, this college offers tidy rooms with fridge and desk in summer, and also the rest of the year if any are not occupied by students. The snag is that reception shuts at 4pm: be there or miss out.

ourpick E-City Matkakoti (☎ 480 897; www .ecitybedandbreakfast.com; Saarenpäänkatu 39; s/d €40/60;

P wi-fi) Tornio's best budget option, this is a friendly guesthouse a block north of the brewery run by a welcoming young family. Cosy rooms feature comfortable beds and colourful fabrics; the shared bathrooms are clean, with good showers, and breakfast includes traditional Finnish porridge.

Kaupunginhotelli (☎ 43311; www.tornionkau punginhotelli.fi; Itäranta 4; s/d €112/129; **P** 🖳 🖳 wi-fi) Tornio's only real hotel has decent facilities, including a small pool, a restaurant, a bar, karaoke and a nightclub. The rooms are attractive, with colourful bedspreads and plenty of natural light (in summer at least), though closer examination might have you calling for a pot of varnish and a tin of paint to touch things up.

Haparanda Stadshotell (☎ 046-9226 1490; www .haparandastadshotell.se; Torget 7; s/d €138/170; **P** wi-fi) Across the river in Sweden, this is the most characterful spot to stay, a beautiful old building that dignifies the centre of the small town. The rooms are decorated in an old-fashioned style and are most commodious. They also offer bargain 'summer rooms' (€31 per person) that come without breakfast or linen included.

Other options:

Camping Tornio (☎ 445 945; www.campingtornio .com; Matkailijantie; tent sites €6 plus per adult/child €4/1, cabins €42-57; 🕑 mid-May–Aug; **P**) About 3km from town, off the road to Kemi. Also boat and bike hire, tennis and a beach.

Gasthaus Tornio (☎ 470 311; www.gasthaustornio .com; Keskikatu 11; s/d €60/76; wi-fi) Central guesthouse with pool table and decent modern rooms.

Eating & Drinking

There is little eating choice in Tornio. In Haparanda, the Stadshotell has a quality **restaurant** (mains €18-26; 🕑 4-10pm Swedish time).

Café Avela (☎ 040-875 9643; Kauppakatu 10; 🕑 9am-5pm Mon-Fri) In a pretty wooden building opposite the bookshop, this unassuming little place is a small cafe and craft shop with a small selection of tasty home-baked cheesecakes and daily salads and soup, good value with a hunk of homemade bread for €3.50 to €4.50.

À La Carte (Itäranta 4; mains €9-25; 🕑 11am-midnight Mon-Sat) Tornio's best restaurant is in the Kaupunginhotelli and its elegant upmarket decor, quality food and this town's lack of other options more than make up for scatty service and an uninspiring name. Dishes come generously proportioned and hand-

somely presented, with tasty smoked salmon and tender meats. Various 'Lapp menus' cost €27 to €48.

OUR PICK Umpitunneli (☎ 430 360; www.umpitunneli .fi; Hallituskatu 15; mains €12-25; 🕑 11am-2am or later, food served until 9.30pm) The 'Dead-End Tunnel' may be a road to nowhere but it's a most enjoyable one, with a huge terrace, plenty of pissed-up locals adding entertainment value at weekends, and large plates of food, from creamy pastas to steaks and Tex-Mex. There are often live bands, or else the humppa (a fast Finnish dance, between a waltz and a foxtrot) music gets going. A classic.

Other options:

Saigon (☎ 430 565; Kauppakatu 13; 🕑 10.30am-7pm Mon, 10.30am-10pm Tue-Fri, noon-10pm Sat & Sun) This Vietnamese place has lunch specials and tasty soups.

Karkiainen (☎ 480 669; Länsiranta 9; 🕑 8am-7pm Mon-Fri, 9am-5pm Sat, noon-5pm Sun) Bakery-cafe with the best fresh pastries, cakes and doughnuts in town.

Getting There & Away

Kemi-Tornio Airport is 18km east of town, and there are regular flights to and from Helsinki. A shared taxi from Tornio to the airport costs €17.

There are a few daily buses from Rovaniemi (€20.50, two hours), although there are more connections (bus and train) via Kemi (€5.90, 45 minutes, more than hourly, less at weekends). Many Tornio-bound buses continue to Haparanda, although the distance is so short you can walk.

From Haparanda, there are buses to Luleå, from where trains run to Stockholm, Göteborg and Kiruna.

AROUND TORNIO
Kukkolankoski

The Kukkolankoski on the Tornionjoki, 16km north of Tornio on Rd 21, are the longest free-flowing rapids in Finland. The length is 3500m and the fall is just under 14m. Kukkolankoski has been a favoured fishing place since the Middle Ages and locals still catch whitefish using traditional long-handled nets. An annual whitefish festival is celebrated on the last weekend of July.

YLLÄS
☎ 016

Ylläs, 35km northeast of Kolari, is Finland's highest skiable fell. On either side of the mountain are the villages Äkäslompolo, prettily set by a lake, and smaller Ylläsjärvi. Both are typical ski-resort towns with top-end hotels and holiday cottages, and shut down substantially in summer, when reindeer roam with impunity. The villages are each about 5km from their respective ski-slopes. The Ylläs area is at the southern boundary of Pallas-Yllästunturi National Park (see p325).

Kellokas Nature Centre (☎ 020-564 7039; kellokas@metsa.fi; Tunturintie 54; ⊗ 9am-5pm Mar-Sep), at the foot of the fell's western slopes, 2.5km from Äkäslompolo, has environmental and geological exhibits on the surrounding area and multimedia displays, as well as maps, information and advice on hiking in the park. Here also is **Ylläksen Matkailuinfo** (☎ 569 996; www.yllas.fi; ⊗ 9am-5pm Jun-Sep), the tourist information centre.

Äkäslompolo's remarkable modern wooden church is the only sight of interest.

Activities

SKIING & SNOWBOARDING

Ylläs (www.yllas.fi) has 37 downhill slopes and 17 lifts, plus special areas for snowboarders. The vertical drop is 463m and the longest run is 3km. Cross-country skiing trails total 250km. Lift passes cost €32/153 per day/week; equipment rental and ski lessons are available. The ski season usually runs from late November to May.

MOUNTAIN BIKING & HIKING

In summer Ylläs is popular with mountain-biking enthusiasts, and you can take your bike up in the **gondola lift** (single/day €5/19; ⊗ Mon-Sat mid-Jun–Sep) to the top of the downhill trails (430m vertical descent). **SportStore** (☎ 040-051 5571; www.sportresortyllas.com), in the Taiga building at the base of the lifts on the Ylläsjärvi side, rents bikes of all types (€15 to €30 per day).

There are numerous nature trails and hiking possibilities. Check the Pallas-Yllästunturi pages on www.outdoors.fi for a list. A couple of long-distance treks head to Olos or Levi (50km to 54km); there are several shorter trails including the 3.5km **Varkaankuru** nature trail, and the 15km **Kiiruna Circuit**, both of which start from the Kellokas Nature Centre. Experienced hikers can walk all the way to Pallastunturi (72km) and from there to Hetta (see p325). Various cross-country skiing tracks crisscrossing the fell also make for good hiking or Nordic walking.

Tours

Various tour operators cluster in Äkäslompolo along the road near the Ylläskaltio hotel. Most are open only in winter, and offer snowmobiling, reindeer safaris, snowshoe walking and husky treks.

Sleeping & Eating

Most accommodation is shut in summer, but there are still plenty of empty cottages around. **Destination Lapland** (☎ 510 3300; www .destinationlapland.com) is the major booker. The **Äkäshotelli** (www.laplandhotels.com) in Äkäslompolo stays open, as does the Fontana spa hotel **Ylläs Saaga** (www.yllassaaga.com) at the slopes on the Ylläsjärvi side. They offer summer rooms for around €75 a twin.

Hotel Ylläshumina (☎ 569 501; www.yllashumina .com; Tiurajärventie; s/d €117/146; ⊗ mid-Aug–Apr; **P** wifi) In Äkäslompolo, near the lake, this welcoming complex resembles a courting willow grouse with its flamboyant wooden architecture. There's full ski service here, and the sauna and outdoor hot tub are great after a day on the slopes. The rooms, set in separate raised buildings, are like apartments, and fit a whole family, with a loft sleeping area and kitchenette. They're considerably cheaper between August and mid-December. The restaurant (mains €17 to €39 plus menus €33 to €60) serves upmarket fare including willow grouse and reindeer.

Between Ylläsjärvi and Kittilä, the **Snow Village** (☎ 565 112; www.snowvillage.fi; s/d €180/240) is built every winter. It's a spectacular complex of buildings including an ice bar in a huge igloo, and sumptuous rooms where you sleep in heavy-duty sleeping bags atop your icy bed.

Getting There & Away

During the ski season, a shuttle heads from Kittilä airport to Ylläsjärvi (€11) and Äkäslompolo (€13.20). Phone ☎ 060-014 919 for bookings.

The nearest train station is Kolari and there are connecting buses to Ylläsjärvi and Äkäslompolo three times a week in the ski season. There's also a weekly bus from Rovaniemi and one from Kittilä.

KITTILÄ

☎ 016 / pop 5967

One of the main service centres for northwestern Lapland, Kittilä is a base or jumping-off

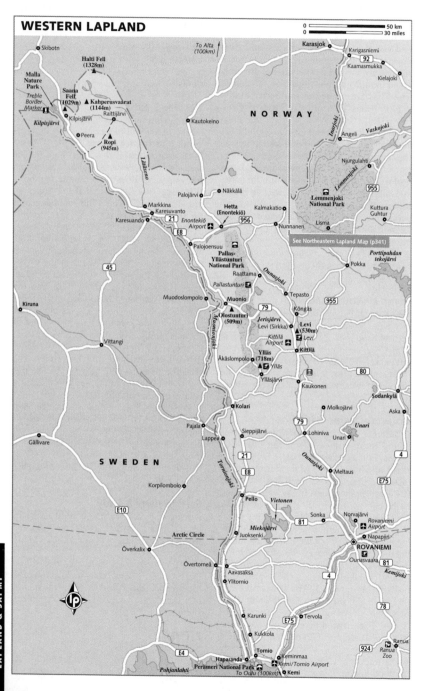

WESTERN LAPLAND

0 — 50 km
0 — 30 miles

Skibotn

Halti Fell
(1328m)

**Malla
Nature
Park**

*Treble
Border
Marker*

Saana
Fell
(1029m)

Kahperusvaarat
(1144m)

Kilpisjärvi

Kilpisjärvi

Peera

Ropi
(945m)

Raittijärvi

Lätäseno

To Alta
(100km)

Karasjok

Karigasniemi

92

Kaamasmukka

Kielajoki

N O R W A Y

Inarijoki

Angeli

Vaskojoki

Kautokeino

Njurgulahti

Lemmenjoki

955

**Lemmenjoki
National Park**

Kuttura
Guhtur

Palojärvi

Näkkälä

Markkina
Karesuvanto

Karesuando

21

*Enontekiö
Airport*

Hetta
(Enontekiö)

Kalmakatio

956

Nunnanen

Lisma

See Northeastern Lapland Map (p341)

E8

Palojoensuu

**Pallas-
Yllästunturi
National Park**

45

Raattama

Ounasjoki

*Porttipahdan
tekojärvi*

Pokka

Pallastunturi

Kiruna

Muodoslompolo

Muonio

Olostunturi
(509m)

Jerisjärvi
Levi (Sirkka)

79

Tepasto

Köngäs

955

Levi
(530m)

Levi

Muonionjoki

Vittangi

Kittilä
Airport

Kittilä

Äkäslompolo

Ylläs
(718m)

Ylläs

80

Ylläsjärvi

Kaukonen

Sodankylä

Gällivare

Kolari

Molkojärvi

Aska

Pajala

Unari

79

Lappea

Sieppijärvi

Lohiniva

Unari

4

S W E D E N

Tornionjoki

21

E8

Meltaus

E75

Korpilombolo

Pello

Vietonen

81

Sonka

Norvajärvi

Ounasjoki

*Rovaniemi
Airport*

E10

Miekojärvi

Napapiiri

Arctic Circle

Juoksenki

ROVANIEMI

Överkalix

Ounasvaara

81

Övertorneå

Kemijoki

Aavasaksa

Ylitornio

4

78

Karunki

E75

Tervola

Kukkola

Ranua

924

*Ranua
Zoo*

E4

Tornio

Keminmaa

Haparanda

Kemi/Tornio Airport

Pohjanlahti

Perämeri National Park

To Oulu (100km)

Kemi

point for the ski resorts of Ylläs and Levi. Although Kittilä is the regional centre, Levi is now, in fact, so popular, that their roles have been effectively reversed.

Gasthaus Kultaisen Ahman Majatalo (☎ 642 043; Valtatie 42; s/d €50/76; P) is a friendly B&B right in the village centre, with breakfast served in your room. **Hotelli Kittilä** (☎ 643 201; www.hotellikittila.fi; Valtatie 49; s/d €95/130; P ⚘ wi-fi) is on the main road: look for the red aeroplane mounted out the front. Rooms are spacious, and there's a sauna and a small pool. The restaurant serves a good buffet lunch (€8.40) and there's dancing and entertainment some evenings.

Daily flights operate between Helsinki and Kittilä as do winter charters from the UK and elsewhere. The airport is 4km north of town. Four to five daily buses run between Rovaniemi and Kittilä (€27.50, two hours). All continue to Levi.

LEVI & SIRKKA
☎ 016

The phenomenal amount of construction that goes on here every summer attests to the boom of the Finnish ski business and Levi's place near the top of the pile. Its compact centre, top-shelf modern facilities and large accommodation capacity mean it hosts many high-profile winter events; it's also a very popular destination for *ruska* season hiking. Though many places shut down, there's enough going on here in summer that it's not moribund, and the great deals on smart modern apartments make this a tempting base from which to explore western Lapland, particularly for families.

Levi is actually the name of the fell, while Sirkka is the village, but most people refer to the whole place as Levi. The ski season runs from November to May, with the busiest period in March and April, when snow is good, temperatures aren't extreme and there's a bit of daylight. In summer and autumn, trekking and mountain biking are the main outdoor activities, while in December overseas charter flights descend bringing families in search of reindeer and a white Christmas.

The **tourist office** (☎ 639 3300; www.levi.fi; Myllyojantie 2; ⏰ 9am-7pm Mon-Fri, 11am-5.30pm Sat & Sun) is behind the tepeelike building on the roundabout in the centre of the resort. The main accommodation booking agency is also here, and staff can book activities such as snowmobile safaris, dog-sled treks and reindeer rides.

At the time of research a new nature centre and exhibition space was under construction halfway up the slope above town; it should be open by publication.

Activities
SKIING & SNOWBOARDING
Levi ski resort (☎ 641 246; www.levi.fi) has 44 downhill slopes and 26 lifts (two gondola lifts and several free children's lifts). Many of the slopes are lit, and stay open until 8pm. The vertical drop is approximately 325m, and the longest run is 2.5km. There are two half-pipes and a superpipe for snowboarders, a snow park and several ski runs for children.

Opportunities for cross-country skiing are also good, with trails totalling 230km, 28km illuminated. On longer ski-treks, you can stay overnight in wilderness huts, which have supplies of firewood.

In the high season (February to early May), lift tickets cost €33/159 per day/week. Single tickets are €4. Skis, snowboards, sleds and snowshoes can be rented and lessons are available.

OTHER ACTIVITIES
In winter there's a full complement of snowy activities from husky, reindeer and snowmobile short trips or safaris, snowshoe walking and ice-fishing. In summer, **canoeing** on the long Ounasjoki that runs from Hetta in the north to Rovaniemi in the south is deservedly popular, as is the **mountain-biking park** (☎ 020-796 0200; www.bikepark.fi) on the ski-slopes: there are decent rigs available for hire and you can take your bike up in the gondola lift; the gravity trails have a drop of 310m. There's also a golf course (green fee €35) and horse riding. The tourist office can book most activities.

Recommended activity operators:

Kinos Safaris (☎ 050-403 2000; www.kinossafaris .com) Winter safaris plus summer canoeing and fishing (rental and trips).

Lapland Safaris (☎ 654 222; www.laplandsafaris.com; Keskuskuja 2) A full range of winter excursions. Closed summer.

PerheSafarit (☎ 643 861; www.perhesafarit.fi) Snowmobile and motor-sled excursions in winter and Ounasjoki canoeing trips in summer.

Polar Speed Tours (☎ 653 447; www.levi.fi/polars peed) Single- or multiday dog-sledding safaris with accommodation in wilderness huts. In summer you can visit the dogs at the Husky Park in Köngäs, 10km northeast of Levi.

THE NORTHERN LIGHTS

The Northern Lights, or aurora borealis, are an utterly haunting, exhilarating and memorable sight, and they are often visible to observers standing at or above the Arctic Circle, which includes a large portion of Lapland. They're especially visible around the equinoxes (late September and March), and are particularly striking during the dark winter; in summer, the sun more or less renders them invisible.

The aurora appears as curtains of greenish-white light stretching east to west across the sky for thousands of kilometres. At its lower edge, the aurora typically shades to a crimson-red glow. Hues of blue and violet can also be seen. The lights seem to shift and swirl in the night sky – they can almost be said to dance.

The aurora borealis has a less famous southern counterpart, the aurora australis or southern lights, which encircles the South Pole. Both are oval in shape with a diameter of approximately 2000km.

These auroral storms, however eerie, are quite natural. They're created when charged particles (protons and electrons) from the sun bombard the earth. These are deflected towards the North and South Poles by the Earth's magnetic field. There they hit the Earth's outer atmosphere, 100km to 1000km above ground, causing highly charged electrons to collide with molecules of nitrogen and oxygen. The excess energy from these collisions creates the colourful lights we see in the sky.

The ancient inhabitants of Lapland believed it was caused by a giant fox swishing its tail above the Arctic tundra. One of the Finnish words for the aurora borealis is *revontulet* (literally 'fires of the fox').

The best website for aurora borealis predictions is run by the University of Alaska: check out www.gedds.alaska.edu/AuroraForecast, change the view to Europe and away you go…

Sleeping

Levi is one of Finland's most popular winter holiday centres and prices go through the roof in the peak season of December, and from February to May. Virtually the whole town consists of holiday apartments and cottages, most of which are available for rental. They typically sleep four to six, have a sauna, a fully equipped kitchen and many other mod cons. In summer, they are a real bargain, costing €45 to €55 per night; in winter €1100 a week is average. **Levin Matkailu Keskusvaraamo** (☎ 639 3300; www.levi.fi; Myllyojantie 2; 9am-4.30pm Mon-Fri, open weekends at busy periods), in the tourist office, is the place to book these.

Hullu Poro (☎ 651 0100; www.hulluporo.fi; ski season d with sauna €100-170, d without sauna €85-115; P wi-fi) The 'Crazy Reindeer' keeps expanding, and now seems like a small city of its own. It has every kind of room you can imagine, with family suites, apartments and rooms with private sauna; there are various restaurants, and a spa complex, though no pool. There are also cabins available on a hostel-basis from May to November.

ourpick Hotelli K5 Levi (☎ 639 1100; www.k5levi.fi; Kätkänrannantie 2; r high season €185-195, rest of year €122-149; P wi-fi) Right opposite the tourist office,

this sleek, modern hotel is Levi's most stylish lodging option. The rooms are excellent; most come with sauna and glassed-in balcony, and those that don't have a Jacuzzi. There are also good family rooms and classy holiday apartments. All rooms feature very comfortable beds and DVD players (free films at reception). Despite the classy design, they haven't forgotten where they are: there's a laundry, mountain bikes and sets of skis free for guests to use, canoes to rent, and a drying cupboard in all the rooms. The restaurant Klaani specialises in Lapp dishes, with several shared platters. Nonguests can use the gym for €6.

Hotel Levitunturi (☎ 646 301; www.hotellilevitunturi .fi; s/d €168/188; P   wi-fi) At the heart of the resort, this place goes on forever and is Levi's best bet if you're travelling with kids. As well as a spa complex, gym and child-friendly eating options, there's an indoor activity centre with bouncy castle, ball pool, golf simulator and pedal cars. Nonguests can use the facilities for a charge. The standard rooms are snug, with wood floors and firm beds.

Eating & Drinking

Most eating and drinking options centre on the four big hotels, which have multiple bars, restaurants and nightclubs, most open only during the ski season and the autumn *ruska* period.

Hotelli Levitunturi (☎ 646 301; www.hotellilevitun turi.fi) The vast interior of this hotel conceals a wide range of grub and nightlife options, including a spot with a live orchestra playing traditional Finnish dancing music. The main restaurant, Luppo (11am to midnight), has a buffet that's €12/21 at lunch/dinner.

Tuikku (☎ 640 240; mains €13-25; ☼ 11am-late Sep-Apr, 11am-5pm Fri-Sun Jul & Aug) Offering panoramic views over the surrounding forests and lakes, this spot is near the top of the fell, accessible by road or ski-lift. During the height of the ski-season it has theme nights: fondue, six-course specials and more.

Hullu Poro (☎ 651 0100; www.hulluporo.fi) Choices include Pihvipirtti (steaks €23 to €45, open September to April), down the road from the main complex, where the €39 steakhouse menu gets you a crack at the cold fish buffet followed by a sirloin, and the year-round Wanha Hullu Poro (mains €11 to €16, open 11am to 11pm) in the original wooden building, serving up tasty food – swordfish and pork belly on the menu last visit – at big wooden tables in a casual atmosphere. The Areena, down the hill, has live music almost every night in ski season, DJs, and dancing on two floors.

Panimo Pub (☎ 010-0430 0400; Levinraitti 1; ☼ 10am-4am) Pints of homebrew and, in summer, a terrace that catches the afternoon sun are reasons to visit this spot by the central supermarket. Downstairs, in the Kellari, big and hearty meals are served year-round (mains €13 to €27, 2pm to 11pm).

Getting There & Away

Sirkka and Levi are on Rd 79, 170km north of Rovaniemi. All buses from Rovaniemi to Kittilä continue on to here, some continuing to Muonio. A bus meets all incoming flights at Kittilä Airport, 15km to the south.

Franchises of the major car hire companies are located at the airport; they will deliver cars to Levi or Kittilä free of charge.

MUONIO

☎ 016 / pop 2363

The village of Muonio is the last significant stop on Rd 21 before Kilpisjärvi and Norway. It sits on the scenic Muonionjoki that forms the border between Finland and Sweden and

is a fine base for summer and winter activities. There are plenty of places to stay around here, and low-key skiing in winter. Most of the town was razed during WWII, but the wooden church, dating from 1817, escaped that fate.

Sights & Activities

The **Kiela Naturium** (☎ 532 280; ☼ 10am-6pm) has a gift shop, cafe, free internet, local fish in a tank and a small nature display. There's also a planetarium with an aurora borealis show (adult/child €10/6).

The local open-air museum, **Muonion Kotiseutumuseo** (☎ 534 317; adult/child €2/free; ☼ noon-6pm Tue-Sat mid-Jun–early Aug) has a collection of prewar buildings with interiors stocked with local artefacts.

Three kilometres south, the excellent **Harriniva Holiday Centre** (☎ 530 0300; www.harriniva .fi) has a vast program of summer and winter activities for individuals or small groups, ranging from short jaunts to multiday adventures. In summer these include guided hikes, canoe and boat trips, horse trekking, quad safaris, and fishing on the salmon-packed Muonionjoki. You can also rent bikes, boats and rods here.

In winter, there are wonderful dog-sledding safaris from 1½ hours (€70) to two days (€530), or trips of a week or longer, perhaps adding reindeer-sledding and snowmobiling to the mix.

Harriniva has the **Arktinen Rekikoirakeskus** (Arctic sled-dog centre) with over 400 lovable dogs, all with names and personalities. A great guided tour of their town (for that is what it is) is €8/5 per adult/child and teaches you plenty about the different breeds of huskies and their characteristics. Prebook it the day before; there are three departures daily. You can also go on summer hikes (€35/20 per adult/child Tuesday and Friday) with a posse of them.

Sleeping & Eating

Lomamaja Pekonen (☎ 532 237; www.lomamajapeko nen.fi; Lahenrannantie 10; s/d €40/55, apt €55-92, cottages €60-85; ℗) In the centre of town, this appealing spot has wee red wooden cabins running up a slope just across from the Muonionjoki and more upmarket apartments and cottages behind them. In summer there's a simple hut (singles/doubles €19/32) as well, and there's space for vans but not tents. They hire canoes, fishing equipment and bikes as well as organising guided trips on the river in summer.

Harriniva Holiday Centre (☎ 530 0300; www.har riniva.fi; s/d up to €120/140, 1-/3-person cabins from €24/36, apt from €95; P ⬚ wi-fi) The Harriniva is a good place to stay. There are simple cabins by the river (nice but plenty of mosquitoes), as well as good hotel rooms and apartments. There's also a good restaurant and bar here; the kitchen is open until 10.30pm.

Kammari (☎ 539 103; www.kammari.com; mains €8-16; ⏲ 2-11pm) By the Hotel Olos (www.lapland hotels.com), at the ski area 6km east of town, this restaurant is the best place for pizzas, steaks, hamburgers and kebabs. It's a friendly spot, with a cosy, intimate dining room.

JHLR (☎ 532 280; ⏲ 11am-10pm) In a homely wooden building in the centre of town, this is basically the only place to eat if you don't have your own transport. It does OK steaks and a lunchtime buffet, and is the place to watch gnarled locals over a beer.

Getting There & Away

Muonio is at the junction of western Lapland's main two roads: Rd 21, which runs from Tornio to Kilpisjärvi, and Rd 79, which runs northwest from Rovaniemi via Kittilä.

There are three daily buses from Rovaniemi (€38.40, 3½ hours) via Kittilä, and services from Kemi/Tornio.

HETTA

☎ 016 / pop 1965

The village of Hetta is the centre of the municipality of Enontekiö, and a good place to start trekking and exploration of the area. It has a large Sámi population and, though a bit spread-out, makes a good stop for a night or two. It's also the northern end of the popular Pallastunturi Trek (opposite).

The **Skierri** (☎ 020-564 7950; www.outdoors.fi; ⏲ 9am-8pm Mon-Fri, 9am-5pm Sat & Sun Jun-Sep, 9am-4pm Mon-Fri Oct-Feb & May, 9am-5pm Mar & Apr) nature centre at the eastern end of town provides information about Pallas-Yllästunturi National Park, and doubles as the **tourist office** (☎ 040-055 6215; www.tosilappi.fi). There's a smart new **exhibition** (adult/child €5/3) on the Sámi and their nomadic history as well as nature displays on the park and a cafe.

In the centre of Hetta is the slender-spired **Enontekiö church** (⏲ 10am-4pm Jun-Sep), built in 1952 with the financial help of American churches. The organ was a gift from Germany. The church has an altar mosaic picturing Christ blessing Lapland and

its people (and reindeer). Opening hours aren't reliable.

A less permanent building is the annual **snow castle**, built in mid-December and lasting until April.

At the junction of the westbound and northbound roads, 2km west of the centre, the market square has a couple of worthwhile shops, **Sámi Duodji Ry** (☎ 040-507 1569; ⏲ 10.30am-4.30pm Mon-Fri), the Sámi handicrafts cooperative, and a local silversmith's workshop, **Hetta Silver** (☎ 040-762 2063).

The biggest festival in Hetta is **Marianpäivä** (feast day of the Annunciation), usually celebrated in March; there are Sámi dances and parties, and the town buzzes with a lot of activity.

Sleeping & Eating

Hetan Lomakylä (☎ 521 521; www.hetanlomakyla .fi; sites €10 plus per adult/child €4/2, 2-person cabins €50, small/large cottages €60/80; ⏲ Mar-Oct) Just near the north–west road junction 2km from the centre, this family-friendly spot has smart, posh little blue-painted cottages with kitchen, sauna and a loft sleeping area, as well as simpler cabins. It's good value and there are various discounts and activities on offer.

ourpick **Hetan Majatalo** (☎ 554 0400; www .hetan-majatalo.fi; hotel s/d €62/84, guesthouse €38/60; P ⬚ & wi-fi) In the centre of town, but set back in its own garden away from the road, this welcoming pad offers two types of accommodation in facing buildings: clean and simple guesthouse rooms sharing bathrooms, and very handsome and spacious wood-clad hotel rooms with good bathrooms and pyramid-shaped skylights. It's an excellent deal that includes breakfast and sauna, and it's even a little cheaper in summer.

Ounasloma (☎ 521 05; www.ounasloma.fi; cottage s/d/q €61/72/94; P wi-fi) This is a friendly family-run place with a series of excellent cottages, some sleeping up to five, others with a capacity of 10, all in a nice little area by the river. They have free boats, bikes and sledges, and hire fishing equipment. They also run ice-fishing, and trips in an unusual sledge-bus pulled by a snowmobile.

Hotelli Hetta (☎ 521 361; www.laplandhotels.com; hostel s/d €72/88, hotel s/d €105/122; ⏲ late Feb-Apr, Jun-Sep, Nov & Dec; P ⬚ & wi-fi) At the eastern end of town towards the visitor centre, this hotel has two classes of room: 'hostel' rooms that have their own toilet but shared shower, and hotel rooms that are spacious, with large beds. They're not stuck-up at all, so sweaty walkers and sodden cross-country skiers get a proper welcome. There are also apartments for rental, and a good restaurant open for dinner only.

Hotelli Jussantupa (☎ 521 101; www.jussantupa.fi; mains €13-25) This unremarkable central hotel has the only restaurant apart from the Hotelli Hetta, and the town's main bar. The basic dishes are rather disappointing, with frozen veg and liberal MSG: they also offer snow grouse in cloudberry-cream sauce for two – overambitious perhaps.

Getting There & Away

Finnair/Finncomm flies to Enontekiö from Helsinki daily from March to May only. The airport, mainly used for winter charters, is 7km west.

Buses from Hetta head out to the main road to Rovaniemi (€46.30, five hours) and Kilpisjärvi (€27.20, 3¼ hours) via a swap-over at Palojoensuu. There's a summer service from Rovaniemi to Tromsø in Norway via Hetta, Kautokeino and Alta. There are also buses to Hetta from Muonio.

PALLAS-YLLÄSTUNTURI NATIONAL PARK
☎ 016

Finland's third-largest national park forms a long, thin area running from Hetta in the north to the Ylläs ski area in the south (see p318). The main attraction is the excellent 55km trekking route from the village of Hetta to Pallastunturi in the middle of the park, where there's a hotel, information centre and transport connections. Experienced trekkers can continue from here to Ylläs, although there are few facilities on that section. In winter, Pallastunturi Fell is a small but popular place for both cross-country and downhill skiing. The longest slope is 2km.

Pallastunturi Luontokeskus (☎ 020-564 7930; pallastunturi@metsa.fi; 🕑 9am-4pm Mon-Fri Jan–mid-Feb, Oct, Nov & May, 9am-5pm daily other times) nature centre at Pallastunturi Fell sells trekking maps (€19), makes reservations for locked huts (€9 per person) and provides information and advice about the region, with AV presentations in several languages. Skierri (opposite) in Hetta and Kellokas Nature Centre (p319) near Äkäslompolo also have keys for the lockable huts.

Trekking Route

The 55km trek/ski from Hetta village to Pallastunturi (or vice versa) is one of the easiest in the country: pretty, flattish, light forest cover with sandy soil. It takes two to four days to complete. The route is well marked, and there are several wilderness huts along the way. The popularity of the trek means huts get pretty crowded at peak times.

Day 1 From Hetta village, you must cross a lake to get to the national park. The boat-taxi costs €5. Walk 7km through a forest to Pyhäkero hut, then ascend to the high Pyhäkero (peak), which is part of Ounastunturi Fell. Then it's 7km to Sioskuru, where there's an open hut and reservable cabin.

Day 2 This section of the trail is mostly treeless plateau with good visibility. You might want to take a detour to Tappuri hut for lunch before continuing to Pahakuru hut (10km). If it's full, continue 1.5km to Hannukuru, the 'capital' of the Pallastunturi Fell area, with an open cabin, a reservable cabin and a sauna.

Day 3 The first leg is 5km over relatively difficult terrain to a *kota* (tepee) where you can cook lunch. Another 7km takes you through pleasant mountains to the small hut of Montelli. If it is full, continue 1km on to Nammalankuru hut.

Day 4 The final day takes you through some magnificent high mountains. There is only one place to stop, a *kota* 2.5km from Nammalankuru. From here, it's a 10km uphill walk to Hotel Pallas.

On to Ylläs It's about 70km from Pallastunturi to the park's southernmost border, by the ski resorts at Ylläs. It's about 21km to the village of Rauhala from Pallastunturi, and then another 11km to the Pahtavuoma hut. Beyond here, there's a *kota* shelter, Kotamaja, and several fireplace points.

Sleeping
WILDERNESS HUTS

Free accommodation along the trail is available in wilderness huts. From north to south:

Pyhäkero This hut is 7km from the lake. There's a gas stove, a toilet and room for five people. In March and April there's also a cafe.

Sioskuru Sioskuru is 8km from Pyhäkero hut and accommodates up to 16 people. There are mattresses, a gas stove, a telephone and dry firewood. There's a rental cabin here also, sleeping up to eight.

Tappuri This nice, newly facelifted hut is 1km off the main path. It accommodates eight people, and has a gas stove and good drinking water from a nearby creek.

Pahakuru This hut is 11km from Sioskuru. It sleeps up to six people, and has a gas stove and a toilet. You can take litter on to Hannukuru when you leave.

FINLAND'S SÁMI

Sámi (sápmelaš in their own language) are the indigenous inhabitants of Lapland and are today spread across four countries from the Kola Peninsula in Russia to the southern Norwegian mountains. More than half of the 70,000 Sámi population are across the border in Norway, while around 8000 reside in Finland, but there are close cultural ties across the borders. The Sámi region is called Sápmi, and about half of Finnish Sámi live in it.

According to stone carvings and archaeological evidence, this region was first settled soon after the last Ice Age around 10,000 years ago, but it wasn't until the beginning of the Christian era – the early Iron Age – that Finns and Sámi had become two distinct groups with diverging languages. The early inhabitants were nomadic people – hunters, fishers and food-gatherers – who migrated with the seasons. They hunted wild reindeer, fished and harvested berries in the summer months, and traded meat, clothing and handicrafts.

Traditions & Beliefs

Early Sámi society was based on the *siida,* small groups comprising a number of families who controlled particular hunting, herding and fishing grounds. Families lived in *kota* – a traditional dwelling resembling the tepee or wigwam of native North Americans. Smaller tents could be easily set up as a temporary shelter while following the migrating reindeer herds, and more permanent ones were overlaid with turf to insulate the fabric and reindeer pelt covering. A 'winter village' system also developed, where groups came together to help survive the harsh winter months. Some groups, like the Skolt, moved several times a year to various seasonal grounds. The advent of mechanisation in the 1950s meant reindeer herders could go out on snowmobiles and return home every night. This ended the need for nomadism and the Sámi became a settled people.

The natural environment was essential to Sámi existence: they worshipped the sun (father), earth (mother) and wind and believed all things in nature had a soul. There were many gods, who dwelled in sacred *seita* places; fells, lakes or sacred stones. The link with the gods was through the shaman *(noaidi),* the most important member of the community. Reindeer were sacrificed to ask for success at hunting and fishing, and, by beating a drum, the shaman went into a trance to travel between the visible and invisible worlds to see if the gods were satisfied. These drums featured drawings depicting life, nature and the gods, usually with the sun as the central image but were mostly destroyed in the 17th century as missionaries forced conversion to Christianity. The drums' characteristic motifs have recently been reborn in Sámi handicrafts.

Traditional legends, rules of society and fairy tales were handed down through the generations by storytelling. A unique form of storytelling was the *yoik,* a chant in which the singer would use words, or imitate the sounds of animals and nature to describe experiences or people. It's still used by the Sámi today, sometimes accompanied by instruments.

Sámi Groups

Five distinct Sámi groups with distinct cultural traditions live in Finland. Vuotso Sámi live around Saariselkä and are the southernmost group. Enontekiö Sámi dwell around Hetta in the west and, with Utsjoki Sámi, who settled from Finland's northernmost tip along the Norwegian border to Karigasniemi, had the strongest reindeer-herding heritage. Inari Sámi live around the shores of Inarijärvi, and have a strong fishing tradition. Skolt Sámi have a particularly poignant story. They originally inhabited the Kola Peninsula around Petsamo, and fled to Finland when the Soviet Union took back control of that area. They number around 600, live around Sevettijärvi and Nellim, and are of Orthodox religion thanks to their Russian roots.

Role of the Reindeer

Reindeer have always been central to the Sámi people's existence. They ate the meat, drank the milk, used the fur for clothing and bedding, and made fish hooks and harpoons from the bones and antlers. Today around 40% of Sámi living in Sápmi are involved in reindeer husbandry; tourism is another big employer.

Originally the Sámi hunted wild reindeer, usually trapping them in pitfalls. Hunting continued until around the 16th century, when the Sámi began to domesticate entire herds and migrate with them. Towards the end of the 19th century, Finland's reindeer herders were organised into *paliskunta* cooperatives, of which there are now 56 in northern Finland. Reindeer wander free around the large natural areas within each *paliskunta,* which is bordered by enormous fences that cross the Lapland wilderness. Each herder is responsible for his stock and identifies them by earmarks – a series of distinctive notches cut into the ear of each animal. There are some 10,000 active earmarks. See p65 for more on reindeer.

Sámi Clothing & Handicrafts

The Sámi have always used the material at their disposal – reindeer furs, antlers and bone, birch and wool – to make utensils, carvings, clothing and textiles. The colourful Sámi costumes, featuring jackets, pants or skirts embroidered with bright red, blue and yellow patterns, are now mostly worn on special occasions and during Sámi festivals.

Sámi handicrafts (including bags and boots made from reindeer hide, knitted gloves and socks, textiles, shawls, strikingly colourful Sámi hats, jewellery and silverware) are recognised as indigenous art. Genuine handicrafts carry the name *Sámi duodji.* Inari is one of the best places to buy them.

Sámi Languages

Sámi languages are related to Finnish and other Finno-Ugric languages. There are three Sámi languages, not very mutually intelligible, used in Finland today. Fell Sámi, spoken by Utsjoki and Enontekiö Sámi, is considered the standard Sámi, while Inari Sámi is spoken by a select few around Inarijärvi. Skolt Sámi have their own language, which includes some Russian loan words, though there are under 2000 regular users. Sámi language is closely linked to cultural identity, taught in local schools and spoken on the radio. Legislation grants the right of Sámi usage in the workplace. There are another seven Sámi languages in Norway, Sweden and Russia.

Local Voice: Heikki Paltto

The reindeer year starts at the beginning of June because the calves that are born around May have to be earmarked. After that marking they are free in the fells for the summer. In autumn we start herding them and decide which are to be killed for meat. To herd them I use an ATV and after the snow falls, a snowmobile. It takes over two months to herd the reindeer and it's hopefully done by Christmas. During the winter we move the reindeer from one area to another because there's not enough food to last them in one place. You should never ask a Sámi how many reindeer they have; it's like asking someone's salary. I wouldn't even tell a close friend. Some people have hundreds, some only have a few.

Our traditions are still important, even to young Sámi. We describe by *yoiking* nature, people, all sorts of happenings, but one never *yoiks* about oneself. Traditional clothes are still important to us; we do wear them, mainly on special occasions. The locations of *seita* places are still re-membered by people, but they don't visit them. And if they do visit them, it's a secret that you wouldn't tell to anybody else.

The Sámi parliament deals with all aspects of Sámi life. We meet four times a year in Inari and are elected by the Sámi people. Our government does listen to us, though that doesn't mean that they do anything. If we want something it is our only channel so in that way it is important. The government asks our advice a lot if they want to know something. That is our main power I suppose. Of course, we'd like to have more!

Though some areas are protected, in parts of Lapland we have big battles with the forestry industry. Some are solved, and some are not. I think the question will never go away; there will always be people wanting to make money from the forest.

Tourism is a good thing for the Sámi people if Sámi people get the results, the benefits from it. That isn't always the case. Where I live, tourism directly benefits the Sámi community, but in other parts the money flows straight out to other places.

Heikki Paltto is a reindeer herder & member of the Sámi Parliament.
As told to Andy Symington. Translation by Eija Kurvi

Learning More

For more information, visit the excellent Siida museum (p340) in Inari or the Arktikum (p308) in Rovaniemi. Siida's website (www.siida.fi) is particularly informative.

Hannukuru Just 2km from Pahakuru, and at the halfway point on the route, these busy huts have room for 24 people. There are mattresses, a gas stove, plenty of firewood and a lakeside sauna. There's also bookable cabin accommodation sleeping up to 24.

Montelli This intimate little hut on the high fells has a fireplace and sleeps four people. It's 12km beyond Hannukuru and 15km from Pallastunturi.

Nammalankuru This large hut is 2km beyond Montelli hut and accommodates 16 people. There is a gas stove, a part-time cafe and fine fell scenery. There's also a rental cabin sleeping up to eight.

Pahtavuoma These two huts are 32km south of Pallastunturi on the route to Ylläs. They are simple, with fireplace. One sleeps three, the other two.

HOTELS

Hotelli Pallas (☎ 323 355; www.laplandhotels.com; s/d €150/180; **P** wi-fi) This noble old wooden place is up in the fells, 50m from the national park information centre, and just what you want to see when you finish your trek. The first hotel in Lapland was built on this site in 1938. There are cheaper rooms in the wooden section, which have their own toilet but share a shower (singles/doubles €67/80 in summer). Some group rooms with bunks and bathroom are also available here. It's got skiing right alongside in winter, and the room prices jump accordingly, but it's good value at other times. There's a nice lakeside sauna (with a winter ice-hole) and a tame reindeer hanging about.

Getting There & Away

A morning bus runs Monday to Friday, plus Saturday in summer, from Muonio (€8.10, 40 minutes) to Kittilä via Pallastunturi. At other times, you'll have to hitch or call a local taxi on ☎ 538 582, or ☎ 040-039 3103.

KILPISJÄRVI

☎ 016

The remote village of Kilpisjärvi, the northernmost settlement in the 'arm' of Finland, is on the doorstep of both Norway and Sweden. At 480m above sea level, this small border post, wedged between the lake of Kilpisjärvi and the magnificent surrounding fells, is also the highest village in Finland. Unless you're just passing through on your way to Tromsøor Narvik in Norway, the main reason to venture out here is for summer trekking or spring cross-country skiing. There are popular walks

to the joint border post of Finland, Norway and Sweden, up spectacular Saana Fell, home to the rough-legged buzzard, and longer treks to Finland's highest fell, Halti (1328m).

Every Midsummer, the folk of Kilpisjärvi put on a ski race at Saana Fell, where the snow may not melt until mid-July. Across in Norway, you can see year-round patches of snow on the mountains.

Kilpisjärvi (www.kilpisjarvi.org) consists of two small settlements 5km apart – the main (southern) centre has the information office, hotel, petrol station and supermarket, and most of the accommodation. The northern knot, 2km shy of the border, has the Kilpisjärven Retkeilykeskus (Kilpisjärvi Hiking Centre) and trailheads.

Information

Kilpisjärven Retkeilykeskus (Kilpisjärvi Hiking Centre; ☎ 537 771; www.kilpisretkeily.fi; ☼ 8am-10pm mid-Mar–Sep) This is a central meeting place for all trekkers. They hire bikes and hiking and skiing equipment. There's also a shop and a cafe here and accommodation close to the main walking routes.

Luontotalo (☎ 020-564 7990; kilpisjarvi@metsa .fi; ☼ 9am-5pm Mon-Fri Mar-Sep, also Sat Apr, May & Jul-Sep, also Sun Jul & Aug) At the southern end of the village, this national park centre is effectively the tourist information office. It has maps, advice on trekking and a nature display.

Activities
TREKKING

The Kilpisjärvi area offers fantastic long and short hikes.

From the Retkeilykeskus, the ascent to slate-capped **Saana Fell** (1029m) takes two to three hours return. A gentle climb through woodland ends abruptly in a thigh-straining 742 wooden steps up the steeper part of the fell. From the top, it's an easier gradient up the angled slate cap to the highest point. When you come down, you can continue right around the base of the fell to make a long loop trail. There's a free wilderness hut at Saanajärvi about 5km from the Retkeilykeskus.

Another Kilpisjärvi classic is the route through **Malla Nature Park** to the Kolmen Valtakunnan Raja, a concrete block in a lake, suspiciously painted Swedish yellow, that marks the **treble border** of Finland, Sweden and Norway. Nearby is a free wilderness hut, where you can stay overnight. It's 11km from the car park 2.5km north of the Retkeilykeskus to the treble border, with a climb through birch forest rewarded with a spectacular route along the Malla hillside, with great lake views below. Apart from a short section picking your way over rocks, it's an easy and rewarding walk in either direction. A side trip takes you up Pikku-Malla, the hill at the northern end of the lake.

A summer **boat service** (☎ 040-066 9392) leaves from just below the Retkeilykeskus at 10am, 2pm and 6pm, dropping you a light 3km stroll from the border marker (one-way/return €15/20, 30 minutes). This allows an easy visit, or to walk one way and cruise the other. The boat returns at 12.30pm, 4.30pm and 8.30pm.

For experienced trekkers, the 54km hike to **Halti Fell** (1328m), the highest point in Finland, is a rewarding, reasonably well-marked, trip. There are simple wilderness cabins along the route, but you should really take a tent. You can get close to it by road through Norway. **Kilpissafarit** (☎ 040-516 1952; www.kilpissafarit.fi) can arrange guided treks there and also runs winter snowmobile safaris.

All trekking routes and wilderness huts around the Kilpisjärvi area are clearly displayed on the 1:100,000 *Halti Kilpisjärvi* map (€19).

SCENIC FLIGHTS

There's a heliport at the southern end of Kilpisjärvi. Sightseeing flights cost around €120 per person with minimum numbers required. For information, call **Heliflite** (☎ 537 743; www.heliflite.fi).

Sleeping & Eating

Lining the main road are several camp sites with cabins. Many places are only open during the trekking season, which is June to September.

Kilpisjärven Retkeilykeskus (☎ 537 771; www .kilpisretkeily.fi; s/d €55/65, 4-person cottages €75; ☽ mid-Mar–Sep) Close to the border but 5km north of the village, this is conveniently close to the trekking routes and the Malla boat. You'll find a range of rooms and cottages here, all with bathroom. There's camping too, but it's more appealing for vans than tents. The no-decorative-frills restaurant dishes up a good all-you-can-eat buffet lunch daily in the high season (€13, from noon to 8pm) as well as breakfasts (€8) and à la carte dishes.

Kilpisjärven Lomakeskus (☎ 537 801; www.kilpis jarvi.net; camping €14 plus per adult €4, cottages €70-200, apt €70-120) This is the best of the clutch of camping 'n' cabins sites in the centre of Kilpisjärvi. It's got a cafe and excellent wooden cottages and apartments with their own sauna, loft bedroom, fully equipped kitchen, TV and video (films at reception). These are great value in summer.

Hotelli Kilpis (☎ 537 761; www.laplandhotels.com; s/d €79/98, 2-/4-bed apt €99/216; ☽ Mar-Sep; **P** wi-fi) This ageing hotel is on the main road in the centre of town, opposite the supermarket. Its rooms are simply appointed, and comfortable, but those in the annexe to your left as you enter are noisy. The 'hostel' rooms (singles/doubles €54/64) share bathrooms, and there are also apartments, more modern and stylish than the main hotel. The restaurant (mains €13 to €26, 5pm to 11pm) is the best around, and serves smallish portions of Lapp-style food, such as a 'Northern Union' of reindeer and salmon (€24). The bar opens from 9pm until 2am and is the town's watering hole.

As well as the hotel and Retkeilykeskus, several of the cabin complexes have their own cafe-restaurant, usually only open during the day. By the supermarket, **Ida-Sofie Café** (☎ 539 229; ☽ 11am-5pm) serves yummy Lappish dishes and snacks.

Getting There & Away

Two daily buses connect Rovaniemi and Kilpisjärvi (€63.70, six hours) via Kittilä, Levi and Muonio, with a connection to Hetta. In summer, one heads on to Tromsø in Norway.

It's a spectacular drive on the excellent sealed road from Muonio to Kilpisjärvi (almost 200km). There are service stations at the small settlement of Kaaresuvanto (where there's a border crossing into Sweden) and in Kilpisjärvi itself. North of Kilpisjärvi, the road continues into Norway and a spectacular ascent through mountains before descending to the fjords.

EASTERN LAPLAND

KEMIJÄRVI

☎ 016 / pop 8882

Kemijärvi, situated on north–south Hwy 5, is many people's first glimpse of Lapland. Its location on a spectacular lake has more to recommend it than any particular sights.

LAPLAND & SÁPMI

The **tourist office** (☎ 020-753 8394; www.kemijarvi
.fi; Vapaudenkatu 8; ☺ 9am-3.30pm Mon-Fri) is in the
centre and, like the **public library** (Hietaniemenkatu
3), has free internet access. Nearby is a bookshop to stock up on English paperbacks; there
aren't too many north of here.

Kemijärvi's attraction is its lake, and
you're best off hiring a bike or canoe and
exploring the countryside around, for
there's damn-all to do in town apart from
admire the 18th-century bell tower by the
modern church and the wooden sculptures
dotted throughout, legacies of the international wood-sculpting festivals. These are
concentrated especially in and around the
Puustelli art centre, which is the festival
display venue.

Festivals & Events

The **Woodcarving Symposium** (www.kemijarven
-kuvanveistoviikot.fi) is held in late June or early
July every odd-numbered year. It attracts
artists from many European countries,
whom you can see about their work. In early
September, Kemijärvi hosts **Ruska Swing** (www
.ruskaswing.fi), a festival of swing music and
dancing. Participants come from around the
world, and there is a special 'Swing Train'
from Helsinki.

Sleeping & Eating

Hietaniemi Camping (☎ 813 640; www.hietaniemicamp
ing.info; Hietaniemenkatu 7; tent sites €5 plus per adult/child
€4/2, cabin r €30-40; ☺ late May-Aug; P) Very close
to the centre on Pöyliöjärvi, a secondary part
of the main lake, this is a small grassy camp
site with not a great deal of privacy if it's full.
Two buildings offer cabin accommodation,
there's a simple cafe, and you can rent bikes
for €10/20 per half/full day.

Lohen Lomakeskus (☎ 040-581 2007; www.lohenlo
makeskus.fi; Lohelankatu 1; dm/s/d €18/35/50, cottages from
€60, apt €125; P) Just beyond the camp site, this
complex offers a variety of sleeping choices.
The cheerful red wooden, green-roofed cottages all come with bathroom, kitchen and
sauna, while the lakefront apartments are even
fancier. In the reception building, wooden bunk
rooms offer plenty of space and value, and simple private rooms share the same kitchen and
bathroom facilities. HI members get a discount.
You can rent canoes and bikes here.

Mestarin Kievari (☎ 322 7700; www.mestarinkievari
.fi; Kirkkokatu 9; s/d €74/84; ☺ food 10.30am-9pm Mon-

Fri, noon-8pm Sat; P ⌨) Kemijärvi's eating and
drinking scene pretty much begins and ends
here, and it's also the better of the town's two
hotels. It's a welcoming spot that'll fortify
you for your onward journey with a variety
of comfortable, fairly unadorned rooms that
differ only slightly in price. Some are in a
newer wing, while others have private sauna;
spacious family rooms with sloping ceilings
sit at the top. The restaurant features mostly
meaty fare (mains €13 to €28), though there
is a vegetarian option, and the lunch buffet
(€10) is very popular with passing traffic. The
pub opens from 10pm.

Getting There & Away

There are buses to Pyhä (€8.80, one hour),
Rovaniemi (€15.10, 1¼ hours), Sodankylä
(€17.70, 1¾ hours) and elsewhere. There's
one daily train to Helsinki, via Rovaniemi
(€13.80, 1½ hours).

SODANKYLÄ

☎ 016 / pop 8982
Likeable Sodankylä is the main service centre for one of Europe's least-populated areas,
which has a population density of just 0.8
people per sq km. It's at the junction of the
main two southbound highways and makes a
decent staging post between Rovaniemi and
the north; even if you're just passing through,
stop to see the wooden church – humble but
achingly beautiful.

The **tourist office** (☎ 618 168; www.sodankyla.fi;
Jäämerentie 3; ☺ 9am-5pm Mon-Fri, 11am-4pm Sat & Sun)
is at the intersection of the Kemijärvi and
Rovaniemi roads. Opposite is the library, with
internet access. Nearby in a small park, the
bronze **statue** of *Reindeer and Lapp* celebrates
reindeer husbandry, one of Lapland's most
important industries.

One of the few buildings in Lapland to survive the Germans' scorched-earth retreat in
WWII is the **old church** (☎ 040-019 0406; ☺ 9am-
6pm Jun–mid-Aug, 9am-5pm Fri-Mon rest of Aug, by request
rest of year) by the tourist office, near the Kitinen
riverside. It is the region's oldest and dates
back to 1689. The church stands in a graveyard encircled by a low wooden fence and is
noteworthy for its decorative shingles and
prominent pronglike standards. The interior
is simple and charming, with gnarled wooden
benches and pulpit, and a simple altar made
from leftover beams. A painting of the Last
Supper from the early 18th century is the

only adornment. The stone church nearby was built in 1859.

Alariesto Gallery (☎ 618 643; adult/child €3/1.50; 🕙 10am-4pm Mon-Fri Jun-Nov, plus 10am-3pm Sat Jul-Sep), in the same building as the tourist office, displays paintings by the famous local artist Andreas Alariesto (1900–89), who favoured a primitive style. There are many images of Sámi life.

Nearby, **Taiga Koru** (☎ 610 507; www.taigakoru .fi; 🕙 10am-5pm Mon-Fri, 10am-2pm Sat) is a jewellery shop famous both for the gold and silver works of goldsmith Seppo Penttinen.

By now you've probably seen reindeer wandering the roads, but if you want to learn more about these vital livestock, **Mattilan Porotila** (☎ 040-018 7877; Meltauksentie 975; adult/child €10/5; 🕙 10am-5pm Mon-Fri), at Riipi, 26km southwest of Sodankylä, is a family-run farm where you can meet and feed the reindeer or go on sleighing trips with them in winter. Phone ahead to arrange a visit.

Arctic Academy (☎ 040-514 2858; www.arcticacad emy.fi; Välisuvannontie; adult/child €11/6; 🕙 10am-4.30pm Jun-Aug) has a pricey, but informative aurora borealis audiovisual show at its Aurora House, 11km southeast of Sodankylä. In winter it arranges various activities including excursions to see the lights.

Sodankylä books out in mid-June for the **Midnight Sun Film Festival** (www.msfilmfestival.fi), which has a comprehensive range of intriguing screenings in three venues.

Sleeping & Eating

Camping Sodankylä Nilimella (☎ 612 181; www .naturex-ventures.fi; tent sites €5 plus per adult/child €4/2, 2-/4-person cabins €36/52, 2-/4-person apt €65/95; 🕙 Jun-Aug; P) Across the river from the town, this camp site has a sauna and good showers as well as a riverside cafe-bar. The cabins, discreetly angled for privacy, are simple but spacious, with a fridge and camp stove; there are also cottage apartments with their own kitchen and sauna. You can hire bikes for €15 per day.

Majatalo Kolme Veljestä (☎ 040-053 9075; www .majatalokolmeveljesta.fi; Ivalontie 1; s/d/tr €42/58/69; P 🖳 wi-fi) Five hundred metres north of the centre, this family-run guesthouse has small but spotless rooms with wire storage units and other comfortable Ikea-type furniture. Guests share decent bathrooms and have use of a lounge and kitchen facilities (there's a big supermarket across the road). Price includes breakfast, sauna, and free tea and coffee.

ourpick Hotelli Karhu (☎ 613 801; www.hotel -bearinn.com; Lapintie 7; s/d €77/100; P 🐾 wi-fi) This central hotel is a great deal, offering buzzy staff, offbeat lobby decor and inviting chambers, with big fluffy beds, grey-wood floors and great modern bathrooms. Some of the rooms have an excellent power steam shower, and single travellers are in for a treat here, as the same rate gets a room with a cute mini-sauna to call your own. You can borrow bikes and ski gear, and the restaurant does steak, salmon, pasta and reindeer in the evenings, and a value-packed €8 lunch.

Hotelli Sodankylä (☎ 617 121; hotsod@hotmail .com; Unartie 15; s/d €90/110; P wi-fi) Looking like a municipal library, this brick place is across the road from the bus station. It's a solid, rather than spectacular, choice, but the rooms are spacious, with trademark Finnish furniture, big windows and a coffee tray. The bar-restaurant isn't exactly humming in summer but the food's good.

Pizza-Paikka (☎ 612 990; Jäämerentie 25; pizzas €6-10; 🕙 11am-10pm Mon-Sat, 11am-10pm Sun) At the northern end of the main strip through town, this place has a pleasant wee terrace and is fully licensed. Pizzas – and only pizzas – are what they serve, but there's a good range, served pan or thin, and yes, there is a reindeer one…

Seita Baari (☎ 611 386; Jäämerentie 20; dishes €6-12; 🕙 9am-10pm Mon-Sat, 11am-10pm Sun, closes earlier in winter) A simple place, with plastic chairs, no frills and a stern but grandmotherly feel, this offers good and inexpensive homemade food, including Lappish specialities such as *poronkäristys* (sautéed reindeer).

Cafe Kerttuli (☎ 624 383; Jäämerentie 11; mains €12-21; 🕙 10am-10pm Mon-Sat, noon-8pm Sun) Cosy and homelike, this is the best eating spot in town, with gingham tablecloths, soups, quiches (try the reindeer-and-mushroom pie), cakes, good coffee and streetside seating. They do cheap lunches and tasty à la carte meals with local vendace and reindeer. Behind is Rooperante, the town's best pub with outdoor seating and a friendly vibe, though, like in any Lapland bar, there are always a few shamblers about.

Getting There & Away

Sodankylä is on the main Rovaniemi–Ivalo road (Rd 4), and Rd 5 from Kemijärvi and Karelia ends here. There are regular buses from Rovaniemi, Ivalo and Kemijärvi. The bus terminal is on the main road.

PYHÄ-LUOSTO REGION
☎ 016

The area between the fells of Luosto (514m) and Pyhä (540m) forms a popular winter sports centre. Most of the area forms part of Pyhä-Luosto National Park, which is excellent for trekking. Pyhä and Luosto, 25km apart, both have ski slopes and are fully serviced resort 'villages'. They make excellent-value, if quiet, places to stay in summer with bargain modern apartments and cottages available.

Orientation & Information
Pyhä is about 14km from the main Kemijärvi to Sodankylä road, while Luosto is the same distance east of the Rovaniemi–Sodankylä road. A good road connects the two resorts, which are 25km apart. Luosto is very compact, while Pyhä is spread out: there are services along the road by Pyhäjärvi, but the main ski slope and accommodation is 3km further west (signposted 'Pyhätunturi').

For information on Pyhä-Luosto National Park and activities such as hiking and fishing, drop by the park's **Pyhätunturi Nature Centre** (☎ 020-564 7302; pyhatunturi@metsa.fi; 9am-5pm), opposite the Pyhätunturi hotel.

Sights
LAMPIVAARA AMETHYST MINE
The **amethyst mine** (☎ 040-052 3924; www.amethyst mine.fi; adult/child €13/8, in winter €15/9; 11am-5pm Jun–mid-Aug, 11am-4pm mid-Aug–Sep, 11am-3pm Tue-Sat Oct, noon & 2pm Tue, Thu & Sat late Nov-late Dec, noon & 2pm daily Jan-Apr), 5km above Luosto, is Europe's only working amethyst mine, and it focuses on small-scale production for jewellery, using low-impact mining methods. There are guided tours (in English by request) on the hour, and you get to have a dig around for your own piece of amethyst. The mine is accessible by forest road from Luosto; follow the signs. If you don't have a car, it's a pleasant hike, or €10 by cab. In winter, you can't get there by road, only on foot, skis, or using the snow-train from Ukko-Luosto parking (adult/child including admission €30/18). Amethyst products are on sale at the mine shop in Luosto.

PYHÄ-LUOSTO NATIONAL PARK
Created in 2005, this 142-sq-km park was a long time in the making, and incorporates

Pyhätunturi, previously the oldest national park in Finland, established in 1938. The core of the park is the long line of fells stretching 35km from Pyhä itself to north of Luosto. There are several peaks around the 530m mark, and winding gorges between them. The most notable sight is the 200m deep Isokuru Gorge by Pyhätunturi.

The park preserves old-growth forest with various endangered plant species, the southern reaches of the Lapland fell ecosystems, and *aapa* (open bog) areas that harbour snipe, bean geese, swans and the occasional golden eagle cruising for prey.

There is a bird-watching tower at the southeastern corner of the park, about 2.5km from the Pyhätunturi Nature Centre. A circular nature trail of 5km takes you there. See opposite for other walks in the park.

Little Aittokuru Gorge, just west of Pyhäjärvi, has a spectacular **gorge theatre**, with frequent performances in the summer months. It's well worth a look even if there's nothing on.

REINDEER & HUSKIES
More or less midway between Pyhä and Luosto, **Kopara Reindeer Park** (☎ 040-0587 9949; www.kopara.fi; 11am-3pm Mon-Fri Jun-Sep, 11am-4pm Jan-Apr) is a good place to meet some reindeer. You can go on a short walk that has information boards on the creatures (€5 per person), and tempt them closer with a feed bucket. In winter, various sledge trips are on offer, from short jaunts (€15) to full-day journeys and longer. The cafe here specialises in blueberry pie in summer and *er* (reindeer soup) in winter.

Nearby, the **Arctic Husky Farm** (☎ 040-027 2714; www.huskysafaris.com) is where the dogs relax all summer gaining strength for winter sledge safaris. You can visit their enclosures at 2pm weekdays from June to August (€5 per person).

Activities
SKIING
At Pyhä there are 10 ski-runs and seven lifts. The longest run is 1.8km, with a vertical drop of 280m. At Luosto, there are seven runs and four lifts, plus a half-pipe and snowboard slopes. The longest run is 1.5km, with a vertical drop of 230m.

Between them, Pyhä and Luosto have over 150km of trails for cross-country skiers, some

40km of which are lit. You can rent equipment and get lessons at either location.

WALKING

Within Pyhä-Luosto National Park there are several marked trails, which, together with the network of cross-country skiing trails, means that walkers are very well provided for. One of the nicest walks is the 35km trail between Pyhä and Luosto, involving plenty of ascents and descents as it climbs from fell to fell. From Pyhätunturi Nature Centre, a 10km loop trail runs to Pyhäkuru Gorge, while from Luosto, a hilly 15km nature trail loops to the top of the fell and around the flatlands and mires on the other side.

There are several huts where you can stay overnight in the national park. The most useful is Huttuloma wilderness hut, which sleeps six. On the Pyhä-Luosto trail, accommodation is possible at Kapusta and Rykimäkuru huts and there's another hut at Yli-Luosto, the end-point of the range of fells and the national park itself.

Tours

LuontoSafarit (☎ 624 336; www.luontosafarit.fi; Orresokantie 1, Luosto) is a friendly agency that has a full range of activities. In summer you can take trips on quads to the amethyst mine or reindeer farm (€65 to €100 per person), or head to the river for canoeing and fishing. In winter there are similar excursions, but on snowmobiles (€100 to €200); there are also exciting multiday trips to the Arctic Ocean.

Sleeping & Eating

Hundreds of cottages, cabins and apartments in the Pyhä-Luosto area make great places to stay. The two main agencies are the excellent **Keskusvaraamo Pyhähippu** (☎ 882 820; www.pyha.fi; open daily, roughly 9am-8pm Nov-Apr & Jul-Sep, 9.30am-5pm at other times) just down the hill from the Pyhätunturi Nature Centre, and **Pyhä-Luosto Matkailu** (☎ 020-730 3020; www.pyha-luostomatkailu .fi; Laukotie 1; 9am-5pm Mon-Fri) on the main road in Luosto. Both offer over a hundred cabins, apartments and cottages that you can book online; Pyhähippu has the advantage of convenient opening hours for on-spec arrivals. For around €50 in summer, you can nab a luxury cottage or apartment for two, complete with sofa, balcony, sauna and fireplace with free firewood, not to mention a fully equipped kitchen and a drying cupboard. Rates increase

sharply in winter, and at peak periods there's a one-week minimum stay (from €600). The hotels also raise their prices.

There are many designated camping areas within a short walk from the Pyhätunturi Nature Centre, and a site for vans by the Luosto ski slope.

Hotelli Luostotunturi (☎ 620 400; www.luostotun turi.com; s/d €120/152, apt €176-220; P □ ☒ wi-fi) The rounded design of this curious hotel is supposed to resemble a reindeer's earmark. Happily, the comforts and facilities on offer are much less difficult to perceive. Most of the spacious rooms have a log-girt balcony, and some have an extra loft-style sleeping space, ideal for families. A new wing has excellent apartments, with a pretty kitchenette and a sauna. There's a pretty indoor pool and various spa treatments. Visitors can use the facilities for €12/7 per adult/child. The hotel also rents bikes.

our pick Hotelli Aurora Chalet (☎ 327 2700; www .aurorachalet.fi; Luppokeino 2; r to €154; May-Mar; P wi-fi) Newly opened at the Luosto slope, this is one of Lapland's most original and stylish hotels and a great deal in summer. All rooms have their own sauna, and many a wood fire; the wide floorboards, warm colours and romantic design create a whole ambience of great creativity, with an old-fashioned rustic air combined with modern comforts. Their activity company can arrange snowmobiling and more.

Hotelli Pyhätunturi (☎ 856 111; www.pyha.fi; s €93-120, d €136-168; P □ wi-fi) Pyhä's major hotel sits halfway up the chairlift at the top of the road. The big bright white double rooms have recycling bags, a drying cupboard and flatscreen TV, and the hotel's restaurant has a great view and is romantically candlelit at night. There are also self-contained chalets available. There's no pool, but a sauna, gym and Jacuzzi will ease those ski-tired muscles. The hotel also rents bikes for €20 a day.

Kerttuli (☎ 624 385; Hartsutie 1; mains €13-21; 2-9pm Oct-Aug, noon-11pm Sep) In the centre of Luosto, this is a cosy place that offers pizzas as well as more intriguing fare such as braised chin of reindeer, roast beef and risotto in its cosy interior.

Getting There & Away

Two daily buses (four in winter) run from Rovaniemi to Luosto (€18, one hour 40 minutes) and Pyhä (€20, two hours): one meets the morning Finnair flight from Helsinki en route. These are the only buses connecting Pyhä and Luosto (€4, 20 minutes).

There are also buses to Pyhä from Kemijärvi (€8.80, 50 minutes) and Sodankylä (€15.10, 1¼ hours), with extra buses put on for the Midnight Sun Film Festival. Call a local cab on ☎ 106 425. The fare between Pyhä and Luosto is €35.

SAARISELKÄ
☎ 016

The bustling, touristy village of Saariselkä (Sámi: Suolocielgi) is a major winter destination for Christmassy experiences, sled safaris and skiing, and in summer serves as the main base for trekkers heading into the awesome Saariselkä Wilderness area. It's more resort than community, but has plenty of accommodation and shops to stock up on trekking supplies and equipment, and high-quality souvenirs.

For information, head for the Siula Centre, just off the main road near the petrol station. Here, there's the **tourist information point** (☎ 668 402; www.saariselka.fi; ⏰ 9am-5pm Mon-Fri), with information left out even when it's closed, and **Kiehinen** (☎ 020-564 7200; www.outdoors.fi; ⏰ 9am-6pm Mon-Fri, 9am-4pm Sat & Sun), a national parks centre with hiking information, cabin reservations, fishing permits, maps and a small nature display.

A couple of hundred metres up the hill, the **Kuukkeli** centre sits at the main entrance to the village and has baggage lockers and postal services as well as the main accommodation agency.

Activities & Tours

Saariselkä is bristling with things to do year-round. Things are most active in winter, with numerous snowy excursions organised by the many activity companies in town. Husky- and reindeer-sledding are understandably popular, with trips of a couple of hours starting at €70. Snowmobiling costs a little more, and there are excursions that combine options, as well as multiday safaris.

In summer, things on offer include visits to Tankavaara (€74 to €89), reindeer farms (€60), Nordic walks in the Urho Kekkonen National Park (€60), canoeing on the Tankajoki (€124), fishing (€67), whitewater rafting on the Juutanjoki rapids in Inari (€49), whole-day rafting on the Ivalojoki

(€168), and various guided walks in the area. All these can be booked at the tourist office or via the hotels. The best hiking is in the Saariselkä Wilderness (p336).

Most operators offer all these activities and also rent mountain bikes and skis:

Eräsetti Safaris (☎ 668 345; www.erasetti.fi; Siula Centre)

Husky Co (☎ 667 776; www.saariselka.fi/huskyco) Pooches and snowmobiles.

Lapland Safaris (☎ 668 901; www.laplandsafaris.com; Riekonlinna hotel)

LuontoLoma/Pro Safaris (☎ 668 706; www.luontoloma.fi) Based at the Tunturi hotel.

SKIING

There are 11 downhill slopes served by five lifts; the longest run is 1300m and the vertical drop is 180m. There's also a freestyle park and some 240km of cross-country trails, some of which are lit. Saariselkä is known for having good snow-kiting conditions, and you can have lessons in this exciting sport. Ski rental costs around €10/50 per day/week, while a lift pass for one/five days costs €29/110 in the peak of the season.

Sleeping

Prices in Saariselkä's hotels are highest during the ski season and *ruska* (late August to mid-September). **Saariselän Keskusvaraamo** (☎ 020-310 000; www.saariselankeskusvaraamo.fi; ⏰ 9am-9pm Mon-Fri, noon-9pm Sat & Sun) is an accommodation service at the bottom of the Kuukkeli centre and can organise a wide range of cabins, cottages and apartments in and around the village. They also rent bikes (€10/20 per half-/full day), mountain bikes (€15/25) and scooters (€40/80).

Here, as in other parts of Finland, the accommodation division of the Forest and Park Service has many rural cabins and cottages for rent. Ask at the Kiehinen information centre, or contact **Villi Pohjola** (☎ 020-344 122; www.villipohjola.fi) directly.

our pick Saariselän Panimo (☎ 675 6500; www.saariselanpanimo.fi; s/d €73/86; **P** wi-fi) The friendly village pub offers good accommodation in a variety of buildings around it, in the heart of Saariselkä. Rooms are spacious and warm, with bathroom, comfortable beds and free wi-fi, and are an absolute steal in summer. A sauna, but no breakfast, is included.

Saariselän Tunturihotelli (☎ 681 501; www.tunturihotelli.fi; standard s/d €118/140, superior €165/197,

2-/4-person apt €176/225; P wi-fi) Now Lapland's largest hotel, this complex sprawls across several buildings including the brand-new Gielas and the Dalmatian-like Paraspaikka but hasn't lost sight of its roots as a solid old place with a warm welcome and excellent service. We'd need the whole chapter to list the numerous grades of rooms and apartments (all but the standards come with their own sauna); the most modern are the superior and junior suite categories. Prices drop in summer and at weekends.

Hotelli Riekonlinna (☎ 559 4455; www.laplandhotels.com; s/d to €135/172; P wi-fi) The sleeping chambers at this sizeable hotel have cheery curtains, nature photos and OK beds. Rates include access to the gym and sauna, but for only €12 extra, you can get a sauna in your room. The rooms all have balconies, but close their door when you leave, else cheeky squirrels will hop in and munch your lunch.

Holiday Club Saariselkä (☎ 6828; www.holidayclub.fi; d/f to €169/194; P wi-fi) In the centre of the village, this spa hotel is most family-friendly and a good choice in winter or summer. There are heaps of facilities as well as leisure activities on offer, two restaurants (one with good-value dinner buffet) and comfortable rooms with balconies. Nonguests can use the spa facilities for €15 (kids €9).

Eating & Drinking

The best restaurants shut in summer, when you are just about wholly restricted to the hotel restaurants. The Panimo brews its own beer and is a cosy, welcoming spot for a drink.

Pirtti (mains €9-22; 11am-11pm) The Tunturi's restaurant is a likeable, family-friendly place that offers light meals such as reindeer wraps and hamburgers, as well as a daily fish special and salmon smothered in hollandaise sauce.

Rakka (mains €13-25; noon-11pm) The Holiday Club's à la carte restaurant has a menu divided into traditional steak-type dishes and 'healthy choices', like tasty roasted salmon on mash, for example, that comes with a rocket and olive-oil salad. Service is slow and wines overpriced, but the food itself is decent value. They also offer pizzas and burgers, though the adjacent buffet restaurant will be more to the kids' liking.

Huippu (☎ 668 803; mains €13-24; 10am-11pm) Situated at the top of the Kaunispää fell by the ski slopes, this restaurant has a spectacular outdoor terrace and cosy interior with a log fire. It's fairly touristy but serves a decent salad buffet as well as well-presented and tasty main dishes with Arctic char and reindeer. It's 2km northeast by road but a nice walk uphill from the village.

In winter and the *ruska* season, several worthwhile eating options open in town:

Petronella (☎ 668 930; mains €16-33; Sep & Nov-Apr) Serves lavish portions of smart Lappish food in a refined, elegant dining room.

Pirkon Pirtti (☎ 668 050; Honkapolku 2; mains €13-24; Sep-Apr) This popular place near the tourist office has a lovely cosy interior with fireplace. As well as tasty pizzas (€8 to €10), it serves delicious Lapp specialities, like reindeer in pepper sauce, at very reasonable prices.

Siberia (☎ 668 143; Saariseläntie 3; mains €19-30; Sep & Nov-Apr) This smart spot sits behind the rainbow screen on the main street and offers quality glassware and a menu with a Russian touch, including borscht and blinis.

Getting There & Away

There are four or more daily buses from Rovaniemi (€43.90, 4½ hours), continuing to Ivalo (€7.80, 30 minutes). Each incoming flight at Ivalo is met by a shuttle bus to Saariselkä (€6.50).

AROUND SAARISELKÄ
Kiilopää

Kiilopää, 17km southeast of Saariselkä, is another major trekking centre for the region, and is an excellent spot to start or finish a hike. Marked trails head directly into the wilderness from here.

Tunturikeskus Kiilopää (Kiilopää Fell Resort; ☎ 670 0700; www.kiilopaa.com; r 1/2 nights to €90/120; P) is an excellent and very professional facility that takes care of all accommodation and services. It rents mountain bikes, rucksacks, sleeping bags, skiing equipment and more. It also sells fishing permits and dispenses sound advice on trekking; guided treks are possible. There are hotel rooms and a cafe-restaurant (packed lunch €6, dinner €13 to €17), as well as a variety of cottages and apartments starting at €65/86 for a two-/four-person apartment in summer, and the **Ahopää hostel** (dm summer/winter €30/37), a comfortable HI-affiliated facility with a kitchen, sauna, laundry and cafe.

The centre has a traditional **smoke sauna** that's fired up on Wednesdays and Fridays from June to August. It's open from 3pm to 8pm and costs €10/5 per adult/child (free if

LAPLAND & SÁPMI

you're staying here). You can rent towels and swimwear here for €4 apiece.

Hotel Kakslauttanen (☎ 667 100; www.kakslauttanen.fi; s/d cabins from €149/188, s/d igloo €147/220, s/d glass igloo €210/266; **P** **⬚** wi-fi) is a large accommodation complex on the main road at the Kiilopää turn-off that comes into its own in winter, when they build the **Snow Village** (☽ Dec-Apr), consisting of igloos to bed down in, and a snow restaurant for your tucker. There are traditional snow igloos (warm sleeping bag provided) as well as swish glass igloos, which are warm inside and give you the chance to watch the aurora borealis from the luxury of your own bed.

Hotel Kakslauttanen is on Rd 4, 11km south of Saariselkä. Kiilopää is 6km east of it. Several daily buses do the one-hour trip between Ivalo and Kiilopää; a bus meets every incoming flight to Ivalo airport. If you are travelling by bus from Rovaniemi, check whether the bus runs to Kiilopää: not all do.

Tankavaara

Back in 1868, a cry went up and started a gold rush to this remote area on the Ivalojoki that saw a community of up to 500 panners seeking their fortune here after an arduous journey. Though people still work claims, Tankavaara these days sees more income from the tourist trade than from the bottom of the goldpans.

The main attraction is the **Kultamuseo** (Gold Museum; ☎ 626 171; adult/child €8/4; ☽ 9am-6pm Jun–mid-Aug, 9am-5pm mid-Aug–Sep, 10am-4pm Mon-Fri Oct-May), which has several parts. Nearest the entrance gate are replica buildings from American goldfields; the nearby smoke sauna and octagonal hut are less flashy but original. Rockhounds will enjoy the gemstone and mineral exhibition despite its neglected air, but the highlight is the main museum, with sections on the Finnish gold rush, and on gold production around the world. A cubic metre of sand is on display along with the sobering 2g of gold it normally contains here. In summer, try your luck and pan for gold (€4 extra, or €20 for a day's licence). Gold-related events and festivals are held in summer, the biggest being the Goldpanners' Festival in early August, which includes the Finnish Goldpanning Championships.

Also here is **Koilliskaira Visitor Centre** (☎ 020-564 7251; ukpuisto@metsa.fi; ☽ 9am-6pm Jun-Sep, 9am-5pm Mon-Fri Oct & Feb-May), with advice on activities and trekking in Urho K Kekkonen National Park. It has top exhibitions on local wildlife, including a display on raptors upstairs, a slide show, a shop and a good selection of maps. Four circular **nature trails** arc out from the centre (1km to 6km); a booklet available from the centre gives good extra information about these routes.

By the entrance to the gold village, **Wanha Waskoolimies** (☎ 626 158; www.tankavaara.fi; daily plates €17; ☽ food 9am-9pm summer; **⬚**) is a kitsch but atmospheric cafe-restaurant that actually predates the museum and serves typical Lapp dishes and wards off the cold with Lapp Schnapps. They have hotel rooms (singles/doubles €40/60) and cabins with (€40 to €60) and without (€30) bathroom facilities alongside. You can also camp here (€12 per night).

Tankavaara is on the main Rovaniemi–Ivalo road 30km south of Saariselkä and 100km north of Sodankylä. All buses pass the village, stopping on request; nonexpress buses actually enter.

SAARISELKÄ WILDERNESS

Saariselkä Wilderness, including the 2538-sq-km **Urho K Kekkonen National Park** and also large tracts of protected forest, extends to the Russian border. It's a fabulous slice of Finland, home to bears, wolverines and golden eagles, as well as many thousands of free-grazing reindeer. This is a highly rated trekking area, partly because of the large network of wilderness huts, but also for the unspoilt beauty of the low fells. You certainly won't be alone in peak season on the most popular routes, but there are plenty of options in this huge and memorable expanse of forest, fell and marshland.

Orientation & Information

The park's divided into four zones, each with different rules. Camping and fires are only allowed in designated places; to minimise environmental impact it is recommended you make use of previously used pitches. In the wilderness zones of Saariselkä (west) and Nuortti (southeast), camping is allowed everywhere except in certain gorges and on treeless areas. In the Kemi-Sompio wilderness zone (east), camping is allowed everywhere.

Although fires (using dead wood) are allowed in certain areas, take a camp stove, as fire bans are common in summer. In most areas, fires are only allowed at designated fireplace zones (these are supplied with firewood).

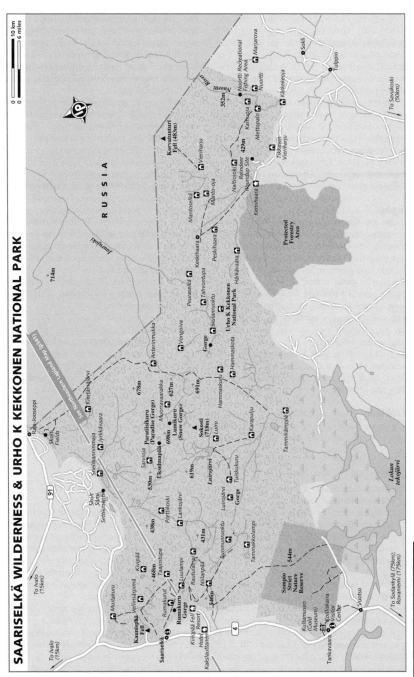

SAARISELKÄ WILDERNESS & URHO K KEKKONEN NATIONAL PARK

There are national park visitor centres in Saariselkä, Tankavaara (Koilliskaira) and Savukoski villages; you can also pick up information at Kiilopää, although it isn't an official information centre. A map and compass are *essential* for the most remote areas of the park.

There are three Karttakeskus maps available for the area. The western part of the park is shown on the 1:50,000 *Saariselkä-Kiilopää* map; the 1:50,000 *Sokosti-Suomujoki* map will take you beyond Luirojärvi; the entire park is shown on the 1:100,000 *Koilliskaira* map. Each map costs €19. The visitor centres also sell a simpler map for day-trip walks (€3).

Sights

There are several natural attractions within the park boundaries, of which **Rumakuru Gorge**, near the hut of the same name, is closest to the main road. **Luirojärvi** is the most popular trekking destination, including a hike up the nearby **Sokosti summit** (718m), the highest in the park. **Paratiisikuru** (Paradise Gorge), a steep descent from the 698m **Ukselmapää summit**, and the nearby **Lumikuru** (Snow Gorge), are popular day trips between Sarvioja and Muorravaarakka huts.

Two historical **Skolt Sámi settlements**, with restored old houses, lie 2km south of Raja-Jooseppi, and 2km west of Snelmanninmaja hut, respectively.

Trekking

There is a large number of possible walking routes in the Saariselkä area. Use wilderness huts as bases and destinations, and create your own itinerary according to your ability: an experienced, fit trekker can cover up to 4km per hour, and up to 25km per day. You will need to carry all food, as wilderness huts in the park are not stocked with supplies; water in rivers is drinkable.

The four- to six-day loop from the main road to Luirojärvi is the most popular, and can be extended beyond the lake. To reach areas where few have been, take a one-week walk from Kiilopää to Kemihaara.

The most remote route follows old roads and walking routes through the fells all the way from Raja-Jooseppi in the north to Kemihaara or Tulppio in the southeast.

Despite its popularity, it can be tough going for the less experienced. Trails – particularly in the eastern part of the park – can be faint or almost nonexistent. Winter ski safaris can become especially dangerous during cold spells, and some areas are only suitable for expert ski-trekkers. Take advice from the park visitor centres on current conditions and route descriptions.

Sleeping

Within the park are 200 designated free camping areas as well as some 40 free wilderness huts. Some of these have locked areas with beds, and there are a few cabins, which must both be booked in advance. The charge is €9 per bed per night; this is on a shared basis. Book beds at any of the park visitor centres.

A few huts close to the main road are for day use only – you can overnight at one of

---

HUT-IQUETTE AND HIKING

Lonely Planet reader Andrew Pitt had this to say on a recent hiking adventure in the Urho K Kekkonen National Park:

'Huts are usually conveniently spaced a comfortable day's walk apart (four to six hours walking – 10km to 20km). Each *laavu* (simple log shelter) is near water, has a wood stove, and anyone can cook inside. In near proximity there are usually pit toilets, camp sites, established fire sites, a supply of dried firewood and occasionally a sauna. The huts have sleeping platforms and/or bunkbeds, and open access. However, should it be busy, etiquette has it that the walkers arriving LAST have first option on sleeping inside as they theoretically have less opportunity to set up camp outside. So carrying a tent is advised – you'll probably sleep better anyway given the high likelihood the hut will be full of mosquitoes by the end of the evening.

'Trails are generally good and well marked, but not always. There are a variety of easy day walks accessible from the villages lining the western side of the park. For longer treks in the park, expect river crossings and be careful to choose the best place to cross. The landscape is undulating and mainly forested but not particularly difficult for confident walkers during the warmer months. A good walking map and a compass are essential. Ski-trekking is popular in winter.'

these in an emergency. You'll need a sleeping bag and mat for the wilderness huts; bookable ones have mattresses. Visitor centres supply maps and details of huts, as does the www.outdoors.fi website.

Getting There & Away

The easiest starting points for treks are Saariselkä or Kiilopää. From Savukoski you can catch a **post-taxi** (☎ 040-730 6484) to Kemihaara village (Wednesday and Friday), 1km from the park's boundary.

The Raja–Jooseppi border station is another starting point for treks, as it takes you directly into the real wilderness; you can get there by taxi-bus from Ivalo.

IVALO

☎ 016 / pop 3500

A small town by most standards, Ivalo (Sámi: Avvil) is a metropolis in these latitudes. With plenty of services and an airport busy with charters at Christmas, it's a useful service centre, but has little to detain the visitor, with Inari's Sámi culture and Saariselkä's plentiful activities so close.

On the main road, **Inarilainen** (☎ 030-624 4120; Ivalontie 7; ☺ 9am-5pm Mon-Fri) has a tourist information point inside. Across the road, there's a **Metsähallitus centre** (☎ 020-564 7701; Ivalontie 10; ☺ 9am-4pm Mon-Fri) with national park information.

Activities

Several husky kennels around Ivalo offer dog-sledding trips in winter. **Kamisak** (☎ 667 736; www.kamisak.com) is 8km south and open year-round. There's a cafe, knowledgeable canine chat, and you can take an informal tour of the husky enclosures and meet the dogs (adult/child €4/2). From November to April, they run safaris that range from a half-day trip to multiday adventures, where participants get their own sleds and are taught how to drive and care for their own team.

If you've always fancied yourself as another Kimi Räikkönen or Marcus Grönholm, pay the **Arctic Rally Team** (☎ 663 456; www.arcticrallyteam .fi; Ivalontie 25) a visit. They organise crash courses (so to speak) in winter driving, rallying and even navigating.

Sleeping, Eating & Drinking

Hotel Kultahippu (☎ 320 8800; www.kultahippu.fi; Petsamontie 1; s/d €72/90; P ⌨ ⌷) In the 'Speck

of Gold' you might still see the odd gold panner stooped pensively over their *tuoppi* (glass) of beer. The rooms are fairly simple and not great summer value, but the riverside location appeals, especially in winter. The spacious restaurant does a €9 lunch buffet, and the pub and club are the main local nightspots (the noise isn't too bad from the rooms though).

Hotelli Ivalo (☎ 688 111; www.hotelivalo.fi; Ivalontie 34; s/d €85/105; P ⌨ ⌷ ⌹ wi-fi) Half a kilometre south of the centre on the main road, the town's main hotel has nondescript comfortable rooms, a sauna and a nice indoor pool. It's worth trying to get a discount in summer, when the rack rate is poor value by comparison with other hotels in the region. They hire bikes to guests; there's also a decent restaurant, pool table and pub, as well as a tour agency.

ourpick Pankkila (☎ 040-354 8337; www.pankkila.fi; mains €13-26; ☺ 11am-9pm Mon-Fri, noon-10pm Sat & Sun) A welcome Ivalo arrival, this former bank building has been lovingly converted into a stylish restaurant, with plenty of natural light and wooden slat screens dividing the tables. The mistranslated menu gives few clues, but dishes such as 'Master of Cheese's Bovine' don't disappoint, and several reindeer dishes, including liver, are on offer. Out the back are excellent apartments (2-/4-/6-person apartments €80/100/160) that are exceedingly modern, spacious and comfortable; some have their own sauna.

Getting There & Away

There are numerous winter charters to Ivalo Airport, and regular Finnair services from Helsinki. The airport is 12km south of Ivalo; a connecting bus meets each arriving flight.

There are a few daily buses from Rovaniemi (€49.80, 4¾ hours) to Ivalo. Car-rental companies with offices at Ivalo Airport (and in town) include Avis, Budget, Hertz and Europcar.

A road runs east from Ivalo to the Russian city of Murmansk, 303km away. Three weekly buses (see p361) travel the distance. The border is crossed at Raja-Jooseppi, 53km from Ivalo. This is also a possible starting point for treks into the Saariselkä Wilderness. The Murmansk bus leaves Ivalo at 3.30pm on Mondays, Wednesdays and Fridays.

NELLIM

This tucked-away village with a population of under 200 is one of the major Skolt settlements and worth a visit for anyone interested in Sámi culture. There's also a significant Inari

LAPLAND & SÁPMI

Sámi and Finnish population and Nellim likes to dub itself as the meeting point of three cultures. Situated on the shores of Inarijärvi some 40km northeast of Ivalo, it has a restored log flume and lumberjack hut as testament to its logging history, and a beautiful wooden Orthodox church built in 1988. **Erähotelli Nellim** (☎ 040-041 5989; www.nellim.fi; Nellimintie 4230; s/d €60/80, 2-/4-person apt €95/135; **P**) offers good little rooms with checked curtains and simple wooden furniture, as well as apartments with sauna and kitchen. They can arrange meals and all sorts of activities. Two buses run Mondays to Fridays between Nellim and Ivalo (50 minutes).

INARI
☎ 016 / pop 550

Though it's Finland's most significant Sámi centre, and one of Lapland's major visitor destinations, you might miss the tiny village of Inari (Sámi: Anár), if you're not paying attention. Don't, for this is the place to begin to learn something of Sámi culture: it has the wonderful Siida museum, as well as excellent handicrafts shops. It's also a great base for heading off to further-flung locations like Lemmenjoki National Park.

Inari is the seat of the Finnish Sámi parliament, and plans have been finalised for a Sámi cultural centre that will hold it, as well as a library and music archive. The village sits on Lapland's largest lake, Inarijärvi, a spectacular body of water with more than 3000 islands in its 1153-sq-km area.

Information

Inari Info (☎ 661 666; www.inarilapland.org; ☺ 9am-6pm Jun-Aug, 10am-5pm early Sep, 10am-5pm Mon-Fri mid-Sep–May) In the centre of the village, this is a goldmine of information and a great place for tips on finding out more about the area and Sámi culture. They rent bikes, kayaks and canoes and have internet access (€2 per 15 minutes).

Sights
SIIDA

One of Finland's finest museums, **Siida** (☎ 665 212; www.siida.fi; adult/student/child €8/6.50/4; ☺ 9am-8pm Jun-Sep, 10am-5pm Tue-Sun Oct-May) should not be missed. It's a comprehensive overview of the Sámi and their environment that's actually two museums skilfully interwoven. The main exhibition hall consists of a wonderful nature exhibition around the edge, detailing northern Lapland's ecology by season, with some wonderful photos and information panels. In the centre of the room is detailed information on the Sámi, from their former seminomadic existence to modern times. In an adjacent hall is a timeline framing Sámi prehistory and history, alongside other world events, and two other halls have excellent temporary exhibitions of Sámi crafts and traditions.

Outside is the original museum, a complex of **open-air buildings** that reflect postnomadic Sámi life. They are mostly original buildings brought here and include farmhouses, storage huts and a courthouse, where miscreants scratched their names on the wooden walls while awaiting a likely flogging. Different Sámi groups are represented, and there are also various artefacts, such as several dastardly traps for bears, foxes and wolves.

Back inside, a theatrette shows pretty visuals of the aurora borealis and Inarijärvi a few times a day; there's also a fine craft shop and a top-value cafe, where the €9.50 lunch gets you a hot dish and free use of the salad bar.

Siida's website is itself worth a mention, for via the 'services' and 'links' menus you can access a series of excellent pages on the Inari and Skolt Sámi cultures among many other treasures.

PIELPAJÄRVI WILDERNESS CHURCH

The *erämaakirkko* (wilderness church) of Pielpajärvi is accessible from Inari by a marked walking track (7.5km one way) from the parking area at Siida. If you have a vehicle there's another car park 2.5km beyond here, up Sarviniementie, from where it's a 4.3km walk to the church. In winter, you'll need snowshoes and a keen attitude to do this. The church area has been an important marketplace for the Sámi over the centuries, with the first church erected here in 1646. The present church was built in 1760, and restored in the 1970s. It's always open. You are invited to open the shutters to get the full benefit of the interior, but close them again after your visit.

Another worthwhile trail in the area leads 9km from Siida to the top of Otsamo fell, where you're rewarded with a great view. There's a day hut here for shelter and cooking.

INARI CHURCH

The **church** (☺ mid-Jun–mid-Aug) on the main street was built in 1952 with American fi-

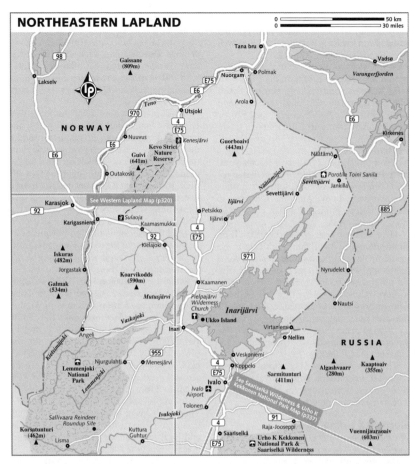

NORTHEASTERN LAPLAND

nancing. It's an attractive A-framed structure with a warm wooden feeling inside. The rather beautiful altar painting by Väinö Saikko depicts a Sámi family, complete with tethered reindeer, meeting Christ in the Lapland wildernesses. Inari Sámi and Fell Sámi are spoken in this church; services are usually on Sunday at 2pm.

Tours

Daily cruises run by **Lake & Snow** (☎ 040-029 5731; www.saariselka.fi/lakesnow) sail on Inarijärvi from mid-June (as soon as the ice melts) to mid-August (€15, two hours). Departures are at 2pm daily, with an additional departure in July at 6pm. Boats leave from the wharf at the Siida car park. The destination is **Ukko Island**

(Sámi: Äjjih), which is sacred to the Sámi. During the brief (20-minute) stop, most people climb to the top of the island, but there are also cave formations at the island's northern end. The same company also organises fishing trips and snowmobile safaris, and in summer can organise quad-bike trips.

Inari Event (☎ 661 666; www.saariselka.fi/inarievent) is run out of the tourist office and is an excellent set-up organising all types of tours and programs with a deep knowledge of local culture.

Two seaplanes parked in the lake serve as air taxis. They also do 10-minute **scenic flights** (☎ 040-039 9906, 040-056 8286; www.konekorhonen.com, www.lentopalvelu.fi) and chartered trips (one to three people €140) around Inarijärvi.

Luontoloma (☎ 668 706; www.luontoloma.fi) organises daily one-hour rafting jaunts on the rapids from the Kultahovi hotel (€25) as well as other watery trips in the region.

Inarin Porofarmi (☎ 673 912; Kittiläntie 1445; www .reindeerfarm.fi) is a reindeer farm that runs sled-trips in winter and visits in summer, with plenty of information on reindeer herding and Sámi culture. The two-hour visit costs €20, or €45 including transport from Inari.

Festivals & Events

The third weekend of January is **Skábmagovat**, an indigenous-themed film festival that in recent years has seen collaborations with groups from northern Russia, Australia, Canada and Brazil. There's enough English content to make it worthwhile.

Held over the last weekend of March or first weekend of April, the King's Cup is the grand finale of Lapland's **reindeer-racing** (www. paliskunnat.fi) season and a great spectacle as the de-antlered beasts race around the frozen lake, jockeys sliding like water-skiers behind them. The semifinals are on Saturday, the final on Sunday, and plenty of betting livens things up. There's also a race for visitors, which degenerates into comedy, as driving a reindeer is harder than it looks.

The last weekend of May is **Ijahis Idja** (www .ijahisidja.fi), an excellent music festival that features groups from all spectra of Sámi music. The name means 'nightless night'.

Sleeping & Eating

Uruniemi Camping (☎ 671 331; www.uruniemi.com; camp sites €14, r €20, cabins €25-50; ☉ Jun-late Sep) This place, 2km south of town, is a well-equipped lakeside camping ground with cottages, a cafe, a sauna and boats and bikes for hire.

Lomakylä Inari (☎ 671 108; www.lomakyla-inari.fi; 2-/4-person cabins €35/45, with bathroom €50/65, cottages with sauna €75-150, camping for 1-2 people €22; ☉ Jun-late Sep; P 🖳) The closest cabin accommodation to town, this is 500m south of the centre and a good option. There's a range of cabins and facilities that include a cafe with internet access (€2 per 15 minutes). Lakeside cabins cost a little more but are worth it for the memorable sunsets.

ourpick Villa Lanca (☎ 040-748 0984; www.villalanca .com; s/d €43/68, with kitchen €53/78; P) Opposite the tourist office, this is Inari's most characterful lodging, with superb boutique rooms decorated with Asian fabrics, feather charms and real artistic flair. The spacious apartments come with fully equipped kitchen, and the cosy upstairs dens have romantic sloping ceilings. Downstairs is a friendly cafe (open 8am to 9pm Monday to Saturday in summer) with coffee, snacks, French wine by the glass, and daily specials (€11 to €13) such as tasty reindeer meatloaf.

Hotelli Inari (☎ 671 026; www.hotelliinari.fi; s/d €65/82; P) In the heart of the metropolis, this has decent rooms with private bathroom, a minibar and TV; it's worth paying a little extra to face the lake (doubles €94), rather than the road. They also have mini-apartments with their own sauna and kitchenette. The hotel's restaurant-bar is the heart of the village and serves burgers and offbeat pizzas (€5 to €9) as well as uncomplicated Lappish dishes (€11 to €19), with little sophistication but plenty of quantity. Look out the windows or gaze from the terrace at the seaplanes' antics and watch the amazing sun at these latitudes.

Hotelli Inarin Kultahovi (☎ 511 7100; www.hotel kultahovi.fi; Saarikoskentie 2; s/d €68/88; P ♿ wi-fi) Just off the main road towards Lemmenjoki, this cosy family-run place overlooks the rapids and has spruce rooms, some with a great river view. Those in the new wing (singles/doubles €105/125) have their own sauna and appealing light-wood Nordic decoration. The waterside sauna is great, and there's a restaurant (open 11am to 11pm) that serves well-presented, tasty Lappish specialities (mains €15 to €28). They use a lot of wild mushrooms in their dishes, and have treats like reindeer carpaccio and local trout, all served with a smile and great views of the Alakoski.

The Siida museum's cafe, **Sarrit** (☎ 661 662), open museum hours, is a great spot to have lunch (11am to 3pm) and also does à la carte options.

Shopping

Inari is the main centre for Sámi handicrafts and there are several studios and boutique shops in the village.

Sámi Duodji Ry (☎ 671 254; Inarintie 51; ☉ 10am-6pm daily Jul & Aug, 10am-5pm Mon-Fri, 10am-3pm Sat Sep-Jun) This place on the main road is the main shop of the Finnish association of Sámi crafts-people. It has a good range of Sámi books and CDs, as well as beautifully crafted silverware and handmade clothing.

Samekki (☎ 671 086; ☉ 10am-4pm Mon-Fri, also weekends mid-Jun–mid-Aug) Down a small lane behind the library is the studio of Petteri Laiti, a famous artisan among Finnish Sámi. The silverwork and handicrafts are very highly regarded; you'll often see the artist at work here.

Inarin Hopea (☎ 671 333; Sillankorva) Opposite the Siida museum, sells hand-worked silver items.

Nativa (☎ 040-748 0984) Opposite the tourist office, this little complex has excellent and original Sámi art and craft shops.

Getting There & Away

Inari is 38km north of Ivalo on Rd 4. Buses run here from Ivalo (€7.20, 30 minutes). Two daily buses hit Inari from Rovaniemi (€52.60, 5¼ hours) and continue to Norway, one to Karasjok and on to Nordkapp in summer, another to Tana Bru. In summer there's also a bus to Kirkenes.

LEMMENJOKI NATIONAL PARK

At 2855 sq km, Lemmenjoki (Sámi: Leammi) is Finland's largest national park, covering a remote wilderness area between Inari and Norway. It's prime hiking territory, with desolate wilderness rivers, rough landscapes and the mystique of gold, with solitary prospectors sloshing away with their pans in the middle of nowhere. Boat trips on the river allow more leisurely exploration of the park.

The launch pad for the park is Njurgulahti, a traditional Inari Sámi community by the river; it's often simply referred to as Lemmenjoki. It's 11km down a turn-off signposted 34km southwest of Inari on the Kittilä road. The village's main festival is the last weekend of July, when there's a gold-panning competition on the Saturday followed by a traditional village dance.

Here, the **Lemmenjoki Nature Centre** (☎ 020-564 7793; ☺ 9am-5pm Jun-Sep) is a small nature centre with displays on the river, maps, walking information, fishing permits, and a powerful set of binoculars trained on a nearby fell. The entrance to the park itself is 1.5km away.

Within the park boundaries, and accessed off the Inari–Kittilä road, 70km southwest of Inari, the **Sallivaara Reindeer Roundup Site** was built in 1933 (although some huts date back to the 1890s) and used by Sámi reindeer herders twice yearly until 1964. Round-ups were an important social event for the people of northern Lapland, usually lasting several weeks and involving hundreds of people and animals.

The corrals and cabins were reconstructed in 1997, and you can overnight in one of the huts, which also serves coffee in summer. Many come here in spring and summer for the top-quality bird-watching on nearby wetlands. To reach the site, park in the Repojoki parking area then follow the marked trail, 6km one way.

Activities & Tours

HIKING

Almost all trails start from Njurgulahti, including a 4km marked nature trail suitable for families. The marked trekking routes are in the relatively small 'basic area' between the rivers Lemmenjoki and Vaskojoki; an 18km loop between Kultahamina and Ravadasjärvi huts takes you to some of the most interesting gold-panning areas. Another route heads over Látnjoaivi Fell to Vaskojoki hut and back, taking you into the 'wilderness area' which has less restrictions on where to camp but no trail markings. For any serious trekking, you will need the 1:100,000 *Lemmenjoki* map (€19), available at the Lemmenjoki Nature Centre.

BOAT TRIPS

In summer, local boat services cruise the Lemmenjoki valley, from Njurgulahti village to the Kultahamina wilderness hut at Kultasatama (Gold Harbour). A 20km marked trail also follows the course of the river, so you can take the boat one way, then hike back. You can also get on or off the boat at the Ravadas falls en route. There are at least two departures a day from June to mid-September (€15/27 one-way/return, 1½ hours to Kultasatama). See below for details of operators.

Sleeping & Eating

There are several places offering camping and/or cabin accommodation, food, and boat trips. Inside the park, a dozen wilderness huts provide free accommodation (another three can be booked in advance for a fee). Several are along the riverboat route.

Ahkun Tupa (☎ 016-673 435; www.ahkuntupa.fi; 2-person cottages €35, 4-person cottages €60-80, log cabins €50, d/q €25/40; ℗) By the water in Njurgulahti, this has rooms, cottages and some further-flung log cabins. They'll let you pitch a tent for pennies. They offer English-speaking river cruises (from €8.40 for a runabout, to €27 for a three-hour return trip to the gold-panning areas) and rent canoes. The restaurant (open 9am to 9pm), does a €9 lunch, has buns with enough cinnamon to season a small nation, and has à la carte salmon and reindeer mains (€13 to €22), including reindeer tongue.

Valkeaporo (☎ 040-039 4682; www.valkeaporo .fi; 4-person cottages €50) A kilometre down the Lemmenjoki turn-off from the main Inari–Kittilä road, with splendid water frontage on spectacular Menesjärvi, this is another good base for river trips on the Lemmenjoki. In addition to smart cottages, good facilities and boat and canoe hire, it offers three-hour trips on the river and all-day gold-panning trips. You can also camp here.

Paltto (☎ 016-673 413; www.lemmenjoki.org; cottages €48-68; P) A kilometre from the centre of Njurgulahti, this home of an active Sámi family has a felt studio selling some extraordinary works of art, as well as comfortable cabin accommodation with sauna and boat. Reader-recommended boat trips are on offer: a half-day that includes reindeer-meeting and Sámi *yoiks* (chants); and a full-day one that adds gold-panning and lunch.

Getting There & Away

There is one taxi-bus on weekdays between Inari and Njurgulahti village; it currently leaves Inari at 3pm, returning at 7.15am (it's a school bus service). In school holidays (ie late June to early August) it leaves Lemmenjoki later, at 1.15pm, giving you time to take the boat trip. Check times in advance with the Inari tourist office. Note that the summer service doesn't appear on the Matkahuolto website. A local taxi service can be called on ☎ 040-039 6312.

KEVO STRICT NATURE RESERVE

The 712-sq-km Kevo Strict Nature Reserve, northwest of Inari, was established in 1956. Within its boundaries you'll find some of the most breathtaking scenery in Finland along the splendid 40km gorge of the Kevojoki (Sámi: Geävu), which also has some decent waterfalls.

Rules for visiting the Kevo reserve are stricter than those concerning national parks: hikers cannot hunt, fish or collect plants and berries, and *must* stay on marked trails. The gorge area is off limits from April to mid-June.

The main trail is 64km long and runs through the canyon, from the Sulaoja parking area 11km east of Karigasniemi on the road westbound from Kaamanen, to Kenesjärvi, on the Kaamanen–Utsjoki road. The trek is rough and takes about four days one way. The Guivi trail separates from the main trail and loops through fell scenery before rejoining further along: it's a 78km journey but has two extra huts en route. You can also walk a round-trip from Sulaoja. See www.outdoors.fi for more details and use the 1:100,000 *Utsjoki Kevo* outdoor map.

Sleeping

You will need a tent if you plan to hike the canyon, as there is only one wilderness hut on this route (there are another two on the Guivi leg). Camping is permitted within the reserve at 20 designated sites.

There are three free wilderness huts along the trail. Ruktajärvi is at the southern end of the gorge route near where the Guivi trail branches off, and Njávgoaivi and Kuivi are on the Guivi loop.

Getting There & Away

The preferred route is from the southwest; catch the Karigasniemi-bound bus from Inari and ask the driver to drop you off at the clearly marked Sulaoja trailhead. From Kenestupa you can catch buses to Inari or Utsjoki/ Nuorgam. The early afternoon southbound bus that passes Kenestupa has a convenient changeover at Kaamasen Kievari to the westbound bus for Sulaoja, allowing you to leave your car at one or the other trailhead.

INARI TO NORWAY
☎ 016

Norway stretches right across the top of Finland, and there are three main routes north from Inari: to the west via Karigasniemi (the most common Nordkapp route); north to Utsjoki; and east to Sevettijärvi. From Utsjoki, you can turn east along the fabulous Tenojoki to Nuorgam, the EU's northernmost village.

Kaamanen

Kaamanen, 25km north of Inari, is the crossing point of the three northern roads. All buses – and most locals for that matter – call in at **Kaamasen Kievari** (☎ 672 713; www .kaamasenkievari.fi; mains €11-25; ⏰ 9am-midnight), a legendary roadhouse a few kilometres north of the Sevettijärvi turn-off and 5km south of the Karigasniemi crossing. It has a cafe, petrol station and hard-drinking bar with pool table, as well as an excellent restaurant serving local dishes such as salmon, whitefish and a top reindeer steak with herb potatoes. They also have rooms and cabins (HI-affiliated), but Jokitörmä, 1km to the south, is better.

ourpick **Hostel Jokitörmä** (☎ 672 725; www .jokitorma.net; camping €13 plus per adult/child €2/1, s/d €32.50/44, cabin/hostel dm €19/22, 2-/4-person cabins €33/54; **P**), on the highway about 24km north of Inari, is a great campsite and hostel. The cabins are small and cosy and look over the river (mosquito repellent is in order in summer). They have a simple stove but no fridge. The adjacent camp sites are grassy, there are good two- and four-person rooms in the main building, and a separate set of cottages, with full facilities (€106 for up to six people). HI members get €2.50 off.

Karigasniemi

The border village of Karigasniemi (Sámi: Gáregasnjárga) thrives on Norwegian trade, and has several supermarkets open seven days a week, bars and restaurants, and a couple of petrol stations, as well as plenty of accommodation catering to fishermen beating the Tenojoki. The locals speak Fell Sámi, the main Sámi language of northern Norway.

A few accommodation choices are in the centre of town, by the border crossing, while others are strung out along the Tenojoki north and south of town.

Kalastajan Majatalo (☎ 676 171; d €60, apt €76-90, cabins €32-36) is in the centre, and offers comfortable rooms and apartments, and simple cabins. The restaurant (mains €15 to €24) serves tasty salmon and is popular with Norwegians fleeing high beer prices.

There's a daily bus from Ivalo to Karigasniemi via Inari and the Kaamasen Kievari. Another bus runs from Rovaniemi to Karasjok in Norway via here. In summer it continues to Nordkapp.

Utsjoki

The border village of Utsjoki (Sámi: Ohcejohka) is strung out along the main road that crosses the Tenojoki into Norway over a handsome bridge. It's an important Sámi community. The river is the main attraction in these parts; head along its banks towards Nuorgam or Karigasniemi and you'll find several picturesque spots with cabins catering to fishing families.

The **tourist office** (☎ 686 234; ☾ 10am-8pm early Jun-late Sep) is on the left just before the handsome bridge to Norway and also has a Metsähallitus information point.

The village hall, **Kylätalo Giisá** (☎ 040-822 8889; ☾ 10am-4pm Mon-Fri, 10am-3pm Sat), has a handicraft shop, cafe and internet access.

Opposite it is the most central camp site, **Camping Lapinkylä** (☎ 677 396; www.arctictravel.fi; cabins €43, tent sites €12; ☾ Jun-Sep), which has a grilli (fast-food outlet), sauna, neat wooden cabins, and plenty of grass underfoot to pitch your tent. They also do fishing trips and rent boats.

A couple of hundred metres up the side road by the Osuuspankki bank, **Hotelli Luossajohka** (☎ 321 2100; www.luossajohka.fi; Luossatie 4; s/d €82/92, superior s/d €100/120; **P**) is the only hotel in the town itself and has decent rooms decked out in blue, smart superior rooms in a new wing, as well as a restaurant and bar; like most places around here, they can organise fishing on the Tenojoki.

Nuorgam & Teno Valley

The 44km road from Utsjoki northeast to Nuorgam (Sámi: Njuorggan), the northernmost village of Finland (N70°4'), is one of Lapland's most spectacular. It follows the Tenojoki, one of Europe's best **salmon-fishing** rivers, and a spectacular sight as its broad waters cut through the undulating dunelike landscape and across sandy spits and rocky banks. Most anglers gather near Boratbokcankoski and Alaköngäs Rapids, 7km southwest of Nuorgam, but there are good spots right along this stretch, and also the other way from Utsjoki, towards Karigasniemi, another beautiful drive following the Tenojoki and the Norwegian border.

Apart from fishing, there's not a great deal to do in Nuorgam, but it's a relaxing spot, and nicer than Utsjoki. The majority of the 200 residents are Sámi. Norwegians flock to the (comparatively) cheap supermarkets, Alko store and petrol stations in town, but the heart of village life is **Nuorgamin Lomakeskus** (☎ 678 312; www.nuorgaminlomakeskus.fi; tent sites €20, cabins/apt €50/100; ☾ Jun-late Aug, plus Mar & Apr; **P** 🖳), which offers camping, cabins and cottage apartments with the works. It sells fishing permits, has a cafe (open until 8pm in summer) with good daily hot meals, and sells the souvenir T-shirt that reads *Nuorgam: Pieni mutta pohjoisin* ('Nuorgam: Small but northernmost'). Book ahead for cabins, as fisherfolk fill them fast.

There are many camp sites and cabin villages scattered by the river between Nuorgam and Utsjoki, and several more on the Karigasniemi road. They cater mainly to fishing parties and are good value. The Utsjoki website (www .utsjoki.fi) has a useful list with map: click on 'Majoituspalvelut'. One good example is **Alakönkään Lomamökit** (☎ 678 620; cabins €40-80; **P**), perched above the Tenojoki 7km from Nuorgam. The spacious cabins are great for families and have simple kitchens with utensils. They share a camp toilet and sauna and shower building, and offer wonderful river views and sounds from this elevated position. There's a grilli-cafe on the main road just below.

Nuorgam is the northern end of a trekking route from Sevettijärvi (see right).

There's a daily bus from Ivalo to Nuorgam via Inari and Utsjoki. A late-evening bus travels from Rovaniemi and on to Tana bru in Norway.

Sevettijärvi

The road east from Kaamanen heads along the shore of spectacularly beautiful Inarijärvi to the village of Sevettijärvi (Skolt Sámi: Ce'vetjäu'rr), in the far northeast of Finland. It's a remote area: the road only got out here in the 1970s.

Sevettijärvi is a major village of the Skolt Sámi, who resettled here when Finland was forced to cede the Petsamo area to the USSR in 1944. About 300 Skolt live in and around Sevettijärvi, which has a church (Orthodox, as the Skolt were evangelised by the Russians back in the 15th century), a shop and bar (Sevetin Baari), and a school, whose dozen-odd pupils are taught in the Skolt language. There's also **Kolttien Perinnetalo** (� 9am-5pm Jun–mid-Sep), a delightful little museum with photos, crafts and memorabilia of the poignant Skolt history. The Skolt traditionally used a system of four seasonal camps, and other nearby buildings show some of this way of life.

Sevettijärvi's namesake lake is predictably picturesque, and has a small sandy beach. It offers good fishing, as does the Näätämöjoki and, of course, Inarijärvi. Sevettijärvi also has some excellent, remote, long-distance hiking trails (see right).

The Orthodox **festival** of St Triphon is celebrated by the Skolt Sámi on the last weekend of August. It starts in Nellim on the Friday, then moves to Sevettijärvi, with celebrations on the Saturday evening and Sunday morning.

Visitors are welcome. As far as the Skolt are concerned, Lapp-dancing is the *katrilli* (quadrille), which you'll see at the festival.

There are a couple of good cabin places in and near town but if you have transport, **our pick** **Porotila Toini Sanila** (☎ 672 509; www.sanila.fi; Sanilantie 36; r €28-44; **P**) is the area's most inviting place to stay. The owners have reindeer and teach at the local school, so it's a good place to learn about the Skolt way of life. A cafe does home-cooked meals, and they have accommodation ranging from simple rooms sleeping up to six to comfortable separate cottages. It's 1km off the main road halfway between Sevettijärvi and the Norwegian border.

Between Sevettijärvi and Inari, at Partakko, **Hietajoen Leirintä** (☎ 673 122; Partakko; cabins €27) has simple cabins in a wonderful position on Inarijärvi. There's a sauna on the lakeshore and boats for rent.

There is a bus connection between Ivalo and Sevettijärvi on weekdays; an extra summer bus runs on to Kirkenes in Norway. There is no petrol station in Sevettijärvi; the nearest is in the border village of Näätämö, 30km northeast.

Trekking Around Sevettijärvi

There's excellent trekking in this remote lake-spangled wilderness. The **Sevettijärvi to Nuorgam** trek is an established route, and the most popular from Sevettijärvi. You'll need the 1:50,000 trekking maps for the area, available at tourist offices throughout the region. You can do the trek in four days, but most people take five or six.

The better of two trailheads is just north of Sevettijärvi, at Saunaranta. You'll see a sign that reads 'Ahvenjärvi 5', and a trekking sign, '12km to Opukasjärvi, 69km to Pulmankijärvi'. There are six mountain huts along the route; from the final wilderness hut you can walk to Nuorgam 18km along a road, or call ☎ 040-037 7665 for the Nuorgam taxi.

Other marked routes from Sevettijärvi include the Saamenpolku (Sámi trail), a circular trail of 87km that loops around to Näätämö and the Norwegian border and back (five to six days). The Inarinpolku is a 100km trek to the fjords of the Arctic Ocean in Norway: allow about five days for this one.

There's a shop in Sevettijärvi, but if you've got transport you might want to stock up on supplies at the supermarket by the Norwegian border at Näätämö, which is much larger and open daily.

Directory

CONTENTS

BOOK YOUR STAY ONLINE

For more accommodation reviews and recommendations by Lonely Planet authors, check out the online booking service at www.lonelyplanet.com/hotels. You'll find the true, insider lowdown on the best places to stay. Reviews are thorough and independent. Best of all, you can book online.

ACCOMMODATION

Finland's not generally a nation of quirky boutique hotels. Solid Nordic comfort in standard rooms dominates rather than whimsical loft conversions or new-agey fabrics. Many accommodation choices open only in summer, usually camp sites or converted student residences.

Sleeping listings in this guide are divided into three price categories, based on the cost of a standard double room at its most expensive (generally midweek outside of the summer season); budget (up to €70), midrange (€70 to €150) and top end (€150 plus).

One of Finland's joys is its plethora of cottages for rental, ranging from simple camping cabins to fully equipped bungalows with electric sauna and gleaming modern kitchen. These can be remarkably good value and are perfect for families.

The double bed is a rare beast in Finnish accommodation; hotel rooms tend to have twin beds that can be pushed together. Family or group rooms are common, and extra beds can usually be added to a twin room at a low extra cost. All hotels and hostels have nonsmoking rooms; some have smoking rooms, which should be requested when booking or checking in.

Camping

Finland's camping grounds are a delight, and have much to offer to all types of traveller. There's one in nearly every town or village, and they tend to offer three types of accommodation. Your average camp site sits by a lake, in a forest, or both, and minimum facilities tend to include a kitchen area, laundry, sauna, playground, boat and bike rentals, a cafe and minigolf (a Finnish addiction). There are pitches and parks for tents and vans, simple cabins, which usually have electric light, bunk beds and a fridge, and larger cottages which come with fully equipped kitchen, TV, sauna, bathroom and separate bedrooms. These can be great value, particularly for families and groups. Most camp sites only open in summer, but the (heated) cottages may be available in winter if you phone ahead.

The website www.camping.fi lists many, but by no means all, camp sites. See also p351 for information on camping cards.

In Finland you can legally pitch a tent in a wide range of places. See p70 for more information.

Farmstays

A growing, and often ecologically sound accommodation sector in Finland is that of farmstays. Many rural farms, particularly in the south, offer B&B accommodation, a unique opportunity to meet local people and experience their way of life. And it's not all about watching grass grow either: plenty of activities are usually on offer, with boats or snowmobiles at your disposal, horses to ride, and the chance to pitch in and help with the harvest.

We list a few farmstay opportunities in the pages of this guide, but there are many more. **ECEAT** (www.eceat.fi) lists a number of organic, sustainable farms in Finland that offer accommodation and, often, a chance to muck in and experience traditional Finnish farming life. Local tourist offices keep lists of farmstay options in the surrounding area; try www.visitfinland.com, which links to a few (click on accommodation), and **Lomarengas** (Map p86; ☎ 09-5766 3350; www.lomarengas.fi; Eteläesplanadi 22, 00130 Helsinki) also has many listed on its website. Some farmstays are independent, family-run affairs, while others are loosely gathered under an umbrella organisation. In general, prices are good – from around €30 per person per night, country breakfast included. Evening meals are also usually available. Your hosts may not speak much English; if you have difficulties the local tourist office will be happy to help arrange the booking.

Guesthouses

A Finnish *matkakoti,* or guesthouse, is a no-frills spot offering simple but usually comfy accommodation with shared bathroom, typically for travelling salespeople. It can be pretty good value, usually includes breakfast, and sometimes rises well above the norm: check out places like Naantali (p227) and Hanko (p123) for some exceptional sleeps in this class.

Hostels & Summer Hotels

If you're travelling alone, hostels generally offer the best-value roof over your head, and can be good value for two people staying in a twin room. Finnish hostels are invariably clean, comfortable and very well equipped, though most are in somewhat institutional buildings.

From June to August, many student residences are made over as summer hostels and hotels. These are often great value, as you often get your own room, with kitchen (bring your own utensils though) and bathroom either to yourself or shared between two.

Some Finnish hostels are run by the Finnish Youth Hostel Association (SRM), and many more are affiliated. It's worth being a member of **HI** (www.hihostels.com), as members save €2.50 per night at affiliated places in Finland. Join in your home country or at the **head office** (☎ 09-694 0377; www.srm.fi; Yrjönkatu 38B, 00100 Helsinki). In Finland the cost is €17 for a year's membership. You can stay at a hostel without an HI card, and there are no age restrictions.

You'll save money with a sleepsheet or your own linen, as hostels tend to charge €4 to €8 for this. Sleeping bags are less acceptable. Most hostels have a kitchen, and many have a sauna.

Hotels

Most hotels in Finland cater to business travellers and the majority belong to one of a few major chains, including **Sokos** (www.sokoshotels.fi), **Scandic** (www.scandic-hotels.com) and **Cumulus** (www.cumulus.fi). **Finlandia** (www.finlandiahotels.fi) is an association of independent hotels, while many others belong to the **Best Western** (www.bestwestern.fi) franchise-style system. They can be quite luxurious, although standard rooms are usually compact and functional. Service tends to be good and the restaurants and nightclubs are often the most popular in town. Hotels are mostly spotlessly clean, efficiently run and always have a sauna, which can be booked for private use. A shared sauna session is usually included in the rate. Most hotels have suites with a private sauna.

Although rack-rates are fairly high, hotels in Finland offer lower rates in summer (from late June to mid- or the end of August), and also at weekends (usually Friday, Saturday and Sunday nights). At that time you can usually get a double room in a reasonably fancy hotel for between €70 and €90. The discount for singles is marginal at all times, so you may prefer to pay the little extra for a twin room, which is usually much larger.

Superior rooms vary in value. In many places they are identical to the standard and your extra cash gets you only a bathrobe and a fancier shampoo. In others, an extra 10 euros can get you 50% more space, views over the town and a private sauna. It's worth asking.

Most hotel rooms have tiny Nordic bathrooms; if you want a bathtub, this can usually be arranged. Many hotels have 'allergy rooms', which have no carpet and minimal fabric.

All Finnish hotels have a large, plentiful and delicious buffet breakfast included in the rate.

Self-Catering Accommodation

There are tens of thousands of cabins and cottages for rent in Finland. They can be booked through tourist offices, starting at €200 a week for two to four people. Two-day rentals are usually the minimum, but camp sites (p347) often have similar accommodation on a per-night basis.

Lakeside holiday cabins and cottages represent the classic Finnish vacation and are a terrific idea if you have a group (or family) and would like to settle down to enjoy a particular corner of the countryside. They are usually fully equipped with cooking utensils, sauna and a rowing boat, although the cheapest, most 'rustic' ones may not even have electricity and require that you fetch your own water at a well. However, this is a true holiday, Finnish style.

Local booking agents are mentioned under individual destinations, and regional ones are listed at the beginning of chapters (the Lakeland chapter particularly, p132). By far the biggest national agent for cottage rentals is Lomarengas (opposite). This agency comes highly recommended for reliability. Another good choice is **Villi Pohjola** (☎ 020-344 122; www.wildnorth.net). This arm of the Forests and Parks Service has cottages and cabins for rent all over Finland, but especially in Lapland and the north.

Wilderness Huts

See p70 for details on huts, shelters and other options on trekking routes.

BUSINESS HOURS

Banks are open from 9am to 4.15pm Monday to Friday. Shops are generally open 9am to 6pm Monday to Friday, and to 3pm on Saturday. Post offices usually open from 9am to 6pm Monday to Friday. Alko stores (the state-owned network of liquor stores) are generally open 9am to 8pm Monday to Friday (sometimes until 9pm on Thursday or Friday), and until 6pm Saturday. Many supermarkets and Helsinki department stores stay open until 9pm or 10pm Monday to Friday and open all day on Saturday and Sunday.

CHEAPER SLEEPER

Hotels in Finland are designed with the business traveller in mind and tend to charge them robustly. But at weekends and during the summer holidays, they bring their prices crashing down to try and lure people who aren't on company expense accounts. Prices in three- and four-star hotels tend to drop by 40% or so at these times, so take advantage. Prices listed in this guide are weekday prices unless otherwise specified.

DIRECTORY

Finns lunch early, so restaurants usually open at 11am, closing at around 10pm, earlier for simpler places. Lunch specials run until 2pm or 3pm. Bars tend to open from 4pm to midnight, later at weekends. Any variations are noted in reviews of establishments throughout this book. Note that when a Finnish restaurant opens, for example, until 11pm, that's the time they expect you to be grabbing your coat and heading for the street, not ordering your food.

CHILDREN

Finland is incredibly child-friendly, and is one of the best places to holiday with kids. Domestic tourism is largely dictated by children's needs, and child-friendly attractions abound. Even potentially stuffy museums often make a real effort to appeal to kids, with simplified child-height information, hands-on activities, or activity sheets in English.

Practicalities

Local tourist information booklets and websites usually highlight attractions with family appeal.

Lonely Planet's *Travel with Children* by Cathy Lanigan is a good source of general information.

Most Finnish hotels and hostels will put an extra bed in a room for little extra cost – and kids under 12 often sleep free. Many hotel rooms have sofas that can fold out into beds or family suites, and hostels often have connecting rooms. The upmarket **Holiday Club** (www.holidayclub.fi) chain of spa hotels is especially child-friendly and camp sites are particularly good, with self-catering cabins good value for families. There are always things to do and other children in these places, and some of the larger ones offer child-minding services or activity programs. Restaurants often have a menu for the kids, or deals where children eat free if accompanied by adults.

Car-hire firms have children's safety seats for hire at a nominal cost, but it is essential that you book them in advance. The same goes for highchairs and cots (cribs); they're standard in many restaurants and hotels, but numbers may be limited.

Entrance fees and transport tickets for children tend to be around 60% of the adult charge in Finland. If this isn't the case, we've included child prices in the text.

Sights & Activities

All areas of Finland have plenty to offer, depending on what appeals. Activities like canoeing and fishing are available almost everywhere, and large towns have a swimming complex that includes water slides, Jacuzzis, saunas and table tennis; excellent for all ages in both summer and winter. See p29 for some destination ideas and p91 for child-friendly Helsinki choices.

CLIMATE CHARTS

Finland is two different places in winter and summer. Summer is reliably dry and hot, but by August things can already begin to get chilly. Winters *are* cold, but the cold is dry. Snow generally first falls in October and clears by the end of March, but in Lapland snow can fall as early as September and stay until late May.

These graphs tell the statistical story; see p17 for a discussion of conditions at various times of year.

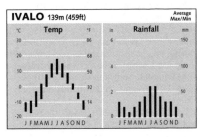

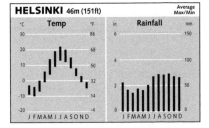

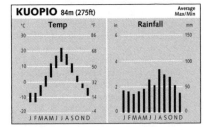

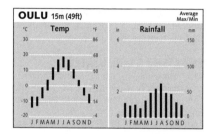

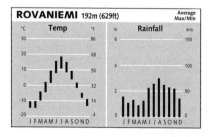

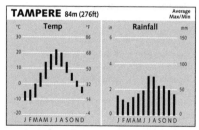

COURSES

See p357 for volunteering opportunities.

Language

There are intensive courses in the Finnish language each summer (June to August) at the universities in Helsinki, Oulu, Lahti, Tampere, Turku, Kuopio and Jyväskylä. For more information contact **Suomen Kesäyliopistot** (☎ 03-214 7626; www.kesayliopistot .fi; Rautatienkatu 26, 33100 Tampere).

The following universities also teach basic courses in Finnish language and culture, with classes typically running either a full term or an intensive period in August.

University of Helsinki Language Centre (☎ 09-1912 3234; www.helsinki.fi/kksc/language.services) Three-month courses from €145. There's even an online course to get you started.

University of Jyväskylä Language Centre (☎ 014-260 3750; http://kielikompassi.jyu.fi)

University of Oulu Language Centre (☎ 08-553 3203; www.oulu.fi/kielikeskus)

University of Tampere Language Centre (☎ 03-3551 6464; www.uta.fi/laitokset/kielikeskus)

University of Turku Language Centre (☎ 02-333 5975; http://kielikeskus.utu.fi)

CUSTOMS REGULATIONS

Travellers should encounter few problems with Finnish customs. Travellers arriving from outside the EU can bring duty-free goods up to the value of €175 into Finland without declaration. You can also bring in up to 16L of beer, 2L of wine and 1L of spirits, 200 cigarettes or 250g of tobacco and 50g of perfume. If you're coming from another EU country, there is no restriction on the value of gifts or purchases for your own use, except for tobacco from new EU member states.

Although technically part of the EU, arriving on or from the Åland islands carries the same import restrictions as arriving from a non-EU country. Check the latest situation on the Finnish customs website www.tulli.fi, at the border crossing or on an international ferry.

DANGERS & ANNOYANCES

Finland is a very safe, nonthreatening country to travel in but there are some potential risks to consider.

Weather extremes, especially in Lapland, can cause unexpected danger at any time of the year. Extreme cold kills lone trekkers almost every winter in the wilderness.

June and July are the worst months for mosquitoes and other biting insects, which are a major nuisance in the country, particularly in Lapland. Insect repellent or those beautiful hat-nets are essential.

In urban areas, violence mostly occurs in association with intoxicated local males, who are normally rowdy rather than particularly aggressive. In more remote spots, long winters and deep thirsts create their fair share of curious characters found propping up the local bars.

DISCOUNT CARDS
Camping Cards

The **Camping Card International** (www.camp ingcardinternational.org) is basically a camping-ground ID. These cards are available from your local camping federation (the website has details) and incorporate third-party

DIRECTORY

insurance for damage you may cause. Most Finnish camp sites offer a discount if you sign in with one.

Camping Card Scandinavia is a similar document, and brings a discount at most Finnish camp sites. It can be ordered (allow three weeks for delivery) from the website www.camping.fi, or a temporary version can be purchased in summer at most camp sites; the cost is €7.

Hostelling Card
See p348 for more information on becoming an HI member. The card also gives discounts on some transport routes.

Seniors Cards
Note that anyone aged 65 or over receives a 50% discount on Finnish trains and 30% on intercity buses. There are also rail passes available for travel within Scandinavia for nationals of any country who are aged over 55; inquire at your local travel agency for information. Seniors with proof of age can also receive discounts at many museums and other attractions.

Student & Youth Cards
The most useful of these is the International Student Identity Card (ISIC), a plastic ID-style card with your photograph, which provides discounts on many forms of transport, reduced or free admission to museums and sights, and cheap meals in student cafeterias – a worthwhile way of cutting costs. Check www.isic.org for a list of discounts by country. Because of the proliferation of fake ISIC cards, carry your home student ID as back-up. Some airlines won't give student discounts without it.

Some discounts are given on age rather than student status. If you're aged under 26, you can apply for the Euro26 card (www.eyca.org) or the International Youth Travel Card (IYTC). These cards are available through student unions, hostelling organisations or youth-oriented travel agencies. There's also the ITIC (International Teacher Identity Card) for teachers and academics, which offers a few similar discounts at some establishments.

The discounts for flashing these cards have reduced due to widespread fraud, and many places don't recognise them at all, but it's always worth a try.

If you are studying in Finland, a Finnish student card will get you megadiscounts on transport and more.

EMBASSIES & CONSULATES
The following is a list of foreign government representatives in Helsinki. Use the Helsinki area telephone code (☎ 09) if calling from elsewhere.

Australia (Map pp80-1; ☎ 4777 6640; australian.consulate@tradimex.fi; Museokatu 25B) This is the consulate; the nearest embassy is in Stockholm (www.sweden.embassy.gov.au).

Canada (Map p86; ☎ 228 530; www.canada.fi; Pohjoisesplanadi 25B)

Denmark (Map p86; ☎ 684 1050; www.denmark.fi; Mannerheimintie 8)

Estonia (Map pp80-1; ☎ 622 0260; www.estemb.fi; Itäinen Puistotie 10)

France (Map pp80-1; ☎ 618 780; Itäinen Puistotie 13)

Germany (☎ 458 580; www.helsinki.diplo.de; Krogiuksentie 4)

Ireland (Map p86; ☎ 646 006; embassy.ireland@welho.com; Erottajankatu 7A)

Japan (Map p86; ☎ 686 0200; www.fi.emb-japan.go.jp; Unioninkatu 20)

Latvia (Map pp80-1; ☎ 476 4720; www.mfa.gov.lv/en/helsinki; Armfeltintie 10)

Lithuania (Map p86; ☎ 684 4880; www.lithuania.fi; Rauhankatu 13A)

Netherlands (Map p86; ☎ 228 920; www.netherlands.fi; Erottajankatu 19B)

New Zealand (☎ 470 1818; paddais@paddais.net; Johanneksenrinne 2) This is the consulate-general; otherwise contact the embassy in The Hague, Netherlands.

Norway (Map pp80-1; ☎ 686 0180; www.norge.fi; Rehbinderintie 17)

Russia (Map pp80-1; ☎ 661 877; http://helsinki.rusembassy.org; Tehtaankatu 1B)

Sweden (Map p86; ☎ 687 7660; www.sverige.fi; Pohjoisesplanadi 7B)

UK (Map pp80-1; ☎ 2286 5100; http://ukinfinland.fco.gov.uk; Itäinen Puistotie 17)

USA (Map pp80-1; ☎ 616 250; www.usembassy.fi; Itäinen Puistotie 14B)

FESTIVALS & EVENTS
See p21 for a calendar of Finland's main festivals and events.

FOOD
The Food and Drink chapter (p57) discusses Finnish food. Restaurant reviews in the book are divided into three price categories: budget (most mains under €15), midrange (most

mains €15 to 25) and top end (most mains over €25).

GAY & LESBIAN TRAVELLERS

Suomi is one of the more tolerant destinations for gay and lesbian travellers; fittingly enough for the nation that produced Tom of Finland. Although there is no parallel to the lively and active gay communities of Copenhagen or Stockholm, Helsinki has a good selection of bars and clubs (see p92), and bigger towns like Tampere and Turku have something on offer. In smaller towns and in rural areas attitudes lag behind a little.

Gay and lesbian couples are officially recognised and have most of the rights of married couples. Information is available from the Finnish organisation for gay and lesbian equality, **Seksuaalinen tasavertaisuus** (HeSeta; Map pp80–1; ☎ 09-681 2580; www.heseta.fi, in Finnish; Mannerheimintie 170, Helsinki).

Useful websites:

http://ranneliike.net Events, links and information.

www.finnqueer.net Online journal discussing issues and news.

www.sappho.net Finnish lesbian site with information and links.

www.z-lehti.fi Finnish gay and lesbian magazine. You can download the Helsinki gay guide from their website.

HOLIDAYS

Finland grinds to a halt twice a year: around Christmas (sometimes including the New Year) and during the Midsummer weekend at the end of June. Plan ahead and avoid travelling during those times. Most hotels and restaurants close over these periods too.

Every town and city in Finland puts on a barrage of festivals between mid-June and mid-August, so accommodation will be tight if you coincide. Vappu (May Day) is another big party day.

Public Holidays

The following are public holidays celebrated throughout Finland:

New Year's Day 1 January

Epiphany 6 January

Good Friday Easter Sunday & Monday

May Day 1 May

Ascension Day May

Whitsunday Late May or early June

Midsummer's Eve & Day Weekend in June closest to the 24th

All Saints Day First Saturday in November

Independence Day 6 December

Christmas Eve 24 December

Christmas Day 25 December

Boxing Day 26 December

School Holidays

Schools are on holiday in summer from early June to mid August; they also are off for a week in late February, a week in late October and two weeks over Christmas. It's traditional for classes to go on school trips in late May and the first few days of June, which can mean that budget accommodation is heavily booked out in some areas.

INSURANCE

Citizens of the European Economic Area (the EU plus Iceland, Norway and Liechtenstein) are entitled to free medical care in Finland (see p371).

For citizens of other countries, travel insurance is a good idea, as it is for anyone who wants to cover theft or loss. Read the fine print carefully as activities like canoeing, skiing etc might not be included.

Worldwide travel insurance is available at www.lonelyplanet.com/travel_services. You can buy, extend and claim online any time – even if you're already on the road.

See p366 for car insurance.

INTERNET ACCESS

Free internet access is widely available in Finland. Every public library in every town has at least one internet terminal (big libraries have up to a dozen) that can be used free of charge. The downside is that there's a time limit – normally 15 to 30 minutes. If you want longer, you may have to book a slot. You're also restricted by library opening hours, which vary but are typically Monday to Friday only.

Many tourist offices have an internet terminal that you can use for free (usually 15 minutes), as do a handful of businesses such as cafes in larger cities. Because of this free access, dedicated internet cafes are not so common in Finland, but you can find them in larger towns, charging around €3 per hour.

If you are travelling with your own computer, things are bright. Wireless internet access is very widespread; several cities have extensive networks and nearly all hotels, as well as

DIRECTORY

many restaurants, cafes and bars offer free access to customers and guests.

Accommodation listings in this guide that display the 🖳 symbol have a computer with internet access available. If wireless internet access is available, the word 'wi-fi' is used. These services may be free or charged.

LAUNDRY

The largest chain of laundries is Sol (www .sol.fi). Though their website is in Finnish, click on 'Yhteystiedot', then 'Pesulapalvelut'. Select a town from the drop-down menu and its location displays on a map. Otherwise, check the local telephone book – laundries are listed as *Pesuloita*. *Itsepalvelupesula* denotes self-service laundrettes, but these are few. Most camp sites and many hostels and summer hotels have self-service laundry facilities. Hotels typically offer (expensive) laundry and dry-cleaning services.

LEGAL MATTERS

Traffic laws are strict, as are drug laws. Fines for minor offences (such as speeding) are based on the offender's income and assets. This system has led to some well-documented and slightly absurd situations where high-flying Finns breaking the speed limit have been fined as much as €170,000! However, foreigners are fined a more reasonable flat rate. Police usually treat tourists politely. See p76 for fishing permits.

MAPS

Almost all local tourist offices offer free city and regional maps that are adequate for finding your way around. Trekking, canoeing and road maps are available from **Karttakeskus** (☎ 020-577 7580; www.karttakeskus.fi; Vuorikatu 14, Helsinki) which produces and sells the largest variety of Finnish maps: you can order via its website. These include road maps, an annually updated road atlas, and detailed maps of all the main walking areas and waterways.

MONEY

Finland uses the euro. Euro notes come in five, 10, 20, 100, 200 and 500 denominations and coins in five, 10, 20, 50 cents and €1 and €2. Euro coins from other countries are legal tender, but 1 and 2 cent coins aren't used here.

See the inside front cover for exchange rates at the time of going to press, and p17 for information on the costs of travel in Finland.

Swedish krona (including coins) are accepted on Åland and in western Lapland, and Norwegian krona can be used in areas near the Norwegian border in northern Lapland.

Cards & ATMs

Finns are dedicated users of credit and debit cards. International cards are accepted and used virtually everywhere – purchasing a coffee with plastic is common. Credit cards such as MasterCard and Visa and debit cards like Maestro and Visa Electron are accepted at most hotels, hostels, restaurants, shops and department stores, and you'll usually need one if you want to hire a car.

Using ATMs with a credit or debit card is by far the easiest way of getting cash in Finland. The ATMs have a name, Otto, and can be found even in small villages. Finnish ATMs accept foreign bank cards with Cirrus, Maestro, MasterCard, Visa, Visa Electron, Plus and Amex symbols. Withdrawals using a foreign ATM incur a transaction fee (contact your home bank for details) so it makes good sense to withdraw a reasonable amount each time. Keep a copy of the international number to call if your cards are lost or stolen.

Moneychangers

The best way to carry and obtain local currency is by using an ATM or credit card, just as most Finns do. Other options are travellers cheques and cash, which can be exchanged at banks and, in the big cities, independent exchange facilities such as **Forex** (www.forex.fi), which usually offer better rates. Finnish post offices also provide banking services and tend to keep longer hours than banks, particularly in remote villages. Airports and international ferries have exchange facilities.

Taxes & Refunds

The value-added tax (ALV), usually of 22%, is included in marked prices but may be deducted if you post goods from the point of sale. Alternatively, at stores showing the 'Tax Free for Tourists' sign, foreign visitors who are not EU citizens can get a 12% to 16% refund on items priced over €40. Present the tax-refund 'cheque' to the refund window at your departure point from the EU (eg airport transit halls, aboard international ferries, at overland border crossings). For more information on VAT refunds contact **Global Refund**

Finland (☎ 09-6132 9600; www.globalrefund.com; PO Box 460, 00101 Helsinki).

Tipping

Tipping is not an essential part of the culture and Finns generally don't, unless rewarding exceptional service. Service charges in restaurants are included in the quoted menu price. You might tell the taxi driver to *'pidä loput'* ('keep the change') but they don't expect it. Doormen at nightclubs and restaurants may expect a small tip, but this is often a mandatory payment in the form of a 'coat charge'.

PHOTOGRAPHY

Despite the digital revolution, film is still readily available, and processing is speedy, fairly cheap and of high quality. A roll of standard 36-exposure print film costs around €7. Any photo shop will happily burn digital photos onto CDs and many will include a CD in the cost of developing a regular film.

POST

Stamps can be bought at bus or train stations and R-kioski newsstands as well as at the *posti* (post office; www.pos ti.fi).

Airmail postcards and letters weighing up to 20g cost €0.80 to anywhere in the world or €0.70 by slower economy rate.

There are also two main rates for international parcels: a 5kg package to Europe will cost €46 to €49 sent priority, and €31 to €35 sent economy, for example. Post offices sell packing material for various size packages.

SHOPPING

On the whole, prices in Finland are lower than in other Nordic countries – which isn't to say that there are any real bargains here, particularly on those items for which Finland is famous: glassware, pottery, woollens and various handicrafts made from pine or birch.

Lappish, or Sámi, handicrafts include jewellery, clothing, textiles and hunting knives, as well as other items made from local wood, reindeer bone and hide, metals and semiprecious stones. Duodji are authentic handicrafts produced according to Sámi traditions. A genuine item, which can be expensive, will carry a special 'Sámi Duodji' label. Sámi handicrafts can be found at markets and shops in Helsinki and throughout Lapland, but for the widest selections visit the Sámi villages of Inari (p342) and Hetta (p324).

Trekkers will want to purchase a *kuksa* (cup) made in traditional Sámi fashion from the burl of a birch tree. These are widely available throughout Finland, at markets and in handicraft or souvenir shops. Quality of workmanship varies, as does price, but the typical *kuksa* costs about €20.

Finnish design is a big attraction, and Helsinki's Design District (p103) is the best place to browse the latest innovations and styles, but the big names, like Marimekko (clothing) and Iittala (glassware) have numerous outlets all over the country.

Local markets are good places to purchase colourful *lapaset* (woollen mittens), *myssy* or *pipo* (hats) and *villapusero* (sweaters), necessary for surviving the cold Finnish winters, as well as *raanu* or *ryijy* (woven wall hangings). A good hand-knitted sweater sells for at least €200. Local folk – particularly in Åland – will often 'knit to order', taking your measurements and then posting the sweater to you in two or three months, once it's finished. It's possible to find cheaper, machine-knitted wool sweaters in Finnish markets, but check the labels – they were probably made in Norway.

It's possible to find bargains on trekking goods such as jackets and down sleeping bags. Chains such as Partio-Aitta and Lassen Retkiaitta specialise in outdoor equipment, but many sports shops, such as Intersport or Kesport, also have good selections.

See also opposite for information on tax refunds for non-EU residents. Most shops will happily arrange postage or delivery to other countries, but this is rather pricey.

SOLO TRAVELLERS

Finland is one of the world's safest places, so travelling alone poses little risk. In smaller hotels and guesthouses, expect to pay 60% to 70% of the double-room rate. Many business-class hotels, however, cynically charge the same price for a single or double room. If this is the case, make sure you get a decent double-sized room for your hard-earned cash.

Many camp sites offer cheaper rates for solo campers, but normally charge the two-person rate for cottages and cabins.

TELEPHONE

Public telephones basically no longer exist on the street in Finland, so if you don't have a mobile you're reduced to making expensive calls from your hotel room, finding a cybercafe and talking over the internet, or tracking down a telecentre, which only really exist in the big cities.

Mobile Phones

The cheapest and most practical solution for telephoning in Finland is to purchase a Finnish SIM card and pop it in your own phone. Make sure your phone isn't blocked from doing this by your home network first. If coming from outside Europe, check with your service provider that it will work in Europe's GSM 900/1800 network.

You can buy a prepaid SIM-card at any R-Kioski shop, which sell them from various network providers like **Sonera** (www.sonera.fi), **GoMobile** (www.go.fi) or **DNA** (www.dnaoy.fi). There are always several deals on offer, and you might be able to pick up a card for as little as €10, including some call credit. You can top the credit up at the same outlets, online or at ATM machines. At the R-Kioski you can also buy cut-rate phonecards that substantially lower the cost of making international calls; there are several varieties, with rates clearly marked.

Phone Codes

The country code for Finland is ☎ 358. To dial abroad it's ☎ 00. The number for the international operator is ☎ 020 208.

TIME

Finnish time is two hours ahead of GMT in winter. When it's noon in Finland it's 2am in Los Angeles, 5am in New York, 10am in London, 7pm or 9pm in Sydney and 11am in Sweden and most of Western Europe. Daylight Saving Time, when clocks go forward one hour, applies from late March to the end of October.

The 24-hour clock is used commonly for transport times, opening hours etc. If you see *Ma-Pe 9-20*, for example, it means that a place is open Monday to Friday from 9am to 8pm.

TOILETS

Toilets in train and bus stations often require a fee of €1 or €2. Other public conveniences cost around €0.40. On doors, 'M' is for men, and 'N' for women.

TOURIST INFORMATION

All major Finnish towns have a tourist office with helpful, English-speaking staff, English-language brochures and excellent free maps. In summer, these offices are often staffed by university students. Most offices publish a miniguide to their town or region and all have a website (which is usually www.nameoftown .fi). Additionally, many offices stockpile brochures, maps and advice for lots of other towns and regions in Finland.

The **Finnish Tourist Board** (Matkailun Edistämiskeskus; MEK; Map pp80-1; ☎ 010-605 8000; www.visitfinland.com; Töölönkatu 11, Helsinki) has a useful website, listing, among other things, overseas points of contact for information on Finland. Their main Helsinki tourist office (p82) is near the kauppatori (market square) in the capital.

TRAVELLERS WITH DISABILITIES

Finland may be the best-equipped country in the world for the disabled traveller. By law, most institutions must provide ramps, lifts and special toilets for disabled persons; all new hotels and restaurants must install disabled facilities. Trains and city buses are also accessible by wheelchair. Some national parks offer accessible nature trails, and Helsinki and other cities have ongoing projects in place designed to maximise disabled access in all aspects of urban life.

In general, the majority of tourist brochures and information booklets give information about disabled facilities, but the best is published by **Rullaten Ry** (☎ 09-805 7393; www .rullaten.fi), which you can order online before leaving home. Another booklet, available at the Helsinki tourist office, focuses just on the capital.

Näkövammaisten Keskusliitto (☎ 09-396 041; www.nkl.fi; Marjaniementie 74, Iiris 00030) is the Finnish national association for the visually impaired. It can give advice on travel in the country, as well as provide details of dedicated holiday centres with a wide range of summer and winter activities on offer.

Kuurojen Liitto (☎ 09-58031; www.kl-deaf.fi; PO Box 57, Helsinki 04001) is the equivalent organisation for the hearing-impaired.

Before leaving home, get in touch with your national support organisation – preferably the 'travel officer' if there is one. They often have complete libraries devoted to travel, and can put you in touch with agencies that specialise in tours for the disabled. One such organisation in the UK is **Can Be Done** (☎ (44 0) 20-8907 2400; www.canbed one.co.uk).

VISAS

A valid passport or EU identity card is required to enter Finland. Most Western nationals don't need a tourist visa for stays of less than three months; South Africans, Indians and Chinese, however, are among those who need a Schengen visa. For more information contact the nearest Finnish embassy or consulate, or the **Directorate of Immigration** (Map pp80-1; ☎ 071-873 0431; www.uvi .fi; Panimokatu 2A, Helsinki).

Visas and information can be obtained at Finnish diplomatic missions (full list at http:// formin.finland.fi).

ESTONIAN & RUSSIAN VISAS

Estonia is also part of the Schengen area; entry requirements are the same as for Finland, and a Schengen visa covers entry to both countries. Check out the website of the **Estonian Foreign Ministry** (www.vm.ee).

All foreigners require a visa to travel into Russia from Finland. Russian visas are best applied for in your home country. If you have to apply in Finland, they take about eight working days to process in Helsinki (you must leave your passport at the embassy) but can take significantly longer. Helsinki tour companies specialising in travel to Russia can usually expedite a visa much quicker, but for a fee.

VOLUNTEERING

There are various opportunities for volunteering in Finland; programs normally include bed and board. Useful websites include:

http://ec.europa.eu/youth The European Commission runs a volunteer program for young people in member states, Youth in Action, with various goals.

www.wwf.fi Finland's branch of the World Wildlife Fund organises summer work camps with specific environmental goals.

www.volunteerabroad.com This page links to various volunteer programs run by not-for-profit organisations in Finland as well as other countries.

www.volunteering.org.au Lists various volunteer programs run by several organisations, including in Finland.

www.wwoof.org Organisation that sets up 'wwoofing' volunteering opportunities on organic farms, with a few choices in Finland. You pay a membership fee to receive the list of participating farms.

WOMEN TRAVELLERS

Finland is one of the safest places to travel in the world. Women often travel alone in the region, which should pose no problems. In smaller towns, and especially in the north, bars can be fairly unreconstructed places, and women sometimes get a bit of nonthreatening but unpleasant hassle from drunk locals.

WORK

Various English-teaching opportunities are available in Finland, but standards are high so experience and good references are essential. Limited summer employment is available, and even those studying in Finland are eligible for a restricted period. Au-pairing is fairly common and organisations set up placements. A good place to start is the website of the **International Au Pair Association** (www.iapa.org), which lists reliable agencies that arrange placements.

Australian and New Zealand citizens aged between 18 and 30 can apply for a one-year working-holiday visa.

For any serious career-oriented work, a work permit is required for all foreigners other than EU citizens. Employment must be secured before applying for the work permit, and the work permit must be filed in advance of arrival in Finland, together with a letter from the intended employer and other proof of employment. Work permits can be obtained from the Finnish embassy in your home country. A residence permit may also be required. For more information contact the Directorate of Immigration (left).

Transport

GETTING THERE & AWAY

Flights, tours and rail tickets can be booked online at www.lonelyplanet.com/travel_services.

ENTERING THE COUNTRY
Passport
EU nationals, Schengen agreement countries, and citizens of Switzerland and small EU affiliates such as Andorra and Monaco can enter Finland with a valid passport or identity card. See p357.

AIR
Finland is easily reached by air, with a growing number of direct flights to Helsinki from European, American and Asian destinations.

THINGS CHANGE...

The information in this chapter is particularly vulnerable to change. Check directly with the airline or a travel agent to make sure you understand how a fare (and ticket you may buy) works and be aware of the security requirements for international travel. Shop carefully. The details given in this chapter should be regarded as pointers and are not a substitute for your own careful, up-to-date research.

It's also served by various budget carriers from several European countries, especially Ryanair and Blue1; check www.whichbudget.com for a complete list. Most other flights are with Finnair or Scandinavian Airlines (SAS).

Airports & Airlines
Most flights to Finland land at **Helsinki-Vantaa airport** (HEL; ☎ 020-014 636; www.helsinki-vantaa.fi), situated 19km north of the capital.

Other international airports include Tampere (TMP), Turku (TKU), Oulu (OUL), Vaasa (VAA) and Rovaniemi (RVN). Other airports in Lapland receive a growing number of winter charter flights from various European countries. The website www.finavia.fi includes contact details and other information for all Finnish airports.

There are good flight connections to Finland from all over the world. Finnair, the national carrier, has scheduled flights to Helsinki from most major cities in Europe, as well as from Bangkok, Beijing, Boston, Delhi, Guangzhou, Hong Kong, Mumbai, Nagoya, New York, Osaka, Seoul, Shanghai, Tokyo and Toronto.

The following airlines fly to/from Finland:

Aer Lingus (☎ 09-6122 0222; www.aerlingus.com)
Aeroflot (☎ 09-659 6552; www.aeroflot.ru)
Air Åland (☎ 018-17110; www.airaland.com)
Air Baltic (☎ 060-002 5831; www.airbaltic.com)
Air Berlin (☎ 080-091 3033; www.airberlin.com)
Air Finland (☎ 010-230 4170; www.airfinland.fi)
Air France (☎ 020-032 020; www.airfrance.com)
Austrian Airlines (☎ 020-386 700; www.austrianairlines.com)
Aviakompania Severstal (☎ 09-6813 8370; www.airport.cpv.ru)
Blue1 (☎ 0600-025 831; www.blue1.com)
British Airways (☎ 09-6937 9538; www.ba.com)
Brussels Airlines (☎ 09-681 1950; www.brusselsairlines.com)
Cimber Air (☎ +45 701 012 183; www.cimber.dk)
Czech Airlines (☎ 09-6937 9545; www.czechairlines.com)
easyJet (☎ +44 870 6 000 000; www.easyjet.com)
Estonian Air (☎ 060-002 5831; www.estonian-air.ee)
Finnair (☎ 060-014 0140; www.finnair.com)
Gotlandsflyg (☎ +46 498 222 222; www.gotlandsflyg.se)

TRANSPORT

CLIMATE CHANGE & TRAVEL

Climate change is a serious threat to the ecosystems that humans rely upon, and air travel is the fastest-growing contributor to the problem. Lonely Planet regards travel, overall, as a global benefit, but believes we all have a responsibility to limit our personal impact on global warming.

Flying & Climate Change

Pretty much every form of motor travel generates CO_2 (the main cause of human-induced climate change) but planes are far and away the worst offenders, not just because of the sheer distances they allow us to travel, but because they release greenhouse gases high into the atmosphere. The statistics are frightening: two people taking a return flight between Europe and the US will contribute as much to climate change as an average household's gas and electricity consumption over a whole year.

Carbon Offset Schemes

Climatecare.org and other websites use 'carbon calculators' that allow jetsetters to offset the greenhouse gases they are responsible for with contributions to energy-saving projects and other climate-friendly initiatives in the developing world – including projects in India, Honduras, Kazakhstan and Uganda.

Lonely Planet, together with Rough Guides and other concerned partners in the travel industry, supports the carbon offset scheme run by climatecare.org. Lonely Planet offsets all of its staff and author travel.

For more information check out our website: lonelyplanet.com.

Iberia (☎ 09-6877 8950; www.iberia.com)
Icelandair (☎ 09-612 6070; www.icelandair.com)
KLM Royal Dutch Airlines (☎ 020-353 355; www.klm.com)
LOT Polish Airlines (☎ 09-6937 9036; www.lot.com)
Lufthansa (☎ 020-358 358; www.lufthansa.com)
Malev Hungarian Airlines (☎ 0600-94484; www.malev.com)
Rossiya Airlines (☎ 09-684 4822; www.rossiya-air lines.com)
Ryanair (☎ 060-016 010; www.ryanair.com)
SAS Scandinavian Airlines (☎ 060-002 5831; www.flysas.com)
Spanair (☎ 09-6151 4135; www.spanair.es)
Swiss International (☎ 09-6937 9034; www.swiss.com)
Turkish Airlines (☎ 010-084 844; www.thy.com)
Ukraine International Airlines (☎ 03-039 203; www.flyuia.com)

Tickets

As with most European destinations, flights are often cheaper if they include a Saturday night stay. One-way flights are rarely good value.

For a simple return trip, online sales work well. Use a price comparison website that simultaneously searches lots of airlines' and travel agents' websites. For more complex itineraries however, these are no substitute for a canny travel agent.

The following are some useful websites for online purchases and price comparisons:
Expedia (www.expedia.com) Reliable online flight agent.
Flightchecker (http://flightchecker.moneysavingexpert .com) Handy tool for checking multiple dates for budget airline deals. The site also contains many tips for finding cheap flights.
Flights.com (www.flights.com) A truly international site for flight-only tickets; cheap fares and easy-to-search database.
Kayak (www.kayak.com) Very comprehensive comparison site.
Kelkoo (www.kelkoo.com) Compares flight prices from several sources.
Opodo (www.opodo.com) Online sales from a confederation of world airlines.
Travelocity (www.travelocity.com) This US site allows you to search for fares (in US dollars) to and from practically anywhere.
WhichBudget (www.whichbudget.com) Up-to-date listings of routes flown by budget airlines.

INTERCONTINENTAL (RTW) TICKETS

Round-the-world (RTW) tickets are sometimes real bargains. They are usually put together by a combination of airlines and allow you to fly anywhere you want on their route systems so long as you do not backtrack. There may be restrictions on how many stops you are permitted and usually the tickets are valid for 90 days up to a year.

Finnair is part of the OneWorld airline alliance with Qantas, British Airways, Cathay Pacific, American Airlines, Iberia, Aer Lingus and LanChile.

Asia

Most Asian countries offer fairly competitive deals, with Bangkok, Singapore and Hong Kong the best places to shop around for discount tickets. Finnair has particularly good connections, flying direct to Helsinki from 11 Asian cities (see p358); it offers competitive fares and a flexible online booking system.

STA Travel (www.statravelgroup.com) is a recommended agent with branches in many Asian countries: find your local page and branches through its portal site.

Australia & New Zealand

From Australia it's at least a two-stage journey to Finland, with an Asian stopover and maybe a European one too. Codeshared Finnair flights leave from Sydney, Melbourne and Perth to Helsinki via Hong Kong, while several other European and Asian airlines can get you to Helsinki via Asia and a European metropolis like Amsterdam, Vienna or Frankfurt.

You may want to consider a round-the-world option, which can work out not much more expensive. These are often the best value from New Zealand.

Useful agencies:

Flight Centre Australia (☎ 133 133; www.flightcentre .com.au); New Zealand (☎ 0800 243 544; www.flightcen tre.co.nz) Has dozens of branches throughout Australia and New Zealand.

STA Travel Australia (☎ 134 782; www.statravel.com .au); New Zealand (☎ 0800 474 400; www.statravel.co.nz) Offices in most major cities.

Trailfinders Australia (☎ 1300 780 212; www.trail finders.com.au) Reliable travel agent.

Travel Online (www.traveline.co.nz) Good New Zealand website for checking flights.

Travel.Com (www.travel.com.au) Australian site that allows you to look up fares and flights into and out of the country.

Mainland Europe

Helsinki is well connected to most European capitals and major cities by a number of air-lines. Particularly good are the connections with Scandinavian and Baltic capitals. The websites listed under Tickets (see p359) offer good prices and comparisons for return fares to Helsinki.

STA Travel (www.statravel.com) has branches in many European nations, while **Kilroy Travels** (www.kilroytravels.com) has branches in Nordic countries and the Netherlands.

Other recommended agents:

France Voyageurs du Monde (☎ 08 92 23 56 56; www .vdm.com); Nouvelles Frontières (☎ 08 25 00 07 47; www .nouvelles-frontieres.fr) Reliable travel agents with online booking.

Italy CTS Viaggi (☎ 199 501150; www.cts.it) Specialists in student travel.

Netherlands Airfair (☎ 0900-7 717 717; www.airfair.nl) Useful flight agent.

Spain Viajar.com (☎ 902 902 522; www.viajar.com) Competitive online agent.

UK & Ireland

From Britain, the cheapest service to Finland is often Ryanair's daily flight from London Stansted to Tampere or Easyjet's London Gatwick to Helsinki service. Apart from these, Finnair/British Airways have daily direct services from London Heathrow and Manchester to Helsinki. Blue1 also connect Heathrow with Helsinki, while Aer Lingus fly there direct twice weekly from Dublin.

Discount air travel is big business in the UK – this is the discount centre of Europe. Advertisements for many travel agencies are in the travel pages of the weekend broad-sheet newspapers, *Time Out,* the *Evening Standard* and the free *TNT* magazine. Shop around – many of the ultracheap fares you see advertised won't be available when you call, but something usually comes up.

Some recommended travel agents:

Ebookers (☎ 0871 223 5000; www.ebookers.com)

Scantours (☎ 020-7554 3530; www.scantours.co.uk) Specialists in the region.

STA Travel (☎ 0871 2300 040; www.statravel.co.uk) Branches across the UK and Ireland.

Trailfinders (www.trailfinders.co.uk) Check the website for the closest branch.

USIT (☎ 01 602 1906; www.usit.ie) Ireland-wide specialists in youth travel.

USA & Canada

Finnair flies direct from Helsinki to New York (around 8½ hours) and, in summer,

Boston and Toronto, but you may find cheaper fares involving a change of flight in another European city. You could fly to London or Frankfurt, for example, and take advantage of the budget airlines.

Popular travel agents:

Flight Centre USA (☎ 1866 967 5351; www.flightcen tre.us); Canada (☎ 1877 967 5302; www.flightcentre.ca) Offices across the USA and Canada.

STA Travel (☎ 800 781 4040; www.statravel.com) Offices in major US cities.

Travel CUTS (☎ 1866 246 9762; www.travelcuts.com) Canada's national student travel agency; offices in all major cities plus a few in the US.

LAND
Border Crossings

There are several border crossings from northern Sweden to northern Finland, and the main highway in both countries runs parallel to the border from Tornio/Haparanda to Kaaresuvanto/Karesuando. There are no passport or customs formalities, and if you're driving up along the border you can alternate between countries.

Between Norway and Finland, there are six road border crossings, plus a few legal crossings along wilderness tracks.

There are nine main border crossings between Finland and Russia including several in the southeast and two in Lapland. They are more serious frontiers; you must already have a visa to cross into Russia.

Bus

It's a long way to Finland by bus from the UK and central Europe – you're unlikely to save much if any money over a plane fare. **Eurolines** (www.eurolines.com) doesn't serve Finland, but may be useful if you plan to visit other Nordic countries en route. There are several bus services to Finland from various cities in Russia, particularly St Petersburg and Murmansk.

NORWAY

There are five daily routes linking Finnish Lapland with northern Norway, some running only in summer. These are operated by **Eskelisen Lapin Linjat** (www.eskelisen-lapinlinjat .com), whose website has detailed maps and timetables, as does the Finnish bus website (www.matkah uolto.fi).

All routes originate or pass through Rovaniemi; the three northeastern routes continue via Inari to either Kirkenes, Tana

Bru/Vadsø or Karasjok. The Karasjok bus continues in summer to Nordkapp (North Cape). On the western route, one Rovaniemi–Kilpisjärvi bus runs on daily to Tromsø in summer, and a Rovaniemi–Hetta bus continues to Kautokeino and Alta.

RUSSIA

There are three daily express buses to Vyborg and St Petersburg from Helsinki, one originating in Turku. There are also three weekly from Lappeenranta. These services are run by Finnish firms in conjunction with Sovavto (www.sovavto.ru) and appear on the Matkahuolto website (www.matka huolto.fi). Other less regular services to Russia are available from Helsinki and other southeastern destinations.

The one-way fare from Helsinki to Vyborg is €41.30 (five hours) and to St Petersburg it's €63.70 (8½ to nine hours). Book at the bus station in Helsinki or the Sovavto Central Ticket Office in the Pulkovskaya Hotel in St Petersburg.

Goldline (www.goldline.fi) runs three weekly buses from Rovaniemi via Ivalo to Murmansk. There are also several local cross-border services in the southeast and, further north, buses across from Kuhmo to Russian Karelia (see p294).

SWEDEN

The quickest route to Finland from southern Sweden is by ferry (see p363). In the north, the main destination is Haparanda/Tornio, twin towns on either side of the border with connecting bus services into both Finland and Sweden.

You can get to Tornio by bus from Stockholm, or you can head to Lulea or Kiruna on the train and get a bus on to Tornio from there.

Tapanis Buss (www.tapanis.se) runs express coaches from Stockholm to Tornio twice a week (€59, 13 hours), and there are daily connections to Tornio from towns in northern Sweden.

Car & Motorcycle

Motorists and motorcyclists will need the vehicle's registration papers, and liability insurance. You may have to contact your insurer to initiate Europe-wide 'Green Card' coverage. A home licence from most Western countries is valid. Contact your local automobile association for details about all documentation.

TRANSPORT

CAR SHARING

Car sharing is a good way of lowering costs and emissions when travelling long distances. Useful websites to search for drivers or to enter your details for prospective passengers are:

■ **www.allostop.net** French site with phone service.

■ **www.autostop.it** Italian site.

■ **www.compartir.org** Spanish site with Europe-wide lifts.

■ **www.freewheelers.co.uk** British site with worldwide lifts.

■ **www.mitfahrzentrale.de** The most useful site. You pay a reservation fee.

See p366 for information about driving in Finland.

RUSSIA
If you plan to drive into Russia, you'll need an international licence and certificate of registration, passport and visa. You must also pay Russian insurance (€40 to €60) on your vehicle – there are offices at most borders, or talk to **Ingonord** (☎ 09-251 0300; www.ingonord.com; Salomonkatu 5C, Helsinki) in Helsinki. At the border you get a temporary permit to drive in Russia. Finnish car rental companies do not allow their cars to be taken into Russia.

Train
The typical route to Finland from most of Europe goes via Denmark and Sweden. There are direct long-distance trains to Stockholm from various major cities in Europe. Train passes give discounts on most ferry routes across to Finland.

ASIA
To and from central and eastern Asia, a train can work out at about the same price as flying, and it can be a lot more fun.

Helsinki is a good place to start your journey across Russia into Asia. Frequent trains run between Helsinki and Moscow (see right), and there are three routes to/from Moscow across Siberia with connections to China, Japan and Korea: the Trans-Siberian to/from Vladivostok, and the Trans-Mongolian and Trans-Manchurian, both to/from Beijing. There's a fourth route south from Moscow and across Kazakhstan, following part of the old Silk Road to Beijing. These trips take several days, often involve stopovers, and prices vary according to the direction you are travelling, where you buy your ticket and what is included.

For details on Trans-Siberian options see Lonely Planet's *Trans-Siberian Railway*.

NORWAY
There is no train service between Finland and Norway.

RUSSIA
There are three trains daily from Helsinki to the Finland Station in St Petersburg, including the sleeper that goes on to Moscow. In 2010 new high-speed trains are scheduled to cut this journey to 3½ hours. Tickets for these trains, which travel via the Finnish towns of Lahti and Kouvola, are sold at the international ticket counter at Helsinki train station. The rail crossing is at Vainikkala (Russian side: Luzhayka).

You must have a valid Russian visa, but border formalities have been fast-tracked so that passport checks are now carried out on board the moving train.

The *Sibelius* and *Repin* are Finnish and Russian trains respectively and run daily from Helsinki to St Petersburg (€54.80, six hours) via Vyborg (€39 to €42, four hours). The *Repin* is a little slower but also offers 1st-class sleeping berths.

The *Tolstoi* sleeper runs from Helsinki via St Petersburg to Moscow (2nd/1st class €93/139, 13 hours). The fare includes a sleeper berth. There are a number of more upmarket sleepers costing up to €350.

Return fares are double, and there are significant discounts for families and small groups. See www.vr.fi for details.

SWEDEN
There is no direct train service between Finland and Sweden, but train passes give significant discounts on ferry and bus connections.

Swedish trains travel no closer than Boden/Luleå; from there take connecting buses (train passes are valid) to Haparanda/Tornio, and on to the railway station at Kemi. Inter-Rail passes cover bus travel all the way from Boden to Kemi.

SEA

Arriving in Finland by ferry is a memorable way to begin your visit, especially if you dock in Helsinki. Baltic ferries are some of the world's most impressive seagoing craft, especially considering they are passenger ferries rather than cruise ships. The big ferries are floating hotels-cum-shopping plazas, with duty-free shopping, restaurants, bars, karaoke, nightclubs and saunas. Many Scandinavians use them simply for boozy overnight cruises, so they can get pretty rowdy on Friday and Saturday nights, when you may need to book in advance.

Services are year-round between major cities: book ahead in summer and if travelling with a vehicle. The boats are amazingly cheap if you travel deck class (without a cabin): they make their money from duty-free purchases. Many ferry lines offer 50% discounts for holders of Eurail, Scanrail and Inter-Rail passes. Some offer discounts for seniors, and for ISIC and youth card-holders; inquire when purchasing your ticket. There are usually discounts for families and small groups travelling together.

Ferry companies have detailed timetables and fares on their websites. Fares vary according to season. Here is a list of operators with their Finnish contact numbers:

Eckerö Line (☎ 060-004 300) Tallinn (www.eckeroline .fi); Åland (www.eckerolinjen.fi)

Finnlines (☎ 010-436 7676; http://passenger.finnlines .com)

Linda Line (☎ 060-0066 8970; www.lindaliini.ee)

Nordic Jet Line (☎ 060-001 655; www-eng.njl.fi)

RG Line (☎ 020-771 6810; www.rgline.com)

Tallink/Silja Line (☎ 060-015 700; www.tallinksilja .com)

Viking Line (☎ 060-041 577; www.vikingline.fi)

Estonia

Several ferry companies ply the Gulf of Finland between Helsinki and Tallinn in Estonia. Since most nationalities don't require a visa and the trip is so quick and cheap, it's a very popular day trip from Helsinki (see boxed text, p109). Competition between the companies keeps the prices low, and if you're heading to Estonia for onward travel it can be cheaper to get a same-day return ticket than a one-way ticket. Car ferries cross in 3½ hours, catamarans and hydrofoils in about 1½ hours. Service is heavy year-round, although in winter there are fewer departures, and the traffic is also slower because of ice. Cancellations occur if the sea is rough; the express boats are more prone to this. Phone the day before to check on sailings in winter.

Ferries are cheapest: Eckerö Line has only one departure daily but is the cheapest with a return fare from €30 to €39 in high season. Tallink, Viking Line and Silja Line have several daily departures (€23 to €28 one way). Vehicle space costs around €20 to €25. On the websites you can easily see which departures are offering cheaper rates.

Catamarans and hydrofoils cost between €29 and €38 one way depending on the company, time of year, time of day and the day of the week, but online deals, advance purchase specials and offers can knock this as low as €18. Linda Line, Nordic Jet Line and Tallink offer these routes. Tallink has vehicle space on its fast ferry (€25 to €38 one-way for standard-sized cars).

Tickets can be booked online, at the ferry company offices in central Helsinki, from the ferry terminal, or from the Helsinki city tourist office (for a hefty booking fee). See p357 for details of Estonian entry requirements.

Germany

Finnlines has a year-round service from Helsinki to Travemünde (from €196 September to May, from €244 June to August one way, plus €100 per vehicle) with a connecting bus service to Hamburg. The faster Star boats (27 hours) are cheaper than the Hansa Class boats (35 hours), which you stay on for two nights.

Tallink/Silja also runs a fast ferry from Helsinki to Rostock (27 hours), with seats costing €72 to €97, and berths starting at €127. Vehicle places are available from €115.

Russia

For information on cruises between Lappeenranta in Karelia and Viipuri in Russia see p167.

Sweden

Stockholm is the main gateway to Finland, due to the incredibly luxurious passenger ferries that travel regularly between Stockholm

TRANSPORT

and Turku or Helsinki. There are two main competing operators, Tallink/Silja Line and Viking Line, with smaller companies operating on certain routes.

The major source of income for these ferry companies is duty-free shopping. Because the ferries stop at the Åland islands, tax-free shopping is possible on board, even though Sweden and Finland are both in the European Union. Thus Swedes and Finns can avoid the high sales taxes in both countries, especially for alcohol and cigarettes. For the traveller, this means ferry companies can afford to keep fares unusually low, and frequently offer discount tickets at laughable levels.

But it's harder for foreign visitors to snaffle cheap Stockholm–Helsinki tickets these days, and passenger-only tickets (ie no cabin) are restricted. The companies don't advertise specials on their English-language pages, so get a Finnish- or Swedish-speaking friend to check their pages for offers.

Viking Line is the cheapest of the two operators, with a passenger ticket between Stockholm and Helsinki costing from €34 to €51 (up to €62 on Friday). In summer you can doss down in chairs or the floor, but an extra cabin ticket is obligatory from September to May: the cheapest berths start at €24.

Tallink/Silja don't offer deck tickets on the Helsinki run: the cheapest cabins start at €122 for the crossing.

It's usually much cheaper to cross to Turku (11 to 12 hours), with tickets starting at €10 on the day ferries. Note that Åbo is Swedish for Turku.

All ferries travelling between Stockholm and Turku call in at Mariehamn in Åland. Viking Lines offers service between Mariehamn/Turku and Kapellskär, Sweden, a small harbour in the northern part of Stockholm province. A connecting bus to Stockholm is included in the price of the ferry.

Eckerö Linjen sails from Grisslehamn, north of Stockholm, to Eckerö in Åland. It's by far the quickest, at just two hours and, with prices starting from €8.90 return, and €11 for a car, it's an amazing bargain. There's a cheap connecting bus from Stockholm, Uppsala or Gävle (Sweden) which is free.

From the main Åland island group it's possible to island-hop across the archipelago to mainland Finland (or vice versa) on free ferries. See p243 for details.

RG Lines sails from Vaasa in Finland, to Umeå, Sweden (€60 to €80 per person plus €65 per car, 4½ hours) almost daily from March to October. Finnlines runs a simpler cargo ferry, which connects Naantali, near Turku, with Kapellskär three times daily (car and driver from €70 plus €30 per person, no foot passengers, seven to eight hours).

GETTING AROUND

A thick book of timetables for all domestic buses and trains is published every year by Edita (www.turisti.fi), based in Helsinki. While all of this information is on the internet, if you like having it at your fingertips, the tome costs €30.

Both bus and rail services have excellent online timetables, and a useful combined journey planner for Finland's public transport network is online at www.matka.fi.

AIR
Airlines in Finland

Finnair is the principal domestic carrier, and runs a comprehensive network from Helsinki, and from a couple of regional hubs. Standard prices are fairly expensive, but check the website for offers.

Special discounts are offered on some routes in summer, and 'snow fares' give big discounts on selected flights between Helsinki and Lapland during nonholiday periods from January to May.

If you book in advance, the budget carrier Blue1 offers the sharpest rates on routes from Helsinki to a range of Finnish cities.

Airlines flying domestically:

Air Åland (☎ 018-17110; www.airaland.com) Flies between Helsinki and Mariehamn on the Åland islands.

Blue1 (☎ 060-002 5831; www.blue1.com) Budget flights from Helsinki to Kuopio, Oulu, Rovaniemi and Vaasa.

Finnair (☎ 81881; www.finnair.com) Extensive domestic network includes flights by subsidiary FinnComm.

Fly Lappeenranta (☎ 020-787 1800; www.flylappeenranta.fi) Flies between Helsinki and Lappenranta only.

Turku Air (☎ 02-276 4966; www.turkuair.fi) Zips between Turku and Åland.

Wingo (☎ 060-095 020; www.wingo.fi) Flies between Oulu, Tampere and Turku.

BICYCLE

Finland is largely a flat country and as bicycle-friendly as any country you'll find, with plenty

TRANSPORT

of bike paths that cyclists share with in-line skaters in summer. The only drawback to an extensive tour is distance, but bikes can be taken on most trains, buses and ferries. Åland is particularly good for cycling. Helmets are required by law.

For more information about cycling in Finland see p71.

Hire

You can hire a bike in nearly every Finnish town, but it's important to bear in mind the type of bikes on offer. Most camp sites and many urban hotels offer bikes for a small fee or for free, but these are made for the job of cycling into or around town, not for ambitious road trips. Better bikes are available at dedicated outlets that we list in the text. Expect to pay around €20 per day or €100 per week for a good-quality road or mountain bike.

BOAT
Lake & River Crossings

Though now superseded in speed by buses and trains, lake and river passenger services were once important means of summer transport in Finland. These services are now largely kept on as cruises, and make a great, leisurely way to journey between towns. It's a real Finnish summer experience.

Apart from two-hour cruises starting from towns such as Jyväskylä, Kuopio, Savonlinna, Tampere and Mikkeli, you can actually cover half of Finland on scheduled boat routes. The most popular routes are Tampere–Hämeenlinna, Savonlinna–Kuopio, Lahti–Jyväskylä and Joensuu–Koli–Nurmes. See Getting There & Away in the relevant town sections for details.

Sea Ferries

Several kinds of ferries operate between various islands and coastal towns, especially near Turku and in the province of Åland. See p224 and p245, respectively, for specific information.

Several cruise companies run boats to interesting islands off the coast, particularly along the south coast. From Helsinki the foremost tour is the short trip to Suomenlinna. Likewise, there are summer cruises aboard historic steamships to mainland towns that may also be reached by car, bus or train. Popular sea routes are Turku–Naantali (p219) and Helsinki–Porvoo (p109).

BUS

The main form of long-distance transport in Finland, especially in remote areas, is the bus. Though more expensive than the train over a given route, the network it covers is far more comprehensive, taking in some 90% of the nation's road system. Buses are comfortable, run on time and are rarely full.

There are two types of intercity bus services: *vakiovuorot* (regular buses) stopping frequently at towns and villages, and *pikavuorot* (express buses) travelling swiftly between cities. Because there are few motorways in Finland, even express buses aren't that fast, covering 100km in less than two hours and 400km in about six hours. The express buses are pricier, but not much more so.

All long-distance bus ticketing is handled by **Matkahuolto** (☎ 020-04000; www.matkahuolto.fi), whose excellent website has all the timetables. Matkahuolto offices tend to work normal business hours, but you can always just buy the ticket from the driver too.

Each town and municipal centre has a *linja-autoasema* (bus terminal), with local timetables displayed (*lähtevät* is departures, *saapuvat* arrivals). Bus schedules change often so *always* double-check – particularly in rural areas where there may be only one weekly bus on some routes.

Departures between major towns are very frequent, but reduce substantially at weekends. In more remote areas, there may be no weekend buses at all. Schedules change during the summer holidays: buses that normally do the school run are struck off, so it can be much harder to move around isolated regions.

Costs

Prices in this guide refer to express services if they are available, or local services if not. Ticket prices are fixed and depend on the number of kilometres travelled; return tickets are 10% cheaper than two one-way fares, provided the trip is at least 80km in one direction. Express buses cost up to €4 more than regular buses. Children aged four to 11 always pay half fare, while there's a 30% reduction for those aged 12 to 16. For student discounts, you need to be studying full-time in Finland and buy a student coach discount card (€6) from any bus station. Proper student ID and a passport photo is required, and the card entitles you to a 50% discount on journeys more than 80km.

TRANSPORT

If booking three or more adult tickets together, a 25% discount applies, meaning good news for groups.

The one-way fare for a 100km trip is normal/express €16.30/19.20. Following are some sample one-way fares from Helsinki:

Destination	Cost (€)	Duration (hrs)
Hämeenlinna	20.90	1.5
Hanko	23.70	2.25
Joensuu	69.30	7.25
Jyväskylä	43.90	4.5
Kuopio	58.10	6.5
Lappeenranta	41.30	4
Oulu	86.00	10-11
Pori	43.90	4
Rovaniemi	108.30	12.5
Savonlinna	52.60	4.5-5.5
Tampere	31.70	2.5
Turku	28.70	2.5

CAR & MOTORCYCLE

Driving around Finland is hassle-free. Finnish drivers are remarkably considerate and polite – rarely will you hear a horn blast in anger and 'road rage' is almost an unknown phenomenon. Finland's road network is excellent and well signposted between centres, although there are only a few motorways, around major cities. When approaching a town or city, look for signs saying *keskusta* (town centre), where you can usually find parking. Only in remote areas will you find unsurfaced roads or dirt tracks, and even these are in good condition. There are no road tolls.

Finland has some of the world's most expensive petrol. Many petrol stations are unstaffed, so you'll need to have banknotes handy for the machine: they don't accept foreign cards. Change is not given.

Driving Licence & Insurance

An international licence is not required to drive in Finland. However, you'll need the driving licence from your home country to bring a car into Finland, or if you plan to rent a car – a passport alone won't suffice. A Green Card (insurance card) is recommended but not required for visitors from most countries that subscribe to this European insurance system. Those who are from countries who do not belong to the Green Card plan will need to arrange insurance on arrival. Insurance is included with car rental.

The Finnish national motoring organisation, **Autoliitto** (☎ 09-7258 4400; www.autoliitto.fi; Hämeentie 105A, 00550 Helsinki), can also answer questions.

Hire

Car rental in Finland is much more expensive than elsewhere in Europe, but between a group of three or four it can work out at a reasonable cost. From the major rental companies a small car costs from €77/320 per day/week with 300km free per day. As ever, there are much cheaper deals online.

While the daily rate is high, the weekly rate offers some respite. Best of all, though, are the

---

DRIVING IN WINTER

Snow and ice on the roads, potentially from September to April, and as late as June in Lapland, make driving a serious undertaking. Snow chains are illegal: instead, people use snow tyres, which have metal studs, or special all-weather tyres. Cars hired at these times will be properly equipped; you can also hire snow tyres from garages and car hire agencies. At this time, the speed limits on major roads drop in winter from 100 to 80km/h and from 120 to 100km/h. Braking distances increase and visibility drops, so caution is the watchword.

Most cars in Finland have a block heater, which electrically heats the engine prior to starting it. Most public car parks have an outlet pole. In really cold weather, you should start heating the engine at least an hour before leaving: many garages have a timing mechanism. Make sure you carry jump leads just in case. Also, the cooling system of the car must have enough antifreeze to cope with the temperatures, and windscreen washer water must also have a high proportion of detergent.

The website www.tiehallinto.fi has a fantastic system of webcams on most main roads in Finland, so you can check what condition the roads are in on your prospective route.

During winter, there are various 'ice roads' that are short cuts across frozen lakes. Once every decade or so, intrepid people even make it out to Åland!

ROAD DISTANCES (km)

	Helsinki	Jyväskylä	Kuopio	Kuusamo	Lappeenranta	Oulu	Rovaniemi	Savonlinna	Tampere	Turku
Jyväskylä	272									
Kuopio	383	144								
Kuusamo	804	553	419							
Lappeenranta	223	219	264	684						
Oulu	612	339	286	215	551					
Rovaniemi	837	563	511	191	776	224				
Savonlinna	338	206	160	579	155	446	671			
Tampere	174	148	293	702	275	491	712	355		
Turku	166	304	448	848	361	633	858	446	155	
Vaasa	419	282	377	533	501	318	543	488	241	348

weekend rates. These can cost little more than the rate for a single day, and you can pick up the car early afternoon on Friday, and return it late Sunday or early Monday.

Car-rental franchises with offices in many Finnish cities include **Budget** (☎ 0207-466 600; www.budget.fi), **Hertz** (☎ 0800 188 777; www.hertz.com), **Europcar** (☎ Helsinki 0403-062 444; www.europcar.fi) and **Avis** (☎ Helsinki 09-859 8356; www.avis.fi). One of the cheapest is **Sixt** (☎ 09-350 5590; www.sixt.fi). There are also local operators.

Road Hazards

See boxed text, p65, for the significant hazards posed by reindeer and elk. This may sound comical, but they can be a deadly danger to motorists.

Road Rules

Most Finnish roads are only two lanes wide, and traffic keeps to the right. Use extreme caution when passing on these narrow roads. The speed limit is 50km/h in built-up areas, from 80km/h to 100km/h on highways, and 120km/h on motorways. *All* motor vehicles must use headlights at *all* times, and wearing

seat belts is compulsory for *all* passengers. The blood alcohol limit is 0.5 grams per litre.

Foreign cars must display a nationality sticker and foreign visitors must be fully insured – see opposite. The Ministry of Transport website (www.lvm.fi) has a downloadable page, Driving in Finland, with more specific details of Finnish road rules. The same document is also available in tourist offices in Finland.

A very important difference between Finland and many other countries is that here, cars entering an intersection from the right *always* have right of way. While this doesn't apply to highways, you'll find that in towns, even when you're on fairly major roads, cars will nip out from the right without looking: you have to give way, so be careful at every intersection. The rule is actually the same in most countries, but intersections tend to be governed by give-way or stop signs much more than they are in Finland.

HITCHING

Hitching in Finland is possible but not an activity for the impatient: expect long waits and pack waterproofs. It's more common in remote areas where bus services are fewer but still unusual. Drivers will ask, *Minne matka?* (Where are you going?), so just tell them your destination. It's a good idea to make up a sign with your destination clearly written on it; looking as much as possible like a backpacker or hiker rather than a ne'er-do-well also helps…

Your greatest friend as a hitchhiker in Finland will be your insect repellent. Mosquitoes can't believe their luck that a large juicy mammal will stand in one place for such a very long time.

LOCAL TRANSPORT

The only tram and metro networks are in Helsinki (p105). There is a bus service in all Finnish cities and towns, with departures every 10 to 15 minutes in Helsinki and other large towns, and every 30 to 60 minutes in smaller towns. Fares are usually around €2.50 to €3, payable to the driver. See individual towns for details of local public transport.

Taxi

The taxi *(taksi)* in Finland is an expensive creature, particularly for short rides. There's a flag fall of €5 in Helsinki, and typically €8 to €10 in other places, and a per-kilometre charge of €1.30. These increase if there are more than two passengers, and there's a surcharge for night and weekend service.

Hail taxis at bus and train stations or pick up the phone; they are listed in the phone book under 'Taksi'. Shared taxis often cover airport routes, and are a common mode of transport in Karelia, Kainuu and, to a lesser extent, Lapland.

TRAIN

Finnish trains are run by the state-owned **Valtion Rautatiet** (VR; ☎ 0600-41900; www.vr.fi) and are an excellent service: fast, efficient and cheaper than the bus. They are the best form of transport between major cities.

There are three main train lines: the Pohjanmaa (West) line runs between Helsinki and Oulu, and continues to Kemijärvi in Lapland; the Karelian route runs from Helsinki to Nurmes via Joensuu; and the Savonian route runs from Kouvola in the south to Kajaani, via Kuopio and Iisalmi. There are car-carriers and sleepers on the longer routes.

VR's website is excellent, with comprehensive timetable information, and some ticket sales. Major stations have a VR office: this is where to buy your ticket, as the automated machines only accept Finnish bankcards. You can pay for tickets over the phone, then pick them up at any R-Kioski newsstand. You can also just hop aboard, find a seat and pay the conductor, but if the ticket office was open where you boarded, you'll be charged a small penalty fee.

Classes

The main classes of train are the high-speed Pendolino (the fastest and most expensive class), fast Intercity (IC), Express and Regional. The first three have both 1st- and 2nd-class sections, while regional trains ('H' on the timetable) are the cheapest and slowest services, and only have 2nd-class carriages.

On longer routes there are night trains with a variety of sleeping choices (see opposite).

Costs

The classes of trains are priced differently (Regional being the cheapest, Pendolino the most expensive), and a supplement is charged for travel on IC and Pendolino trains.

Children under 17 pay half fare and children aged under six travel free (but without a seat). A child travels free with every adult on long-distance trips, and there are also discounts for seniors, local students, and any group of three or more adults travelling together.

If you purchase your ticket from the conductor after boarding from a station where the ticket office was open, a €3 'penalty' is charged (€6 on Pendolino), but this can be worth it if there's a queue in the station and the train's about to leave.

A one-way ticket for a 100km express train journey costs approximately €15 in 2nd class. First-class tickets cost 50% more than a 2nd-class ticket. A return fare is about 10% less

TRAINS WITHIN FINLAND		
Destination	**Cost (€)**	**Duration (hrs)**
Joensuu	56.30	5¼
Kuopio	53.10	5
Oulu	66.20	7-9
Rovaniemi	77.70	10-12
Savonlinna	51.70	4½
Tampere	26.90	2
Turku	26.90	2

than two one-way tickets. See the box, p368 for sample one-way fares for 2nd-class IC travel from Helsinki.

SLEEPING BERTHS

There are two types of sleeping carriage currently in operation. The traditional blue ones offer berths in one-/two-/three-bed cabins,

and cost a flat rate of €44 for a single berth (with a 1st-class ticket), and €22/12 per person for double/triple berths, in addition to the cost of an ordinary ticket.

The swish new sleeping cars offer single and double compartments in a double-decker carriage. There are cabins equipped for wheelchair use, and, on the top floor, ones with

MAJOR RAILWAY ROUTES

0 — 200 km
0 — 120 miles

Kolari

Kemijärvi

ROVANIEMI

Kemi

OULU

Vihanti

Kontiomaki

Kajaani

Ylivieska

Kokkola

Iisalmi

Nurmes

Lieksa

Vaasa

Kuopio

Seinäjoki

Joensuu

Pieksämäki

Häapamäki

Varkaus

Parkano

Jyväskylä

Savonlinna

Jämsä

MIKKELI

Pori

Orivesi

Parikkala

Kokemäki

Tampere

Toijala

HÄMEENLINNA

Imatra

Loimaa

Lahti

Kouvola

Lappeenranta

Riihimäki

Vainikkala

To Vyborg,
St Petersburg
& Moscow

TURKU

Salo

Kerava

Karjaa

Kotka

HELSINKI

Hanko

TRANSPORT

ensuite bathroom. Berths in a single compartment cost €49 to €54 (with a 1st-class ticket), in a two-person compartment €26 to €31.

The above prices increase sharply at winter weekends and during ski holiday seasons.

BICYCLES
See p71 for details on transporting bikes.

CAR
Some trains transport cars from the south to Oulu, Rovaniemi and Kolari – which is handy if you've brought your own vehicle and are keen on exploring Lapland. From Helsinki to Rovaniemi, the cost (except during weekends and holidays in the winter season) is €218 to €242 for a car plus a cabin that accommodates one to three people. All fares are detailed on the VR website.

Reservations
Seat reservations are included in the ticket price on all trains except regional services. Advance reservations are not mandatory, but are advised for travel in summer.

Train Passes
There are various passes available for rail travel within Finland, or in various European countries including Finland.

EURAIL PASSES
Eurail (www.eurail.com) now offers a good selection of different passes available to residents of non-European countries, which should be purchased before arriving in Europe. Some of the passes offer discounts for under-26-year-olds, or for two people travelling together. The Finland Eurail Pass gives you three/five/10 days' 2nd-class travel for €128/169/230 in a one-month period within Finland. The Eurail Scandinavia pass gives a number of days in a two-month period, and is valid for travel in Denmark, Sweden, Norway and Finland. It costs €232 for four days, up to €361 for 10 days. A similar, but cheaper, pass includes just Sweden and Finland. The Eurail Global Pass offers unlimited rail travel in 20 European countries for up to three months, but is only worth having if Finland is part of a trip involving a great deal of rail travel in Western Europe.

FINNRAIL PASSES
A national rail pass, the Finnrail Pass (www.vr.fi), is available to travellers residing outside Finland and offers a similar deal to the InterRail and Eurail passes though, at the time of writing, was slightly more expensive. The pass is good for three, five or 10 days of travel within a one-month period. The Finnrail Pass may be purchased from the VR travel agency Matkapalvelu, at major train stations in Finland, or from your local travel agency before arrival in Finland. The cost for 2nd-/1st-class travel is €129/192 for three days; €171/256 for five days; and €232/347 for 10 days. As with any pass, you need to plan your trips wisely to make it pay.

INTERRAIL PASSES
If you've lived in Europe for more than six months, you're eligible for an InterRail (www.interrailnet.com) pass. InterRail has scrapped its complex zonal system and now offers two passes valid for train travel in Finland. The InterRail Finland pass offers travel only in Finland for three/four/six/eight days in a one-month period, costing €109/139/189/229 in 2nd class. The Global Pass offers travel in 30 European countries and costs from €249 for five days' travel in any 10, to €599 for a month's unlimited train travel. On both these passes, there's a 33% discount for under-26s.

Both Eurail and InterRail passes give a 50% discount on Viking and Tallink/Silja ferries between Sweden and Finland.

Health

CONTENTS

Health-wise, there's very little to worry about while travelling in Finland. Your main risks are likely to be viral infections in winter, sunburn and mosquito bites in summer, plus typical travellers complaints like foot blisters and an upset stomach.

BEFORE YOU GO

INSURANCE

EU, EEA and Swiss citizens are entitled to free medical care in Finland, but you should carry proof of this entitlement. This comes in the form of the European Health Insurance Card (EHIC), which has replaced the E111 form in most EU countries.

If you don't fall into this category, a travel-insurance policy is a good idea. Some policies offer a range of medical-expense options. There is a wide variety of policies available, so check the small print.

Some policies exclude 'dangerous activities', which can include skiing, snowmobiling and trekking. You may prefer a policy that pays hospitals directly rather than you having to pay on the spot and claim later. If you have to claim make sure you keep all documentation. Some policies ask you to call back to a centre in your home country where an immediate assessment of your problem is made.

Although EU citizens are covered for medical care, you may want to consider travel insurance to cover loss/theft.

IN FINLAND

AVAILABILITY & COST OF HEALTH CARE

An *apteekki* (local pharmacy) – of which there are many in all Finnish cities and towns – or neighbourhood health care centre *(terveyskeskus)* are good places to visit if you have a minor medical problem and can explain what it is. Visitors whose home countries have reciprocal medical-care agreements with Finland and who can produce a passport (or sickness insurance card or EHIC for those from EU countries) are charged the same as Finns for medical assistance: this ranges from €11 to €22 for a visit to a doctor. Hospitalisation costs €26 per day, and the charge for day surgery is €72. Those from other countries are charged the full cost of treatment. Tourist offices and hotels can put you in touch with a doctor or dentist; in Helsinki your embassy will probably know one who speaks your language.

TRAVELLER'S DIARRHOEA

Simple things like a change of water, food or climate can all cause a mild bout of diarrhoea, but a few rushed toilet trips with no other symptoms is not indicative of a major problem.

Dehydration is the main danger with any diarrhoea, particularly in children or the elderly as it can occur quite quickly. Under all circumstances fluid replacement (at least equal to the volume being lost) is the most important thing to remember. Weak black tea with a little sugar, soda water, or soft drinks allowed to go flat and diluted 50% with clean water are all good.

ENVIRONMENTAL HAZARDS

Cuts & Scratches

Wash well and treat any cut with an antiseptic such as povidone-iodine. Where possible avoid bandages and Band-Aids, which can keep wounds wet.

Food

Finnish food is of a very high hygiene standard. Mushroom- and berry-picking is a favourite pastime in this part of the world, but make sure you don't eat any that haven't been positively identified as safe.

Hypothermia

If you are trekking in Lapland or simply staying outdoors for long periods, particularly in winter,

HEALTH

be prepared for the cold. In fact, if you are out walking or hitching, be prepared for cold, wet or windy conditions even in summer.

Hypothermia occurs when the body loses heat faster than it can produce it and the core temperature of the body falls. It is surprisingly easy to progress from very cold to dangerously cold due to a combination of wind, wet clothing, fatigue and hunger, even if the air temperature is above freezing. It is best to dress in layers; silk, wool and some of the new artificial fibres are all good insulating materials. A hat is important, as a lot of heat is lost through the head. A strong, waterproof outer layer (and a 'space' blanket for emergencies) is essential. Carry basic supplies, including food containing simple sugars to generate heat quickly and fluid to drink.

Symptoms of hypothermia are exhaustion, numb skin, shivering, slurred speech, irrational or violent behaviour, lethargy, stumbling, dizzy spells, muscle cramps and violent bursts of energy. Irrationality may take the form of sufferers claiming they are warm and trying to take off their clothes.

To treat mild hypothermia, first get the person out of the wind and/or rain, remove their clothing if it's wet and replace it with dry, warm clothing. Give them hot liquids – not alcohol – and some high-kilojoule, easily digestible food. Do not rub victims, but instead allow them to slowly warm themselves. This should be enough to treat the early stages of hypothermia. The early recognition and treatment of mild hypothermia is the only way to prevent severe hypothermia, which is a critical condition.

Insect Bites & Stings

In Finland, the mosquito breeding season is very short (about six weeks in July and August), but the mosquitoes make good use of the time. They are a major nuisance in most parts of Finland, and those in Lapland are particularly large, fierce and persistent.

The best way to handle the mosquito problem is through prevention. From June to August, travellers are advised to wear light-coloured clothing and avoid highly scented perfumes or aftershave. Use *ohvi* (mosquito repellent) liberally; the 'Off' brand seems to be particularly effective. If you have a mosquito net, use this too. There are net hats available in sports shops; if you don't mind how absurd they look these are useful for treks and outdoor activities.

When all else fails and the pesky suckers have had their piece of you, look for Etono, a concentrated antihistamine salve that is sold in stick form, for relief from bites. It is available at most pharmacies.

Parasites
TICKS
You should always check your body if you have been walking through a potentially tick-infested area – this includes rural areas of the Åland islands and in any forested areas – as ticks can cause skin infections and other more serious diseases. If a tick is found, press down around the tick's head with tweezers, grab the head and gently pull upwards. Avoid pulling the rear of the body as this may squeeze the tick's gut contents through the attached mouth parts into the skin, increasing the risk of infection and disease. Smearing chemicals on the tick will not make it let go and is not recommended.

Snakes

The only venomous snake in Finland is the common viper *(kyy),* and human deaths from viper bites are extremely rare. All snakes hibernate from autumn to spring. To minimise your chances of being bitten always wear boots, socks and long trousers when walking through undergrowth where snakes may be present.

Sunburn

You can get sunburned surprisingly quickly, even through cloud, or in subzero temperatures. Use sunscreen, hat and barrier cream for your nose and lips. Calamine lotion or Stingose are good for mild sunburn. Protect your eyes with good-quality sunglasses, particularly if you are going near water, sand or snow.

Water

You can drink the tap water in all Finnish towns and villages, and it's usually delicious. Always be wary of drinking natural water; Finland's lakes and rivers are more polluted than they may appear. A burbling stream may look crystal clear and very inviting, but there may be pulp factories, people or sheep lurking upstream. Many trekkers in the wilderness of eastern Lapland claim that springs there are safe to drink from without purifying – use your own best judgment as to whether you'd care to follow that advice. The simplest way to purify water is to boil it, use a water filter, or to add purification tablets.

Language

CONTENTS

The Finnish language is a distinct national icon that sets Finland apart from all its Western European neighbours. It is not a Scandinavian language, nor is it related to any of the Indo-European languages. There are, however, many loan words from Baltic, Slavic and Germanic languages, and many words are derived from English. It is a Uralic language belonging to the Finno-Ugric family, and is closely related to Estonian. It also shares common origins with Samoyed and languages spoken in the Volga basin of Russia. Linguists have even recognised similarities between Finnish and Korean grammar. The most widely spoken Finno-Ugric language is Hungarian, but its similarities with Finnish are few.

There are some six million Finnish speakers in Finland, Sweden, Norway and Russian Karelia. In Finnish, Finland itself is known as *Suomi*, and the language as *suomi*. With 15 cases for nouns, and at least 160 conjugations and personal forms for verbs, it is not an easy language to learn. There are no articles (a, the) and no genders, but the word for 'no' *(ei)* also conjugates.

Fortunately, staff at most tourist offices and hotels are fluent English speakers; bus drivers and staff at guesthouses, hostels and restaurants may not be – though they'll often fetch someone who can help. Finns who speak Finnish to a foreigner usually do so extremely clearly and 'according to the book'. Mistakes made by visitors are kindly tolerated, and even your most bumbling attempts will be warmly appreciated. A

final note: in Finnish, **ä** is pronounced as in 'bat', and **ö** is pronounced 'er', as in 'her' (with no 'r' sound). These letters are the last two in the Finnish alphabet. Lonely Planet's *Scandinavian Phrasebook* is a handy pocket-sized introduction to Finnish, Swedish and other languages of the region.

ACCOMMODATION

I'm looking for ...	*Etsin ...*
the youth hostel	*retkeilymajaa*
the campground	*leirintäaluetta*
a hotel	*hotellia*
a guesthouse	*matkustajakotia*

What's the address?	*Mikä on osoite?*

Do you have a ...?	*Onko teillä ...?*
(dorm) bed	*vuodepaikkaa*
cheap room	*halpaa huonetta*
single room	*yhden hengen huonetta*
double room	*kahden hengen huonetta*

for one night	*yhdeksi yöksi*
for two nights	*kahdeksi yöksi*

How much is it ...?	*Paljonko maksaa ...?*
per night	*vuorokausi*
per person	*yhdeltä henkilöltä*

Does it include	*Sisältyykö hintaan*
breakfast/sheets?	*aamiainen/lakanat?*
Can I see the room?	*Voinko nähdä huoneen?*
Where is the toilet?	*Missä on vessa?*
I'm/we're leaving now.	*Olen/olemme lähdössä nyt.*

Do you have ...?	*Onko teillä ...?*
a clean sheet	*puhtaat lakanat*
hot water	*kuumaa vettä*
a key	*avain*
a shower	*suihku*
sauna	*sauna*

CONVERSATION & ESSENTIALS

Good day.	*Hyvää päivää*
Hi!	*Hei/Moi/Terve!* (less formal)
Goodbye.	*Näkemiin.*
Bye!	*Hei hei!* or *Moi moi!* (less formal)
Good morning.	*Hyvää huomenta.*
Good evening.	*Hyvää Iltaa.*

Thank you (very much).	Kiitos (paljon).
You're welcome.	Ole hyvä.
Yes.	Kyllä/Joo.
No.	Ei.
Maybe.	Ehkä.
Excuse me.	Anteeksi.
I'm sorry.	Olen pahoillani.
How are you?	Mitä kuuluu?
I'm fine, thanks.	Kiitos hyvää.
Where are you from?	Mistä olet kotoisin?
I'm from ...	Olen ... -sta
What's your name?	Mikä sinun nimi on?
My name is ...	Minun nimi on ...
I'm a tourist/student.	Olen turisti/opiskelija.
Are you married?	Oletko naimisissa?
Do you like ...?	Pidätkö ...?
I like it very much.	Pidän siitä paljon.
I don't like ...	En pidä ...
May I?	Saisinko?
I understand.	Ymmärrän.
I don't understand.	En ymmärrä.
Does anyone speak English?	Puhuuko kukaan englantia?
How do you say ... (in Finnish)?	Miten sanotaan ... (suomeksi)?
Please write it down.	Voitko kirjoittaa sen.

EMERGENCIES

Help!	Apua!
Go away!	Mene pois!
Call a doctor!	Soita lääkäri!
Call the police!	Soita poliisi!
I'm allergic to ...	Olen allerginen ...
penicillin	penisilliinille
antibiotics	antibiooteille

NUMBERS

½	puoli
1	yksi
2	kaksi
3	kolme
4	neljä
5	viisi
6	kuusi
7	seitsemän
8	kahdeksan
9	yhdeksän
10	kymmenen
11	yksitoista
12	kaksitoista
100	sata

1000	tuhat
1,000,000	miljoona

PAPERWORK

Surname	Sukunimi
Given names	Etunimet
Date of birth	Syntymäaika
Place of birth	Syntymäpaikka
Nationality	Kansallisuus
Male/Female	Mies/Nainen
Passport	Passi

SHOPPING & SERVICES

Where is the/a ...?	Missä on ...?
bank	pankki
town centre	keskusta
embassy	suurlähetystö
entrance	sisäänkäynti
exit	uloskäynti
hospital	sairaala
market	tori
police	poliisi
post office	posti
public toilet	yleinen vessa
restaurant	ravintola
telephone office	Tele-toimisto
tourist office	matkailutoimisto

I'd like to change ...	Haluaisin vaihtaa ...
some money	rahaa
travellers cheques	matkashekkejä
I want to make a telephone call.	Haluaisin soittaa puhelun

I'm looking for ...	Etsin ...
the chemist	apteekkia
clothing	vaatteita
souvenirs	matkamuistoja

How much is it?	Mitä se maksaa?
I'd like to buy it.	Haluaisin ostaa sen.
It's too expensive.	Se on liian kallis.
Can I look at it?	Voinko katsoa sitä?
I'm just looking.	Minä vain katselen.

Do you have ...?	Onko teillä ...?
another colour	muuta väriä
another size	muuta kokoa

big/bigger	iso/isompi
small/smaller	pieni/pienempi
more/less	enemmän/vähemmän
cheap/cheaper	halpa/halvempi

TIME & DATES

When?	*Milloin?/Koska?*
today	*tänään*
tonight	*tänä iltana*
tomorrow	*huomenna*
yesterday	*eilen*
all day	*koko päivän*
every day	*joka päivä*

Monday	*maanantai*
Tuesday	*tiistai*
Wednesday	*keskiviikko*
Thursday	*torstai*
Friday	*perjantai*
Saturday	*lauantai*
Sunday	*sunnuntai*

January	*tammikuu*
February	*helmikuu*
March	*maaliskuu*
April	*huhtikuu*
May	*toukokuu*
June	*kesäkuu*
July	*heinäkuu*
August	*elokuu*
September	*syyskuu*
October	*lokakuu*
November	*marraskuu*
December	*joulukuu*

What time is it?	*Mitä kello on?*

It's ... o'clock	*Kello on ...*
1.15	*vartin yli yksi*
1.30	*puoli kaksi*
1.45	*varttia vaille kaksi*

in the morning	*aamulla*
in the evening	*illalla*

TRANSPORT

I want to go to ...	*Haluan mennä ...*
How long does the trip take?	*Kauanko matka kestää?*
Do I need to change?	*Täytyykö minun vaihtaa?*

Where does ... leave from?	*Mistä ... lähtee?*
What time does ... leave/arrive?	*Mihin aikaan lähtee/saapuu ...?*
it	*se*
the boat/ferry	*vene/lautta*
the bus/tram	*bussi/raitiovaunu*
the train	*juna*
the plane	*lentokone*

The train is ...	*Juna on ...*
delayed	*myöhässä*
cancelled	*peruutettu*

airport	*lentoasema*
bus station	*linja-autoasema*
left-luggage locker	*säilytyslokero*
one-way	*yhdensuuntainen*
platform	*laituri*
return (ticket)	*menopaluu (lippu)*
station	*asema*
ticket	*lippu*
ticket office	*lipputoimisto*
ticket machine	*lippuautomaatti*
timetable	*aikataulu*

I'd like to hire a ...	*Haluaisin vuokrata ...*
bicycle	*polkupyörän*
car	*auton*
canoe	*kanootin*
rowing boat	*soutuveneen*
guide	*oppaan*

Directions

How do I get to ...?	*Miten pääsen ...?*
Where is ...?	*Missä on ...?*
Please show me (on the map).	*Näyttäisitkö minulle (kartalta).*
Is it near?	*Onko se lähellä?*
Is it far?	*Onko se kaukana?*
(Go) straight ahead.	*(Kulje) suoraan eteenpäin.*
(Turn) left.	*(Käänny) vasempaan/vasemmalle.*
(Turn) right.	*(Käänny) oikeaan/oikealle.*
at the traffic lights	*liikennevaloissa*
at the next/second/third corner	*seuraavassa/toisessa/ kolmannessa risteyksessä*
here/there	*täällä/siellä*
up/down	*ylös/alas*
behind/opposite	*takana/vastapäätä*
north/south	*pohjoinen/etelä*
east/west	*itä/länsi*

LANGUAGE

Glossary

You may meet many of the following terms and abbreviations during your travels in Finland. Throughout the country you will often hear the words *järvi* (lake), *lampi* (pond), *saari* (island), *ranta* (shore), *niemi* (cape), *lahti* (bay), *koski* (rapids), *virta* (stream) and *joki* (river). Unless otherwise noted, all entries are Finnish and, as noted in the Language chapter (p373), ä and ö come at the end of the Finnish alphabet.

aapa – open bog; mire
ahma – wolverine
aitta – small wooden storage shed in a traditional farmhouse, used for guests
ala- – lower, eg in place names; see also *yli, ylä-*
apteekki – pharmacy
asema – station, eg *linja-autoasema* (bus station), *rautatieasema* (train station) or *lentoasema* (airport terminal)

baari – simple restaurant serving light lager and some snacks (also called *kapakka*)
bruk – early ironworks precinct (Swedish)
-by – village (Swedish); as in Godby (in Åland) or Nykarleby (in Pohjanmaa)

etelä – south

feresi – traditional Karelian dress for women, formerly worn daily but now worn only on festival days

gamla – old (Swedish)
grilli – stand or kiosk selling burgers, grilled sausages and other greasy snacks

hamn – harbour (Swedish)
hirvi – elk (moose)
huone – room

ilta – evening
ilves – lynx
itä – east; *itään* means 'to the east'

jokamiehenoikeus – literally 'everyman's right'; every person's right to wilderness access
joki – river
joulu – Christmas
Joulupukki – Santa Claus
Juhannus – Midsummer
juna – train

järvi – lake
jää – ice

kahvila – cafe
kahvio – cafeteria-style cafe, usually more basic than a *kahvila*
kala – fish; *kalastus* means 'fishing'
Kalevala – the national epic of Finland; *Kalevala* is Elias Lönnrot's 19th-century literary creation, which combines old poetry, runes and folk tales with creation myths and ethical teaching
kalmisto – old graveyard, especially pre-Medieval or Orthodox
kantele – Karelian stringed instrument similar to a zither
kapakka – see *baari*
karhu – bear
Karjala – Karelia
katu – street
kauppa – shop
kauppahalli – market hall
kauppatori – market square (usually just referred to as *tori*)
kaupungintalo – city hall
kelkka – sled or sledge; see also *moottorikelkka*
kesä – summer
kioski – small stand that sells sweets, newspapers, phonecards, food items and beer
kirjakauppa – bookshop
kirjasto – library
kirkko – church
kiuas – sauna oven
koski – rapids
kota – Sámi hut, resembling a teepee or wigwam (from the Finnish word *koti*)
koti – home
kuja – lane
kuksa – Sámi cup, carved from the burl of a birch tree
kylpylä – spa
kylä – village
kyrka – church (Swedish)

laavu – Sámi permanent or temporary open-air shelter, also used by trekkers
lahti – bay
laituri – platform (for buses or trains); wharf or pier
lakka – cloudberry
lampi – pond, small lake
laiva – ship
lappalainen – Finnish or indigenous person from Lapland; this is a contentious term in some parts of the

north, and many indigenous people will only refer to themselves as Sámi

Lappi – Lapland, a province and a popular term, usually applied to the land north of Oulu; it's better understood as roughly the area between Rovaniemi and Sodankylä; north of this is the Sámi region called Sápmi, which many consider the 'true Lapland'; see also Sápmi

leirintäalue – camping ground

lentokenttä – airstrip or airport (terminal: *lentoasema*)

linja-auto – bus (informally called *bussi*)

linna – castle

linnoitus – fortification

lippu – ticket

lounas – lunch

luontopolku – nature trail

lähtevät – departures

länsi – west

lääkäri – doctor

maatila – farm

majoitus – accommodation

maksu – payment, charge, fare

Matkahuolto – national umbrella company managing the long-distance bus system

matkakoti – guesthouse, inn; also called *matkustajakoti* (traveller home)

matkatoimisto – travel agency

Midsummer – (or Juhannus) longest day of the year, celebrated at the end of June, beginning on Friday evening *(Juhannusaatto)*. Saturday, Sunday and Monday following are also serious holidays when Finland is basically closed.

moottorikelkka – snowmobile (Finns often call these 'snow scooters' in English)

muikku – vendace, or whitefish, a common lake fish

museo – museum

mustamakkara – mild sausage made with cow's blood, black-pudding style

mäki – hill

mökki – cottage

Napapiiri – Arctic Circle

niemi – cape

Norja – Norway

olut – beer

opastuskeskus – information centre, usually of a national park

pikkujoulu – 'Little Christmas', an informal party arranged by companies or schools leading up to Christmas

pirtti – the living area of a Finnish farmhouse; a word often affixed to a rustic restaurant or tourist attraction

pitkospuu – boardwalk constructed over wetlands or swamps

pitopöytä – major pig-out buffet table

pohjoinen – north; also *pohjois-*

polku – path

poro – reindeer, a generic term for the common, domesticated variety

posti – post office, mail

Praasniekka – also *Prazniek*; Orthodox religious festival that sometimes includes a *ristinsaatto* to a lake, where a sermon takes place

pubi – pub serving strong alcohol and very little food

puisto – park

pulla – cardamom-flavoured bun, the classic Finnish pastry

pääsymaksu – entry fee

raatihuone – town hall; see also *kaupungintalo*

raja – border

ranta – shore

rautatie – railway

ravintola – restaurant, but also a bar

retkeilymaja – hostel

revontulet – Northern Lights, literally 'fires of the fox'

ristinsaatto – an annual Orthodox festival to commemorate a regional saint, involving a procession of the cross

roskakori or **roskis** – rubbish bin

ruoka – food

ruokalista – menu

Ruotsi – Sweden

rupla – Russian rouble

ruska – gorgeous but brief period in autumn (fall) when leaves turn red and yellow

rådhus – town hall (Swedish)

Sámi – the term for most indigenous people in the north of Finland; see also *lappalainen*

saari – island

saapuvat – arrivals

sairaala – hospital

Saksa – Germany

Sápmi – the area where Sámi culture and customs are still active; it is a quasi-legal territory covering the far north of Finland as well as parts of northern Sweden, Norway and Russia

satama – harbour

savusauna – 'smoke sauna'; these have no chimney but a small outlet for smoke

savuton – nonsmoking

seisovapöytä – buffet; see also *pitopöytä*

SRM – Suomen Retkeilymajajärjestö, or Youth Hostel Association of Finland

stad – city or town (Swedish)

suljettu – closed

suomalainen – Finnish, Finn

Suomi – Finland

syksy – autumn

sähköposti – email
sää – weather

talo – house or building
talvi – winter
Tapaninpäivä – Boxing Day
tavarasäilytys – left-luggage counter
teltta – tent
tie – road
torget – market square (Swedish)
tori – market square; also called kauppatori
tsasouna – small chapel or prayer hall used by the Orthodox faith
tulva – flood
tunturi – a northern fell, or large hill, that is treeless on top (as opposed to the less dramatic, tree-covered *vaara*); most of Finland's fells are in the Sápmi area, where many are sacred to the Sámi
tuomiokirkko – cathedral
tuoppi – beer-glass

uimahalli – indoor swimming pool
uimaranta – swimming beach

vaara – danger; low, broad hill (typical in Lapland Province and North Karelia)
vaellus – trek (verb *vaeltaa*)
valtio – State or government
vandrarhem – hostel (Swedish)
vapaa – free, available
varattu – reserved
vaunu – train carriage or wagon
vene – boat
Venäjä – Russia
vero – tax
vesi – water (generic form: *vettä*)
vessa – toilet
virasto – state or local government office building
Viro – Estonia
viisumi – visa
vuode – bed
vuorokausi – 24 hours (abbreviation: vrk), eg for rentals
vägen – road (Swedish)

WC – toilet (also vessa)

yli, ylä- – upper; see also *ala-*

The Authors

ANDY SYMINGTON
Coordinating Author; The Lakeland; Tampere & Häme; Oulu, Kainuu & Koillismaa; Lapland & Sápmi

Andy, author of the previous edition of this guidebook, first visited Finland many years ago more or less by accident, and walking on frozen lakes with the midday sun low in the sky made a quick and deep impression on him, even as his fingers froze in the -30°C temperatures. Since then they can't keep him away, fuelled by a love of the *Kalevala*, huskies, saunas, Finnish mustard, moody Suomi rock and metal, and, above all, of Finnish people and their beautiful country.

GEORGE DUNFORD
The Culture, Food & Drink, Helsinki; South Coast; Karelia; Turku & the Southwest; Åland; Pohjanmaa

Finland has long been the dream destination for George after first encountering it through its wonderfully intrepid people. Several visits gave him a deeper love for the destination, but this time he got to have a genuine sauna at a summer cottage, skirt the Russian border and rock out amid passing ocean liners at Turku's Ruisrock. A freelance writer, George has written for various publications including *Wanderlust*, *The Big Issue* and *Life Coach*, as well as kookier Lonely Planet titles such as *The Big Trip* and *Micronations: The Lonely Planet Guide to Home-Made Nations*. He wrote Lonely Planet's first blog and blogged most of this Finland trip at http://hackpacker.blogspot.com.

Behind the Scenes

THIS BOOK

This 6th edition was updated by Andy Symington and George Dunford. The 1st edition of Finland was researched and written by Virpi Mäkelä. Markus Lehtipuu and Jennifer Brewer updated the 2nd and 3rd editions respectively. Paul Harding updated the 4th edition and Andy Symington updated the 5th edition. This guidebook was commissioned in Lonely Planet's London office, and produced by the following:

Commissioning Editors Fiona Buchan, Ella O'Donnell, Jo Potts
Coordinating Editors Katie O'Connell, Shawn Low
Coordinating Cartographer Owen Eszeki
Coordinating Layout Designer Wibowo Rusli
Managing Editor Lauren Hunt, Sasha Baskett
Managing Cartographers Shahara Ahmed, Mark Griffiths
Managing Layout Designer Laura Jane
Assisting Editors Victoria Harrison, Anne Mulvaney, Alan Murphy
Assisting Cartographer Corey Hutchison
Cover Designer Mary Nelson Parker
Project Managers Chris Girdler, Craig Kilburn
Language Content Coordinator Quentin Frayne

Thanks to Riika Åkerlind, Imogen Bannister, Lucy Birchley, Sally Darmody, Barbara Delissen, Mark Germanchis, Geoff Howard, Trent Paton, Andy Rojas, Brad Ryan, Laura Stansfeld

THANKS
ANDY SYMINGTON

Many thanks to cheery coauthor George Dunford for the teamwork on this project and to Fiona Buchan, Jo Potts, Ella O'Donnell and the Melbourne team for running it from the LP end. Particular thanks for proofreading and Finnish support go to Riika Åkerlind, whose assistance with the previous edition was also invaluable, and to my family for their encouragement. I am indebted to numerous helpful people that I met along the way, particularly in tourist offices, and owe thanks to many Finnish friends for kindnesses and hospitality: Gustav, Marja and Mirjam Schulman, Auli, Benita and Riku Åkerlind, Kile Flink & Krisse Lundqvist, Iain, Teija, Jonah and Alex Campbell, Tiina Mikkonen and more. Thanks also to Andrew Burns for the company and Andrew Pitt for passing on his hiking experiences. Special thanks too, go to Jorma Hynninen, and, for various reasons, thanks also to the F-Body Club Finland, Timo & Anne Harju, Satu Natunen, Harri Pohjolainen, Santa Claus, Heikki Paltto, Eija Kurvi, Jan Pedersen and other people who picked up a Lapland hitchhiker.

GEORGE DUNFORD

Kiitos paljon to my serkku, Päivi Rissanen, easily Finland's greatest ambassador. Thanks to Raili

---

THE LONELY PLANET STORY

Fresh from an epic journey across Europe, Asia and Australia in 1972, Tony and Maureen Wheeler sat at their kitchen table stapling together notes. The first Lonely Planet guidebook, *Across Asia on the Cheap*, was born.

Travellers snapped up the guides. Inspired by their success, the Wheelers began publishing books to Southeast Asia, India and beyond. Demand was prodigious, and the Wheelers expanded the business rapidly to keep up. Over the years, Lonely Planet extended its coverage to every country and into the virtual world via lonelyplanet.com and the Thorn Tree message board.

As Lonely Planet became a globally loved brand, Tony and Maureen received several offers for the company. But it wasn't until 2007 that they found a partner whom they trusted to remain true to the company's principles of travelling widely, treading lightly and giving sustainably. In October of that year, BBC Worldwide acquired a 75% share in the company, pledging to uphold Lonely Planet's commitment to independent travel, trustworthy advice and editorial independence.

Today, Lonely Planet has offices in Melbourne, London and Oakland, with over 500 staff members and 300 authors. Tony and Maureen are still actively involved with Lonely Planet. They're travelling more often than ever, and they're devoting their spare time to charitable projects. And the company is still driven by the philosophy of *Across Asia on the Cheap*: 'All you've got to do is decide to go and the hardest part is over. So go!'

SEND US YOUR FEEDBACK

We love to hear from travellers – your comments keep us on our toes and help make our books better. Our well-travelled team reads every word on what you loved or loathed about this book. Although we cannot reply individually to postal submissions, we always guarantee that your feedback goes straight to the appropriate authors, in time for the next edition. Each person who sends us information is thanked in the next edition – and the most useful submissions are rewarded with a free book.

To send us your updates – and find out about Lonely Planet events, newsletters and travel news – visit our award-winning website: **lonelyplanet.com/contact**.

Note: we may edit, reproduce and incorporate your comments in Lonely Planet products such as guidebooks, websites and digital products, so let us know if you don't want your comments reproduced or your name acknowledged. For a copy of our privacy policy visit lonelyplanet.com/privacy.

enduring separation, pyjama-ed grouchiness, misspelled drafts and Suomi-obsessed rants.

OUR READERS

Many thanks to the travellers who used the last edition and wrote to us with helpful hints, useful advice and interesting anecdotes:

Richard Bevan, Ann Bullen, Iris Burghuber, Leslie Burnett, Christopher Culver, Sissi Deiwick, Blanca Díaz, Claudia Fennel, Stefanie Franz, Johanna Frigård, Ludovica Galeazzi, Peter Grencis, Kirstie Hamilton, Ricarda Hechtl, Liedy Hendriks, Chris Hodge, Robert Holder, Dave Johnson, Emmi Jormalainen, Deirdre Keary, Eva Kondla, Selina Kreiselmeier, Peter Lee, Adrian Legge, Sally Leppala, Chris Lewis, Judy Lijdsman, Kati Löytty, Lynda Mason, Ursa Mekis, Rebekka Mustonen, Anja Nopanen, Rolf Palmberg, Antonis Papoutsidakis, Jennifer Pike, Marilyn R Pukkila, Minna Puustinen, Michael Raffaele, Vitali Reif, Eleonora Rivolta, Ernesto Robledo, Matthew Ross, Jose Ruivo, Marcela Salamanca, Barbara Sheerman-Chase, Karl Stouthuysen, Narpaier Thresh, Hester Van Toll, Enid Vincent, Jan Weerd, Susanne Weinberger, Bernard Willems, Iris Woitschell, Nick Woodhams, Annie Wragg, Manuele Zunelli.

ACKNOWLEDGMENTS

Many thanks to the following for the use of their content:

Globe on title page ©Mountain High Maps 1993 Digital Wisdom, Inc.

Internal photographs p4 Raili Ojala-Signell; p10 (top) F1online digitale Bildagentur GmbH/Alamy; p11 Jon Sparks/Alamy; p45 All Pattern Photos, Minna Kurjenluoma, 2008 © Minna Kurjenluoma; p47 Aarikka; p48 Aino Huovo/Artek; p49 Anna Watson/Alamy; p50 Onitsuka Tiger shoe © Janne Kyttänen; p51 Harri Koskinen © Genelec; p52 Jan Suttle/Alamy. All other photographs by Lonely Planet Images, and by David Tipling p5, p6 (top), p7, p10 (bottom); John Borthwick p6 (bottom), p8 (bottom); Lee Foster p8 (top); Wayne Walton p9, p12; David Borland p46.

Ojala-Signell, for the best Juhannus accommodation not included. A glass of champers to Pia Juutilainen. *Kiitos* to all at Helsinki Tourism particularly Laura Itävaara & Piipponen Tiina. Special thanks to the generous Mikko Von Hertzen, Paola Suhonen, Ari Peltonen and Disco Ensemble, plus all at Ruisrock.

A hearty thanks to Andy Symington for sterling coordination, plus Paul 'Hards' Harding for previous editions. Thanks to travel companions Donna Wheeler and Sally O'Brien. Cheers to Carolyn Bain for moral (and mental) support. A husky puppy is in the mail for Rose Mulready, but Jane Ormond gets a round on Mr Lao. And biggest thanks to Nikki for

BEHIND THE SCENES

Index

INDEX

GreenDex

GOING GREEN

Finland in general has a very high regard for the environment, and though ecotourism isn't a buzzword, the truth is that most businesses here are quite responsible. We've selected the following sights, sleeps, eats and more as having demonstrated something extra; for solid commitment to environmental education, for striving towards carbon neutrality, for favouring organic produce and 'slow food', or for contributing to the survival of local cultures and communities.

It's by no means a comprehensive list, and we're in a continuous process of increasing our sustainable travel content, so we'd greatly appreciate your feedback for future editions at www.lonelyplanet.com/feedback. For more information about Lonely Planet's commitment to sustainable travel, go to www.lonelyplanet.com/responsibletravel.

MAP LEGEND

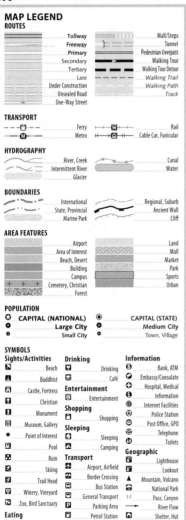

ROUTES

- Tollway
- Freeway
- Primary
- Secondary
- Tertiary
- Lane
- Under Construction
- Unsealed Road
- One-Way Street
- Mall/Steps
- Tunnel
- Pedestrian Overpass
- Walking Tour
- Walking Tour Detour
- Walking Trail
- Walking Path
- Track

TRANSPORT

- Ferry
- Metro
- Rail
- Cable Car, Funicular

HYDROGRAPHY

- River, Creek
- Intermittent River
- Glacier
- Canal
- Water

BOUNDARIES

- International
- State, Provincial
- Marine Park
- Regional, Suburb
- Ancient Wall
- Cliff

AREA FEATURES

- Airport
- Area of Interest
- Beach, Desert
- Building
- Campus
- Cemetery, Christian
- Forest
- Land
- Mall
- Market
- Park
- Sports
- Urban

POPULATION

- ✪ CAPITAL (NATIONAL)
- ◉ CAPITAL (STATE)
- ● Large City
- ● Medium City
- ● Small City
- ○ Town, Village

SYMBOLS

Sights/Activities
- Beach
- Buddhist
- Castle, Fortress
- Christian
- Monument
- Museum, Gallery
- Point of Interest
- Pool
- Ruin
- Skiing
- Trail Head
- Winery, Vineyard
- Zoo, Bird Sanctuary

Eating
- Eating

Drinking
- Drinking
- Café

Entertainment
- Entertainment

Shopping
- Shopping

Sleeping
- Sleeping
- Camping

Transport
- Airport, Airfield
- Border Crossing
- Bus Station
- General Transport
- Parking Area
- Petrol Station
- Taxi Rank

Information
- Bank, ATM
- Embassy/Consulate
- Hospital, Medical
- Information
- Internet Facilities
- Police Station
- Post Office, GPO
- Telephone
- Toilets

Geographic
- Lighthouse
- Lookout
- Mountain, Volcano
- National Park
- Pass, Canyon
- River Flow
- Shelter, Hut
- Waterfall

LONELY PLANET OFFICES

Australia
Head Office
Locked Bag 1, Footscray, Victoria 3011
☎ 03 8379 8000, fax 03 8379 8111
talk2us@lonelyplanet.com.au

USA
150 Linden St, Oakland, CA 94607
☎ 510 250 6400, toll free 800 275 8555
fax 510 893 8572
info@lonelyplanet.com

UK
2nd fl, 186 City Rd,
London EC1V 2NT
☎ 020 7106 2100, fax 020 7106 2101
go@lonelyplanet.co.uk

Published by Lonely Planet Publications Pty Ltd
ABN 36 005 607 983

© Lonely Planet Publications Pty Ltd 2009

© photographers as indicated 2009

Cover photograph: Tourist on a reindeer ride, Lapland, Melba/Alamy.

Mixed Sources
Product group from well-managed forests and other controlled sources
www.fsc.org Cert no. SGS-COC-005002
© 1996 Forest Stewardship Council